WOMEN'S STUDIES IN INDIA

WOMEN'S STUDIES IN INDIA
A READER

Edited by

MARY E. JOHN

PENGUIN BOOKS

PENGUIN BOOKS
Published by the Penguin Group
Penguin Books India Pvt. Ltd, 11 Community Centre, Panchsheel Park,
New Delhi 110 017, India
Penguin Group (USA) Inc., 375 Hudson Street, New York, New York 10014, USA
Penguin Group (Canada), 90 Eglinton Avenue East, Suite 700, Toronto,
Ontario, M4P 2Y3, Canada (a division of Pearson Penguin Canada Inc.)
Penguin Books Ltd, 80 Strand, London WC2R 0RL, England
Penguin Ireland, 25 St Stephen's Green, Dublin 2, Ireland
(a division of Penguin Books Ltd)
Penguin Group (Australia), 250 Camberwell Road, Camberwell,
Victoria 3124, Australia (a division of Pearson Australia Group Pty Ltd)
Penguin Group (NZ), 67 Apollo Drive, Rosedale, North Shore 0632,
New Zealand (a division of Pearson New Zealand Ltd)
Penguin Group (South Africa) (Pty) Ltd, 24 Sturdee Avenue, Rosebank,
Johannesburg 2196, South Africa

Penguin Books Ltd, Registered Offices: 80 Strand, London WC2R 0RL, England

First published by Penguin Books India 2008

Anthology copyright © Centre for Women's Development Studies 2008
Introduction copyright © Mary E. John

Pages xi–xvi are an extension of the copyright page

10 9 8 7 6 5 4 3 2 1

ISBN 9780143063773

Typeset in Adobe Garamond by SÜRYA, New Delhi
Printed at Baba Barkhanath Printers, Haryana

CONTENTS

≈

3. History

4. Development

12. Sexualities

13. Literature and Media

SOURCES AND COPYRIGHT
ACKNOWLEDGEMENTS

~

Most excerpts in Women's Studies in India: A Reader *have been published before. The editor and the publisher are grateful for permission granted to use the following material.*

In Section 1 (New Beginnings)

Neera Desai, 'From Accommodation to Articulation: Women's Movement in India,' in *Visibility and Power: Essays on Women in Society and Development,* ed. Leela Dube, Eleanor Leacock, Shirley Ardener (New Delhi: Oxford University Press, 1986), 287–99. Vina Mazumdar, 'Making of a Founding Text.' Excerpts from *Indian Journal of Gender Studies* 5, no.1 (1998), 87–88, 98–103. K. Lalita, 'Women in Revolt: A Historical Analysis of the Progressive Organisation of Women in Andhra Pradesh,' in *Women's Struggles and Strategies,* ed. Saskia Wieringa (1988), 54–68. Gower: Aldershot. Madhu Kishwar and Ruth Vanita, 'Initiatives against Dowry Deaths.' Excerpts from *Manushi* July-August (1979), 15–17. Manimala, 'The Bodhgaya Struggle.' Excerpts from *Manushi* (Jan-Feb 1983), 2–16. Asok Mitra, 'Implications of Declining Sex Ratio in India's Population,' in *The Enduring Conundrum: Essays in Honour of Asok Mitra,* ed. N. Krishnaji and Vina Mazumdar (New Delhi: Rainbow, 2001), 143–98.

In Section 2 (Politics)

Gail Omvedt, '"Socialist-Feminist" Organizations and the Women's Movement.' Paper presented at the National Conference, on a Perspective for a Women's Liberation Movement in India, Bombay, November 1980. Nandita Gandhi and Nandita Shah, 'The Question of Autonomy,' in *The Issues at Stake: Theory and Practice in the Women's Movement in India,* (New

Delhi: Kali for Women, 1992), 273–321. Narayan Banerjee, 'Grassroots Empowerment 1975–1990: A Discussion Paper.' CWDS Occasional Paper no. 22, Centre for Women's Development Studies, New Delhi, 1995. Manoranjan Mohanty, 'The Concept of 'Empowerment,' *Economic and Political Weekly* (17 June 1995), 1434–38. Sharmila Joshi, 'Interview with Satyabhama 'Nani' Lawand.' In *And Who will Make the Chapattis?* A Study of All-women Panchayats in Maharashtra, ed. Bishakha Dutta (Kolkata: Stree, 1998), 32–62. Nivedita Menon, 'The Elusive 'Woman': Feminism and the Women's Reservation Bill,' *Economic and Political Weekly* (28 October 2000), 3835–44. Indu Agnihotri, 'The Fourth World Conference on Women: A Report from China,' *The Indian Journal of Gender Studies* 3:1 (1996), 111–25.

In Section 3 (History)

Uma Chakravarti, 'Beyond the Altekarian Paradigm: Towards a New Understanding of Gender Relations in Early Indian History,' *Social Scientist* 16, no 8 (August 1988), 44–52. Saleem Kidwai, 'Of Begums and Tawaifs: Women of Awadh', Indian Association for Women's Studies Newsletter 2, no. 3 (December 2007), 30–32. Jasodhara Bagchi, 'Positivism and Nationalism: Womanhood and Crisis in Nationalist Fiction—Bankimchandra's *Anandamath,*' In *Ideals, Images and Real Lives, Women in Literature and History,* ed. Alice Thorner and Maithreyi Krishnaraj (Hyderabad: Orient Longman, 2000), 176–89. J. Devika, 'Introduction' to *Her–Self: Early Writings on Gender by Malayalee Women 1898–1938,* trans. and ed. J. Devika (Kolkata: Stree, 2005), xix–xxxi. V. Geetha, 'Periyar, Women and an Ethic of Citizenship,' *Economic and Political Weekly* 33 (25 April 1998). WS 9–15. Maitrayee Chaudhuri, 'Citizens, Workers and Emblems of Culture: An Analysis of the First Plan Document on Women,' *Contributions to the Indian Sociology* 29, no. 1& 2 (1995), 211–34. Ritu Menon and Kamla Bhasin, 'August Anarchy', excerpts from *Borders and Boundaries: Women in India's Partition* (New Delhi: Kali for Women, 1998), 33–45. Stree Shakti Sanghatana, 'Pramila Tai,' in *'We were making history': Life Stories of Women in the Telengana People's Struggle* (New Delhi: Kali for Women, 1989), 96–120.

In Section 4 (Development)

Maithreyi Krishnaraj, 'Women's Work in the Indian Census: Beginnings of Change,' *Economic and Political Weekly* (1–8 December 1990), 2663–72. Bina Agarwal, 'Why do Women Need Independent Rights in Land?' Excerpt from *A Field of One's Own: Gender and Land Rights in South Asia* (Cambridge: Cambridge University Press, 1994), 27–45. Saheli, Sabala Sangh, Action

India, Disha, Women's Centre, FAOW, Awaz-e-Niswan, 'Broader issues for Discussion,' in *Development for Whom? – A Critique of Women's Development Programmes*. A Report on the Women's Development Programme in Rajasthan with Specific Focus on Ajmer District, October 1991, 24–26. K. Saradamoni, 'Women, Kerala and Some Development Issues,' *Economic and Political Weekly* 29, no. 9 (26 February 1994), 501–09. Mary E. John, 'Feminism, Poverty and Globalization,' in *Social Movements in India: Poverty, Power and Politics*, ed. Raka Ray and Mary Fainsod Katzenstein (New Delhi: Oxford University Press, 2005), 107–34. Nirmala Banerjee, 'How Real is the Bogey of Feminization?' *The Indian Journal of Labour Economics* 40, no. 3 (1997), 427–38. Kumud Sharma, 'Women in Struggle: A Case Study of the Chipko Movement,' *Samya Shakti* 1, no. 2 (1984), 55–62. Vandana Shiva, 'Decolonizing the North.' Excerpt from *Eco-Feminism* (New Delhi: Kali for Women, 1992), 264–76.

In Section 5 (Violence)

Kalpana Kannabiran, 'Rape and the Construction of Communal Identity', in *Embodied Violence, Communalising Women's Sexuality in South Asia*, ed. Kumari Jayawardena and Malathi de Alwis (New Delhi: Kali for Women,1996), 32–41. Sudesh Vaid, 'Politics of Widow Immolation,' *Seminar* 342 (February 1988), 21–23. Malavika Karlekar, 'Domestic Violence,' in *The Oxford India Companion to Sociology and Social Anthropology*, ed. Veena Das (New Delhi: Oxford University Press, 2001). 1127–57. Susie Tharu, 'The Impossible Subject: Caste and Desire in the Scene of the Family,' in *Signposts: Gender Issues in Post-Independence India*, ed. Rajeswari Sunder Rajan (New Delhi: Kali for Women, 1999), 187–203. Urvashi Butalia, 'Speaking Peace: An Introduction,' in *Speaking Peace: Women's Voices from Kashmir*, ed. Urvashi Butalia (New Delhi: Kali for Women, 2002), ix–xxiv.

In Section 6 (Law)

Upendra Baxi, Vasudha Dhagamwar, Raghunath Kelkar, Lotika Sarkar, *An Open Letter to the Chief Justice of India*, 4 Supreme Court Case Finder (Jour) 17, New Delhi, 1979, 1–5. Flavia Agnes, 'Family Courts: From the Frying Pan into the Fire?' *The Lawyers* (September 1990), 4–12. Nandita Haksar, 'Human Rights Lawyering: A Feminist Perspective,' *Engendering Law in India: Essays in Honour of Lotika Sarkar*, ed. Amita Dhanda and Archana Parasher (Lucknow: Eastern Books, 1999), 71–88. Ratna Kapur, 'Sexcapades and the Law,' *Seminar* 505 (September 2001), 40–53. Prem Chowdhry, 'Enforcing Cultural Codes: Gender and Violence in Northern India,' in *A Question of Silence? The Sexual Economies of Modern India*, ed. Mary. E .John and Janaki Nair (New Delhi: Kali for Women, 1998), 332–67. Mohan Rao, 'The Two Child Norm and Population Policy'. Mss.

In Section 7 (Education)

Partha Chatterjee, 'Women and the Nation: The Trouble with Their Voices,' from *The Nation and its Fragments Colonial and Postcolonial Histories* (New Delhi: Oxford University Press, 1994), 135–57. Tanika Sarkar, '*Strishiksha* or Education for Women,' from *Words to Win: the Making of Amar Jiban, A Modern Biography*, (New Delhi: Kali for Women, 1999), 67–81. Department of Education, 'Education for Women's Equality,' National Policy on Education, 1986. Kumud Pawde, 'The Story of my Sanskrit,' (translated by Priya Adarkar) in *Poisoned Bread: Translations from Modern Marathi Literature*, ed. Arjun Dangle (Hyderabad: Orient Longman, 1993). 96–106. Karuna Chanana, 'Gender Inequality in Primary Schooling in India: The Human Rights Perspective,' *Women's Link* 4 (Oct-Dec 1998), 2–12. Zoya Hasan and Ritu Menon, 'Creating an Enabling Environment,' in *Educating Muslim Girls: A Comparison of Three Cities*, ed. Zoya Hasan, Ritu Menon, (New Delhi: Women Unlimited, 2005), 144–67. Dipta Bhog, 'Gender and Curriculum,' *Economic and Political Weekly* (27 April 2002), 1638–42.

In Section 8 (Health)

Veena Shatrugna, Nirmala Soundarajan, P. Sundaraiah, Leela Raman, 'Backpain, the Feminine Affliction,' *Economic and Political Weekly* (28 April 1990), WS-2–6. Vineeta Bal, Vani Subramanian and Laxmi Murthy, Saheli, 'Contraceptive Research: Is there a Gender-Neutral Approach?' (New Delhi: Saheli). Mss. Imrana Qadeer, 'Reproductive Health: A Public Health Perspective,' *Economic and Political Weekly* (10 October 1998), 2675–84. Shodhini, 'Our Health Our Heritage,' in *Our Lives Our Health*, ed. Malini Karkal, Coordination Unit-India, World Conference on Women, Beijing, 1995, 168–79. Bhargavi Davar, 'Our Mind Our Madness,' in *Our Lives Our Health*, ed. Malini Karkal, Coordination Unit-India, World Conference on Women, Beijing, 1995, 161–67. Anita Ghai, 'A Disabled Feminism?' Paper presented at XIIth National Conference of the Indian Association for Women's Studies, University of Lucknow, 7–10 February 2008.

In Section 9 (Household and Family)

Devaki Jain and Nirmala Banerjee, Introduction to *Tyranny of the Household: Investigative Essays into Women's Work* (New Delhi: Shakti Books, 1985). Rajni Palriwala, 'Economics and Patriliny: Consumption and Authority within the Household,' *Social Scientist* 21, no. 9–11 (Sep-Nov 1993), 47–73. Jaya Srivastava, 'Widows of November 1984,' in *Widows Abandoned and Destitute Women in India*, ed. Pramila Dandevate et al. (New Delhi: Radiant Publishers, 1989), 63–67. Amita Tyagi Singh and Patricia Uberoi, 'Learning to 'Adjust': Conjugal Relations in Indian Popular Fiction,' *Indian Journal of Gender Studies* 1, no. 1 (1994), 93–120. Brinda Karat, 'On the Uniform Civil Code,' from *Survival and Emancipation: Notes from Indian Struggles* (New Delhi: Three Essays Collective, 2005), 163–73.

In Section 10 (Caste and Tribe)

Ruth Manorama, 'The Downtrodden among the Downtrodden,' *Dalit Solidarity*, ed. James Massey and Bhagwan Das (New Delhi: SPG Publications, 1992), 165–76. Sharmila Rege, 'Introduction' to *Writing Caste, Writing Gender: Dalit Women's Testimonios* (New Delhi: Zubaan, 2006), 1–8. Annie Namala, 'Dalit Women: The Conflict and the Dilemma,' Paper presented at Workshop on Dalit Women, Anveshi Research Centre for Women's Studies, Hyderabad, 1995. Leela Dube, 'Caste and Women,' in *Caste: Its Twentieth Century Avatar*, ed. M.N. Srinivas (New Delhi: Penguin Viking, 1996), 1–27. Virginius Xaxa, 'Women and Gender in the Study of Tribes in India,' *Indian Journal of Gender Studies* 11, no. 3 (2004), 345–67. Tiplut Nongbri, 'Ethnicity and Gender: Identity Politics among the Khasi,' in *Development, Ethnicity and Gender: Select Essays on Tribes in India*, (Jaipur and New Delhi: Rawat, 2003).

In Section 11 (Communalism and Religion)

Radha Kumar, 'The Shah Bano Case.' Excerpts from *A History of Doing: An Account of the History of the Women's Movement and Feminism, 1800–1990*, (New Delhi: Kali for Women, 1993), 160–71. Flavia Agnes, 'Women's Movements in a Secular Framework: Redefining the Agendas,' *Economic and Political Weekly* (1994), 1123–28. Gabriele Dietrich, 'Women's Movement and Religion,' from *Women's Movement in India, Conceptual and Religious Reflections: Selected Essays* (Bangalore: Breakthrough Publications, 1988), 128–49. Kumkum Sangari, excerpt from 'Politics of Diversity: Religious Communities and Multiple Patriarchies,' *Economic and Political Weekly* (30 December 1995), 3381–89. Tanika Sarkar, 'Pragmatics of the Hindu Right: Politics of Women's Organisations,' *Economic and Political Weekly* (31 July 1999), 2159–66.

In Section 12 (Sexualities)

Kumkum Roy, 'Unravelling the Kamasutra,' in *A Question of Silence? The Sexual Economies of Modern India*, ed. Mary E .John and Janaki Nair, (New Delhi: Kali for Women,1998), 52–76. Janaki Nair, 'The Devadasi, Dharma and the State,' *Economic and Political Weekly* (December 1994), 3157–67.

Sex Workers' Manifesto, Theme paper of the First National Conference of Sex Workers organised by Durbar Mahila Samanwaya Committee, Yuba Bharati Krirangan (Salt Lake Stadium), Calcutta, 14–16 November 1997. Campaign for Lesbian Rights, 'Lesbian Emergence.' Excerpts from *A Citizens' Report*, August 1999, New Delhi. Shohini Ghosh, 'The Troubled Existence of Sex and Sexuality: Feminists Engage with Censorship,' in *Image Journeys: Audio-Visual media & Cultural Change in India*, ed. Christiane Brosius and Melissa Butcher (New Delhi: Sage, 1999), 233–59. Rinchin, 'Querying Marriage and Family,' *Economic and Political Weekly* (19 February 2005), 718–20.

In Section 13 (Literature and Media)

Nabaneeta Dev Sen, 'Alternative Interpretation of the Ramayana: Views from Below,' Fourteenth JP Memorial Lecture, Centre for Women's Development Studies, New Delhi, 2001. Susie Tharu, 'Binodini Dasi: An Actress in the Drama of Public Modernity in India,' *Contributions to Indian Sociology* 33, no. 3 (1999), 581–86. Rajeswari Sunder Rajan, 'Life after Rape: Narrative, Rape and Feminism,' from *Real and Imagined Women: Gender, Culture and Postcolonialism* (London: Routledge, 1993), 64–82. Vasanth Kannabiran and Volga, 'Telugu Feminist Poetry Today.' Unpublished. Tejaswini Niranjana, 'Integrating Whose Nation? Tourists and Terrorists in 'Roja',' *Economic and Political Weekly* (15 January 1994), 79–80. Kalpana Sharma, 'The Medium is the Message,' *The Hindu*, 13 August 1995. Sonia Bathla, 'Gender Construction in the News Media.' Occasional Paper no. 37, Centre for Women's Development Studies, New Delhi, 2002.

PREFACE

~

The longer it takes to complete a particular work, the greater the debts one accumulates. This volume is no exception. Spanning over a decade, from the time when the idea of bringing together recent writing on feminism and women's studies was first articulated to its present fruition, I am most indebted to friends and colleagues at Anveshi Research Centre for Women's Studies, the Centre for Women's Development Studies and the Women's Studies Programme at Jawaharlal Nehru University. They have provided stimulating contexts for exploring the world of women's studies in all its diversity and transformations.

I am particularly grateful to all the contributors for having readily agreed to be part of this volume, including in excerpted form. The original sources of their articles have been acknowledged separately, and I hope readers will be inspired to read them in full.

But for the labours of many individuals, this volume would never have seen the light of day. Swapna Guha at CWDS and Kanchan Mann at JNU helped in the arduous task of typing many of the articles. Usha Wali was invaluable in corresponding with contributors and publishers. Poulomi Pal went beyond the duties of research assistant in the final stages of production. Madhushri and Deepa Singhal at the CWDS library responded with amazing swiftness to every request.

For their support and responses to this volume, warm thanks to Inderpal Grewal, Malavika Karlekar, Vina Mazumdar, Nivedita Menon and Tejaswini Niranjana.

It was V.K. Karthika at Penguin who enthusiastically initiated this project, and R. Sivapriya who saw it through. I am very grateful for their unfailing interest and support. The Sir Ratan Tata Trust provided a subsidy towards production costs for which I am also thankful.

Finally, Satish Deshpande and Apoorv Avram have known the direct effects of work that never seemed to end. The joy of its completion is one we can fully share.

Mary E. John
April 2008

INTRODUCTION

⁓

This anthology brings together writings spanning the last thirty years, an extraordinarily vibrant period in the history of independent India. The rise and spread of a remarkably new field of knowledge, focusing on women, their lives and their struggles, has been witnessed from the mid 1970s. Today, the field is indeed a vast one, having extended its reach into—and indeed beyond—every conventional discipline. At the same time—and this will surely surprise many readers—conceptions about women's studies continue to be remarkably elusive and confusing. Is women's studies about becoming feminist? (But wouldn't this be a matter of personal politics?) Is it an academic discipline like sociology or the study of literature? (But where does one find departments of women's studies?) Or is women's studies primarily engaged in outreach and advocacy on women's issues? (But aren't these the concern of NGOs or perhaps the state?) Indeed, whom is women's studies for? Rather than answer these questions directly, this introduction will examine how these and other questions have been part and parcel of the very making of women's studies.

Where should one begin? Thanks to the kinds of mammoth investigations undertaken by women's studies scholars themselves, we have records of women's writings going as far back as 600 BCE (Tharu and Lalita 1991, 1993). More commonly, public debates about women and their status take us to the nineteenth century. This was the century of social reform, a process led overwhelmingly by men, although some women gained access to the public sphere by the time that century closed. The language of rights and equality is first heard in the early decades of the twentieth century, as were terms like feminism, whether claimed or repudiated by women themselves. Thus, for instance, Sarojini Naidu, equally famous for her political activism, oratory and lyrical poetry, addressed the All India Women's Conference as their President in 1930, where she also explicitly said that she was no feminist. (In her view, feminism implied an admission of women's inferiority compared to men, which she contested.) In 1950, the ratification of the Constitution of India made equality between men and women a fundamental right. Our story, however, begins somewhat later.

The history of the nation after independence is just beginning to be written—its institutions and peoples, its political processes, and the ideas and debates that pervaded them all. One such very recent effort, running to 900 pages and released to considerable public acclaim, has a few obligatory pages on the subject of women. The institutions responsible for the first report on the status of women in India (which we will discuss shortly) are incorrectly described, with no mention whatsoever of the national committee that authored it. Instead, a summary report subsequently produced by the Indian Council of Social Science Research (ICSSR) in 1975 has been taken to mean that the ICSSR was the original sponsoring institution. (Indian Council of Social Science Research 1975). Nothing further is heard till the women's movement makes a sudden and isolated appearance towards the end of the book, a good two decades after its emergence: while discussing the declining female–male child sex ratio figures of the 2001 Census, a passing mention is made that 'there was also a vigorous feminist movement' (Guha 2007, 471, 629). Obviously, periods can be opened up in many ways to scrutiny. The perspectives and experiences of those who helped found a critical field like women's studies and the many challenges they and others have since encountered in their journeys into the present offer as interesting a commentary on our recent intellectual and social history as any other seemingly more comprehensive approach.

The first national crisis and the birth of women's studies

A necessary place to start would be the early 1970s. It is now widely acknowledged that the late 60s and early 70s marked the first major turning point in the social and political history of post-independent India. The ethos of legitimacy that accompanied the creation of the new nation state had worn thin in two decades, with growing criticism and public protests, in many places and in several forms. Spiralling urban unemployment, food shortages and drought raised fundamental doubts about the Nehruvian model of planned development and Indira Gandhi's Congress rule. A new level of political engagement became palpable not only with political parties ranging across the ideological spectrum mobilizing support, but because seemingly apolitical groups were taking to the streets. There are accounts, for instance, of how students and housewives in states like Gujarat agitated against rising prices, corruption and hoarding, and even forced the state government to resign. Young people—students, doctors, scientists and many others—left their urban contexts to join groups and struggles in rural areas, such as those of Bhil adivasis in Maharashtra, and militant left-wing peasant organizations in Bihar, Bengal, Andhra Pradesh and Kerala. Gandhian-inspired activism took the form of the first organization of women workers—the Self-Employed Women's Association (SEWA)—in Ahmedabad in 1974. Trade union activism reached an unprecedented peak when an estimated one million railway employees brought the railways to a halt in a nation-wide strike for three weeks in 1974. According to historians of the women's movement, Nandita Gandhi and Nandita Shah, 'It was in these alternative development activities, mass struggles and agitations that middle class and working class women participated in great numbers and with militancy' (19).

This growing economic and political crisis, largely directed against the state, constituted the most visible roots of what, by the early 1980s, became a democratic upsurge on several fronts, including a women's movement in its own right. Other processes, however, were also set in motion in the early 1970s, that were less well known, but equally significant for understanding the emergence of women's studies and its complex relationship to the women's movement and to the state. In 1971 the Government of India set up a Committee on the Status of Women in India (CSWI) by a resolution of the Ministry of Education and Social Welfare. Members of this committee were given the task of putting together a comprehensive review of the rights and status of women, with a special focus on education and employment, against the backdrop of the constitutional, legal and administrative provisions available. The aim was to provide recommendations 'which would enable women to play their full and proper role in the building up of the nation'. The CSWI had no idea that the document they were to prepare was meant to represent India at the United Nations international women's year gathering in Mexico scheduled for 1975. (In fact, the initial directive and several reminders by the UN to the Indian government might never have yielded anything significant, but for the active intervention of Phulrenu Guha, minister of social welfare.)

As academics, social workers, policy makers and parliamentarians who were squarely the beneficiaries of national development, the results of their researches into the social, legal, educational, economic, and political status of women came as a major shock to the committee members. For the report entitled *Towards Equality* showed that—with the important exception of middle class women's entry into education, which had expanded enormously after independence—the condition of the vast majority of women had been deteriorating since the 1950s, often at an accelerated pace. Whether it be the first discovery of a declining sex ratio, women's exclusion from the processes of capitalism and modernization, the status of legislative reforms amongst different communities, or the tiny numbers of successful contestants in state and national elections—the picture that emerged was grim. No severer indictment of the state and its claims of progress for the new nation and its citizens could have been anticipated.

The very experience of undertaking this study led to a deeper questioning among some of the members of the committee. How had their belief in the constitutional guarantees of gender equality and the very education they had received rendered processes of women's marginalization invisible in the first place? As member-secretary of the CSWI, when political scientist Vina Mazumdar recounted the effects of those years for herself, it was not personal experiences of gender discrimination, or even a particular affinity for feminism, but rather the unrest she felt about the roles being played by university teachers and researchers that exerted the strongest influence in her life.

The earliest impetus for setting up women's studies in the Indian context therefore came from a generation of social scientists who became more critically aware of their own location within higher education. Recall that these were the early 1970s, years of growing radicalization, with women participating in a range of struggles, but (with a few exceptions that we will discuss in the opening section of this volume) not yet a time when women's issues had gained public recognition and a space of their own. This means that the first explicit naming of women's studies, which took place in 1974 in a women's university, *preceded* the onset of a fresh phase in the women's movement in India. Neera Desai, a sociologist in the SNDT Women's University in Bombay, recalls the identity crisis she experienced as someone carrying forward the by now uncontroversial legacy of social reform—the education of women. In the context of her growing dissatisfaction with the university's ambivalent approach to modernizing courses, while fostering a conservative upper caste vision of women's domestic role, the disturbing findings of the *Towards Equality* report provided the push for realizing that women's lives themselves, especially those of poor rural women, needed recognition and transformation. In order to achieve this, a research unit of women's studies came to be established in 1974. A fundamental shift was thus inaugurated—from women as subjects to be educated to 'women' as new subjects of investigation and study. 'A theoretical view of systemic women's subordination was not yet on the horizon, but women's studies was already being identified as an instrument of change' (Krishnaraj 2004, 87).

Barely had the CSWI report been published and the first fledgling university-based research centre set up, when the larger climate of social upheaval and political unrest was met with the declaration of a state of Emergency in 1975 by the Congress government under Indira Gandhi, who had been touted as India's first woman prime minister. Democratic rights were suspended, and scores of people, including many women, imprisoned without trial. Others were forced to go underground and carry on their resistance under vastly altered circumstances. The irony of the situation should not be lost on us—while one arm of the state exhibited its repressive powers in no uncertain manner, the other allowed *Towards Equality* to make its way to the United Nations international meet, with all its negative findings in place.

Equally telling of the complicated relationship between women's studies and the state was the first institutional response by a government body to the challenges thrown up by the report. The ICSSR, the country's apex research body established in 1969, began a sponsored programme on women's studies in 1975, with a broad mandate that included the generation and analysis of data to uncover significant trends in women's position, the development of new perspectives in the social sciences and the revival of the debate on the women's question (ICSSR 1977a, 1977b). As Vina Mazumdar tells this story,

> The ICSSR's research programme in Women's Studies was conceived as a counterpoint to the declaration of National Emergency in June 1975. The late Prof. J.P. Naik, then Member-Secretary of the ICSSR, called me back from leave within a few days after the Emergency had been declared . . . 'Let us concentrate on women. I do not think the political implications of such research will be immediately understood by the powers that be. I am doubtful if we shall be permitted to do anything else. (1990, 5)

The multi-pronged programmatic framework set by the ICSSR clearly demonstrated the significance of women's studies—not confined to the collection of data, but openly making a claim on the social sciences and for political engagement. And yet, as Rekha Pappu has observed, an implicit assumption lurks in the above account, whereby, 'women's studies was regarded as an *alibi* for political activity. What was it about women's studies that made it political and yet safe? Why was it non-threatening in ways that other areas of study wouldn't have been? Was it only the newness of the field that made it acceptable?' (2002, 224). While the situation of the Emergency brought these contradictions into sharper relief, the subject of women continues to invite a variety of responses. A common view at the time was to approach women's issues as quintessentially *social* problems, harking back perhaps to the era of social reform itself, and to conceptions of the low status of women, which tend to engender attitudes of upliftment rather than critique.

Women's studies and the women's movement

These ambivalent frameworks notwithstanding, there is no gainsaying the uniqueness of the origins of this 'women's studies movement', as many have called it. After the lifting of the Emergency in 1977, these significant beginnings were able to join other forces, especially a burgeoning women's movement, as more and more groups sprang up, bringing new issues into public debate as struggles intensified. The first section in this volume provides some examples of the 1970s period of synergy between women's studies and a newly emerging women's movement. After its publication, the *Towards Equality* report—hardly a document destined to gather dust in government departments—galvanized many feminists and activists and was hailed as a founding text for the movement itself. On their part, the authors of the report later came to recognize some of the limitations and absences in their own understanding and in the terms of reference set for them by the government. (See Vina Mazumdar's contribution in the opening section.) Above all else, both the movement and women's studies shared a common driving force—that of inaugurating a change of vision compared to the past, whether this be past struggles, earlier perspectives on women or the dominant orientations of academic research.

Thus, Nandita Gandhi and Nandita Shah described the emerging phase of the movement as being 'also concerned with violence against women, although not with the earlier issues of sati and ill-treatment of widows, but with rape and wife battering; with marriage, but not widow or child marriages, rather divorce, maintenance and child custody; with legislative reform, not the enactment of more laws but in amendments and with the implementation of the existing ones; with education, not merely spreading educational facilities but attacking sexist and stereotyped textbooks, with equality, not only equal rights, but equal opportunities to work and with equal pay' (1992, 21). New perspectives and issues were therefore constantly in focus. The situation was not very different in early reviews of women's studies.

Vina Mazumdar and Kumud Sharma produced the first discussion on the scope of women's studies in 1979, "Women's Studies: New Perspectives and Challenges". Questioning the large-scale neglect of women in the social sciences against the backdrop of the history of social reform, the political mobilization of women during the nationalist struggle and the constitutional guarantees of equality, they drew attention to the range of work just coming out, especially studies that challenged older theses on the role of 'tradition' or 'culture' to account for women's low status. Instead, they called out for more studies on women's participation in agriculture, in the urban informal sector, the effects of modernization, women's declining political representation, the nature of contemporary socialization processes, and so on, to argue strongly for a 're-examination of conventional theories and strategies for women's development' and a recognition of 'the complexity and the magnitude of problems of women and development' (16). In their introduction to the first textbook on women's studies, Neera Desai and Maithreyi Krishnaraj did not pull their punches in indicting the elite bias of earlier research, whether through scriptural studies that 'glamourised' the position of women in early Indian history, or in PhD theses that worried over the 'role conflict' of the modern middle class working woman, (a prominent sociology topic of the 1960s, we are told) (1987, 7).

Already in 1980 women's organizations came together for the first national conference on a perspective for the women's movement in India, held in Bombay. In the following year the same city hosted the first national conference on women's studies, which evoked a similarly overwhelming response from almost four hundred delegates. On the one hand, the contrasts are evident—the women's movement conference was the culmination of a coalition of groups, organizations and individuals, spearheaded by the autonomous Bombay-based Forum against Rape, who wished to take forward the nationwide protests sparked off by the publicity surrounding a police rape, the Mathura case. The women's studies conference was hosted by the SNDT Women's University, with broad-based support from a range of government institutions, ministries and various agencies, to 'initiate the long overdue process of incorporation of women's experiences and women's roles in academic studies' (National Conference 1981, 3). Where the movement conference concentrated on organizational issues and on chalking out an agenda to combat violence, the deliberations of the women's studies meeting emphasized agendas of research and the critique of syllabi.

On the other hand, it is very important to recognize degrees of overlap if not convergence. Many of the papers in the movement conference could have been presented at the other venue or vice versa, and indeed, some of them were. A major paper at the movement conference "On Socialist-feminist Organizations and the Women's Movement" (included in this reader in the section on politics) might have been a discussion paper in the women's studies sub-theme on the role of organizations and institutions. A presentation on the revival of sati in Rajasthan in the women's studies sub-theme on women and the law could have been part of the strategizing on issues of violence at the women's movement meeting. Pioneering papers on women and health were presented at both venues.

The interesting issue here is therefore how we ought to think about the relationship between women's studies, the women's movement and questions of education. One must keep in mind that major participants and leaders in both were college and university teachers, students and researchers. Moreover, subsequent women's studies conferences were hardly ivory tower affairs, and took on themes that reflected on and sought to intervene in the most urgent issues of the day. We have seen the extent to which even state bodies were compelled to take notice. In other words, all accounts suggest that women's studies enjoyed some degree of state support and a close connection to a vibrant movement. The more difficult and elusive part of the history of women's studies lies elsewhere—in trying to assess the impact of women's studies on the system of higher education itself. The agenda set at the first women's studies conference could not have been more unambiguous: Women's studies was a critical perspective, not a discipline, least of all a special topic, requiring articulation in every discipline, institution, in all studies and at all levels. This was an extraordinarily ambitious mandate, proof of the confidence and energy of the moment, where visions were totalizing in scope. No less than the chairperson of the University Grants Commission, Madhuri Shah, who inaugurated the conference, referred to separate women's studies programmes and courses as a 'temptation'. 'The ideal state would be reached when women's concerns, perceptions and problems have been so internalized by different disciplines at different levels of the educational process, that there will be no need for promoting women's studies separately' (National Conference 1981, 10). The dominant mood was one that voiced the idea of setting up autonomous centres or degrees in women's studies as a move to be opposed, however tempting it might appear to some.

Here, then, is an answer to some of the questions raised at the very beginning of this introduction. The identity of women's studies has been so confusing to many in the Indian context because it was not envisaged as a separate field of study but addressed to the academic community as a whole. Unlike in other parts of the world, notably the United States, where women's studies was emerging as a powerful autonomous force in higher education due to feminist pressure, we come across no one here who was interested in setting up departments of women's studies. The demand was for intervention into and transformation of education, and the place from which to undertake this was higher education. It is only with the benefit of hindsight that we can detect some of the contradictions this position entailed.

There are few signs that these problems were sufficiently apparent at the time. For one thing, women's studies found its first institutional home in centres such as SNDT or in the ICSSR, followed by others such as the Institute of Social Studies Trust (1980), the Centre for Women's Development Studies (1980) and the Anveshi Research Centre for Women's Studies (1985). It is not accidental—being in some cases a deliberate choice—that these were primarily if not exclusively *research* centres, set apart from the everyday life and structures of university and college departments. Research itself was often envisaged as a form of outreach, linking a politically aware class of women and men within higher education to the lives and realities of women outside. The belief and hope was that research and activism would become increasingly connected, whether through influencing state policy, or in relation to the women's movement. The 1980s period of growth of women's studies was thus fuelled by this widely expressed need for new knowledge about women, articulated by everyone concerned—the state, international bodies, academics and activists. While differences emerged over what kinds of perspectives and scholarship were required, one comes across no voices of dissent regarding the general mandate and scope of women's studies.

Women's studies and education

We now come to the more intractable aspects of the development of women's studies, namely its impact on the educational system. The 1981 women's studies conference had already undertaken a review of syllabi and courses being offered in a number of universities across the country. It was widely agreed that the absence of women in most of these courses contributed strongly to an unquestioning attitude and an acceptance of gender subordination in society. Any effort to change ways of thinking therefore required changing what was being taught. Senior-level bureaucrats, administrators and a number of university vice chancellors were amongst those present, with the UGC chairperson also playing a proactive role. In 1983 Madhuri Shah sent out letters to all universities to incorporate women's studies in their research, teaching and extension activities. Going by the extremely unsatisfactory response, Shah commented that 'the universities had not applied their minds to the issues of restructuring of courses or curriculum development as a part of taking note of the new knowledge. Only a broad based movement to develop women's studies within the general educational system could initiate a process to prevent future injustice in the context of the marginal position of women in education' (cited in Desai, Mazumdar et al 2004, 63). Further meetings ensued, culminating in lobbying with the Ministry of Education itself. By 1986, when the new National Policy of Education was finalized, the document not only referred to education for women's equality and empowerment, but specifically mentioned the role of women's studies in achieving this. (See the reading from the NPE document in the section on education in this volume.)

At the level of the very highest bodies of the state therefore—the University Grants Commission and the Ministry of Education—it was possible to make a difference. Existing accounts have emphasized the lack of political will to make universities treat women's studies with greater seriousness. And yet, how exactly was the problem envisaged? Where was the 'broad based movement to develop women's studies within the general educational system' that Madhuri Shah spoke of at the time? It is here that we must pay closer attention to the priorities that came to dominate the women's movement and indeed, women's studies itself, in the years that followed. We also have to ask ourselves whether the nature of the challenge before women's studies was sufficiently appreciated.

Strange as it might seem at first glance, education was *not* a priority in the 1980s, and this was true for the women's movement and among many of those who were effectively contributing to women's studies. In a tone of disappointment and regret, Neera Desai has recently reflected on this situation, commenting on the absence of questions of education in the women's movement (in contrast to the pre-independence period), as well as in the major women's studies conferences hosted by the Indian Association of Women's Studies (IAWS), established in 1982: 'Varied issues have been taken up so far including health, communalism, culture, environment, survival strategies, public policies, globalisation and many other aspects of women's lives ... [but] the patterns of education, trends in the spread of education, structural features or state policy on education have hardly been questioned or made main themes of conferences' (2002, 34) The agendas set at the first women's studies conference notwithstanding, powerful currents of political engagement and new social movements, including the women's movement, were drawing people out of their institutional locations into battles over civil rights, critiques of the law, development policies, the role of the state, and so on. The list of challenges only kept growing. For activists in the women's movement in particular, organizational issues and engagement with the law were prominent—education was not throwing up major problems nor was it seen as a site of radical change.

We have already seen how women's studies began its career with a strong focus on new research. Less noticeable was that the emphasis on research did not require a direct confrontation with institutional and disciplinary structures. After all, the main activity of universities and colleges was (and is) teaching, a dimension which remained marginal within women's studies till the 1990s, (a matter we shall come to later). In any event, the earliest efforts in curriculum development emphasized the need for new materials, thus effectively placing emphasis on the need for more research. In retrospect, this is how education could recede from view. On its part, research constituted a new form of action, whether in the hands of well-established scholars, young teachers, or activists outside academic structures altogether. To give some instances from the early 1980s, EIWIG (Economists Interested in Women's Issues Group) came together as a network following up on the sub-theme on development at the women's studies conference. One of their first products was a collection of essays *The Tyranny of the Household: Investigative Essays on Women's Work.* (See the essay in the section on family and household in this volume.) Their stated aim was to be an intradisciplinary forum using economic and statistical techniques for highlighting gender-based inequality, especially for state bodies like the Planning Commission. Coming from a different academic location, an interdisciplinary seminar on women and culture hosted by Indraprastha College for Women in Delhi in 1981 hoped to shed light on the 'tenacity' of culture in history, given the problems thrown up by the women's movement and the lack of understanding compared to the 'more quantifiable areas of economic status, health facilities, education and the like' (Sangari and Vaid 1985, 24–25). In the city of Hyderabad, a major project of the women's organization Stree Shakti Sanghatana was to broaden and question existing accounts of the Telengana People's Struggle (1946–51) through recovering the voices and experiences of its marginalized women members. Making its first political impact in Telugu, the volume of interviews became available to English readers some years later. (See the excerpt on Pramila Tai in the section on history.) The Centre for Women's Development Studies (CWDS), established in 1980, deliberately chose to focus on rural women and use the tools of action-research to disprove common explanations of such women's 'backward consciousness' and 'passivity'. Rather, the role of intermeshing institutions in rendering these women's rights inoperative and the lack of knowledge about possible options became the bases for generating new insights (CWDS 1986, 14). These are but scattered examples to illustrate the multiple streams of new research and writing on women that characterized the early 1980s, developing in many more directions in the years that followed.

It is this kind of work—disciplinary, interdisciplinary and often transdisciplinary—that effectively constituted women's studies, whether the term 'women's studies' was explicitly claimed or not. We should now be in a better position to recognize the diffuse nature of women's studies, as scholars and activists responded to a range of issues and from many locations. Moreover, we can also begin to appreciate that the mandate not to develop into a separate field often worked *against* the inter- and anti-disciplinary modes of inquiry employed by women's studies. It was not obvious how women's studies was meant to transform existing structures of higher education, when, as we know, the university system is not just organized around discrete disciplines, but is also deeply hierarchical across disciplines, with the sciences at the top, economics further down, and the lower rungs of the ladder occupied by the other social sciences and humanities. While much of the new writing on women was effectively made possible by raiding the academy, this was hardly a reciprocal relationship. Disciplines were not about to give up their boundaries, indeed, were usually less rather than more open to change. Many of these issues came to the fore in a seminar conducted by CWDS in 2001: "Engendering Disciplines, Disciplining Gender?" (see John et al 2001). And yet, certainly by the 1990s, something had moved. Women and gender concerns could now be found within development debates, the history of colonial India was significantly 'recast' (Sangari and Vaid 1989; Krishnamurthy 1989), mainstream sociologists felt compelled to react to the presence of feminism in their midst (Beteille 1995; Gupta 1995), and in the case of literature, critiques of its foundations produced a crisis in the discipline itself (Joshi 1991; Sunder Rajan 1992; Tharu 1997).

The 1990s: Marking a new conjuncture

How, then, should we look upon the struggles and achievements since then? There are several reasons why an overview is not possible, and not only because we do not have enough critical distance. First of all, the extraordinary spread in the field defies any assessment—the pieces in this reader are the veritable tip of the iceberg. In the early 1980s, the women's studies centre at SNDT brought out some of the first publications in women's studies and by the movement. Feminist publishing houses like Kali for Women, and some journals subsequently took the plunge—while *Manushi* grew directly out of the women's movement as early as 1979, the *Economic and Political Weekly* began biannual special issues on women's studies in 1985, and the in-house publication of the CWDS *Samya Shakti* transmogrified into the *Indian Journal of Gender Studies* in the 1990s. Today there is no publisher that does not bring out books under 'Gender'.

More importantly, though, a series of processes with their beginnings in the 1980s, but whose effects became palpable to most only in the 1990s, have changed the face of the nation, shifting the very ground on which we thought we stood. In 1990, the government sought to implement the Mandal Commission Report on reservations for the Other Backward Classes (OBCs) in government services and higher education. The decision was greeted with massive protests including immolations by students, forcing the closure of several universities and colleges in north India for a year. In 1991, a new economic policy was announced under pressure from the International Monetary Fund and the World Bank, which envisaged dismantling the era of development planning in favour of 'irreversible' processes of liberalization, globalization and privatization of the economy. In December 1992, the demolition of the Babri Mosque at Ayodhya, followed by unprecedented communal riots in several cities, provided the most violent public demonstration of the political ideology of Hindutva. The point is not that these and other unanticipated developments, including regional movements, sprang from nowhere. For the women's movement, in particular, the first critical encounter with communalism took place around the Shah Bano case in 1986. (See the section on religion and communalism in this volume.) Rather, it is the conjunctural effect of all these processes and events in the 1990s that created a rupture with the nationalism of the Nehruvian era, *including the frameworks of the 1970s within which women's studies first emerged*. Since the 1990s, secularism, state welfare and socialism, caste, sexuality and the nation are all in the process of being rethought (and this is not an exhaustive list), thus changing the terms of prior debates and strategies. *Even more pertinent is that all these developments have gradually brought education back onto the agenda of social movements, compared to its relatively marginal role before.* I do not think that the significance of this has been sufficiently appreciated, whether by those specifically concerned with women's studies or, indeed, by the much larger number of intellectuals and activists engaged in progressive social and political change. The battles over Scheduled Caste and OBC reservations, the erosion of state support for the so-called social sector, and, indeed, the discovery by the Hindu Right that not just elite institutions, but schooling and the mundane production of textbooks are critical for securing ideological consent, have—each in their own way—turned the field of education into sites of struggle.

Whether fortuitous or not, it is in this transformed context that women's studies has effectively come of age. We have frequently focused on its founding mandate to be a critical perspective and not a discipline. In practice, women's studies developed in countless ways, less in any concerted effort to create a new paradigm or transform institutions, than to respond—however unevenly—to issues thrown up by the movement and to understand the conditions of women's marginalization in myriad spheres. In 1986, ongoing pressure on the UGC produced the first institutional results. Centres of women's studies were to be established in select universities, to function as 'catalytic agents' through a range of activities—research, extension and teaching. Beginning with four centres (in the universities of Kerala, Punjab, Delhi and the Banaras Hindu University), the number had expanded to twenty-two by 1997, and has burgeoned into sixty-six barely a decade later, with the promise of many more to come. Women's studies cells were also established in a few undergraduate women's colleges in Delhi. Meanwhile, university teachers taught some of the first courses on women in the form of optional papers, such as in the departments of sociology in Delhi University, Bombay and Jawaharlal Nehru universities in the 1980s, and through an interdisciplinary paper on the social construction of gender at the University of Hyderabad in the early 1990s.

Institutionally, these developments have led to a significantly new moment in the evolution of women's studies. The establishment of UGC-supported women's studies centres was seen as the culmination of a 'long struggle for legitimacy' by founding figures like Vina Mazumdar and Neera Desai. Through the 1990s, the guidelines for these centres were periodically revised in an effort to provide them with some flexibility and stability, while reiterating the mandate of women's studies' interventionary role within education. At the same time—and this is surely not unconnected to the new economic order and its reduced vision of higher education—the UGC women's studies scheme came to be formally identified with non-formal education in a climate of ongoing uncertainty and financial fragility, with the most meagre of resources at its disposal. One such centre began its life in a converted cycle shed, another found itself suddenly ejected from the department that first welcomed it. The incredible spate of growth in the number of these centres coupled with their real marginality has created a situation today where the future of women's studies as a whole can be conflated with their particular struggles. Perhaps unintentionally, a recent volume of essays on women's studies consists of eleven case studies of UGC centres, three studies of centres outside the university, with just three accounts of individual scholars and no discussion of the university system itself (Jain and Rajput 2003). Even more telling is that both the foreword by the UGC chairperson and the introduction to the book refer in passing to women's studies as a 'discipline'. What, then, of the original mandate? Have we come full circle?

I think not. It would be truer to say that the current moment is forcing unresolved issues and differences into the open. Claims of women's studies being a discipline should be seen for what they are—as demands for recognition. More importantly, three decades down the line, the battle lines have shifted—whatever be its location, women's studies is now involved in problems of institutional *reproduction* as distinct from its inception. The 1970s and 80s were a period of expansion in higher education, as departments added to their faculty, new universities were established and research centres consolidated themselves. Institutions of higher education could assume ongoing state support. Unlike the already established disciplines, therefore, women's studies is coming of age at a moment today when state support of higher education is in some jeopardy—at least where the less 'marketable' social sciences and humanities are concerned—and certainly cannot be taken for granted. The growth of a project culture increasingly dependent on foreign funding, where issues like 'gender mainstreaming' are emanating from NGOs rather than universities, is also shaping the present.

Equally significant for this new moment is that teaching is moving out of the margins. Interestingly, questions regarding the nature and scope of women's studies that could be left unresolved when research was the primary objective, must be confronted when pedagogy and course structures are at issue. In the last few years the subject matter of women's studies has entered the system of higher education in a number of universities and colleges through the introduction of optional papers, foundation courses, as a component of a general course, and even through the introduction of degrees in women's studies. It is here that differences are most apparent—while some university departments have created spaces for special papers or sections within compulsory courses, a few women's studies centres have found themselves pushing for full-fledged degrees, both in response to student demand and in an effective bid to carve out their own futures. These initiatives are still in their early stages, and there is no telling in advance as to what actually gets taught under the rubric of women, gender or women's studies. Some recent reviews from western and southern India point to the need for much wider debate on issues of curriculum development and feminist pedagogy (Rege 2006; S. Anandhi and Swaminathan 2007). Many of us, both teachers and students, can indeed vouch for the fact that the women's studies classroom can be very different from a conventional disciplinary space (Uberoi 1989; Chaudhuri 2002; Niranjana 1997), yet questions of pedagogy remain least examined in our context. A critical stage has clearly been reached, with all its attendant possibilities and dangers.

Why this book?

This reader on women's studies is a direct response to the current conjuncture and the challenges we are faced with. Spanning the 1970s to the present, the essays brought together offer a series of glimpses into what can perhaps best be called a problem field—that is to say, a field composed of issues and problems—rather than a discipline. Without making any claims to comprehensiveness, this volume nonetheless hopes to open up significant issues in the many arenas of thought and action that scholars, teachers and activists have defined for us. The modules or sub-themes chosen are, once again, not exhaustive, but indicative of the complexity of the field, which simply cannot be fitted neatly into disciplines or sub-disciplines. While the first sub-theme is introductory, the others—politics, history, development, violence, law, education, health, household and family, caste and tribe, communalism and religion, sexualities, literature and the media—are loosely thematic, though not in any discrete sense, since they are deeply enmeshed in one another. The articles themselves span the gamut of research essays, commentaries, documents and even manifestos, while their authors can be identified in several ways—by discipline (history, economics, literature), by organization or institution (autonomous women's group, NGO, political party, trade union, research centre), by profession (as writers, lawyers, journalists, doctors), or simply as part of the women's movement. Some pieces have been anthologized elsewhere, others have not been published before. Taken together, they demonstrate not just how vast the field has become, but also how contested it continues to be.

The challenges ahead

This anthology bears witness to the diverse pulls and pressures that are constitutive of women's studies as a site of research, action and teaching today. By virtue of its location within the academy (and in other kinds of institutions), women's studies is *both* a critical and a normative force. Its marginal location (whether within a discipline or in a centre of its own), however difficult to live with, is also a vantage point of the utmost value. We must never lose sight of the founding idea that women's studies be interventionary in character, which translates into an ongoing negotiation with existing systems of knowledge production, however problematic or even hostile they might appear. There are no short cuts in the kinds of struggles a feminist historian, literary critic or political scientist may have to wage, even as degrees of acceptance or moments of recognition may differ.

This also means that women's studies has frequently been trapped between false options, as though having some degree of autonomy in a quasi disciplinary mode and being a perspective across disciplines were inherently contradictory, requiring resolution in either/or terms. Rather, the future development of the field will depend more than ever before on inhabiting multiple institutional sites and building links between them. At the same time, we need some space of our own to further develop critical vocabularies, theories and methodologies. There have been too few full-fledged engagements with notions of feminism, gender and patriarchy (as a starting list), and too easy an alignment with 'women' as a simple category, requiring no further elucidation.

Much has been said about the marginal location of women's studies. However, from its inception right up to the present, there has been too little engagement with the uniqueness of its formation. What other examples can one offer where an openly political and non-neutral field was provided a place within the educational system? The trajectories of Marxism and labour studies, for instance, were interestingly different. New areas such as Dalit or minority studies are only just emerging. Does this mean that women's studies has been favoured in some way? Many would disagree. Some years ago, for instance, an unofficial draft of a fresh set of guidelines for the Tenth Plan (2002–07) for UGC women's studies centres revealed that the centres were to be renamed as 'women and family studies centres'. The overall tenor of the guidelines was even more problematic—increasing centralization and control by state agencies was being sought in the name of a 'convergence' of activities with state institutions. Theoretical and academic endeavour was devalued, as women's studies was asked to take a more 'practical' approach to improving the status of women in the country. Letters of protest were immediately drafted to the chairperson of the UGC, and the IAWS was particularly active in raising questions in the media (IAWS 2003; Bagchi 2003).

These are real dangers. In this case they were successfully fought and the guidelines swiftly withdrawn. Evocations of an embattled status, however, do not diminish the existence of margins within women's studies itself and the need to acknowledge them more fully. The communalization of society, heightened caste cleavages and the ravages of globalization are not just subjects of study, they structure the very world of education that women's studies is embedded in. In this situation, it is not fortuitous that women's studies is effectively located at the very apex of the system of higher education with English as our effective means of communication. The fact that right-wing forces stole the march on us several years ago by identifying education as a site for waging ideological battles only means that we have little time to lose. We live in difficult times, when cynicism, fatigue, and defensiveness loom large. Renewal will only happen when 'invisible' women and men, girls and boys, on our margins have a greater stake in what we do.

This volume provides a window on the many journeys undertaken, none of them finished. As we can see, there was never a 'golden age' for women's studies—its very beginnings surrounded by a sense of crisis, and the absence of a history to build on. Many more generations are part of the struggle today; new issues are being raised. Not all of them have even found a place in this collection—consider questions of men and masculinities, amongst others. More than ever before, then, it is our readiness to be a force of critique, to raise questions where answers are not forthcoming, that will take these unfinished journeys forward.

References

Agarwal, Bina. 1994. *A field of one's own: Women and land rights in India.* Cambridge: Cambridge University Press.

Arya, Sadhana, Jinee Lokaneeta and Nivedita Menon, ed. 2001. *Feminist Politics: Struggles and Issues.* (In Hindi.) New Delhi: Hindi Medium Implementation Board.

Bagchi, Jasodhara. 2003. "Letter to the editor: women and family studies." *Economic and Political Weekly*, 38, 46.

Beteille, Andre. 1995. "Feminism and academia: Changes in theory and practice." *Indian Journal of Gender Studies* 2, 1: 111–113.

Centre for Women's Development Studies. 1986. *Six years and forward.* New Delhi: CWDS.

Chatterjee, Partha, ed. 2002. *Social science research capacity in South Asia.* New York: Social Science Research Council.

Chaudhuri, Maitrayee, 2002. Learning through teaching the sociology of gender. *Indian Journal of Gender Studies* 9, 2: 245–61.

Desai, Neera. 2002. Reflecting back, forging ahead: Issues before women's studies. In *Between tradition, counter-tradition and heresy: Essays in honour of Vina Mazumdar*, ed., Lotika Sarkar, Kumud Sharma and Leela Kasturi. New Delhi: Rainbow Publishers.

Desai, Neera and Maithreyi Krishnaraj. 1987. *Women and society in India.* Bombay: Ajanta.

Desai, Neera and Vibhuti Patel. 1989. *Critical review of researches in women's studies, 1975–88.* Bombay: SNDT University.

Desai, Neera and Vina Mazumdar, 2003. From women's education to women's studies: A long drawn struggle for legitimacy and influence. In *Narratives from the women's studies family*, ed., Devaki Jain and Pam Rajput. New Delhi: Sage, 44–77.

Gandhi, Nandita and Nandita Shah. 1992. *The issues at stake: Theory and practice in the women's movement in India.* New Delhi: Kali for Women.

Government of India. 1974. *Towards Equality.* New Delhi.

Government of India. 1986. *National Policy of Education.* New Delhi.

Guha, Ramachandra. 2007. *India after Gandhi: The history of the world's largest democracy.* New Delhi: Picador.

Gupta, Dipankar. 1995. Feminification of theory. *Economic and Political Weekly* 30, 12: 617–20.

Indian Association of Women's Studies. 2003. Newsletter of August 2003.

Indian Council of Social Science Research. 1977a. *Programme of women's studies.* New Delhi: Indian Council of Social Science Research.

——. 1977b. *Critical issues on the status of women: Suggested priorities for action.* New Delhi: Indian Council of Social Science Research.

Jain, Devaki and Nirmala Banerjee, ed. 1985. *The tyranny of the household: Essays on women and work.* New Delhi: Shakti.

Jain, Devaki and Pam Rajput, ed. 2003. *Narratives from the women's studies family.* New Delhi: Sage.

John, Mary E., Smita Tewari Jassal and Vasanthi Raman. May 2001. Seminar on women's studies: A report. *The Book Review* 26, no. 5: May, 14–15.

Joshi, Svati, ed. 1991. *Rethinking English: Essays in literature, language, history.* New Delhi: Trianka.

Krishnamurthy, J., ed. 1989. *Women, work and survival in colonial India.* Delhi: Oxford University Press.

Krishnaraj, Maithreyi. 2003. Blazing a quarter century trail: Research centre for women's studies, SNDT University. In *Narratives from the women's studies family,* eds., Devaki Jain and Pam Rajput. New Delhi: Sage, 81–114.

Kumar, Radha. 1993. *A history of doing: An illustrated account of women's movements and feminism in India, 1800–1990.* New Delhi: Kali for Women.

Mazumdar, Vina and Kumud Sharma. 1979. Women's studies: New perspectives and challenges. *Economic and Political Weekly* 14, 3, 113–20.

Mazumdar, Vina. 1990. Women's studies in India. In *Women's studies in the emergent Indian scenario,* ed. Bharati Ray. Calcutta: Calcutta University, 4–9.

National Conference on Women's Studies. 1981. *Report of the first national conference on women's studies, 20–24 April 1981.* Bombay: SNDT University.

Niranjana, Tejaswini 1997. Questions for cultural politics. In *Subject to change: Teaching literature in the nineties,* ed. Susie Tharu. Hyderabad: Orient Longman, 125–33.

Pappu, Rekha. 2002. Constituting a field: Women's studies in higher education. *Indian Journal of Gender Studies* 9, 2: 221–34.

Rege, Sharmila, ed. 2006. *Sociology of gender.* New Delhi: Sage.

S. Anandhi and Padmini Swaminathan. 2007. Making it relevant: Mapping the meaning of women's studies in Tamil Nadu. Working paper no. 198, Madras Institute of Development Studies, Chennai.

Sangari, Kumkum and Sudesh Vaid, ed. 1985. *Women and culture.* Bombay: Research Unit for Women's Studies, SNDT University.

Sangari, Kumkum and Sudesh Vaid, ed. 1989. *Recasting women: Essays on colonial India.* New Delhi: Kali for Women.

Stree Shakti Sanghatana. 1989. *We were making history: Life stories of women in the Telangana people's struggle.* New Delhi: Kali for Women.

Sunder Rajan, Rajeswari, ed. 1992. *The lie of the land: English literary studies in India.* New Delhi: Oxford University Press.

Tharu, Susie and K. Lalita, ed. 1991 and 1993. *Women writing in India: 600 B.C. to the present.* 2 volumes. New Delhi: Oxford University Press.

Tharu, Susie, ed. 1997. *Subject to change: English literary studies in the nineties.* Hyderabad: Orient Longman.

Uberoi, Patricia. 1989. Some reflections on the teaching of sociology of gender. *Samya Shakti* 4 & 5: 279–89.

1

≈

NEW BEGINNINGS

The first cluster of essays in this anthology depicts the range of influences—whether 'grass-roots' or state-initiated, academic or activist—that found expression and transformed the face of post-independence India during the 1970s. They address the questions: What kinds of struggles characterized the rebirth of the women's movement in the course of the 1970s? What were the institutional processes involved? As we saw, the explicit idea of 'women's studies' was first articulated within a women's university in 1974 in response to the new times: the rise of numerous social and political struggles in urban and rural locations across the country, a growing international feminist movement, and, most importantly, the findings of the *Towards Equality* report.

We begin this section with the reflections of Neera Desai, who became the director of the first women's studies centre at the SNDT Women's University in Bombay in 1974. In this excerpt, she is particularly concerned to explain the decline in the women's movement after independence, and its subsequent re-emergence as a fresh political force in the 1970s and 80s. In her view, both the enormous legitimacy enjoyed by the newly formed nation state in carrying forward the promises of the nationalist movement, and the perceptible advantages that most women from the major pre-independence women's organizations experienced as members of a growing middle class, provide clues. By gaining access to new educational opportunities, even appearing to straddle the demands of family and public life better than western women, Desai speculates that these women did not find it necessary to raise women's issues. It therefore required the crises of widespread unrest, spiralling prices and the imposition of a State of Emergency in 1975 to shatter complacency and create the conditions for new perspectives to emerge.

The shocking and unexpected findings of worsening trends on many counts that came to light in the report *Towards Equality* published for the United Nations year of women in 1975 contributed in no small measure towards disturbing the complacency alluded to by Neera Desai. The report was hailed by both women's studies and the women's movement. The excerpt reproduced here has been taken from a collective review commemorating twenty years of *Towards Equality*. On this occasion, and with the benefit of hindsight, Vina Mazumdar questions some of its shortcomings, both in the terms of reference set by the government and in their own approaches. Issues of violence, many aspects of women's health, and the politics of diversity, for instance, were not on the horizon when the report was conceptualized.

Central to the political moment of the 1970s was the radicalization of a younger generation of women, particularly as students and teachers, though in the early years very few women's groups existed. K. Lalita provides an account of one of the exceptions, the Progressive Organisation of Women (POW) in Hyderabad, formed in 1974. Spearheaded by a small number of women students with close links to left political groups, she describes how they came to experience the need for a separate women's organization. The forms of their campaigns and the issues they took up—against dowry, 'eve-teasing' (as the daily sexual harassment faced by women on city roads and buses used to be called), and especially their protests against obscenity in films—came, she says, 'as a bolt from the blue' to many residents of the city. Spreading from the state capital to nearby towns, the POW suffered a decisive blow with the declaration of the Emergency.

The next essay by Madhu Kishwar and Ruth Vanita takes us to Delhi after the lifting of the Emergency and to the first campaigns against dowry murders in 1979. The sudden death due to burning of young wives had hitherto been viewed as accidents or put down to suicide. That these could be murders as a culmination of dowry harassment from in-laws only came to light as the result of the report of a women's group and subsequently became a rallying point for urban-based organizations in many places. Feminist intervention resulted in far-reaching media attention and fundamental changes in investigative procedures, medico-legal documentation and the law. In this account published in the inaugural issue of the journal *Manushi*, the writers vividly contrast effective demonstrations in local colonies which attracted wider public participation, with counter-experiences of campaigns that never materialized due to the extreme hostility they encountered, especially from women. Already at this inaugural stage, therefore, the authors record the divisions and conflicts among women that challenge easy conceptions of collective struggle or a common identity.

While POW and the dowry campaigns were urban based, the Chhatr Sangharsh Yuva Vahini, inspired by Jayaprakash Narayan's call to 'total revolution', offers an example of political mobilization in rural areas. The excerpt from Manimala's account of the birth of the organization in 1977 and their subsequent work among landless labourers in Bodhgaya district of Bihar is also testimony of women activists' ability to give direction within a larger organization. It took several years of struggle to be able to articulate women's rights to land in a context of male landlessness and dispossession, and it was only because of the active and even angry demands raised by the local women themselves that their claims could be partially realized. Of the many unresolved issues they subsequently faced, one is worth highlighting— when Manimala asked these women who would subsequently inherit their land, they replied that it would go to their daughters-in-law, not their daughters.

When thinking about the beginnings of women's studies, it is tempting to concentrate solely on the efforts of women, whether as activists or in the academy. The final essay by Asok Mitra on the deteriorating sex ratio (the ratio of the number of women compared to men in a given population) is an important example of the contributions made by male social scientists in discovering patterns of gender discrimination during this formative period. It was in the late 1960s and 70s that demographers like Pravin Visaria and Asok Mitra first noticed the long-term secular decline in the sex ratio using census data. In this essay Asok Mitra shows clearly why arguments like the under-counting of women cannot be sustained, and why questions of active discrimination against girls and women not only have an answer in demographic evidence but must be adequately explained.

Whether written in the thick of struggle or in the mode of a retrospective assessment, each of these essays is a window onto the 1970s. Further essays in this volume will reveal how foundational these beginnings turned out to be, as the interface between the women's movement and women's studies deepened. Twenty years after *Towards Equality*, it was possible for someone like Vina Mazumdar to critique the understanding they possessed in the early 1970s. This would become equally true of most, if not all, of the issues introduced here. Subsequent events and scholarship have led to new debates, fresh insights as well as rethinking. Thus, for instance, the 1950s and 60s are no longer thought of as the 'silent period' in the women's movement, as new scholarship on the fall-out of the partition of the subcontinent, the workings of the Hindu Code Bill and other issues come to light. Madhu Kishwar, for one, has changed her position on the anti-dowry agitation in a series of articles in *Manushi*, while others hold on to the need to oppose its alarming spread. Further developments since the 1970s are also producing revised perspectives on the declining sex ratio. Today it is the role of new technologies in selectively eliminating the female foetus that has taken centre stage, while women are beginning to outlive men at the other end of the life cycle.

Pointing to such changes by no means diminishes the significance of the 1970s, but demonstrates the political challenges involved in negotiating women's issues as activists and scholars, which are never closed or settled once and for all. The themes in this volume attempt to show how much has been achieved and yet how much remains to be done.

≈

FROM ACCOMMODATION TO ARTICULATION: WOMEN'S MOVEMENT IN INDIA
Neera Desai

Introduction

[. . .] A disturbing aspect of the social situation in India is the slow erosion of concern for women's issues [after independence]. In the decades preceding the attainment of national independence, prior to 1947, there was an outstanding record of women's participation in political struggle and through it of articulating their rights. Particularly until the early seventies, there has practically been no concerted action towards achieving the goal of equality. How is this inaction to be explained? Why have the women leaders chosen to accept and acquiesce? Has their prevailing mood any linkages with the nature of development?

Women's movement in post-independence India: Accommodation and passivity

The dawn of independence in 1947 generated a great deal of hope and optimism in the people. Now that the enemy was driven out of the country, the Indian people could dream of prosperity and justice. Free India adopted a constitution which recognized equality of both the sexes. In the field of economic development, India opted for a mixed economy, with a great emphasis on rapid industrialization. It was also visualized during this period that prosperity in one sector, or one class, would gradually spread to all others. The early fifties saw the enactment of several legislations which established formal equality and removed social disabilities. Some women, who had taken an active part in the freedom struggle, were elected or nominated to legislative bodies, or occupied other positions of power and social esteem. In short, the immediate impact of political freedom was the generation of hope and confidence among women regarding their future. There was no need, it was felt by many, of an active women's movement to press their demands.

Another important factor which affected the contours of the women's movement was the emergence of new India as a welfare state. As a part of the policy of establishing a democratic welfare society, in 1953 the government established a Central Social Welfare Board with a nation-wide programme for grants-in-aid for certain specific activities. Many of the prominent women social workers were associated with this organization either at the Centre or in the states. Several voluntary organizations and women's associations began to rely on the grants received from the Board. As a result they lost some of their spirit and vigour of the pre-independence phase and the nature of their activities was shaped by the programmes for which grants were available. Women's development was thought to be confined to education, social welfare, and health by the Planning Commission. The main thrust was on the expansion of girls' education, rural welfare services, and condensed courses for adult women. The Health services for women mainly concentrated on the provision of services for maternal and child welfare, health education, nutrition, and family planning. Besides, in every plan the proportionate allocation for social services was declining, and this was the sector which was subjected to heavy cuts in times of crisis. As mentioned by the Committee on the Status of Women (1974, 308), 'The order of priorities upto the Fourth Plan has been education, then health, and lastly other aspects of welfare because it was generally assumed that all other programmes will benefit women indirectly, if not directly.' The continual absence of concern for increasing the earning power of women has given women's economic needs a low priority value. This approach of the ruling group had its impact on the activities of women's organizations. They considered women as beneficiaries of economic development and not as active participants in it. Hence women's organizations during this period, of nearly a quarter of a century, ran literacy classes, adult education centres and nursery schools, and aided nutrition programmes for pre-school children. As for the economic improvement of women, the organizers of these institutions felt that giving them some sort of training in crafts was enough. Hence many of them ran tailoring, embroidery, and other classes. Having sewing machines in a women's organization was considered a great achievement.

These trends, as well as the nature of economic development which took place in India, gave the best pay-off to urban middle and upper class women. Since the leadership of the women's movement in the pre-independence period was primarily in the hands of these classes, the implications of their advantaged position, in terms of the development of the women's movement, were very serious. Another factor which had serious implications for the development of the women's movement was planning based on a mixed economy, which helped the tertiary sector in the earlier period. The increasing entry of women in higher education, and the pressure of a rising standard of living within the middle class, raised their entry into the employment market.

The upper and middle classes were the beneficiaries both of higher education and new employment opportunities. The academic and medical professions which were most liberal in accommodating an increasing number of qualified women within their ranks, helped to strengthen the illusion of a rapid improvement in women's conditions and the achievement of equality by them. Many of these women were happy that they were successfully playing a dual role, unlike their western counterparts. Of course, they had relations and inexpensive domestic help. Several of them suffered the strains of the dual role but not always the conflict, because many a time they were getting the best of both the worlds. On the one hand they were able to work and feel satisfied that they were 'using' their education, and on the other hand they were able also to accord a high priority to the needs of the family.

In short, the operation of these politico-economic factors after independence generated a complacency in the minds of women of this class and they easily adjusted to the traditional value of accepting a subordinate role in the family. These were the women who had earlier articulated the demands for equality. When they accepted the path of acquiescence and complacency, the women's movement experienced a setback. Being the beneficiaries of development, these women not only did not lead any movement but, on the contrary, gloried in the traditional subordinate role under the guise of 'India's Cultural Tradition'. The various findings about the deteriorating condition of women notwithstanding, even today they are not ready to accept that there is any need for concerted action around women's issues. They feel that they are better off than their western sisters because their marriage tie is not as fragile as in the West and family feeling is stronger in Indian society. Hence some of these women, who continue to hold high positions in women's organizations, do not recognize the need even for consciousness raising. Further, they believe that there is no discrimination in employment and they are also convinced that most women work not out of necessity but to get some extra money. They do not take any lead in pressing for legislation to improve the working conditions of women or even for starting day care centres. In fact, their sensitivity to the injustice suffered by lower class women is so blunted that they are not ready to even raise a mild protest against the atrocities suffered by the latter. This elite leadership has its counterpart in the academic world as well. Many studies undertaken on middle class working women or on the status of women have been blind to the real situation.

End of acquiescence?

The passivity or accommodation to the new situation, referred to above, lasted till the seventies. The stagnation of the economy after the sixties, the growing agrarian unrest in states like Tamil Nadu, Maharashtra, Kerala, Andhra Pradesh and the rapid rise in the prices of necessities, led to a growth of interest in some of the left parties to take up issues centering round women. Women's Organizations such as Shramik Mahila Sangathana (The Working Women's Organization) took up the issues of rising prices of essential goods, adulteration, and empty hearths. The Anti-Price Rise Movement in 1973 was a united front organization of women belonging to CPI(M), Socialist Party, Congress, and even non-political middle class housewives.

The economic hardships of the rural masses have also drawn the attention of some political parties. While pressing for better working conditions for peasant women, issues like wife beating, alcoholism, dowry, and sexual harassment from upper castes were also given attention.

The publication of the Report of the Committee on the Status of Women, on the eve of the International Women's Year, drew attention to some of the alarming facts with regard to employment, political participation and health status of Indian women. The International Women's Year and the Decade provided opportunities for analyzing Indian women's real status.

Many of the studies have shown that the adoption of modern farming methods, new cropping patterns, and new technology have affected female labour adversely. The commercialization of markets and the increasing role of capital and wholesale dealers in trade have virtually eliminated the traditional role of women in trade and commerce. The modernization of the fishing industry and the large scale organization of dairying are instances in point. The displacement of female labour through the introduction of new technology as in the case of handweaving in the textile industry, indicates that the labour market, as it is operating, is not neutral between men and women.

Besides these setbacks, one of the most depressing phenomena in evidence is that of more and more women working in the unorganized sector, where they are being forced to accept lower wages. Nirmala Banerjee has described succinctly how entrepreneurs, in order to reduce their cost of production, resort to a sort of 'putting out' system, thus making women workers suffer in terms of wages, working conditions and inhuman existence.

Women are finding it harder to get jobs than men in every discipline among the higher educated.

In short, during the last decade some currents have been generated which have drawn the attention of some of the sensitive sections of the society to the suffering of women and efforts have started, though not in a systematic manner, to organize women against their economic, social, and personal oppression.

The major shift in the women's movement which is nascently developing is that the leadership is now being slowly transferred to young college-educated women, and the problems of women of lower middle class and weaker sections are becoming the concern of this group. The increasing number of cases of wife beating and wife burning over dowry, and atrocities against the 'untouchable' (Harijan) and tribal women, have induced some of these groups to organize women for a struggle. As a consequence, various groups with radical perspectives have emerged. Though they are not very stable, many of them take up a militant socialist feminist perspective, and do not restrict their activities to economic and political issues but also take up social issues like dowry and rape.

Conclusion

In the post-independence period, the development strategy initially benefited middle and upper class women, who, being beneficiaries, did not assume the leadership of a strong women's movement. In fact, they appeared to have blinkers with regard to women's problems. The limited changes that had taken place looked significant, if not unbelievable. Things, it appeared, had started to move. The realization that it was a false start came later.

The problem is now viewed in a new perspective. Our development strategy has conferred little benefit on women. The emergence of a women's liberation movement in the West has encouraged some sections of women in India to fight for equality and justice. Myths with regard to the high status of Indian women are being exploded and protests are being raised against the use of woman as a sex symbol. Of course, this trend is still not very powerful, but the failures in the field of economic development are likely to draw women into the movement in increasing numbers.

～

THE MAKING OF A FOUNDING TEXT
Vina Mazumdar

Background note

The Committee on the Status of Women in India (CSWI) was constituted by a resolution of the ministry of education and social welfare, Government of India on 22 September 1971 with Dr. Phulrenu Guha, then union minister for social welfare as chairperson. The committee was set up to review the changes in Indian women's status that were expected to result from constitutional equality, governmental policies and social reform since independence. Vina Mazumdar, who joined the committee in 1973, was appointed as the new member secretary.

What impact did the committee's findings have on its members and on society? Are the findings the same or different from the issues confronting the women's movement today? What are the issues that were left out by the committee and what were the main questions it sought to ask? To what extent did the committee stick to its terms of reference or were they redefined in the course of its work? What was the committee's conceptual framework?

1994 marked the passage of 20 years since the CSWI submitted its report. On this occasion the Centre for Women's Development Studies (CWDS) in collaboration with the Nehru Memorial Museum and Library organized a one-day meeting to which members of the committee and those associated with the investigations were invited to reflect on the many questions raised by the report, to evaluate its achievements and limitations, and to delineate the tasks that lie ahead for the women's movement.

The meeting sparked off collective reflection and individual recollection, it also captured the tensions and spontaneity as well as the planning that went into the report. Excerpts are presented below: [. . .]

Quite accidentally, the notes I prepared for this meeting begin by saying that the committee's terms of reference were clearly indicative of the loss of the political perspective on the issue of gender equality within the government. One can elaborate on the phrase 'political perspective' by referring to the Gandhian perspective or to the demands of the pre-independence women's movement . . . Despite the reference in the very opening statement of the resolution of the Government of India constituting this committee according to the constitutional provisions relating to the rights and status of women, the word 'political' was completely missing from the terms of reference. Instead the entire emphasis was on social status, education and employment.

Second, there was an assumption in the terms of reference that the problems were primarily in rural areas rather than in urban areas. Today, I have to ask the question, was the *Bharat sarkar* (Government of India) unaware of the escalating problem of dowry? It had enacted the Dowry Prohibition Act in 1961 under pressure from various women's organizations. But having enacted the law, was it completely unaware of how rampant the problem was? Didn't members of parliament as well as administrators suffer due to dowry demands? We may say that they were ignorant—even the committee remained ignorant about the problem of dowry-related violence. We were told about harassment, even physical torture. We heard about young women committing suicide before marriage because they felt they would become burdens on their families who would have to find dowries for their marriages. But we didn't hear about any one murdered for dowry after marriage. So this was something that had not entered our perspective at all.

Third, regarding education, the committee was asked to find out only the factors responsible for the slow progress of women's education in some areas. I am glad that Phulrenu Guha raised the issue of 'illiteracy'. The word 'illiteracy' was missing in the terms of reference. The committee was constituted on 22 September 1971. Provisional figures of the 1971 Census, out in April, reported a female literacy rate of 18.4 per cent as against a rate of 39.8 per cent among males. Even then the problem of illiteracy did not even enter the terms of reference. Many members have referred to the irrelevance of education: I beg to differ. I would use the term 'the content and method of education'. Perhaps we are speaking from hindsight because this is one of the areas in which the women's movement in the post-1975 period has paid a lot of attention. The committee itself can be thanked for this as many of its members came from the field of education, as well as Naik Sahib (J.P. Naik) who headed the task force on education. I would refer to the last paragraph of the chapter on education where we asked why the educational system, which in our opinion is the most powerful socializing force, had failed to meet the challenge of equality, and why it had failed to promote the value of equality. Today, if I were to write that chapter, I would pick up Phulrenudi's point—namely, that rights also mean responsibility. Did our educational system promote a sense of social responsibility?

In the economic and social spheres, the committee was asked to survey only discrimination in employment and remuneration, and the problems of housewives and mothers in further education and employment. You will forgive me if I use a typically Bengali expression, a pet phrase of my deceased *bua* (paternal aunt), who left a deep impression on me: 'The foundation is not there and you are talking about building further structures' (*Atham nai tar thatham ache*). Sakina [Hasan] raised the issue of health. We could not find adequate data. We were not even asked to look at women's health. It is not even mentioned in the terms of reference. The word is missing. Consequently, no task force for health was set up. However, the committee was asked to survey the implications of the population policy and family planning programmes on women's status. Fortunately for us, there was a concluding term of reference which was open-ended. The committee was allowed to suggest any other measures to enable women to play their full and proper role in building the nation. I still wonder who was responsible for making it open-ended. [. . .] When you get this term of reference alongside the rest, there is a disjunction. There is talk about social status, housewife, mother and discrimination, and then suddenly the absence of the word 'political' hits you, after which you come to this term of reference 'how are women to play their full and proper roles in nation-building'. Obviously that term of reference had been drafted by someone with a very different vision.

Last night I was going through our submission letter (produced when submitting the report). I do not remember what we had in mind when we were writing that letter. [. . .] I was quite taken aback last night while looking through our letter to find the statement: 'Any assessment of the status of women cannot be made outside the social framework.' We had indeed based our enquiry keeping in mind the diversity and inequality that prevail in our society. Was it intuitive or mere accident, I wonder? The committee had grasped that there was a difference between diversity and inequality. Over the decades that difference has become increasingly clear. But I am afraid that those of us who became active in the women's movement gave so much priority to fighting the equality issue, (I'm not trying to wish that away—it was necessary) that our neglect of the diversity issue is one of the reasons why we have to listen to the points raised by Sakina today. Why is it that Sakina has to come and tell us today that the status of Muslim women remains so low? Why haven't we taken it up? I am trying to interpret all the mistakes—perhaps our perspective was narrow, perhaps we were over-committed to a one-front cause and neglected other equally major issues as a result.[. . .]

But how things evolve! I have become a convert to the theory that verbal communication plays only a minor role. A great deal of communication takes place through body language, eye-to-eye contact. We were touring Himachal Pradesh. We began in Simla and met large groups of women like us—middle class, educated and urban—and heard the same old story, the same moans and groans. We travelled right across Himachal, stopping at villages for impromptu meetings. In one of these meetings I was sitting on the ground in the midst of women in an effort to make them feel more relaxed when I realized how mistaken I was—these women did not need any assurance. They knew what they had to say and say it they did. They said, 'Ask the Himachal sarkar (government) on whose labour the state economy depends. On the men's? Most of the men are emigrants—either *faujis* (employed in the army) or working in the plains.' A succession of similar meetings gave us the first clue. Sitting in the car driving back we thought: How are we going to define status? Status means different things in different contexts. That was the beginning. Then the committee decided to set up a drafting committee. This drafting committee was to draw up and put before us an approach.

The committee imposed a self-denying ordinance on itself: not to be influenced by any other country reports or any feminist literature and philosophy. Urmila Haksar's pet words used to be, 'We have been given a fact-finding task and fact-finding we are going to do, so that nobody has the chance to accuse us of being biased by external influences.' We were all staunch nationalists so that argument appealed. We also refused to reopen the equality debate, despite Naik sahib's suggestion that we look into questions such as: Does equality mean identity or similarity? Does it mean that women do all the things that men do? After all, men cannot do all the things that women do. We refused to reopen this debate because we adopted a very firm position on the Constitution. [. . .] We did not critically examine the Constitution. We put a lot of emphasis on the Constitution as a deliberate departure from the inherited social, economic and political systems. Today you can say that the committee made its ideological position fairly clear, but (and this is a confession from a person who taught political science for sixteen years), our understanding of political dynamics was appallingly weak.

How did we interpret inequality? We related it first to the variety of social, economic and cultural inequalities inherent in our traditional social structure, making specific references to caste, class and community. Second, we related it to the increasing forces of disparity through structural changes in the economy, and in our discussion we talked about the two-way effect of modernization through education and other processes of social transformation. This understanding of the two-way effect of modernization had come from the committee's understanding of highly differentiated forms of tradition and modernity in roles and opportunity structures. Leela [Dube] provided us with a mass of literature and made us read about things we had never thought of before—kinship systems, descent systems—so that there were no pretensions left that I was knowledgeable about this country. Since modernization had made so little effort to combat either the hierarchy of the Indian social structure or the inequalities inherent and emanating from that structure, the process of sanskritization continued unabated. More concretely, since the message of the Constitution—equality of rights, justice, etc. had not reached those who were expected to benefit the most from these values, social acceptance of constitutional prescriptions remained negative. The few efforts at social engineering which had been initiated by governmental planning (today we can call them efforts at social development) were not only inadequate but also exceedingly half-hearted.

Lastly, with regard to defining status in terms of roles, I must mention that Leela added a sentence to the chapter stating that status is realized through roles. I don't think I understood then—I had to learn so much from so many sources—about law, sociological concepts, social anthropology. But we did write all this in. This is where the committee had run into massive contradictions in the evidence that came to us—between women's roles that were socially perceived, accepted and recognized and the real, actual, varied and multiple roles that women in different classes played. We had the perceptions but we did not have the concepts, the language or the theory to fully articulate these perceptions and what thousands of women across the country were trying to tell us. So we used common-sense explanations. We talked about the invisibility syndrome and explained it by referring to colonialism, the eternal enemy. We referred to the urban, middle class bias of planners and social scientists and identified the state, the intelligentsia, in general, and the educators and analysts, in particular, for their blindness and indifference to the declining conditions of the majority of women. We did use the declining sex ratio as a composite indicator of this broad process of increasing women's subordination or marginalization. But we failed to see that our rejection of the modernization process as an unmixed blessing was also a critique of the dominant development paradigm.

This failure to put the blame and responsibility squarely on the development paradigm, I find unpardonable today. Because it was pointed out to me and I failed to recognize it. After a meeting in Nagaland Lotika [Sarkar] asked, 'What is this development all about? Who is more developed?

Those women we met in the city yesterday or the women in the village? I find the villagers more developed.' Urmila and I agreed but we still did not assess it. On hindsight, perhaps our self-denial ordinance and the refusal to look at the experiences of other countries was not altogether a good one. We were becoming too inward looking and this contributed to our failure to grasp the effect of global forces on the phenomenon we were trying to understand and record. [. . .]

The one definite outcome of those shocks was an acute sense of unrest about the roles we ourselves as teachers, researchers, political and social activists had played. How had we justified our equally privileged roles and status? What had we done with our political rights? For me personally, the question was even more acute. How was I going to face my dead mother who on the day I joined school told me, 'If you allow your thinking and mind to remain confined within the boundaries of me, my husband and my children, the older you grow, the smaller your mind will become. You are getting a chance to be educated, a chance we never had, I see education as a constant process of widening your mental horizons and social concerns.' What answer was I going to give her for having remained so socially unconcerned and so mentally ignorant despite the highfalutin education which she made sure I got? The shame and wonder has increased a thousand-fold by discovering the speed with which poor women associate rights and any kind of power or influence they might acquire with social responsibility.

The Committee on the Status of Women in India did not and could not produce an ideology of its own. It made its position clear but did produce a perspective and a challenge. The women's question in India had to be defined adequately. And this time from the bottom up. This could only be done by reviving, renewing and recreating the movement and reshaping India's history. The question remains, who will take the responsibility? [. . .]

≈

WOMEN IN REVOLT: A HISTORICAL ANALYSIS OF THE PROGRESSIVE ORGANIZATION OF WOMEN IN ANDHRA PRADESH

K. Lalita

Historical context

[. . .] Osmania University of Hyderabad, the capital of the state of Andhra Pradesh, was no exception to the general conditions that prevailed in Indian universities. It was full of corruption, opportunistic politics and violent elements (hired thugs or musclemen used by the politicians). From 1971 onwards, under the leadership of a few individuals, seminars, debates and discussions took place to raise the consciousness of students. This process slowly took shape as an organization which started mobilizing students not only around their own demands, but also on issues such as the price rise of basic commodities. This group was radical, professing scientific socialism as the only solution to all problems.

At the national level, a similar political situation prevailed. There was a massive Railway Strike in July 1974, which almost succeeded in bringing the day-to-day administration of government to a standstill. [. . .] The economic and political crisis made the government unstable and as a result a State of Emergency was proclaimed in 1975. [. . .]

A new women's movement in Andhra Pradesh

Out of this atmosphere of struggle all over the country emerged a group of about six to ten women students of the Osmania University who keenly felt the clash between the traditional values inculcated at home and the progressive ideas they came into contact with at the university. Women who go to college or university encounter society in one of its most sophisticated forms, but their socialization at home, in the family, prepares them for marriage, motherhood and traditional patterns of work at home. For these women, the contrast between their traditional feminine roles, and competitive academic life was felt as extreme and irreconcilable. For instance, they were expected to be at home by 5 o'clock in the evening, and were not allowed to go out alone. Such restraints made them conscious of their real status in society, and the double standards applied to them.

College should be a place for self-development in a woman's life just as much as in a man's. Unfortunately, this is not true for women in India. The early social reformers who advocated education for women had to repeatedly reassure society that this would not be subversive, insisting that an educated wife would be an asset to her home, could bring up her children better, and would serve the family more faithfully. A certain amount of 'freedom' is given to women going to colleges, but this is not independence. This realization of double standards resulted in an initial struggle by these women in their own homes, where they had to counter family standards of women's behaviour. Although the root cause for the origin of the women's movement was the oppression they faced at home, the immediate political context was the radicalism of the student movement in Andhra in the early 1970s, which served to channel and give direction to the movement for women's emancipation. This has parallels with the women's movement in the West which broke out in the late 1960s during the anti-Vietnam war demonstrations and was closely connected with the student movement.

The small group of women students of Osmania University mostly came from upper-middle and middle-class families. They were active in extra-curricular activities such as debates, seminars and discussions and consequently possessed a higher degree of self-confidence than other women students. On the whole, they were very vocal and militant. This group was inspired not only by women's liberation movements all over the world, but also by the radical student struggles in Andhra and they were determined to follow the path of study and struggle: study so that they could understand the nature and causes of oppression better, and struggle so that they could emancipate themselves.

In August 1973, an anti-price rise campaign was led by the Progressive Democratic Students of the University. The group of women we are discussing not only took part in it but actively mobilized some women's colleges for the campaign. This was the first ever public participation of women students in a campaign, which left an impact on both the women and the men. The women felt the necessity of an organization to bring everybody together under one banner for a united struggle. The group continued to conduct regular discussions on general problems, and on national and international political issues, to acquaint women with the conditions of the people in India and the rest of the world. Discussions continued for five months with between forty and fifty women students taking part in these meetings. In December 1973, after a violent clash between reactionary, communal students (belonging to organizations like the Rastriya Swayamsevak Sangh (RSS) and Akhil Bharatiya Vidyarthi Parishad (ABVP)), and the progressives, ten of the latter were unjustly rusticated from the University. Immediately, the issue was taken up by the progressive group and a movement developed all over Telangana (comprising nine districts of Andhra Pradesh) against the rustication of these ten students. This time, again, the women's group cooperated with the students in conducting the campaign, distributing leaflets and holding small meetings, mainly in the women's colleges. On the whole, however, although there was enthusiasm among all the women students, they did not come out in large numbers to participate in demonstrations or processions conducted by the students. The experience gained in this anti-rustication campaign, however, helped the group to think seriously about the prospects for a women's organization.

At the beginning of 1974, for almost two to three months, discussions were held by the activists of the women's group among themselves, and with other progressive organizations of students, writers and others. The principal response of male students was that it was anti-Marxist to have a separate women's organization; that women are not a class by themselves; that only an economic revolution would ultimately and automatically emancipate women, and hence that there was no need for a separate women's organization. By virtue of personal friendship with some of the progressive male students it was easier for some women to convince this particular section of the necessity of a separate women's organization. From the time of the anti-price rise campaign in 1973, there were differences among groups of students belonging to progressive sections as to the methods of organizing support.

At this stage, the women activists sympathized with the Marxist-Leninist groups but did not belong to any particular group, except for one person who was a member of the Marxist-Leninist party. This may be one of the most important reasons for the fact that the group was not so deeply influenced by the left-wing group's thinking.

During discussions the women held among themselves, they felt that first they had to understand the different trends in the women's movements before they would be able to identify with one. The main trends that were recognized by them were: radical feminism, liberal feminism and socialist feminism. Though there was not much information available on this categorization, the group more or less followed a tradition common among left-wing students of finding it necessary to categorize movements. The literature available to the group at that time was Betty Friedan's *Feminine Mystique*, Shulamith Firestone's *Dialectic of Sex*, Germaine Greer's *Female Eunuch* and Simone de Beauvoir's *Second Sex*. Based on this literature, a common understanding of the broad categorization of the feminist movement into liberal, radical and socialist strands was arrived at.

The group felt that those who advocated equal rights for women, not through change but by reforming the capitalist system, could be categorized as 'liberal feminists'. Those who advocated a sexual revolution, making the contradiction between men and women an antagonistic one, could be called 'radical feminists'. The group felt that women's oppression under male domination was very much part of the overall oppressive capitalist and feudal system; hence, a women's movement should be organized as a part of the people's movement against this exploitative system. They concluded that the correct line was that of the 'socialist feminists', which they used to refer to themselves.

Formation of the progressive organization of women (POW)

At a city convention held on 29 September 1974 an organization called the Progressive Organization of Women (POW) was formally established. A formal organizational structure was instituted with office-bearers such as president, vice-president, general secretary and treasurer. POW branch committees were formed at the college level with local students and one of the POW activists. The seminar, editorial, cultural activities and library committees were formed. Realizing the need for involving working women in POW, a *bastee* (slum) Service Committee was also formed. The activists insisted on the need for an autonomous organization. Though they stressed the support they received from their male comrades—the progressive students belonging to Progressive Democratic Students Union (PDSU)—they felt that women as individuals were not taken seriously. But once they were organized and had a united section of women behind them, they would be. They were very clear that they would work together with male comrades but would never merge with them. [. . .]

The activities of POW

The first issue to be taken up by the group of activists in Hyderabad was the dowry system which is prevalent mostly in the middle and upper classes. As the group had its beginnings among middle class women, amongst whom this issue is one of the most salient personal problems, this was not surprising. They felt that this problem, like all social problems, should be seen as having its roots in the exploitative social system. For more than two weeks the POW agitated among students, both men and women, distributing leaflets and going into offices and factories to arouse consciousness on the evils of the dowry system. The leaflets pointed out, through a detailed exposition of dowry problems, the necessity of its abolition for the emancipation of women, and for the emancipation of all oppressed classes and sections of society, linking its abolition to the creation of socialism. In almost all the colleges and offices, protest meetings were held. At a public meeting, over 700 women, mostly college students, turned up. Such a large participation of women had never been witnessed before. This was followed by a unique procession, which marched to the Secretariat, the seat of the state government, with a variety of slogans ranging from 'Dowry Down Down', and 'Jo Dowry Mangega Vo Kunwara Reh Jayega' (those who demand dowry shall remain bachelors), to 'Fight for Socialism'.

This issue brought hundreds of women together and they began to understand what it was to organize on the basis of issues directly affecting themselves.

The anti-dowry campaign was followed soon afterwards by a city convention, when POW was officially formed and given an elaborate organizational structure. The following month of October 1974 witnessed the anti 'eve-teasing' campaign. 'Eve-teasing' is a phrase describing the humiliation and molestation of women on the streets, a common feature in Indian cities. It is sexist, related to a conflict between the 'modern' values of a growing capitalist system and sex-repression in the Indian family. When the secretary of POW was assaulted and humiliated by ruffians belonging to a communal organization with a 'religious' chauvinist slant, the challenge was taken up by the POW. It was the first organization in Andhra Pradesh to fight back against the sexist behaviour of men. POW organized its executive committee meeting, and in just one day mobilized women students for action. The students boycotted classes and attended a mass rally where all forms of feudal oppression were condemned from the platform. Then they marched in an extremely lively procession to the vice chancellor's lodge, contained him in a 'gherao' circle, and demanded strict action against all eve-teasers. Pent-up anger from years of eve-teasing surfaced in the campaign. [. . .]

Around this time there had been a gradual increase of obscenity and pornography in Indian films and advertisements. In January 1975, a militant anti-obscenity campaign was taken up by the POW. 'Women—Revolt Against Slavery'; 'Ban Obscene Literature'; 'Destroy Obscene Posters'; 'Smash Obscene Culture'; 'Struggle for Socialism'; these were some of the slogans ringing in the ears of people in the city area. This campaign came as a bolt from the blue for the public in the city.

Within a week of taking up the issue, three processions were organized, covering the major parts of the city. Obscene film posters were tarred with black paint, cinemas where obscene films were showing were picketed, and some pornographic books were burnt on the roads in front of bookshops. At many places, the women climbed up over high bill-boards and explained the POW perspective in fighting against the exploitation of women as sex objects to the gathered public. On one occasion there was a confrontation with the police, but the women refused to disperse even at the risk of arrest. The public was cooperative and sympathetic and quite a few people walked out of theatres even after buying tickets, to express solidarity with the cause of POW. But there were also those who booed and ridiculed the women in the processions.

For quite some time, a spate of letters from the public in the newspapers had been condemning the movement for being of a western women's liberation type. But there were also many that were appreciative and encouraging. Later, at a public meeting, an extremely lively and responsive audience listened to various speakers who exposed the vulgarity of existing culture and the causes for the degradation of women, pointing the way to emancipation.

The POW also participated in the anti-price-rise movement in February–March 1975, in response to the state-wide call given by the Progressive Democratic Students Union (PDSU) which many organizations and trade unions supported. Propaganda was disseminated on an unprecedented scale in colleges, factories, slums, buses and theatres. But travellers and factory workers were indeed very surprised to find young women asking them to protest and fight against the price-rise.

On 21 and 22 February the POW organized two *'Thali-beating'* processions. Hundreds of women from various slums marched with empty plates and spoons to show their anger against rising prices. 26 February was observed as Black-Day, and all students and employees wore black bands as a protest against inflation, unemployment and corruption. A mass rally was held.

The Progressive Women's Movement did not remain confined to Hyderabad. Hearing about the POW, women from all over the state wanted to start a similar organization in their own towns, at the district and sub-district level. After October 1974 the movement slowly spread all over the Telangana Region. Most of these committees took up the anti-dowry campaign as their first task. In the town of Warangal, (a district headquarters) in January 1975, over 8000 attended a meeting on this theme and 3000 women marched in the procession. What was most striking was the fervour and seriousness with which they took up the women's progressive cause everywhere. In some small towns the women organized POW activities on their own, without help from Hyderabad.

The POW had stressed continuously that there could never be a strong women's movement unless they had a strong base among the labouring classes. As part of a regular programme, the POW extended its activities into the slums. The problems these women faced were those of naked exploitation, working long hours in factories for a pittance, or at home without status or salary, without any maternity leave, without child care facilities, and tied down by patriarchal customs and traditions.

Through work started by the *Bastee* Service Committee, POW succeeded in mobilizing many members in these slums. Regular activities and discussions were conducted. In one area, the POW led various demonstrations and processions, demanding basic facilities. On 26 February 1975, POW led a demonstration to the municipality board to protest against the proposed demolition of huts in an area called Picket. This demand was acceded to and demolition averted. On 21 March 1975, over 600 women marched to the municipality board to demand water, lighting and a sewerage system. In the face of this determined front, promises were made by the authorities. When they remained mere promises, over 150 women of POW 'gheraoed' the executive engineer of the municipality board, who pleaded inability to grant even these minimum facilities. Subsequently, on 12 May, slum dwellers marched in a procession of over 1000 people to the Secretariat to press for their demands. [. . .]

1975 was declared International Women's Year. POW took up the issue of exposing the government's response to this year, which was to hold seminars and conferences, largely attended by the wives of ministers and officials, who were hardly aware of the conditions of the majority of working women, urban and rural. 'Does a single woman prime minister or a few women doctors and lawyers prove that Indian women are liberated? What about those millions of Indian women, illiterate, ignorant and suppressed helplessly by feudal customs and traditions?' These were the major questions raised by the POW members.

While exposing the hypocrisy of the ruling classes which sought to continue their exploitative rule by abusing International Women's Year, POW proclaimed solidarity with its aims. A number of meetings and seminars were organized, explaining why it was necessary to recognize the struggles that were being conducted in the West as well as the East: What was the path to emancipation, and what was the responsibility of Indian women in achieving it?

A campaign was conducted and delegations were sent to the chief minister, but this time the number of women who participated was quite low both because of the general atmosphere of political terror which by that time had become increasingly repressive, and the restrictions imposed on them by their individual college principals.

The emergency and its effects on POW's organization

The crisis in the economic and political sphere in the country led to the proclamation of the State of Emergency in June 1975, when many national leaders and hundreds of others were imprisoned. Curbs were imposed on the press, and the government ordered the censorship of all material published.[. . .]

During the State of Emergency, the activities of the POW were drastically curtailed because of intimidation by the police. The president of POW was arrested in a district town on charges that she was suspected of being involved in anti-social activities. Detained in a police lock-up cell for eighteen days, she was humiliated, beaten up and ill-treated by police officers. Later, she was detained under MISA (Maintenance of Internal Security Act). [. . .] Soon after the president's arrest, POW brought out pamphlets protesting against her arrest and torture and condemning the government for its double standards. On the one hand, it repressed an organization which was devoted to the women's cause and; on the other hand, held seminars and conferences to talk about women's causes. But no action was taken.

At the beginning of 1976, two more POW activists were arrested under MISA. Practically all the activities of the organization came to a halt. With just one issue completed, the organ of POW, *Stree Vimukti*, was stopped and the movements of the organizers and activists of POW were paralyzed. POW almost disintegrated.

By the time the State of Emergency had been declared, 80 per cent of the organizers of POW had become members of the Marxist-Leninist Party. This was one of about twenty-six political parties and groups banned by the government at this time. Anticipating arrests, the main organizers of PDSU, POW and the Marxist-Leninist Party decided that they should try to evade arrest by going underground. [. . .] As a result, the police succeeded in intimidating the general members of POW, and branding the organization itself as the front organization of an underground party. It meant that the organization became illegal at a stage when the majority of POW members did not understand what Marxist-Leninist politics were, nor the 'necessity' of an underground organization. This was a mistake committed by POW organizers, bringing about its rapid disintegration.

Reflections on the POW

From this rich experience of a specific women's movement, which thrived for a short period, lessons should be drawn.

In the initial stages of the movement, by virtue of being the first ever militant women's movement in Andhra Pradesh, the POW had a great impact. People in general, and women in particular, responded in an extremely enthusiastic manner, understood and supported the movement. Campaigns were conducted rapidly in many districts within six months from the time POW started functioning.

One of the reasons for the 'successes' of POW is that many of the issues it took up, such as dowry, eve-teasing, and obscenity, were directly relevant to its middle-class members and sympathizers.

More generally, the women gained the experience of organizing themselves on the basis of their own issues, which gave them a new confidence. This experience of POW also brought a realization to many that they were wrong to believe that an economic revolution would ultimately and automatically emancipate women, and hence, that there was no need for a separate women's organization. When POW was being formed, there was criticism from all sections of the Left that this was a deviation from the main struggle for revolution, and was in imitation of the West. But later the necessity for a separate women's movement was proven. The way POW took up issues which were relevant to the people they mainly worked with, and the way they conducted campaigns rapidly, attracted many people and the movement spread into districts outside the city and even to some other cities of India. This showed that as a separate autonomous women's group, POW was more successful in drawing out masses of women students than mixed student groups were, with the result that some of the other radical student groups were toying with the idea of forming separate women's organizations, apart from POW.

Another success of POW was its effect on the attitudes of many people in progressive organizations, which underwent a gradual change. As one of POW's office-bearers put it, without a group behind it a woman's word would not have carried any weight. The political parties and the male student groups would not have taken women seriously if they had not been constituted as an organized force.

POW lacked enough cadres who were prepared to devote all their time to the organization, and it was not given enough time to consolidate itself. To continue the organizational build-up, the women had to fight constantly against their traditional, orthodox middle class families, which very few of them were prepared to do. Thus, the expanded POW suffered from lack of sufficient full-time cadres who could have maintained the tempo of growth of the organization and its activities after the various campaigns.

Apart from this, the group more or less followed an *issue-oriented approach*, concentrating upon successive spectacular campaigns. It was not really able to concentrate on theoretical work, discussions among members and self-reflection. It could have tried to concentrate and consolidate its work, instead of regularly undertaking campaigns. For instance, after the anti-obscenity campaign, it could have worked consistently with the people, until the government took steps to ban obscene posters, films and advertisements. After the anti eve-teasing campaign, it could have formed into groups to take action against eve-teasers and people who harass and humiliate women. It is true that none of these problems would have been solved unless the exploitative system was destroyed, which is the basis for all forms of oppression. *But to awaken people's consciousness, when the long-term objectives of socialism are so difficult to comprehend*, it is necessary for an organization to fight more consistently for its immediate demands.

Further, POW did not survive long enough to develop a base among the working masses and train cadres from their ranks. Without taking into consideration the preparedness of the women to participate in political struggle, it exposed itself to repression by regularly associating with left-wing student organizations, which gave the repressive agents of state power, the police, an excuse to intimidate the POW members, branding the leadership as leftist. Ultimately, by going underground and becoming 'illegal', the main organizers of POW attracted even more repression after the State of Emergency was introduced. All these factors prematurely evoked state repression when the organization was still too weak to withstand such an assault. This was the reason for its disintegration during and after the State of Emergency.

There is another important point I wish to make here. The POW stated its belief that a women's movement should be 'firmly entrenched in a strong, working-class movement'. But now, with the experience we have gained, it is felt that this position implies either waiting until such a movement evolved, or working towards a similar movement first and putting the women's question aside for the time being. The question which then comes to mind is: *Is there a need for a specific middle class women's movement?* POW has shown that there was a similar need, and that much could be achieved, but due to the Marxist-Leninist orientation of POW, the struggle had to assume a 'proletarian' base, which was sought in the *bastees* or slums. One is left wondering what middle class women can do 'for' slum women (or peasant women) unless they have first broken the sexist and patriarchal fetters which keep them down.

～

INITIATIVES AGAINST DOWRY DEATHS
Madhu Kishwar and Ruth Vanita

Instead of the usual three-line item, the newspapers carried a full report: Tarvinder Kaur, 24, of Model Town, Delhi, had died of burns. While she watched TV on the evening of May 17 [1979], her mother-in-law poured kerosene on her clothes and her sister-in-law set her afire. Inspite of Tarvinder's dying statement to this effect, the police registered a case of suicide. Her father said she had been under constant pressure to get more dowry from her parents so that her husband could expand his motor spare parts business.

Tarvinder's mother cried but not alone. Many women in Delhi cried out with loud voices against the murder of young Tarvinder. On June 1, a large group marched through the streets of the middle class colony where her in-laws lived. It was a mixed group—from students and teachers to working women and housewives of all ages with their children.

Shouting angry slogans—'Punish the murderers of Tarvinder', 'Stop burning brides', 'Women will not put up with any more atrocities', 'Do not give or take dowry'—they marched to the house where Tarvinder was burnt to death. Her in-laws stayed behind closed doors. But as the group approached, an old relative of theirs, seated in the courtyard, read out verses from the Granth Sahib, trying in vain to outshout the demonstrators.

Another relative came out to speak to the press. He said that the husband's family had not demanded more dowry since the girl had brought enough of it. 'She brought everything you can want—a television set, sofas for the drawing room, clothes . . . What do we need more for? We have a flourishing business . . .' He said that a case of murder had been registered (this was not true) and the girl's husband and in-laws had been interrogated by the police. 'What more do these people want?' he asked. 'Do they want their lives?'

What women want was again forcefully brought out on June 12, when a women's organization, *Nari Raksha Samiti,* organized a large procession to Parliament, where a memorandum was presented to the home minister. There were working women, housewives with babes in arms, some burkah-clad women and washerwomen from many miles away. A man came all the way from Punjab to voice his protest. His sister was reportedly burnt to death by her husband just fourteen days after marriage.

The placards read: 'Arrest the killers of women', 'We will never give dowry nor let women burn'. They advocated reform of the marriage system: 'All marriages must be registered', 'Severely punish bigamists', and 'Do not make divorce laws more stringent'.

What was highly significant in both these demonstrations was that they swelled with passers-by and people coming out of their houses to join in. In fact, those who poured in spontaneously far outnumbered those brought by the organizers. At Model Town, people were so eager to read the leaflets headed 'Women are not for Burning', that even after they were all exhausted, the demands kept coming.

This action by women was given wide publicity in the press and on TV. The Delhi State Mahila Federation held a women's public meeting on June 26. A resolution was passed urging the government to make dowry a cognizable offence. Also, if a girl dies within seven years of marriage, a postmortem should be conducted, as is the law in Punjab. When girls are driven to suicide, the cases should be treated as constructive murder.

July dawned with new forms of anti-dowry agitation. A young couple, both from Delhi, Premlata and Vijay Narang, were engaged to be married. At the time of the engagement the boy was given 'advance dowry' (sagan) worth Rs 15,000. This included cash and goods like a TV and a sewing machine. The demands, however, kept growing every day. On May 25, two days before the wedding day, when the girl's relatives went to the boy's house to give the invitation cards for distribution, they were confronted with the demand for a scooter. Says Premlata's uncle: 'We came home and discussed the matter till two o'clock at night. Finally we decided, "If we meet this demand, another will come up—there is no end to it. And such people cannot keep the girl happy."' So the engagement was broken off, but the money was not returned by the Narangs.

Premlata's family had read in the papers about the anti-dowry demonstrations. They approached the *Nari Raksha Samiti* and decided to organize a demonstration outside the boy's house to disgrace him and demand their money back. Usually, when an engagement breaks off, the girl's family try their best to conceal the fact, because they fear that people will suspect the girl's character and it will be difficult to get her married.

The courage of this family was truly remarkable. They brought their women onto the streets to openly proclaim that the engagement had been broken due to the greed of the boy's family, thus for once taking the offensive and shaming the boy. Another significant feature of the protest was its direct anti-dowry tone. Usually, the girl's family dare protest only when the girl has died, and it is the murder, not the dowry in itself, that is condemned.

Premlata's family and their supporters, with the women in the forefront, collected outside Vijay Narang's house at 10.30 a.m. on July 1. Vociferous slogan shouting—'Why did Vijay not marry? For a scooter.' 'Vijay Narang, shame on you', 'Vijay will never get a wife', 'Vijay will never marry', 'Down with dowry', 'Shame on those who demand dowry'—brought neighbours out of their houses to sympathize. Some narrated how the Narangs had already broken off two earlier engagements after taking large sums of money, and thus were running a regular 'business' with their son's eligibility as capital!

The procession marched round the area. Some of the demonstrators suddenly took up the cry 'Collect alms for Vijay's scooter', and two of them began to carry around a cloth as if asking for money, while a third held up the photograph of Vijay and called on spectators to see the 'beggar'. Later, Premlata's uncle said she would get married but there was no question of dowry now. She would be given the clothes and jewels already prepared for her, no more. The only dispiriting part of the affair was the passivity of the girl herself. When asked what her opinion was, the uncle proudly said, 'She is a very homely girl. She never opens her mouth.'

Parents who have despairingly let the deaths of their daughters go uninvestigated, because they knew only too well the callousness of the authorities, or who have been fighting lone battles for months, found a sudden rallying-point when the recent protests took place. They came in contact with each other and felt a certain renewal of hope.

Like Mr Nair with his bag full of xeroxed letters describing his daughter's death, which have been submitted to so many authorities and received no reply. Like Ms Chadha whose life and whose consciousness have been transformed after her daughter's murder—she's now fighting not just her daughter's case, but actively participates in all anti-dowry protests, even bringing her younger girl along with her!

Yet it is other women, other mothers like these, who burn their daughters-in-law. This most disturbing reality was brought to sharp focus when some members of a women's organization went for a demonstration which failed to materialize.

While the family which was being demonstrated against remained behind closed doors, dozens of men, women and children streamed out of neighbouring houses. They were aggressive: 'Why have you come here? Ask us the facts. We know.'

The men sneered: 'What will these interfering busybodies do? They've been hired to come here for five rupees each. The police will pass judgement, not they.' The women swarmed around. They shouted each other down: 'She locked herself in a room and killed herself. What is the use of education when parents don't teach their daughters how to behave in their husband's house? Cursed be such education!'

'But why did she kill herself?'

'How do we know? Nowadays, girls can't put up with the smallest thing—they get into a temper.'

'And how is it no one heard anything?'

One hardfaced old hag raises her hands to the sky: 'God knows where she got such fortitude. She burnt to death without uttering a cry.'

Another advises us: 'Teach your daughters patience. Girls must learn to bear everything patiently.'

A newly married woman grins: 'What is it to do with us? Forget it.' Her friend agrees: 'The one who had to die has died. What's the use of making a noise about it?'

The viciousness on their faces is like something in a nightmare; would seem exaggerated on the stage or screen. The local police arrive—obviously in league with them. And horror of horrors! For once, there is no difference between the brutal expression on the faces of policemen and citizens.

As we walk away, a young housewife smiles menacingly from her doorway: 'So you've come here to fight? Come along, we'll teach you a lesson!' We stare at her, speechless. She waves her hand: 'Go to hell,' and pours out a stream of abuses.

An old man sitting at the doorstep glares at us, folds his hands: 'Go, go, please go.' The whole neighbourhood is out in the street, murder written large on their faces. Concentrated hostility in the air like the heat before the storm. Someone whispers that four dowry deaths have taken place in this locality in the space of a year.

What is it that has turned these women against each other—mother-in-law against daughter-in-law, sister against brother's wife? Is it the fear that the precious male, the son, will turn away and love his wife, leaving his sister helpless, neglecting to pay her dowry? Is it the necessity to extract as much as possible from the daughter-in-law so that the daughters can be married? How does the same mother who is humiliated by her arrogant son-in-law, who trembles for her daughter's happiness in an alien home, find it so easy to tyrannize and torture her son's wife?

As long as we women are divided against ourselves, as long as we see ourselves not as women but as some man's wife or mother, our struggle is hopeless. We are our own destroyers.

We look to men for salvation—we hope for good husbands, brothers who will protect us (however badly they may be treating their own wives).

The woman who has been degraded, beaten, insulted through a whole lifetime takes her revenge on her helpless daughter-in-law—perhaps the first person who is in her power, whom *she* can beat and insult. How can her bitterness be transformed into a constructive protest, a collective rather than a personal anger?

Above all, how can a woman who has never been recognized as a valuable human being learn to value others, how can she who has never known tenderness, feel tender to human life? Why should not she, whose silent screams have gone unheard, turn a deaf ear to the shrieks of the girl burning next door, or in her own kitchen?

She has been made to think of this as 'normal', 'a woman's fate'. Religion, the films, her elders, her own and her mother's experience—all tell her that if a woman is unhappy, nothing can be done about it. It must be her own fault. And she who has been denied happiness and freedom, grudges them to her daughter-in-law, who may be educated, employed, who has access to a world she has never seen. She grudges them even to her own daughter. Most mothers are viciously rigid in denying their daughters the liberty they themselves were not allowed: 'I never had such freedom. Why should you complain?' How can a systematically deadened mind and heart be brought to life?

Our problem is too complex, the task of women's organizations too vast for any simple solution to be put forward. Our agitation to help ourselves realize our predicament, has to be a sustained one and permeate every aspect of women's lives—not remain just sporadic outbursts of anger in issue-to-issue demonstrations. The narrow cultural and social world of women which extends only to the market place, the temple and the Hindi film must be enlarged. We need new instruments of consciousness raising if women are to stop seeing themselves as belonging to various families, to various men, and begin to see other women as sisters—even though not born of the same biological parents.

~

THE BODHGAYA STRUGGLE
Manimala

The year 1974 saw the emergence, in different parts of the country, of people's movements against rising prices, miseducation, unemployment and corruption. Young people who stood outside any party affiliation massively participated in these movements. In the course of this struggle, Jayaprakash Narayan felt the need for a youth organization which would keep away from the politics of power and devote itself to the struggle for a 'total revolution', an organization that would struggle for a complete change in the system. Chhatra Yuva Sangharsh Vahini was born in January 1975, with membership restricted to people under thirty years of age. From 1975 to 1977 it devoted itself to working for the movement's programme and helping build public opinion against the autocratic tendencies of the ruling Congress party.

The principles accepted by Vahini activists as the basis of their political understanding were: 1) Sangharsh Vahini activists will not contest elections; 2) Vahini will work for total revolution by peaceful methods; 3) Vahini activists will live among the landless people of Bodhgaya, will adopt their ways of life, eat the same food as they do, and live as members of their families. [. . .]

Searching for a direction

After the 1977 elections, in which the Congress party was defeated, the Sangharsh Vahini had to decide its long-term strategy for total revolution. In the beginning most of the young people who came into the organization were not dogmatically committed to any particular political doctrine or ideology. Having liberated themselves from the old quarrels and contradictions between different isms, they sought a better way of analyzing the present social system to help them decide on a more effective strategy for the political struggle. On 17 and 18 January 1978, a meeting of the Bihar state committee of the Vahini was organized in Patna city, and was attended by forty-eight men and two women. Even though two out of fifty is a very small number, it was a significant development. Prior to this, even though large numbers of women had been participating in people's struggles, they never played any part in policy-making. It would not be an exaggeration to say that this was the beginning of the search to find ways to make it possible for women to play an active decision-making role in the people's struggles in Bihar in this decade. A special feature of the Vahini has been effective participation of women at every level, even though there were never as many women as men in the Vahini's decision-making bodies.

The main focus of discussion at the Patna meeting was to decide the basic issues of struggle, to identify crucial areas in which the movement must concentrate its activity, and to chalk out a strategy for action. We agreed between us that only those issues with the potential to shake the social system to its roots would be considered basic. Hence the struggle for land was identified as the main issue for the current action programme. The perspective adopted was that those who labour productively on the land should have rights over it.

There was also much debate over the last issue we discussed. Even though we all agreed that the focus of our thinking and action would be on the most oppressed (*antim jan*, the last person), our definition of the most oppressed remained unclear. It was agreed that in our attempt to create a new nucleus for the new organization, we would identify the most oppressed as those who labour but at the same time do not exploit the labour of any other individual or class. According to this thinking, we came to see the landless labourer as the focus of our organization.

This initial discussion gave our actions a certain direction. However, even at this stage some important issues were left out. For example, in the definition of the most oppressed, it was easy to see clearly that we must include those who labour themselves, but it was not as clear how it would be possible to exclude all those who exploit the labour of others. Labour has many forms and so has its exploitation. One kind of productive labour, that performed by both women and men in the fields, is subject to exploitation by the owners of the land. Then there is the labour performed by half of the population—household labour, which is considered unproductive. Women perform this labour and men, even men who labour on the fields of the landlord, exploit this labour of the women. The organization was not sensitive enough to be able to acknowledge the significance of both types of exploitation. During our discussion, we stuck to a very worn out and conventional definition of labour, within which household labour has been given neither any economic nor any social value. We concluded that it was enough to begin with a broad consensus that the focus of our organization would be the landless poor and their struggle for their rights over the land. The issue of women's exploitation was passed over. Since, in creating the organization and deciding on the main issues, we overlooked the specific nature of the exploitation of women, inevitably both the organization and the struggle came to be dominated by men.

It was, however, recognized that in present-day society women are doubly exploited, that they are treated as second-class citizens, and that they will have to struggle to win their basic human rights. In this struggle, the people's movement will need to lend them support. We thought that we could begin the fight with the struggle for land, and then the fight against the many other inequalities in the social, cultural, political and educational realms would ultimately become linked up with the struggle for land rights, leading to a movement for total change. But there was no clarity about how the different forms of inequality involving exploitation were related to one another. Therefore, without any analysis that unified and organized the issues more systematically, the struggle for land became not just the focal point of our efforts, but our total struggle. The other issues usually got taken up or left behind according to the conditions laid down by the struggle for land.

Thus, with limited clarity, but prepared to take the risk of learning from our own experience, the Vahini activists began their struggle in the second week of March 1978. Bodhgaya was chosen as the area to try out our strategy, since 12,000 acres in this area were believed to be under the control of one *math*. We felt that it would be easier to organize the landless labourers in this district because there was only one landowner with whom we could enter into a direct confrontation. In other districts we would have had to deal with landowners of varying categories, and labour conditions might also have differed from one landholding to another. [. . .]

What is just distribution?

By October 1981 the government had identified 1000 acres of land as illegally possessed by the math, and some of this land was redistributed among the landless labourers in Kusha, Munesarpur, Chakla, Jayarampur, Parsawa, Gosai Pesra, Kurmawa, Lebra and other villages. At this time, the Vahini brought out a pamphlet criticizing the government distribution policy. It stated that we would prepare a list of allottees and present it to the government. This list would be legal and just. It was declared that if the government continued distributing land in an unjust manner we would resist by organizing *gherao* of the concerned officials. It also stated that in land distribution 'we will give priority to landless labourers, those without means of subsistence, the disabled, widows, and small peasants'. The Vahini activists accordingly prepared lists in which women, except for widows, were not included. These lists created two categories of those who were eligible to receive land. To be eligible, a man had to be landless or without means of subsistence. But a woman was eligible only if, first, she was married and widowed, and, second, she belonged to a family in which the men were landless. The reality is that most women are landless, even if their husbands own land. This was not recognized; a women's eligibility was made to rest on her relationship to a man, living or dead. Also, the implication of this categorization was that for a man to be without land and for a woman to be without a man, that is, a widow, were identical situations. Some women activists were infuriated when land distribution began on this pattern. Since even when the movement made such a small gain it was completely usurped by men, we wondered what would be the shape of the society which would emerge from this kind of class struggle.

When the issue was raised and discussion started, most of the Vahini activists acknowledged that this kind of distribution was wrong in principle, and that it proved how strong was the hold of male ideology on the movement. However, many *saathis* asked: 'What difference does it make in whose name the land is registered? After all, it is for both husband and wife.' We replied: 'If it doesn't make a difference, then put it down in the woman's name. Why argue over it? And secondly, if it makes no difference who owns the land, then why not let it continue to be owned by the Mahant? Why don't we fight for better wages, about which he had offered to negotiate? Why do we insist on the transference of land ownership from the Mahant to the landless, if it makes no difference in whose name land is registered?' Some *saathis* also argued that raising this question would weaken class organization and unity. To this we replied that equality can only strengthen, not weaken, an organization, but if it does weaken our unity, that will mean that our real commitment is not to equality or justice but to transfer of power, both economic and social, from the hands of one set of men to the hands of another set. Some activists, including some women, also argued that since women marry and go to their in-laws' homes, it is not possible for the land to be in their names. To this we answered that the right of women to land was perhaps the one crucial issue which could simultaneously shake up all the social and economic institutions including the oppressive institution of marriage and the family. If we do not acknowledge the legitimacy of a man–woman relationship founded on inequality, why should we assume that a woman must leave her home and go to her husband's home to provide heirs for his family and continue his line? Perhaps the only way to resolve the dilemma is that the land should not belong to individuals but should be the collective property of all the villagers who toil on it. We felt that to shirk the question of women's right to land would be to shirk the 'total revolution' to which we were committed, and replace it by the desire merely to improve the labourers' life conditions, instead of bringing about vital change in the system as a whole. In practice, however, no systematic attempt was made to collectivize the land.

The village women were discontented by their exclusion. The women of Pesra said: 'We were in the forefront of the fight, carrying our children in our wombs and in our arms. We went to jail and faced the *lathis*, we also did all the housework. But when the land was distributed, we were pushed back, we didn't even come to know by what rules the land was distributed.'

It was also observed that after the land distribution there was a greater imbalance in the relationship between men and women. There were more incidents of drunkenness and beating. In the course of quarrels, men were heard saying: 'Get out of the house, the land is mine now.' All this led women to feel that after such a long struggle to get land, they were left without ground to stand on. Women in almost every village expressed their anger at this injustice, and categorically demanded that land be given in women's names.

Women assert their land rights

In February 1982, the Vahini held its Bihar state conference in Mehsi in East Champaran. There too, the women activists who had come from Bodhgaya criticized this inegalitarian policy and demanded that women be given land in their names. Since it had now been proved that carrying ahead the class struggle without the participation of half the class, the women, was not possible, the human rights of this half had to be conceded. A decision was taken that land would be accepted in women's names wherever redistribution was yet to take place.

There was a great deal of angry debate among the villagers. The women in Pesra said: 'Fine, let the block development officer come here. We will snatch the measuring tape from his hand and measure out the land ourselves.' The men asked: 'How can you cultivate the land on your own? Who will plough it for you?' The women replied: 'Well, who will harvest your crop in that case? We are ready to cultivate the land with hoes instead of ploughs, but we want it in our names.' In Piparghati, the women declared that they would not let the land be distributed at all, if it was to be given to men only.

We then discussed whether land should be given jointly in the names of both husband and wife. Some of us felt that this would tie down the woman completely. She would be unable to leave the man if she wanted to, because leaving him would mean leaving the land. We felt that land should be given in the names of women alone. We said that if we are truly committed to equality, the men should atone for years of domination. So far, whatever little property they had was owned by the men whether it was a hut or livestock. Now, therefore, the first round of land distribution arranged should be in the names of women, just as the reservation policy, for instance, works in favour of harijans and other groups oppressed for centuries. In the next round, land could be given to men so that there would be equality. Though some Vahini activists were not in agreement, most of the villagers, including the men, felt it was fair, and agreed to it.

In Beeja and Piparghati villages, lists giving the names of women and widowers were drawn up. It was rewarding to observe that the men had also realized the importance of this principle and were committed to it. They too felt that what was happening was significant. In Piparghati, however, the district officer refused to distribute land in the names of women, and insisted that a list of men's names be drawn up. His only argument was that the land must be given to the head of the family, and in India the head of the family is the man, not the woman. He also said that women would go away to their in-laws, hence they could not own land. The villagers unanimously refused to take the land in the men's names. The women organized a *gherao* of the officer, and the men, too, agreed that since we are fighting for equality, nothing should be accepted on the basis of inequality. Some of the Vahini activists were perturbed and said that the land should be taken in someone's name so that at least a crop could be raised. But in spite of unemployment and near starvation in this village, none of the people agreed to accept land in the names of men. In villages where women got land, I asked them who would inherit the land. They said they would give it to their daughters-in-law, not to their daughters.

Stalemate continues

Thus, the stalemate with the government continues. In the meantime, internal conflicts broke out in the organization and the village activists decided that from now on they would conduct the struggle on their own. Vahini activists who belong to the area will from now on conduct the struggle but outsider activists should not come to intervene at the local organizational level. One or two Vahini activists were opposed, saying that the village activists are not yet in a position to conduct their own struggle. But who was to decide who was capable or not? Since they feel capable, we must agree. One of the main activists was expelled from Vahini for bungling. Some others have of their own accord gone to work in other areas. The struggle continues with small ups and downs, but it is not as intense now; there has been no new phase. Only 1000 acres of land were distributed, although 3000 had been captured originally. The villagers have not been able to plough the rest of the captured land even though they are not allowing the Math to plough it either. The rest of the property remains with the Math. A total of 26 *kachheris* have been closed down as a result of the economic losses and the pressure caused by the land movement. These *kachheris* are deserted and some of them are falling to pieces. From 1978 to 1981, the Bodhgaya Math has suffered a loss of about two crore rupees. [. . .]

~

IMPLICATIONS OF DECLINING SEX RATIO IN INDIA'S POPULATION

Asok Mitra

The steadily deteriorating ratio over the last one hundred years and particularly since the beginning of the current century of females to males in the Indian population has been the subject of much speculation and investigation. In this discussion, the word sex ratio will be used to denote the number of females per 1000 males of any particular population. When the censuses began in the second half of the last century, the deficit of females was, not without plausibility, attributed to incomplete enumeration in the first few censuses, particularly in the northern and northwestern regions of the country. It must, however, be borne in mind that when the first non-synchronous series of censuses was taken, Bengal (which then included Bihar and Orissa and Bangladesh) showed a ratio of 1001 females to 1000 males, while Mysore showed a ratio of 994 and Madras 990. The Central Province of those times showed a ratio of 965. These were all higher than the accepted probable sex ratio at birth of between 960 and 930. The region of old Uttar Pradesh showed a ratio of 875 while Oudh showed 928 and the Punjab, which then included the whole of modern Punjab, Haryana, Himachal Pradesh, Chandigarh and Pakistan, showed a sex ratio of 835. [. . .]

It can be argued with some confidence that the census undercount of females probably worked itself out in various parts of the country between 1901 and 1921. Nobody has yet argued that the quality of the census count may have deteriorated from 1921 onwards, particularly in respect of females. Such a possibility seems unlikely particularly after the abandonment of the one-night census counts after 1931. The sample post-enumeration checks conducted in 1951, 1961 and 1971 betray little discrimination against the counting of females. The course of decline in sex ratio is not erratic but steady and staircase like. As we shall see, the growth rates and birth and death rates do not throw any serious doubt on the magnitude of reported counts of the sexes. It is, therefore, difficult to attribute the decline to an increasing undercount of females.

On the other hand, *purdah*, which was once held responsible for the undercount of females as well as the shortness of female lives, has steadily diminished in many areas, or at least, has not intensified. There were speculations in the early census reports of a peculiarly high masculinity at birth in India, which have not been borne out by prolonged and searching investigation. The masculinity at birth is still of the order of 104 to 107 male births per 100 female births. There were speculations again on race, climate, season of gestation (the seasonality of births in India favouring the spring and autumn), food (the 'farinaceousness' of Indian meals (excess of starch) presumed to favour masculinity, but no point was made of the lack of protein in the meals of growing and adult females causing deterioration in the health), consanguineous marriages (which oddly enough prevail even today in many of those areas where the sex ratio is above par) and polyandry (which obtains in very limited areas of India). There has been longstanding evidence of female infanticide in the northwestern and Rajputana regions, against which the British government took certain steps, and also among the hill tribes of Orissa. In the past few decades the all-India and state census reports have paid varying emphasis on the following possible causes: (a) female infanticide; (b) greater neglect of females specially at the earlier ages; (c) premature cohabitation and child bearing coupled with unskilled midwifery; (d) hard work for females particularly among lower income groups which constitute the bulk of the nation; and (e) general adverse conditions of climate, nutrition, ventilation, house accommodation and the like.

Table 1 brings out the widening gap between males and females in the last 70 years. From a difference of only 3.4 million in 1901 the excess of males has been steadily and rapidly increasing each year. On the contrary, widening of the gap seems to have dramatically accelerated since 1951. The female death rate which was lower than the male death rate in 1901 overtook the latter substantially in 1911 and has never looked back. What is more, the difference between the female and male death rates reached its highest in 1961 to the extent of 2.9 per thousand. The ratios of sex- and age-specific mortality rates in Table 8, extracted from the All India Age and Life Tables for 1941–50, 1951–60 and 1961–70, will be found very revealing.

This table gives an idea of the extent of neglect that normally attends female babies and young girls from birth to about age 9, and the pace at which this selective neglect has been growing between 1941–50 and 1961–70 compared to male mortality. The normal experience of most countries is that the higher masculinity at birth is rapidly reduced by a higher rate of male mortality at age 0, male infants being naturally more vulnerable than females at that age, and as male and female babies proceed through life, their ratio is quickly adjusted to par. This seems to have been the experience of India, too, in earlier decades, although there may be reason to suspect that earlier actuaries may have been biased in their calculations by the study of age smoothings in European countries. All the same it will be worth recalling the figures of past decades up to age 5 (see Table 3).

Table 3 supplements Table 2 and serves as a foil to the pattern of change that has come about in 1941–1970 against the background of 1881–1930. For example, we find from Table 3 that in the earlier period 1881–1930 the mortality of female babies in each of the ages 0 to 5 was in each decade substantially lower than that of male babies, except for ages 4 to 5 in 1901, where the former was slightly higher. Not so in the later period of 1941–1970 as we see in Table 2. A very substantial change had occurred in the course of 1931–50, for, except for age 0, the mortality of females at each of the ages 1 to 9 was notably higher than that of males for each of the census years in the period 1941–50 to 1961–70. The two streams of mortality rates tend to get even with each other only as late as age 9, but even at this point the female mortality rate suggests an edge over the male rate. In 1951, female mortality at age 15 was notably lower than the male mortality rate at that age but this favourable picture was reversed in no uncertain terms, particularly in 1971. The rate of female mortality between ages 15 and 45 has been higher for every year of life and female mortality emerges as lower than male mortality only as late as age 50 onwards. Even here the 1961 rate of female mortality at age 50 is marginally higher than the male rate.

This is the all-India picture. What is even more distressing is that the southern zone, which has traditionally been fortunate in having had a higher sex ratio over the decades, has been rapidly shedding this advantage and exhibiting higher female mortality particularly since 1931. In other words, the sex differential has improved in favour of males. [. . .]

As matters now stand, it is in the age group 49 and above that women's longevity improves over that of men. What improvements, apart from termination of childbearing, contribute to this phenomenon will have to be investigated. It is possible that women's share in strenuous manual work declines in this age group, while her authority at home and over disposable income improves.

To investigate more fully whether certain socioeconomic behavioural protective mechanisms that operated in the society and the household up to say 1901 have been breaking down since 1901, and whether this break down has accelerated since 1951, it seems desirable to undertake mapping what conditions still prevail in the four southern states of India and two or three states of northeastern India, conditions that still safeguard a favourable sex ratio in those regions but are lacking or disappearing in other states of India. On the other hand, whether the improving record of agricultural productivity in the northwestern states is going to establish an abiding relationship with the recently improving sex ratio in that region. In that region improved agricultural yields and withdrawal of women from field work through upgradation of social status may be (i) conferring more leisure; (ii) more food; (iii) more share in processing work at home, improving the value-added component; (iv) more side business like processing, weaving, knitting, etc., (v) more share in livestock and animal husbandry leading to greater food intake, leisure, and command over disposable income in Rajasthan, Haryana, Punjab as well as in Kerala, Karnataka and even in Gujarat or western Uttar Pradesh.

It looks as though in recent decades the socially and economically productive role of women has been yielding place more and more to their biological reproductive role which in turn is reducing their social and economic value.

Among the areas to be investigated the following deserve attention:

1. The protean effects of the dowry system;
2. The various traditional and modern patterns of distribution or allocation to women of earned and disposable income;
3. On account of growing monetization, whether women are being exposed more and more to discriminating wage competition and losing those areas of employment and sustenance which traditionally had belonged to them and given them status, disposable income, authority and leisure;
4. Whether wage discrimination between men and women is widening through widening of skill and technology gap between men and women in manual and blue collar work, and whether women are being relegated more and more to the worst of heavy manual, low paid jobs requiring longer hours of work than before;
5. Whether men are usurping women's occupations;
6. Whether women's access to disposable income or authority over spending family income is deteriorating over time, whether higher social status is leading to withdrawal from field work and more income by male members is constricting women's share or proportion of income, and whether actual sources of income in family enterprise are being denied to women;
7. Whether increasing urban population, district by district, clustered zone by clustered zone, is leading to deterioration in sex ratio, by exposing more women to insecure, low paid urban jobs;
8. Whether the varying patterns of arduousness in crop cultivation, wheat, rice, maize, millets, etc. have varying patterns of toll on female lives of differential mortality among females both in infancy and in adult age;
9. The relationship between deteriorating sex ratio and educational standards—rural and urban;
10. The relationship between deteriorating sex ratio and social, public health and medical welfare availability and accessibility;
11. The relationship between sex ratio and industrial and occupational distribution of female workers in selected districts of high deterioration;
12. The nature of sex ratio deterioration in districts in which most of the women are in the traditional employment sectors and districts in which a sizeable number of women are in the modern sector. Whether this deterioration has been stemmed in the modern sector.

[. . .]

Table 1: Population of Males and Females 1901–1971 (in 000s)

	Population of males	Population of females	Difference between males and females	Sex ratio F/M	Decade growth rate of male	Decade growth rate of females	Estimated death rates for previous decade per 1000		F/M
							Male	Female	
1901	120911	117485	3426	972	-	-	50.4	49.9	-0.5
1911	128385	123708	4677	964	6.18	5.30	46.6	48.2	+1.6
1921	128546	122775	5771	955	0.13	-0.75	52.8	53.5	+0.7
1931	143055	135922	7133	950	11.29	10.71	35.2	37.7	+2.5
1941	163825	154835	8990	945	14.52	13.91	27.2	29.4	+2.2
1951	185528	175560	9968	946	13.45	13.39	28.8	30.2	+1.4
1961	226293	212942	13351	941	21.97	21.29	20.5	23.4	+2.9
1971	284049	264110	19939	930	25.52	24.03	-	-	-

Compilation: Various Censuses of the Registrar General

Table 2: Ratio and Age Specific Mortality Rate of Males to Age Specific Mortality Rate of Females, All India 1941–50, 1951–60, 1961–70

	1951	1961	1971
0	1.09	1.11	1.04
1	0.76	0.83	0.84
2	0.74	0.83	0.73
3	0.76	0.82	0.76
4	0.80	0.82	0.83
5	0.83	0.81	0.74
6	0.86	0.81	0.73
7	0.89	0.81	0.72
8	0.92	0.27	0.74
9	0.96	0.83	0.81
10	1.00	0.86	0.88
15	1.27	0.94	0.79
20	1.34	0.95	0.72
25	1.05	1.00	0.84
30	0.84	0.63	0.93
35	0.80	0.64	0.91
40	0.83	0.79	0.82
45	0.91	0.92	0.90
50	1.03	0.99	1.03
60	1.15	1.09	1.09
70	1.18	1.17	1.03

Source: Official Life Tables of the Registrar General.

Table 3: Ratio of Age Specific Mortality Rate of Males to Age Specific Mortality Rate of Females at Ages 0 to 5, 1881–1931

	0	1	2	3	4	5
1881	1.17	1.18	1.16	1.14	1.12	1.10
1891	1.14	1.11	1.09	1.06	1.04	1.02
1901	1.10	1.02	1.05	1.06	0.97	1.26
1911	1.02	1.06	1.07	1.07	1.01	1.05
1931	1.07	1.06	1.11	1.15	1.18	1.17

Source: Official Life Tables of the Registrar General.

2

~

POLITICS

Singling out 'politics' as a specific theme within this anthology surely calls for an explanation. After all, doesn't the idea of a distinct political sphere contradict the women's movement's contestation of conventional political boundaries and women's studies' own non-neutral stance? Slogans such as 'the personal is political' derived their power by displacing the focus from the public realm as the only domain of meaningful political action, especially that of the state. On the other hand, a remarkable feature of the Indian situation is that no particular institution or site was privileged when the women's movement and women's studies emerged as public forces: the first national campaign around rape was against custodial rape, involving the criminal assault on women by the police, thus squarely confronting not just the power, but the patriarchal collusions of the state (see Section 5 on Violence and Section 6 on the Law). Dowry and the murders committed in its name were approached both as violence within the family and as the product of modern economic forces; an essential dimension of rural women's security was to demand that they must have rights in land. The list could go on. In this sense, all the themes in this volume, from technical discussions of women's work to the most intimate realms of women's sexuality, are inextricably political, since they all question existing structures of gender and power.

Even more than the other sub-themes in this volume then, this section cannot stand alone. Against the backdrop of the volume as a whole, its specific purpose lies in seeing how the existing field of politics has been explicitly addressed by the women's movement and women's studies. There are illustrative texts on forms of political organization, controversies over women's empowerment, debates on political representation and reflections on feminist internationalism.

The opening contribution in this section is a presentation by Gail Omvedt at the first National Conference of the Women's Movement held in Bombay in 1980. What, she asks, should be the political approach of new women's groups that identify themselves as socialist-feminist? (The Progressive Organisation of Women included in the previous section would be an example.) Omvedt makes a distinction between mass-based grassroots organizations, working full-time in rural and urban areas, closely linked with political parties or other political organizations, and small socialist-feminist middle class groups, who, she feels, have a special role to play in developing a perspective for the women's movement within larger working class struggles. Omvedt's intervention is thus an exploration of how political and ideological connections between feminist and left organizations can be forged, offered at a very early stage of the new women's movement. The contrasting perspective of the next essay, an excerpt from a longer chapter by Nandita Gandhi and Nandita Shah, reflects on the demand for an 'autonomous' women's movement. The call to autonomy among numerous women's groups that emerged in the 1980s was fuelled both by the desire for alternative forms of support to the kind enabled by political parties, and by the belief that such spaces provided common ground to ideologically diverse women. Gandhi and Shah go on to discuss the many challenges these groups faced, from questions of openness and informal membership to democratic functioning and allocation of work. Notice, however, the overlapping concerns in both these discussions— Omvedt is searching for a distinct, if not autonomous, role for socialist-feminists within a wider left-identified struggle, while Gandhi and Shah see autonomous spaces as a platform to bring together otherwise politically differentiated feminists. It is worth emphasizing that—till the rise of Hindutva and the new policies of economic liberalization in the late 1980s and 90s— questions of autonomy, political ideology and party allegiance amongst women's groups were fought out principally in relation to the state and its power, and with left-identified political parties.

The next pair of essays takes on the contested concept of 'empowerment', a term that shot into prominence in the 1990s and is now ubiquitous among a host of institutions claiming to work for women. In its common deployment, empowerment has been used to describe processes whereby relatively powerless groups are able to overcome their subordination and so gain some measure of control over their lives. Narayan Banerjee begins his article by emphasizing the characteristics of third world contexts where the economic and cultural obstacles facing the vast majority of women are simply too immense to expect them to organize on their own. Empowerment, then, implies the necessary presence of an 'external intermediary' for change to be possible. In his essay the two main intermediaries are identified as non-governmental and governmental, and much of the discussion centres on contrasting and conflicting views of their roles and functions. Banerjee also reserves a special place for research, since it was feminists and scholars who criticized existing models of empowerment, and questioned many of the assumptions that were made about the women who were being targeted and organized. While Banerjee nonetheless speaks of empowerment as an enabling process, Manoranjan Mohanty approaches the concept from a different angle. In his view, the concept of empowerment is a questionable term being currently promoted by state governments, at international summits and by growing numbers of NGOs. The contradiction lies in the claims being made to 'empower' people at a time when current policies are fundamentally undemocratic—hence it becomes imperative to uncover some of the disabling meanings that the term carries with it.

Along with the discourses and institutions of empowerment, women's relationships to the state have been simultaneously reoriented since the 1990s with the emphasis on women's political representation and new global discourses of governance. In India this took the enormously significant form of linking the revival of local self-government or decentralization, with a special reservations policy, whereby one-third of all seats in local bodies, whether rural or urban, were reserved for women. With considerable variation across states (for example, Karnataka had already implemented a 25% reservations policy in the 1980s, and Kerala actually devolved major finances to local bodies through the concept of the People's Plan), there is no way of offering an overall perspective on the entry of over one million women into political office across the country since the mid 1990s. The essay included here is taken from a larger study of rural Maharashtra, unique because of the presence of all-women panchayats. In this interview by Sharmila Joshi, readers get a glimpse of the views of Satyabhama 'Nani' Lawand, who became sarpanch of her panchayat in Bitargaon village in 1989. She shares her role as undisputed leader of the panchayat, the new 'knowledges of the world' women thereby acquired, as well as harder problems relating to the different worth of sons and daughters. The questions and responses reflect back 'our' assumptions about gender equality as well as 'Nani's' political journey. The excerpt from an essay by Nivedita Menon introduces readers to the subsequent demand for a similar reservations policy at the state and national levels in order to counter the extremely low presence of women members of legislative assemblies and parliament (MLAs and MPs). The Women's Reservation Bill has been the site of much struggle, debate and opposition, and is yet to be passed. Her discussion brings the wider context of the 1980s and 90s into the picture to show how the different strands in arguments for and against the women's reservation bill cannot be understood purely as a gender issue but are centrally about caste as well.

The final contribution to this sub-theme is by Indu Agnihotri, which offers an account of the last major world conference on women. The 4th UN Conference held in Beijing in 1995 brought together tens of thousands of delegates worldwide in a country whose communist history had hitherto made it relatively 'closed', especially to the West. Agnihotri's account of her experiences at the meeting indicate the extraordinary energy and strong organizational focus that prevailed during the conference, around issues ranging from new economic policies and religious fundamentalism to violence and sexuality, among others. Countering dominant media representations of the event, she records her sense of the contributions and interest taken by the Chinese delegates in particular, who both contributed to the workshops and wished to make the most of the opportunity. Subsequent accounts by Chinese scholars have attested that the Beijing Conference has marked a new phase in their history of women's issues and feminism, and thus offers an interesting counterpoint to our own.

The many questions raised by the contributors in this section are indicative of how activists and scholars have addressed the political field through the realm of the state, organizational and ideological orientations, women's access to power, and local and international political structures. Obviously, this is only a partial list, and there is much more to be said on these and related issues concerning citizenship, rights and politics. Taken together, the essays are also indicative of certain shifts and changes from the 1970s to the present that require more debate and analysis around questions of autonomy, approaches to the state, forms of political mobilization and the relationship of the women's movement to other movements. Compare earlier debates on autonomy and women's organizations with subsequent discussions on the comparative roles of the state and NGOs. Has the demand for autonomy been inherited by the NGO sector? Consider also the general distance amongst women's organizations from the electoral process in the 70s and 80s—even left-oriented groups were discussing their relationships to mass-based forms of mobilization. With full support being given to women's participation in panchayati raj and so much rallying behind the Women's Reservations Bill, what might be the consequences of the greater readiness to wield state power through demands for women's political presence? Subsequent sub-themes will revisit these and related questions of politics, by opening up the domain of history, the frameworks of development, the crisis of communalism and secularism, the politics of the family, caste and tribe, and sexuality.

'SOCIALIST-FEMINIST' ORGANIZATIONS AND THE WOMEN'S MOVEMENT
Gail Omvedt

Introduction

These notes will discuss the question: What is the role of middle-class Marxist 'socialist-feminist' women's liberation organizations in helping build a broad women's movement in India?

Since 1974 there has been an upsurge of women's participation in militant, agricultural labourer, poor peasant and working class agitations as well as broader movements like the anti-price rise movement. This participation has resulted in bringing forward the issue of women's oppression and the need for liberation and the full involvement of women in mass movements. Along with this process, a number of radical women's groups have developed. These latter have the following characteristics:

1. Broadly they differ from the traditional party women's fronts in taking a militant 'socialist-feminist' perspective, that is, they bring forward the oppression of women as a central feature and take a radical liberationist stand on demands for full equality; at the same time they are aware and insist that the women's movement should be guided by a working class (or scientific socialist) perspective and be a part of the movement of all oppressed classes.
2. While they continue to raise economic and political issues, they also differ from traditional women's fronts in seeing 'cultural' issues to be of crucial importance, for instance dowry and marriage issues. They also view 'housework' as a broader economically crucial issue and not simply a trivial matter. There is often a new consciousness about democratic style of work, etc.
3. They are middle class (petty bourgeois) in social composition.
4. They have not been the conscious creation of any political party—though members may be linked to political parties.
5. They have been relatively unstable, temporary.
    Examples: POW (Hyderabad), Purogami Stri Sanghatana (Pune), Stri Mukti Sanghatana (Bombay), Feminist Network (Bombay), Samta (Delhi), Stree Sangarsh (Delhi).

In discussing the role of these organizations, it is important not to 'identify' them with the entire women's movement—they are not grassroots mass organizations, they may not be the central organizations which will help to build a women's movement. At the same time I believe they have a very special and important role to play.

Growth of a women's movement in India

A prior question should be dealt with first: How do we visualize the process of development of a genuine women's liberation movement in India—a movement with a real base among the masses of toiling women?

In Indian conditions, a *spontaneous* growth of women's organizations (outside of a few middle class urban centres) does not take place among the masses of rural and urban working women and working class women. (There are numerous reasons: the lack of productive work and hence economic independence, the associated continuing strength of a feudal type of family structure, etc.) Nevertheless a genuine movement can be organized. It will develop, based on organizations in bastees, factories, villages, through the following process: In connection with an organization that takes up a fight around all the problems of peoples' lives, women can begin to come forward, coming out of their homes to fight perhaps on neighbourhood issues (water facilities, etc.), on social issues such as drunkenness, perhaps in support of a strike, on any number of issues. These may not immediately be 'women's issues' as such and may not at first involve a 'women's liberation' consciousness. But in the process of coming out of their homes, demonstrating and developing their own initiatives and decision-making power, establishing in practice their equal role, the women's consciousness will develop, political consciousness may develop and a grassroots women's organization can be established in which such working class or rural poor women play a leading role. As such genuine mass-based organizations grow, develop in numbers and in strength, there can begin a process of women from such organizations coming together, developing further their political consciousness and women's liberation consciousness, and on this basis a real leadership can develop from among working class, agricultural labourer and poor peasant women themselves. Along with middle class women of the cities and towns, as such organizations develop and come together in demonstrations, conferences, etc., an *organization centre* for a genuine women's liberation movement will be created. It will be a centre that is not imposed from above and consisting of a small number of politically conscious middle class women going out to organize the masses— but a centre that develops out of the democratic self-expression, organization and struggle of the masses of women themselves.

Such a process of developing a centre is *different* from a middle class Marxist organization thinking of itself as a centre and going out to 'build a mass base'. It is also *different* from representatives of party fronts and all other existing organizations coming together and taking themselves as a centre to build up some mass movement.

The process described above of course requires political guidance and leadership. Building up organizations in slums or villages requires continuous, day-to-day work. People who do such work do not do so on an ad hoc basis but under the guidance of a political group (whether this is a party or political organization of another type); they do not work as individuals but in a collective and disciplined way. In the same way, the process of building up and bringing together a genuine women's movement will require leadership (ideally that of a revolutionary party). And in both cases the leadership does not come from a 'women's group' but from a political organization including both men and women. (To put this another way, the *basic* force in building up a women's movement will not be a women's organization, but a revolutionary organization of both men and women. Similarly I think it is incorrect to debate about whether 'working class women' or 'rural women' or whatever are the 'vanguard'—the vanguard in building up a women's movement is the working class. That is, men play a role—and must be brought to recognize this role.)

Now it can be said that those women who are most committed to women's liberation should take as their priority the building up of such organizations based on toiling women. But the question still remains: What can be the role of existing 'socialist-feminist' organizations in such a process? In regard to this question, two basic points should be added: (1) Not every middle class woman who is committed to revolution and women's liberation can work full time, most in fact cannot; at the same time such politically conscious middle class women do have special talents and resources which can aid the process of building a Marxist (working class based) women's liberation perspective before the people: such a perspective will not exist immediately as the 'line' (principles of unity) of the women's organizations (because of their nature and the existing level of consciousness of the participants). (2) Similarly, because ongoing tendencies to male chauvinism do exist, the need for women's liberation and dealing with women's issues on all fronts will have to be fought out—by both men and women—internally within the political parties/groups that are guiding the local organization work.

It has to be added that such organizations are still extremely rare and the process of developing such a genuine women's liberation movement has barely begun. What we see at present are a cluster of socialist-feminist groups on the one hand, and on the other a number of middle class (i.e. bourgeois feminist) organizations and party women's fronts which *mobilize* (rather than organize) women.

The role of socialist-feminist organizations

I believe that socialist-feminist groups should work on the following principles: They should *not* try to 'organize women', they should not aim at being 'organizing centres' or a nucleus of a developing women's movement; they should not try to become themselves mass organizations of women. A natural tendency for women in such organizations is to say: 'We must organize women, we must build up our mass base among working class women,' etc.

I believe this is a mistake. (This is self-criticism since it was also my own view three years ago). It is true that we should go among toiling women—the question is how. It is true that a working class–based, rural poor–based movement must be built. But who will build it and how will it be built? These are different issues. As organizations, middle class socialist-feminist organizations cannot and *should not* try to be organizing centres for such work. Many of their members, as individuals, may be doing part-time or full-time work in slums, etc. But this work will be guided by/directed by the political group responsible (or the political group to which they are committed) and cannot be done under the *authority* of a middle class women's organization, however progressive or revolutionary its ideology may be. Instead, such organizations should be *political organizations* of a particular type, organizations of activists, not mass organizations. Their goal should be to help build up a women's liberation movement linked to the revolutionary struggles of the toiling masses—but their role in that process should be to *present before the masses a political line of women's liberation,* i.e., a line which links women's liberation to the fight for revolution, and to spread this as much as possible among the masses of working women and men, rural women and middle classes, and party and union activists.

This is primarily a task of political propaganda—though this will take a variety of forms, from marches, demonstrations, satyagrahas and gheraos if necessary (which at this stage and in the case of these organizations are important for their *communication* or political propaganda aspect more than immediate direct results), to exhibitions, cultural programmes, writing articles, pamphlets, leaflets, etc.

For example, if such a group prepared a slide show and took it around—to villages, factory areas, slum neighbourhoods, wherever invited, presenting a developed and class-oriented view of women's oppression and women's liberation, this will serve the function of developing consciousness and at the same time provide important help to whatever local group is working and has invited them. The exact results of such a programme (i.e. a one-time visit by the organization with its slide show and women's liberation message) may not be immediately seen and in fact will depend on whatever local group is working, but such a campaign can be of great use. We can also see here the double function of a socialist-feminist group: political propaganda and providing services (aid) to grassroots-based organizations.

Problems of 'political' conflicts often come up when socialist-feminist organizations (or members of such organizations) make mass contact. That is, socialist-feminist organizations contain members of varying Marxist/left perspectives, and unions or other groups who provide mass contacts sometimes have different Marxist/left perspectives. Thus suspicions arise that (a) 'they' do not want to let us have access to people in their unions or organizations, or (b) 'they' are simply 'using' the women's organizations as an excuse for doing their own separate political propaganda, etc. etc. I think that such suspicions/tensions can be eased somewhat if we take the following principles to guide our work: (1) Though people may have varying political perspectives, when working *under* the auspices of a socialist-feminist women's organization, they should put forward only the line agreed on as the line of that organization and not their separate/developed party, political line. (2) There should be a general attitude of support, not criticism, to all left (using 'left' deliberately in a broad sense) organizations, party, trade union, etc. (3) At the same time, members of socialist-feminist organizations who go to different villages, slums, factories, etc. have a *right* to make contact with the toiling women they meet, to maintain those contacts, and if they wish, to return and discuss any kind of political or social issues with these contacts. To put it differently, parties/unions have no inherent right to close off their masses from any broader political discussion—the only thing is that this must not be done under the auspices of women's organization work. (In this case the women's organization will be 'used' only to make contacts; still many parties/ organization may fear that such contacts will result in harm to them and so not invite us for women's political propaganda work—but I think still that there will be countless areas that are open.)

Thus socialist-feminist organizations should take part in both working class movements and broader women's movements (eg. in women's united front activities in which party women's organizations and/or middle class feminist groups also participate), but in doing so they should always maintain their separate identity, always strive to put forward their own political line (in a democratic way, without bureaucratically imposing it), and they should not dissolve their identity in the process of doing such front work. (In fact a primary objection to the theme that such organizations should 'build themselves up as mass organizations' is that when they try to do so under existing conditions they inevitably play down and dissolve their socialist-feminist identity).

Along with such direct political functions, its members and those it mobilizes can also provide *service functions* for those doing grassroots work with women (they can help with cultural programmes, access to the media, aid at times of repression, etc.) and they can mobilize young women who are becoming radicalized, encourage such women to go into direct organizing work with the masses, and even give suggestions for such work (but not direct it).

Such socialist-feminist organizations, then, should be political organizations with a broad agreement around a common political line, generally one of 'socialist-feminist' women's liberation. (What the level of political agreement can be exactly will have to be seen. This can be worked out in the process of drafting a manifesto or whatever. I think there should or will be a general broad agreement about the nature of class society, the need for a revolutionary transformation of that society, the need for overthrowing the old state/society and establishing a new one, the leading role of the working class and rural toiling masses, the need to constantly bring forward and take up women's issues as well as issues of caste and other forms of oppression within the whole process, and so forth. In other words, there can probably be a fairly strong degree of shared political commitment, though of course this is not at the same level as the full political line of a party. There will and should be room for people of different but broadly revolutionary political commitments to work together.) Their goals, then, should be to go among the masses but not to organize them directly, rather to put forward a line of women's liberation, build up a mass consciousness concerning the reasons for women's oppression and the way in which to fight that among vanguard sections of the masses but also as widely as possible, and so to help prepare for the building of a truly revolutionary women's movement.

It can be added that though the work of political propaganda is a limited one (people speak of 'mere propaganda' work!), still there is a burning need for it at this stage. Intensive grassroots organizations will for a long time remain limited to enclaves: there is a need to think of a way to direct and influence the growing turmoil among women at a mass level. Women are being mobilized and are coming out—but only for immediate 'economic' issues and generally by parties and groups which do not put forward a liberationist women's perspective (aside from the issue of whether they put forward a general revolutionary perspective). This by itself is insufficient— that is, such forms of mobilization by themselves will not give birth to a women's *movement*. Similarly, coming forward merely on anti-dowry issues, protesting against cultural degradation, resistance to being bound to the home, is by itself insufficient. The need is to link all of these together. The established parties, often caught up in union work or in the requirements of their alliances with bourgeois parties, very frequently lack the time, resources, or imagination to do such simple work of *prachar*—there is an absolute lack of simple pamphlets (or plays, slide shows, exhibitions, etc.) which put forward such a perspective in language which is understandable and attractive to lower class women. Where such material exists (the songs already written, for examples, are very valuable and invariably awaken tremendous response), it is still limited in its reach. This kind of work, then, should be done—and can be done—by socialist-feminist organizations.

These notes have been written after a good number of discussions, so I have a lot of people to thank for the ideas here, though they are my responsibility. I hope the discussion can be carried forward with critiques, revisions, suggestions, filling in the gaps, etc. I would also suggest that in the process it is now important to involve male comrades in the discussion! So that the 'women's movement' does not remain limited to women or seen as the responsibility only of women!

$\sim$

THE QUESTION OF AUTONOMY
Nandita Gandhi and Nandita Shah

[. . .]

Unity in diversity?

Women have often formed political platforms and alliances with mainstream parties. The 1980s however saw the birth of several autonomous women's groups. In 1979, for example, the Forum Against Rape, Bombay, was informally created by women who had come for a discussion on the open letter written by four lawyers against the Supreme Court judgement or what came to be called the Mathura rape case. Saheli, in New Delhi, was started by a group of eight women who had protested together in several dowry murder cases. 'We began to feel strongly that the women's movement had to provide an alternative support structure for women . . . We did not start with a manifesto. Too many groups had fallen apart on ideological differences before they could even get started. There were (and are) different levels of feminist consciousness in our group but all of us share a common concern' (Saheli 1985). Many such groups proliferated, mainly in urban areas in different parts of the country. Some, like the Nari Nirjatan Pratirodh Manch, Calcutta, brought together a range of women, from sympathizers of the ruling Communist Party of India (Marxist), to different Maoist groups, socialist-feminists and activists of voluntary agencies. The Mahila Utpidan Birodhi Sangarsh Samiti, Ranchi, brought together Maoist sympathizers and apolitical housewives.

Ideological heterogeneity exists in politics too but is set aside by the willing submission of the majority to the party line which, the majority believes, analyzes the present political trends and helps in planning strategy. Here, experimentation or debate is not encouraged, rather, what is stressed is adherence to tenets and policies. What probably made women activists of the 1980s more amenable to submerging their political differences and making common cause in the 'autonomous' movement was the realization that no political party had understood or realized the latent militancy and consciousness of women which had so resoundingly revealed itself throughout the 1970s. Perhaps it was necessary for women to distance themselves from traditional, accepted theories and practices, draw on each other's political experiences, to go back to the subjective and rethink their positions and actions. This gave them a collective strength, a spirit of militancy and a fresh approach to theory which became so evident that left organizations were forced to take cognizance of these groups.

However, there were also some unforeseen consequences. While some activists left these groups because of ideological differences, others felt that maintaining such diversity meant a reluctance to have any ideological debate within the group. In Pennuramai Iyyakam, Madras, some of the younger members complained that the older ones were not interested in an ideological debate with them. The older members felt often that theory, which was developed outside the group, became a reference point and influenced its working. In many groups, discussions begin with an issue and end with strategic planning; theory may find a place, but theoretical discussions are mainly confined to women engaged in research. There have not been many attempts to devise ways of breaking the theory/practice divide and forming alternatives so that different women can hold theoretical discussions. A study circle formed by Shakti, a Bombay-based resource centre, to discuss analytical concepts such as patriarchy, feminism and its various streams, had to close down for want of people.

Conferences and discussions, especially large ones, consciously confine themselves to empirical findings and experiences for maximum participation, while smaller meetings are often viewed as elitist or irrelevant. As a result, most groups have produced papers which mainly recount their activities and describe campaigns, programmes or events. Women's groups cannot neglect to formulate their own theory and praxis. If the collective cannot do so as a group, it will require individuals from among its own members to do this work. Another way this difficulty can be overcome is through a coordinated effort by women's studies researchers and academics.

Formal and informal members

What makes one a member of an organization? Informal bodies usually have no restriction on membership, their dues are nominal, there are no party identity cards and no statutory attendance. Some members prefer not to attend meetings, others come only for demonstrations, others may be interested in particular campaigns. One woman proclaimed herself a member of a group because she felt she needed a group identity at a conference! In April 1983, some women, tired of the FAOW's (Forum Against Oppression of Women, Bombay) ad-hocism, asked for the formalization of the group into a federation with representatives and voting rights. The majority of the group rejected the proposal as they felt that, as an agitational group, the FAOW should be open to whoever wanted to be part of it and was willing to work on the basis of collective decision making. In practice this discouraged women belonging to political parties or groupings who could not take decisions in their individual capacities, that is, without referring back to their party. For Saheli, New Delhi, the question of dual identity came up in a different way. 'Due to certain circumstances, support for individual women is what Saheli got known for and before its other activities were fully developed . . . At a personal level, it did pose a dilemma: to get absorbed into the task of helping individuals or to carry out other issue-oriented activities and campaigns . . . Some members chose to resolve this dilemma by taking on campaign work in other organizations. For the rest of us it meant having a reduced collective strength and practically no choices' (Saheli 1988). Some of the older members saw no contradiction in having a dual membership in Saheli and in other groups because Saheli was an open organization and also because they felt their work in other groups aided rather than hindered Saheli's functioning. In the ensuing heated debate, it was decided that no member of Saheli could have dual membership, which prompted five of its older members to leave the group. What makes an organization 'open' and how does such openness help or hinder its members and their efficiency? Some claim that an open policy gives ample opportunity for anyone who would like to join in or propose an action. 'There is no exclusion of any woman from whichever part of the world, whichever group she may come from. A genuine lack of caste/class/ political/religious bias and a true spirit of cosmopolitanism is something even the most ardent critics of the FAOW have appreciated' (FAOW, 1985). But there have been problems too. Journalists and researchers have attended the group's meetings and given distorted versions without understanding the context or background of decisions and actions. Some have given press statements on current topics which the majority have not discussed or agreed upon. Most important and disturbingly, such an open door policy has not encouraged a growth in membership. On the other hand, semi-open bodies too have lost members as well as the input of those from other groups who may want to give some of their time and energy. Perhaps collectives need to reconsider their membership policies.

Sachetana, Calcutta, which also works as a collective, has worked out its own method: they have retained the more conventional method of formal application, recommendation and acceptance of a new member by the group. This is based on their conviction that women should consider their membership and involvement in a group seriously and consciously. This gives them a sense of identity, responsibility and commitment. Formal membership also eliminates the problem new women may have in joining a group. They need not depend on older members or 'cultivate' them to be accepted into the group.

Subtle hierarchies

Collectives have rejected hierarchies; they oppose the belief that there are some people with leadership qualities who ought to carry the responsibility of leading others. The leader, seen as a superior, talented person, can exercise considerable power over his or her followers. Collectives see this as an unequal, often oppressive relationship that denies others the room to develop their abilities and ideas. It is hoped that by removing the official post of a leader and decentralizing the structure each member will be able to relate to the other equally as well as assume the collective responsibility of leadership. It is easy to banish leaders and an administrative hierarchy but more difficult to maintain a non-hierarchical structure because of the presence of the subtle, invisible forms of hierarchy. In a group of volunteers, for example, there may be some who can afford to spend more time, take more responsibility and therefore have more access to people and decision-making. Women with full-time jobs and/or family responsibilities, who may be equally committed, feel hesitant to intervene or opine on issues or actions. Sometimes, full-time or paid workers had an edge over the part-time volunteers. In other groups, volunteers, because of their non-remunerative 'social work' based on notions of altruism or sacrifice, were given a special status with no accountability. Then there are groups within groups which usually consist of people who have certain things in common such as education, social class, tastes, language or a political tendency. They can at the same time be friends who share similar ideas and values and/or political comrades. This can be both a help and a hindrance to the group. For example, work allocation is often easily executed if people are personally close, but this can also lead to the formation of an inner circle which can become an elitist force and which often has control of the decision making.

Most groups function so casually that they unconsciously follow procedures which prohibit free access to information. The combination of experience and information which founder members usually have can sometimes become the basis of hierarchy and power. Decentralization does not mean the complete rejection of procedures such as writing minutes and maintaining reports, rather it should mean the development of other, newer, methods. The problem of hierarchy most sharply comes up in deciding a salary structure. According to the concept of collective functioning, each member should get paid an equal amount.

Organizationally we need to ask whether a uniform salary structure is possible given that skills and experiences differ. Flavia Agnes, one of the founder members of the Women's Centre, Bombay, says that the group battled with this problem for almost three years. The centre had followed a policy of employing women in distress who needed work as full-timers, volunteers and part-time workers. But it was not easy to decide how each worker should be paid. The idea of a need-based salary structure was rejected because women perceived their basic needs according to their class and education. A middle class woman for example, would find it difficult to live in a low rent *chawl*, or she may aspire to an expensive education for her children. The concept of seniority in terms of the number of years spent with the organization had its own problems: it could mean a disparity which need not be commensurate with people's skills, while differential incomes for different inputs were also not acceptable all round. Another dimension of this problem is the question of commitment to the women's movement. Should women's groups recruit their staff from the movement or should they also include professionals? Women from the movement and those from social work schools not only have different perspective but different expectations of social/job mobility and salaries. For them, political commitment and expertise are not mutually exclusive. Nonetheless, it is true that women's groups have traditionally shied away from discussing details such as working hours, salaries, holidays, increments and other job conditions. But these form an important part of a harmonious working relationship. More discussion is necessary on these important issues as the survival and effective functioning of the group will depend on it. It has become increasingly clear that it was idealistic to imagine that there could be complete equality within a group. There are class, caste, cultural differences: some women have more stamina, others more time and fewer responsibilities, some have special skills or personality traits. The collective had set out to provide a space for the participation and development of the capabilities of all women. On the basis of our experiences, we need to ask again: if we want a leaderless structure how are we going to undertake all the functions usually performed by the leader? Secondly, can we have rotating leaders or convenors who are more accountable to the group? Can we prevent the abuse of leadership by acknowledging everybody's contribution, by sharing access to money and information as well as teaching and sharing skills?

Allocation of work

All organizations require a division of work in order to be able to function. Such categorizations often become rigid and prevent people from learning and developing their skills. They also place a value tag on each type of work which prevents mobility or promotion. Conventional organizations usually follow the job hierarchy which exists in society: for example, leaders perform high profile jobs such as public speaking, representation; educated middle class members might be involved in theorizing or debating; grassroots level activists usually mobilize people, organize demonstrations or do administrative work. The professed aim of the collective is to break these divisions and share work equally among the members. Instead, this often leads to problems: tasks are not completed on time, correspondence may or may not be prompt, and, occasionally, someone takes charge and pulls up everyone when the level of disorganization gets unbearable (Saheli 1985).

As a magazine, *Manushi* could not afford to be leisurely about time. They found that from a group of 30 women with differing commitments and ideology, some took on specific tasks, others did [too] but often did not meet their commitments and eventually the burden fell on a core group. This group then asked why those who did not work should have any say in the decision making. Immediately after its first issue, there was a heated and disturbing controversy in which *Manushi* split and reconstituted itself (Manushi Prakashan 1987). However, what is also clear is that tasks are assigned to those who have some experience. This then leaves the less interesting tasks for others to pick up, thereby reinforcing hierarchies. Another aspect of shared responsibilities is the pressure on members of the group to undertake tasks they may not be comfortable with. Those who have never theorized before are asked to write papers because everyone should express themselves. Or those who had never climbed a public platform in their lives are firmly though gently asked to deliver lectures. In many groups women are often so apprehensive of task rotation that they disappear when they know their turn is coming round. Others find that their special talents like writing or acting are often simply ignored by the group. A good orator will not be asked to speak because she may seem to be taking over this important task. Ironically, task rotation in its literal sense can itself become oppressive for individuals.

Usually the load of work in collectives has not permitted the problems of work rotation and distribution to surface. Accountability has been an issue which has often led to quarrels and splits. Voluntary work done over and above a regular, full-time job often means it has been hastily performed. Collective members are hesitant to pull up such defaulters, for who can say who is responsible and make evaluations for paid as well as unpaid members. This persistent dilemma is central to the survival of collectives.

The group decision-making process

To break the hierarchy between decision makers and administrators, informal and collective groups decided against executive or elected bodies and involved all their members in the decision-making process. Soon enough it was noticed that collective decision making, especially in large groups, tended to either become painfully long (too many issues being handled in too short a time) or ineffective (delayed or repeatedly changed). Groups were then impelled to establish procedures for decision making which would not prevent them from being open to people and their involvement.

For example some groups set up sub-groups which could meet, decide and implement programmes thus leaving the larger group to act as a policy-making group. *Manushi* made a definitive link between work responsibility and decision making. 'Despite much unpleasantness, it was decided that in future only those women who were willing to make a regular time commitment and take on specific responsibility would be involved in the decision making process. Others were welcome to give as much casual help as they wanted, but could not insist on taking part in every decision making process' (Manushi Prakashan 1987). Some groups which started informally later formalized their decision-making structures by co-opting serious and committed volunteers into a central body. Members of the formal body of the Women's Centre, Bombay, who were accountable to the charity commissioner wondered why a collective method should place more responsibility on them. They asked all those interested in decision making to join the formal group and share responsibilities as well as policy decisions.

Differences between group members in terms of their personalities, class, political experience, etc. also play an important part in the level of their participation. Newer members may need time to think or prepare before they make up their minds. We were once in touch with Maitreyi, Bombay, a seven-member research and training group which takes almost all its decisions unanimously. A group of like-minded people? Perhaps, but its composition pointed to another factor. One of them, a pioneer in the women's movement, is vocal, resourceful and performed most of the group's administrative work and also suggested programmes. The rest were professionals who did not have her experience or time. Such a lopsided division of work and responsibilities created a situation in which she became the mainstay of the organization and its unofficial leader, and by virtue of this, dominated the decision-making process. And views that were different from hers were unconsciously avoided or rejected. For decision making to be truly collective and equal, it seems that not only is a common background of skills, political experience and time a prerequisite, but also respect and value for each other's views which overcomes the various differences between women and encourages each to be fully involved in the group and its processes. [. . .]

References

Forum Against Oppression of Women (FAOW). 1985. Sharing our Problems in the FAOW—its organizational structure and functioning. Paper presented at the conference on Perspectives for Women's Liberation Movement in India, Bombay.

Manushi Prakashan. 1987. *Manushi.* New Delhi.

Saheli. 1985. *Saheli the first four years.* New Delhi: Saheli.

Saheli. 1988. 7th anniversary brochure. New Delhi: Saheli.

∾

THE ENABLING PROCESS OF EMPOWERMENT
Narayan K. Banerjee

[. . .] Some major debates still continue to revolve around the enabling process of grassroot-level empowerment. The initial debate originated from the concept of empowerment itself. Admittedly, the use of the concept of empowerment has greater relevance and application to 'third world' countries which were characterized by high levels of poverty and feminization of poverty, low female literacy, invisibility of women and strong patriarchal and community values. Because of these characteristics practically nothing was expected to evolve on its own as an enabling process from within the poorest, most powerless class of women. There are hardly any instances to show that indigenous or spontaneous organization of poor women has occurred in this country—except in one or two isolated cases—in response to certain specific issues directly affecting a section of women in specific locations. It was clear therefore that empowerment was possible only through external intervention of some kind. This seems to have been accepted as an appropriate approach in the context of the nature and condition of the target population, the conceptual content of empowerment and the immensity of the task involved.

One major issue that surfaced fairly early concerned the appropriate 'time' and 'space' available to poor women for organizational work, tied as they are to their increasing labour obligations with diminishing autonomy and cultural worth: How was the process of organizing to begin? Both non-governmental intermediaries and government agencies lacked accurate, detailed information about the life styles, work patterns, mental capacities, etc. of poor women, especially in the context of agro-climatic and occupational diversity. Several research studies indicate that many efforts at grassroot empowerment initiated by NGOs or the government started with pre-conceived assumptions about, for example, the sexual division of labour, or women's powerlessness and passivity.

This information gap—especially on patterns of labour allocation within the household, social values as interpreted at the level of the family, defining women's options, and the connections between such values/options and the production process—began to be partially met in the latter half of the eighties. A fair amount of such information has been gathered by social action groups now playing an active role in women's empowerment. Other fallouts from this development are: (i) attempts to narrow the gap between research and action at the individual or institutional level, and (ii) increasing consciousness of social responsibility among researchers, and the erosion of the theory of academic neutrality among a section of social scientists in this country.

There was another consideration in the adoption of the induced organizational approach for women's empowerment. It is believed that women's power is limited because their authority rarely extends beyond the limits of small family units, and even within them it is usually circumscribed by cultural norms and often legal structures. Established feminist theory on the public–private dichotomy argues that sexual equality is promoted by involving men in the domestic sphere and by drawing women out into public life. When men's authority is invested along with women's in the family and household, and the women embrace the wider community, the legitimacy of the power of both sexes is more nearly equal.

In the context of grassroot empowerment then, an analysis of domestic and public space assumes great importance. Considering the fact that a great deal of diversity and heterogeneity exists in this country and that research in this area is still theoretically and conceptually rather weak, it will be premature to delve into this area just now. However, it should suffice to say that the success or failure of grassroots empowerment is to some extent related to the whole concept of this sexual geography. One could easily hypothesize that the collective empowerment process succeeds with really poor women—whose livelihood occupations have never, i.e. traditionally, been restricted to the 'private' domain. On the other hand, women from a somewhat higher family status, being more used to economic dependence on the family and some form of social seclusion, may find an identical approach more threatening/intimidating, at least initially.

The second debate, albeit largely operational, actually originates from the previous one described above. It throws up the following questions: (a) How/who will initiate the mobilization of poor women? (b) How can such organizations be sustained? (c) What is the role of the intervening/intermediary group/institutions/persons? (d) What changes characterize the relationship between the women at the grassroots and the interventionists? All these issues in this wide spectrum of debate have not been very systematically addressed yet, and opinions vary among interventionists, and within the women's movement itself.

While trends during the period indicated increasing acceptance by the government of the need for non-governmental intermediaries, debates on this question continue without any clear consensus. The response of the state during the post-1975 period in its attempts to organize women at the grassroot level cannot be said to have been consistent and/or efficient. For instance, the two schemes launched by the government viz. STEP and DWCRA aimed at strengthening the socioeconomic base of rural women through a group approach, awareness generation and provision of support services. The schemes also provide for the training of functionaries in basic concepts and approaches in programme planning so that they are able to understand the concepts of participatory development and group approach whose ultimate objectives are empowerment and women's equality. The schemes have been implemented both by government and non-governmental intermediaries. While generalizations are risky on the basis of impressions, it is generally believed that while in the case of government agencies the emphasis was more on quantity (number of groups organized), in the case of NGOs it was quality. The primary goals of the latter were and are true participatory development, awareness of wider concerns, cohesiveness of groups organized and entry of such groups into wider sociopolitical issues.

The awareness generation programme of the Central Social Welfare Board and the Mahila Samakhya Programme of the Ministry of Education are other examples of the government's attempts towards empowerment. While the first programme is almost totally dependent on NGO intermediaries, the second programme involve both government and NGO intermediaries. Both the programmes are contextually similar as well as dissimilar, but neither seem to be specific to grassroot women's immediate needs in the sense that they are unlikely to be sustainable in the long run. Issues are being currently approached in an isolated manner. In other words, both the programmes need extensive and immediate support from other programmes for a strong foundation and group cohesiveness, and subsequent continuous interaction for several years to put women on the path of empowerment. It is unrealistic to devise a time-bound/single dose programme for poor women's empowerment.

Doubts concerning the efficacy of such interventions at the micro level with government support or by the government itself in some areas, have intensified due to certain fallouts in the recent past. For example, there is evidence to show that although at the policy level many state governments agreed to transfer land (good, bad, wasted) to grassroot women's groups, at the operational level hurdles and harassment became prominent. This has been the experience of intermediaries working with poor women in Gujarat and Rajasthan. SUTRA—a voluntary organization in Himachal Pradesh— ran into problems while implementing an awareness generating programme against alcoholism through women's groups. In Andhra Pradesh, motivated by the textbook materials of the National Literacy Mission, scores of neo-literate women joined together to close down village liquor shops and waged war against drunkards, liquor dealers and even their own husbands. Curiously enough, the same state which made a public policy of enabling grassroot women's empowerment was trying to oppose these attempts by women as liquor contributes to state revenue. The Andhra Pradesh government is reported to have gone further by attempting to censor the textbooks which contain such positive messages. There have been attempts also to dub these movements as part of caste or class movements, ignoring the fact that the cries of women's groups are being smothered and their empowerment jeoparadized. In the end, the women's movement is faced with the question of the sustainability of grassroot groups supported by and/or organized by the government, and rightly suspects the genuineness of government attempts at grassroot empowerment.

In 1980, when seven national women's organizations presented a joint memorandum to the Government of India, recommending major policy thrusts needed for women's empowerment (AIWC—1980) the majority of the organizations ruled out any active role by the government in organizing women at the grassroots. There was a distinct unity on the issue despite ideological diversity. Some organizations were willing to take resources from the government but preferred to do the organizing themselves. Some had objected even to the acceptance of resources.

A section of the women's movement, which claims complete autonomy from the state and political parties, also debated on the issue of taking government resources to work for grassroot empowerment. These autonomous groups based their objection on both ideological (the state represents the repressive power of the dominant class and is, therefore by nature incapable of supporting the empowerment of the poor and oppressed) and pragmatic ('we would get co-opted by the state') grounds.

Defenders of state support for the empowerment/organization approach have argued all along that:

(a) women's powerlessness at the local/micro level cannot be eliminated without legitimate and powerful support;

(b) it is the state's constitutional responsibility to provide this type of support;

(c) only state-sponsored programmes could achieve adequate spread across the country and arrest the neglect, marginalization and increasing impoverishment of women; and

(d) it is the only way to publicly register and acknowledge poor women's rightful claim to a share of national development and resources.

The National Commission on Self-employed Women and Women in the Informal Sector (NCSW) (1988) also argued squarely for governmental support to organizations of poor women. The argument is justified in a situation where few organizations exist, and on the ground that non-governmental intermediaries are too few in relation to the size/needs of the target population, and that poor women's own efforts are practically non-existent due to no fault of theirs. NCSW also demanded that the state should help initiate a network of grassroot level organizations as 'development is basically about the people' and as equality has been guaranteed for women by the Constitution. In any case—the concept of empowerment was already a part of government policy, though its universality was still under debate in 1988. On the basis of nearly five years of experience of DWCRA, the Department of Rural Development of the Government of India suggested to the Cabinet in 1987 that the 'group approach' should be adopted for all women covered under IRDP as well. Acceptance however did not follow—despite the NCSW's recommendation.

Even if it is agreed that (i) the organizational approach, (ii) the need of an external intermediary, and (iii) state support through intensive policy articulation and appropriate programme backup are prerequisites for women's empowerment in this country, all problem areas will still remain. The issues of sustainability, the nature of transformational developments, adjustment mechanisms, and the direction etc. of grassroot organizations and resultant degree of empowerment cannot be tackled immediately. The state will continue to have an advantage over non-governmental organizations in that it can lay claim to a continuity that is denied to other forms of organizations.

What is critical today is the need to formalize and ensure some longevity to the organizations that have emerged all over the country, on the foundations of women's informal or formal networks, around issues, programme activities, or sociopolitical relations. They need to be identified and mobilized through research, documentation, information/experience sharing, etc. to widen their base.

An ideological consensus in the political life of this country for grassroot women's empowerment as a comprehensive strategy, as opposed to the current partial, fragmented thrusts for narrow political or departmental gains, is a fundamental priority. Grassroot women may be socially or occupationally divided, *but as a class they do represent certain secular values and demonstrate the basic instincts of sharing, reciprocal help and responsiveness to reach out to others in similar conditions. These noble human traits of poor and illiterate women hold great hope and potential.*

Experiments in different corners of the country, under diverse situations, have yielded enough evidence to show that the pathological situation created by poverty, illiteracy, marginalization, subordination, invisibility and social disabilities is not an impediment to poor women's mobilization. Approaches to grassroot empowerment, therefore, have to be synergic in nature, and should not be viewed as points of arrival but as components of the process itself. It has to be a combined process of external promotion and internal initiatives. The 'target' women must experience development from the very outset.

Conclusion

Grassroot empowerment also needs to be viewed from the standpoint of the share of grassroot women in the women's movement per se. While there is little doubt that the vitality of the Indian women's movement owes a great deal to the pressures generated from the grassroots, it would be far more difficult to answer the question: How far has the women's movement been able to carry the grassroots? What has been largely achieved is representation by intermediaries of the views and issues of grassroot women. To induct grassroot women as vocal and active participants in the women's movement is the challenge of the nineties. The relationship would be of mutual interest. The current political situation makes this imperative, as with the deepening national crisis and increased violence, the constructive efforts of over a decade could be washed away overnight.

∾

ON THE CONCEPT OF 'EMPOWERMENT'

Manoranjan Mohanty

For about two decades since the mid 1960s there was a plea to put 'politics in command' and accordingly growth models and development strategies were assessed. Even though there was no consensus as to the political criteria for evaluating development policies, still certain values such as freedom and equality were put at the core of this exercise. While the preoccupation with growth was questioned, the 'political essence of progress' was emphasized. With the upsurge of the women's movement and other social movements, the pursuit of freedom and justice was put in more concrete terms and the development process was scrutinized on the basis of such political parameters. It is in this process that the term 'empowerment', i.e., giving power to a certain unprivileged sections of society, came to be used.

In the 1990s, however, the milieu is one of 'economics in command'. Growth of production, modernization of technology and management issues are supposed to be the central goals of development in the contemporary age of 'structural adjustment programmes'. Liberalization and privatization of the economy and its integration with the global economy are advocated essentially on the grounds of developing production. Actually, in China, the Deng Xiaoping regime, while launching the reforms in 1978—which were launched on their own and not on the initiative of the World Bank—explicitly rejected the talk of 'politics in command'. They had announced that the focus during the new period was on 'economic construction'. The Indian government has tried to project the new economic policies as representing a consensus, hence being 'above politics,' citing the policies of the non-Congress governments in the states. What is interesting is that, along with the stress on production, a commitment to what is called 'empowerment' of the people is usually reiterated. The old formulation of 'growth with social justice' is now gone; it is 'development with empowerment' now.

Ostensibly, empowerment as an objective of economic development should be a welcome addition to the democratic discourse. After all, oppressed groups ranging from unorganized workers and poor peasants to tribal people, dalits and women have been engaged in a struggle for power and should normally judge the development process in those terms. Whether development projects had led to their pauperization and subjugation was the issue raised by the various movements of displaced people and ecological movements among others. So when documents of the UN summits as also the declarations of the national governments eloquently stress their commitment to the empowerment of the people, the normal reaction is one of positive glee among the democratic forces. However, the context of the popularization of this term 'empowerment', the framework of globalization which underlies it, make it a questionable concept.

Discourse of world summits

As an illustration, let us take up the documents related to the World Summit for Social Development held in Copenhagen on March 6–12, 1995 where 'empowerment' figures prominently as an objective. The Declaration signed by the heads of the states and governments says the following:

> We affirm that in both economic and social terms, the most productive policies and investments are those which empower people to maximize their capacities, resources and opportunities. (United Nations 1995)

The Declaration and the Programme of Action have many such statements which clearly link up empowerment with economic globalization. This statement also implies that empowerment as such—even in the sense it is used here—is not the goal, but something to be understood in the context of production and investment. At another place there is a little more focus on empowerment:

> Recognise that empowering people particularly women, to strengthen their capacities is a main objective of development and its principal resource. Empowerment requires the full participation of people in the formulation, implementation and evaluation of decisions determining the functioning and the well-being of our societies. (United Nations 1995)

There is a certain definition of 'empowerment' suggested in this statement as 'strengthening their capacities' which can be achieved through 'full participation of people in . . .' Strengthening of capacities is, of course, crucial to the liberation of the oppressed. But is it possible to achieve that without removing the structural constraints on their capacities? Such a definition does not imply liberation from the bondages which have historically constrained fuller realization of human potential in the case of the deprived sections. Such constraints operated at various levels including the socioeconomic structure, ideology and political process which the omnibus concept of 'empowerment' does not capture. Then there are processes of exploitation which encompass the entire society, some which afflict several sectors or groups, yet others which target specific classes, castes, ethnic groups and others. The revival of the dalit movement in India with a new momentum in the 1980s and 1990s has brought out this aspect abundantly. Without a relevant disaggregation, the autonomous significance of specific struggles is not acknowledged nor is an appropriate interconnection established. Hence 'strengthening their capacities' boils down to an over generalized, albeit noble, statement of intent with little political value to the oppressed.

As for the meaning of 'full participation of people', it has to be read together with the first commitment of the Declaration which talks about creating an enabling environment—economic, political, social, cultural and legal environment. The heads of states and government announced their first commitment thus:

> Provide a stable legal framework, in accordance with our constitutions, laws and procedures, and consistent with international law and obligations which includes and promotes equality and equity between women and men, full respects for all human rights and fundamental freedom and the rule of law, access to justice, elimination of all forms of discrimination, transparent and accountable governance and administration and the encouragement of partnership with free and representative organizations of civil society. (United Nations 1995)

There is further commitment to people's participation through 'decentralization open management of public institutions, and strengthening of the abilities and opportunities of civil society and local communities to develop their own organizations, resources and activities'.

The emphasis is on participation through the existing institutions or by building 'representative organizations of civil society'. In other words, those who advocate replacement of the prevailing institutions are either outside the civil society or are denied the right to participate since that might upset the 'stable legal framework'. Stress on law and order is an integral part of the contemporary strategy of liberalization and globalization. The Deng Xiaoping regime has often proclaimed: 'Without stability there would be no growth.' They had for that reason brutally suppressed the youth demonstration at Beijing's Tiananmen Square in June 1989. In most of the third world countries a combination of coercion and manipulation has accompanied structural adjustment policies.

'Empowerment', 'civil society' and 'democratization' form the new package of liberalization discourse which on face value respond to the long-standing demands of struggling groups. In practice, however, each of them has been given a restricted meaning and has been oriented to serve the present global drive of western capitalism. Civil society, for example, has come to mean those organized groups who pursue their demands in the pluralist democratic process. So the objective of the dominant western forces is to promote interest group politics to take part in the bargaining process while the state maintains law and order. The state in the third world has become inefficient, corrupt and bureaucratic, therefore civil society should take over the task of development—that is how the argument runs. [. . .]

A disabling concept

Many scholars and activists of some social movements have uncritically accepted the use of the term 'empowerment' partly because of the global discourse which actually is the western discourse. Non-governmental organizations (NGOs) have been the first to accept this discourse. They seem to think that by using this term they answer the usual criticism that the NGOs accepted the prevailing power structure within which they pursued developmental functions. They would rather be known as part of 'grassroots movements' interested in 'social transformation'.

There is considerable debate going on in India on the character of NGOs and grassroots movements. It is important to differentiate among non-governmental efforts, each of which has its own specific character and value. At least three can be identified: (1) extension activity assigned by the government; (2) developmental activity that may or may not be supported by the government, where the organization exercises autonomy to the extent of criticizing government while the latter tolerates it. These are groups marked by their permissible dissidence; and (3) sociopolitical activity which seeks to transform the prevailing system and therefore is open to suppressive measures by the government.

For similar reasons the governmental agencies have also picked up this term to establish that programmes such as the National Literacy Mission, the many women's development schemes or Panchayati Raj aim at 'empowering' the people, especially women, poor peasants, etc. In fact, several models of 'empowerment' are being popularized. See, for instance, the Government of India's country paper for the Copenhagen Summit which has a section on 'Empowering the People: Models of Mobilization'. It talks about the poor being empowered to be able to help themselves and breaking social, economic, cultural and psychological barriers to convert them from being 'passive recipients of government programmes' to 'active participants and managers of their own affairs' (GOI 1994). Here is a description of empowerment which involves 'organizing them into informal groups, formal associations, trade unions, cooperatives, etc. for exerting collective pressure, articulating demands and effectively participating in the decision-making process with the ultimate objective of building foundations of individual and collective self-reliance' (GOI 1994). All this is no doubt necessary and desirable. But it is also the method by which the politics of the oppressed and the poor is restrained and channelized by dominant forces in society. Their right to struggle is circumscribed by these forms of political bargaining. The state is assumed to be an impartial arbitrator trying to 'enable' the poor to pursue these forms of politics. One has to only point out the growing role of the state in pursuing authoritarian measures to maintain law and order and restrict trade union rights to provide a stable environment for liberalization. Thus instead of allowing the oppressed to expand their realm of political struggle this notion of empowerment actually limits it.

In this process, the alliance of the government and the NGOs is playing a strategic role. The India Country Paper says: 'The non-government/voluntary organizations can provide great help in this process, particularly providing the support structure needed for such groups, and associations and liaising between them and the government are sensitized to an organized approach to development' (GOI 1994). It is true that because the governmental machinery has proved to be inefficient and often corrupt, there is a preference to rely on the NGO sector. The UN agencies, multinational corporations, foreign foundations and other funding agencies now insist on involving the NGOs for this reason. But when 'empowerment' is mediated by this alliance of government and NGOs, it has serious political implications. It may have the normal tendency to co-opt people's movements and their cadres, curb their struggling power and capacity for carrying on autonomous campaigns. This is why there is currently considerable disenchantment with NGO activity and even more questioning of the government handing over resources to NGOs for delivery among the people. If there are inadequacies in the accountability of governmental agencies, there are even more constraints to make the NGOs answerable to people. [. . .]

Many human rights activists have apparently adopted the term 'empowerment' unaware of its implications. The liberal discourse on rights had facilitated this because rights of the individual or a group can be realized, according to this viewpoint, if the concerned individual or the group has the power to take part in decision making. Therefore, institutional functioning is stressed as an essential part of democratic politics. Hence, empowerment becomes a cherished goal. Of course, institutional functioning is a crucial component in a democracy. The question is how to make institutional procedures positively contribute to the substantive exercise of power.

The concept of 'empowerment' puts excessive emphasis on formal institutional arrangements. Women are empowered by the provision of 33 per cent reservation in the panchayats. The Scheduled Castes, Scheduled Tribes and the Other Backward Classes are 'empowered' by reservation in legislatures and services. These are only minor 'though necessary' measures for transforming the power structure in society. Much more needs to be done in redistributing productive assets, in employment, education and other spheres. By providing reservations, the rulers claim that they have 'empowered' the dalits and adivasis—a claim that is questionable as is abundantly exposed by the contemporary dalit and adivasi movements. In fact, the concept itself implies that an external agency has 'given' power to or 'empowered' another section—a patronizing idea rather than power redistributed through a process, including a process of struggle. [. . .]

The new political discourse has tried to appropriate the pedagogy of the oppressed by focusing on concepts like 'empowerment'. But it is difficult to subdue the democratic upsurge of the 20th century which has experienced the anti-colonial struggle, the great social revolutions and the social movements both old and new. This concept has to contend with concepts like liberation, freedom and equality—ideas in pursuit of which much sacrifice has been made in the history of humankind.

Bibliography

United Nations. *Declaration of the World Summit for Social Development.* Geneva: United Nations, 1995.

Government of India. *India Country Paper for the UN Summit on Social Development,* New Delhi: Government of India, 1994.

~

INTERVIEW WITH SATYABHAMA 'NANI' LAWAND
Sharmila Joshi

Till October 1994, Satyabhama, whom the villagers called Nani (imprecisely meaning elder sister), was sarpanch of Bitargaon. Nani headed Bitargaon's panchayat of nine uneducated women, which was constituted for five years on 25 October 1989. The residents of Bitargaon [a village in Solarpur district] might never have agreed to an all-women panchayat if male-dominated panels in the past had worked effectively. For several five-year terms, the village had a joint panchayat with Shingewadi, a neighbouring village. It is not clear, from the villagers' accounts, who first started considering alternatives such as an all-women panchayat. The processes could have been simultaneous: of Nani, an exceptionally spirited and articulate woman, believing such a panel would work and trying to convince other women to participate; of the village patriarch Dadasaheb Patil offering his support for the panchayat; and of the village gram sabha endorsing the proposed experiment.

Nani, now possibly in her sixties, had lived a rebellious existence; she was used to taking independent decisions. When her husband died after two years of marriage and the birth of their son, Nani decided to ignore community strictures that barred Maratha women from tilling the land. Not only did Nani yoke the bullocks and plough the land to ensure it was not usurped by her brother-in-law, she also dressed up like a man to go to the grains market at Kurduwadi during harvest time for many years. [. . .]

Q: When you decided to have an all-women panchayat, you gathered all the other women. They mustn't have been so courageous then?

A: Then I nagged these women. Enough of this fear. I'm there with you. You follow me. Speak where I speak. Agree to a thing when I say 'yes'. We will stand for the election. Let's see what happens, who says what! See, later you may be cowed down. 'What will my husband say, what will my mother-in-law say?' You may get scared, but you should not, at all. If any calamity comes, I'm there, if there is no calamity even then I'm there. But you should always come behind me. They agreed. 'If you're there Nani, we're totally with you.' Then I approached Patilbhau, and put before him the proposal. 'Bhau I wish to enter politics. If you give your wholehearted permission, then we will stand.' He said, 'If you have the daring, do it. If you want to stand, you want to be sarpanch, then we've nothing to say.' No one else wanted to be [sarpanch]. All of us were together. No one speaks before Bhau.

Q: But even before this you've worked in the gram panchayat, didn't you?

A: Fifteen years. As a member. Group panchayat. I was in it for fifteen years.

Q: What work did you do there? There must have been men as well?

A: Yes, there were men. They would do everything. Why would I ask for anything there? I would simply go and sign.

Q: Then how did you come to participate in it?

A: Bhau made me stand for that panchayat. Old Bhau told me to stand at that time. 'You do talk, you're bold. People tremble to speak. When you're there, women will have courage, there will be reform.'

Q: You also wanted to be part of it?

A: Very much. When I got Bhau's permission, I became fully active. Everyone was happy. Old people as well as children. There wasn't any jealousy, or bad feelings about me in anyone's heart, or bad looks. No, never. From the beginning.

Q: But how did you make the women understand?

A: I told them not to remain under pressure, we should get information, find out what is going on in the world. We must know what is going on in the world. Leave behind the old ways. We should think of the betterment of our sons, daughters-in-law, and of their children. Can't we even get to understand what and how things are done in the world? Why won't it be done if we do it? What can be done by me? A big gunny bag can be lifted only if all come together. Can I do it just by myself? Whatever is, is of God Pandurang. He gave me wisdom, knowledge, he supported me throughout. I haven't done anything. He turned my earthen things to gold.

Q: Why do you think women usually remain suppressed?

A: Because they have no information. They don't even know how to buy four annas of cumin seeds. They only go on toiling in the fields. Do they know anything beyond that? Any knowledge of the world, what things are required to be done. Do they know anything of this? Their husbands bring things home, they know how to make *bhaji-bhakari* (vegetables and chapati) and serve them, that is all they know. Where do they go inquiring in the village, in the office, in the market, purchasing things? They know nothing . . . won't they remain suppressed?

Q: **By whom?**

A: Say, by the husband, by the house, by the world. But we shouldn't remain under pressure. Why should we? We eat of our own making. Why should I be scared of you?

Q: **But why did you want to have only women in the panchayat?**

A: The men have done most things till today. They move around a lot, go here and there. Can't we do the same? If we can't, then we ask them how to keep accounts and so on. We had adamantly decided not to take them then. What for? Do they teach us anything properly? Thus, we didn't keep any contact with them whatsoever. These men have addictions, pay bribes, eat up money, destroy work; then they come up with excuses. Here work wasn't done, this didn't happen, that couldn't happen. Who is going to ask them anything? Can a woman do so? They would say, 'Do you know anything? Do you understand anything?' Why should we compromise? Their way is very annoying and different. So are their intentions. We saw no reason to take them. We decided our own members and decided to work by ourselves.

Q: **In the beginning did any man oppose or laugh at you?**

A: No, no one. The acceptance was total, you see. There were fireworks to celebrate.

Q: **After the panchayat was formed what was the first work you took up?**

A: Our first work? Was it the office? The first school? The one which we showed you. Another one is being constructed. Also the office. Yes four schools. Yes, drainage as well.

Q: **Who decided that the beginning should be made with the school?**

A: We ourselves decided. Do the children have a school? They used to get soaked. Then the school was closed. Then their studies suffered. If it got cloudy, they would go early.

Q: **Why did you give so much importance to the school? You had a shortage of water as well.**

A: See, the importance of education is growing. Either the dowry is more, or the education is more. If the girl is educated, then the boy approves, if the boy is educated then the girl approves. They inquire whether the person is educated. Then shouldn't we provide for the school? [. . .]

Now I'll discuss how we do not have the right to be self-dependent, how we do not get education. I'll hold discussions next time. But in the villages people are ignorant, I tell you. There should be knowledge. Our Marathwada has remained backward because of this lack of knowledge, they never think of self-dependence or education, or improvement or about the difference between men and women, that's for certain.

Q: You're not educated, even then you have done so much. You showed so much boldness. If you were educated, do you think it would have made a difference?

A: There would've been bright light. Education is so important. Earlier I had only two eyes.

Q: Even then you did so much.

A: That's with my head. It makes the difference. Things happen if you act. We should show them by doing something. If they say don't use the plough, then use it.

Q: Your husband is no more. But when the other women started working in the panchayat, did any change take place in their houses?

A: No, nothing changed. No mother-in-law or father-in-law or husband said any bad words. If you have to go somewhere or if you are called, then you go; if not then you work in the fields, or in the house. No one said anything.

Q: But was there any change or at least a thought like, now that women are working outside, in the panchayat, so some husbands could work in the house?

A: Husbands doing housework.

Q: Yes, why don't they?

A: Husbands and housework?

Q: Yes, now that women work outside.

A: There are other people in the house, they take over when we go out.

Q: But don't you think husbands should? A woman does look after the housework as well as outside work.

A: No, we can't say. Our men won't be able to. These modern, educated boys do. But from the earlier generation, they won't sweep with a broom or cook or won't do anything in the house, they will come, dine and go. They won't think of cooking because the woman has gone out.

Q: What do you think of that?

A: Nothing.

Q: Do people in the village still want only sons?

A: Some people do wish to have a daughter. After four sons they say now we will have a daughter and then we will go for the operation. My own sister waited and waited to have a daughter. After getting four sons, finally she underwent an operation thinking if she took a further chance she might get another son.

Q: After having sons, why do they want to have a daughter?

A: A girl is needed to weep, to bring her back home for Diwali.

Q: She is required for weeping? What do you mean?

A: To cry when we die, to weep saying, 'O, my mother has died, my mother has died.' A daughter cries, and makes the village cry. A son never cries, he doesn't get it. He simply hangs down his head. There's a difference between their love, therefore a daughter should be there. A daughter has more affection for her parents. And she makes the entire society weep and feel the loss.

Q: Why can't the sons weep?

A: They do not get tears. They weep but only in a low voice. That's the difference between their love. Girls have more affection. She goes out, she leaves the house, she has no right here. Yet the difference is there.

Q: So for these reasons, to weep and for festivals a daughter is wanted. What does she do in festivals?

A: What does she do? She comes at the time of Diwali, she graces the festival. At Panchami time she goes to dance, we give her bangles, some money, a saree and some gifts. The festival is complete with her presence. A son should be there as a lamp, a creeper plant. There is expansion when a son is there.

Q: What is the meaning of 'expansion'?

A: He gets married, gets children, as the creeper grows. The girl goes out, if there is no son, what remains? Nothing. The house is locked and deserted. Who will be there? The daughter goes away, then who remains? A boy is the light of the family.

Q: Does it mean that a girl is like darkness?

A: Darkness. A girl is like the shade of a tamarind tree, a boy is like that of a mango tree. Mango is sweet and tamarind is sour. And because of the boy the family expands.

Q: But do you agree with these thoughts and beliefs about a girl and a boy?

A: Yes, I do.

Q: But don't you think that these belittle a girl? Seeing the girl as an outsider, a tamarind tree and so on? What does she lack for her to be considered of less importance?

A: She belongs to others, she is not ours.

Q: Why doesn't she have anything of her own?

A: She doesn't have anything. Who is going to give her any land or property?

Q: I know she is not given any property, but why so? What's the reason?

A: It's been like that from the beginning. If from the beginning it had been that the girl gets two acres and the boy gets two acres, then it would have continued like that even today. But custom has always had it the other way round.

Q: Do you think it should be changed?
A: How does it matter how I feel it or how you feel? The entire system should change. If the raj changes, all will change.

Q: But do you feel that it should change?
A: If I alone feel that, will they agree?

Q: Whether it's accepted or not is another thing.
A: Then, yes. A girl and a boy are the same. Both are born from our womb, they are the same, we should treat them equally. At least if two portions are given to him, one could be given to the girl. At least a quarter should be there for the girl.

Q: Are such things—for instance that the girl should have a right over land, rights of a woman, that she is in no way less, that she is also a human being like a man and so on—are these things ever discussed among you or in the panchayat?
A: This topic could never be kept on the agenda. When we discuss, it is about work which should be done. What's the point of just discussing and talking?

Q: Because it's not likely to happen, it shouldn't be discussed?
A: Yes, since it won't happen, it should not be discussed. If we say something, then the words should be respected.

Q: Isn't there any point in discussion? Shouldn't things just be discussed?
A: No, we don't wish to.

Q: See, you're the sarpanch, you do a lot of work. Your case is different. But the rest of them, do you think that because they've become members of the panchayat they have got more power? Take the case of Mastudbai, the chamar, what power did she get?
A: She got a little power.

Q: Over what?
A: About liquor.

Q: But later no one did anything. So what power did she really get?
A: Power means that the people obeyed. The fact that people respect what she says pleases her. No one drinks now, there is no trouble. That is power. Comfort to her heart that no one drinks. That much power. That much satisfaction in her mind. That the villagers feel they ought to obey her. That the power is in a woman's hands, they have to listen to her.

Q: Now that you're the sarpanch, what according to you should your commitment to the village be? Or to the women? Or to yourself?
A: Not to myself. It should be for the good of the village, of the poor, and for the betterment of women. Women should be informed about various

things. They should be told that unless they move about, mix with people, they won't know how things are, how the atmosphere is. Let them say anything behind our backs, or criticize us, we should walk ahead. We shouldn't retreat. [. . .]

~

THE ELUSIVE 'WOMAN':
FEMINISM AND THE WOMEN'S RESERVATION BILL
Nivedita Menon

[. . .]

Gender and caste since 1980s

What were the developments between 1974 when women's movement activists in the Committee on the Status of Women in India rejected reservations for women in parliament, and 1996, when almost the same representatives of the women's movement demanded such reservations? What were the shifts in the two intervening decades that would explain this change? In the years that passed, there were two significant developments in Indian politics. One had to do with challenges to the legitimacy of the national integrity argument. By the mid-1970s, the legitimacy of the post-independence elites had begun to erode with the economic and political crisis precipitated by the failure of development planning. There was a resurgence of militancy in every section of society. Critical questions were arising as to whose interests were being protected by the 'integrity' of the nation state. By the mid-1980s, various regional movements were challenging the inherited idea of Indian nationhood, and backward caste assertion had begun to transform the nature of the political arena and the composition of the Lok Sabha. Yogendra Yadav (1999) points out, 'The influx of lower orders into the field of democratic contestation has . . . [made] it respectable to talk of caste in the public-political domain. The emergence of social justice as a rubric to talk about caste equity [and] political representation of castes and communities . . . is a distinct achievement of this period.'

The other development was that women had emerged as a significant force in politics. Women had been at the forefront of the movements against corruption and price-rise that preceded the imposition of the Emergency. The 1980s saw the emergence of vocal and visible autonomous women's groups which placed feminist issues firmly on the public agenda—dowry, rape, violence against women. At the same time it was clear that women were underrepresented on representative bodies. Already by the time of the National Perspective Plan 1988–2000, therefore, there was both an acknowledgement of women's militant participation in politics as well as of their absence in decision-making bodies. Vina Mazumdar, who was member secretary of the Committee on the Status of Women in India (CSWI), points out how as 'daughters of independence' her generation had been critical of special representation, but gradually 'we have found our understanding of nation-building changing radically' (Mazumdar 1997). By 1996 then, the 'daughters of independence' had come to acknowledge that abstract citizenship was only a cover for privilege, and that difference had to be acknowledged.

However, the point I would emphasize here is that the emergence of women as a significant group in Indian politics is only one of two factors shifting the consensus on women's reservations. The other, the transformation of the caste composition of parliament and the growing presence of backward castes through successive elections, is an equally significant development. I will argue that these two very different (even opposed) sets of concerns—feminist and upper caste—tied in at this particular conjuncture to produce the sudden general acceptability of women's reservations.

Is the WRB only about 'women'?

The career of the Women's Reservations Bill in parliament is striking for the high drama and rhetoric of women's rights that has accompanied it. The passionate opposition to the bill being generally characterized by its supporters as anti-women and phrases decrying the derailing of the bill are illustrative—'a predominantly male parliament developed cold feet' (Rai and Sharma 2000); 'Sansad par kabiz purush satta'; 'Parliament was divided into men and women, the former all opposed to the Women's Reservations Bill'; 'Parliament is like an all-male club and I feel like an unwanted intruder'; 'Caste-based arguments in defence of male domination'. Similarly, speculating about the reasons why political parties who supported the reservations of seats for women in local bodies are reluctant regarding similar legislation at the parliamentary level, Shirin Rai and Kumud Sharma wonder, 'Could it be that enhanced representation of women in the national parliament spells a far greater and immediate challenge to the gendered status quo within the party political system?' or conversely, 'Is it that the patterns of quota systems in India have shown that elite based strategies of empowerment are less helpful to groups seeking greater recognition than those based on grassroots institutions?' (Rai and Sharma 2000). In other words, is it the case that political parties resist the bill because they fear it will empower women too much or too little? However, as Rai and Sharma unravel the actual arguments of the protagonists and antagonists of the bill, it becomes clear that while the protagonists make their arguments in terms of gender justice, the arguments against the bill come from two opposed positions—they stem either from opposition to reservations in general or from a belief that reservations for women should be extended to other disempowered groups (the quotas within quotas position). The arguments against, in other words, are not 'anti-feminist'. In spite of their own evidence, however, the writers continue to frame their discussion in terms of whether mainstream political bodies have 'embraced the gender justice agenda' or not.

It is now evident that to continue to understand the bill in terms only of attitudes to women would be a partial exercise at best. Rather, I would argue that when we tease out the strands in the debate, we find two sets of arguments for and against. There are feminist (or at least, pro-women) arguments for and against reservations for women, and (implicitly or explicitly) caste-based arguments for and against.

A feminist case for reservations is made in terms of the need for affirmative action to redress the situation of women. This argument comes from Left parties and women's groups. A characteristic statement of this kind is that made by Vasanth and Kalpana Kannabiran, long-time activists of the women's movement. 'Women's participation in the political process is critical both to the strengthening of democratic traditions and to their struggle against oppression.' But they are obstructed in such participation by 'power relations that . . . operate at many levels of society from the most personal to the highly public'. It is necessary therefore to appropriate spaces in mainstream political arenas and reshape them (Kannabiran 1997). A CPI(M) MP expresses another facet of this strand when she argues that while the reservations policy per se is not democratic, it is nevertheless necessary to rectify existing imbalances. Thus, it is a partial measure, but one that is unavoidable if women are to participate effectively in politics (Bhattacharya 1997). Similarly, an editorial of *ML Update,* the weekly bulletin of CPI (ML), states that while 'formal equality in law hardly brings equality in society', the WRB is important as 'the moot point at this stage is to recognize women in their entirety as an oppressed category in an otherwise male dominated society.' More importantly, the bill 'may prove catalytic to their larger entry in the political arena' *(ML Update 1998).* The feminist argument for reservations is thus made in terms of creating equality of opportunity in order to make real the formal equality given by the constitution.

What could be called a pro-women case against reservations is made by Madhu Kishwar, the editor of *Manushi* (which calls itself 'a journal about women and society'), and by the Shetkari Mahila Aghadi (SMA), a peasant women's organization founded in 1986. Their broad argument has to do with the concern that reservations will only bring to the fore the 'biwi-beti brigade'. The SMA in an 'Open Letter to MPs', signed by Gail Omvedt among others, said that quotas for women 'is being pushed by women in the creamy layer'. Omvedt too, opposes the WRB, terming one of the most disturbing aspects of the debate around it, 'the way it seemed to set (mainly upper caste) feminists against (mainly male) OBC leaders' (Omvedt 2000).

The SMA prefers to put up all-women panels for panchayat elections as the experience of reservations in panchayats in Maharashtra has not been favourable—relatives of established male leaders are fielded, and there has been no impact at all on inefficiency and corruption. It suggests a more fundamental transformation in the election system, the introduction of three-seat constituencies, with each voter having three votes, one of which has to go to a woman. One seat is to be for the woman with the highest votes from among women candidates. (SMA 1997).

Kishwar too originally backed the proposal of the SMA although now she has come up with a separate proposal (endorsed by Omvedt in a different form) [. . .] Kishwar believes that reservations are unnecessary because 'our country has a well-entrenched tradition whereby any party, politician or public figure who tries to bad mouth women in public or opposes moves in favour of women's equality is strongly disapproved of. Hence, compared to many other parts of the world, it is relatively easy to get legislation favouring women passed in India' (Kishwar 1996). This is an amazing statement—a cursory look at newspapers would reveal that extremely patriarchal and sexist, at best protectionist, views of women are routinely publicly expressed in the course of rape trials and election campaigns, in police statements on violence against women, and the like. These are contested only by women's groups and women's wings of political parties, usually of the Left. As for legislation favouring women, Kishwar's is a surprisingly naïve understanding of Indian politics, and of how and why laws get passed. Take for instance, the right to abortion which she cites as an example. The Medical Termination of Pregnancy Bill was introduced as a population control measure in 1971 and the debate in parliament was entirely within those terms. It is not surprising therefore that only two MPs opposed it. Abortion was not being discussed as a question of women's right over their bodies, but on the contrary, as a measure necessitated in order to achieve lower population growth. In the context of countries of the global south where 'overpopulation' is presented as the reason for poverty, state control of fertility is the problem for feminists, not the illegality of abortion. Therefore, the fact that this right took 'decades of struggle in the west' while it was 'enacted in India without a fight', as Kishwar puts it, has to be understood very differently. In other words, the passing of apparently 'feminist' legislation has to be located also in the context of the compulsions of ruling elites in order to understand the complex dynamics involved. Eventually, however, Kishwar concedes that 'our democracy has failed to include women in its purview', partly due to the Gandhian legacy which saw women's role in politics as self-sacrifice rather than as a bid for power, and more recently, because of the increasing corruption and criminalization associated with politics (Kishwar 1996).

I term SMA and Kishwar's position as a 'pro-women' critique of reservations because their objections arise from focusing on women's interests, which they believe would be better served by other measures. The next set of arguments, which I term 'caste-based', take positions for and against reservations explicitly or implicitly, in term of caste. The most reviled, explicitly caste-based opposition to women's reservations has been the derogatory reference of Sharad Yadav to the 'short-haired' women who would over-run parliament. While this has been understood as a misogynist statement, we must see it also as expressing a legitimate fear that reservations for women would radically alter the composition of parliament in favour of upper classes and upper castes—the term 'parkati mahilaen' in this context drawing upon a common stereotype of westernized and elite women. Of course this stereotype is sexist and misogynist, but that is not really the point here, because surely we are under no illusion that all the support for women's reservations comes from those who actively contest and reject such stereotypes. Rather this kind of opposition to the bill in its present from has to be recognized as arising from the politics of caste identity.

The idea of reservation for an undifferentiated category of 'women' has been uniformly denounced by politicians and writers speaking for backward castes and dalits. At its most explicit, such an argument attacks the bill as an upper caste ploy to stem the rising tide of lower caste men in politics (Dhanda 1989). In this context, we must take into account the experience of women's reservations in panchayati raj institutions. Studies in Gujarat and Karnataka have confirmed that the entrenched power of the dominant castes has been strengthened by women's reservations. It is not surprising then, that OBC and dalit leaders are highly suspicious of the WRB. In an interview, Mayawati, the Bahujan Samaj Party leader, demanded that there should be 50 per cent reservations for women, and within this, separate reservations for backward castes and minorities. Mulayam Singh Yadav of the Samajwadi Party has consistently opposed the bill, saying that in its present form it is anti-minority and anti-dalit.

Most interestingly, Uma Bharati of the BJP, herself from a backward caste, has taken a position opposed to that of her party's. Unlike Sushma Swaraj, the upper caste BJP leader most vocal in support of the bill, Uma Bharati makes a clear feminist argument for reservations, while asserting that a backward caste or dalit woman is doubly oppressed, and so should have a place within the quota. Characteristically, Uma Bharati does not grant a quota for Muslim women, even while conceding that they are among the most oppressed, for 'in a secular constitution, there can be no place for reservations based on religion'. This could push the country toward theocracy. She does not however, reject the idea of reservations for Muslims altogether. Her solution is instead to give reservations to Muslim caste-groups included in the Mandal OBCs, for example, julahe, bunkar, ansari. Thus, in a move which challenges BJP's nationalist Hindutva perspective, she decisively privileges caste identity. It is this split within the party that keeps the BJP from pushing through the bill, rather than mere 'hypocrisy' about gender justice, as many commentators have suggested, for I am persuaded that hypocrisy is all-pervasive in politics, and cannot be treated as an explanatory device.

Within the caste-based opposition to the bill I would place another strand—a defence of abstract citizenship against any kind of affirmative action. That is, an anti-reservation position in general. It is significant that this position is not taken by any political party, and is expressed only by individual commentators in the media. Thus for example we have an editorial in *The Indian Express* which says that the pandemonium in parliament over the bill 'is a sorry vindication of this newspaper's traditional position that affirmative action is a wrong headed idea. Once unleashed, it perpetuates and propagates itself in the most divisive ways. Is Parliament to be parceled into lots of the historically oppressed, leaving the rest of mainstream India to its own devices?' Chandan Mitra bemoans the fact that 'Already the vicious specter of casteism has begun haunting the party system' and feared the degeneration of parliament to a 'caste panchayats' union'. Reservations for women would lead to demands for reservations for other groups, and 'instead of moving towards the 21st century and age of virtual reality, we have been dragged back into medievalism'.

This last anti-reservation position opposing the bill is an interesting counterpoint to the final position I present—the (implicitly) caste-based support for women's reservations. These two apparently contradictory positions, one rejecting reservations in toto and the other supporting women's reservations while rejecting caste-based reservations, represent similar interests. It is when we examine the latter that we move more directly towards the suggestion I made earlier, that upper caste concerns and feminist concerns tie in at this historical moment on this question. This position pushes for the passing of the bill and flatly rejects the demand for further quotas. Within this last position I would place the BJP and the Congress. While within the BJP there is considerable contestation of the official party line rejecting 'quotas within quotas', as we have seen, any debate within the Congress is muted. The party seems reconciled to the loss of its earlier dalit and Muslim base, and is pushing for the bill in its present form.

Madhu Kishwar takes heart from the fact that the very same people who opposed the Mandal reservations for OBCs have accepted reservations for women 'with apparent grace and enthusiasm'. For her this is further proof of the great women-friendly traditions of India (Kishwar 1996). As a political analyst one cannot help but note, however, that the fearsome future that Chandan Mitra and *The Indian Express* editorial outline is precisely what a blanket 33 per sent reservation for women hopes to prevent. That is, an immediate filling of 33 per cent of seats with women would certainly change the class and caste composition of parliament back in the short term, to one more comfortable for our elites, which clearly considers itself to be 'the mainstream', as opposed to the 'historically oppressed', as the editorial quoted above unabashedly declares. As Vasanthi Raman points out, OBCs and Muslims, given their numerical strength as well as their social location, pose a greater threat to upper castes than SC/STs, about whom some complacency was still possible (Raman 1999).

Within the broad feminist camp, the suggestion of 'quotas within quotas' has received mixed responses. As Gail Omvedt points out, by now the stark antagonism between OBC and feminist leaders is easing (Omvedt 2000). Most women's groups accept the principle of quotas within quotas, but while some groups are prepared for a redrafting of the present bill to include such quotas; others, like the Left groups, continue to insist that the bill must be passed first, and further quotas can be worked out later.

This survey of positions on the WRB throws into relief a set of interrelated questions about (a) 'women' as the subject of feminist politics, (b) citizenship in postcolonial democracies, and (c) the idea of political representation. This is about women and the women's movement on the one hand and women and the nation state on the other, with representation as the category mediating both relationships. [. . .]

References

Bhattacharya, Malini. September 1997. Democracy and reservations. *Seminar* 457, 23–24.

Kannabiran, Vasanth and Kalpana Kannabiran. 1 February 1997. From social action to political action: Women and the 81st amendment. *Economic and Political Weekly*, 196–97

Kishwar, Madhu. 26 October 1996. Women in politics: Beyond quotas. *Economic and Political Weekly*, 2867–74

Mazumdar, Vina. 1997. Historical soundings. *Seminar* 457, 14–19.

Omvedt, Gail. 12 September 2000. Women and PR. *Hindu.*

Rai, Shirin and Kumud Sharma. 2000. Democratising the Indian parliament: The reservations for women debate. In *International perspectives on gender and democratisation,* ed. Shirin Rai. Macmillan: London, 149–165.

Raman, Vasanthi. 11 December 1999. Women's reservations and democratisation: An Alternative Perspective. *Economic and Political Weekly*, 4393–95.

Shetkari Mahila Aghadi. June 1997. Reservation on reservation. *Communalism Combat.*

Yadav, Yogendra. 21–28 August 1999. Electoral politics in the time of change: India's third electoral system, 1998–99. *Economic and Political Weekly*, 2393–99.

∾

THE FOURTH WORLD CONFERENCE ON WOMEN:
A REPORT FROM CHINA

Indu Agnihotri

In the history of world conferences on women, the Beijing meet shall stand out for its reassertion that women's struggles are integral to the mounting challenge to the existing world order, and that women's issues could not be segregated from larger issues related to development. It has also become clear that women's struggles in various countries are not disaggregated and dissipated. Beijing and Huairou reaffirmed the vitality of the women's movement. [. . .] With the collapse of the socialist bloc it became clear that the struggle for women's rights was up against political forces which were pushing the agenda in favour of fundamentalism and tearing out of context the very goals sought to be achieved. At Nairobi a clear attempt was made to deflect from a systemic perspective of issues, focusing instead in a fragmented and ineffectual way on particular manifestations of women's oppression. Gender sensitization and training were being bandied as panaceas while it became clear that the women's movement itself did not set the agenda.

In Beijing, the initiative rested clearly with the movement. The failure of the developed countries to cope with the crises in world capitalism was brought out by pointed critiques of the gamut of liberalization strategies and trade agreements including from within the developed world itself, drawing attention to the effects of the 'dismantling' of the welfare state. This provided the backdrop to a consolidated critique from the perspective of the international women's movement. It showed the relevance of the international political context in the framing of any meaningful women's agenda, rather than its being based on a mere biologically based sisterhood. This is not to understate the domination of the advanced west in the international political configuration which was apparent right from the preparatory stage of the conference and in the selective nature of accreditation given to non-governmental organizations (NGOs). Here the influence of the donor agencies was clear. The first world dominated in terms of the presence of their governments and in the say that the first world–based donor agencies had in deciding who went to Beijing. The gap between the aspirations articulated by the movement and the commitments governments were willing to make remained, nevertheless.

The significance of the conference lay in moving towards a build up of alliances which spilled out of strictly 'women's issues', reflective of a shift in the prevailing attitude towards the direction of global change. This was completely missed out in media coverage of the event. The dominant media representation seemed to endorse the trivialization of women's issues which were also restrictedly seen as confined to the right to abortion, fight against rape, sexual abuse and so on. Further, these were projected as being delinked from international issues.

This approach was surprisingly abandoned when it came to China-bashing, the other dominant trend in media coverage of the meet. The grounds on which China was picked out as an 'inappropriate venue'(its capabilities in hosting the meet, its record of human rights violations: female infanticide, forced abortion, Tibet and state censorship) reflected the hostility towards China. What was more surprising was the uncritical acceptance of this bias by the media of the third world, which even though not always shared by the journalists present, was carried over through western news agency copies used by the Indian newspapers. To those who were present in Beijing–Huairou, China showed that it was more than capable of hosting the meet: the arrangements made in terms of accommodation and transport facilities were excellent. It needs to be pointed out that these arrangements were made even for those on a tight budget, a fact glossed over by the strident critics of the venue. As far as apprehensions about surveillance and security go, it was clear that it was largely restricted to procedural requirements of such a large meet and did not infringe on delegates' freedom of movement or speech. Pamphlets of all kinds were freely distributed and demonstrations were held at the forum site every day.

Finally, the belief that violence and crimes against women are a third world problem was belied by the various personal testimonies by women from developed countries of the first world in the public hearings on 'women's rights as human rights' in Beijing itself. [. . .] Along with others, the United States has yet to ratify the Convention on Elimination of Discrimination against Women (CEDAW). The violence that multinational companies generate in Mexico across the US border in the lives of the Makiladoras was very revealing. To single out China for a pointed attack was clearly a motivated political strategy. This, however, is not to imply that China or other socialist countries should be overlooked when assessments are made of the denial of women's rights/human rights.

The issues: Structural adjustment programmes (SAPs) and the implications of globalization

Critiques of the current stage of capitalist development were mounted from different standpoints throughout the forum. There was near unanimity over the havoc wreaked on women's lives by SAPs and globalization strategies. There were over 300 workshops dealing with economic issues which indicated the effects of international trade agreements on national policies and the role of international funding agencies. Notions that peace, equality and development could take place in the prevailing ethos of the global economy was questioned by delegates from Latin American, Asian and African countries and Denmark,

Canada, the Scandinavian countries, and Ireland, especially given the complicity of the north in the development of the arms industry and the interference in the democratic processes of the south. Across the board women emphasized that women are not a monolithic category, that the indignities heaped on them had their roots in economic and political structures, as these were not neutral *per se*, and that material realities had a crucial bearing on their lives.

The feminization of poverty figured as a major theme. The International Association of Feminist Economists organized a series of panel discussions which put women's property rights, control over land and resources and challenges posed by globalization on the agenda. Strategies and struggles against SAP were also focused on. The implications of new laws regarding intellectual property and the threat to the environmental balance were specifically discussed in many sessions, also with specific reference to the hazards of the consumption and production patterns of the developed countries.

In a workshop organized by the Women's International Democratic Federation (WIDF) the dominant perspective of participants leaned to the left. It was reiterated that 60% of the world's rural population were women, and 2/3 of the poor are women and that half a million women die every year due to maternity-related problems. A delegate from Cuba noted the effect of the economic blockade on Cuba, which is tantamount to the denial of Cuba's sovereignity as a nation. A representative of the All China Women's Federation, affirmed that in China too the brunt of the new 'open' policies was faced by women. A delegate from erstwhile East Germany spoke of the problems faced by her people after the re-unification in terms of education, housing and other social and welfare issues.

Religious fundamentalism

A consolidated opposition to religious fundamentalism was clearly sought to be built in the forum. This was heartening in the wake of the organized presence of the Christian and Islamic fundamentalist groups for the meet. There was a formidable presence of large numbers of female supporters of both these and what became clear to all was the close coordination amongst them. Unlike the general impression being conveyed amongst activists of an Islamic fundamentalism, at Beijing the orchestrated and combined opposition mounted by the Holy See and Islamic fundamentalism led by Iran was very visible. The latter even threatened their own country women who did not agree with them. The fundamentalists attacked women activists as being godless, non-feminine, anti-family, unnatural and attempted to portray the Virgin Mary as a feminist and a religious symbol. [. . .]

It was also clear that to eulogize the concept of 'woman as agent' in a decontextualized and depoliticized sense was dangerous. Hereby, beliefs and practices of an exclusivist genre are sought to be sanctified on the basis of 'differences' and women are projected as being active participants in the perpetuation of such ideologies. In fact the presence of such a large number of women upholding religious fundamentalism in an international conference on women points to the insidious manner in which the feminist facade of fundamentalism operates. Unable to present an outright anti-woman face given the reality that women's struggle for their rights is rooted in their everyday experiences, fundamentalism has tried to adapt itself to many modern agendas and even cites 'cultural difference' as the basis for deflecting criticisms. Doubtless, cultural differences do exist and need to be taken into account. However, it does not necessarily follow that cultural frameworks become the paradigm within which these issues are to be confined. The most significant question lies in analyzing the precise basis of gender inequality which is systemic. Culturally relativist stances and the defence of traditions on the plea of plurality lead to selective tinkering with some aspects of women's existence, without undermining the systemic basis of this existence. [. . .]

Violence against women

Judging by the importance given to discussions on violence against women, it was clear that despite the number of action programmes focusing on different aspects of violence, the issue continues to remain an important one for the women's movement. If anything, there seems to be an intensification of mental and physical violence against women in the recent past. A plenary session organized at Huairou consisting of public hearings of personal testimonies before a panel of judges revealed the gross violation of women's rights at all levels. It underscored the fundamental view that women's rights are human rights and that the inability of the state to safeguard the rights of citizens is a violation of the state's commitments and responsibilities towards women. These hearings were the culmination of efforts begun in Vienna in 1993. Radhika Coomaraswamy, UN's special rapporteur on violence against women, placed the preliminary findings of a report on domestic violence. The proceedings highlighted, in general, the different aspects of violence: domestic, child abuse, rape in situations of war and strife, dalit women's oppression in India, violence arising out of power situations—at the work place, due to class and social structures, violence emanating from moral precepts, against lesbianism, the sufferings of the Korean 'comfort women', and so on. The state, whether liberal democratic or authoritarian, was equally implicated in the denial of civil rights and justice to women. More than anything else, the session made it clear that all societies were guilty witness to problems on this count and not merely a few societies from the south. The testimonies also drove home the point that while patriarchy was a crucial element in oppressive structures, in their fight for equality women were also confronting institutions and structures which perpetuated other forms of inequality and injustice. However, sexual abuse and assault remained the common form of attack, cutting across territorial boundaries.

Legal strategies

The women's movement has consistently engaged with the law both as an institution reflecting dominant attitudes as well as an instrument that can effect change. [. . .] A tradition of legal activism exists which emphasizes that law cannot be treated either as a given nor as static, even as specific sections and clauses are invoked for implementation. There were workshops at Beijing on the rights of women under different laws, more particularly personal laws. Judicial bias also came in for criticism. There were also discussions on the strategies to expand the horizons of laws and legal concepts in the workshop 'Basic Laws—Basic Needs'. One argument advanced by a participant from the Caribbean region was that talk of legal rights is rendered meaningless unless enabling conditions are created for the actual exercise of these laws. Equality cannot be secured merely by provision of legal guarantees. In the discussion on CEDAW, attention was drawn to the fact that no follow-up legislation had been brought forward to advance the implementation of the concerned clauses after the signing of the convention by several nations. Furthermore, in many countries countervailing laws continued to exist alongside CEDAW, and in some cases even new laws had been passed which were violative of CEDAW in letter and spirit. The All India Democratic Women's Association (AIDWA) delegate cited the example of the Muslim Women (Protection of Rights of Divorce) Bill, 1986, which continues to be in force, despite being challenged in court and, by all accounts, being violative of both CEDAW and the provisions on fundamental rights enshrined in the Indian constitution. Participants pointed out that the convention lacked teeth and could not be implemented. Also, that the reporting procedure was extremely deficient. Countries like India could get away by merely ratifying the convention and subsequently violating it. In a workshop on women's rights in Nepal the manner in which majority fundamentalism was practised was discussed. Participants highlighted how Nepali women suffer under the brahmanical Hindu laws of Manu, for example, in Nepal bigamy is valid, the second marriage is not void. The maximum penalty imposed, if at all, is that the bigamist goes to jail for a few months.

Health, reproductive rights and sexuality

The context for the discussions on reproductive rights was the Cairo conference held in 1994. At Beijing, fundamentalists, Islamic and Christian, were well-organized. Activist groups from the south were also well-prepared to challenge the Cairo draft which seemed to push population 'control' measures through social policies which made contraceptives proven to be hazardous as part of an aid package . [. . .] Battle lines were drawn on two fronts: one favouring reproductive rights along with the availability of long-acting barrier method contraceptives as part of a more comprehensive health policy; the other focusing on the autonomy argument, pushing for freedom of choice against repressive social policies based on fundamentalist precepts represented by Vatican and Islamic fundamentalism.

Sexuality, which is only beginning to surface as an issue in the women's movement in India, was high on the agenda of a sizable section in Beijing. Despite reservations about the single-point nature of the sexual rights agenda, often at the neglect of other related problems, there was recognition of the sexual rights issue as a part of human rights. Indian laws, though regressive in many aspects, remain silent on the issue of lesbianism though discrimination and fear of discrimination prevail.

Role and functioning of UN agencies

At a plenary organized in Huairou the role played by UN agencies in advancing the cause of women's empowerment and gender equity strategies came up for discussion. Representatives of various UN organizations such as the UNFPA, UNIFEM, UNICEF, and UNDP reported on the manner in which women had emerged as a target group in agency programmes/projects. The status of women within the agencies was commented on and observations made on the success of training programmes to focus on gender issues. However the panelists resisted being drawn into discussions regarding the positions being advanced in UN documents and the extent to which these advanced the fight for gender equality. When attention was drawn to the fact that the UN could perhaps be lending itself to what was seen as a 'retreat' and that the history of the UN was now being talked of only as of Rio, Cairo and Copenhagen whereas important documents such as the Alma Ata one were being consigned to the archives as pre-history, this was seen as 'negative assessment'. For the record, it must be mentioned that the UN programme had put pressure on some governments to specially focus on women. As a prominent functionary in the UN rightly asserted, 'in the UN when equality is achieved it will be not only for women but for the organization as a whole'.

Funding, NGOs and donors

The functioning of NGOs and their relationship with donor agencies came up in discussions. Many took positions which were critical of donors and funding agencies. Questions were also raised about the role of donor agencies and the attempts to influence agendas and NGOs which were accepting funds. This aspect becomes particularly crucial in the light of the preparatory process of the UN conference where donor agencies were very influential. Countries need to make financial commitments in relation to their own gross domestic product (GDP). But budgets and the decision as to who got to the conference and who could speak was also a question of money. At least half of the delegates to the NGO forum were US and Canada based. Japan, China and Thailand too had a large presence.

The extended preparatory process has to be critically reviewed. Many activists could not make it to the conference. There is a pattern to the networks that have been built up. For the first time the Indian government was forced to have a mediated relationship with its own NGOs through an Inter-agency Facilitating and Coordinating Bureau, which itself is a creation of the donor agencies. This pattern was repeated in Beijing. Briefings and meets at the official UN conference could only be organized through such established networks. Furthermore the NGOs and NGO caucuses are based in the first world: their heads and spokespersons are largely from there. Though a token presence of others may be seen, they are not always allowed to voice their opinions. [. . .]

China in the conference

The All China Women's Federation (ACWF) conducted several discussions, and meetings of its own members to ensure full participation of its own delegates in the World Conference. Although the language barrier surfaced all through, one gathered that many of the Chinese participants followed the line of argument during discussion though they seemed hesitant to express themselves in English without the help of an interpreter.

ACWF delegates could be seen attending a wide range of workshops and their desire to keep up with the debates could be seen in their eagerness to get copies of pamphlets/literature being circulated. It was clear that they were interested in the issues thrown up in the course of discussions and were not going to miss the opportunity that the UN conference offered. Sometimes they were very forthcoming in private conversation and in discussions on SAP and liberalization policies. Their interventions made it clear that they too were keenly following the debate on SAP and women, and monitoring the impact of these policies on women in China. Apart from participating in thematic workshops, the ACWF had itself organized several panel discussions/workshops. Many of these were on the theme of women's education and literacy, an area in which they have amassed a great deal of experience. Indian participants in these workshops found that the Chinese delegates brought into these sessions a very live concrete experience based on their work, offering insights into the question of obstacles faced in the effort to advance women's education. However, one of the most largely attended sessions where Chinese participants displayed a great deal of enthusiasm was on the theme of business entrepreneurship and women in China—which sums up the current mood of the society.

At the same time, what struck all the participants from outside was the tremendous confidence Chinese women displayed in their dealings with foreign participants and their male colleagues. Their spirit and their eagerness to know more went a long way in making the conference a success. It is also notable that even in the middle of such hectic activity, senior delegates/office-bearers of ACWF found time to meet with delegates from different parts of the world and exchange information about status, the impact of globalization and trends affecting women. The fact that they could take time off to extend such warm hospitality was also at the same time a gesture of friendship towards the women of the world.

The challenge of the nineties

The dismantling of the socialist bloc was evident in the waning of the peace movement. The Peace Train group from Helsinki had problems coordinating itself, leave alone linking up with the others. The presence of Japan was marked in the peace initiatives. The Peace Tent was the centre of many activities.

The WIDF-organized workshops on the post-socialist scenario included some interesting discussions on women's rights in the eastern bloc countries. Awareness of the post-Soviet unipolar reality was strong among the Palestinians. Many of these delegates were using this conference to regroup and take stock of the specific challenges faced by them. Delegate after delegate pointed but how they were finding it difficult even to meet given the disturbed situation 'back home'. As one Croatian put it in a discussion on women's studies, there is far greater talk of women's rights now that the earlier climate of an 'ideology of equality' no longer existed.

It is important to note that while critiques of capitalism and opposition to imperialism were forthcoming from varied quarters there were no alternative 'models' being advocated. It was as if activists had realized that for the moment coming to terms with this phase of globalization was the issue at hand and that the economic agenda of conservatism was not entirely divorced from the aggressive political stance being adopted by fundamentalism. Recognition of this double-edged sword was a first step towards stemming the tide of conservatism and asserting that the women's movement was a significant component of the forces working towards structural transformation. The search for allies as well as the need for joining hands with other forces fighting for social change was expressed over and over again: in the discussions, in marches, in the graffiti and in the music women made, the songs they sang, hoping that the notes would reach their brothers and sisters who could not all join them in Beijing.

3

≈

HISTORY

For the women's movement and women's studies, history has been a very special disciplinary domain and site of struggle. Beginning in the early 1980s, feminists from a range of fields, and, indeed, from outside the academy itself, took issue with the historiography of every period. The interface between history and 'the women's question' offers a particularly revealing instance of a double relationship—the shaping power of 'mainstream' history on the concept of 'women', on the one hand, and feminist interrogations of this legacy, on the other. One of the more fascinating aspects of feminists' repeated incursions into history has to do with how questions thrown up by current events opened up hitherto neglected or lost pasts.

We begin this cluster with a classic essay by Uma Chakravarti, who discusses why the study of ancient India (which dominated the discipline in its early stages) was unique in the special emphasis accorded to women of the Vedic period. The most divergent schools, colonial and nationalist, whose characterizations were otherwise opposed, saw 'Vedic India' as holding the key to an understanding of the subsequent history of the subcontinent, including its present condition. Chakravarti establishes how this idea was first developed in the nineteenth century, and critiques the work of the historian Altekar, in particular, whose views went well beyond the confines of his profession to constitute the general 'common sense' of our time. Feminist historians have, in the last two decades, provided fresh perspectives on the significance of gender and patriarchal relations in different parts of the subcontinent during this early period. This reader offers an illustration in the section on sexuality, where Kumkum Roy locates the *Kamasutra* in its own time and ours, to reveal extraordinary transformations in the course of its many translations.

The elevation of the ancient period, with its roots in the dynamic of colonial rule, also led to areas of comparative neglect—of alternate sources of study to Sanskritic and brahmanical texts, and of the medieval period especially. Though no essay has been included here, we must mention feminist investigations into the legacy of women-saints and poets who were active in the bhakti movements from the eighth century up to the seventeenth century in many regions, who spoke out against elaborate ritual and ascetic withdrawal in favour of personalized forms of devotion, and who composed in local languages for ordinary people. The overall paucity of research on this period, however, (including from feminist perspectives), and in spite of a rich archive, is yet to be rectified.

The study of the colonial era marks a watershed in the history of the subcontinent. Feminists have been at the forefront of recognizing how pivotal this period has been in establishing frames of reference for approaching the nature of tradition and modernity, colonialism and nationalism, and indeed the question of history itself. Women have been critical in the concern over their rising or falling 'status', in the emergence of 'rights', and in the making of the nation. We are still in the process of 'recasting women' (to deploy the title of a path-breaking collection of essays *Recasting Women: Essays in Colonial History*) in the genealogies of social reform, the rise of nationalism, the histories of caste, class and community, the 'civilizing mission' of colonialism, and the development of regions. These efforts have rarely rested with contributing the subject of women to a genderless narrative, but have questioned prior concepts of gender themselves. As a result, feminist scholars are both uncovering the silences and problematic assumptions of the 'mainstream' while also challenging one another. Our next essay by Saleem Kidwai provides glimpses into gender relations that the growing colonial power could only label 'degenerate'. Awadhi culture in cities like Lucknow during the eighteenth and nineteenth centuries defies periodisation into 'medieval' or 'modern' as we hear about the power wielded by its begum rulers; the development of a new genre of Urdu poetry known as rekhti; and innovative religious rituals at court, all of which transgressed colonial (and, later, nationalist) norms of gender and sexuality.

Colonial Bengal has occupied a prominent place in the history of the women's question—in the first campaigns over the abolition of sati and for widow remarriage, in the controversies over women's education and age of marriage, and in the subsequent shifts in the agendas of nationalism. Two discussions (by Partha Chatterjee and Tanika Sarkar) on the significance of these nineteenth century developments in the first woman's autobiography have been placed in the section on education, though they obviously belong here as well. Here we offer an early essay by Jasodhara Bagchi on the work

of the much-cited nineteenth century intellectual Bankimchandra
Chattopadhyay. Themes of womanhood, reinventions of a Hindu past and
the first national confrontations with colonial rule come together in her
analysis of his Bengali novel *Anandmath*. Tracing Bankim's closeness to the
ideas of the founder of scientific positivism, Auguste Comte, she shows just
what happens to Comte's relatively harmonious principles of transition into
a new society based on order and progress, when these ideas are transposed
into a context of colonial domination and alienation. Bankimchandra's novel
is suffused with a sense of crisis and deep threat, and, women, who provide
the 'heart' in Comte's scheme, become 'symbols of the ravaged order and the
resistance to such ravages'. Far from remaining within the cultural spaces of
literature, Bagchi goes on to point out how, in just a few decades, Bankim's
work was to provide a basis for the most extremist forms of militant Hindu
nationalism.

The next essay takes us into the early decades of the twentieth century.
This intense and turbulent period, witnessing the rise of political nationalism
against colonial rule, has frequently been associated with the relative invisibility
of women's issues, compared to the public debates and battles of the previous
century. However, this misleading—if not erroneous—picture is progressively
being redrawn to make room for the numerous ways in which women were
mobilizing themselves or being mobilized, and in a diversity of regions. A
major concern from the point of view of history, therefore, has to do with
the selective ways in which certain figures and moments have been remembered,
while others were effectively lost after independence, only to be rediscovered
afresh very recently. A good example would be Sarojini Naidu, celebrated in
school textbooks as the 'nightingale of India', but hardly known for the
power of her political oratory and active role in the Indian National
Congress. Moreover, it is not merely women who have been slighted by
memory and history. V. Geetha's essay on E.V. Ramaswamy Naickar or
Periyar, leader of the non-Brahmin Dravidian movement in Madras, is part
of a larger intervention, provoked by the painful experience of the absence of
this legacy when it was needed most—the redeployments of caste in national
and regional politics after the anti-Mandal agitations of 1990 against
reservations for the Other Backward Classes in government services. Even
more buried from view was the relevance of Periyar's caste-based critiques of
gender and sexuality. In this discussion, V. Geetha compares Periyar to the
much more familiar figure of Gandhi, both of whom privileged what she has
termed 'the inter-linked realms of consciousness, communication, sexuality
and identity'. The break with Gandhi after 1925 arose out of Periyar's
opposition to religion, caste and gender inequality, and resulted in a full-
fledged campaign against Gandhian and Congress-led nationalist politics.

The history of what is now Kerala is also being radically revised. Much,
perhaps too much, has been claimed on behalf of Malayalee women, both

historically and in the present. The essay by J. Devika, taken from her introduction to a collection of writings and speeches by Malayalee women (from the 1890s to the 1930s), opens a window onto a founding generation of feminists, their worlds and their demands. Not unlike V. Geetha, J. Devika's project has been one of rediscovery and translation, but her challenge has been to place in better perspective the emancipatory potential of these 'foremothers'. While the decline of this highly creative period of activism after the 1930s is yet to be explained, J. Devika argues against uncritical acclaim, by drawing attention to these women's active participation in the making of a new and problematic 'order of gender'. The shaping power of this legacy in contemporary Kerala society is just being unravelled.

In spite of the dominance of Nehruvian nationalism from the 1940s into the postindependence decades, even those feminist efforts carried out directly under the eye of Jawaharlal Nehru for the nation-to-be, have not necessarily lived on. A telling case is the fate of the report on women by one of the twenty-nine sub-committees established in 1938 by the National Planning Committee for independent India's future development. Maitrayee Chaudhuri's discussion of the report—*Women's Role in a Planned Economy* (WRPE)— prepared by some of the most well-known and highly placed women of the time, and the very first of its kind, illustrates the range of concerns and political ideas that had gained prominence among women's organizations by the 1940s. More than anything, it evokes the hopes this generation placed on what the future nation would bring to women—as workers, citizens and 'emblems of culture'. Chaudhuri's analysis lays bare the conflicting forces visible in the making of the text, where liberal individualism, radical socialism and questions of tradition all jostled for space. Economic rights, in particular, dominated the report. Could the complete disappearance of this report after independence, (only to be discovered much later in the 1990s), be an aspect of the acquiescence and withdrawal of women's organizations put forward by Neera Desai in the first essay of this volume?

In the essays chosen so far, feminists have raided the archives, and retrieved and reinterpreted texts, both well-known and forgotten. The years surrounding independence have also been approached with the tools of the oral historian, and here, too, feminists have been pioneers. The last two contributions to this section on history provide deeply disorienting images of the fruits of nationalism and the power of the Indian state. Ritu Menon and Kamla Bhasin have been instrumental in changing our relationship to independence by forcing into view the suppressed dimensions of the partition of British India into India and Pakistan. It is through people's experiences and memories of the event, as these were shaped by larger forces, including the policies of the newly installed government of India, that the extent of the communalization of society at that moment can be gauged. Their project has shown how unresolvable the partition of the subcontinent turned out to be in the lives of many women who were among the millions of migrants crossing a now divided Punjab, and what happened to those who got separated from their families and began another life in the 'hostile' community, only to then be subjected to recovery operations by the government of India. In the excerpt reproduced here, Menon and Bhasin describe the 'August anarchy' unleashed at the time of partition, and how one might begin to understand the extent of the violence that accompanied—or perhaps caused—the migration of Muslims out of India, and Sikhs and Hindus out of Pakistan. This study, too, could be called a history of the present—initially set in motion by the anti-Sikh riots of 1984 in the city of Delhi (which brought back memories of the violence of partition for those who lived through it), and then by the rising tide of communal aggression against Muslims that has been sweeping across the country since the late 1980s.

The final essay is a selection from a larger project of oral history by the women's collective Stree Shakti Sanghatana, and represents an intervention in the political history of communism in India. The testimony of 'Pramila Tai' (one of sixteen women whose life histories were recorded and translated by this women's group in the 1980s) takes us to the years before and after independence, as they were lived and remembered by those women who actively participated in the communist-led peasant struggle in the region of Telangana in Andhra Pradesh, 1947–1951. For the feminist collective this project involved taking issue with the patriarchal biases of the Communist Party and the repressive actions of the Indian state, while also confronting the ideologies structuring these women's own sense of their self-worth. Pramila Tai's remarkable account also recovers a radical strain in the national movement, now largely reconstructed as Gandhian or Nehruvian. The extraordinary heterogeneity among women's organizations and the Congress-backed coalitions that were possible while opposing the rule of the Nizam, stand in stark contrast to the subsequent isolation she experienced as a communist forced to go underground and then face imprisonment under the newly formed state.

These essays have not been chosen with a view to provide a representative, much less a comprehensive picture of how feminist scholars and activists have claimed the domain of history. There is now a huge corpus of work available, and far too little of it has been acknowledged here. My much more limited aim has been to give readers some glimpses into how history has been a critical resource in the women's movement and women's studies, with profound implications for understanding contemporary events and in feminist battles on the ground.

≈

BEYOND THE ALTEKARIAN PARADIGM: TOWARDS A NEW UNDERSTANDING OF GENDER RELATIONS IN EARLY INDIAN HISTORY

Uma Chakravarti

Discussion on the status of women has a unique position in the writing, teaching and learning of early Indian history. Further, some of the conclusions of this discussion have actually found their way into the syllabi of school and undergraduate courses. For whatever it is worth, there is some information on women in almost every textbook on ancient India. This kind of information does not occur in any other course of history (medieval or modern), since there has been no tradition of a separate discussion on the status of women. The uniqueness of the situation made its point while I was correcting examination papers some time ago. A question on the main features of the later Vedic civilization resulted in a spate of answers dealing with the position of women. It was clear that to most students one of the important indices of a civilization was the position that women occupied in it. This general understanding is based on an informal debate that took over 150 years to crystallize and percolate down to a large number of people among the upper classes in India.

The existing material on women in early India, however, has a seriously limiting dimension to it, especially when we consider the negative effect that such work has had on a real understanding of women in history. It might therefore be worthwhile to explain why the first historians undertook studies of the status of women, why they remained confined essentially to ancient India, and also review the state of the existing literature so as to evaluate the worth of available studies. This will, in turn, help us outline the kind of work that needs to be done in the future.

The women's question took a central place in the early stage of the national movement. The socioreligious reform movements of the nineteenth century advocated a reform of Hindu society whose twin evils were seen as the existence of caste and the low status of women. All the major reformers of the time attacked the practice of sati, child marriage and enforced widowhood, and this was a common platform whether the reformers belonged to the Brahmo Samaj in Bengal, the Prarthana Samaj in Maharashtra or the Arya Samaj in northern India. The preoccupation with these questions was derived, at least in part, from the dominance of Sanskritic models in the nineteenth century, since the major thrust in the debate came from within the upper sections of the Hindu community. The above-mentioned characteristic has survived in the women's question even in contemporary times where the study of the identity of women is based almost entirely on Sanskritic models and the myths conditioning women.

Another feature which has significant consequences for the general debate on the status of women is that both the proponents of the reform as well as the opponents of the reform looked back to the ancient texts as the source from which both groups took their positions and invoked the sanctions of the Shastras in putting forward their arguments. This naturally necessitated a study of the position of women over the course of history. The deciding factor in the debate between the liberals or progressives and the conservatives was the relative antiquity of the source from which they were quoting. The older the source the more authentic and authoritative it was considered. [. . .]

Since traditional work on the status of women in India exists entirely within the context of Hinduism, it is heavily preoccupied with religious and legal questions such as the right to widow remarriage, the existence of the institution of Niyoga, the right to property for women, the origin and development of the institution of Stridhana, the right of the childless widow to adopt and so on. On the religious front there is an obsession with the right of a woman to perform religious sacrifices either by herself or with her husband, as also with her interest and involvement with the pursuit of religious goals. The social position of women is usually concerned with the inclusion or exclusion of women in public assemblies and their right to education. On the whole, the perspective on women is confined to seeing them within the context of the family. It is the status of women within the family, and primarily in the relationship of wives to husbands with which the traditional writers were concerned.

Another feature of the traditional writing on the position of women is that they were based entirely on brahmanical sources. Even if these sources are considered to be reasonably authentic, which I have reason to doubt, they carry the problem of (a) an inherent bias of the brahmanas, (b) reflecting the precepts of the brahmanas rather than the actual practice of the people, and (c) confining themselves to the upper castes. At best, the existing work can be termed as a partial view from above. How unsatisfactory such unconditional reliance upon brahmanical sources has been will be clear further on in this paper.

The analysis of the position of women in ancient India has also been coloured by the fact that almost all the works have been written by scholars who would fall within the nationalist school of history. Writing at a time when Hindu social institutions were being subjected to fierce criticism by a generation that was imbibing western education and western values, these scholars worked hard to show that the position of women had been high in the ancient past. The contemporary evils reflecting the low position of women were responsible for the Hindu sense of inferiority in relation to their ruling masters. As a reaction, Hindu scholars argued that the evils were only a temporary aberration and could easily be eliminated. The general thrust of the work has therefore been to demonstrate that the status of women was very high in the Vedic period; according to this view there was a general decline afterwards, reaching rock bottom with the coming of the invaders, especially the Muslims, who abducted Hindu women and violated them, and these circumstances resulted in the development of such evils as purdah, sati and female infanticide. This view has become widely prevalent since it appears regularly in popular literature and vernacular journals. But we must point out that it is only an extension of traditional academic research.

Here is a fairly representative example from the pen of a woman scholar:

> The tenth and the eleventh centuries saw the advent, and later, the firm establishment of Muhammadans in this country. When Hindu culture came to clash with a culture far different from its own, the leaders of society began to frame rules and laws to safeguard their interest—specially the position of women. Rigorous restrictions were placed on them . . . We find at this stage child marriage firmly enforced. The death of a widow was preferred to her falling into evil hands. Hence self-immolation of a widow was enjoined by the law codes giving the unfortunate victim the hope of heavenly bliss. Such and several other customs were introduced which curbed the freedom of women to a very large extent. This was done perhaps to save her from the foreigners and to preserve the purity of the race. (Shastri 1959)

Similarly, R.C. Dutt, the well-known nationalist historian and the first to present a coherent account of ancient Indian civilization and of women, writes: 'Absolute seclusion and restraint (of women) were not Hindu customs. They were unknown in India till Mohammedan times . . . No ancient nation held their women in higher honour than the Hindus' (1972).

Such a sweeping view is untenable if one looks at the past without the tinted spectacles of the present. Even if one were to confine oneself to brahmanical sources there is enough evidence to show that women of the upper castes did not have access to the public domain by the early centuries of the Christian era, and that Manu and other law givers recommended early marriage for girls. Sati itself was associated with women of the ruling classes, as is evident from the seventh century account of Harsha's early career. The structure of institutions that ensured the subordination of women was complete in essentials long before the Muslims as a religious community had come into being. The Muslim bogey was a convenient peg to explain the origin of all oppressive practices. It was particularly convenient for those who did not wish to see the structural framework of institutions that governed gender relations in early India mainly because it was the same framework that governed women even in contemporary society. The term 'patriarchy' was hardly used, and even when it did stray into an occasional historian's writing, it was a neutral term, completely divested of the power factor inherent in it; successfully depoliticized thus, it lost its real import.

The cultural encounter between England and India in the nineteenth century, which was the context for the emergence of nationalist historiography, shaped the focus and the thrust of writing on women in early India. The injury to the Hindu sense of superiority resulting from the unfavourable comparison between Hindu women and western women, which was common throughout the cultural encounter, was so marked that it led frequently to an inversion of the 'Vincent Smith syndrome'. Vincent Smith's position was a general contempt for everything Indian. If he was faced with visual and incontrovertible proof of something worthwhile in Indian culture he would immediately attribute it to Greek influence. Historians writing on the position of women in ancient India reversed the argument by invariably trying to point out that nowhere else in the ancient world were women held in such high regard as in the India of 3000 years ago. They specially revelled in comparisons with Greece and Rome as in the passage below:

> The historian of India who has studied the literature of the ancient Hindus will have no hesitation in asserting that never in the most polished days of Greece and Rome were women held in such high regard in those countries as in India three thousand years ago. (Dutt 1972)

Similarly, the historian Altekar surveys the condition of women in ancient Greece, Rome and Palestine, and then reiterates that the position which women occupied at the dawn of civilization during the Vedic age was much better. The need of the nationalist historians to resurrect examples of the lost glory of Indian womanhood has led to a selective focus on certain aspects of the ancient texts. [. . .]

The best known and most internally coherent nationalist work on women is Altekar's study on the position of women in Hindu civilization. His work is based primarily on brahmanical sources and outlines the position of women from earliest times right up to the mid 1950s when the Hindu Code Bill was under consideration. Altekar's work represents the best that is available to us by way of women's studies in history, but it also shows up very sharply the limitations of the traditional approach. Although the work unravels in detail the entire body of opinion of the law makers on such areas as the education of women, marriage and divorce, the position of the widow, women in public life, proprietary rights of women, and the general position of women in society, it is steeped in the nationalist understanding of the women's question. Further, his overwhelming concern is with women in the context of the family and one almost gets the feeling that the status of women needs to be raised in order to ensure the healthy development of the future race of India. In this he was reflecting the opinion of nationalist writers from the second half of the nineteenth century who placed tremendous importance on the physical regeneration of the Hindus.

A survey of Altekar's work will indicate the limitations inherent in his approach. His theoretical framework is spelt out in the very first page of his work. According to him,

> One of the best known ways to understand the spirit of a civilization and to appreciate its excellence and realize its limitations is to study the history and status of the position of women in it . . . The marriage laws and customs enable us to realize whether men regarded women as market commodities or war prizes or whether they realized that the wife is after all her husband's valued partner whose cooperation was indispensable for *happiness* and *success* in family life. (1987; italics mine) [. . .]

Altekar's programme for women, despite his apparent liberality and sympathy for them, was to view women primarily as stock-breeders of a strong race. This view is particularly noticeable in his suggestions about women's education. In Altekar's programme of reform, women were to be educated enough but in doing so one had to ensure that no undue strain was placed on them. He expressed his fears thus: 'As things stand today, girls have to pass the *same* examinations as boys and to learn house-keeping at home as well, all the while having less physical strength than their brothers. This certainly puts too much strain upon them and *is injurious to the future well-being of the race.*' (1987; italics mine)

Establishing the high status of women was the means by which 'Hindu' civilization could be vindicated. This was the finished version of the nationalist answer to James Mill's denigration of Hindu civilization published a century ago; the locus of the barbarity of Hindu civilization in Mill's work (*A History of British India*) had lain in the abject condition of Hindu women. By reversing the picture, Altekar was attempting to lay Mill's ghost aside. But it was easier to provide a general picture than to deal with a variety of customs oppressing women that still obtained in the early twentieth century. Altekar was thus forced to provide explanations for existing biases against women. For example, he attempts to explain the Hindu preference for a son over a daughter by advancing a psychological argument, as in the passage below:

> If a cruel fate inflicted widowhood upon the daughter, the calamity would break the parent's heart. Remarriage being no longer possible parents had to see the heart-rending pain of seeing their daughter wasting herself in interminable widowhood . . . Parents had often to pass through the terrible ordeal of seeing their daughters burning themselves alive on the funeral pyre of their husbands. To become a daughter's parent thus became a source of endless worry and misery . . . As a natural consequence . . . passages about the undesirability of the birth of a daughter become more numerous. (1987)

Altekar is particularly weak in his attempts at relating the status of women at a given point of time with social organization as a whole. Thus, early Vedic society, which did not as yet have a noticeable concentration of power, or a well-developed institution of kingship, is the context for Altekar's unnecessary explanation for the absence of queens. Since Altekar is convinced about the high status of women in the Vedic period, he feels he has to account for why we do not hear of women as queens. Thus he is constrained to suggest that, 'Aryans were gradually establishing their rule in a foreign country surrounded on all sides by an indigenous hostile population that considerably outnumbered them. Under such circumstances queens ruling in their own right or as regents were *naturally unknown*' (1987; emphasis mine).

Similarly, Altekar has a facile explanation for why women did not own property. According to him, 'Landed property could be owned only by one who had the power to defend it against actual or potential rivals and enemies. Women were obviously unable to do this and so could hold no property' (1987).

In his inability to see women within a specific social organization and/or to recognize the patriarchal subordination of women, Altekar was not unique. Like others he was reflecting a deeply internalized belief in biological determinism and therefore in the physical interiority of women.

Very occasionally, however, Altekar shows flashes of insight into the socioeconomic context within which women's subordination was achieved. For example, in his analysis of the causes for the 'fall' of the status of the Aryan women, Altekar suggests a connection with the subjugation of the sudras as a whole. He argues that the Aryan conquest of the indigenous population and its loose incorporation as members of a separate varna had given rise to a huge population of semi-servile status. In such a situation Aryan women ceased to be producing members of society and thus lost the esteem of society. But even as he makes this broadly contextual explanation, Altekar is insensitive to the crucial distinction between the participation of women as producers and participation in terms of controlling production. Thereafter Altekar's semi-historical insight is unfortunately lost and popular prejudice takes over. Like the ancient brahmanical law givers, he appears to have a horror of sudra women:

> The introduction of the non-Aryan wife into the Aryan household is the *key* to the gradual deterioration of the position of women . . . The non-Aryan wife with her ignorance of Sanskrit language and Hindu religion *could obviously not enjoy the same religious privileges as the Aryan consort*. Association with her must have tended to affect the purity of speech of the Aryan co-wife as well. Very often the non-Aryan wife may have been the favourite one of her husband, who may have often attempted to associate her with his religious sacrifices in preference to her better educated but less loved Aryan co-wife. This must have naturally led to grave mistakes and anomalies in the performance of the ritual which must have shocked the orthodox priests . . . Eventually it was felt that the object could be gained by declaring the whole class of women to be ineligible for Vedic studies and religious duties. (1987)

This facile argument was, in Altekar's view, the key factor in the decline of the status of women. Altekar is completely obtuse to other historical explanations. The possibility that the sudra woman, whom he regards as a threat, could have contributed to a more dynamic and active kind of womanhood for Hindu society would not even occur to Altekar because his focus is on Aryan women (regarded then as the progenitors of the upper caste women of Hindu society) and in his racist view, sudra women counted for nothing. The most important consequence of Altekar's limited repertoire of biological and psychological explanations was that the logic of the distorted social relations between men and women is completely obscured. The kind of explanations offered by Altekar might appear to be astoundingly trivial to us today. But it is important to remember that, by and large, nationalist historians were content to restrict historical explanations to cultural factors while writing about ancient India. This was in contrast to their focus on economic and social factors while discussing British rule in India.

In summing up the nationalist historiography on women in early India, we might draw attention to the fact that the Altekarian paradigm, though limiting and biased, continues nevertheless to influence and even dominate historical writing. In essence, what emerges from the mass of detail he accumulated is the construction of a picture of the idyllic condition of women in the Vedic age. It is a picture which now pervades the collective consciousness of the upper castes in India and has virtually crippled the emergence of a more analytically rigorous study of gender relations in ancient India. There is thus an urgent need to move forward and rewrite history, a history that does justice to women by examining social processes, and the structures they create, thus crucially shaping and conditioning the relations between men and women. Just as Altekar displaced Mill in his work, it is time we realized that despite Altekar's substantial contribution we must lay his ghost aside and begin afresh.

References

Altekar, A.S. 1987 (reprint). *The Position of Women in Hindu Civilisation.* New Delhi: Motilal Banarsidass.

Dutt, R.C. 1972 (reprint). *A History of Civilisation in Ancient India.* New Delhi: Vishaal Publishers.

Shastri, Shakuntala Rao. 1959. *Women in the Ancient Laws.* Bombay: Bharatiya Vidhya Bhavan.

OF BEGUMS AND TAWAIFS: THE WOMEN OF AWADH
Saleem Kidwai

Commentators and historians often label the culture of Awadh decadent and effete; along with licentiousness and hedonism, the presumed effeminacy of its men is generally a primary indicator of this supposed decadence. The assumptions behind this labeling derive from Victorian notions of propriety and masculinity; women's agency does not figure prominently in the perspective of those who label cultures in this simplistic way. But if it is mentioned, women's agency may be seen as the obverse of male emasculation, and thus strengthen the stereotype of a cutlure's decadence.

Women played a very important role in the politics and culture of Awadh, and this I would argue, was a sign of the culture's strength rather than weakness.

Two women, Nawab Begum and Bahu Begum, were responsible for Lucknow becoming the capital of nawabi Awadh. Wielding power, both real and symbolic, from the original capital at Faizabad, they also played an important role in the survival of Awadh as an independent successor state to the Mughal empire.

Sa'adat Khan was a Mughal governor (nawab-wazir) of the subah of Awadh. In 1722, he became independent and decided that the governorship would thenceforth be hereditary. He moved from Lucknow, the Mughal capital and established his new capital at Faizabad. He married his daughter Aliya Sadr un Nisa to his sister's son who succeeded him as Nawab Safdar Jung (1739–54). As daughter of the first nawab and the only wife of the second, Aliya was known as Nawab Begum. Her son Shuja ud Daulah, the next Nawab (1954–75), was married to Amat uz Zehra, the daughter of a powerful Persian courtier at the Mughal court. Amat came to be known as Bahu Begum.

Awadh was a pretender to the glory of the Mughal state. Yet, while Mughal politics featured only one Nur Jahan who became a power centre of consequence, Awadh, at its very inception, saw two strong women exercising considerable clout at court. They were rich, hard working, economically independent and expert at court intrigue as were most courtiers. Both were personally very wealthy because of the dowries they received as personal gifts, including jewellery and personal valuables, horses, elephants, retainers and troops, as well as ownership of revenues from vast tracts of fertile land. Both maintained their own independent establishments and a bureaucracy of women, men and eunuchs. Even though they were in purdah, they held regular court and conducted business through an elaborate, theatrical protocol whereby they were neither seen nor heard, yet were overpowering presences. They controlled closely the administration of their assets. Nawab Begum would write in a very fine hand and sign and seal important orders herself. Bahu Begum did not write, but dictated and signed orders. Bahu Begum is reported to have had a force of ten thousand trained and well-armed troops, good horses, elephants and a fleet of boats.

In 1764, Shuja ud Daulah lost a decisive war against the British at Buxar. As a result, the Company helped itself to his kingdom and imposed punitive damages. The state treasury was emptied, yet there was not enough to meet the demands. Bahu Begum helped him out from her treasury, and his mother, Nawab Begum, chipped in with two million rupees in cash. Having spent so much of her money to save a truncated state, Bahu Begum subsequently got involved in managing the state finances. Neither woman allowed herself to be bullied by anyone, be it husband, son, grandson or Company.

When Shuja ud Daulah died, Bahu Begum was instrumental in ensuring the succession of her son, Asaf ud Daulah (1774–98), despite the Company's opposition. Among other things, the British considered Asaf ud Daulah incompetent because he was fat and of unconventional temperament; they also alleged he was a pederast because he was homoerotically inclined. Nor would he play the role that the British had scripted for the nawab. Once he became nawab, however, Asaf ud Daulah came into conflict with his mother and grandmother who had both come to represent power at Faizabad. To escape the court dominated by them, he shifted the capital back to Lucknow in 1775.

Public spats ensued between the nawab and the two Begums over money, and the Company eagerly got involved. It decided that the power of these women had to be destroyed. Warren Hastings, the governor-general, accused them of conspiring with the raja of Banaras to revolt, and launched a violent attack. In 1781, both women were arrested and imprisoned. Their aides were tortured, their establishment ravaged and looted, and the occupants humiliated and assaulted. So vicious was the attack that even the brazen Company was embarrassed at the way Hastings had treated the begums. Hastings was impeached after Edmund Burke denounced him in Parliament. Hastings's trial lasted from 1787 to 1794 when he was acquitted. The East India Company paid some of his legal costs.

Nawab Begum lived till 1795. Bahu Begum died in 1815 after witnessing the succession of three nawabs who followed her son. She kept herself abreast of developments at court even though she was in Faizabad. She set up a unique trust, to which she left her entire personal wealth. The trust gave pensions in perpetuity to her dependents.

Beginning with Nawab Asaf ud Daulah who shifted the capital to Lucknow to escape the influence of his mother and grandmother, Lucknow became both a museum and a stage of Awadhi culture. It also grew into an exciting supermarket for the finest in crafts and talents. The best artists, poets and courtesans moved to Lucknow. There was an enormous spurt of creativity. Patronage became a hallmark of elite culture.

Asaf ud Daulah, dubbed the 'debauched-jester' by the British, deprived of nearly all his political power by unfair treaties, inaugurated the cultural and economic renaissance of Lucknow. He undertook elaborate architectural projects as public work schemes. Lucknow came to outshine contemporary Lahore, and even Delhi. It was only economically that the colonial cities— Bombay, Calcutta and Madras—were more prosperous.

Two cultural developments of this period are of special interest. Both are cited when Awadhi culture is labelled debauched for its sensuality. One was the appearance of Rekhti, a genre of Urdu poetry written mostly by men but in the voice of women. Rekhti is the feminine of Rekhta, as Urdu was originally called. Though primarily associated with three important Rekhta poets—Rangin (1755–1835,) Jurrat (1748–1810) and Insha (1756–1835)— who had settled in Lucknow, Rekhti was written by many others, including women, and became popular. Ruth Vanita (2000) has argued that the language and idiom of Rekhti is similar to erotic love poetry in other northern Indian languages. Rekhti became notorious because of explicit poems about female sexuality, including same-sex attractions and love-making. Similar poems, with male-homoerotic content have long been part of the larger body of Urdu poetry, and some leading poets have contributed to this 'vulgar' genre, yet Rekhta, unlike Rekhti, suffered no disrepute.

Rekhti chapti-namahs (female same-sex narratives) were used to brand all of Rekhti as pornographic and therefore an embarrassment to literary tradition. However, Rekhti was subversive in far more serious ways. The Urdu ghazal had superbly mastered the technique of not gendering lovers although indicators were often provided. The nouns were mostly gendered masculine. Rekhti removed all ambiguity by gendering the verbs. Some Rekhti poets further transgressed notions of gender by donning feminine attire during public recitals. Their performances were very popular at mushairas.

Because Rangin, the 'founder' of Rekhti, was unabashed in admitting that he drew from the language of courtesans in whose company he spent a considerable amount of time, it was assumed that all Rekhti was inspired by the same source. The chapti-namahs probably had a strong kotha linkage. However, much of Rekhti depicted everyday lives within the zenana. It was populated with female relatives including in-laws, friends, neighbours, maids, husbands, lovers and sometimes even children. Its language was drawn from within these respectable establishments where women, particularly servants, spoke many dialects. Its concerns were deemed mundane when compared to the mysticized romance of the Urdu ghazal. However, to classify this genre as misogynist or voyeuristic is self-defeating reductionism. Researching its 'mundaneness' is bound to be more fruitful.

Notions of gender were also transgressed at the court in Lucknow through religious ritual. The Mughal rulers were Sunnis. The nawabs being Shia, Shi'i religious rituals supervised by begums evolved at the court. Many begums were devout and generous to religious causes. They built private and public imambaras and patronized religious scholars. Badshah Begum, wife of Ghazi ud din Haider (1814–27) led the way in instituting innovative religious rituals.

Along with the Prophet and his family, the twelve imams are deeply venerated by Shias. Ali, the Prophet's son-in-law, was the first imam. Badshah Begum decided to personify the wives of the next eleven and have them live around her. Beautiful, well-born young ladies were chosen and given appropriate historical names. They were set up in luxury, and played their part in rituals surrounding the birth and death of imams. They were decreed achhuti (untouched/untouchable), because of their purity. Badshah Begum also decided which of these virgin faces she wanted to see first thing each morning. They were not allowed to marry, with the exception of one who escaped through clever devotional intervention when she dreamt that the imam had divorced her.

Regular in her daily devotions, Bahu Begum was sometimes possessed by the djinn of her husband and would go into a trance. She would get dressed, sit on the throne, and sway her head as female musicians performed for her. Her son, Nawab Nasir ud Din Haider (1827–37), got further involved in his mother's innovations. The notion of achhutis stayed intact. However, he showed his own personal devotion by participating in the commemoration of the birth of each imam by playing the expectant mother. Befitting arrangements for the auspicious child-birth would be made and the 'pregnant' nawab would go into labour; eventually a bejeweled doll would be placed in his arms, and he would receive all the post-natal indulgence he had earned.

This royal attitude to gender naturally affected the elite. Juan I. Cole (1997) points out that many other elite men who started dressing and behaving like women as a sign of religiosity were from families where devout wives had started claiming to be achhutis.

The royal harem too underwent a change. The nawabs were married to high-born women, but being Shia, they were also allowed temporary wives. The size of the harems increased substantially. The number of concubines too increased as the empire of the nawabs neared its end. Among the wives and concubines, there were many former tawaifs.

The tawaifs, who supposedly inspired Rekhti, were the second interesting feature of this period. They are considered another marker of Awadhi culture's decadence and feminization. Though the obvious origin of the tawaif was sex work, by the eighteenth century many of them had transformed themselves into successful public performers; some were recognized as artists and were in a position to decide on whom to bestow sexual favours. The developing culture of Awadh suited the tawaifs. Patronage was available and liberal. Smart professionals that they were, they were also known for their mobility. Many tawaifs moved to Lucknow to set up establishments. Pretty fortune seekers replenished their ranks.

To become successful tawaifs, young girls were rigorously trained in literature, music and dance and the art of conversation. Unrelated tawaifs, often from different religions, lived in independent establishments called kothas (literally, top floor). Male relatives, attendants and musicians lived on the ground floor. The kotha was also the salon where they performed or entertained clients. Children lived with them as did many dependants. The entire establishment was ruled by a matriarch-like figure.

The public perception of a kotha has been completed distorted by *mujra*-numbers in big budget Hindi films. However, one cinematic image is very telling. This is the first shot of the kothas in *Pakeezah*, soaked-in-pink and dripping with attar. It scans a curly skyline of kothas with their delicate architecture and pastel colours, lining both sides of a busy, commercial street. Each kotha is dazzlingly alive with light, music and dance. They are open to the sky, the air and the street. In one of these, Sahib Jan sings and dances coquettishly to *Inhin logon ne*, complaining about all those who 'outraged' her modesty by having anything to do with her dupatta—the tradesman who sold it, the dyer who dyed it pink and the policeman who pulled it off her in public. Sahib Jan is a virgin and remains so till the end of the film.

While it may appear over-the-top, this one shot shows the profusion, prosperity, energy and openness of the kothas. The kothas prospered due to extravagant patronage. As artists, the kothewalis were alive to creativity around them were tuned into musical and literary developments. Soon they became the main performers of kathak and singers of love lyrics. They often performed at the same gatherings as their seniors and their peers and were close to the literary and artistic mainstream. Since men from different backgrounds, including merchants and neighbouring territorial chieftains, visited their kothas, they were also well tuned into what was happening around them. They were well networked and could even swing royal appointments.

Kothas had two common features with the establishments of the two begums. They were prosperous, and independently controlled by women. They were also viewed with suspicion by the Company. As a group, the tawaifs became one of the first victims of Queen Victoria's government's policy of retribution after the *ghadr* of 1857 was crushed. Veena Talwar Oldenberg (1997) has found tax records showing that the tawaifs were among the richest citizens on record and the largest tax payers. She has also highlighted colonial policy towards them. The British considered them deeply complicit in the events of 1857–58 and treated them the way they treated armed resistors. Tawaifs were suspected of providing financial and logistical help to the rebels. Their establishments were ransacked; their valuables, their urban and agricultural property and their other business ventures were confiscated.

British fury at the tawaifs was partially understandable because it was a former tawaif who helped make it so difficult for the Company to recover Lucknow. This was Begum Hazrat Mahal, one of the wives of the last Nawab Wajid Ali Shah who had been exiled to Calcutta in 1856 when Awadh was annexed. Wajid Ali Shah had wives in the hundreds but he was allowed to take only a dozen with him. Begum Hazrat Mahal was one of the many he left behind in Lucknow. The rebels approached many begums who had sons with a legal claim to the throne to provide symbolic leadership to the resistance. None agreed. Begum Hazrat Mahal, a junior wife, having stipulated that she would be the regent of her minor son, volunteered and soon became one of the main leaders of the resistance.

Hazrat Mahal, a tawaif, had been sold to talent scouts for Wajid Ali Shah's harem, the *Pari Khana* (fairy house). The Pari Khana had an elaborate hierarchy. Entrants entered as attendants but were proclaimed paris or fairies once they were allowed to sing and dance. If they became concubines, they also became begums and if they bore the nawab a child, they were given the highest title of mahal. Mahak Pari (fragrant fairy) turned into Hazrat Mahal when she reached the top rung.

Begum Hazrat Mahal took very seriously her role as representative of a dynasty of nawabs, and defender of their honour. She proclaimed her son emperor, helped fortify Lucknow, travelled extensively rallying support, dealt with other rebel leaders and participated in planning strategies. A non-combatant herself, she appeared personally with her troops at battles. Allegations about her personal liaisons, or even the paternity of her son, could not stop her from being recognized as the leader who had royal legitimacy backing her, for even Bahadur Shah Zafar recognized her son as nawab. When Lucknow fell, Begum Hazrat Mahal continued to fight. Eventually, she reached Nepal and was offered refuge by the raja, whom she had had dealings with earlier. She was offered a pension if she returned but she refused and instead countered Queen Victoria's proclamation as Empress of India, with one of her own, affixed with the royal seal, from exile. She died in Nepal, probably in 1874.

References

Cole, Juan I. 1997. Shi'ite noblewomen and religious innovation in Awadh. In *Lucknow: Memories of a city*, ed. Violette Graffe. New Delhi: Oxford University Press.

Oldenburg, Veena Talwar. 1997. Lifestyle as resistance: The case of the courtesans of Lucknow. In *Lucknow: Memories of a city*, ed. Violette Graffe. New Delhi: Oxford University Press.

Vanita, Ruth and Saleem Kidwai, eds. 2000. *Same-sex love in India: Readings from literature and history*. Hampshire and London: Macmillan.

~

POSITIVISM AND NATIONALISM: WOMANHOOD AND CRISIS IN NATIONALIST FICTION— BANKIMCHANDRA'S *ANANDAMATH*

Jasodhara Bagchi

I

The second half of the nineteenth century in Bengal, often characterized as the Bengal Renaissance, saw a major break in the narrative form. Under the spectacular leadership of Bankimchandra, the novel was properly launched as the dominant fictional prose narrative, fit for the consumption of the newly educated *literati*. Prior to this, throughout the middle decades of the nineteenth century, there had been a systematic campaign by the 'modernizing' section of the rulers about the need to reform the existing popular literature in Bengal. In their programme for 'improvement' of the newly formed 'middle class' Bengali, the proselytizing zeal of the Christian missionaries found an ally in the rationalism of the 'progressive' Utilitarians when they pleaded against the undesirable 'popular' narratives, mostly Purana-based, leaning towards the 'uncouth' 'otherworldliness' of Hindu superstitious myths. [. . .]

The Bengali novel, when it first emerged in the second half of the nineteenth century, went far beyond these pleadings for reforming popular taste in literature. What the colonial educator saw as a somewhat mechanical programme for raising the consciousness of the subject race soon bore rich aesthetic fruit in the novels of Bankimchandra. Born in 1833, Bankimchandra Chattopadhyay died in 1894. His life span thus almost exactly coincided with that of a late Victorian aesthete like Walter Pater, to whom he offers a striking contrast. No recluse cloistered within the walls of an Oxford College, Bankimchandra was a public servant in colonial India, deeply involved with the workings of a society that was becoming acutely conscious of foreign domination. Subscribing to the view of August Comte, the founder of Positivism, that culture was an index of society, novel writing was, for him, a part of the social obligation of an intellectual in a colonial society facing the strictures against the poverty of culture produced and consumed by his own class. One of the first graduates of Calcutta University, well versed in law, in which he took a degree from Presidency College in 1869, he served the British government as a deputy magistrate. His commitment to the art of novel writing developed from the debates that were going on around him in which the fictional narrative was singled out for its absence of naturalism and human content. He obviously felt a moral obligation to forge ahead and create a literature that was suitable for the educated reader of Bengal. In his search for a suitable literature, Bankim, it should be noted, avoided a mechanical polarization between tradition and modernity. He found deep sustenance from his discriminating reading of the Sanskrit 'Kavya' literature as well as the grand structure of its epic narratives. At the same time, he was equipped, like his Victorian contemporaries, with all the latest developments in social philosophy. Right through the seventies, when he was building up the main structure of the novel form, he was using the writings of Comte, JS Mill, Herbert Spencer and Buckle in his penetrating critiques of society, which he published in his own periodical *Bangadarshan.* Bankim's art of novel writing owed a great deal to this pervasive social concern, a concern that was born of a deep historicism and an agonizing search for individual selfhood. It is this which perhaps accounts for the moral *fiat* often associated with an unchanged traditional society that tends to make its presence felt in the novels of Bankim. This should not be considered a flaw in the narrative structure of Bankim's novels. The presence of social order, however threatened from outside and from within, is as essential a component of Bankim's narrative as the suffering individuals who have to act out their tortured lives within the dictates of traditional society. It is the juxtaposition of the unchanging and the changing within Indian society that produced this magnificent crop of fictional narratives.

From the beginning, Bankim used certain Romantic presuppositions about the 'expressive' power of literature as the basic precondition of his use of the vernacular as the medium of expression. He said, 'We are not English-haters, we dislike neither the English people nor the English language . . . English is a great language, it is a mine of jewels. The more it is studied the better' (Das 1984, 45). But the 'expressive' powers of a foreign language, Bankim felt, could not match that of the native tongue. 'A single great idea communicated to the people of Bengal in their language circulated among them in the language that alone touches their heart, vivifying and permeating the conceptions of all ranks, will work out grander results than all our English speeches and preachings will ever be able to achieve' (Das 1984, 96–97). According to Sisir Kumar Das, the most recent biographer of Bankimchandra, this passage quoted from an English essay published in 1870, 'can be described as a manifesto of his plan to foster a new spirit of enquiry among the people of Bengal'.

The 'manifesto' part of it echoes the older prescriptions of the rulers about 'popular literature' that we have seen before. But the claim of 'expressiveness' made by Bankim deserves special attention.

The language that alone *touches their heart, vivifying and permeating the conceptions* definitely suggests the foundation of a national, though not a fully-fledged nationalist, consciousness. It is in this spirit that the poignancy of the later Swadeshi songs may be located, a spirit that was again much in evidence nearer our times during the recent upsurge in Bangladesh in 1971. An essentially Romantic poetics becomes the vehicle of the new identity that was both individual and society specific. Referring to De Quincey's famous distinction, Sisir Das sums up Bankimchandra's literary programme: 'it will be a literature of power as well as a literature of knowledge'. In a colonial society, however, where the intelligentsia was waking up to the acute contradictions of colonial domination, 'power' came to acquire a dimension not conceivable by De Quincey. Specially in his last novel when he interprets the crisis of his own society with the help of a reawakened sense of a threatened Hindu order, Bankim throws overboard John Stuart Mill's cautious expressivism when he had claimed in his 1833 essay that 'The truth of poetry is to paint the human soul truly; the truth of fiction is to give a true picture of life' (Das 1984, 119).

For Bankim, who felt himself to be a man of the moment, such distinction between poetry and fiction was of little consequence. His effort was to raise the new consciousness by interpreting science, history and religion with the help of the vivifying power of language, sensitive enough to express the incommunicable (*a-vyakta*). Bankim's own claim about the epic or *'mahakavya'* which incorporates the intensity of the lyric in the largeness and externality of the human action finds a 'modern' shape in the complex and challenging structure of his novels.

II

Bankim's art of novel writing accompanied his vigorous analysis of society. Of all the European social philosophers to whose writings he makes frequent references it was Auguste Comte who provided him with the most interesting problematic as it came to be structured in his late novels. In most popular accounts of the influence of Positivism in nineteenth-century Bengal, it is vaguely suggested that it was a philosophy that emphasized the importance of scientific observation by questioning all metaphysical absolutes. According to this partial view, the influence of Positivism on Bankimchandra was to be seen most prominently in the years when he was editing his journal *Bangadarshan* in which appeared his major analyses of society as also his articles on science and scientific outlook. Positivism is given credit for the spirit of observation and the exploration of society that marked the social novels of his middle period in the 1870s. It is also believed by some that the Bankimchandra of the later novels—*Anandamath, Debi Chowdhurani* and *Seetaram*—turned away from the modernizing tendency of Positivism to revive the traditional Hindu consciousness that coloured the militant section of the swadeshi nationalists.

This is, however, a superficial and a misleading account both of the reception of Positivism in Bengal and also of the complex blending of tradition and modernity in the emergent consciousness of nationalism. In order to understand the deep sense of crisis that produced the Gothic splendour of these late novels, it will be necessary to take a closer look at this system of philosophy called Positivism and to suggest ways of its assimilation into the nationalist consciousness in Bengal.

Comtean Positivism originated in post-revolutionary France in the early decades of the nineteenth century, when various theories of social reconstruction were being launched. Auguste Comte, who was a brilliant teacher of mathematics in the Ecole Polytechnique, broke away from the social philosopher Saint-Simon, whose secretary he was for a while. In formulating his own blueprint of a new society he tried to combine two trends of social reconstruction that were vying with each other and which appeared to be sharply polarized. The first pointed towards commerce, capital, the newly emerging powers of the proletariat, to a society, in other words, that was fully industrialized. The other was represented by the Legitimist De Maistre or the Romantic poet Chateaubriand, and looked backwards to the Catholic, feudal, hierarchical order. Hence the motto with which Comte captured his social vision was Janus-faced: it was order and progress. He believed in the Law of the Three Stages. The progression was from theological to metaphysical to positive. The aim of Positive philosophy was, to quote John Morley, to advance the study of society into the third of the three stages to remove social phenomena from the sphere of theological and metaphysical conceptions (*Encyclopaedia Britannica* 234).

The final stage of Positive harmony was going to be reached through *'pouvoir spirituel'*, a spiritual power which will be distinct from any temporal authority, nor will it be like the Catholic priesthood, for the benefit of any existing class. Unlike Fichte, Comte did not have faith in the *savants* or the scholars. He envisaged a wholly new class in whom the future spiritual power will reside and which will appear spontaneously out of the voluntary assent of men's minds to positivist doctrines.

Another marked feature of Comteism, especially in the later years, was the shift towards the Affective side (as contrasted with the Intellectual side) of human nature in his plan of social regeneration. This was inspired by his sublimated love for Clothilde de Vaux, a letter-day Beatrice to Comte's Dante. Not united in wedlock in this life, she continued to inspire Comte after her death with a glorified image of womanhood. In the works Comte wrote after 1848 he insisted upon the necessity of submitting the Intellect to the Heart. Comte's mistrust of the scholarly or professional pursuit of classics or science made him plead for the subordination of the Male Principle of Intellect to the Feminine Principle of Heart. From this came about the peculiar positivist cult of womanhood, which, in its turn, drew upon the cult of the Virgin Mary. Being cut off from the mainstream of the analytical tradition of classics and science, women in his society stayed closer to the Catholic reaction and preached the subordination of politics to morals.

In a harmonious scheme of social regeneration, both the underprivileged partners of the male patriciate, that is, the women and the proletariat, are accorded a place of special importance. Without their willing cooperation, Comte is perspicacious enough to realize, the precarious balance of the industrial society is likely to topple.

The movement can have no great force until women give cordial support to it; for it is they who are the best representatives of the fundamental principle on which Positivism rests, the victory of social order over selfish affections. On philosophers rests the duty of giving logical coherence to this principle and saving it from sophistical attacks. Its practical working depends upon the proletary class, without whose aid it would almost always be evaded. But to maintain it in all its purity, as an inspiration that needs neither arguments nor compulsion, is the work of women only (Comte 1957, 232).

III

Of all the models of social regeneration that arrived from the west in the second half of the nineteenth century, Comte's programme had its special appeal to the ambivalence latent in the nationalist consciousness that was coming into being around this time. It enabled the Janus-like intelligentsia of nineteenth-century Bengal to look backwards to the order of the golden age of the Hindus recreated by the Orientalists of the two previous generations and, at the same time, to look forward to the progress of modernization generated by British rule. There was, however, a specific feature about the positivist programme, not adequately noticed so far, that recommended this model to the emerging nationalist ethos. This was its anti-imperialist stance. [. . .]

IV

The late novels of Bankimchandra, far from being a recantation of his early belief in scientific Positivism, are a fuller response to the total ambience of the positivist ideology of order and progress. This is the phase of his life when he entered into fresh debates with his positivist nationalist friend Jogendra Chandra Ghosh and wrote *Letters on Hinduism*. This was part of his *engagement* with the Hindu order recreated by the Orientalists, reinterpreting it in order to redefine the self-image of the upper caste Hindu intelligentsia. This re-definition did not preclude the benevolence of the British rule of progress. As in the positivist utopia, so in Bankim's programme of national regeneration, the notion of *order* was the order of progress. This is the phase when he wrote the positivist life of Krishna and his ethical religious dialogue *Dharmatattva* in which he laid down the ethical foundations of a revived Hindu order, purged of all the dross. This carefully constructed Hindu order was a superb 'invention of tradition' that Bankim reconciled with the tortuous sense of 'progress' generated by British rule, which he could not but welcome. It will hardly be an exaggeration to say that foreign domination and its manifestation of 'progress' brought about the need for an 'order' that had to be located in the Hindu past. (Hence the appositeness of the model of the Renaissance, with Muslim rule standing for the dark ages.)

However, it is due to the menacing presence of colonial domination that Comte's vision of 'order and progress', when transmitted into nineteenth-century Bengal, did not produce an image of a harmonious transition to a new society; it produced, on the contrary, a sense of interlocking crisis. If one has to understand the nature of this crisis in Bankim's nationalist consciousness, it will never be sufficient to read his social writings alone. The crisis that is latent in this last phase of Bankim's social thought leaves its real impress in the non-naturalistic structure of his late fiction. The Gothic gloom and the sense of sublimity resulting from it carries the Romantic impact of these late novels far beyond the mere expressivism with which I had opened this discussion. In the late novels of Bankimchandra, more particularly in *Anandamath*, order and progress are not discussed in terms of social analysis, nor in naturalistic psychological terms. In these novels, broad historical canvases are lit up by the lurid glow of a vengeful, often mythologized, order threatened from within and without. Despite its confusing signals, *Anandamath* uses important ingredients of positivist utopia, in order to create this parable of the nationalist confrontation. Consistent with the mood and temper of Comte's writings, womanhood becomes the emblem of this threatened order of nationhood. Comte's goddess of humanity acquires a new dimension as the Devi who is the motherland. 'Bande Mataram', originally composed as an issue of *Bangadarshan*, found its explosive context within the narrative of the novel. In a situation undreamt of by Oscar Wilde, life proceeded to imitate art in the eruption of militant Hindu nationalism nearly two decades after the novel had been written; Bande Mataram became the unifying mantra of a real nationalist struggle of extremist swadeshi.

[. . .] Much of the appeal of the novel arises out of the deep sense of crisis born out of a threatened order. The icon of this order is the Devi/motherland, her resplendent past, her wretched present and her radiant future, a trope of obvious appeal for a rising nationalist consciousness.

What should be noted, however, is that the defence of this violated order is assigned by Bankim to another kind of order, this time the monastic order of the 'Santans' (the sons of mother) based in Anandamath, the eponymous monastery. In his presentation of this secret order, Bankim appropriated the *modus operandi* of the 'little tradition' of religious sects that operated among the downtrodden and immiserized toiling masses. The immediate model of this monastic order of rebels may have been, as R.C. Dutt reminds us, the Sannyasi rebellion of 1772. The other inspiration may have been the anti-British uprising organized by Vasudev Balwant Phadke. The immediate occasion of this revolt was a terrible famine in western India, echoed in the novel as the devastating famine of 1769; Phadke went about rousing people in the garb of a sannyasi. What Bankim imported into his historical sources was the organized brotherhood as a recreated order. This may be seen as a striking adoption of Comte's *pouvoir spirituel*, a spiritual order conceived outside the pale of established priesthood. Despite their cultivation of violent heroism, the predominant note of this resistance is one of bhakti or absolute submission. The heroic action on which this novel is built is thus founded on a preponderance of heart. Their extreme vow of renunciation is a manifestation of Comte's altruism, taken out of its European context of piety into the more fundamentalist defence of order as Devi and order as motherland. An 'inverted' Hindu theocracy, cleaned up in order to defend the motherland suffering under alien rule, is Bankim's answer to its invocation by many conservative anti-colonial positivists in Bengal. From being a blueprint for a peaceful transition to an industrial society, Positivism is transformed into a vehicle of a fight for a heroic age that has to be retrieved by sacrifice. In the process, the Comteist glorification of womanhood also undergoes a sea-change. Instead of being conceived as a corrective of heart to the action of the male patriciate, womanhood in *Anandamath* becomes both a symbol of the ravaged order and of the resistance to such ravages. Moreover, woman is presented both in the demonic role of a potential temptress and as a daimon or a guardian angel who helps the male Santan in the fulfilment of his vows.

The gothic aesthetic effect of the novel thus arises from the affective contributions of the feminine image. In the adaptation of the mythology of the Shakti (power conceived as a feminine force), Bankim successfully appropriated some of the folk practices into his elitist nationalist consciousness. But the heroic act of resistance is played out against the usual domestic relationship that Bankimchandra explores in his novels. The effective part of the social narrative is split into two. Bankim, with all his traditionalism, subscribes to the 'refined' Victorian ideal of womanhood, which has two faces: the partner in marriage, conceived as a 'sahadharmini', and its 'other', that is, the temptress. In these two roles she makes and breaks homes as well as polity in the social and historical novels of Bankimchandra. In the late novels this stereotype is given a distinctive turn. Throughout the last phase of his novel writing, when Bankim was distinctly preoccupied with the heroic obligations of preserving a Hindu order, he threw up one after another of these images of women who have defied the normal canons of femininity in order to join the resistance against the crisis in the order. Bankim has given an above-ordinary proportion and almost demonic power to women in his late novels to convey the heightened sense of crisis in the societies presented in these novels.

Anandamath presents a world that ranges between the settled habitat of padachinha and the surrounding forest. Likewise the women in the novel belong to these two realms. Kalyani, the wife of the prosperous householder Mahendra, belongs to the 'enclosed space' of a settled homestead. The ravages of famine, recreated from authentic historic sources in the novel, drive her out of her village into the dangers of the forest outside. The other woman, Shanti, belongs to the forest. When the male patriciate is roused to heroic action by the clarion call of sacrifice for the defence of one's motherland, the two women range themselves on two different sides. Kalyani, the domesticated wife, becomes the temptress and Shanti, the outlandish wife, becomes the real 'sahadharmini', the partner in religion. Kalyani thinks of herself as an obstacle in the way of her husband's vow of celibacy. In a scene of euphoria she releases Mahendra from the ties of home by drinking poison. Even when she is revived, almost miraculously, by the Santan Bhabananda, she becomes, against her wishes, a snare and a temptation. Bhabananda has to atone for his lapse by dying a hero's death. Kalyani is rewarded for acts of self-denial by being restored to her home (now a flourishing base for the manufacture of defence armament), and her husband and child.

It is in creating Shanti that Bankim delinks wifehood from the 'enclosed space' of domesticity. Like Kapalkundala in the early novel of that title, Shanti belongs naturally to the forest. But the heroic struggle for liberation of the motherland gives an outlet to Shanti's unusual energy—an outlet that was not present in Kapalkundala's life. Shanti is left free to contribute the full strength of her affective self to the heroic life of her sannyasi husband. Brought up, like Kapalkundala, outside the pale of normal domesticity, Shanti decides to perform her wife's role by the side of her ascetic husband Jibananda by donning the male sannyasi's disguise and fighting by his side. This dynamic uplift that Bankim gives to the traditional quietist role of a 'sahadharmini' greatly contributes to the patriotic euphoria of the novel that overwhelms any loyalist message that Bankim may have introduced in it. Shanti, for instance, is seen to tackle the British soldiers with admirable panache. The ease with which Shanti unhorses the English Lindley and rides away on his horse could put any modern feminist to shame. In another of the late novels of Bankimchandra, the female bandit heroine Debi Choudhurani has to revert to her earlier identity and make her compromises with domesticity. Unlike her and unlike Sree, the torturous chaste temptress in Bankim's last novel *Sitaram*, Shanti in *Anandamath* remains a fighter to the last and refuses to go back to domesticity. When Jibananda dies after his heroism had induced the Santans to go back to the fight and totally crush the enemy, Shanti finds his corpse. After Jibananda is brought back to life by the supernatural presence of the healer, Shanti induces him to renounce the garb of a sannyasi because they have won the battle and do not want a share in the kingdom. Instead, she accompanies Jibananda on their 'great departure' (mahaprasthan), somewhat reminiscent of the final journey of the Pandavas. While Draupadi was a mere camp follower of her five husbands, the first to fall on the way, the neo-positivist heroine of Bankim marches abreast with her fellow traveller husband in their joint quest for the welfare of the motherland. Their final departure though depicted in supernatural terms is seen as the last act in the heroic defence of the motherland.

> *Then the two arose, hand in hand they disappeared on that moonlit*
>   *night into infinity.*
> *Alas, will the like of them ever appear again?*
> *Sons like Jibananda, daughters like Shanti?*

The restoration of order in the torturous situation of a colonial society transforms the man–woman relationship into an allegory of heroism that crosses the boundaries of naturalism. The novel begins to aspire to the condition of the epic.

References

J.C. Ghosh, 'Literature and Drama: Bengali' in O' Malley (ed), *Modern India and the West*, London 1941.

Das, Sisir Kumar. 1984. *The Artist in Chains.* New Delhi: New Statesman Publishing, 1984.

Comte, Auguste. 1957. *A General View of Positivism,* trans. J H Bridges. New York: Centenary Publication, Robert Speller and Sons.

Encyclopaedia Britannica 6. 9th edn. Edinburgh: Adam and Charles Black.

~

PERIYAR, WOMEN AND AN ETHIC OF CITIZENSHIP.
V. Geetha

Placing Periyar

From his earliest days in public life, Periyar was wary and contemptuous of politics, the realm of power, contention, manipulation and machinations, of office, honours and authority. When he launched the Self-Respect Movement in 1925, he consciously chose to work in what we today refer to as civil society. Then, this was a restricted space, held captive to colonialist 'native' intelligentsia. This colonial subject, male, upper caste and middle class, on his way to becoming a nationalist, dominated civic life in the Tamil country as elsewhere; a civic life, devoted to ideas, agitations, meetings, mobilization of men and resources which engaged the colonial state in a vigorous dialogue, confronting it with its professed commitment to progress and freedom. These articulate and earnest men fashioned for themselves a sober, solemn subjectivity, anticipating an ideal of citizenhood, which, in the years to come, would find its most lofty expression in the Constitution of free India. But in the 1920s and 1930s, this ideal was only in the making and was subject to the attractions of that curious admixture of politics and piety which Gandhi embodied in his person and utilized to justify his practice. The colonialist (nationalist) subject's dream of a modern, free nation was riddled with fantasy and nostalgia, elements which were crucial to Gandhi's vision of free India, of a Hind Swaraj.

Periyar, iconoclastic, sensitive to caste as a system of inequality and cruelty, was initially a fellow traveller with these dreamers of modern India: he was much influenced by the Gandhi of the mid- and late-1920s, inspired by the ideals of non-cooperation and constructive work. However, he inflected the Gandhian ideal in his own terms. As he wrote in the very first issue of his remarkable weekly, *Kudi Arasu*:

> A sense of self-respect and fraternity must arise within human society. Notions of high and low amongst men should disappear. A sense of the unity of all humankind must dawn in each of us. Communal confrontations must cease to be. In the course of propagating these ideals, we will not hesitate to take on friend or foe if they range themselves against us and criticize us through word and deed. (Anaimuthu 1974, xxiv)

Periyar's re-reading of Gandhi was particularly evident in his definition of untouchability. It is clear from his pronouncements of this period that he held the abolition of untouchability to be contingent on the attainment of self-respect by the 'adi dravidas'. Thus, he would imprecate, rage, cajole and persuade adi dravidas to fight an oppression which inhered as much in their felt lowliness, as it did in those social and economic structures which utilized their labour and cast them aside as untouchable (*Kudi Arasu*, 24 May 1925; 21 June 1925). Periyar also made it clear that the liberation of other non-brahmin castes lay in the liberation of the adi dravidas (Anaimuthu 1974, 404). This anti-caste, egalitarian vision sustained Periyar's work and thought, even after he broke faith with Gandhi. This happened in 1927, after Gandhi had expressed at a public meeting in Mysore his faith in the norms of 'varnadharma'. Periyar had been uneasily aware of Gandhi's peculiarly convoluted arguments about caste and untouchability, and *Kudi Arasu* carried a courteous but firmly-voiced criticism of Gandhi's stance in this respect in late 1925. The critic, one Pandit Dharma Deva Siddhanta

Alangarar, had remarked that by endorsing 'varna' differences, Gandhi was creating obstacles in the way of the one objective dear to his heart: the abolition of untouchability (*Kudi Arasu,* 13 September 1925).

After 1927, Periyar undertook a systematic, relentless campaign against the Mahatma's politics of piety on the one hand and, on the other hand, chose to work in those very spaces Gandhi had recognized as pertinent, both for the transformation of Hindu (and by implication, Indian) subjectivity and the dawning of Hind Swaraj. These were spaces constituted by the interlinked realms of consciousness, communication, sexuality and identity. To re-work and reclaim these spaces for a radical utopia, Periyar founded the Self-Respect Movement in 1925 and worked hard to advance a counter to both the lures of the Gandhian Congress as an institution and nationalism as an ideology. He rejected the latter's claims as the ethic of our times and chose, instead, to create a social and cultural movement of revolt—against caste, brahminism, religion and the rule of men over women. Periyar's antagonism as well as affiliation to Gandhi needs to be understood if we are to map the coordinates of his distinctive ethic. Besides, Periyar's life, world view, practice and ideas represent, in their complex articulation with one another, an experience, a consciousness, a politics that modern India did not choose and, as such, indicate choices which the so-called makers of modern Indian consciously eschewed and actively cast aside.

Where Gandhi looked to an abiding and deeply felt religious faith, experienced by him, at least, as an ineffable inner voice, an instruction from a morally sensitive conscience, to sustain political and social activism, Periyar trusted to reason. Defined by him as an intelligence which sought to splice apart and critically examine all sorts of phenomena, this reason existed in his lexicon as an adjunct of a fearless, questioning self; which was determined to claim its autonomy and dignity in a society which, for centuries, had subjected either to the brahmin's cunning power, divisions of caste and to notions of intellectual and ethical lowliness. Describing his epistemology, as it were, he once observed that he had always tried to go beyond appearances to get at the truth behind phenomena. As far as he was concerned, it was his power of rationality which helped him do this (Anaimuthu 1974, 2009). It was for this reason that Periyar praised and upheld the example set by the Buddha. He remarked that the Buddha had counselled men to use their minds and follow the dictates of their intelligence. He had also asked men to exercise their freedom to reject what their rational minds could not comprehend or accept, such as heaven, hell, salvation and differences between human beings, such as brahmin, shudra and panchama (Anaimuthu 1974, 307).

What was 'truth' to Gandhi, directing him to offer satyagraha in various instances, was sophistry to Periyar: for, as he observed, the 'truths' which the Mahatma claimed for his own cannot be considered given and universal. For Periyar, truth was essentially relative and subjective and he did not imagine that there existed a surefire test that would help one ascertin what was truth and what was not in any given instance. The 'triumph of truth', Periyar argued, represented, more often than not, a triumph of cunning and authority. For one was as likely to submit to a regimen of truth, as to be convinced of it. For his own ideas, Periyar made no absolute claims and insisted they were to be accepted or discarded by subjecting them to rational and critical scrutiny at various moments in time. If Gandhi rested his 'truth' in a transcendence he believed to exist, Periyar refused to rest his arguments in anything but the claims of the oppressed in the here and now (*Kudi Arasu*, 6 September 1931).

Where Gandhi demanded penitence and sacrifice, as for example, with the practice of untouchability, and insisted that only a morally active and repentant self can bring about social reform, Periyar advocated resistance and struggle, often urging his self-respecters to bring to the fore those antagonisms and contradictions in caste society and act on them. This was particularly evident in Periyar's remonstrance to the adi dravidas. Rather than appeal to their felt lowliness he sought to provoke their sense of defiance and anger. He upbraided them for referring to upper caste men as 'swamis', and for letting themselves be convinced that their physical condition—of dirt, ill-health and sickness—was because they had not worked enough to lift themselves out of their misery (Anaimuthu 1974, 56). He implored them to look to and understand the system which required their labour and therefore kept them confined to a position of abject lowliness (Anaimuthu 1974, 71 –72).

Where Gandhi communicated through complex metaphors drawn from the language of faith and devotion, appealing to the meditative self, Periyar spoke as a pedagogue, a teacher, who sought to expound ideas and encourage discussion, debate and dialogue. Periyar was given to concluding his addresses with an entreaty: his listeners were to think through whatever they had heard at the meeting and decide for themselves if there were reason and justice in the things which had been told them.

Where Gandhi looked to Tolstoy, the righteous prophet, Periyar invoked Socrates; to the 'ashram' with its experiments in truth, was counterpoised the 'agora', that public and civic space to which all manner of people could claim access and rights. The Self-Respect Movement in fact caused the agora to come into existence for hundreds of ordinary people; adi dravidas and women not only attended self-respect meetings in large numbers but took part and addressed the movement's several conferences.

Gandhi's piety and transcendence committed him and the Indian National Congress to a politics which commanded mass devotion, but, which, in the final analysis, was dictated by the hegemonic demands of a multi-layered Congress leadership and the material interests of a confident and growing bourgeoisie (Ghosh 1989, 1995). Periyar's reason and commitment to the agora of the here and now left him with a constituency that was shifting, and which existed as a whole only in terms of that large and complex non-brahmin historic bloc Periyar attempted to build and re-build. Sometimes this bloc appeared divided and internally inconsistent, as when rich non-brahmins found themselves being criticized for their class biases by young self-respecters committed to socialism. At other times, there ensued arguments between believers and atheists; between those who were convinced of the cultural worth of saivism and those who felt all religious ideas and institutions were inexorably brahminical. Yet, Periyar's catholic non-brahminism and his anti-caste mission held this unwieldy bloc together, especially at those strategic and crucial moments when the larger interests of all non-brahmins were at stake, as during the anti-Hindi agitations and when the Congress ministry—formed after the 1935 elections—tried to impose an educational system that would allow youngsters to practise the caste vocation of their fathers. For Gandhi, for all that piety and faith, the here and now of politics proved determinate, whereas for Periyar, committed to the present and scorning transcendence, the future seemed to hold infinite promises.

Gandhi imaged the socially conscious and active subject of history as a devout upper caste Hindu, essentially noble and pious, who, of his own volition, would surrender his privileges and usher in change, conferring, as it were, equality and self-respect on those whom, until recently, he had imposed his logic of difference and exclusion. This subject was to attain his own in history through a conscious re-making of his subjectively through specific acts of penance and sacrifice. He had to discover the untouchable in himself, suffer his indignity as his own and thereby cleanse himself of disgust, prejudice, fear and hatred. Likewise, by spinning, wearing khadi and working with his hands, he was to acknowledge and make his own the labour and life of the Hindu peasant and weaver. At another level, he was expected to reexamine his sexual identity, since it was a particular deployment of masculinity, premised on desire, its satiation and the eruption of desire again, which forced men to think dark thoughts, bred incontinence in all aspects of life and, thereby, urged them onto unethical action. The 'brahmacharya vrata', which Gandhi counselled to his male disciples, why even to Congressmen, rested on a particular vision of femininity: if men were to renounce desire, and forswear the excess and violence which desire propelled into existence, women had to rework the terms of conjugality. They were to transform the passive virtues, conventionally associated with them, patience, sacrifice, rectitude and suffering, into active ones and use them in the cause of the nation. Women, for Gandhi, were the ideal satyagrahis, natural political subjects in the Gandhian narrative of satyagraha. They were not to be bound by their domesticity, but neither were they to discard their duties. In effect, they were to assume responsibility for the nation, as they did for the home and family.

Periyar worked with and through different notions of identity and sexuality. For him the lowest of the low in caste society, adi dravidas and women, were the natural subjects of history. But their emancipation and self-fulfillment in history were possible only if the entire social order of caste was stood in its head. That is, Periyar did not trust to the enabling power of individual consciousness alone to bring about transformation. Consciousness was for him always already collective. Entire communities of the oppressed, all those non-brahmin communities which stood shamed and humiliated by brahminism and caste, and women everywhere, were to create their own history, by responding in anger, in defiance and in unison, in full knowledge of what held them in thrall to an unjust social order. On the one hand, this meant a renunciation of caste with all its privileges, an abjuring of that religious faith which legitimized caste and a re-making of society along non-hierarchial lines. On the other hand, this required a remaking of masculine and feminine subjectivities, so that the much desired self-respect, mutuality and freedom Periyar sought out as the defining premises of his utopia, could be grounded in primary human relationships. Thus, reason and critique, desire and freedom, mutuality and reciprocity constellated into a figuration for Periyar, in which could be traced those new structures of feeling he wished to cultivate in his fellow beings. For him, the emergence of a social order rested as much on such structures of feeling as they did on transformed material structures and social relationships. [. . .]

References

Anaimuthu V., ed. 1974. *Periyar E Ve Ra Sinthanaikal* (Thoughts of Periyar). 3 volumes. Tiruchirapalli: Sinthanaiyalar Kazhagam. (Translations by the author.)

Ghosh, Suniti Kumar. 1989. *India and the Raj 1919–1947: Glory, shame and bondage*. Vol. 1 & 2. Calcutta: Bagchi.

≈

HER-SELF: GENDER AND EARLY WRITINGS OF MALAYALEE WOMEN

J. Devika

Writing to C.W.E. Cotton, agent to the governor of the Madras Presidency in response to his inquiries regarding a certain Lakshmikutty Amma from Travancore (Tiruvitamkoor), M.E. Watts, the dewan of Travancore, remarked: 'This clever young Nair lady has got on by her own efforts. She is headstrong, mannish and full of the perfervid spirit that espouses lost causes'. The young lady in question was the daughter of a retired senior official in the Travancore Education Department, and had taught at Queen Mary's College, Chennai

(Madras), before she proceeded on leave to London for studies in 1926. There she is said to have completed her studies in a year and then set off all by herself on a tour of Europe, with the help of friends, she claimed. Watts observed that Lakshmikutty had made friends with K.M. Panikkar and prominent Britishers sympathetic to the cause of Indian independence, and that her antecedents made her rather suspect. Watts had been informed that early in the 1920s, as a schoolteacher in Trivandrum (Thiruvananthapuram), she was deeply interested in Gandhi and non-cooperation, and even tried to popularize these subjects among her pupils. He remarked, however, that now she was on her way back to Trivandrum, the best place to cool her ardour (Watts and Cotton 1928).

The picture of Lakshmikutty Amma, which emerges from this official correspondence, matches almost exactly with the caricature of the 'speech-making woman' etched by the well-known Malayalee humorist Sanjayan in the 1930s (Sanjayan 1970). This figure, too, is stridently assertive, eager to take the stage against male dominance at the slightest provocation, 'mannish' to say the least and, in the last reckoning, pretty harmless. For all her tumult, she evokes but a few tremors, which turn out to be not as dreadful as it may have seemed.

This was how the first generation of Malayalee feminists was represented in their heyday, by writers located in very different fields of Malayee society in the late 1920s and 1930s, only to be wiped out of collective memory a few decades hence. Though not all of them were authors, many engaged with the emergent public sphere in early twentieth-century Kerala on behalf of a collectivity of 'Women', assuming that all women had in common certain interests, inclinations and so on, which made them important to society, and certain rights, which society had to concede. Of course, some were remembered, with a curious sifting powerfully in place. Anna Chandy, for instance, continued to be remembered, not as a powerful feminist intellectual, which she indeed was, but as a 'woman-achiever'; Lalitambika Antarjanam continues to be much lauded not for her powerful critique of individualizing modern gender, and her feminist reconstruction of it, but as the epitome of a very non-disruptive Motherliness. Some, of course, were almost entirely erased: B. Bhageeraty Amma, who had edited for twenty years what may arguably be called one of the leading magazines for women in early twentieth-century Kerala, and was an acclaimed public speaker of those times, is little remembered. The articles [I have] collected were all published between the 1890s, when these women began to air their views in the emergent Malayalee public sphere, and the late 1930s, after which they go into an odd decline, yet to be fully explained.

However, I would not like to present these authors as a brave generation that lost out against modern patriarchy, as a prominent author has (Saradamoni 1999). The fact that they stayed well within the framework of modern gender as it was presented in late nineteenth/early twentieth-century Malayalee society, committed to the goal of sexual complementarity it promised, can hardly be overlooked. By 'modern gender', one would mean *(a)* the presupposition of the division of the world into 'public' and 'private' domains, appropriate for men and women respectively, who are seen to possess distinctly sexed 'dispositions' that direct them to the spaces deemed right for them; *(b)* compulsory heterosexism; *(c)* a strong claim to represent the 'natural' foundations of human social order, with the cautionary rider that for this 'natural' aspect of humanity to manifest in society, a great deal of social activity, ranging from legal interventions to training through modern education, is necessary. The established jati (caste)-based social ordering in Kerala, which valued *jamma-bhedam,* or difference in birth, came to be repeatedly denounced in the late nineteenth century, from a range of sites, including the missionaries, and the newly educated elite.

In these denunciations, an alternative was posed, often implicitly. This is what I would like to call 'the order of gender', an ideal form of social ordering projected into the future (and re-discovered in the 'past' as well, in the imaginings of 'Golden Ages' of, for example, Indian/Hindu society), in which the only unsurpassable social division would be of gender. The division between men and women also implied two distinct social domains deemed 'naturally-ordained' for them, the public and the domestic. The 'order of gender' was to be sustained through the complementary exchange of gendered capacities, men as industrious producers in the political, economic and intellectual fields, and women as efficient and active overseers of the domestic domain. While material sorts of authority were largely assigned as male, a certain sentimental and moral authority, that was to work not through force and violence but by the gentle power of persuasion—of words—was designated Womanly. Modern education, then, was set the task of 'developing' the 'natural' (gendered) capacities inherent in specific bodies to shape 'internalities' that would help the modern Individual, the product of such training, to conform to idealized modern gendered subjectivities. The individual, thus believed to be culled out of the traditional order and shaped through modern institutions, or in another language, 'freed from bondage to tradition', was always and already implicated in a modern collectivity. Modern gender was to mediate this implication made. Firstly, it was asserted that women, by nature, deserved to have a thoroughly active supervisory role within the home; not as passive domestic labourers but as active agents overseeing not only the materials but also the souls within the home. Woman as the guardian of the home and hearth was to exist in a relation of complementarity with Man, whose proper domain was deemed to be the public, within the spheres of political power, wealth creation and intellectual production. By the late 1920s, this argument had gained significant diffusion in the Malayalee public sphere, enthusiastically taken up by almost all the community reform movements in Travancore, Cochin (Kochi) and Malabar. Many of the first-generation feminists were active propagators of this new active domestic ideal for women (for instance, Ayesha Mayan and K. Chinnamma). By the 1920s and 1930s the new domestic ideal was also refurbished by the inclusion of money-making activities, such as cottage industry, minor farming, animal husbandry, and so on. Secondly, by the late 1920s, many of these women-intellectuals claimed that the boundaries that separated the modern home from the world outside were becoming increasingly blurred. Earlier, the modern home was envisaged as a site that worked best with the power of 'gentle words, emotions, prayers, devotion and tears'; it appeared most obviously to be the space of Woman, who seemed naturally equipped to exercise such power. Now, however, with an increasing number of institutions seeking to rely upon such power, rather than upon the use of physical violence—such as schools, hospitals, philanthropic institutions, local bodies—it was argued that women's 'special capacities' had a relevance outside the home. Thus, it could be argued that the Womanly might no longer be identified with a certain space, but with a certain form of power. Many first generation feminists based their arguments in favour of paid employment for women outside the home on this claim. Thus they were hardly asking for unconditional freedom of life-choices for women; with rare exceptions, they were demanding an expansion of women's space without challenging the claims regarding the 'quintessential qualities of Womanliness'.

Moreover, this second claim was not necessarily made *against* the first. K. Chinnamma, perhaps, illustrates well how a woman, who had herself entered much larger social concerns, ardently espoused the ideal of a taxing modern domesticity which demanded eternal vigilance over children from women and women alone. These were determined efforts to carve a specifically 'Woman's domain' that straddled the domestic and (ever-expanding) parts of the public, in various fields ranging from politics to literature, without jeopardizing a certain hallowed Womanliness. Forceful arguments in favour of recognizing women as a group with distinct political interests were also made in the late 1920s (the editorial of the *Vanitakusumam* is a good example of such strong appeals), very often coupled with their 'special' significance.

The flip side was of course the idea that women needed to be more self-disciplined, industrious and responsible than men. This followed on the heels of the idea that women were natural disciplinarians, and hence were the custodians of social order and morality. Throughout the late-nineteenth and early twentieth centuries, reflections on building a new 'modern' self had insisted upon a distinction between *swatantryam* (self-means for survival) and *tantonnittam* (doing-as-one-pleased). The former was valued, the latter condemned, and these were linked in a binary relation. Swatantryam meant also the capacity to conform to ideal modern gendered subjectivities, to 'attain' Womanhood or Manhood, and did not mean the simple absence of all forms of coercion. It would not be off the mark to claim that through all these decades, educated Malayalees have got used to identifying 'freedom' with an active agency which is economically productive and congenial to the interests of, mainly, the family. This has been especially so for freedom has hardly been attentive to the gender divide. One has to merely refer to the representations of 'women's progress' in the 'Kerala model' literature to see how this idea has remained unchallenged within academics: indeed it remains one of the most powerful props to the 'Kerala model' itself. It is certainly true that these women intellectuals had to engage in prolonged and charged debate with modern men in the public sphere and were often marginalized as unrealistic rabble-rousers. However, the extent of their differences with male reformers should not be exaggerated.

This, however, is not to belittle the political significance of these writings. [. . .]

As someone who grew up seeing political/intellectual docility as a necessary requirement for coming under the sign of Woman in Kerala, I was awestruck by the marvellous deploying of reason, humour and rhetoric in these writings (many of which were actually speeches) to dismantle older forms of patriarchy, even to ferret out what appeared to be the vestiges of it in emergent institutions. Nor were they blind to emergent advantage to men, shaped often within reformism that claimed to liberate women. [. . .]

A common strategy is to plumb a given text for its internal contradictions and omissions, acknowledged or unacknowledged, and to lay bare the interests underlying it as those of patently non-modern male dominance. [. . .]

Another familiar strategy is to point to developments in the western world, especially those in the women's movements there, to argue for active social agency for women here. [. . .]

Thus even as I maintained a conscious wariness against setting up intellectual foremothers, I could not help listening enraptured to the 'fantasy-echo' so aptly named by the historian Joan W. Scott in her attempt to understand how feminists of different generations, with often diametrically-opposed concerns, are able to 'connect' (Scott 2001). As translator, I found myself grappling with several new ideas: many of these writers had indeed 'named' forms of gender oppression rampant in the Malayalee society I grew up in, for which I had no name. The most telling instance was Anna Chandy's coinage *Adukkalavadam,* which translates as 'Kitchenism', which refers to the belief that women's legitimate space, all said and done, is indeed the space of domestic labour.

Yet it is crucially important to see what is excluded from the Womanhood that is imagined in these writings. The elitism inherent in much of this writing is something I would not like to conceal at all: racism and even a pathological concern over blue blood is often present, even if in an oblique way. Indeed, even as the Womanly domain was being opened up and widened at tremendous effort, it immediately created other spaces that were 'non-Womanly'. For instance, the nominated representative of women in the Cochin Legislative Council was vociferously arguing in 1929 that women should be prohibited from the production and sale of liquor. Women who were far removed from modern education, women of the labouring classes and less-privileged groups are present in these writings only as junior members at best, as aspirants for full membership in Womanhood, who had to be guided into it under the tutelage of women with adequate cultural capital. A recent study of the constitution of the female workforce in the cashew industry in Kerala (Lindberg 2001) reveals the extent to which the women of the poorer classes with little access to modern education were separated from the first-generation feminists. For them, modern gender began to shape everyday life not so much through their heightened exposure to new ideals and aspirations, as through governmental interventions in wage-fixing and so on. However, one of the pieces is an appeal to the 'Hindu Women of Kerala', actually, to the *savarna* women, asking them to join the Vaikam Satyagraha against the restrictions of movement imposed on the lower castes in the roads around the Vaikam temple, to help alleviate the disabilities of their lower caste sisters (Vatakkecharuvil P.K. Kalyani). In her attack on T.K. Velu Pillai, Anna Chandy questions his reduction of all Malayalee women to those of the matrilineal castes, and presents an alternate construction, of a Malayalee Womanhood separated by caste differences, but united by the common experience of oppressive traditional restrictions and mistreatment. That, perhaps, indicates the limits of the inclusiveness of Womanhood as conceived by the first-generation feminists, remaining as it was within the ambit of modern gender that presupposed the public–private divide as expressing a gendered delineation of social space. [. . .]

References

Watts, M.E. M.E.Watts to C.W.E. Cotton, 13 January 1928, 317/877, Bundle no. 18, *Confidential Files,* Tiruvitamkoor, Kerala State Archives.

Sanjayan (M.R. Nair). 1970. *Sreemati Taravath Ammalu Amma—Oru Anusmaranam.* (Taravath Ammalu Amma—A Remembrance). N.p.

Saradamoni. K. 1999. *Matriliny Transformed.* New Delhi: Sage.

Scott, Joan W. 2001. The evidence of experience. *Critical Inquiry* 17 (Summer): 773–97.

Lindberg, Anna. 2001. Experience and identity: A historical account of class, caste and gender among the cashew workers of Kerala, 1930–2000. Lund: Department of History, University of Lund.

∽

CITIZENS, WORKERS AND EMBLEMS OF CULTURE: AN ANALYSIS OF THE FIRST PLAN DOCUMENT ON WOMEN

Maitrayee Chaudhuri

I

The scope of the sub-committee report: Woman's role in planned economy

On 16 June 1939, the National Planning Committee (NPC) appointed the Sub-Committee on Woman's [SCW] Role in Planned Economy (*WRPE* 27). The *WRPE* is a comprehensive account of the status of women in India of that period. It is also an outline of a plan for changing the status of women in independent India. [. . .]

Entitled *Woman's Role in Planned Economy,* the 265-page SCW report contains a preface and an introduction by K.T. Shah, who was also the editor of the other reports produced by the various sub-committees. The main text is divided into three principal sections: Section 1 on the individual status of women, has four chapters, namely, 'Civic rights', 'Economic rights', 'Property rights' and 'Education'. (Why the chapter on 'Education' does not have 'rights' appended to its title we do not know.) Section 2 on the social status of women has two chapters, entitled 'Marriage and its problems' and 'Family life'. Section 3 on miscellaneous issues begins with a chapter entitled 'Miscellaneous', dealing with caste, widows, widow remarriage, widows' home, unmarried mothers, abortion, illegitimate child (*sic*), prostitution and traffic, women and children (*sic*) prostitutes, commercial prostitutes, courtesan and temple prostitutes. Then follows the 'Summary statement of policy' (chapter 8), and the 'Summary of recommendations'. The final chapter contains the resolutions of the NPC on the report of the SCW. [. . .]

The *WRPE* is a kind of hybrid sum of institutional and discursive practices bearing on the nation, family, class, gender, religion and community. We have here divergent languages, often encapsulating antithetical worldviews. We have images of a liberal nationalist worldview, jostling with visions of cultural revivalism and socialist utopias. The hegemony of the liberal nationalist view is finally established, though not without a concerted struggle with the other views. The *WRPE* reflects the basic ideological thrust of its time. It contains the ideas of the grand narratives of the West, which had such a powerful impact on the English-educated middle class, but which were interpreted in the specific context of colonialism, a context peculiarly gifted with the potential of endowing new meanings. This potential of transformation is, of course, located in the very process of the skewed development of colonialism.

This paper can in no way do justice to the report. Reading it today, almost sixty years after the SCW was constituted, reading it in the light of the issues which the women's movement has raised in the last few decades, it is remarkably contemporary. To mention but a few of the issues which were widely debated in the *WRPE* then, and which have continued to be debated since, the report considered: the nature of household labour and the need to recognize its value (*WRPE* 104); the rights of the unmarried woman; the irrelevance of legitimacy for determining the rights of children so far as the state is concerned (204); and even issues like 'identical moral standards' (38).

The *WRPE* is also remarkable as a well-documented status report, the first of its kind, based entirely on primary investigation in an era when such exercises were not the order of the day; and on women, an area where paucity of data continues to be a major problem. This idea itself is based on an understanding of the complex ways in which the lives of women are structured by the economic, social, political, cultural and religious spheres, thereby grappling with the perplexities of the woman's question in Indian society. In this respect, the report puts many studies on women in India of the late 1960s and 1970s in a poor light. [. . .]

While the socialist model is the one which is most frankly advocated, emphasis on key liberal concepts like 'citizenship' (*WRPE* 36–38), the 'individual as the primary unit' (153) and 'private property' (118) runs through the *WRPE*. This is but one of the lines of conflict regarding political options. The other discernible tension is that between the avowed aim of the *WRPE* which reaffirm the past, the gendered nature of the family and the role of traditional religion.

The SCW, like the other sub-committees of the NPC, was trying to outline a society based on secular principles. That this was not an issue likely to pass uncontested is clear in the report not only from the manifest mention of differences (*WRPE* Appendix I, 232), but also from the manner in which issues such as the Uniform Civil Code (229–31) are presented, and in evidently ambiguous views regarding religion. [. . .]

The SCW accords the individual woman an unequivocal centrality, but what is significant is that the aspects of the individual accorded the highest premium are those of the 'useful citizen' and 'the productive worker' (*WRPE* 36). The underlying assumption is that this usefulness and productivity of the individual is to be evaluated in terms of her contribution to the making of the nation. While societal barriers in the way of women's progress are sought to be pushed back, the retreat of society and the celebration of the individual are not absolute. For now the nation state emerges as the central actor and the question of women's individual progress becomes a question of the nation's progress. For instance, on education the *WRPE* writes:

> All restrictions which prove a handicap to the *free and full development of woman's personality* shall be abolished. (*WRPE* 219, emphasis added)

On health, we have:

> Any steps taken to protect the health of the women workers should *not be considered as for their exclusive benefit only*, but as taken *in the interests of the whole nation*. (209, emphasis added)

On widowhood:

> We are strongly opposed to widowhood being considered as a perpetual condition and every effort should be made by education, social reform and even legal reform, to put an end to the evils that result from such condition. We desire that the widow, instead of being the *nation's liability* be turned into a [*sic*] *useful member of society*. (182, emphasis added)

On birth control the document notes that 'from the national point of view, birth control is very important' (175) and,

> From the eugenic point of view the Indian stock is definitely deteriorating for want of proper selection as well as due to poverty, malnutrition, etc., factors which are detrimental to the nation's health. (175) [. . .]

The interest of the whole nation is itself understood in the particular sense of 'growth', the basic value underpinning modern social thought. This is reflected in the chapter on 'Civic rights' which argues: 'In order to help woman to become a useful citizen and *productive worker* she must be assured of her fundamental rights' (*WRPE* 209, emphasis added). Apart from the obviously utilitarian vision that informs the *WRPE*, we have a certain prioritization of the nation as a collective unit. Social organizations other than the nation are seen as hindrances to the growth of the individual.

> The rigidity of the caste system has affected the *individual rights of man and woman*, by preventing them from marrying outside the caste and thereby limiting their choice. (117, emphasis added)

And,

> Marriage from a rational view point can no longer be a divine dispensation but a voluntary association of two *individuals* with rights and obligations attached to it. (153, emphasis added)

What we have is a hierarchical placement of the community (caste, religion) at the base (understood as a legacy of the past and therefore transitional until a point when the nation becomes the community), the individual (understood as citizen and worker), and, finally, the overarching state.

> Individual families will and should continue, but as far as the State is concerned, the *individual* must be the basic unit to which consideration should specifically be given. (221, emphasis added)

The *WRPE* reflects this emphasis in content, balance and form. It is significant that Section 1 dealing with 'individual status' is spread over 114 pages (35–150), including 72 pages (45–117) devoted to 'Economic rights', while Section 2 concerning 'social status' was limited to 46 pages (151–97). Despite the neglect of women in agriculture, the report's detailed investigation on women's economic life and role is of special significance in relation to planning in independent India, for the very idea of the woman as a productive worker was subsequently eclipsed in state and academic discourse except with reference to the new middle class working woman. It was only in 1974 that the Committee on the Status of Women in India raised the matter of the invisibility of women workers, and only as recently as the 1991 Census that a concerted attempt was made to both redefine women's work and communicate to the people a more comprehensive understanding of 'work'. [. . .]

Special mention is made of the invisibility of work done in the precincts of the 'home' and the need to recognize household work.

> A great many women will confine their activities to the home, in any event, a great part of their work will be done in the home. This home work, though not recognized in terms of money value, is an essential contribution to the social wealth of the State and should be recognized as such. The aggregate of social wealth under a planned economy will include all kinds of work, whether rewarded in money value or not. (200)

As mentioned, we have a substantive thrust on 'Economic rights', and an empirical focus on working class women, but an ideological tilt in favour of bourgeois rights—the right of women to hold private property (*WRPE* 118), the right of citizenship and the individual woman's right to choose (37). On the one hand the liberal view contains the socialist position; on the other the nation state contains the individual. [. . .]

Returning to the issue of marriage, the SCW disapproves of the idea of the 'sanctity of marriage' and writes that in 'the new social order that we are planning, it will therefore be the State which will lay down and enforce the law of marriage and for the State, therefore, marriage will only be a civil contract' (*WRPE* 153). But this is followed by:

> This, however, does not mean that religion will be a taboo or that the State will not recognize any marriage which is not performed under the civil law of the State. It only means that, for the purposes of protecting the rights and enforcing the obligations of the parties concerned who enter into marriage, the State will not recognize any marriage which is not performed under the civil law of the State. (153)

This clarification about the relationship envisaged for the still unborn Indian nation state and religion suggests that the SCW was responding to reservations that were probably being raised at that time, and an attempt is made to introduce a caveat that all religions are not to be dismissed, but only those which are 'doctrinal':

> The domination of religion—the doctrinal religion—has done much harm to the individual in the past and continues to harm him today wherever such domination still exists. With the growth of a rational outlook on life such a domination is bound to go. (153)

The remedy for the 'diversity of laws which exists today is a common civil code including inheritance, marriage and divorce laws, which should be optional to begin with but universally enforced' within a 'reasonable period of its passing into Act' (*WRPE* 217).

The addition of the word 'optional', even if it is only to begin with, reflects the kind of opposition such moves were generating. The SCW itself bears witness to the dissenting voices. A note on this subject states that 'considerable discussion took place on this resolution' (*WRPE* 229), and that a great deal of disagreement was expressed. The other issues on which differences were expressed were on resolutions on divorce, on property rights for women and on recognition of the rights of the illegitimate child.

A sharp schism divides what the SCW overtly set out to do—the 'drastic recommendations' (*WRPE* 32) to bring in the new social order—and what it eventually does. The shift does not appear in the text as a retreat, but only as an adjustment for a transitional period. [. . .]

The spirit of optimism, progress, enlightenment and equality, images of the brave new order, 'of man and woman, comrades of the road, going forward together, the child joyously shared by both', 'a reality' which cannot 'but raise the manhood and womanhood of any nation', are tangibly present in the *WRPE* (33). The new times are special times, where all 'superstitious beliefs' will be abandoned in the 'new social order' in which the 'searchlight of reason' (153) would be shining.

On the other hand, the language used when deliberating on the constraints on implementing the recommendations is matter-of-fact, pragmatic and cautious. The actual recommendations are straightforward but their substance is diluted both by the subsequent elaboration of specific recommendations, and by the repetition of the phrase 'transitional period' (or words to that effect) in reference to the phase 'before the new measures actually come into effect'.

For instance, we have a long explanation about the actual intention of the proposed marriage reforms:

> In advocating divorce, our desire is not to break up the home but to make marriage more happy, and, therefore, more stable. If we turn to the evidence of writers like Pammine Halle, Beatrice and Sidney Webb and others, we find that even in Russia where the experiment of divorce under easy conditions was tried, it has resulted actually in strengthening the bond

of marriage. It does not follow therefore, that by conceding the right of divorce to women the State will be undermining the foundations of marriage, and, therefore, of society. It will rather, we think, help to make the foundation more secure. (*WRPE* 164)

This is a far cry from the view that, with the state taking over certain responsibilities, the twin institutions of the 'family' and 'private property' would be rendered 'as unnecessary as they are objectionable today' (240); or that 'private property is the root cause of many inequalities' (118); or that 'in planned society the basic unit would be the individual'. [. . .]

The *WRPE* clearly retreats from its initial views on the issues of marriage reforms, of divorce (164), of the adoption and maintenance of children (230), and of the role of religion in the making of laws (227–31). Not surprisingly, these issues all pertain to the private, domestic sphere. In the section on the analysis of labour, the *WRPE* breaks the public/private dichotomy. In the discourse on family reform, this dichotomy is reaffirmed.

I have two possible explanations for this. The first is that the identity of 'Indian womanhood', resting on the attributes of motherhood and other qualities connected with domesticity, is class based. The working class woman is seen entirely in terms of production (as in the 72 pages on 'Economic rights'). Not so the middle class woman. While the need for her economic independence is recognized (*WRPE* 105), her responsibility to 'create a cultural environment in the home for the proper nurture of the children' and not 'merely to cook, wash and attend to the needs and comforts of the family' is emphasized to improve the low standards of life in the country (104). These differential role expectations draw attention to the ways by which class is itself gendered.

The second explanation for the selective gendered analysis of the public/ private split can be traced to certain limits to the production paradigm, even if production is taken to be both 'production of things' and 'production of life'. Recent feminist philosophy has asked whether 'the concept of production, which is based on the model of an active subject transforming, making and shaping an object given to it' can adequately comprehend traditionally female activities such as child-rearing and care-giving, 'which are so thoroughly intersubjective' (Benhabib 1987, 2). The *WRPE* attaches great 'national' significance to these activities (104) but thereby also reifies them, alienating them from the subject. [. . .]

Significantly, all the twenty-seven members of the SCW, including Chairperson Rani Lakshmi Rajwade, were women. The disparate views, the patriarchal resistances, the 'drastic recommendations', the eugenic view, the contestation and the eventual hegemony of the liberal model in the analysis have to be attributed to them. Since I do not see the theorization of hegemony as contradictory to the theorization of resistance (they are in fact part of the same project), I would not hesitate both to acknowledge the hegemonic project of the *WRPE* and yet to argue that the other resistive strands within the *WRPE* open up a new space for the woman's question, even if the possibilities thus opened up are foreclosed in the text.

References

Benhabib, Seyla. 1987. The generalized and concrete other. In *Feminism as critique*, ed. Seyla Benhabib and Drucilla Cornell. Oxford: Blackwell/Minneapolis: University of Minneapolis Press, 1–15.

Woman's role in planned economy, 1947 (WRPE). (The sub-committee on women's role in planned economy). Bombay: Vora.

~

AUGUST ANARCHY

Ritu Menon and Kamla Bhasin

The Hindustan–Pakistan Plan was announced on June 3, 1947 whereby a new entity called Pakistan was created, of which West Pakistan was to comprise the Muslim-majority provinces of Sind, the North-West Frontier Province, and 16 districts of Punjab; the remaining 13 districts of undivided Punjab were to be part of India. Although the exact boundary line between the two countries had still to be determined by the Boundary Commission, the exchange of populations started taking place much before August 15.

Even earlier, however, in November 1946 in fact, Jinnah had suggested such an exchange, referring to the exodus of Hindus from Noakhali after the riots there in August. People were already on the move, he said, and it would be prudent to devise some mechanism for their smooth and safe transit. In December 1946, Raja Ghazanfar Ali Khan referred to increasing communal unrest and said the transfer of populations was a necessary corollary to the establishment of a Muslim state. Even Akali leaders changed their minds after the Noakhali riots, and Sardar Swaran Singh, leader of the Panthic Assembly Party, said in July 1947 that such an exchange was the only solution to the problem of violence against minority communities on either side of the redrawn borders. Only the Congress thought that the sporadic violence that had occurred was temporary; and Mahatma Gandhi unequivocally rejected the very idea:

> It is unthinkable and impracticable. Every province is of every Indian, be he Hindu, Muslim or of any other faith. If won't be otherwise, even if Pakistan came in full. For me any such thing will spell bankruptcy of Indian wisdom or statesmanship, or both. The logical consequence of any such step is too dreadful to contemplate. Is it not bad enough that India should be artificially divided into so many religious zones? (Rai 1965: 102)

To give Congress leaders their due, however, the unworkability of the idea was apparent: religious minorities were scattered all over the country, there were towns and villages even in Muslim majority provinces that had very large numbers of Hindus and Sikhs, those left behind would be more vulnerable than ever, and in any case, transfer of power was what had been agreed to, not transfer of populations. So, although people had begun moving out of villages as early as March 1947, much before the announcement of the Plan, the Partition Council nevertheless passed a resolution on August 2, 1947 to 'arrest further exodus and encourage the return of people to their homes'. (Rai 1965:102)

The Boundary Commission announced its awards on August 16. Within a week, about one million Hindus and Sikhs had crossed over from West to East Punjab, and in the week following, another two and a half million had collected in refugee camps in West Punjab. By November 6, 1947, nearly 29,000 refugees had been flown in both directions; about 673 refugee trains were run between August 27 and November 6, transporting more than two million refugees inside Indian and across the border. Of these, 1,362,000 were non-Muslims and 939,000 were Muslims. Huge foot convoys, each 30–40,000 strong, were organized by the Military Evacuation Organization and the East Punjab Liaison Agency to move the bulk of the rural population, especially those who still had their cattle and bullock-carts with them. The estimate is that in forty-two days (September 18 to October 29), twenty-four non-Muslim foot-columns, 849,000 strong, had crossed into India. Migrations varied in size and composition as well as in mode of transit. Some people moved in stages, first from small hamlets to larger communities, and thence to local transit camps; others travelled directly from the big cities by rail or air to the other side of the border. Families might leave together or in batches, depending on how permanent they thought the move was going to be. Many simply locked up their houses, entrusted their neighbours with the keys, and left with the assurance of returning. Others knew there would be no going back; and still others made the move, stayed for a while, and then returned.

As the violence increased, however, the migrations took on an urgent and treacherous character: convoys were ambushed, families separated, children orphaned, women kidnapped—whole trainloads massacred. By the time the exodus was finally over, about eight to ten million people had crossed over from Punjab and Bengal—the largest peace-time mass migration in history—and about 500,000–1,000,000 had perished. The exchange, at least as far as Punjab was concerned, was as nearly equal as can be imagined: the total non-Muslim population of Punjab in 1941 was 4,357,477, the total Muslim population, 4,286,755.

No one, they say, foresaw either the rivers of people that would flow from one part of Punjab to the other, or the blood that would be shed as they were killed in their tens of thousands. By the first week of March 1947, rioting, arson and looting had broken out in Punjab, beginning with the central districts of Lahore, Amritsar, Ferozepur, Ludhiana, Sheikhupura, Gurdaspur, Sialkot, Montgomery, Lyallpur, the countryside. The violence was, by most reckonings, organized and systematic: Hindu and Sikh shops and businesses were singled out for burning and looting in West Punjab, Muslim property and homes in East Punjab. Allegations were made by both sides of the active involvement of political leaders, the Muslim League and the Jamaat, the National Guards, demobilized soldiers of the Indian National Army (INA), the Hindu Mahasabha and the Rashtriya Swayam Sewak Sangh (RSS), with all claiming only to be acting in self-defence. Muslim leaders complained to Evan Jenkins, then Governor of Punjab, that Dr. Gopi Chand Bhargava and Lala Bhimsen Sachar were encouraging communal violence in Amritsar. They said the Muslim League had been non-violent for 34 days while the non-Muslims became violent on the first day of their agitation. [. . .]

Suspicion and mistrust ran deep, exacerbated by inflammatory pamphlets put out by both sides. One, with a picture of Jinnah, sword in hand, declared:

> *Be ready and take your swords! Think you, Muslims, why we are under the Kafirs today. The result of loving the Kafirs is not good. O, Kafir! Your doom is not far and the general massacre will come.* (Khosla 1949: 52-53)

Meanwhile, in a secret letter to Mountbatten dated April 9, 1947, Evan Jenkins warned of an organized attack by Sikhs against Muslims, and an appeal made by Giani Kartar Singh and Master Tara Singh for Rs 50 lakhs towards a 'War Fund'. A pamphlet in Gurmukhi exhorted:

> *Oh, Sikhs! Read this and think yourself, what have you to do under the circumstances? In your veins there is yet the blood of your beloved Guru Gobind Singhji. Do your duty!* (Jenkins 1947)

Calls to take up arms had their predictable consequences. Between March 1947 the official figures for deaths in disturbances in Punjab were 3,410–3,600, and the loss of property, Rs 15 crore.

Official versions of the violence in Punjab put out by India and Pakistan, post-Partition, detail its occurrence district by district, village by village, mohalla by mohalla, and trace its progress towards the 'August Anarchy' which marked the announcement of the Boundary Commission awards. Swarna Aiyar (1995) has given us an almost bogey by bogey account of the great train massacres that were a feature of every train that carried fleeing refugees from one side of Punjab to the other in the weeks between August 9 and September 30, until the Refugee Specials were arranged. [. . .]

Foot convoys were ambushed, with escorts sometimes joining the mobs and shooting indiscriminately; one such convoy, nearly six miles long, which left Lyallpur on September 11, 1947 was attacked several times during its journey, and of the five thousand refugees, one thousand perished. Kidnappings and abductions were widespread; one account has it that in Narnaul in Patiala State, 16,000 Muslims were killed and 1,500 women abducted. Lorries and trucks were not spared either, and as late as July 1948, travelling by road in West Punjab was wholly unsafe.

The scale and intensity of the violence in Punjab continue to horrify us even today, virtually paralyzing any effort to fully comprehend its meaning. The extreme difficulty experienced by all those who have attempted to 'write' Partition violence finds its mirror-image in the difficulty which most commentators have in offering an adequate explanation for it. Nor is there any agreement on its primary causes. Early writing generally accepts that much of it was organized and orchestrated by law enforcement agencies and their functionaries, by willing henchmen of various quasi-political organizations, and a communalized bureaucracy. There was not so much a breakdown of law and order, as a suspension of it: brutality was allowed. Had this not been the case, few would have been motivated enough to leave their homes and lands and livelihoods, and resettle in a new country. Time and again, in the course of our interviews we were told, 'governments change, even rulers may change, but people are never exchanged'. They were forced out of villages and towns by the ferocity of attacks on them, creating enough terror to banish any doubt or possibility of reconciliation. Why else would thousands from Patiala have resettled in faraway Sind? From faraway Peshawar in Dehradun?

The economic factor has also been considered a powerful motivator; so, agricultural labour was amenable to violently dealing with landowners, debtors with money lenders and traders, and assorted adventurers and opportunists who quickly saw a short-cut to betterment. Forty years later in Karnal, Gyan Deyi said, 'It was our own labour, people who worked on our land, they attacked us. Our own people did this.' Economic considerations persuaded many who were propertied to accept conversion to one or other religion in order to retain their assets. Yet, according to other analyses, organized violence and economic factors, though important, cannot sufficiently account for the brutality; for them a good part of the explanation lies in cultural and psychological factors, and in the abiding nature of prejudice and deep-seated antagonism. Latent in 'normal' times, it erupts with extreme virulence during communal conflict and remains lodged in collective memory, to surface with renewed intensity in the next round. 'Cultural memory,' says Sudhir Kakar, 'is a group's history freed from rootedness in time—it is as much imagination as the actual events that go into its construction' (Kakar 1995:37) In his view, the retelling of Partition violence is the primary channel through which historical enmity is transmitted; the 'truth' of these accounts lies not in their veracity but in the 'archetypal material they contain'. The particular forms this violence takes—disfigurement, mutilation, disembowelment, castration, branding—are part of its pathology and must be recognized for their symbolic meaning. The brutal logic of reprisal thus realizes its full potential, with all parties to it fully cognizant of their role. In its own way this theory seeks to restore volition and 'agency' to the actors and resists the passivity that more instrumentalist explanations assign to them, although, as Veena Das has noted, 'there is no contradiction between the fact that, on the one hand, mob violence may be highly organized and crowds provided with such instruments as voters' lists or combustible powders, and on the other, that crowds draw upon repositories of unconscious images to spur them on' (Das 1990, 28). The exchange of violence that reprisal entails is justified by what some social scientists have called the language of feud. In this consideration, feud may be defined as 'a pact of violence' between social groups in such a way that the 'definition of the self and the other emerges through an exchange of violence'. In this exchange, victims of feud are simply 'bearers of the status of their group, the means through which the pact of violence continues to be executed' (Das and Nandy 1985, 179).

In our own time, analyses of ethnic violence in Bosnia, especially, but also in Sri Lanka, Sudan, Chechnya and Rwanda, see a strong link between ethnicity or religion-based territorial vivisection and ethnic 'cleansing'. Nationalist fratricide is part of the partition of countries when that partition is caused by the collision of two fundamentally opposed nationalist imaginations. Partitions in South Asia—India–Pakistan, Pakistan–Bangladesh, Tamil Eelam, among them—are the archetype of nationalist fratricide, the 'conflict of people of a common cultural heritage in competition as "nations" for control over land and government' (Francisco 1996, 227).

Marking the body

Women occupy a special place—and space—in such enactments of violence. Our own interviews with several women, survivors of the violence and the displacement, as well as with those who worked on their recovery and rehabilitation over an extended period of time, corroborate but also expand and elaborate upon what is found in written accounts. Our attempt here is to look at the violence that women were subjected to, both at the hands of men of the other community and within their own families, and to demonstrate how these diverse, yet linked, kinds of violence formed part of a continuum of violence that began pre-Partition and continued into the early fifties. A careful consideration of such violence, specific though it may be to a particular historical moment and to communal conflict, may enable us to gain some insight into the more mundane violence and abuse that form part of the everyday experience of many women. It is also our hypothesis that the dramatic episodes of violence against women during communal riots bring to the surface, savagely and explicitly, familiar forms of sexual violence—now charged with a symbolic meaning that serves as an indicator of the place that women's sexuality occupies in an all-male, patriarchal arrangement of gender relations, between and within religious or ethnic communities.

The most predictable form of violence experienced by women, as women, is when the women of one community are sexually assaulted by the men of the other, in an overt assertion of their identity and a simultaneous humiliation of the Other by 'dishonouring' their women. In this respect, the rape and molestation of Hindu, Sikh and Muslim women before and after Partition probably followed the familiar pattern of sexual violence, and of attack, retaliation and reprisal. What may be remarkable is the exultation that accompanied it. Stories of women been stripped 'just as bananas are peeled', and being made to parade naked in the market-place; or of being made to dance thus in gurudwaras; of being raped in the presence of their menfolk, recur both in written accounts and in our interviews. The civil surgeon of Sheikhupura, for example, testified to the Fact Finding Team mentioned earlier, on the violence in Guru Nanakpura on August 26, 1947 and said that, 'women and young girls in all forms of nakedness' were brought to his hospital; 'even the ladies of the most respectable families had the misfortune of having undergone this most terrible experience. The wife of an advocate had practically nothing on when she came to the hospital.' And the medical doctor at the refugee camp in Jhang testified as follows:

> Apart from the injured from Jhang-Maghiana town (following the violence of August 26, 1947) over 500 seriously wounded persons were brought to the refugee camp from adjoining villages. One of the cases that I treated was of a woman from village Chund Bharwana who was the wife of a railway porter. One of her hands was chopped off above her wrist and then she was thrown into the fire, as a result of which her lower portion got burnt. But she escaped from there and was then thrown into a well with her two daughters and one son. She was taken out of the well later on and brought to the refugee camp.

Among the chief types of injury inflicted on the wounded, the same doctor cites 'amputation of breasts of women', and adds that 'six such cases of chopped-off breasts were brought to the refugee camp and all of them proved fatal'.

Very large numbers of women were forced into death to avoid sexual violence against them, to preserve chastity and protect individual, family and community 'honour'. The means used to accomplish this end varied; when women themselves took their lives, they would either jump into the nearest well or set themselves ablaze, singly, or in groups that could be made up either of all the women in the family; the younger women; or women and children. The Fact Finding Team recorded that in Bewal village (Rawalpindi district) during the massacres of March 10, 1947, 'many women and girls saved their honour by self-immolation. They collected their beddings and cots in a heap and when the heap caught fire they jumped on to it, raising cries of 'Sat Sri Akal'!

And the story of 90 women of Thoa Khalsa (Rawalpindi) who jumped into a well on March 15, 1947 is too well known to bear repeating.

Similar accounts abound but it is not our purpose here to repeat the litany of horror; it has been amply documented and can be easily located. Nevertheless, as we read and heard these reports, and as today we read and hear about similar violence in Meerut, Surat, Bhagalpur, Ahmedabad, we begin to discern some specific features of 'communal' crimes against women: their brutality, their extreme sexual violence and their collective nature. The range of sexual violation explicit in the above accounts—stripping; parading naked; mutilating and disfiguring; tattooing or branding the breasts and genitalia with triumphal slogans; amputating breasts; knifing open the womb; raping, of course; killing foetuses—is shocking not only for its savagery, but for what it tells us about women as objects in male constructions of their own honour. Women's sexuality symbolizes 'manhood'; its desecration is a matter of such shame and dishonour that *it has to be avenged.* Yet, with the cruel logic of all such violence, it is women ultimately who are most violently dealt with as a consequence.

Each one of the violent acts mentioned above has specific symbolic meaning and physical consequences, and all of them treat women's bodies as territory to be conquered, claimed or marked by the assailant. Some acts are simultaneous or continuous (they may begin with stripping and culminate in raping, branding or tattooing); they may take place in public—market-places, temples or gurudwaras, the latter two signifying the simultaneous violation of women and sacred space—or privately, but with families as witness. Tattooing and branding the body with 'Pakistan, Zindabad!' or 'Hindustan, Zindabad!' not only mark the woman for life, they never allow her (or her family and community) the possibility of forgetting her humiliation. In the deep horror of its continuous and forever present recall of brutality, this particular violation has few parallels. In the context of Partition, it engraved the division of India into India and Pakistan on the women of both religious communities in a way that they *became* the respective countries, indelibly imprinted by the other. Marking the breasts and genitalia with symbols like the crescent moon or trident makes permanent the sexual appropriation of the woman, and symbolically extends this violation to future generations who are thus metaphorically stigmatized. Amputating her breasts at once desexualizes a woman and negates her as wife and mother; no longer a nurturer (if she survives, that is), she remains a permanently inauspicious figure, almost as undesirable as a barren woman. Sudhir Kakar, in his exploration of how communities fantasize violence, says that sexual mutilation figures prominently:

the castration of males and the amputation of breasts 'incorporate the (more or less conscious) wish to wipe the enemy off the face of the earth' (Kakar 1990: 37) by eliminating the means of reproduction and nurturing.

Stasa Zajovic, analyzing the mass rape of women in Bosnia-Herzegovina, says that as a result of rape 'the female womb becomes occupied territory' (Zajovic 1994, 36). In Serbo-Croat, she continues, the term 'cleansing' is popularly used for abortion, but abortion takes on a particular political significance in circumstances such as these. The idea of polluting and cleansing applies especially to women's bodies. In the process of rehabilitating women, post-Partition, many were regularly submitted to 'medical check-ups' to eliminate the possibility of their bearing the enemy's children and 'polluting the biological national source of family'. Thus is a woman's reproductive power appropriated to prevent the undesirable proliferation of the enemy's progeny. Worse, the female body itself can be made to seem as if it has turned traitor.

The violence against women during Partition cannot be separated form the violent hostility that erupted between Hindus and Muslims at that time. The repertoire of violence on all sides included profaning everything that was held to be of sacred and symbolic value to the other—from pigs and cows slain in front of mosques and temples, to the circumcision of non-Muslim men, and the forced consumption of beef by Hindus—and this extended to sexually violating their women. The preoccupation with women's sexuality formed part of the contract of war between the three communities, and in our view, was of an even greater order of magnitude than circumcision or forcible conversion and marriage. So powerful and general was the belief that safeguarding a woman's honour is *essential* to upholding male and community honour that a whole new order of violence came into play, by men against their own kinswomen; and by women against their daughters or sisters and their own selves. [. . .]

References

Aiyar, Swarna. 1995. "August Anarchy": The Partition Massacres in Punjab 1947, in *South Asia: Journal of South Asian Studies*, vol. 34, pp.13-36.

Das, Veena, ed. 1990. *Mirrors of violence: Communities, riots and survivors in South Asia*. New Delhi: Oxford University Press.

Das, Veena and Ashis Nandy. 1985. Violence, victimhood and the language of silence. In *Contributions to Indian Sociology* (n.s.), vol. 19, no. 1., 177–95.

Francisco, Jason. 1996. In the heat of fratricide: the literature of India's Partition burning freshly. *Annual of Urdu Studies* 2, 227–50.

Jenkins, Evan. 1947. Note dated 4 April 1947. Confidential papers and reports. London: India Office Library.

Kakar, Sudhir. 1990. *The colours of violence.* New Delhi: Viking.

Khosla, G.D. 1949. *Stern reckoning: A survey of the events leading up to and following the partition of India.* Delhi: Oxford University Press.

Rai, Satya. 1965. *Partition of Punjab.* Bombay: Asia Publishing House.

Zajovik, Stasa. 1994. Women and ethnic cleansing. In *Women against fundamentalism* 5, vol.1, 36.

~

PRAMILA TAI

Stree Shakti Sanghatana

I spent my childhood in an orphanage in Bombay. I remember telling the Vietnamese that land once sold out and replanted does not take root. That was true of me too. Even as a child I was always thinking I was not like ordinary children—I kept thinking all the time. Then in 1939 when the war broke out and Gandhiji started satyagraha, I read all about it. I did not have any ideology but I read everything I could get hold of. I read Adhikari's article. He explained why satyagraha was not the way either for my country or for mankind. That was the beginning. In 1942 I came to Hyderabad. I was the headmistress of Bansilal High School for Girls. Then I came in contact with the Communist Party. It was a banned Party and its literature was not easily available, but somehow I managed to read some literature and thought, this is my way, this is the only way my country and humanity also can be saved. So I studied a little before I got drawn towards this. I came also because of my personal misery which attracted me towards the miserable.

I studied by myself and worked as headmistress of this school. B.A., M.A., all this I did on my own. I did my B.A. and M.A. from Benares. I came to know that Benares University was allowing women, working women. So I did my Intermediate from there. Later on I did my B.A. also. Of course I did my M.A. after I came out of jail in 1952. Somehow it was a necessity for me. I never went to any college. Bansilal was the first Hindi medium school. At that time Hindi was also considered anti-Nizam though it was not—the sahukars and the rajahs were old lackeys of the government—but still that feeling was there. When I came here [to Hyderabad] from Bombay I was just a matriculate.

I left this school in 1943. I worked only for one and a half years because I joined the Communist Party in 1942. The Party saw my ability and my devotion and took me into the district committee immediately. Naturally I had to leave the school to become a full-timer of the Communist Party. I was the only woman. There were no women's committees. Only afterwards all these women came. Remember, those were days of the war. There were some Congress women, women in the government also—Princess Niloufer and Princess Dureshawar. They used to give air raid precautions training. They asked me to help. First I said I wouldn't join them. Then I thought to myself: How else will I get contact with people? I didn't know anybody except my school children. I started with my children's mothers. Then I met all of them in their localities. Later there were also the Congress programmes—spinning and weaving. Then I started going from locality to locality, I started meeting women. Of course these were the issues which were not really issues touching our lives—women's problems like education. There was no education.

I remember we used to go from house to house. They thought I was trying to get their wives into this. Then came the Navjivan Mahila Mandal. This Navjivan Mandal, it was separately there and we had this programme. It was war time and economic problems were most pressing. I do not know how far it was correct or not. Princess Dureshawar issued rations of 13 kgs jowar per rupee for widows. So house to house I went and issued coupons. With so many students and teachers I used to do this type of work. We organized cheap and fresh milk and sold it against coupons. Princess Niloufer was the president and I was the secretary. We had two shops, one in Sultan Bazaar and one in Begum Bazaar. Of course this was there, but our daily routine was visiting localities and households, and finding out problems. Many women whose life was a drudgery, who were thrown out of the house, took shelter with us. Sometimes we used to help them with getting jobs, or getting married. We had all this at Navjivan Mandal.

In 1943 or so, the government wanted to introduce rationing. There was no rationing. In two days it had to be organized. Without ration cards you couldn't get any ration. How were we to do it? The Communist Party approached the government. We said: 'We will help you with the distribution.' The government refused. So we went on behalf of Navjivan Mandal. We got nearly 4000 cards. We did that. It was the time of the national movement. In Navjivan Mandal we had all ranis, rajahs. National feelings were the main thing—we were all working for national salvation. The RSS women were also there, Congress women were also there, non-political women were also there. The main feeling was that we were serving women and that we were serving the national cause.

How this Navjivan Mandal work helped Party work is a question which may interest you. I used to go and meet these women to talk to them. I also carried pamphlets and other Party literature in my bag, if I found anyone interested or inquisitive I gave them this material. That is what I used to do. Of course the other people would come to know, but what could they do. Our Navjivan Mandal alone had more than 2000 members from all Hindi-speaking communities. And for Telugu speaking people we had Andhra Mahila Sabha, because the language problem was there, you know. Here we

had Marathi, Gujarathi, Marwadi—all these. You know Vasudeva Nayak—
a real Congress man—once he asked his wife, 'Don't you people quarrel in
your committees?' She said, 'No, we never quarrel, we have a programme.'
That is true. In our Navjivan Mandal we had a programme and we used to
follow that. We never took our communist literature there. After all what is
the communist programme? To organize the masses, to awaken them—it is
not just reading or distributing. That won't help. I have some experience.
This mass work helped me a lot.

When the Party was banned, I had to support myself. Where could I go?
I had no relatives here. It is the mass organization, my women's organization,
my school teachers—it is they who supported me—why me? —not only me,
but the Party, for five years, giving me shelter, helping me economically also.
And it was . . . I don't boast . . . it was not just these people but unorganized
people who also helped me. Consciousness was there. Conditions were there
. . . How did we fight against the Nizam? It was not just the Communist
Party. It was the United Front—all the way. Rich landlords were also with
us. It was not just our credit. It was the conditions of the time—and the
organizing skill of the Communist Party.

It was like this. Whatever programme there was, we used to first discuss
it—Andhra Mahila Sabha members, Congress women. We used to meet
earlier and discuss things. Like that we used to have joint action (NMM and
AMS). For example, when the Suryapet firings on students took place; we
organized a meeting at—what was that place—yes, it was Dilshad Talkies, I
think. The meeting was banned but we all joined. Congress women also,
Navjivan Mahila Mandal also, Andhra Mahila Sabha also—and there were
other small women's organizations like Karnataka Mahila Sabha and other
language organizations. We had almost everybody except for the Muslim
women—very few Muslim women joined us. The majority wouldn't come.

You know, All India Women's Conference was there. We used to
participate in AIWC programmes also. All of us. Well, those who didn't want
to come didn't come. [. . .]

When Mahendra was a student, Osmania University was boycotted by
all Hindu students. He went to Shantiniketan. You know the leftist atmosphere
there. He left college and started working in the Iron and Coal mines in
Berampur. When the Armed Struggle started he was asked to come back.
'We want our comrade back,' they said. By the time he came here Maqdoom
had gone outside the state. None of the leaders were left. Mahendra was new
to the place. He didn't know all the people or the places. I used to help him.
But when the question of my shelter came up he said, 'We cannot provide
shelter for you.' I was the last person to go underground. I had provided
shelter for everybody. Well, Mahendra said, 'We can't help you.' So I
thought I would have to go to Bombay. I had only one relative in the whole
world. This was in 1946, I felt very bad. We are in the movement—and in

the thick of movement I had to leave the place. I didn't like it at all. As I told you, I had so many contacts all over the city, there was not a lane, not a place where I was not known. So I immediately got shelter. I arranged my shelter and arranged shelters for other people also. During that underground period Mahendra came to know what I was. Why did he ask me to go away, you ask. Well, he was a new person here and did not know many people— and generally, you know, [smiling] women are a handicap.

In 1946 I went underground. I was told there was an arrest warrant for me. In 1951 I was arrested. I was married in 1947 while I was underground. Yes, we had to ask the Party for permission. I don't know what they said. Sundarayya and all this big committee was there and I had no chance to meet them. But suppose I am in their place. What would I think? That these two people want to join their lives. So, what are the plus points, what are the minus points? How will they be able to pull on? I'm sure they would have thought of all these things. They would have considered the personalities— it was an intercaste marriage—whether the persons would be able to stand the onslaught. Especially since we are in the thick of the movement. Whether we will be able to withstand all this rough weather. Anyway they did not raise any problem.

Let me tell you about organizing girls. First thing, locality-wise it's very difficult. One had to go to the schools. Nowadays when we organize students we raise all the other questions also: political, economic and so on. But then it was not so. Then it was the women's position—tomorrow we have to enter into the new life—how? What do we know about it? What should we do? We must have freedom. We should not marry a person who demands dowry. Then, fighting against oppression. At that time also these were the main things. [. . .]

I used to move around with my comrades' sons wearing my shorts—half pants and half shirt—tying something in my hair. I used to take off my specs and go around with Mahendra because he did not know anybody. For instance, when Aruna Asaf Ali came for the first time, she wanted to meet our comrades. He didn't know where to go and how to meet them. So we used to go on cycles. We never had these scooters then. I used to sit with him—that's how we got acquainted. No, I did not ride alone. I knew cycling but I had no strength like that. I was a very thin person. So I could pass off for a man very easily. Even police fellows never suspected—except [for] your voice there is no difficulty.

You ask whether I felt that I was treated like one of the men? Whether I was given important responsibilities? Of course, of course. What could they do. When all the important leaders had gone away, who was there to look after the Party office and the Party work? I was there. They had full confidence. Here, you know in the Communist Party, it is the capacity that is recognized. It was like that with me also. I had to fight for it. I had to show my ability. I will give you some examples. We used to stay in Begum Bazaar. Our meetings always used to take place at night—in Sultan Bazaar. I used to go alone. I would never ask any comrade to come with me. Now I might request someone to come, but in those days, oh, never. You have to show your calibre. That is there. Not only here. Everywhere in the world. You find in the other countries also very few women coming into leadership. In fact once Lenin was asked why it is so. And his answer I always remember. He said that woman, when it comes to fighting against the enemy, she fights tooth and nail, but when it comes to fight her own kith and kin then she succumbs. Then she hasn't got that stamina. We have to remember this and we have to prepare our cadre accordingly. I don't think that it is the fault of women that they do not show the calibre. No, no, not at all. See, if the conditions are favourable to them, and even then they do not come forward, then it can be their fault. But generally the conditions are not there. In the world of women's organizations also, I have seen. Very few women come forward as leaders. Men also have not overcome that supremacy, is that not?

I never lived in a commune, but I organized them. Really there was no time for comrades to cook or do house work. We needed to engage a boy to do the cooking. Mahendra and Jawad would be the first ones to come and eat always. They could eat anything—even stones. You see, organizing ourselves into a commune is different. But that was a very difficult time, we had no time, spare time. One example I would like to give. Once I attended a conference at Jangaon, the Jangaon Kisan Sabha, the first time I went out to a village in Telangana. I think it was in 1942 but it would have been '43 or '44. I can't remember. I did not know the language but I wanted to attend the conference. People were coming—men and women—they were coming, pouring in thousands. You can't imagine such a thing today. Only one idea struck my head. I asked Comrade Ravinarayan Reddy, 'These masses are getting awakened. But where is our organization? Can we organize them?' Because of mass enthusiasm they are coming, they had faith in us. But we had no organization. To that extent our Kisan Sabha was not capable of holding them together or educating them. It was a mass upsurge at that time. To this day we must always remember, if the organization does not stand the mass upsurge, it creates a lot of problems. [. . .]

You ask what I felt when the Armed Struggle was called off. Well, it was difficult to meet to discuss what to do. What do you call him—B.N. —I don't know him by any other name—used to come to our shelter. The last time he came, Mahendra and he had a discussion. I said it was not good to discuss things so loudly, but for both of them, the heat was too much. I only listened—because I was an ordinary person—they were big leaders. I was a district committee member, they were state committee members. And what was I doing? Generally working and feeding the comrades. Anyway . . . that is there, that recognition will come to you only after you are gone from this world. So long as you are here, there will not be any recognition. Anyway . . . what was I saying. Huh, so they were discussing the Armed Struggle— whether to withdraw or not. B.N. said that the squads were working and that the people supported them and fed them and . . . like that he defended himself. I said, well even a dakoo (dacoit) gets these things. In Madhya Pradesh even a dacoit would get support. People do have sympathy. This is not the criterion. In the earlier period the people participated in the movement—that is how it was, exactly. That is why we used to say it is a people's movement. But in the last phase, because the United Front itself broke up—it was the Nehru military that came. So naturally, Congressmen— we can understand it politically also—naturally Congressmen's sympathy went away. The big landlords went that side and how many remained with you? I just said this. Mahendra of course said, 'You do not know all these details, why do you want to butt in?' I said 'Why not? I would like to voice my opinion whether you like it or not.' He was with us—but you know, a man wants to show—that he is . . . Even now, even now you will find [the same thing]. Where are *we*? Will anyone believe that I would do so much work even though I did not have much strength? I can even do it now. It is there in me. But, [softly] it is the men's world today. [. . .]

When did I stop working actively in politics? After coming out of jail, I had taken up a job. To meet women you have to go in the afternoons only. We decided that those who are able to work, should work, and we would give them our experience and support if necessary. But after coming out from jail the things were not so smooth. I really felt suffocated coming out from jail and taking a job. In 1952 we were released and a case was going on till 1953. Then the case was withdrawn, and we were free. But my political work, social work and educational work slowly . . .

Why did I withdraw, you will ask. Well, sometimes it was the conditions; then there is the question of time also. Sometimes help from your comrades is also important. If somebody could have helped and understood me then I could have done much more work. Did men feel suffocated in the same way as I did? I don't know. Because you asked me the question I told you what I felt. I said the Party was shattered—but not in that sense. The whole Party was in jail. For instance, because of the Armed Struggle nobody—not even I—could get a house. Nobody would give us a house. Some were afraid; some mocked at me. 'Why do you want a house?' they asked, 'Russia will give you money.' We found two rooms here in this locality and later I moved in here. These people also didn't like us in the beginning. But I have been staying here for the last twenty-six years. [. . .]

Why didn't the Party think of any programmes? Did they lose many activists like me? [Pause] Please don't make me answer this question. I can't answer this . . . Maybe the time will come when one can answer this question. This is an organizational question. Time has to answer it. It is better we don't speak about it.

I do trade union work now. There are two unions—one is Royal Laboratories in the small-scale industrial estate. It is a pharmaceutical factory. I am the president of that union. The majority are women. The other factory is Bharat Metal Works. They make small boxes. I have been president of these two unions since 1969. The workers are illiterate. They have very little understanding about unions. We organized their demands and looked into their problems and we started taking up issues: economic demands, working conditions—that type of thing. About my point of view—about educating them also, about raising their understanding of society and of the country— that I haven't succeeded in much— [very emphatic] that needs contact with the locality. That is the main thing. [. . .]

There is an event that might interest you. There was a girl from the forest region—so to say. She was arrested and was put into the same jail as I was. Her name was Mallamma. I was alone on one side of the building. There was a big open space and the criminals were put on the other side. This girl was put along with the criminals. I asked that she should be kept with me. They refused to do so. Later I had to go on hunger strike to get her to stay in my cell. She was the daughter of a wage labourer. She did not even know how to name the days of the week: Sunday, Monday . . . She had never eaten rice either, only drunk ganji water. She came from such a low strata. But what did she learn from the squad? Equality. That I am a communist and you are a communist, so we must have equal rights. Her other education was nil. It was a very unhappy situation. I mean it was a hell of a life. Hell. Both of us were together, but I couldn't sleep. She would always quarrel with the other women and then they would pull each other's hair and tear clothes. Then I had to intervene and say please don't, otherwise they would be punished again. All these things were also there. Political education is also very necessary . . .

I told you in the last phase, how anxious I was when they talked so loudly about the struggle. Other people had also told us that our house was being watched—to be careful. All my shelters had become exposed. I packed everything—guns and cartridges. There were three full bags of cartridges. I was listening carefully all the time. There were vehicles passing, but I didn't suspect anything. Suddenly, at 6 o'clock they knocked at my door. With that knock I understood that the game was over. I opened the door. Policemen. Welcome. For nearly two to three hours they raided the whole locality, not just one house. So there was no chance of escaping. I understood this. All these inspectors knew me. [. . .]

They kept me in the police station for thirty-five days. Policemen would come, peep and see what I was doing. I used to just walk up and down. What could I do? It was terrible. Being in the jail is one thing, but police custody is terrible tension. For me there was no physical torture but mentally what tension! [. . .] It gives you a shock when so many people come in suddenly.

We don't know what they will do. But they only threatened me. I have seen this Adivamma—she was tortured: her feet were broken. They used to put chains on her feet and stand on them, press, dance—so many horrible things they used to do.

Did I take up activities like buying guns for the Party or transporting them, you ask. Transporting, of course. I was the key person here. Buying was difficult. Transporting without a woman was difficult. We used to have closed rickshaws. We used to carry the guns with us in this way. It was not necessary to wear burkahs, but we had a purdah over the rickshaw. Even Hindu women used to have purdahs. These kayasth women, marwadi women and others. I was never afraid.

I used to remember all the heroes of my time and get courage. I was very proud and brave. I will be completing seventy now. My health does not permit me much—I have spondylitis—otherwise I wouldn't keep quiet . . . let this not be the last meeting, come again.

4

~

DEVELOPMENT

Development has occupied a unique place in the history of the women's movement and the inception of women's studies. Till recently most people assumed that the economic significance of women was heralded by the new perspectives of the 1970s and 80s. However, as we saw in the discussion of the report *Women's Role in a Planned Economy* in the history section, already during the 1940s the radical hopes of pre-independence feminists centred on women as the economic citizens of the future nation. That this document finds no subsequent mention in India's history, with rural women instead being addressed through the techniques of 'family management' in the Community Development Programme of the 1950s and 60s, has yet to be adequately explained. A critique of this moment has been definitive for Indian feminism.

With the 1970s and into the next decades, India's development path was targeted from a range of perspectives and locations. While *Towards Equality* used the lens of women's declining economic status to some effect at the national and international levels, others prioritized grassroots organizing, whether in conjunction with left political parties or through forming independent women's associations such as the Self-Employed Women's Association (SEWA, established in 1974), which drew from Gandhianism to work with women vendors and petty producers. Explorations of working women's lives, the relationships between gender and poverty, the 'inner' domain of the household, the problems of public policy, among others, occupied a new generation of scholars and activists, not all of whom were necessarily professional economists. The 'opening up' of the Indian economy to international markets after forty years of state-led development represents only the latest of challenges.

This theme begins with a discussion of efforts to change the Indian Census. Maithreyi Krishnaraj's account of her project on women's work is indicative of the confluence of forces—the building up of women's studies, the politics of making the labour of women visible, the strategy of influencing policy through national statistical data, and the support of UN agencies such as UNIFEM—that has frequently characterized the field of women and development. Above all, her article demonstrates the extraordinary levels of complexity that attend a seemingly simple and objective activity like work, and why issues relating to the range of work that women do can be so critical and yet so difficult to resolve. The next essay by Bina Agarwal—an excerpt from her larger study—makes the proposal that it is women's rights in property rather than in employment that has the greatest potential to transform women's lives. In South Asia this translates for the majority into control over land, and Agarwal defends her thesis in welfare and efficiency terms for the economy as a whole, as well as how land rights for women would empower them in relation to men.

The impact of national and global concern over women's role in the development process in India has been regionally quite diverse. The next two pieces take a critical look at two 'models'—one in the northwestern state of Rajasthan and the other in the southern state of Kerala. In 1984, the Women's Development Programme (WDP) was launched in parts of rural Rajasthan, one of India's so-called 'Bimaru' states—undeveloped, drought-prone and marked by strong upper caste norms of female seclusion. Instead of the usual emphasis on employment generation, this innovative programme focused on awareness raising and communication, through village-level workers or sathins, and made a remarkable impact within a few years. The article 'Development for whom?' was written by women's organizations in the wake of the subsequent backlash by the state of Rajasthan against the very programme it had helped initiate—today the WDP is but a hollow shell of its former self. The concluding section of their essay reproduced here focusses on the contradictions of state-led empowerment and the perils of cooption for the women's movement. In sharp contrast, Kerala has been held up as a 'model' for the rest of modern India, precisely because of the celebrated status of empowered Malayalee women, and in spite of low levels of economic development. A historical critique of gender relations in early twentieth century Kerala was provided in the history section. The article here by K. Saradamoni articulates another perspective on contemporary Kerala, by raising serious doubts about the emancipatory potential of present-day education, work opportunities, the small family norm and women's consciousness itself. Far from embodying the special history or culture of Kerala, she believes that Kerala has internalized others as models. Whether in a 'backward' or an 'advanced' state, therefore, feminists have uncovered fundamental problems in dominant paradigms of 'women and development'.

The next pair of essays concerns globalization, the new paradigm or era of development officially inaugurated in India in 1991. As is well-known by now, the economic policies of globalization and liberalization seek to shift attention from the state's fundamental role in the development process to the hitherto constrained potential of markets for generating growth. Both the women's movement and women's studies took shape at a time when the most critical institution to address was the Indian state. How, then, have feminists responded to the new paradigm and its claims, especially in relation to struggles against poverty? The essay by Mary John discusses the range of reactions and positions that have been adopted, from outright rejection to qualified acceptance. While not enough attention has been paid to the frameworks undergirding such diverse positions, the present moment is throwing up challenges that globalization discourses have not addressed so far. The next essay by Nirmala Banerjee takes on the theme of the feminization of work. Evidence of a worldwide increase in the share of women workers in the economy in recent decades has been one strand in ongoing debates on the relationships between globalization and women. Banerjee's paper works at two levels—firstly it demonstrates some of the problems inherent in the general literature that argues for and against the feminization thesis, and, secondly, it looks more closely at the situation in India. Not only have employment opportunities in manufacturing actually shrunk for women in our context, but increases in sectors such as agriculture have not been accompanied by changes in the sexual division of labour or even in enhanced wages. Her conclusion, however, is not to make universal claims about the impact of globalization, but to emphasize the contradictory potential of work opportunities outside the home, which are doubtless exploitative, but also make new collective experiences possible.

Development is an all-encompassing term, and in our context cannot be separated from questions of the environment. Indeed, a complex politics of naming is involved in movements against dispossession and for sustainable livelihoods, locally and internationally, especially when it comes to arguments about women's special role in these contexts. The final pair of essays investigates the interface of development, nature, and the environment. Kumud Sharma opens up India's early and much celebrated Chipko movement of the 1970s and 80s in the Himalayan foothills to closer scrutiny. What were the decisive moments in this struggle, where women opposed the felling of trees for commercial gain, which cannot be seen only from the angle of gender? Her essay argues that it is in the mechanics of political mobilization and especially in the absence of an institutional link to the local panchayats that the strength and weakness of this movement needs to be understood. In her contribution 'Decolonizing the North' Vandana Shiva seeks to dismantle the latest form of the 'white man's burden', namely, the effective recolonization of the South in the name of protecting the environment. Instead of viewing poverty and overpopulation as the causes of environmental degradation, Shiva argues that the dominant logic must be reversed—it is the North that is most in need of decolonization, from their economic frameworks of unsustainable growth, to the omnipotence of science over all forms of knowledge. The latest struggles over biodiversity and intellectual property rights require new international social conventions that must question the largely shared perception that the white man is a privileged species upon whom the future of the rest of the world's people and the earth itself depends.

From local models of women's empowerment and national statistical systems to the new global order, feminists have changed the ways in which work, economic activity, the role of the state and markets, and the gender relations that undergird all of these, are approached today. Clearly there are differences in the perspectives being advocated here, and it is not obvious that they would diminish in the years to come. Even if consensus is not in sight, and many feel that current global trends are only exacerbating inequalities on a world scale, the force of these essays lies in the many ways in which women have something to say about the hardest questions of development, and are willing to make arguments about issues many believe are beyond question.

∼

WOMEN'S WORK IN INDIAN CENSUS: BEGINNINGS OF CHANGE

Maithreyi Krishnaraj

There has been a growing concern about the inadequacy of our national data systems to capture women's work and the resulting undercounting of it. [. . .]

I

More than in any other area it is in recording women's role in the economy that the most serious distortions take place in India. Problems of unemployment, poverty and destitution are ostensibly the stated concerns of development policy in most third world countries. However, there is as yet not enough recognition that these above problems are also gender-specific. For any serious effort to alleviate these conditions and prevent their further aggravation would require a particular focus on the women of poor households. Micro studies have yielded new insights in this area that bear to be given weight by policy-makers. For the framing of development policies, national level statistics is the principal data input, but this is severely impaired by the undercounting of women, both as workers and as those available for work. This lacuna in the data system cannot but affect the very conceptualization of schemes and programmes instituted to help the poor among the women. For this we need to know (a) what proportion of rural (and urban) women may be counted as workers, (b) what proportion of women not so counted are available for work, (c) for what period are rural women (both those included as workers and not so included) willing to work and available for work. To these basic questions our data systems are unable to give unambiguous and accurate figures.

The first and foremost barrier is the central question of what is work or gainful economic activity, especially when we are dealing with women's work. Despite worldwide debate and discussion we have yet to successfully resolve this problem.

On the one hand, macro data systems are attuned to treating only remunerative aspects of work as 'work', deriving this concept from advanced economics that have wage work as the dominant form. Transposed to insufficiently industrialized, agrarian economies of the third world where subsistence production or production of survival needs by the household are met by own production and hence do not enter the exchange network, this basis of what constitutes economic activity produces serious anomalies. This bypassing of economically relevant activities that are not readily associated with remuneration affects women more seriously because they tend to be more concentrated in this sector. On the other hand, women report themselves as non-workers because they tend to regard what they are engaged in as 'domestic responsibilities' and therefore outside market related or remunerated work. Even activities that yield income may get ignored if women engage in them for short periods of time or intermittently or because these activities are wedged in between other domestic chores. [. . .]

II

Indian women are engaged in two kinds of work: one that produces an income and the other that does not. The former in turn has home-based work and work outside the home. Even within the latter, there are many components that are not 'pure' domestic work like cooking, cleaning, child care but encompass post-harvest processing, livestock maintenance, gathering of fuel, fodder, water and forest produce, unpaid family labour in the family farm or family enterprise and so on.

As the situation of women became a focus of national and international concern and a variety of proposals, programmes and policies were advanced or designed for the benefit of women, the call for reliable statistics on women became more insistent. This appeal is reiterated in three significant documents: The World Plan of Action for the Implementation of the Objectives for the

International Women's Year and in the Programme of Action for the second half of the United Nations Decade for Women. In particular, the Plan of Action adopted in 1975 gives high priority to data collection and analysis on all aspects of the situation of women. In paragraph 170, the plan requests the United Nations to prepare an inventory of the social and economic indicators for the analysis of the status of women. The Programme of Action also recommends that 'All data collecting agencies should give a sex and age breakdown of any information they gather, wherever relevant (and that a) set of statistical indicators should be established by which progress towards equality between the sexes can be monitored.' More recently, the United Nations International Research and Training Institute for the Advancement of Women (INSTRAW) has declared its major objective as that of improving the availability and promoting the use of national and international indicators and the related basic statistics concerning women. [. . .]

III

Women's economic activity in the recent Indian census

The economic questions in the Indian Census adopt definitions of work more suitable to advanced industrial economies where work for wages (i.e. market-oriented work) is typically the norm. As mentioned earlier, this is inappropriate for economies like India and the third world in general where there is large non-monetized, non-market production of a subsistence nature and where women tend to be concentrated in this sector. Even where women are doing work which is market-oriented, the special characteristics of women's work make such work 'invisible', as for example, home-based piece rate workers. The Census concept of 'work' overemphasizes production for exchange and although it does include some non-market production for own consumption such as cultivation where men are also involved, it excludes by a strange logic other types of production for own consumption such as livestock maintenance (done mostly by women) and hence these figures do not correspond with the non-market output in the national accounts. In field studies and in the observed discrepancies between the National Sample Survey (NSS) and the Census, causes of underestimation of women's productive activity have been identified as arising out of ideological and conceptual biases. According to the 1981 Census only a little over 13 per cent women are shown as workers, whereas the Report of the National Commission on Self-employed Women, *Shram Shakti* (1988), states that 89 per cent of women workers are in the 'unorganized sector'. The ideology that all women are primarily 'housewives' and whatever work they do is marginal and secondary to that of men pervades the data system from the formulation of the schedule design to actual data collection and reporting. Conceptually, the multiple roles played by women at different levels of economic life are not perceived because of the definition of work as 'for pay or profit'. There are in fact seven categories of work performed by women in rural and urban India. These are (i) wage and salaried employment, (ii) self-employment outside the household for profit, (iii) self-employment in cultivation or household industry for profit, (iv) self-employment in cultivation for own consumption, (v) other subsistence activities in allied sectors like dairying, other livestock rearing such as poultry, goats, pigs, etc. and fishing, hunting and cultivation of fruit and vegetable gardens, (vi) activities related to domestic work, such as fetching fuel, fodder, water, forest produce, repair of dwellings, making cowdung cakes, food preservation, etc., and (vii) domestic work such as cooking, cleaning, care of the children, the aged and the sick.

The present definition of work as 'for pay or profit' covers only (i) to (iii). Though cultivation of crops for own consumption is included, it excludes pre- and post-harvest operations, which peasant women carry out within the domestic premises, particularly by upper social groups where outdoor work for women runs against social norms. It is also often the case that men may 'supervise' or just own land and be regarded as cultivators while the women who in men's absence or un-involvement actually carry out all the operations may be termed as family helpers. This has consequences for women's status, for the 'cultivator' has more rights than a family helper. It is in a patriarchal society a value loaded term. A major fuzzy area relates to the concept of 'head of household' which is culturally defined and does not reflect the fact that in many cases, it is women who bear the sole or major part of the economic burden of the household. The Census in fact specifically instructs the enumerator to accept whosoever is reported as 'head' by the respondent. Another distortion is in household industry. In many household industries, women are engaged in 'preparatory processes' (e.g. weaving, pottery, tanning). If at all they are included, they appear as secondary or marginal workers. Finally the Census excludes production for consumption items other than particular crops and excludes activities (v) and (vi) in which mostly women are engaged. Among wage workers, home-based piece rate workers are inadequately covered. [. . .]

IV

Improvements introduced in 1991 census

There have been certain improvements over the questionnaires for 1961, 1971 and 1981, namely:

(i) a longer reference period (9–12 months) has been used. This is expected to better capture the subtleties of women's seasonal and intermittent labour-force activity in the agricultural and informal sector;

(ii) 'seeking work' has been changed to 'availability of work';

(iii) in order to reflect the earning capacity of the self-employed, a distinction has been made between recipients of income and unpaid family workers;

(iv) a gender-wise break up of data on heads of households has been included for tabulation;

(v) introduction of the clause 'including unpaid work on farm or family enterprise' has been added in parentheses to the question 'Did you work any time at all last year' in the individual slip that classifies the population into workers and non-workers.

V

The Research Centre for Women's Studies (RCWS) at SNDT Women's University had convened meetings of experts during 1989 which included the representatives from the Regional Directorate of Census Operations, Maharashtra, on changes that could be incorporated in the Census. [. . .] The participants at the preparatory meeting had been asked to come up with specific written suggestions. These were discussed and recommendations made accordingly. [. . .]

VI

The scope of the UNIFEM project was as follows:

(i) to improve the data on women's economic activity within the parameters already set for the 1991 Census by the Registrar General's office on Census operations. This would be done by adding such explanations and probing questions to the set of economic questions in the instruction manual to enumerators so that enumerators become aware of the gender bias operating in society in perceiving women's work which is heavily conditioned by cultural values;

(ii) to launch a campaign of public awareness with respect to women's work by highlighting their invisible work.

As regards the modification of the instruction manual, this was with reference to the Second Pre-test Manual for 1991 Census and focused on the individual slip.

Comments by the participants

The Census data was extremely unreliable on work participation of women. The all-India figure of a little over 13 per cent work participation for women and of 2.3 per cent for the women of Punjab were such gross underestimates and out of alignment with reality, proving that the problem was not one of statistics but one of perception. The quality of the Census data hinged on how enumerators handled the questions and how respondents interpreted them. Hence, it is of utmost importance that the concepts behind the questions be clarified. Concepts such as work, household work, female heads of households, piece rate work, wage work, self-employment, seasonal work, part-time work, marginal work, etc. The Census question 'Did you work anytime at all during the last one year?' needs to be clarified for the enumerator that the respondent should understand the question to mean not only earning money but also contributing labour to family farm or business. This has been included in parentheses but should carry an adequate explanation in the manual. Secondly, the category 'housework' being ambiguous, care should be taken that piece rate work or activities allied to agriculture done within the household premises do not get categorized as 'housework'. If, as suggested by the draft recommendations, the response to the question 'Did you work at all anytime during the last year?' should be entered only after fully eliciting answers to subsequent questions, would it not be advisable to place it at the end? The participants felt that even though the Census question included anyone who worked even for a day as 'worker', there was no provision in the Census to net the multiplicity of activities that women do, which cannot be nearly captured by the terms 'main activity' and 'marginal activity'. In any case, separate tabulation of marginal workers giving not only sex-wise but activity-wise divisions would be useful.

Home-based piece rate workers are not covered separately in the present Census. Women are represented in large numbers in this category and are severely exploited because of lack of protective measures under existing legislation, which cover only categories of workers clearly identifiable as working for a particular employer. Piece rate workers who are home-based often work for chains of sub-contractors who are not technically 'employers'. We need reliable data on this category of workers for instituting proper policy measures. One way in which home-based piece rate workers could be covered was by introducing a fifth code under household industry under the present four-fold class of workers—employer, employee, single worker and family worker. Informal sector work such as piece rate work occurs in rural and urban areas, and falls into three categories—own account work, self-employment, piece rate work on sub-contracting basis and wage or time rate.

Piece rate work carried out at home does not include things like beauticians' work, secretarial assistance in family enterprises, etc. Doubts were raised by some participants on the feasibility of introducing a new code 'piece rate home-based workers' under household industry within the existing questionnaire. Generally, no enumerator asks this question to informants but determines the status of a worker from the answers to previous questions. It might help if the enumerator is persuaded through special instructions to identify the status of a worker through probing questions.

Some discussion took place on the concept of the head of household. We have to be clear on whether we are talking of female supported or female headed households. Female supported can be considered to imply that women are chief economic providers. The enumerator should in dealing with economic questions be sensitive to women who are de facto economic providers and that there are cultural connotations of leadership as wielding authority that lead to men being labelled as heads. In our society even if a woman bears the major economic responsibility she does not necessarily enjoy the authority to make decisions for the household. In countries like Canada, the term has been dropped. A via media solution could be to tabulate female heads of households separately and include adult male absent households. This of course presents a difficulty, for female economic responsibility can coexist with the presence of husbands or other adult males who may not be earning for whatever reason.

There was general agreement among the participants that the phrasing of explanations in the pre-test manual tends to overemphasize women's household work. In several places, it is stated, 'women reinforce the cultural perception of women as doing only household work which again is seen as not work'. The Census collects a lot of data on households but does not tabulate data by household as a unit. Such a tabulation is necessary.

Training for Census enumeration was expected to begin in June 1990 and end in September 1990. These training programmes would be organized in development blocks and tehsils. District census officers would train lower level officials who in turn would train the actual enumerators. Participants recommended that women's studies centres and women's groups in different universities could play a useful role in these training programmes. Women's organizations could also be involved. UNIFEM, in addition to a poster, could produce a film and give it wide publicity. The proposed poster, it was suggested, should be designed by an agency sensitive to women's issues in addition to professional competence in designing as such. The training programmes for enumerators should be supplemented by suitable addition to household duties . . .' Household work can be done by men also. Secondly, whenever a woman is a worker, she is always doing it in addition to household duties, and this does not need a specific mention. This orientation programme was for tabulators, editors and coders. One participant felt that the training of enumerators or an improved manual alone was not enough because the census enumerators in rural areas, being local school teachers, have preconceived ideas and their previous knowledge and information about individuals and households act as a deterrent in obtaining actual and unbiased data. It is important, therefore, that the supervisors be more careful, observant and vigilant. Pilot studies to test new methods were advocated by all.

Based upon the detailed suggestions put forward, the modifications were adopted and the final recommendations were sent to the Registrar General of the Census in the first week of February, 1990. The instruction manual for the 1991 Census brought out for enumerators for filling up the household schedule and individual slip has incorporated only some of the recommendations.

VI

UNIFEM has prepared a poster depicting the range of women's work and this would be reached to every enumeration block. Spots on Doordarshan have been prepared to highlight women's work. The Research Centre for Women's Studies (SNDT) has placed articles in popular journals and regional language papers. More than thirty women's organizations have been contacted in Maharashtra requesting their help in the training of enumerators. It is to be seen whether all these efforts result in better results in the 1991 Census. [. . .]

∽

WHY DO WOMEN NEED INDEPENDENT RIGHTS IN LAND?

Bina Agarwal

Economic analysis and policies concerning women have long been preoccupied with employment, to the neglect of a crucial determinant of women's situation, namely, the gender gap in command over property. This is especially (but not only) true in analysis relating to South Asia.

It is argued here that the gender gap in the ownership and control of property is the single most critical contributor to the gender gap in economic well-being, social status and empowerment. In primarily rural economies such as those of South Asia the most important property in question is arable land. [. . .]

The importance of South Asian women having independent rights in arable land rests on several interconnected arguments which can be grouped into four broad categories: welfare, efficiency, equality and empowerment.

(a) The welfare argument

To begin with, especially among poor households, rights in land could reduce women's own and, more generally, the household's risk of poverty and destitution. The reasons for this stem partly from the general positive effect of giving women access to economic resources independently of men; and partly from the specific advantages associated with rights in *land* resources.

Consider first the general case. There is considerable evidence of intra-household gender inequalities in the sharing of benefits from household resources. For instance, in large parts of South Asia a systematic bias is noted against women and female children in intra-household access to resources for basic necessities such as health care, and, in some degree, food. This is revealed in gender differences in one or more of the following indicators: malnourishment, morbidity, mortality, hospital admissions, health expenditures and female-adverse sex ratios (females per 100 males), although the evidence on food allocation *per se* is less conclusive. The extent of this anti-female bias varies regionally, but it exists in some degree almost everywhere, particularly as revealed by the sex ratios which are female-adverse across all of South Asia, except Kerala in southwest India. The bias is strongest in northwest India, Pakistan and Bangladesh, and much less stark in south India and Sri Lanka where the sex ratios, although still female-adverse, are closer to parity.

Further, notable differences have been found in how men and women of poor rural households spend the income under their control: women typically spend almost all their incomes on the family's basic needs; men usually spend a significant part on their personal needs (tobacco, liquor, etc.). [. . .] A corollary to these gender differentials in spending patterns are research findings which suggest that children's nutritional status tends to be much more positively linked to the mother's earnings than the father's (Kumar 1978).

In other words, the risk of poverty and the physical well-being of a woman and her children could depend significantly on whether or not she has *direct* access to income and productive assets such as land, and not just access *mediated* through her husband or other male family members. For female-headed households with no adult male support, the link between direct access to economic resources and physical well-being needs no emphasis. Such households constitute an estimated (and by no means negligible) 19–20 per cent of all households in India and Bangladesh.

Moreover, a woman's economic status cannot be judged adequately by the economic status of her family. Even women from rich parental or marital homes can be economically vulnerable without independent resources in case of marital breakdown or widowhood. In parts of western and northwestern India, not uncommonly, women—divorced, deserted or widowed—can be found working as agricultural labourers on the farms of their well-off brothers or brothers-in-law. Elsewhere, in east India and Bangladesh, there are many cases of women, married into prosperous households, being left destitute and forced to seek wage work or even to beg after widowhood. 'This fact,' as Omvedt (1981, 21) observes, 'perhaps . . . more than any other, shows the essential propertylessness of women *as women.*'

Within this general argument for women's independent access to economic resources, the case for their having effective rights in *land* is especially strong. Consider, for a start, the relationship between a household's access to land and poverty. In India, in 1982, an estimated 89 per cent of rural households owned some land, and an estimated 74 per cent operated some. In Bangladesh, in 1978, the percentage of rural households owning some land (arable or homestead) was 89, and those owning arable land was 67.

In Sri Lanka, in 1982, 89 per cent of agricultural operators owned some land, including home gardens. Although, given high land concentration, the majority of these households across South Asia only have marginal plots, they face a significantly lower risk of absolute poverty than landless households: a negative relationship between the incidence of absolute poverty and land access helps in both direct and indirect ways. The direct advantages stem from production possibilities, such as growing crops, fodder, trees or a vegetable garden (unless of course the land is of very poor quality), or keeping livestock, practising sericulture, and so on. In addition, land provides indirect benefits, such as increasing access to credit, helping agricultural labour maintain its reserve price and even push up the aggregate real wage rate, and, where the land is owned, serving as a mortgageable or saleable asset during a crisis. Moreover, for widows and the elderly, ownership of land and other wealth strengthens the support they receive from relatives by increasing their bargaining power within the household . As an old man put it: 'Without property, children do not look after their parents well' (Caldwell et al 1988, 191).

However, given the noted biases in the intra-family distribution of benefits from household resources, exclusively *male* rights in land, which would render the *household* less susceptible to poverty by some average measure, will not automatically benefit all its members. And on grounds of both women's and children's welfare, there is a strong case for supporting women's effective rights in private or public land, independently of men. Although such rights are especially important as a poverty-alleviation measure for women in poor rural households, they are also relevant for those of better-off households, given the risk of poverty following marital breakdown faced by all rural women.

It needs emphasis here that the welfare case for women's land rights stands even if the plot is too small to be economically viable on its own. Indeed, those opposing female inheritance in land often emphasize that women might end up inheriting economically nonviable holdings. In my view, this could be a problem where cultivation is seen as the *sole* basis of subsistence, but not where land-based production is one element (although a critical one) in a *diversified livelihood system*. For instance, a plot of land which does not produce enough grain to economically sustain a person or family could still support trees or provide grass for cattle. Moreover, although forced collective farming is likely to be inefficient, cases of people voluntarily cooperating to undertake land-based joint productive activities also exist.

Of course, as the countries of South Asia develop and the industrial and service sectors expand, arable land would become less significant as a source of livelihood and a form of property. But today, the majority of South Asia's population still depends on agriculture as a primary or an important supplementary source of sustenance. To this may be added the dependence on village common land and forests for fuel and other basic necessities, even among villagers whose income derives mainly from the non-farm sector. In none of the South Asian countries do projections predict a rapid absorption of labour (especially female labour) into urban industry in the foreseeable future. Furthermore, since it is predominantly male workers who migrate from rural to urban areas, women's dependence on the rural/agricultural sector remains greater than men's. Although the rural non-farm sector holds potential, its record in providing viable livelihoods has been mixed: there are some regions and segments of high returns/high wages (such as the Indian Punjab), but many others that are characterized by low returns and low wages. In particular, women's non-farm earnings (to the limited extent this has been studied) appear characteristically low and uncertain. Hence, although there is clearly a need to strengthen women's earning opportunities in the non-farm sector, especially by ensuring their entry into its more productive segments, for most women non-farm livelihoods cannot substitute for land-based livelihoods, although they could supplement them. It is also noteworthy that those who do well in the rural non-farm sector through self-employment are usually those who have land as an asset base. Effectively, therefore, land will continue to occupy a place of primacy in South Asian livelihoods in general, and female livelihood systems in particular, for quite some time. [. . .]

(b) The efficiency argument

Tracing the likely efficiency effects of women having land rights is much more difficult than tracing the potential welfare effects. Consider the issue situationally.

In several contexts, women are operating as household heads with the primary and sometimes sole responsibility for organizing cultivation and ensuring family subsistence, but without titles to the land they are cultivating. For instance, due to long-term male out-migration many women are serving as *de facto* household heads, especially but not only in the hill regions of the subcontinent. Or widows are cultivating plots given to them from joint family estates (as part of their inheritance claims to their deceased husbands' lands), but the plots are still in their in-laws' names. Again, tribal women cultivating communal land rarely hold titles to their fields, which are typically given out by the state only to male farmers. Titling women in these circumstances and providing them infrastructural support could increase output by increasing their access to credit, and to technology and information on productivity-increasing agricultural practices and inputs (in the dissemination of which both a class and a gender bias prevail). Land titles could both motivate and enable women to adopt improved agricultural technology and practices and hence increase overall production. This is not dissimilar to the argument made in land reform discourse favouring security of tenure for tenants to encourage technical investments in land by increasing the tenants' incentive and capacity to invest.

A more general issue, however, is the likely efficiency effect of women inheriting land. Female inheritance is often opposed in South Asia on the grounds that it will further reduce farm size, increase land fragmentation, and thus reduce output. Is this fear valid? The efficiency implications of female inheritance can be separated analytically into three: a farm-size effect—the average size of ownership holdings will be lower than if only men inherit; a land-fragmentation effect—fragmentation could increase insofar as the land is parcelled out to heirs, say, according to land quality; and a gender transfer effect—some of the land which would have gone only to men would now go to women.

The concerns surrounding the farm-size effect are similar to those arising from redistributing land from big to small farmers on farm output, on the adoption of new technology and on marketed surplus. Those opposing redistribution argue that the impact would be negative on all three counts. However, existing evidence from South Asia indicates otherwise. For instance, small-sized farms typically have a higher value of annual output per unit cultivated area than large-sized ones: this inverse size-productivity relationship which was strong in the 1950s and 1960s (the pre-green revolution period) has sustained in the post-green revolution period, even if somewhat weakened, as studies for India, Bangladesh and Pakistan bear out. Small farmers have adopted the new technology in most areas where large farmers have done so, although after a time lag; and the evidence on marketed surplus does not bear up to the sceptics' claim that this will decline because small farmers will tend to retain a larger percentage for self-consumption. In any case, an improvement in the consumption of the poor in the farm sector cannot, in itself, be seen as an inefficient outcome. Indeed, a dietary improvement among the very poor may add to labour productivity.

The existing evidence thus gives no reason to expect that land distribution in favour of women would reduce output on account of the size effect. And the problem of land fragmentation again is not unique to female ownership, but can arise equally with male inheritance: in both cases it calls for land consolidation. There could of course be a negative output effect, insofar as women usually face the earlier noted gender-specific disadvantages as managers of farms, when operating in factor and product markets. But again the answer lies in easing these constraints by institutional support to women farmers, rather than in disinheriting them.

Indeed the experience of non-governmental credit institutions such as the Grameen Bank in Bangladesh suggests that women are often better credit risks than men. Also, supporting women as farm managers would enlarge the talent and information pool; and in very poor households allocating resources to women could increase their productivity by improving their nutrition.

The provision of land to women could have other indirect benefits as well, such as reducing migration to cities, both by women themselves and by family members dependent on them; and increasing farm incomes in women's hands, which in turn could generate a higher demand for non-farm goods that are produced locally and labour intensively, thus creating more rural jobs.

(c) The equality and empowerment arguments

Equality and empowerment concerns, unlike welfare and efficiency considerations, stem less from the implications of land access or deprivation in absolute terms, and more from the implications of men's and women's *relative* access to land, and they affect particularly women's ability to challenge male dominance within the home and in society.

The equality argument for land rights can be approached in several different ways, but two aspects are especially important here. One is the larger issue of gender equality as a measure of a just society, in which equality of rights over productive resources would be an important part. Two, there is the specific aspect of equality in land rights as an indicator of women's economic empowerment and as a facilitator in challenging gender inequities in other (e.g. social and political) spheres. In the present discussion, the links between gender equality in land rights and women's empowerment are specially important. But first, what is meant by empowerment? The term has been used variously (and often loosely) in academic writing and by social action groups across the world, including South Asia. In the present context, it could be defined as *a process that enhances the ability of disadvantaged ('powerless') individuals or groups to challenge and change (in their favour) existing power relationships that place them in subordinate economic, social and political positions.* Empowerment can manifest itself in acts of individual resistance as well as in group mobilization. Entitling women with land could empower them economically, as well as strengthen their ability to challenge social and political gender inequities.

A telling illustration is provided by the Bodhgaya movement in Bihar in the late 1970s, in which women and men of landless households jointly participated in an extended struggle for ownership rights in the land they cultivated, which was under the illegal possession of a local *math* (a temple-monastery complex). During the struggle, women raised a demand for independent land rights, not only for reasons of economic security but also because this impinged on marital relations. They feared that if land titles went only to husbands, wives would be rendered relatively even more powerless, and vulnerable to domestic violence. Their fears proved correct. Where only men got titles there was an increase in drunkenness, wife-beating and threats: 'Get out of the house, the land is mine now' (Manimala 1983; excerpted in the section 'New Beginnings' in this volume). Where women received titles they could now assert: 'We had tongues but could not speak, we had feet but could not walk. Now that we have the land, we have the strength to speak and walk.' Similar responses were noted in China, when the Chinese Communist party promulgated the Agrarian Reform law in 1947, which entitled women to hold separate land deeds for the first time.

Land rights can also improve the treatment a woman receives from other family members by strengthening her bargaining power. Although employment and other means of earning could help in similar ways, in the rural context land usually offers greater security than other income sources—at the very least, a space of one's own. In the Bodhgaya case, for instance, the women were already wage labourers and were therefore not economically dependent; but their husbands were still able to threaten them with eviction. It is notable too that the Bodhgaya women saw intra-household gender relations being affected not just by their own propertyless state, but by their remaining propertyless while their husbands became propertied. In other words, land titles were important to women not only for improving their economic well-being in absolute terms (the welfare argument), but also for improving their *relative* bargaining position vis-à-vis their husbands: their sense of empowerment within the home was linked to economic *equality*.

Outside the household as well, land ownership can empower women by improving the social treatment they receive from other villagers, and by enabling them to bargain with employers from a stronger fall-back position. Land ownership is also widely linked to rural political power. Of course there can still be social barriers to individual women's participation in public decision-making bodies, even for women endowed with land, but land rights could facilitate such participation. Group solidarity among women would also help. For instance, an individual woman with landed property may find it difficult to assert herself politically or socially in the village, especially where social norms dictate seclusion, but a group of women acting in unity could do so. (Here there could be some congruence of interests even between women of diverse class and caste backgrounds.)

Indeed, in a limited sense, collective action may itself empower women by enhancing their self-confidence and their ability to challenge oppression, although in a larger sense it is a *means* to empowerment, wherein empowerment lies not only in the process of challenging gender inequity but in eliminating it. And collective action is likely to prove a critical means for effecting change towards greater gender equality in land rights.

(d) Practical versus strategic gender needs

While each of the above arguments for women's independent rights in land is important, are they of comparable weight? Or do some merely serve to further what have been described as 'practical' gender needs, while others serve 'strategic' gender needs? This distinction between practical and strategic needs, first made by Molyneux (1985) and elaborated by Moser (1989), is worth exploring since it also appears to define where, in public policy itself, a line is drawn on questions of gender. Practical gender needs, as defined by these two scholars, are the needs of basic subsistence (such as food, health care, water supply, etc): to satisfy them does not challenge women's position within the gender division of labour; strategic gender needs, they argue, are those that would help overcome women's subordination, including transforming the gender division of labour, removing institutionalized forms of discrimination, such as in rights to own and control property, and in establishing political equality. In these terms, land rights would fall under strategic gender needs.

However, the apparent analytical neatness of this distinction is confounded when examined from the perspective of *practice,* on several counts. First, certain strategic gender needs, such as for land rights, are also, in specific contexts, necessary for fulfilling practical gender needs, as evidenced from the welfare and efficiency arguments spelt out earlier: for instance, land titles for poor rural women may be a necessary component for improving female nutrition and health. At the same time, we also noted the significance of land in 'empowering' women to challenge unequal gender relations within and outside the home. In other words, the case for women's land rights has both a welfare-efficiency ('practical') component and an empowerment ('strategic') component.

Second, even meeting subsistence needs often requires challenging existing political-economic structures. For instance, a demand for wage increases by poor women workers is a practical need in that it would improve their living standards, but it is strategic in that it challenges existing production relations and requires confronting the opposition of employers. Third, and relatedly, the same process, viz. group organization, is often necessary for fulfilling both practical gender needs (such as increasing women's wages), and strategic gender needs (such as struggling for land rights). Fourth, action in pursuit of 'practical' needs may easily turn into action to meet 'strategic' needs. Group organization around economic issues often opens the door for women to question other aspects of their lives. For instance, poor women organized into groups for the better delivery of credit or other economic programmes by the Grameen Bank in Bangladesh, or the Bangladesh Rural Advancement Committee (BRAC), or the Self-Employed Women's Association in north India, have in many cases also been able to challenge gender violence or restrictive social practices such as female seclusion. Indeed, even to participate in group meetings often requires women to overcome social constraints, or to negotiate childcare responsibilities with husbands and other family members.

In other words, the *process* of fulfilling 'practical' gender needs cannot always be delinked from that of fulfilling 'strategic' gender needs. That it is often more 'politic' to couch gender concerns in terms of practical rather than strategic needs, because welfare and efficiency arguments resonate more with state planners, should not detract from this linkage.

We might of course ask why welfare and efficiency arguments resonate more with state planners. Part of the answer certainly lies in the fact that these arguments (especially those concerning welfare) focus especially on poor women and can be subsumed within the poverty-alleviation component of planning, with special targeting towards 'the most vulnerable' groups, identified as women and female children. But part of the answer must also lie in deep-rooted notions of appropriate gender relations shared by many men who make and implement policy, for whom empowering women to transform those relations into more equal ones would appear inappropriate and even threatening to existing family and kinship structures. Hence, it is easier to push for changes where the goal appears to be to give poor women a slightly better deal, than where the goal is to challenge basic inequities in gender relations across classes. It is also the case that programmes for health and nutrition are more readily perceived in welfare terms than programmes which call for gender-redistributive land reform. It is not a coincidence that *land rights* have yet to become a necessary component even of women directed poverty-alleviation programmes.

References

Caldwell, J. C. et al. 1988. *The causes of demographic change: Experimental research in South India*. Wisconsin: University of Wisconsin Press.

Kumar, S.K. 1978. Role of the household economy in child nutrition at low incomes. Occasional paper no.95, Department of Agricultural Economics, Cornell University.

Omvedt, Gail. 1981. Effects of agricultural development on the status of women. Paper prepared for the International Labour Office Tripartite Asian Regional Seminar on Rural Development and Women, Mahabaleshwar, India, April 6–11.

Manimala. 1983. Zameen Kenkar? Jote Onkar! Women's Participation in the Bodhgaya Land Struggle. *Manushi* 14.

Molyneux, M. 1985. Mobilization without emancipation? Women's interests, the state, and revolution in Nicaragua. *Feminist Studies* 11, no. 2, Summer.

Moser, C.O.N 1989. Gender planning in the third world: Meeting practical and strategic gender needs. *World Development* 17, no. 11.

~

BROADER ISSUES FOR DISCUSSION: WOMEN'S DEVELOPMENT PROGRAMME, RAJASTHAN

Saheli, Sabala Sangh, Action India, Disha, Women's Centre, FAOW, Awaz-e-Niswan

A. The nature of the state and its role in women's development

As a welfare state, the government has the responsibility of ensuring the resources required for the development of the entire population, including women. Yet, in contrast to development plans for other sections of the population, government emphasis with respect to women is not on policy measures, resource allocation or redefining development but on awareness raising, organization and mobilization—or, in other words, on struggle as opposed to development. With such a definition of development a bizarre situation has been created where the struggle is no more against the establishment but is militating with state support—what is the new target?

1. Why is the government viewing women's development in terms of developing consciousness and organization? Why do its programmes with respect to their oppressed sections lack such an orientation even today?
2. Why are these efforts on the part of the government occurring simultaneously with active efforts on the part of political parties of all shades to woo women as a constituency?
3. Is it not important to critically put into context the role of the government vis-à-vis women? Do we not consider the present status of women to be an outcome of the broad policies of the government followed since independence? Are the WDPs, Mahila Samakhyas, etc., really the corrective steps which go beyond raising the propaganda value for the government?
4. Does the government have a role to play at all in the 'struggle' considering that women's problems are not limited to the family but arise as much out of the larger society and maldevelopment therein?

5. When the organization for struggle is local and fragmented, is it not going to always get subverted by the broader policies of the government? That is, in the case of vertical programmes, such as the family planning programme, will they not take precedence over the aspirations of the people?

6. Will a government takeover of women's organizing potential not subvert any future attempts at organizing women? Will the government not act as a depoliticizing force, considering that politicization of women will cause a lot more questions to be asked which the government is in no position to answer?

7. In a nutshell, are these programmes not akin to being a management/owner sponsored trade union of workers?

8. Are there certain areas of development which concern women and where the government can be a facilitator without being an organizer, i.e. provision of support services, legal aid, etc.?

B. Women's movement and the government-sponsored women's development

While there is a relatively long history of non-government organizations (NGOs) undertaking the implementation of government-sponsored programmes, the entry of women activists in direct government programmes is a more recent phenomenon. While the possibility of reaching out to large numbers of women has attracted many an activist, the entry of activists has also provided such programmes with much needed legitimacy. The implications of this direct alliance have far-reaching consequences.

1. Has the state consciously chosen to use progressive symbols and jargon to blur the contradictions between its own interests and those of the people?

2. Do the concerned activists feel that they can influence such programmes to their own ends even while providing immediate legitimacy to the government?

3. Will the influence not work both ways? How are the stands of the activists likely to be diluted in the interest of the 'programmes'? For example, the question of forced separation of sexuality from fertility in the health project of WDP, and readiness to deal with fertility alone, in direct contrast to constant feminist attempts at linking the two.

4. Is it not in the interest of the ruling classes to subsume the class question under gender concerns and to direct energies away from major structural contradictions in society? Are the activists in government programmes not unwittingly abetting such a process?

C. Multinational sponsorship of women's development

Since the women's decade, funds for women's development have increasingly poured in from the very sources whose character is not necessarily pro-people or pro-women. Increasingly, these funds have also been used to support activists, voluntary agencies and governmental programmes. The most convenient explanation has been that this support is being made available because of the growth in the women's movement in the west. While somewhat true a decade ago, this does not explain continuing flow of funds at present.

Within the movement, this question has been debated back and forth in extremely heated exchanges between those who accept funds and those who do not. All the same there is a great need to understand some issues.

1. Why are funding agencies endlessly supporting women's programmes?
2. Why is it that with respect to women the stress has been on conscientization, mobilization, etc., as opposed to tangible development?
3. What is the relationship of first world and third world feminists? Is there any attempt at influencing the issues and the priorities?
4. In the aid agencies, how is women in development related to population control- theoretically and programmatically?

D. Implications of NGO structure and functioning

Not only in terms of issues has the government adopted the jargon of the women's movement, it has also adopted an organizational form where the strength of the bureaucracy has been replaced by the weakness of NGO structures. The lack of distinction between employer and employee has not meant increased democracy but has given all powers to the top functionaries to act in completely arbitrary and unjust ways. The pay structure is exploitative just as in many NGOs existing on government or funding-agency grants. The right to unionize is non-existent because the workers are deemed to be 'volunteers'.

As such, associating with such programmes has also meant supporting unfair labour practice with justification on grounds of at least ameliorating abject poverty. How far is such a position tenable?

E. Questions before the women's movement

Collaborating with the government to advance the movement has been one clear option for some organizations and activists. While no movement can flourish in isolation, no movement is likely to flourish without an ideology clearly spelt out. At present, the movement is in its nascent stage and has to contend with a very sophisticated opposition. Clearly, we do not face suppression—we face co-option. We also have a movement which is extremely amorphous and has obfuscated certain differences among women in the name of universal sisterhood. We are continuing to form alliances within the movement with individuals and organizations of all sorts 'aurat honey ke natey' (on grounds of their simply 'being women'). This may have been the only way out in the beginning—but now we have acquired an image larger than life and a legitimacy which has spurred even the most reactionary elements, such as the BJP, into action.

1. Is this not the time to take stock and develop a clear strategy?
2. Why should the movement feel responsible to reach the largest number of women in the shortest time? Is it not at the same time equally vital to be choosy about collaborations as well as programmes?
3. Why has the movement not systematically questioned the government and its intentions vis-a-vis women? This needs to be analyzed in the context of the women's movement's visible critiques and suspicion of the established left.

The questions raised in this report are of relevance to all people working in autonomous groups, mass organizations and NGOs, whether collaborating with the government or not. This is in context where the government is offering the enticement of stability and outreach to all of us through all kinds of programmes due to its awareness of loss of its own credibility among people. As individuals and organizations concerned with the have-nots, it is our responsibility to debate these questions before entering into/continuing our collaboration with the government.

It is equally vital that we raise wider debates to support/oppose specific programmes of the government. We feel that debating these questions in the context of this report will be the beginning.

∾

WOMAN, KERALA AND SOME DEVELOPMENT ISSUES
K. Saradamoni

Kerala, with her enchanting stretch of backwaters, and the soothing greenery which becomes marked as soon as one enters the state, together with a literate, educated and politically alert population, offers some features distinct from other states. But of late the state has acquired the status of a special case or model which has succeeded in raising the physical quality of life of the people even with a relatively low per capita income. This attracts a large number of researchers, media persons and others, particularly from the developed countries to see, study, photograph or video the place and people. This idea has entered the thinking of at least a section of the educated Keralites. As a result it is not uncommon to see reference to the 'paradox' or 'dilemma' of our development in their writings and speeches. [. . .]

Sex ratio

One of the most widely publicized indicators about Kerala women's status is the sex ratio which was 1032 and 1040 according to the census of 1981 and 1991, respectively. Moreover, Kerala was the only state in India where women had a favourable sex ratio not only in these two censuses, but in every census since 1901. [. . .]

Family planning, literacy and falling infant mortality

A few decades back it was not unusual for a Kerala woman to give birth to four, five or even more children. But in recent decades this has fallen to two. There are couples who are content to have one child and some who opt to have none. We come across such a phenomenon among the educated middle class in big cities and metropolitan areas. In Kerala, the acceptance of small family norm is practically by all, irrespective of rural–urban, rich–poor, or literate–illiterate differences. The female literacy rate is often projected as the single important cause for this success in Kerala. However, we have to recognize that other states in the country too have relatively high literacy rates. Even in 1981 Goa, Mizoram, Andaman–Nicobar Islands, Chandigarh, Daman–Diu, Delhi, Lakshadweep, Pondicherry, etc. had more than 50 per cent female literacy. By 1991, Himachal Pradesh, Maharashtra, Nagaland, Tamil Nadu and Tripura too reached that level. The achievements of Gujarat (48.50), Manipur (48.64) and Punjab (49.72) too are not insignificant. This relatively high rate of female literacy is not reflected in the manner in which infant mortality is falling or the small family norm is accepted in these states.

To understand the Kerala phenomenon, it would be worthwhile to examine some of the changes the state witnessed during the decades prior to independence. At that time the present state of Kerala comprised the princely states of Cochin and Travancore, and the Malabar province of the Madras presidency. In sequence or intensity, there were differences between the three areas in the manner in which these changes took place. But in all the three areas they covered changes in land relations, family and kinship, and rules binding them and, above all, in the social and economic distances and rigidities which the caste system imposed. The social and political movements of the period not only accelerated changes, but instilled in the average Kerala person a new sense of individual freedom and dignity. Though the slogans of freedom and equality are not yet fully realized, the sense of pride which the ordinary Keralites imbibed has given them ideas of a 'better life'. To understand the present-day Keralite it would be useful to have a glimpse of the denials which were the lot of the low castes. Caste and customary practices had rigid prescriptions regarding dress, food, style and size of house, personal names, etc. For example, names like Sridevi, Padmanabhan, Narayan were Chirutha, Pappu or Nanoo for the low castes, which sometimes included the Nayars, too. Today nobody can deny anyone the right to wear any kind of dress or own any type of house provided she or he has money. If the 'poor' or 'low caste' wears synthetic fabrics or indulges in wasteful expenditure in the name of house construction or marriages, it is in a sense a protest against the earlier denials and also their ability to imitate the rich and the upper castes. As a result, the exploited and the oppressed, particularly the women among them, are keen that their children should not experience a life of humiliation, want and uncertainty which used to be their lot. They look towards education as a helping hand.

There is an economic reason too behind this, which is not recognized. It would be wrong to think that India's rural poor have no dreams and desires about their children. The endless struggles to meet their day-to-day needs and the oppressions they face do not leave them time or confidence to think of them or to express their hopes. At their subhuman level of existence they do not incur much additional expense when a new child is born. On the other hand, that child too can contribute towards family sustenance. At a very tender age the elder child starts taking care of the younger ones. Cutting grass, fetching fuel wood and making cow-dung cakes for domestic consumption as well as for sale to purchase daily needs are work women all over rural India are engaged in, whether they have other income-earning work or not. In these tasks the children, particularly girls, join their mothers. In addition to these, we can find region-specific tasks in which also women and girls are engaged. In West Bengal, I have come across women catching small quantities of fish from the running water around paddy fields using fishing rods. Women in some areas collect edible leaves and flowers. Girl children in addition to learning these from their mothers are invariably found gleaning for grain in harvested fields. Rural Kerala has lost all these tasks. A poor child in Kerala has the option to be a domestic help in a well-to-do house, remain idle or run away from home. It is a combination of all these factors that makes the Kerala women accept the small family. Not many from among the poor have succeeded in seeing their children realize their hopes. Yet they believe that a few years of schooling would be helpful in the long run. This is one reason why many mothers do not resent it when their daughters do not learn any of the traditional skills. In Kerala a 'secure' job is equated to an 'office' job because people realize that such jobs alone can free them from worklessness and insecurity.

Small families are not a heaven, and Kerala has started experiencing this. We shall touch upon that later.

Kerala women have undoubtedly contributed to the 'success' of the government's population policy, though they may not be aware of that. It is also true that they are unaware of the possible ill-effects of the various contraceptive methods they use to prevent pregnancy. We have not come across any individual woman or women's group demanding details about the different contraceptives, where they were developed, on whom they were tested and results of monitoring, if any, and asking that monitoring should begin if it has not so far been done. Even doctors admit that oral contraceptives in the long run can lead to serious problems, including heart ailments. But the media, including Doordarshan, give wide publicity to the pills. Big hoardings inform people that anti-pregnancy pills are freely distributed in the government hospitals. While we were talking about this, a young college-going daughter of doctor parents said that doctors are aware of the possible dangers of the various contraceptives. But the number that would be adversely affected will not be big when our population is taken into account. She might have heard this at home or among the doctor friends of the family. However, most women are not aware of this and are by and large made to believe that all contraceptives are totally safe. [...]

Education

Kerala occupies, as we have seen, pride of place in the literacy map of the country. The literates include women and scheduled castes and scheduled tribes who are found to lag behind in most parts of the country. Achievements of Kerala women in the higher levels of education are also 'impressive'.

It cannot be said that women are kept out of the education system simply because they are women. In fact, an average Kerala girl today may be spending more time in the name of education than her mother would have and most other girls elsewhere in India. Education in Kerala today is regular studies in school/college plus private tuition in a teacher's home, which has come to be believed as inevitable. 'Tutorial' or coaching institutions do thriving business and attract large numbers of students, both girls and boys, particularly those who fail. The number of girls who try to acquire some kind of skill by joining ITIs and institutions where typewriting, short hand, etc, are taught is not small. Currently, the trend is to join 'computer courses'. What do all these put together equip the girl for? It shows that the number of girls who are in need of work and income is large. At the same time it cannot be said that the woman is made more independent, self-confident with ideas about her place, role or responsibility in life or in the world at large. It may not be off the mark to say that the education system has a major role in making her conform to accepted societal norms and definitions. [...]

Marriage and family

A noticeably growing tendency among the well-to-do, particularly in the urban areas, is the sense of urgency parents display in the matter of their daughters' marriage. Nearly 90 per cent of marriages in Kerala are 'arranged' marriages. Here I am not trying to make a distinction between 'arranged' and 'love' marriages. Most marriages in well-to-do families are arranged through the thriving matrimonial columns of newspapers and journals. As a result, many of the marriages are not among families that knew each other or between cross cousins as used to be the practice among certain communities. Many marriages are arranged at short notice to suit the convenience of bridegrooms who come from abroad. Many among the young women would be in college or university trying to complete a degree or diploma course. This can include professional courses like medicine, engineering, agricultural or computer science. Apart from the young women's ability to get admission, the parents' ego is also satisfied in these achievements. It is hard to believe that the parents or the present Kerala society motivate them for anything beyond that. The message that is given to the growing up girl is to see marriage as the most important and essential act in life. [. . .]

In this context we have to remember that Kerala has made a relatively speedier transformation from joint families to nuclear families. That is, many women who could find support and living space in the matrilineal joint families as a matter of right have to fend for themselves or be at the mercy of not-so-willing siblings and relatives. If employed they stay in hostels or at home. But whose are these homes? How do they fare in the employment market? Here again we do not come across studies on the women under discussion and their economic wherewithal, including employment.

However we have some data which reflect the employment/unemployment situation in the state. According to the 1981 census, Kerala ranked 15 in female work participation rate in the descending order. The highest was Nagaland (42.46) and lowest Punjab (2.27). Kerala has been experiencing a sharp decline in opportunities in the areas where women in large numbers were finding employment. Agriculture, particularly paddy cultivation, cashew and the coir industry, handloom, etc. have been facing systematic decline. A section of the women are absorbed by the expanding construction and quarry works. Where do the others go? In private conversation one hears of increasing prostitution in the state. Incidentally, an article published recently in the Malayalam weekly *Mathrubhumi* has mentioned male prostitution which is increasing in the wake of tourism. It will not be wrong to say that no concerted effort has been taken to tackle the problem of unemployment in the state. The authorities look upon migration, both within India and outside, as a solution. The hazards associated with it are borne by the concerned persons.

Table 13: Sex Ratio Among Total Population and Selected Categories of Workers in Rural and Urban Areas, India and Kerala, 1981

Population and categories of workers	INDIA			KERALA		
	Total	Rural	Urban	Total	Rural	Urban
Population	934	952	880	1032	1034	1021
Total workers (main and marginal)	351	410	149	382	405	227
Main workers	253	289	132	321	338	245
Marginal Workers	5245	5756	1715	1030	1087	703
Non-workers	1583	1583	1584	1561	1559	1593

Source: Census of India, 1981, Part-II-B(i), Statement 12

Table 13 gives some interesting aspects of Kerala's female employment. As far as total workers are concerned, Kerala fares well when compared to the all-India figures and the urban situation is above the all-India level. In the case of main workers too, the Kerala experience was better than that of all-India, both under rural and urban categories. Under 'non-workers' too Kerala is almost near all-India level. The shocking differences between Kerala and all-India comes under 'marginal' workers. Main or marginal work does not mean work continuously done or on any permanent basis. The figures under marginal work are indicative of the gross non-availability in Kerala of odd work which is available elsewhere in India, the earnings (kind or cash) from which are very important for the survival of these women and their families. [. . .]

We cannot ignore in this connection the changes that have come about in people's notions of work or employment. They know the difference between uncertain jobs with irregular income and regular salary-earning permanent or semi-permanent jobs. While this awareness is welcome, they are not able to convert it into practice as opportunities are highly restricted. Poor Kerala women look for sweepers' jobs in government or private concerns, while Tamil immigrants occupy or create certain types of work and earn a rather regular income. One hears a lot on self-employment, but Kerala is yet to make a breakthrough in this in a big way. [. . .]

Growing consumerism

Women's status cannot be seen in isolation from several other developments in the state. Nor can any society's progress be measured without seeing how women are placed within it, the freedom and opportunity they get to participate in all areas and at all levels of its functioning, and their awareness about themselves and society. We have so far examined some of the acknowledged areas related to people's well-being. However, these alone cannot give us a picture of present-day Kerala. We have to examine the growth of consumerism and its impact on the people, increasing violence, and changes in attitude.

Exposure and contact with the wider world and the money that follows are among the reasons for the present onslaught of consumerism in the state. Kerala has had contact with countries far and near from ancient times. Even earlier in the present century Keralites had gone to seek jobs in the old Persia, Ceylon, Burma, Malaya, etc. But the current exodus is different in size and quality. The times have changed. World economic relations and technology too have witnessed unbelievable changes. Glittering consumer goods are produced on a mass scale, which anyone with money can buy. Though some of us use consumerism as a dirty word, production and use of consumer goods have come to be associated not only with better living, but also higher status. For this reason, most of our migrants to the Gulf countries bring many things which are not essential for our life. A large number of people are indulging in this wasteful expenditure at the cost of essentials like good food, education and health care. This certainly is not a phenomenon limited to Kerala.

Conclusion

Can we say that Kerala is a model? Jeffrey (1993, 217) says that Kerala is 'no model', but offers 'lessons'. Yes, but lessons for whom, for others to follow or for us to rethink? What are the lessons for those of us who vote for the latter? Every forward or progressive step Kerala has taken has thrown up problems before the state and no serious attempt has been made to understand them in their totality. Education and the educated unemployed, land reform legislation which did not include production, productivity or employment in its agenda, political awareness and individual or group rights without the essential sense of responsibility both at individual and collective level are just a few examples in this context. Kerala has the essential ingredients of what we have always believed necessary for women's 'emancipation'—literacy and education, freedom from inhibitions against women's education and employment, right to own property including land or house and to have savings in her own name, freedom to vote and also to contest elections. But Kerala women are far from being emancipated. Besides, some of the superficial freedoms they enjoy act as blinkers. The main reason for this is the way in which Kerala society is changing primarily as a result of official development policies. Though balanced regional development is an accepted goal, regional identity, resources, needs and culture never got ingrained in the development models. In fact diversity has no place in our development. On the other hand, uniformity is emphasized and very often it is seen as unity. The messages first came from cosmopolitan India, and now they come from global centres. They are introduced through developmental programmes, the administration, education and the media. Ideologically this means acceptance of the superiority of the message giver. On the other side, the message receiver develops a sense of inferiority. This started with colonialism.

So what is happening is not that Kerala has become a model, but that Kerala has accepted and even internalized others as models. This has first happened in Kerala mainly because the educated, politically alive, yet unemployed people are receptive to new ideas and styles to which they are exposed more and more. They do not 'cling' to 'tradition', as in the rest of India. This is a process and has penetrated into our world view and thinking. We have in general an uncritical view towards developments around us. The demographers are happily emphasizing the demographic transition in the state which is following the pattern of the 'developed' countries. Referring to the high suicide rate in the state, a recent article states that 'this high rate of suicides is a common phenomena in the development process . . . The suicide rates in most developed countries are comparatively very high'. The logic behind these kinds of arguments itself needs to be examined. At a time when we begin to think of 'alternative' and 'decentralized' development, it is natural that we should emphasize diversity in development, and that diversity should not be superior and inferior.

Kerala has many challenges before her. The people have to be roused, as during the social reform movement days, to take up these challenges. They include instilling in us a new sense of purpose and the fearlessness to question dogmas and break away from the shackles of subservience, consumerism, greed, frustration and cynicism and generating among us a sense of pride and confidence in our collective destiny. I am one who believes that Kerala has the potential to rise to the occasion, but which woman or man will kindle the light?

References

Jeffrey, Robin. 1993. *Politics, women and well-being.* New Delhi: Oxford University Press

∼

FEMINISM, POVERTY AND GLOBALIZATION
Mary E. John

[. . .]

With the 1990s, the quieter liberalization measures begun in the mid 1980s led to India's first serious balance of payments crisis of 1991. This in turn resulted in the announcement of a New Economic Policy involving a comprehensive programme of economic reform aiming towards structural adjustment in all sectors, thus fundamentally revising, if not undoing, more than four decades of development planning. First publicly initiated when the Congress returned to power in 1991, these policies were subsequently taken forward under the coalition government headed by the Bharatiya Janata Party which took control in 1996. 'Economic facts' should not, however, blind us to the transformed larger ideological climate by virtue of which a country like India, as a relative latecomer to the processes of stabilization, structural adjustment and liberalization, has entered the contested terrain of globalization.

As successor ideologies, liberalization and globalization appear as deeply contradictory, indeed, even as negative paradigms. Their economic rhetoric consists of a retreat from the productive and welfarist dimensions of the state in favour of market- and export-led growth, and the creation of a culture built around consumption. The fact that other third world nations have referred to their time of economic restructuring during the 1980s as 'the lost decade' and that our new models—the Asian Tigers—witnessed major crises during the very years when India began to globalize, has accentuated two things—the extraordinarily intense modes of ideological reconstruction of the new Indian global citizen being deployed today (acutely visible in the heightened place occupied by the media in everyday life), and the severe erosion and loss of authority of alternate paradigms, especially with the collapse of the socialist bloc. What does all this mean for a social movement such as the women's movement? [. . .]

In a recent article reviewing India's 'micro-movements' from the 1970s to the present, D.L. Sheth has argued that the very onset of globalization has revitalized the entire spectrum of social movements (many of whom had become moribund or routinized after the initial elan of the 1970s), and is even producing a 'high degree of convergence on a wide range of issues concerning globalization' (Sheth 2004, 47). There are many fascinating and informative aspects to Sheth's account. However, having rightly seen how the entry of globalization has become the new frame of reference and target for numerous social movements (including the women's movement), this slides into the problematic claim that a 'counter-discourse' of converging positions is consequently in the making. The multiple strands of the women's movement illustrate the extent to which divergent and contrary positions have actually been hardening in recent years. Even when allowance is made for the fact that these positions often focus on different dimensions of liberalization and globalization, their range is truly remarkable, while they are all feminist, and committed to social justice. Compared to the extensive debates within the movement on issues such as the question of a uniform civil code, or over reservations for women in local self-government and in parliament, similar public debates have not taken place over the immensely critical nature of the new conjuncture of 'globalization'. Whether positions are being adopted unequivocally or with considerable uncertainty, it is time that they are reflected on at greater length. No discussion of poverty takes place today without reference to globalization, its discourses, policies and institutional restructuring.

The most frequently heard and strongest voices within the women's movement have condemned and attacked the New Economic Policies right from their inception a decade ago. Their basis is that globalization can only inaugurate a widening of disparities across and within nations and regions, leading to a deepening of processes of impoverishment for the majority. The special sufferers here will be poor women, for such women will have to increasingly bear the disproportionate burdens arising from the unequal allocation of resources and poorer self-care, even as they work harder to make up for falling real incomes, reductions in social welfare, and the privatization of services. As women take on multiple jobs, their daughters will either follow them, or take charge of the household, thus being debarred from an education. Greater levels of stress will also lead to a worsening of men's ability to cope, which then takes such forms as growing violence or increased desertions. Following this line of argumentation, large sections of the women's movement, not only those coming from the left, have been mobilizing repeatedly against economic reform, whether it be over disinvestment of the public sector, conditions of work in export processing zones, or food security subsidies.

In order to show how seriously they viewed the announcement of the New Economic Policies in 1991, the Indian Association of Women's Studies devoted its 6th national conference in 1993 (a three-day event held every two years with plenaries and simultaneous sessions) entirely to the theme of the 'New Economic Policy and its Implications for Women'. While numerous consultations have followed, actual in-depth studies of the consequences of the new policies in the lives of women are just beginning to appear. One of the earliest efforts was by activists and scholars in Bombay, who questioned claims in favour of the feminization of the labour force during structural adjustment, by showing that major manufacturing industries in the city of Bombay have in fact been retrenching women at unprecedented rates since the 1980s (Shah et al 1994). A parallel critique of the feminization thesis has been levelled by Nirmala Banerjee. (See her essay "How Real is the Bogey of Feminization?" in this section.)

Less visible in the concerted attacks against liberalization have been the frameworks and perspectives being deployed by those who oppose the current regime. In my view, the absence of self-reflexivity about their ideological frames of reference constitutes a major impediment that is blocking the advancement of such oppositional agendas. As I mentioned earlier on, it is never enough, especially not today, to think that facts somehow speak for themselves. What, then, are the ideological subtexts fuelling current opposition, and whom do they address? The major problem here is that these oppositional voices invariably speak from positions that have precisely lost their authority in the present climate. They either stem from the era of developmentalism and economic nationalism that has lost out in the current conjuncture, or hark back to an even earlier time, to a cultural past free from all forms of capitalist and imperialist domination. This has also led to the situation where Marxists, whose frameworks continue to be pinned to state-centred welfare and socialist planning, share a common platform with eco-feminists such as Vandana Shiva, whose opposition to multinational capital arises from a fundamentally different world view, one based on the desire to preserve the indigenous local knowledges and pre-modern relationship to nature that she imputes to third world women farmers. A series of phases of globalization—colonization by Europe, the universalization of production and consumption in the name of 'development', and finally, the current trade treaties focused on biodiversity and genetic resources—are opposed by Shiva to the potential of 'decentralized agricultural communities', which are somehow without hierarchies—whether of ecology and economics, domestic or commodity production, natural or human economies, or relations of gender. As the result of the coming together of such incommensurable frameworks, there is a definite air of eclecticism in some of the current oppositional rhetorics being deployed. This adds to the problem of coming across as speaking not from the present but from the past.

In comparison, the voices of those who have offered some kind of qualified acceptance to globalization, though often couched in a more tentative or speculative language, nonetheless appear to gain simply by virtue of being more rooted in the present. Here again, positions are quite diverse. A figure like Madhu Kishwar, for example, seems to be basing her assent to the current economic regime less out of any careful assessment of its claims than from her opposition to any state-centric—or what she identifies as western-inspired—world view, whether of development or women's empowerment. In a set of proposals canvassed in *Manushi*, she wishes to set in motion a 'freeing up of the entrepreneurial skills of the people' especially women, who have been made dependent and prevented from taking their place in the public sphere of the economy due to an over-bloated, over-centralized bureaucracy, and a larger culture of criminalization and violence (Kishwar 2001). From a very different perspective, the Marxist-feminist Rohini Hensman views the greater integration of the world economy as a necessary stage in the evolution of global capitalism. She goes further to assert that this demands a correspondingly international level of intervention and struggle, whether through the promotion of coordinated class actions by globally disenfranchised workers or by taking advantage of international standards such as the highly controversial WTO directive to link trade with labour standards in developing nations like India. The anti-globalization agenda does not make sense for groups like women workers in third world contexts, she goes on to argue, who have potentially more to gain through 'concerted action to shape the global order in accordance with a women's agenda for justice and equity as well as caring and nurturing ... Can a socialist feminist vision of an ideal world include national boundaries maintained by nationalism, with its potential for developing into fascism, imperialism and war?' (Hensman 2004, 1034). The weakness in her otherwise cogent account has to do with her audience—neither the international working class nor transnational feminist groups are particularly visible today. (It is the anti-globalizers who seem to be steadily gaining in global visibility—most recently at the third social summit organized in Mumbai, India in January 2004, which included several feminist organizations. And yet, there have been some telling reformulations in the rhetoric deployed at these meetings—calls for a movement of 'counter-globalization' and opposition to 'imperial globalization' rather than direct opposition to globalization per se may well be indicative of a nascent political formation critical of both nationalisms and certain versions of globalization.)

The third example of qualified support to globalization comes from the work of Gail Omvedt, and is surely the most provocative. Omvedt has argued that globalization and the new economic order may actually help those very groups whom the development era effectively marginalized. Her analysis is based on the expectation that globalized markets will, on the one hand, rein in the Indian bourgeoisie, its unviable monopolies, and the inefficient upper caste state bureaucracy, and, on the other hand, give the small farmer a better global price for produce which was previously underpriced due to state intervention. As she has put it polemically, 'if the choice is between a high caste capitalist Indian economy with a highly privileged all-male workforce ... producing steel or automobiles, and a relatively labour-intensive multi-national linked company in a rural area employing women [or lower castes, in leather trades, fruit and vegetable production and so on] then we will prefer the multinational' (Omvedt and Gala 1993). This argument (which shares common ground with some feminization arguments elsewhere) begs as many questions as it raises, the most important of which would be the following: Are these hitherto marginalized groups—peasants, dalits, backward castes and women— socially positioned to take advantage of globalization, and on what basis can we expect the hitherto dominant urban classes and castes to lose out in the current realignments taking place?

My final example of a different voice is that of SEWA, the Self-Employed Women's Association, as mediated by its leaders Ela Bhatt and Renana Jhabvala. The history of SEWA goes back to the early 1970s, and grew out of its founder Ela Bhatt's formative experience as a Gandhian with the Textile Labour Association in Ahmedabad. SEWA describes itself as a trade union of poor, self-employed workers, and has a membership of over 200,000 women. Its main centres are in Gujarat, though there are newer ones in a few other states as well. Their approach to women's issues is one of economic empowerment—the 'second freedom' Bhatt believes is India's struggle after political freedom was won in 1947—by providing the necessary economic and financial security to women workers in the informal or unorganized sector, through a system of cooperative banking, maternal and child care, and most recently, through an insurance programme set up in collaboration with insurance companies. I would call their response to liberalization one of pragmatism. Recognizing that the living standards of the poor may well have declined after structural adjustment was initiated and that the hitherto secure entitlements of the organized sector may also get eroded, they wish to take the 'positive' approach of creating the necessary social security systems that could potentially address the needs of the vast majority of the country's workers. In contrast to the public sector and the private sector (the backbone of India's experiment with a mixed economy during the development era, and towards whom all national policies have been aimed) they have mooted the concept of 'the people's sector'—unorganized labour and self-employed producers in rural and urban India, subjects of neglect, yet on whom the economy effectively depends (Jhabvala 2000). With their emphasis on women's economic agency, processes of decentralization, increased levels of financial and managerial participation by the 'beneficiary' population, and the reduced role of the state, it is perhaps not surprising that SEWA has been picked up as a model by international agencies such as the World Bank, and not just for third world countries, but even for first world nations who are themselves seeking to dismantle their welfare systems in favour of neo-liberal policy orientations. SEWA is therefore at the hub of a number of highly contentious issues. What are the elisions underwriting the liberal concept of women's 'economic agency' and greater efficiency in managing poverty, and what dangers does this portend for the future? [. . .]

What other emergent processes have accompanied the rise to dominance of the ideologies of globalization? We have come a long way from the technicist battles over the determination of poverty during the 1970s that focused on the appropriate measurements of calorie intake for determining below poverty line populations. And yet, the power of economic ideologies is such that material concepts of disadvantage, lack of entitlements and unmet basic needs continue to dominate contemporary debates. Furthermore, there has been a tendency during the last decade to uphold struggles over poverty in opposition to those being raised in the name of so-called 'identity politics', especially in the wake of the re-emergence on the national stage of the politics of caste and community. Such misgivings have been voiced in the women's movement as well. To my mind, this polarization blocks the chance of actually transforming our understanding of poverty itself. It could be argued, and I am going to do so here, that one of the failures of the developmental era was its inability to account for inequalities and hierarchies such as those based on caste and community, other than as residues of the past. It therefore required major national crisis points—the anti-Mandal agitation of 1990 against the implementation of reservations for the Other Backward Castes in administration and higher education, the demolition of the Babri Masjid in 1992 and the anti-Muslim riots that followed, and the rise of new regionalisms, amongst others—for hitherto largely invisible structures of disparity based on caste, community and region to gain some measure of recognition in their own right. One of the potential gains of the last decade, therefore, would be to acknowledge that the *multiple inequalities of the present* must be taken into account (rather than transcended or sought to be bypassed) in ongoing struggles against poverty. For the women's movement—already accused of having 'divided' prior struggles by introducing questions of gender—the way forward may not be easy. But it is not for nothing that contemporary studies of poverty have begun to notice that dalits, major sections of the backward castes, tribals, Muslim minorities and female headed households practically exhaust the categories of the poor. Feminists will have to play their part to turn such lists into live zones of coalition building.

It would, however, be exceedingly naïve to suppose that the deprivation and marginalization experienced by these groups would somehow act as a natural magnet drawing them together as a majority, whether socially or politically. It is not for nothing that recognition of the 'cultural' dimensions of poverty is emerging at a time when the nation has witnessed the revival of a very different majoritarian project, that of Hindutva. Recent developments in states as different as Uttar Pradesh and Gujarat are but an indication of how the most vicious conflicts can take place between groups adjacent to one another in strictly economic terms. Moreover, there is a longer history of anti-reservation *resentment* whereby the small but never invisible members of lower castes within the middle classes have not been allowed to forget who they are, a strategy that has been reproduced to deadly effect in the successful destruction of lives and livelihoods of all classes of Muslims in Gujarat. The current agenda of the Hindu Right to produce a Hindu Rashtra by incorporating sections of the most backward castes, dalits and tribals within its fold cannot be countered by purely economistic conceptions of deprivation. And yet, as the extraordinary results of the just concluded Lok Sabha elections of 2004 would indicate, the aggressively marketed 'India Shining' campaign of the BJP, which—more than anything else—sought to make the poor invisible if not irrelevant, has backfired in a way no one predicted beforehand.

The diversity in the experiences and forms of poverty in India today may thus require unlearning inherited ways of conceptualizing our underdevelopment, which the women's movement can only ignore at its peril. Perhaps this is still less controversial than the final issue I would like to raise, one that is bound to be more debatable since it involves going beyond the 'poor'. To put it most provocatively, has the heavy emphasis on representations of poverty—at the cost of a parallel understanding of class dynamics—also become one of the weaknesses of the women's movement? Poverty and class continue to be conflated with one another (not unlike the conflation of women and gender) and to the detriment of *both*. Class analysis—that is to say, analysis that focuses on the non-poor as well as the poor—has seen no significant advancements in the last few decades.

The major aspect of class analysis that is urgently in need of redressal centres on the intermediate classes and castes, which, for lack of a better description, I will call the non-poor. An indispensable dimension of such analysis would include patterns of mobility across class fractions, processes that enable some groups to move out of poverty and possibly gain some measure of prosperity, while others strategize to prevent themselves from 'falling'. Isn't it curious how little we wish to know of such trends? Now it could of course be argued that since a movement must have its priorities, the problems of the non-poor cannot be expected to figure very highly. However, such a shortsighted approach has come home to roost today. As far back as the first shocked discovery of the prevalence of dowry murders amongst urban lower middle class families almost three decades ago, there has been evidence of *greater* gender biases in families beyond the pale of dire need. In more recent years considerable anxiety has emerged over the worsening of female–male sex ratios, which are sharpening outside the classes of poor, leading to speculations of the 'paradox' of the 'prosperity effect', the negative effects on women of fertility decline, and the mismatch between measures of 'backward' districts according to economic and gender indicators. The results of the 2001 Census in particular, where child female/male ratios in the 0–6 age group have dropped precipitously in many districts of the most economically advanced states of the country, especially in urban areas, have led to dystopic speculations of various kinds. (The worst state averages for 2001 are Punjab (793), Haryana (820), Gujarat (879) and Himachal Pradesh (897), and the all-India figure is 927 girls per 1000 boys.) There is every reason to believe that these are not isolated patterns but a potential sign of things to come, as men and women make 'choices' under conditions of limited gains and potential losses in an expanding, increasingly competitive economy. And yet, analysis is still largely impressionistic, mobilization quite weak and often not sufficiently sensitive to the genuine problems involved. The women's movement often appears caught in a kind of cleft stick—denouncing poverty and the 'evils' of the new consumerist culture in one and the same breath. Sometimes the question is posed: If poverty is bad for women, could prosperity be worse?

Perhaps, then, the way forward may have little to do with actually getting the right perspective on 'globalization'. Feminism must, on the one hand, realize that its future is tied up with the multiple languages of poverty and disparity that are straining to be heard. On the other hand, even at the cost of overload, there are no stopping places where gender loses its urgency— 'success' stories in class terms are not being mirrored in the egalitarian life-chances of sons and daughters. [. . .]

References

Hensman, Rohini. 6 March 2004. Globalization, women and work. *Economic and Political Weekly* vol. 34, 1032–39.

Jhabvala, Renana and R.K.A. Subramanya, ed. *The unorganised sector: Work security and social protection.* New Delhi: Sage, 2000.

Kishwar, Madhu. 2001. Laws, liberty and livelihood: Towards a bottom-up, woman friendly agenda of economic reforms. *Manushi* 122. 8–12.

Omvedt, Gail and Chetna Gala. October 1993. The new economic policy and women: A rural Perspective. *Economic Review.* 15–18.

Sheth, D.L. 3–9 January 2004. Globalization and the new politics of micro-movements. *Economic and Political Weekly.*vol.34, no.1, 43–48.

Shah, Nandita et al. 30 April 1994. Feminization of the labour force and organizational strategies. *Economic and Political Weekly.* vol.24, no.18, WS-39–48.

~

HOW REAL IS THE BOGEY OF FEMINIZATION?

Nirmala Banerjee

The phrase feminization of work in the sense it is being used now was probably first employed systematically by Guy Standing of the ILO (Standing 1989). The article included data from various countries at different stages of development; it showed that, since about the mid-sixties, there has been a widespread trend towards a higher share of women workers in the labour force of both developed and developing countries. In his comments, the author had argued that the trend did not augur well either for the women workers or for the working class as a whole. Since then, several studies have put together similar data for different countries and most of these appear to share the apprehensions voiced by Standing. For India too, this has been a recurring theme in the writings of several authors since it adopted the new economic policies of an open economy (Ahmed 1994; Shah et al 1994;

Ghosh 1996). This has created some confusion in the debates on women and development; for a long time, we had been lamenting the fact that development of the kind that was taking place in market economies the world over throughout this century had continuously destroyed the work opportunities of women. If now the next phase of development has brought a reversal of those tendencies, then why is it not to be regarded as a welcome change?

This confusion is perhaps rather naïve, but it has not really been addressed in the burgeoning literature on this theme. Obviously, those writing in this vein were not just being capricious—they have put forward reasonable grounds for fearing the process. Feminization, as they see it, can come about in either of two ways. First, it may happen through women replacing men in the jobs that were previously held by the latter. The motive of employers in doing so presumably would be to downgrade the average terms of employment from the standards enjoyed by men to the level usually given to women. The fact that women's average earnings are consistently below those of men is well established for most countries. So, if women do come to replace men in the latter's jobs without a concurrent increase in the total number of jobs in a given economy, the aggregate earning of workers as a class would be sharply reduced. Alternately, feminization could be the result of a development in which the additional jobs go to women on terms similar to those normally offered to women workers in that case, the average standard of working conditions in the economy would worsen and the share of the working class as a whole in the additional value added would be less than the level enjoyed by it so far. The entire process, moreover, would mean that, though their employment opportunities increase, women continue to work under the same kind of insecure and poor working conditions as before.

Both the possibilities outlined here are no doubt grim, especially in the context of India where over thirty per cent of households were still under the poverty line at the time when India went in for a structural adjustment programme. However, I want to argue that the analysis by Standing and others has paid too little attention to the diverse economic factors that have affected women's relative employment in different economies. Their arguments rest mainly on drawing analogies between the apparently similar employment trends in different countries without tracing back the history or the causal links in each case. Following this lead, the scholars who have been analyzing the recent trends in women's work in India have focused selectively on those sectors, however small in the Indian context, where the trend towards feminization had been more pronounced in several other countries. In the process, they have ignored some very serious and persistent problems of Indian women workers. Also, even in those selected activities, their concern about the feminization of the workforce has stemmed largely from an outsider's viewpoint, and has taken little note of the way the workers themselves view the situation. [. . .]

The Indian case

In India, there has been a gradual shift over the last decade or more towards policies for a more open economy; the 1991 policy declaration was more of a formalization of that phenomenon than a radical shift to a new outlook. However, available macro-statistics indicated that, *in India, in a period of relative liberalization of the economy, the trends in women's employment pattern were, if anything, in the reverse direction.* The share of women in the rural workforce had been increasing in the 1970s; but in the late 80s, it went down from a high of 36 per cent in 1983 to about 34.5 per cent and had remained there till 1993–94. There was a slight rise in women's share in the urban workforce, which according to Visaria, reflected mainly the growth in women's rate of urbanization (Visaria 1996). With that, the fall in their share in the country's overall workforce from 1983 to 1993–94 was small, but nonetheless it was a fall. [. . .]

If we look at this sectorally over that period, if there was any increase in work opportunities for rural women, then it was in agriculture. State-wise analysis of census data shows that, in states where women's activity rates had increased during the1980s, it was almost always due to an increase in agricultural work for them and vice versa. Their employment in the secondary sector [of manufacture] fell drastically in almost all states. Work opportunities in the secondary sector for urban females (who form only a small proportion of the total female workforce) also shrank significantly; but they did make significant gains in the tertiary sector [of services]. [. . .]

The model behind the theme

Feminization has generally been linked with the globalization of different economies. Opening up the country's economy to unrestricted multilateral trade and foreign capital investment increases the level of competition faced by the country's producers in domestic as well as foreign markets. Simultaneously, there has been a shift in the composition of trade, especially between developed and the faster developing countries, towards a greater share of manufactures especially of the footloose kind, i.e. of the kind in which no country has a natural advantage. Among the producers who compete in these keenly competitive markets, there is a strong presence of multinational companies which move their capital from country to country in search of relatively cheap labour. In order to keep their labour costs down, these employers impose a very strict and exacting work schedule on their workers. Also, because they want to keep open the option of moving their capital whenever they find a greater cost advantage elsewhere, the companies are generally unwilling to offer the workers long term, protected work contracts. In most countries it is only the women who would be willing to take up those kinds of jobs; therefore in countries which join this competitive trade regime with the participation of multinationals, the workforce of the export-oriented manufacturing industries comes to be dominated by women workers.

It is worth noting that the entire process rests on the assumption that, even with a fairly fast rate of economic growth, there is little or no change in the basic nature and working conditions of the jobs that are assigned to women in a given economy. Nor is there a change envisaged in the social ideas about the sexual division of labour. [. . .]

Flexibility and organization

The model assumes that in the countries undergoing this process, legislations for the protection of labour would hitherto be dismantled to give flexibility to employers in the use of labour. The resultant labour contracts would be of the sort that usually are offered to women and this would discourage male labour from entering. However, with the dismantling of labour laws, just as women would not get special benefits, men too would not be able to demand better work contracts on grounds of their united strength. In that case, employers would be free to choose precisely those workers who they think can do the work efficiently and according to their specifications. There is really no reason why these should necessarily be women.

Alternatively, it is possible that even if labour laws continue to apply to the formal, factory sector, efforts will now be made to reduce their sphere of application. The literature under review argues that, with the new economic policies, employers will try to reorganize production through more decentralized, subcontracted units where they can avoid the extra costs imposed by labour laws. This is supposed to induce feminization of the workforce because, once again, these poorer work conditions would find a readier acceptance among women workers.

If such cheaper options were available and considered efficient by the entrepreneurs, it is difficult to understand why these were not already in use even before globalization triggered off the process. In actual fact, long before the Indian economy had begun to open up, many firms here had been systematically following this policy. It is well-known that, as far back as the 1960s, the Indian-owned textile mills of Ahmedabad and Mumbai had begun to farm out their weaving work to decentralized powerloom units. Similarly, a recent study by the Workers' Research Centre (Mumbai), has shown that, in the early 1970s, the multinational pharmaceutical firms of the Bombay/ Thane belt started to farm out the work on their consumer product lines to smaller units run under Indian ownership. These subunits, whose products are sold under multinational labels, are located away from the high-wage, industrialized belt and the terms of employment they offer are nowhere comparable to those in the parent units. But their workforce has always been entirely a male one (Shah et al 1994). It is worth remembering that, in the 1950s, these same MNC units had given a lead to the entire country by expanding women's employment in their modern manufacturing industries; but, for the last twenty years, they themselves have stopped recruiting women and are currently busy persuading the remaining women employees to accept a golden handshake and go. The Philips company too has been following a similar policy at least since the beginning of the 1980s for the work of assembly of their consumer electronic products. These MNCs had sought out such cost-cutting measures even though they had long enjoyed patents and monopoly rights in the production of several of their products. Therefore, there is no reason to believe that it is only global competition that induces flexible work contracts or that it will necessarily increase women's employment at the cost of men's. [. . .]

Footloose industries and exports

The across-country generalization about export-led growth in women's employment rests mainly on the assumption that the products of the exporting industries are of the footloose variety. It is true that, for most countries with fast growing exports, the structure of exports comprises goods in whose production no country need have any natural advantage; so any country can compete in the export market provided it can supply goods of required quality at competitive rates. Most countries have tried to get that competitive edge mainly by keeping down their labour costs.

However common this trend, it cannot be assumed to be universal. In fact, India's exports even after the 1990s are still a very different kind of mixture. Indian merchandise exports include a number of commodities in which the country's relative advantage lies in its traditional skills, and not merely in providing cheap labour of any kind. In 1994–95, fabrics, garments, gems and jewellery and handicrafts together accounted for about 3/4th of India's manufactured exports. All these items were known mainly for the distinctive use of India's traditional crafts in their manufacture.

This is not to deny that India's comparative advantage even in these industries lies mainly in the low wages paid for the skills that go to make the exports distinctive. Indeed, one reason why the emphasis is on traditional skills is that, compared to their sale value, they come so cheap. But, in order to continue those exploitative practices, it is essential that the traditional relations of power are not unduly disturbed. If these are traditionally skills of male artisans, then the wider marketing and increasing demand for the products generally means more work for the men who possess the traditional skills. In a labour-surplus economy, there is possibly an excess supply of those workers as well; so, in the short run, the process would not call for inducting a new section of the labour force, such as women, into those industries.

There is no reason to expect that to happen in the long run either. Along with its traditions of skills India also has long traditions of skill training through families and *ustads*. Other systems of reproducing the skills will not necessarily be more efficient or cost effective. If now those traditional ways were to pass the skill from men to young boys and men, then the process need not generate jobs for women at all. The Indian garment industry provides the best example of how this process has been working in India. Calcutta has traditionally housed a vast supply of very skilled garment makers who have their own traditions of training apprentices and organizing production. In a recent study, I have discussed how these Calcutta producers, with their very competitive prices and quick deliveries, have been able to build up within a short period of 10–15 years a huge all-India market for readymade garments for women, men and children. The entire workforce of this thriving industry happens to consist of Muslim males (Banerjee 1995a). Reports say that the fast expanding export-oriented garment industry around Delhi also uses predominantly male artisans who hail from the cities of Uttar Pradesh. This is in sharp contrast with the practice the world over of identifying the garment industry, particularly in its recent globalized phase, with female labour. [. . .]

What is happening to women's work in India?

As we saw before, there are as yet no signs of feminization of the Indian workforce and there are no obvious reasons why this should take place in the coming years. What then is the outlook for women's work? Do we rejoice because Indian women are not being subjected to the dangers of such international exploitation? Or do we start worrying afresh about the fact that our struggles for women's economic empowerment for the last twenty years have brought little change in their situation?

We should, above all, examine the changes that are taking place on the ground both at macro and micro levels. Macro data show that, in recent years, there were two noticeable developments in women's work experience whose combined upshot is mixed. Firstly, additions to women's employment in the last decade and a half have been confined mainly to agriculture. Between 1981 and 1991, census figures show that more than 80 per cent of the new jobs generated for rural women were in the agricultural sector. However, this increase in women's employment has remained confined to five states (Andhra Pradesh, Madhya Pradesh, Maharashtra, Tamil Nadu and Uttar Pradesh): between them they accounted for about 2/3rds of the women agricultural workers in 1981 as well as in 1991. In these states, women have been the traditional mainstay of three crops—paddy, sugar cane and cotton. A further intensification in their cultivation over this period was probably the main factor behind the additional work days for women. So far, there are no signs of any change in the technologies of cultivating these crops; so, when cultivation is intensified, women get more work.

But while paddy cultivation in West Bengal has become equally intensified, there has not been a corresponding increase in women's employment there. On the other hand, in Punjab and Haryana, for wheat cultivation, along with the intensification of cultivation, there have been some technological changes in the machinery used. There, women's agricultural employment has actually shrunk. It appears that women get additional work in agriculture only in those locations and operations where there is a well-established tradition of their participation. [. . .] Secondly, among women agricultural workers, the relative share of cultivators has been rising since 1971. This shift, however, has not brought a real change in women's role in agriculture. Whereas male cultivators spent only about 3 per cent of their work days on manual field tasks in cultivation, the equivalent figure for women cultivators was 36 per cent. This means that actually, most women cultivators are probably still working as unpaid family labour; since 1971, rural men, specially those with small holdings, have tended to move out of agriculture, leaving women to cultivate the family plots. This does not appear to mean that women are given the powers to market the crop or to alter the use of the land. From another angle, we see that even with increasing agricultural employment for women, the difference between male and female wage earnings in agriculture had in fact increased from 1977–78 to 1987–88.

At the micro level, findings of a small study that we recently conducted in the Hooghly district of West Bengal may provide a few useful indications of the kind of changes that were taking place (Sachetana 1997). The study examined the work experience of women in four industries with a long history in that region. These were agriculture, handlooms, jari work and textile mill work. Women had always been involved in these either as unpaid family labour or as wage workers (casual or regular).

We found that, in the last ten years, women had broken through the traditional taboos on their occupations; they were now to be found working as weavers or paid labour processing yarn for powerloom weavers. This was also true of the jari workers who were now trying to form their own cooperative to cut out the middleman and work directly for the order-givers. Similarly, in agriculture, even caste Hindu or Muslim women were now working as casual labour particularly in crops like potato, vegetables and flowers. However, as in textile mills, they were generally to be found working on operations with relatively primitive technologies. For example, in weaving, they were being given the family handlooms to work on when men had moved to powerlooms. In jari work, they were engaged in simple, repetitive operations; in mill work, they had found a few openings in the modernized rayon mills and were still working on the manual operations in jute mills. It appeared that most of these operations where women had recently found an entry were poised for a change through the challenges of modern technology and may become obsolete in a short while.

Their work in agriculture too was relatively more precarious because the crops depended heavily on support from public agencies providing timely infrastructural facilities like water, storage, electricity, etc. Since this assurance was difficult for small farmers to obtain from the state, women's work opportunities varied widely from season to season. Altogether, while the sexual division of labour and ideas about a women's proper role may be changing in times of household hardship, ideas about women's inherent capabilities were more difficult to alter.

Feminization and empowerment

The last question in this debate is, if feminization of the workforce were to take place, would it necessarily be empowering for women? Of the two current views on this issue, that of Standing and his friends is that feminization does little to reduce women's subordination and may even enhance it. The other point of view has been put forward, among others by Sen (1990), and claims that wage work increases the bargaining power of women in the household and the economy and is therefore empowering. Both these, I feel, need to be heavily qualified.

The Standing position is essentially a sweeping and logically weak generalization from limited and defective data. It is, in addition, very much an outsider's view in so far as it ignores the initial position of the women concerned and the reasons why they have the low supply price that employers are looking for. Condemning the employers alone does nothing to reduce the initial vulnerability of those women. Nor is the state, at least in India, capable or willing to challenge the patriarchal norms which treat women basically as a flexible family resource rather than as a person with independent rights and priorities. The supply price of women's labour is lower because they enter the labour market more handicapped by family responsibilities and their lack of assets. This is as true of the domestic servants of Calcutta as of the garment factory workers of Dhaka. [. . .]

The Standing position also takes no note of the dynamics of this process although it is essentially discussing a fast changing economic background. However exploitative the Bangladesh factory conditions for women, they gave them an unprecedented chance to come out from the close monitoring by their families and to live among their peers. This breaking of traditional norms is perhaps the main contribution that employment in modern factory industries can make for women. In a faster developing country like the Republic of Korea which otherwise is an extremely patriarchal society, women were also able to use their visible numbers in the public domain to get important concessions from their employers, the state and their social system.

Sen (1990), on the other hand, starts from an explicit recognition of women's low bargaining strength within their households. He lists the various factors that determine its level. The important one in these is the breakdown of well-being, which he defines as follows: 'given other things, if the breakdown position of one person was worse in terms of well-being, then the collusive solution, if different, would be less favourable on his or her well-being' (Sen 1990, 135). In other words, if one party to the bargain feels that she would be worse off breaking the existing pattern and living separately, then her bargaining strength in the initial position will be less. Taking a cue from there, whether or not a women's position improves by getting into wage work should be assessed in terms of how far it makes it possible for her to strike out on her own on the strength of that income.

The problem is, in most cases, that the initial position of the woman at the entry to the labour market is such that her expected income from the work is poor and uncertain; it is by no means sufficient for her to live singly. Added to that are the problems associated with the society's reaction to women who seek divorce or try to find a living on their own. Therefore, at least in South Asian countries, women are rarely able or willing to walk out of the marital home. In that case, wage work outside the house increases her work load because she is not in a position to bargain with the others about sharing her housework. Perhaps the jobs in the export factories, however exploitative they might be, at least give women an opportunity to find a way of living with other women and to draw strength from them in her deals with the family. So, unlike what Sen has claimed, I do not think that work by itself would always give women the necessary bargaining strength; but factory work, especially when it brings women into close contact with others in a similar situation, may well do so.

References

Ahmed, I. 30 April 1994. Technology and feminization of work. *Economic and Political Weekly*, vol. 29, no. 18.

Banerjee, N. 1995. Labour, institutions and the new economic order in India. In *Institutions and industrial development: Asian experiences,* ed. Lauridsen, L. Occasional paper no. 16, International Development Studies, Roskilde University, Denmark.

Ghosh, J. 1996. Macro-economic dynamics and female employment: India in the Asian context. Paper presented at the seminar on Gender and Employment in India, organized by the Indian Society of Labour Economics and the Institute of Economic Growth, New Delhi.

Sachetana. 1997. *Report on the study of women's work and SAP.* Department of Women and Child Development of India, no. 409, New Delhi.

Sen, A.K. 1990. Gender and cooperative conflicts. In *Persistent inequalities,* ed. I. Tinker. Oxford University Press, Oxford, New York.

Shah, N. et al. 30 April 1994. Structural adjustment, feminization of labour and organisational strategies. *Economic and Political Weekly*, vol. 24, no. 18.

Standing, G. 1989. Global feminization through flexible labour. *World Development*, vol. 17, no. 7.

Visaria, P. 1996. Level and pattern of women's employment in India, 1911–1994. Paper presented at the Seminar on Gender and Employment in India, organized by the Indian Society of Labour Economics and the Institute of Economic Growth, New Delhi.

~

WOMEN IN STRUGGLE:
A CASE STUDY OF THE CHIPKO MOVEMENT
Kumud Sharma

The debate on women's role and participation in popular movements had raised several questions regarding organizational and leadership issues, nature of struggle, mobilizing mechanisms and strategies, perspectives on micro issues in relation to larger political processes and ideological dimensions.

The question arises: What does 'participation' mean? Do women's activities in larger movements always have a politicizing effect? What are the linkages between women's participation in the political process and the emergence and growth of the ideology of the women's movement? Why is it that women have always responded to 'crisis issues' and then retreated to the mundane issues of daily existence? Does the nature of politics and political institutions deter women from active participation? Do women play a significant role in less conventional politics? What is the role of childhood socialization in political achievement? What are the relationships between women's participation in movements, the material conditions of their existence and the ideology of gender? Any attempt to answer these question involves looking into wider issues of women's role in social and political life. [. . .]

The context

The Uttar Pradesh Himalayas consist of eight hilly districts, collectively known as Uttarakhand. About 93% of the hill population is rural with a per capita income which is nearly half of that in Uttar Pradesh. Tehri and Uttar Kashi in Garhwal are two of India's poorest districts. The economy of the region is primarily agricultural and pastoral.

The forest area ranges between 37.95 to 47.2 per cent, and including Panchayati forest covers about 60–63 per cent of the entire region. However, unofficial figures estimate that about 50% of this area is degraded and nearly eight per cent of the total area is facing severe soil erosion. Official statistics put the total area under forest as 64% of the total geographical area. It is estimated that out of this only 40 percent is really under forest cover. The Uttar Pradesh hills have conifers and broad leafed forests rich in timber and medicinal herbs.

For more than a century, developments in this region and injudicious interference with its ecosystem have brought about major ecological transformations affecting the lives of the people. Some of the major problems plaguing the region are heavy male migration to the plains and the proverbial 'money-order economy' to bridge the subsistence gap, excessive commercial exploitation of the forest for defence and development needs, construction of river valley projects, industries and communication links creating an acute scarcity of fuel and fodder, overfelling of trees causing floods, soil erosion and land slides affecting agricultural productivity.

By the fifties, the forests in the foothills of the Himalayas were wiped out. After the 1962 Indo-China conflict, a network of roads and communication links opened the whole area to timber contractors who indulged in rapacious felling of the forests. In 1978, the Uttar Pradesh government deforested large areas in the Doon Valley to rehabilitate persons displaced by the acquisition of land for the construction of Tehri Dam in Garhwal. The growing pressure of human and bovine populations is playing havoc with the fragile ecological balance in this region. Various enquiry committees in the last decade have detected irregularities and in one of the official documents of the Uttar Pradesh forest department it was stated that 'due weight in the past has not been given to considerations of ecology and environment while sanctioning leases or actually conducting mining and quarrying operations in pursuance of the sanctioned leases. This needs to be effectively corrected forthwith. A set of guidelines needs to be evolved in this regard in consultations with the ecologists and environmentalists and the same should be rigorously enforced'.

The Uttar Pradesh Forest Corporation was set up in 1970 to replace the contractor system by public sector undertakings and forest cooperatives. However, the corporation is guided more by its financial viability rather than by any social purpose. The forest department claims that there are no differences in the basic objectives of the department and the organizers of the 'save forest' movement in terms of conservation and involving local people. But it would appear that this is not always true. For instance, the corporation appears to be grappling with the problem of its identity as a commercial or welfare organization and the conflicting expectations different groups have of it. Thus, reacting to the demand made by one of the Chipko activists for a complete moratorium on fellings, the department expressed the difficulty experienced by them in building an organization of a commercial nature in the teeth of opposition from the private sector, which then expected it to switch over from commercial to welfare and conservation work.

The genesis of the Chipko movement lies in the shortsighted forest policies followed by the British Raj and, after independence, by the Indian government (with a slight remodelling of the old system). No attempt was made to evolve a new system of forest management taking account of the pressing needs of forest dwellers. The state government in April 1959 appointed the 'Kumaon Forest Fact Finding Committee' to look into the grievances of the hill people and make recommendations to the government. The Forest (Conservation) Ordinance 1980, converted into an Act in 1981, took away any authority of the state government to de-reserve any 'reserved forest or use of forest land for non-forest purpose'. In 1982, it was announced that the Forest Act of 1927 would be replaced by a comprehensive Indian Forest Bill. However, due to strong reactions from people it has been shelved.

The genesis: Finding the strategy with women

Women shoulder the major burden of subsistence agriculture and cattle care, in addition to the drudgery of bringing fuel, fodder and water from long distances and their other domestic responsibilities. The economically non-viable fragmented land holdings are managed by women with little help from men. More then 95% women are cultivators in the Garhwal region. Forests provide an important resource base for goods and services, minor forest produce, firewood, medicinal herbs, fruits, etc. With the overexploitation of forest produce, fodder and fuel collection is becoming a full day's job for many women.

Firewood is obviously the biggest challenge in the absence of alternative energy sources and yet new energy technologies, i.e. improved wood stoves, bio-gas, etc have not made any headway because women are seldom involved in these exercises.

In 1973, a non-violent agitation against deforestation took shape in Garhwal to protest against the exploitative, commercial policies of the government. Describing Chipko as a civil disobedience movement, a forestry economist thinks that its 'modus operandi' is somewhat histrionic and involved physical interference with felling operations by embracing each marked, condemned tree in a desperate bid to rescue it from the lethal strokes of the axe-men. Despite its turbulent political genesis and boisterous mode of regimentation, its ideals are patriotically motivated and help in focusing attention on the crisis in Indian forestry.

The official viewpoint on the genesis of 'Chipko movememt' has a very different explanation to offer:

> Notwithstanding the significance of the name and the fact that initially the movement manifested itself in the form of protest against felling of trees by the forest contractors in government forests, its roots lay in the intense

feeling amongst the local people that they are not getting sufficient advantage out of the benefits flowing from the forest resources, the only worthwhile resources in the area, and even the contracts for its exploitation are secured mostly by the outsiders and they have been victim of neglect and exploitation.

Since 1977, voluntary agencies in this area have been pressing for a total moratorium on the felling of trees in this area. The incident that sparked off action in 1972–73 was the allotment of asti trees to a large sports goods manufacturing company while permission to cut a few asti trees to make agricultural implements for the village people was denied to a local organization.

The basic issue behind the first agitation in 1972–73 was the monopoly of the forest contractors and an assertion of local people's rightful share in the forest resources. The success gave a fillip to the movement. Questioning the entire system of forest management created awareness about the environmental degradation, thus broadening the perspective of the movement. The movement which originated from narrow economic issues developed into an environmental movement and since then has moved beyond the conservation dimension into a social movement through its afforestation programme.

It was women's action in Reni village in 1974, which added a new leaf in the history of the Chipko movement by forcefully bringing home the point that women have high stakes in protecting the forests. It also created an awareness among the local leadership concerning women's potential role in the movement. Till then women were never thought of as initiators but only as supporters who needed to be made aware of the problems and motivated to lend their support. The action of Reni came as a surprise to the male leadership. It has since then been publicized as a women's movement, as women are the real strength behind it.

> Notwithstanding the divergent opinion of the leaders (of the movement) the real strength of the movement are the women of the region. Except for a few organized events as at the Rampur Phata or Henwalghati, the Chipko Movement essentially consists of a string of spontaneous confrontations in which none of the so-called leaders were present. Women, acting entirely on their own rose up on the spur of the movement. While in Reni (Chamoli district) the protest was against a timber contractor, in all other cases the protest was against their own cash-hungry men, who could not care less if the forest was destroyed while their women had to walk for many more miles to collect their daily load of fuel and fodder.

Two faces of Chipko

Women's active participation in the movement has been acknowledged and written about. The narratives of a series of incidents that took place between 1973–83 are anecdotal and give an impression that women's participation in the movement was sporadic, basically in response to the immediate crisis, whether they were mobilized by Chipko activists or to save the forest from which they drew sustenance. Historical research is gradually digging up evidence of the crucial role women have played in peasant and workers' movements by providing vital support even in the radicalization of the movement. The loss of their traditional rights and privileges has often brought women into open confrontation if there is a rallying point for action.

Within the movement two alternative patterns of women's protests emerged. Even six years after the genesis of the movement women in many remote villages remained untouched by the ideology of the Gandhian organizations spearheading the movement. However, their reaction to the issue of deforestation was strong even without mobilization. Women may not understand the 'economics of the scientific management of the forest', but they are poignantly aware that the problems of their daily living are tied up with the destruction of forests. They are already conservation conscious. Fuel, fodder and water are women's issues. Energy issues are critical for women who have to keep the home fires burning.

In a remote village women fought not only the bureaucracy but also their cash-hungry men in the local panchayat who had agreed to sell the only forest in the vicinity to the state government for it to be converted into a potato farm. In recent years, evidence of increasing conflict between Mahila Mandal Dal (a grassroots organization of women) and the local panchayats is surfacing, causing C.P. Bhatt, at a recent seminar, to say that when it came to women's issues, panchayats were as bad as the bureaucracy. Women have asked why they are never consulted before a decision is taken to auction the forest, though it is they who collect forest produce. It is not only the decision-maker's concepts of development activities and the women's concept of development that is different, but there is also a gap between men's and women's interests. This issue emerged in one of the eco-development camps organized by a local organization where men wanted to plant 'fruit trees' while women wanted 'fuel and fodder trees'.

There is an increasing awareness among women of the continuing degradation of the natural environment. If we look back at this decade of development is there cause for optimism? A decade back the initiators of the movement would have found it a laughable idea to call Chipko a women's movement. Today it is known nationally and internationally for the crucial role women have played in the movement. Were the demographic and economic circumstances responsible for women emerging as a new interest group as they were the worst victims of the changing environment? Why then were they by-passed in organization-building efforts? Why did local women's organizations not make any successful bid in local power structures? Understanding many of these issues needs a deeper investigation into the nature of women's subsistence activities, nature of the production process, and the social and economic options within the family framework.

An analysis of events that took place in different parts of the Garhwal region suggests that in areas which were inaccessible or relatively isolated and where there was no organizational base for the mobilization of women, the action was spontaneous. In such cases the action resulted in a sharp conflict between women and men and between women and the local panchayats. During our interviews with Chipko activists from Garhwal, it was reported that whenever women take initiative in such matters, the male ego is hurt and they become hostile. From Henwalghati and Muniki Reti (a village near Rishikesh) several such incidents were reported.

The movement has not only sharpened conflicts between women and men but also between different economic strata. In Reni village when men returned to the village and heard of the heroic struggle of women, some of them who had hoped that the contract would bring them jobs and some cash inflow totally disapproved of the women's action. Their wrath fell on Gaura Devi who led the action. Only a small group of women supported her. But this apart, the very success of their action has divided the women coming from different strata. On our visit to Reni we could sense the tensions among the members of the Mahila Mangal Dal. In many cases the unity among women was fragile as the priorities of women from different sections were different. In her own style Gaura Devi told us about the large number of people who interviewed her and how this made women jealous of her. Some women asked why others too had not been given the same recognition for their contribution as had Gaura Devi.

Some very pertinent issues that were raised spontaneously by women have not been taken up either by the government or by any voluntary agencies who are leading this ecological conservation movement. Some of these deal with their representation in village panchayats, the fact that they should be consulted before any decision is taken either for deforestation, afforestation or about development activities. As far as the local panchayats are concerned, these continue to function without women's representation in total defiance of the provision in the Uttar Pradesh Panchayat Act which requires that if women are not elected then at least one/two women should be coopted/nominated as full members. One aspect that needs to be probed further is whether there exists a close relationship between women's activism and the process of politicization. Women who begin activism under the general banner of movements begin to develop some consciousness regarding women's issues. [. . .]

If one looks at the women who have taken active part earlier in the prohibition movement in the 60s and later in the Chipko movement and have participated on a more sustained basis, one finds that these are mostly older women in their forties and fifties, widows or single women. This was true both at Gopeshwar and at Reni. On the basis of such scanty evidence it is difficult to suggest any links but there is a strong suggestion that the structure of families and the age and sex-specific nature of family responsibilities could be a worthwhile dimension for an analysis of women's roles in the movements. Women's family labour remains their over-riding responsibility. Young married women are more constrained by their family responsibilities and kin-based authority patterns. Most of the analyses of the role of women in movements have tended to neglect the family and work dimensions. The mystification of women's experiences within the family, obscures the conflict of interests between the sexes in the sharing of resources, responsibilities, rewards and power. The strengthening of the patriarchal family through legal and economic policies has implications for women moving into conventional politics.

There is a sharp difference in women's and men's participation in popular movements. The social control mechanisms in a society which place a heavy premium on conformity by girls to sex mores makes it difficult for young unmarried girls in the rural areas to participate actively. The fear of rejection and conflict within the families is much greater in the case of young women than in the case of older women who wield more authority and have less work responsibility at home. Conversely the participation of young men in the movement has radicalized the movement. These asymmetrical response patterns in women's and men's participation in the popular movements and the nature of constraints need to be probed further.

The Chipko movement has given women a strong forum to articulate what obviously are women's concerns. However, their participation has not helped them in their own struggle against oppression although claims have been made that it is a 'feminist' movement.

~

DECOLONIZING THE NORTH
Vandana Shiva

The white man's burden is becoming increasingly heavy for the earth and especially for the south. The past 500 years of history reveal that each time a relationship of colonization has been established between the North and nature and people outside the North, the colonizing men and society have assumed a position of superiority, and thus of responsibility for the future of the earth and for other peoples and cultures. Out of the assumption of superiority flows the notion of the white man's burden. Out of the idea of the white man's burden flows the reality of the burdens imposed by the white man on nature, women and others. Therefore, decolonizing the South is intimately linked to the issue of decolonizing the North.

Gandhi clearly formulated the individuality of freedom, not only in the sense that the oppressed of the world are one, but also in the wider sense that the oppressor too, is caught in the culture of oppression. Decolonization in the North is also essential because processes of wealth creation simultaneously create poverty, processes of knowledge creation simultaneously generate ignorance, and processes for the creation of freedom simultaneously generate unfreedom.

In the early phases of colonization, the white man's burden consisted of the need to 'civilize' the non-white peoples of the world—this meant, above all, depriving them of their resources and rights. In the later phase of colonization, the white man's burden consisted of the need to 'develop' the third world, and this again involved depriving local communities of their resources and rights. We are now on the threshold of the third phase of colonization, in which the white man's burden is to protect the environment, especially the third world's environment—and this, too, involves taking control of rights and resources. [. . .]

Ethical decolonization

From the democracy of all life to man's empire over nature. Most non-western cultures have been based on the democracy of all life. As a schoolgirl, one lesson I learnt in the Hindi class was that human beings are part of *Vasudhaiva Kutumkam* or the earth family. As a part of the earth family, one participates in the democracy of all life. Rabindranath Tagore, our national poet, wrote that the peak of Indian culture consists in its having defined the principles of life in nature as the highest form of cultural evolution:

> The culture of the forest has fuelled the culture of Indian society. The culture that has arisen from the forest has been influenced by the diverse processes of renewal of life which are always at play in the forest, varying from species to species, from season to season, in sight and sound and smell. The unifying principle of life in diversity, of democratic pluralism, thus became the principle of Indian civilization.

As a source of life, nature was venerated as sacred, and human evolution was measured in terms of the human capacity to interact in harmony with her rhythms and patterns, intellectually and emotionally. In the final analyses, the ecological crisis is rooted in the mistaken belief that human beings are not part of the democracy of nature's life, that they stand apart from and above nature. For example, Robert Boyle, the famous scientist who was also the governor of the New England Company, saw the rise of mechanical philosophy as an instrument of power not just over nature but also over the original inhabitants of America. He explicitly declared his intention of ridding the New England Indians of their absurd notions about the workings of nature. He attacked their perception of nature 'as a kind of goddess', and argued that 'the veneration, wherewith men are imbued for what they call nature, has been a discouraging impediment to the empire of man over the inferior creatures of God'. 'Man's empire over the inferior creatures of God' was thus substituted for the 'earth family'.

This conceptual diminution was essential to the project of colonization and capitalism. The concept of an earth family excluded the possibilities of exploitation and domination, therefore a denial of the rights of nature and nature-based societies was essential in order to facilitate an uncontrolled right to exploitation and profits.

Scientific missions combined with religious missions to deny rights to nature. The rise of the mechanical philosophy with the emergence of the scientific revolution was based on the destruction of concepts of a self-regenerative, self-organizing nature which sustained all life. For Bacon, who is called the father of modern science, nature was no longer Mother Nature, but a female nature, to be conquered by an aggressive masculine mind.

While the ethical aspect of the ecological crisis can be traced to the white man's self-perceived burden as the only species with rights, the white man's burden is again seen as instrumental in solving the problems of the ecological crisis linked to the idea that the North's ethical discourse is generously expanding to concede rights to other peoples and other species. Most importantly, simultaneous with a pervasive Eurocentric assumption that an ethical expansion of rights to include nature in all its manifestations is taking place, is a blindness to the diminution and alienation of nature's rights at deeper levels than ever before, and a shrinkage of poor people's right to survival. This split is best exemplified in the area of biodiversity. While on the one hand, biodiversity conservation is ethically justified on the grounds of the intrinsic value and rights of all species to exist, developments in biotechnology are predicated on the assumption that species have no intrinsic worth. Species are being robbed of their rights. And since the ethics based on the democracy of all life makes no distinction between rights of nature and rights of human communities, this new violation of the rights of nature is intimately linked to the violation of rights of farmers, tribals and women as knowers and users of biodiversity. [. . .]

Economic colonization:
The growth of affluence, the growth of poverty

Two economic myths facilitate a separation between two intimately linked processes: the growth of affluence and the growth of poverty. Firstly, growth is viewed only as growth of capital. What goes unperceived is the destruction in nature and in people's subsistence economy that this growth creates. The two simultaneously created 'externalities' of growth—environmental destruction and poverty creation—are then causally linked, not to the processes of growth, but to each other. Poverty, it is stated, *causes* environmental destruction. The disease is then offered as a cure: growth will solve the problems of poverty and the environmental crisis it has given rise to in the first place. This is the message of World Bank development reports, of the Bruntland report, *Our Common Future* and of the UNCED process.

The second myth that separates affluence from poverty is the assumption that if you produce what you consume, you do not produce. This is the basis on which the production boundary is drawn for national accounting that measures economic growth. Both myths contribute to the mystification of growth and consumerism, but they also hide the real processes that create poverty. First, the market economy dominated by capital is not the only economy; development has, however, been based on the growth of the market economy. The invisible costs of development have been the destruction of two other economies: nature's processes and people's survival. The ignorance or neglect of these two vital economies is the reason why development has posed the threat of ecological destruction and a threat to human survival, both of which, however, have remained 'hidden negative externalities' to the development process.

Modern economics and concepts of development cover only a negligible part of the history of human interaction with nature. For centuries, principles of sustenance have given human societies the material basis of survival by deriving livelihoods directly from nature through self-provisioning mechanisms. Limits in nature have been respected and have guided the limits of human consumption. In most countries of the South, large numbers of people continue to derive their sustenance in the survival economy which remains invisible to market-oriented development. All people in all societies depend on nature's economy for survival. When the organizing principle for society's relationship with nature is sustenance, nature exists as a commons. It becomes a resource when profits and accumulation become the organizing principles and create an imperative for the exploitation of resources for the market. Without clean water, fertile soils, or crop and plant genetic diversity, human survival is not possible. These commons have been destroyed by economic development, resulting in the creation of a new contradiction between the economy of natural processes and the survival economy, because those people deprived of their traditional land and means of survival by development are forced to survive on an increasingly eroded nature.

While development as economic growth and commercialization are now recognized as the root of the ecological crisis in the South, they are, paradoxically, offered as a cure for the ecological crisis in the form of 'sustainable development'. The result is that the very meaning of sustainability is lost. The ideology of sustainable development is, however, contained within the limits of the market economy. It views natural resource conflicts and ecological destruction as separate from the economic crisis, and proposes a solution to that crisis in the expansion of the market system. As a result, instead of programmes of gradual ecological regeneration of nature's and the survival economy, the solution prescribed is the immediate and augmented exploitation of natural resources with higher capital investment. Clausen, as the president of the World Bank, recommended that 'a better environment, more often than not, depends on continued growth'. Later, Chandler further renewed the argument in favour of a market-oriented solution to ecological problems, believing that viable steps toward conservation can come only through the market.

Economic growth is facilitated through overexploiting natural resources, and this, in turn, creates a scarcity of those resources. Economic growth cannot help in the regeneration of the very spheres which must be destroyed to enable economic growth to take place; nature shrinks as capital grows. The growth of the market cannot solve the crisis it creates. Further, while natural resources can be transformed into cash, cash cannot be transformed into nature's ecological processes. But in nature's economy, the currency is not money, it is life. The neglect of people's economy and nature's economy is also linked to the failure to recognize production in these domains. In the self-provisioning economies of the South, producers are simultaneously consumers and conservers, but their production capacity is negated, and they are reduced to mere consumers. An illustration of this approach is the World Bank, World Resources Institute (WRI), International Union for the Conservation of Nature (IUCN), and World Wildlife Fund (WWF) programmes on biodiversity conservation. In such proposals, economic value is divided into the following categories:

* consumptive value: value of products consumed directly without passing through a market, such as firewood, fodder and game meat;
* productive use value: value of products commercially exploited; and
* non-consumptive use value: indirect value of ecosystem functions, such as watershed protection, photosynthesis, regulation of climate and production of soil.

An interesting value framework has thus been constructed which predetermines analyses and options. If the South's poor, who derive their livelihoods directly from nature, are only 'consumers', and the trading and commercial interests are the only 'producers', it follows quite naturally that the South is responsible for the destruction of its biological wealth, and the North alone has the capacity to conserve it. This ideologically constructed divide between consumption, production and conservation hides the political economy of the processes which underlie the destruction of biological diversity. Above all, it denies the South's role as the real donors to the North, in terms of biological resources, most primary commodities, and even in terms of financial resources. The first myth that needs to be abandoned in the decolonization of the North is that goods and finances flow only from the industrial economies to the South. In fact, in the 1980s, the South's poor countries have been massive exporters of capital. The net transfer of resources from South to North is US$50 billion per year. If the plants, germ plasm, cheap cassava, soya beans, fish and forest products that the South 'donates' to the North—insofar as the low commodity prices for these items reflect neither their environmental nor social value—are added, the reverse flow of resources is much greater. The South's poverty is generated through the very processes that generate the North's affluence.

Intellectual colonization:
The growth of knowledge, the spread of ignorance

Never before has human knowledge increased exponentially at such a high rate—never before has our ignorance about our world been deeper. And the ignorance has largely been created by the explosion of scientific knowledge.

When we consider the complexity and inter-relatedness of the cycles by which Gaia maintains her balances, the massiveness of the disruptions which we now impose on her, the primitive quality of the scientific materials by which we attempt to decipher her clues, then truly we can speak of a man-made ignorance, criminal or pitiful, depending on your point of view, in our relations with Gaia. A system of knowledge which enforces the 'ignorance of ignorance' has been assigned the prime place in creating the modern world. Science has been called the engine of growth and progress. On the one hand, contemporary society perceives itself as a science-based civilization, with science providing both the logic and the impulse for social transformation. In this aspect science is self-consciously embedded in society. On the other hand, unlike all other forms of social organization and social production, science is assumed to be value neutral and universal and thus is placed above society. It can neither be judged, questioned, nor evaluated in the public domain. As Sandra Harding has observed:

> Neither God nor tradition is privileged with the same credibility as scientific rationality in modern cultures ... The project that science's sacredness makes taboo is the examination of science in just the ways any other institution or set of social practices can be examined.

While science itself is a product of social forces and has a social agenda determined by those who can mobilize scientific production, in contemporary times scientific activity has been assigned the privileged epistemological position of being socially and politically neutral. Thus science takes on a dual character; it offers technological fixes for social and political problems, but absolves and distances itself from the new social and political problems it creates. Reflecting the priorities and perceptions of particular class, gender or cultural interests, scientific thought organizes and transforms the natural and social order. However, since both nature and society have their own organization, the superimposition of a new order does not necessarily take place in a faultless and orderly fashion. There is often resistance from people and nature, a resistance which is externalized as 'unanticipated side effects'. Science remains immune from social assessments, and insulated from its own impacts. Through this split identity the 'sacredness' of science is created.

The issue of making visible the hidden links between science, technology and society and making manifest and vocal the kind of issues that are kept concealed and unspoken, is linked with the relationship between the North and the South. Unless and until there can be social accountability from the structures of the science and technology, and the systems to whose needs they respond, there can be no balance and no accountability in terms of relationships between North and South. This need for accountability will be extremely critical, more so than ever before, in the biotechnology revolution. In the absence of binding international conventions that create ethical and political boundaries, the biotechnology revolution will increase the polarization between the North and the South and the rich and poor. The asymmetrical relationship between science, technology and society will become further skewed as one part of society has a monopoly of the knowledge and profits linked to the biorevolution, and the rest of society is excluded from the knowledge and benefits, while being forced to bear the ecological, political and economic costs. Without the creation of institutions of social accountability and social control, the South will become the laboratory, providing the guinea pigs and the dump yards for all the risks that are to come, while the benefits flow to the industrialized North. In fact, this has already started to happen; it is not a fear of the future, we are facing it already.

The UNCED process, instead of challenging the sanctity of science and technology and rendering these structures more transparent, actually makes technology more opaque, more mystical and magical. The environmental crisis was precipitated by the view that nature was inadequate, and that technology could improve on it. Now it seems that the dominant view is to propose the disease as the medicine, and 'technology transfer' has become the magical cure for every ecological illness.

To question the omnipotence of science and technology's ability to solve ecological problems is an important step in the decolonization of the North. The second step is linked to a refusal to acquiesce to the growing, pervasive power of 'intellectual property rights'. Even while the South still labours under the burden of older colonization processes, new burdens of recolonization are added. The General Agreement on Tariffs and Trade functions similarly to the old East India Company in demanding freedom for the North's financial and industrial interests and denying the South's citizens the freedom of their rights to survival—rights which are to be treated as 'non-tariff' trade barriers that interfere in global trade. As in the earlier phases of colonization, the South's original inhabitants are to be robbed of their rights as citizens to make way for the stateless corporations' rights as super-citizens in every state. Trade and plunder merge once again, especially in Trade-Related Intellectual Property Rights. The land, forests, rivers, oceans, having all been colonized, it becomes necessary to find new spaces to colonize because capital accumulation would otherwise stop. The only remaining spaces are those within—within plants, animals and women's bodies.

The construction of 'intellectual property' is linked to multiple levels of dispossession. At the first level, the creation of the disembodied knowing mind is linked to the destruction of knowledge as a commons. The Latin root of *private* property, *privare*, means 'to deprive'. The laws of private property which rose during the fifteenth and sixteenth centuries simultaneously eroded people's common right to the use of forests and pastures, while creating the social conditions for capital accumulation through industrialization. The new laws of private property were aimed at protecting individual rights to property as a commodity, while destroying collective rights to commons as a basis of sustenance.

Trade negotiations are a strange place for products of the mind to be discussed. Yet that is precisely what has happened with the rich countries of the North having forced the so-called TRIPs onto the agenda of the Uruguay Round of multilateral trade negotiations being held under the auspices of GATT. The multinationals of the North are sending their representatives to each country to ask for stricter intellectual property protection for everything that can be made in their laboratories. And with the new technologies, that includes life. From the MNCs' perspective, intellectual property rights are essential for progress and development. Those countries which do not have them are accused of putting national interest above 'internationally' accepted principles of fair trade. They insist that the assertion of intellectual property rights is essential in order to stimulate investment and research.

On the other hand, countries in the South, such as India, have adapted their patent laws to promote technology transfer and defend themselves against subjugation. They have modified patent terms, excluded vital sectors such as food and health from monopoly control and strengthened compulsory licensing by stipulating that patents must be used in local production processes or the patent rights will be forfeited.

During the 1960s and 1970s, these discussions took place through the United Nations system. But in the 1980s, the rich countries decided that the intellectual property discussions should be transferred from the UN, where the world's majority rules, to GATT, where the minority from the industrialized North effectively rules. The South's patent laws, designed to protect the public interest against monopolies, are no longer seen as a tool for development, but as a cover-up for economic embezzlement. The US international trade commissions estimate that US industry is losing anything between US$100 and 300 million due to 'weak' patent laws. If the stricter intellectual property rights regime demanded by the US takes shape, the transfer of these extra funds from poor to rich countries would exacerbate the current debt crises of the South ten times over. The MNCs, from which citizens need protection, are to have new power to monitor markets. The industrialized countries want bolder controls, seizure and destruction of infringing goods, imprisonment, forfeiture, criminal sanctions, fines, compensation and the like.

While market power is the apparent motivation for this drive to privatize and own life itself, the social acceptability of the changes derives from a world view that continues to see the white man as a privileged species upon whom other species (including other peoples) depend for survival and value.

The earth and the South have paid heavily for 500 years of the white man's burden. Probably the most significant step in striving towards re-establishing an earth community is the recognition that the democracy of all life is inconsistent with the idea that this beautiful planet is the white man's burden. Unlike the mythical Atlas, we do not carry the earth; the earth carries us.

5

~

VIOLENCE

When the women's movement burst forth onto the public stage in the years following the Emergency, it did so most dramatically under the banner of 'violence against women'. The issues they raised were both international and local, new and old. Campaigns against rape, for instance, were a feature of many women's movements across the world. Others, like the phenomenon of dowry deaths discussed in the introductory cluster, appeared distinctively Indian. Feminists interrogated widely shared assumptions about tradition and modernity when they discovered how much a product of contemporary forces the revival of sati in a state like Rajasthan could be; other scholarship challenged existing accounts of social reform by recasting the history of sati abolition in colonial Bengal.

The subject of violence throws up major questions in the context of this volume. As all the essays in this section will demonstrate, issues of violence against women have been difficult to name and recognize, whether shamed into invisibility, rendered inconsequential, or, on the contrary, transformed into acts of public religiosity. The problem has also been compounded by silences in women's studies, its initial failure to intervene and force the issue onto the academic agenda. Recall Vina Mazumdar's reflections from the opening cluster of essays, where she wonders why issues of violence (including dowry harassment) were not on their horizon when they prepared the *Towards Equality* report. Indeed, neither the dominant frameworks of 'the status of women' nor those of development and political economy more broadly, allowed for questions of violence until these were raised by activists. Even in a discipline like sociology, where women and gender find a prominent place in family, kinship and marriage, violence was not a recognized theme. In other words, forms of violence did not have an academic 'home' (unlike, say, politics, development and so on) and, for a long time, feminist scholarship lagged behind the work and involvements of activists. Another issue worth reiterating here is that it would be a mistake to equate violence with domestic violence, and it would be just as problematic to think that men are the only aggressors and women only victims. This was painfully learnt in the first campaigns against dowry deaths by in-laws. (See "Initiatives against Dowry Deaths" by Madhu Kishwar and Ruth Vanita in the first section.)

This cluster of essays begins with the first public campaign against rape that took place in the city of Hyderabad in 1978. Rameeza Bee, a visitor to the city with her husband, was brutally raped by four policemen and her husband murdered when he protested against their actions. A huge public outcry ensued as thousands of Hyderabadis attacked the police station, armed police were brought in, followed by gheraos, firings and a city-wide bandh. President's rule was required to quell the agitation. In the opening essay Kalpana Kannabiran investigates the unfolding of the legal case against the policemen, and shows just how—in spite of their evident guilt—they were exonerated. Rameeza Bee was turned into a 'prostitute', an unreliable Muslim woman who did not know the tenets of Islam, so that the actual rape itself could be dismissed as a non-issue. More than anything else, the collusions of the state apparatus were starkly laid bare. This came to a head in the Mathura Case a year later, which is discussed in the section on the law.

The next article by Sudesh Vaid focuses on sati. When Roop Kanwar, a young widow from a well-to-do family, committed sati in the village of Deorala in Rajasthan in 1987, the event triggered not only a major mobilization of conflicting forces, but also widespread and acrimonious debate among academics and activists. This turned into a battle that focused as much on the actual circumstances of her death (which began to look more and more like murder) as it did on what should be the frameworks of analysis for feminist politics. In relation to the general point made earlier about the overall lag in scholarship on the subject of violence, sati turns out to be an exception. Already in the early 1980s, feminists like Sudesh Vaid and Kumkum Sangari had explored the 'live' world of sati worship and its contemporary popularity in regions of Rajasthan, so that the widespread support that the Roop Kanwar incident subsequently evoked, however shocking, could not be dismissed as medieval barbarism. In the essay reproduced here, Vaid contextualizes the postindependence history of the Shekhawati region in particular, to reveal the range of interest groups and the combination of economic, social and cultural stakes fuelling the politics of widow immolation.

In a review article on domestic violence, Malavika Karlekar highlights the dearth of scholarship as well as the tendency to privilege marriage-related forms of violence in the existing literature. She proposes instead a 'life cycle' approach, beginning with the early prevalence of gender discrimination, including female infanticide and the selective abortion of female foetuses (foeticide), right up to the gender biases of old age. The sections of her review essay reproduced here focus on neglected forms of child abuse, and problems of reducing the multiple aspects of marital violence to dowry alone. The essay that follows shows how feminist literary criticism can illuminate the terrors of domestic violence in remarkable ways. Susie Tharu comments on the short story 'Mother' by the dalit writer Baburao Bagul, originally written in Marathi in the 1960s and made available in English translation in 1992. Revisiting many of the dominant themes opened up by the women's movement—widowhood, abuse, impoverishment—Tharu argues that the dalit movement, and especially the domain of dalit literature, offers a profound challenge. Within and beyond the scenes of the 'domestic', the perspectives of caste and untouchability reveal how the everyday structures of violence spell forms of annihilation in the relationships of *all* the characters inhabiting this dalit family—father, mother and, even, son.

The final contribution is by Urvashi Butalia and it takes us into present-day Kashmir. Since the late 1980s, Kashmir has come to represent the violence of unremitting conflict, as demands for self-determination appear lost amidst the myriad groups, the involvements of Pakistan and the counterinsurgency of the Indian security forces. Drawing parallels with the situation in the Northeast and in war-torn Sri Lanka, Butalia questions the invisibility of women in most accounts of the region, even though they are among the worst victims of the loss of life, assault and insecurity that people are living with. Her own project in the region has been to demonstrate the suffering of women (as well as their participation in the conflict), in order to explore the much more difficult question of what 'peace' might mean.

Today, therefore, we are a long way from the silences of a generation ago. It is clearer now that no phase of life or space is protected from violence; references are made to the violence of structures and not just individuals or groups, as phrases like 'the violence of development' have shown. Scholarship so far has been rather uneven and hesitant. At the same time, questions of violence recur in all the subsequent themes in this volume, indicative of further perspectives and fresh challenges in thinking about and struggling against the many ways we live in crippled worlds.

∾

RAPE AND THE CONSTRUCTION OF COMMUNAL IDENTITY
Kalpana Kannabiran

Rameeza Bee was eighteen years old when she was gang-raped by four policemen, one Hindu, and three Muslim, and her husband beaten to death, in 1978. There was public protest over her rape and the death of her husband, Ahmed Hussain. The police treated the angry crowd as an unlawful assembly and opened fire indiscriminately, resulting in further loss of life. After the firing, a commission of enquiry was set up with a sitting judge of the Andhra Pradesh High Court, a Muslim from a fairly affluent feudal background, being appointed to constitute the one-man commission. This was the time when the Bhargava Commission was enquiring into so-called 'encounter' deaths during the Emergency. (In 1975, Prime Minister Indira Gandhi declared a National Emergency in India to counter 'terrorist' activity and 'lawlessness'. A repressive eighteen months followed, during which all access to judicial redress was blocked, and there was total suspension of civil and democratic rights.) The terms of reference of the commission were confined to the assault on Ahmed Hussain, the causes of his death and the rape of Rameeza Bee.

By itself, a commission of enquiry is inquisitorial in nature and cannot pronounce an enforceable judgement. The state government did not take any steps to assist the commission in the conduct of the enquiry apart from providing the infrastructure. There were no instructions from the home secretary to the police department to assist the commission in procuring witnesses, etc.; on the contrary, the government went out of its way to shield the delinquent policemen. As a result, the police department tried to exploit the bias against Rameeza Bee on account of her alleged 'prostitution', and against Ahmed Hussain who they alleged was a pimp. No effort was made to prove that she was not raped. The forensic experts had been bought over and the Special Branch had intervened in the preparation of the postmortem report on Ahmed Hussain which said that he died of cardiac arrest. Justice Muktadar found the policemen guilty of the offences of rape, assault and murder with a common intention to commit all three. He recommended that they be prosecuted. An investigation was conducted and chargesheets filed against them. The accused then moved the Supreme Court of India on the plea that since a sitting judge of the AP High Court was the one-man commission of enquiry, his subordinate judiciary was likely to be biased in his favour. The matter was transferred to the district judge of Raichur, Karnataka state, who acquitted the policemen. This was made possible because the evidence recorded in a commission of enquiry cannot be used in a prosecution. At this point a women's group, Vimochana of Bangalore, filed a review petition and compelled the state government to proffer an appeal, which was dismissed.

Official discourse on Rameeza's rape

What was Rameeza's background? To quote her:

> When I was a young girl I was married to a person. I do not remember how old I was at the time of my first marriage. I do not remember how long I

was married to my first husband, but I left him about a year and a half ago. I reached puberty about a month and a half ago from today ... My first husband did not like me and I did not like him. I left my first husband and got married to Ahmed Hussain. I was in love with Ahmed Hussain before I reached puberty ... Both Ahmed Hussain and I used to go for agricultural labour.

Rameeza Bee was picked up by two policemen while her husband was answering a call of nature. In her cross-examination, set up by the commission of enquiry to investigate the case, this act of her husband's which had no bearing on the case whatsoever became a crucial factor, as is evident from Rameeza's replies:

> I did not tell Mr. Bari that my husband went into a graveyard for purposes of answering the call of nature. Where my rickshaw was standing I saw a graveyard ... I do not know whether Muslims respect Muslim graveyards or not. I do not know whether the Muslims put flowers on the graves and whether they perform fateha and I do not know that Muslims consider it a bad thing in desecrating the graveyards by answering calls of nature or urinating there.

Rameeza was not the only one to be subjected to questions regarding her knowledge of Islam. Malan Bi, mother of the deceased Ahmed Hussain, also had to defend herself against accusations of procuring girls for brothels. An important part of Malan Bi's cross-examination, however, had to do with the validity of Rameeza's marriage to Ahmed Hussain from the standpoint of Islamic law:

> I know that according to the principles of Islam a marriage cannot take place unless the nikah is performed. At my marriage, nikah was performed. No nikah was performed at the marriage of Rameeza Bee to Ahmed Hussain, but before four respectable persons, garlands were exchanged and betel nuts distributed. I know that in Islam the relationship between a man and a woman without the performance of a nikah is illegal. I do not know whether my brother Imam Saheb is keeping Sambakka without performing any nikah with her.

Demonstrating the illegality of Rameeza's marriage on the one hand, and furnishing proof of her complicity in and links with prostitution on the other, served to prepare the ground for the argument that her rape did not constitute a violation of any kind—either of her person or of the law—and that being a prostitute rationalizes rape, which then ceases to be an offence.

The crucial testimonies for the defence in Rameeza's case were those of Qutubuddin and a couple of women who asserted that Rameeza was, like them, a prostitute by profession. The testimonies of both women point very clearly to the fact that they were set up by the police. Qutubuddin, the uncle of Ahmed Hussain's first wife, Shahazadi Bi, says in his testimony,

I work as a mason wherever I get a job . . . I have given up my mason's job and am now selling fish and mangoes. The Transport Minister telephoned Ali Saheb, Panchayat Board member, and he contacted me to get all this information.

And what is the 'information' he procures?

Rameeza Bee had married another person about two years ago . . . I learnt that she was married a second time at Mandlam . . . Why should I now say as to how many men Rameeza Bee got married to and with whom she had been living? I got to know that she got married to a man named Noor Ahmed. I personally do not know anything about the second marriage of Rameeza Bee with Noor Ahmed. It is all hearsay. I do not know whether Rameeza Bee got married to Ahmed Hussain . . . The character of Rameeza Bee is wayward. I have only heard and did not see about the behaviour or bad character of Rameeza Bee. I heard that she was friendly with the son of one Sattar. And also she was friendly with Rahmatulla. I have not seen Rameeza Bee with these people at all.

According to Ahmed Hussain's first wife, Shahzadi Bi, however:

My husband was a mason. While working as a mason, he started the business of selling stones. My husband was never acting as a pimp or indulging in immoral traffic. My mother-in-law was working as a midwife in Nandikotkur. I came to know of my husband's death through Qutubuddin. Qutubuddin also told me that the government is giving a compensation of Rs 2000. A policemen had also come to my house. Qutubuddin brought me to Hyderabad for filing the petition . . . I do not know what language the petition is in. I also did not say anything about Rameeza Bee. If she says she does not lay claim to the compensation given by the government, but I am entitled to the compensation. I am quite happy . . . They brought me here representing that they will get me Rs. 2000.

Although Shahzadi Bi's testimony exonerates Rameeza and Ahmed Hussain and Malan Bi, and is clearly based on facts, it was marginalized in the trial. The entire evidence for the case was built around the fact that Rameeza Bee was a prostitute, or that she had, in any case, married so many times that the fact of rape itself was inconsequential.

Further, from the point of view of the state, non-conformity on the part of Muslims to the tenets of Islam justifies the aggression perpetrated on them by the state in collusion with the dominant community. Conformity to Muslim religious law in this case is defined and assessed by the state and its agencies, not by the minority community. The agencies of the state were therefore communalizing an issue that had nothing to do with religion. Before going into the complicity of the state in legitimizing majority domination, there is a further dimension to this entire case that needs elaboration. Among the political parties that supported Rameeza, were the Left groups and the Majlis Ittehadul Mussalmeen, which is a Muslim fundamentalist organization. It would be useful to look briefly at the history of this organization.

Unlike the rest of Andhra Pradesh, Hyderabad before independence was a princely state governed by the Nizam, part of the British Paramountcy. The Nizam's state of Hyderabad spanned most of the Deccan Plateau, with a total area of approximately 82,000 square miles. It had a predominantly Hindu population, while Urdu-speaking Muslims accounted for 12 per cent of the entire population of the state. Feudal ownership of land by the zamindars and their proprietorial rights over peasants made Telengana an area with the greatest feudal exploitation in the Nizam's government. In 1947, when the Indian Union declared independence, the Nizam refused to join the Union and instead attempted to establish Hyderabad as an independent state. At this point, the Ittehadul Mussalmeen, which started in 1927, became active through its paramilitary wing, the Razakars. The Ittehadul Mussalmeen was set up to protect the political and cultural rights of the Muslims and to ensure their continued dominance. Between 1940 and 1946, the organization had built up a corps of armed volunteers who had been given regular military training. These armed volunteers were the Razakars who let loose a reign of terror in the city and rural areas immediately after independence, to continue what they perceived as Muslim hegemony. In September 1948, the Indian government sent in the Union Army, forced the Nizam to surrender and disbanded the Razakars. A revived Majlis Ittehadul Mussalmeen was now supporting Rameeza.

One argument, and a quite valid one, given the history and politics of the Majlis, is that the Majlis was trying to communalize the issue. Far more significant, however, is the fact that the interest of the Majlis in the case put the state on the defensive, and Rameeza, quite literally, became the ground on which the battle for hegemony was fought all over again. And we know by now that this battle had a long and tortuous history in Hyderabad. I would contend that the arguments of the defence and the rhetoric of the Ittehadul Mussalmeen addressed and reinforced each other, and the fact of Rameeza's rape or Ahmed Hussain's death was lost in the process. The entire experience—the defence, the marginalization of protest and the marginalization of the recommendations of the commission—is a lesson in minority experience.

Understanding Rameeza's experience

Although it is impossible to generalize from one instance, the Rameeza Bee trial brings into focus important issues pertaining to the functioning of state apparatuses in India and the norms that govern them. These norms are set by the majority community, that is upper caste Hindu, and no Muslim woman (or dalit woman as we see in instances of upper caste violence) can register any grievance especially against the agencies of the state.

While theoretically, the power to set up norms for governance undoubtedly rests with the state, we are speaking here of a situation that is far more complex than appears to be at first sight. To begin with, although secularism is the basis of the Indian state, a consideration of national communal politics and nationalism both in the colonial and postcolonial periods unearths serious contradictions between professed ideology and practice in India.

After Partition, policy-makers in India defined secularism not merely as a separation of religion and politics, but as a separation of religion from public affairs, and insisted that religion remain a private matter for the individual. Alongside this effort there was also a keenness, especially on Nehru's part, to win the confidence of the Muslims who were still feeling besieged by the events surrounding Partition. The common civil law was therefore set aside; religion was separated from politics, but not from law—which in fact was more crucial to the secular identity of the state. The Muslims also perceived secular law as a threat to their interests, a continuation of their already grave dispossession. The loss of privileges and dim material prospects were reinforced by the communal atmosphere that prevailed in the country and its effect on Muslims. For one thing, their loyalty to the country was suspect. With Hindu communalism and militancy finding a raison d'etre in the massive influx of refugees from west Punjab and east Bengal, there was a greater and more vigorous insistence on Muslims to prove that their sympathies did not lie with the secessionists in Kashmir or the Razakars in Hyderabad.

For the minorities, as for the Indian state, compensation for material dispossession could be sought through the exercise of control over women. This was made relatively easy by enshrining freedom of religion as one of the fundamental rights in the Indian Constitution. The corollary of the right to freedom of religion was that each community in India would continue to be governed by its own personal laws. These laws govern all matters relating to the family—marriage, divorce, custody and guardianship, succession and inheritance, and adoption. So while we have the elegantly enunciated ideal of secularism, on the one hand, political practice in India, the politics of the Indian National Congress as well as that of the major national parties, has been structured along communal and caste lines, to the extent that hierarchies within, say the Congress, have more often than not, replicated hierarchies outside. In this context, the Indian state, which with minor exceptions has been constituted by the Congress throughout the postcolonial period, has absorbed the dominant upper caste Hindu norms of the Congress, along with the ideal of secularism. This is demonstrated in instances where, although the agencies of the state itself are not directly responsible for acts of violence, their complicity with the aggressors is established by refusing to press charges against those of the dominant group responsible for the violence. This, as I have asserted elsewhere, is also true for dalit women.

What implication does this have for women? Let us take Rameeza's instance. She was a victim of gang-rape. First she had to prove that she was not a prostitute; second that she was not a woman of loose character who had married several men before cohabiting with Ahmed Hussain; third, that she was in fact legally married to Ahmed Hussain; fourth, that she was a good Muslim and knew and respected the tenets of Islam, as presented by the Hindu state and so on. The fact of rape in her case is lost in a maze of considerations that in no way disprove the rape: on the contrary, they effectively justify it.

Given the fact that women are trapped in battles of identity and that their access to secular criminal and civil justice is limited in serious ways by the aggressive identity politics that is legitimized by the state we, as feminists, need to comprehend the complexity of the situation. A serious consequence of the official definition of secularism is that it places women firmly within the family and community. In doing this it denies them equal citizenship and access to democratic, civil and criminal justice systems; and by legitimizing male control within the family and community, it pushes all those women who cannot be placed within the family outside the purview of law, thus sanctioning all manner of aggression against them without providing any access to democratic justice. This denial of access has serious consequences for all women, especially family women: all that needs to be done in instances of aggression or rape in their case is to prove that they are not the property of any man—that they are prostitutes. And a prostitute, or worse still, an independent single woman, by definition, has no constitutional or democratic rights in this society.

~

POLITICS OF WIDOW IMMOLATION
Sudesh Vaid

The Shekhawati region, which lies close to Jaipur district, has in the post-independence period witnessed a deliberate and organized effort to revive the practice of widow immolation. At present the region consists of Sikar and Jhunjun districts, but both administratively and culturally, it earlier embraced a wider territory.

What is notable is that during neither the medieval nor the colonial period was this region particularly known for this practice. The Shekhawat chieftains paid tribute to the Amber (Jaipur) rulers, to whom they were linked as a branch of the ruling Kachwaha clan. There are few instances of the burning of ranis and other women of the zenana on the death of Amber rulers. One of them even tried to totally abolish the practice. Again during colonial rule, from the recorded instances of sati in the Rajputana Agency during 1818–1873, it appears there were very few satis from this area.

It was the Marwar (Jodhpur) and Mewar (Udaipur) rulers who gave wide sanction to widow immolation, and made it virtually an institutionalized practice to be observed on the death of the ruler or leading chieftains. Through Col. Ludlow's efforts, in fact, Jaipur was the first of the 18 states of the Rajputana Agency to abolish sati and make it a penal offence (1846). At that time, leading Shekhawati chieftains had given their public assent to the abolition legislation. Though there must have been sporadic incidents of sati, the small decayed memorials to medieval or colonial period satis in the area indicate that the practice had ceased to have socio-religious significance attached to it.

The present revival has been led by the three upper castes of the area— the rajputs, mahajans and banias (drawn from sub-castes belonging to the local agarwal trading community), and brahmins, bhats and charans, who were earlier dependent on the patronage of the rajput rulers. The significant role of the brahmins, bhats and charans may not be very overt at present, but it is necessary, nevertheless, to pay attention to these groups. The brahmins as priests, and the bhats and charans as bards and geneaologists, were important caste and social groups who invested widow immolation with heroic valour and religious merit. The former gave it religious sanction while the latter gave it a place within the 'glories' of family history and rajput 'custom' and 'tradition'.

But the relationship of these groups to the rajput rulers and thakurs was not simply one of dependence. They were landowners, thanks to the extensive practice of making land grants to temples and to individual priests and bards. (In fact, entire villages of brahmins, charans or bhats are still to be found.) On these three castes rested the legitimacy of the power of the rajputs. Apart from their role in the political sphere, they were important in the social sphere and in family life. They regulated and maintained clan and caste superiority, arranged matrimonial alliances and played a determining role in the lives of women, particularly the rajput male *veerta* was the combined making of these groups, with all its prescriptive implications for rajput women—namely to uphold its 'feminine' counterpart, jauhar and sati. This investing of sati with material valour was carried, via Col. Todd's romantic narratives of such events, to the Indian middle classes in other parts of the country and has formed a staple of Hindu cultural nationalism from the late nineteenth century onwards to the present times.

Along with the rajputs, after the abolition of the princely states and the jagirdari and zamindari system of land relations, these caste groups are no longer in a position to economically and socially exploit other social and caste groups as they did in the pre-independence era. Some have joined various middle class professions, both in the rural and urban areas, but, through caste and family networking, they are lending support to the rejuvenation of the practice of sati. It is not accidental, for instance, that the so-called 'living sati' at Devipura (prevented in 1985) asked for instructions from a guru at Triveni temple located at a stone's throw from the village, that a guru from the same temple was also associated with a sati at Hathideh (1977), or that a priest who officiated at the sati at Jhadli (1979) and wrote booklets in honour of the 'satimata' had links both with the Hathideh family and the Triveni math. It may be noted that Deorala is located only a few kilometres from the math.

Let us turn now to the other groups involved—the mahajans and the rajputs. The former do not appear to have had a dominant role during earlier periods, though there are a number of instances of sati from this community in medieval times. This is not surprising, as the leading mahajans were close to the durbar and, as financiers and administrators, had various honorific titles conferred on them by the ruler. Further, due to the *ijara* system prevalent in the Jaipur area, they had a firm base in the agrarian economy. As traders, moneylenders and bankers they were close to village-level thakurs. Both the ruler and the thakurs wooed them to set up commercial centres within their territory, thereby creating a network among them within the entire region. Among such centres were Ramgarh, Sikar, Lakshmangarh, Fatehpur, Nawalgarh and Jhunjunu.

But it was the colonial period, often termed, 'the golden age of the banias', which gave a tremendous boost to the fortunes of both impoverished banias and rich mahajans. The opening of the Delhi–Calcutta railway route in 1860 saw thousands of agarwals from this region spread all along the Gangetic belt to Assam, Bengal, Orissa, and further into Burma and parts of Southeast Asia. Calcutta soon became the headquarters of marwari capital amassed through cotton, jute, oilseeds and opium trade as well as through banking and speculation. As is well-known, the Burrabazar area of Calcutta, which recently saw demonstrations and a bandh call by pro-sati marwaris, is the business locality dominated by traders from this and other areas of Rajasthan.

The Shekhawati traders prospered with the advent of independence and now head some of the leading industrial and business houses of the country. Among them are the Jhunjunwalas, the Khaitans, the Poddars, the Kanodias, etc. Although these industrialists and businessmen have ceased to have the local economic interests they previously had in the pre-independence era, they maintain links with Shekhawati through the huge sati temples they have set up in the region.

The most well-known of these is of course the Rani Sati temple at Jhunjunu, commemorating a medieval Agarwal sati. A legend has now been created concerning this sati whose insignificant memorial has been transformed into a huge marble temple complex sprawling over many acres. Apart from the main shrine to Narayani Devi, daughter of a trader from Hissar, now termed 'Rani', are twelve smaller shrines named, for want of their original names, after various goddesses of the Hindu pantheon. Although some building had started in the earlier decades of the twentieth century, it was in the post-independence period, notably from the fifties on, that the huge temple complex, still undergoing expansion, acquired its present shape. During the same period the annual mela was started, which coincides with the first Rajput sati in Sikar district (1954), of which more later. A Rani Sati Girls Primary School with 175 students was started in 1961, near the temple. In 1986 a new section to the temple and a fifty-one kilo gold *kalash* were added. In addition, a month long Shashtra Chandi Mahayagya was conducted by a large number of priests. The state governor was one of the notable VIPs to bless the activities.

The Rani Sati Sarva Sangh is the managing trust of the temple, and its several branches throughout the country and abroad had by 1983 set up no less than 105 Rani Sati temples in different towns and cities. The devotees of this new devi cult naturally maintain that they are only worshipping a family sati. But their lavishing crores of rupees for temple building activity on mouldering medieval sati mounds as well as on cremation sites of fresh victims in the vicinity, no matter of which caste, belies their claims. In the past three decades, it is these temples with their annual melas, booklets, posters, *jankis,* cassettes, etcetera which have been pumping a refurbished ideology of sati and *nari dharma* into the area. It is noteworthy that all the incidents of sati have taken place within an hour or two of Jhunjunu temple, which lies close to Udaipurvati tehsil across the border in Sikar district.

Udaipurvati was and continues to be the stronghold of the Shekhawati Rajputs. During the 1930s, it was the contesting ground for the conflict between the Rajput landowners and the jats, the principal cultivating caste in the area. During the fifties, the Rajasthan Land Reform and Resumption of Jagirs Act (1952, amended 1954) provoked an anti-land reform agitation headed by the Kshatriya Mahasabha, comprised of ex-rulers and big jagirdars. On its coming to a favourable settlement with the government in 1954, the agitation was withdrawn, to be immediately followed by the agitation of the Bhuswami Sangh, representing the interests of the small landholders. Like the Kshatirya Mahasabha, the Bhuswami sangh mediated its anti-land reform agitation through a potent cultural ideology combining rajput 'identity' and militant Hinduism.

For the rajputs and their dependent caste groups, land reforms were a threat both to their economic and social power. The *thikanedars* (big jagirdars) had not only civil and judicial powers, but police functions as well. Thana rights and privileges were commonly bought by sub-grantees, often clansmen and relatives of the principal thakur. Under the *kath* system they were entitled to impose fines and punish offenders with a range of cruel physical tortures. The loss of coercive powers to collect agrarian and non-agrarian levies affected not only the large landowners, but also the sub-infeudatories down to the holder of one or two bighas of land. The non-agrarian levies numbered as many as twenty-nine in many areas, including, for instance, levies like '*baiji ka hath kharach*' (contributions towards the marriage of a thakur's daughter often levied from her birth), '*mataji ki bhent*' (presents for the thakur's mother), '*karaj kharach*' (levies on the death of a thakur's relative), etc. Such rights gave the most impoverished rajput a sense of solidarity with his richer clansmen and a stake in his caste identity.

The Shekhawati region not only had the jagirdari system but also the *bhoomichara* system of land tenure; the *bhoomias* deemed their land personal property, not a grant from the local ruler or thakur. However they also styled themselves 'jagirdars'. Due to the principle of equal division of land among male heirs followed among the Shekhawats, barring a few exceptions, there has been extreme fragmentation of land over the past two centuries. Many of the *bhoomias,* for example, have tiny land holdings. As such they need to supplement their incomes from non-agrarian sources. Some have taken to business and academic professions, but right from the colonial period when the Shekhawati Brigade was formed, they have joined the army in large numbers. They have been recruited into the police force. As such the military and police service gives them a sense of continuing their 'martial' tradition as 'kshatriyas'. It is such Shekhawats who rallied to the call of the Bhuswami Sangh. Notably, along with the ex-army man, Danta Singh, another leading figure in the Bhuswami Sangh was Bhairon Singh Shekhawat, a *bhoomia* who had been a police inspector in Jammu state.

It is such middle class leaders that were recently able to mobilize thousands of small *bhoomias* for 'religious dedication' in the defence of 'ancient rights to the soil'. The leaders addressed tens of thousands of lathi-bearing saffron-clad rajputs with exhortations to remember that their ancestors had fought for 'dharma' and that their women had committed jauhar. Thus the jagirdars and bhoomias fought the economic and social interests through the ideology of the erstwhile rajput ruling class. They claimed for themselves the 'tradition' and 'heritage' constructed by local bards and by nationalist historians—of Rana Pratap of Mewar and Chittor, of the 'heroic rajputs' defending Hindu dharma and the 'motherland', and the 'heroic rajpootni' committing jauhar and sati.

The agitation came to an end by 1956. That it had a tremendous role in preparing the social soil for sati in this area can be seen from the fact that the first sati here occurred in 1954, and the expansion of the Jhunjunu temple started around the same period. Some details of this sati are worth noting as they provide an insight into the making of the practice and ideology of sati now current in the area.

Thought the incident took place in a village, Madhav-ka-vas, both the victim herself and the family were by no means uneducated. Taradevi, belonging to a rajput chauhan family of Hissar, had studied up to standard VIII. Her father was a subedar in the army and her maternal uncle is headmaster of a school in Hissar. Both his daughters, in fact, are teachers. The uncle, moreover, seems to have travelled widely. Taradevi was married to Ugam Singh, a Shekhawati rajput and younger son of the village thakur. Her elder sister was already married to Ugam Singh's older brother. Herself childless, she had arranged her younger sister's marriage into the family, possibly with an eye to adopting her children. Taradevi, during her eight years of married life, had two daughters but only one son. The son, presently sole trustee of the temple, went to high school in Kanwat. When her husband died after a 40-day illness, Taradevi's son was only two years old, and her infant daughter barely twenty-two days old.

The official family version is that Taradevi made up her mind to commit sati at the suggestion of her dying husband. On his death, she did not shed any tears and personally chose a site for the cremation on family land near the entrance to the village, in front of which runs a railway line. She dressed herself in bridal finery, asked that information be spread in the village, and led the procession. She also personally instructed the pundit in the performance of various rituals. The procession was accompanied by band-baja and her relatives, carrying swords, 'protected' her during the procession and at the cremation site. The arthi or bier was carried by minor children of the family, the sati asked the two-year-old son to touch the pyre, which lit itself.

A few hours before her death, Taradevi miraculously bestowed a well on the village. She raised her hand and a well sprang up in the courtyard. Thousands flocked to see the young woman's immolation, a bazaar sprang up, a temple trust was immediately formed. An annual mela is being held at Madhav-ka-vas since 1955, for which an otherwise unscheduled stop of the train facilitates the coming of devotees and commerce. The temple and rooms for pilgrims were funded by rajputs and businessmen and the ex-rulers of Jaipur and Jodhpur, along with important politicians, have visited the marble temple and lent support to its activities.

It is clear that the perpetrators of the crime well knew that it is against the law and that due care was taken to have minors perform a crucial part of it. Taradevi's three brothers-in-law and the pundit who performed the *havan* were arrested shortly after the event, but no one was convicted. In fact, stories of miracles prominently tackle the problem created by what little police action was taken. Reportedly, handcuffs fell off the offenders' wrists three times, the son of the SI fell ill, and the sati devi appeared in a dream to warn him against 'harrassing' her relatives. The local police officer and the collector, 'awed' by these sundry miracles, themselves reverently worshipped the 'sacred' spot. An unbeliever among the railway officials was immediately sent a divine warning through a minor accident on the railway tracks. What about the normal humane feelings of compassion at a human being suffering the tortures of fire? This too was conveniently taken care of. Taradevi's mother in a dream asked her daughter how she could have borne the pain of live burning. The daughter replied with serenity that she had not suffered at all, the fire was like bathing in water, an '*agni snanan*'.

In this particular case, inheritance appears to be an underlying motive for carrying out the sati. Taradevi's father-in-law's land was equally divided between his four sons. Before the event occurred, some land had already been allocated to tenants under the land reform laws, for which the family later received government compensation. What was divided among the sons was still substantial, about a 100 bighas each. The choice of the site not only secured a certain amount of land from government appropriation, but also secured it for Taradevi's children, and for her childless sister, who became their guardian. On Taradevi's death, the inheritance of two brothers could thus be consolidated for the single son and heir, and family disputes averted. Notably, the maternal uncle who played a pivotal role in setting up the temple, nominated the infant son as its sole trustee. When the sati's elder sister herself became a widow nine months later, rumours immediately circulated that she had not wept, a 'sign' that she too would commit sati. She had to send an urgent message to her father, who sought police intervention. She escaped her sister's fate through armed police accompanying the bier to prevent a second immolation. Had she too been burnt, the property would have devolved upon the two surviving brothers.

Later satis in the area have tended mainly to come from impoverished families in strained circumstances. It must be emphasized here that all the victims were burnt by the in-laws, and the natal family was never informed before the event. The *sasural* family is clearly the principal in perpetrating the crime. In this they are abetted by the village *mukhia* and elites. What makes sati different from the other related crime of burning a daughter-in-law is that the murder is a public event, 'endowed' with religious sanctity, invoking the 'kshatriya tradition' of 'heroic death' and 'glorious Hindu womanhood'. Through it emerges a reinforcing of *pativrata dharma*. In the hagiographical accounts constructed about the sati, the victim is made into an exemplar of a dutiful, pious daughter and *bahu* and symbol of conjugal love and sacrifice. Thus the oppressed are made to furnish a victim, whose 'willed' death serves to keep other women in patriarchal subordination in their daily lives.

The present iconography of sati in the area, the trishul, embodies the convergence of several interest groups and ideological currents—assertions of a 'glorious' rajput communal identity, aspirations to kshatriya status by the business community, militant Hindu revivalism, the attempt to have hegemonic control by the upper castes—all fuelling a reassertion of patriarchal norms of women. Hence the fury of the onslaught against those who protest the mystification of this crime. The well-orchestrated propaganda emanating not only from the Dharm Rashka Samiti but from a wide spectrum of pro-sati ideologues in the press and the universities attests to the deep stakes—economic, social, cultural—that the revived practice of sati in the Shekhwati region has for the postcolonial upper and middle class in rural and urban India. A new configuration of caste/class social forces has appeared, but it is obfuscating its interests as it wears the mask of an 'ancient' and 'timeless' anti-women practice. It is utilizing existing structures of religious belief and ritual to gain mass support, thereby projecting a micro-level phenomenon of a small area as 'Hindu' and even 'Indian' culture. In this it has raised the most dangerous of mythologies of femininity that the democratic movement in the post-1947 period has had to struggle against.

⚬

DOMESTIC VIOLENCE
Malavika Karlekar

Introduction: Definition of violence

[. . .] There is surprisingly little material available in the form of books or academic essays or papers on the entire issue of violence against women in India; despite the fact that a battery of statistics and reports made available by official sources and the media reinforce the view that this form of gendered violence is fast becoming a feature of daily living in contemporary India, it has yet to become a priority area of research. Further, of what is available, about half relates to violence within the family (Vyas 1996). In Patricia Uberoi's (1995) opinion, this silence is explicable by a certain hesitance in subjecting the family and its intimate relationships to scrutiny; at the same time, if there is any data base on the nature and kind of violence that goes on behind locked doors, it has become available largely due to the activists of NGOs, those in the women's movement and the police. [. . .]

Put simply, violence is an act of aggression, usually in interpersonal interaction or relations. It may also be aggression of an individual woman against herself, such as suicide, self-mutilation, negligence of ailments, sex determination tests, food denial and so on. Basically, then, violence brings into question the concept of boundary maintenance and a sense of self as well as a perception of another's autonomy and identity. It implies that when the body—and indeed the self—is vulnerable to violation, individuals have a very different notion of 'what is one's body and what is done to one's body' (Litke 1992, 174). Indian scholars in the field of women's studies have emphasized the dynamics of power and powerlessness involved in a violent act. It is a coercive mechanism 'to assert one's will over another, to prove or to feel a sense of power' (Litke 1992, 174).

Given that violence is not limited to any single group, 'it can be perpetuated by those in power against the powerless or by the powerless in retaliation against coercion by others to deny their powerlessness' (Poonacha 1999). Further, Govind Kelkar situates violence against women 'in the socio-economic and political context of power relations'. She feels that the view that violence is 'an act of illegal criminal use of force' is inadequate and should include 'exploitation, discrimination, upholding of unequal economic and social structures, the creation of an atmosphere of terror, threat or reprisal and forms of religio-cultural and political violence' (Kelkar 1991, 1).

This wide definition of violence finds resonance in a hierarchical society based on exploitative gender relations. Violence often becomes a tool to socialize family members according to prescribed norms of behaviours within an overall perspective of male dominance and control. The family and its operational unit, the household, are the sites where oppression and deprivation of individual psyches and physical selves are part of the structures of acquiescence: often enough, those being 'moulded' into an acceptance of submission and denial are in-marrying women and children. Physical violence, as well as less explicit forms of aggression, are used as methods to ensure their obedience. At every stage in the life cycle, the female body is both the object of desire and of control. [. . .]

The abused child

An area in which there is little available research is that of child abuse within the home. This includes sexual aggression, beating, as well as extracting hours of labour from children who should be in school or at play. Nonetheless, nearly all available studies have shown that children are victims of substantial abuse of a physical, psychological, and emotional nature (MARG 1996). In part, this abuse is caused by the life situation of families, where, for instance, children become part of the labour force due to poverty. Recent studies have shown that, in absolute terms, child labour is on the increase, particularly for those who work as marginal workers. For girls, the expansion has been dramatic in both rural as well as urban areas. Neera Burra (1995) has divided child labour into four categories—those who work in factories, workshops, and mines; those who are bonded; street children; and children who form part of the familial labour force. Working in inhuman conditions, often for a pittance, children are abused at work and within homes where their earnings become the property of their parents. Not unexpectedly, then, child labour has become an emotive issue resulting in a sense of moral outrage in the international community and the concomitant boycott of products using this form of labour; however, banning child labour is a simplistic response to a much deeper problem, which lies embedded in structures of power, availability of alternatives and schooling, as well as the overall immiseration of at least a third of the population. For those children who do not work for a wage but contribute to the family workforce, leisure, education, and anything remotely regarded as the rights of the child need to be defined keeping in mind the cultural specificities of notions of childhood, play, learning, and consequently exploitation and abuse.

Apart from the physical burden of working before the body is ready for it, children are often enough subjected to beatings and lashings in a range of situations. Amarjit Mahajan and Madhurima (1995) have argued that punishment per se does not constitute violence; however when an act of punishment involves substantial injury, it is no longer legitimate punishment but violence against a defenceless child. In a study carried out in a village in Haryana, 200 children in the age group 7–14 years were interviewed. The majority came from landless families, and 97 per cent of fathers preferred physical punishment. However, the reasons for punishment were different: 72 per cent of the landowners punished the children for non-compliance with family norms and standards of discipline; for the landless, the major concern was with unwillingness to work—for 'when the child shirked work, he was given severe punishment' (Mahajan and Madhurima 1995, 86). It was also this category of children who were injured more often in the course of punishment. Most parents, irrespective of their background, felt that there were positive consequences associated with beating. On the other hand, the study found that routinely abused children started hating their parents, became more obstinate, and a few even ran away from home.

In 1982, a study of 1000 victims of child abuse, (Dave 1982) found that 81 percent could be classified as victims of physical abuse, 7 per cent of what the authors call physical neglect, 9.3 per cent of sexual abuse, and 2.7 per cent of emotional abuse. None of these categories can be treated as exclusive and it is important to note that studies of this kind are extremely difficult to undertake, particularly so in the area of sexual relations where the overall attitude of secrecy and suppression that governs any discussion or reference to sex makes it difficult to come to definite conclusions on the extent of sexual abuse of children. Yet, of the available figures, of almost 10,000 reported rapes in 1990, an alarming 25 per cent are of girl children below the age of sixteen, and about a fifth are of those under ten. A recent analysis done by the Crimes Against Women Cell, Delhi Police, points out that of the 381 rape cases registered between January and August 1997, 270 or almost 75 per cent of the victims were in the age range 7–18 years. Only fifty-seven of the rapists were unknown to the victims. Most were immediate neighbours; ten girls were raped by their fathers; and three by stepfathers (*Pioneer* 1997).

Such alarming figures are indicative not only of the sexual vulnerability of the girl child in and around her home, but also of a social climate which encourages her violation. In an interesting presentation at a seminar on child rape organized by the National Commission for Women (NCW) in New Delhi, in October 1992, Sobha Srinath from NIMHANS, Bangalore, pointed to an important, though perhaps little thought about, fact: a young child below the age of ten need not always be aware that her sexual violation is in fact qualitatively different from thrashing and abuse: it is only with the onset of puberty that she becomes aware of her sexuality. In fact, in an environment where physical contact, both affectionate and abusive, by relatives of both sexes is not uncommon, child rape needs to be viewed a little differently from the rape of a post-pubertal girl.

Not unexpectedly, families rarely talk about the rape of their young daughter; when the rapist is a father or a brother, the chances of reporting are even lower. Members of voluntary organizations said that a mother would often suppress and wish away the event, not only because of a sense of shame and outrage, but also out of fear of reprisals from her husband, son, or other relatives (NCW Seminar, October 1992, personal observations). In 1992–93, there were eight cases of rape and molestation reported by mothers to the Crime Against Women Cell in Delhi; officials at the cell pointed out that this as significant development as hardly any such instances were reported earlier. At the same time, wives expected the police to merely caution their husbands, filing a case against them would be unheard of (Wadhwa 1993). If there is a silence around the sexual violation of the girl child in the family, this is equally true of cases of sodomy and abuse of the male child. [. . .]

Violence in the conjugal home

Marriage continues to be universally regarded as essential for a girl, in India, irrespective of class, caste, religion,and ethnicity, as control of her sexuality and its safe transference into the hands of the husband are given prime importance. [. . .]

An important part of the power relationship between spouses and indeed their families relates to dowry and its ramifications. In the Indian context, the preference for structural asymmetry between the two families and the consequence burden of gift giving on the bride's family strengthens inequality. Anthropological studies, particularly of north Indian marriage and kinship patterns, indicate that hypergamous unions establish a permanent asymmetry in gift giving and presentations. Here the notion of property in marriage acquires another meaning: not only is the in-marrying girl viewed as the property of her husband if not of the conjugal family, but also, the event marks the unequal flow of goods and even property between the two kin groups. Based on her fieldwork in North India, Ursula Sharma has argued persuasively that dowry, or what the bride's family gives to the groom's family at the time of hypergamous marriages, is 'a concrete form of property in which members of the household, both men and women, have different kinds of interest and over which they have different kinds of control' (Sharma 1984, 62). Important for later analysis is the communal aspect of dowry, nor is it a one-time transaction: ritual occasions, festivals and indeed any minor pretext result in more demands being made on the daughter-in-law's family.

In India, there is a tendency to club most marital violence under the overall heads of 'dowry', 'dowry deaths', and 'dowry violence'. This categorization glosses over the other causes of violence which pervade the familial context. However, to argue that dowry is not always the cause behind marital discord is not to ignore the fact that it is one of the major factors responsible for domestic violence. While keeping this fact in mind it is necessary to work towards a fuller understanding of the institution of dowry and its impact on inter-family relationships. Madhu Kishwar feels that oppression of wives for bringing inadequate dowry is one more excuse for using violence against them: in other words—and in fact evidence from other countries has indicated as much—even without the additional 'attraction' of dowry, inter-spousal violence is endemic. She has also pointed out that dowry payments in themselves do not transform girls into burdens but rather 'dowry makes daughters "burden-some" only because daughters are unwanted to begin with' (Kishwar 1986). For instance, middle class parents who save to pay lakhs as capitation fees for sons in medical or engineering colleges do not view them as burdensome; but similar sums set aside for daughters' marriages are regarded differently.

Though it is difficult to be categorical on the background of those either harassed or killed for dowry, it is clearly a phenomenon on the increase among all social categories. In a study of dowry victims in Delhi, Ranjana Kumari (1989) commented that 'dowry has become inseparably interlinked with the general status of women in our society'. Her study shows that in a sample of 150 dowry victims, one-fourth were murdered or driven to commit suicide, and more than half, that is, 61.3 per cent, were thrown out of their husband's house after a longdrawn period of harassment and torture. Dowry-related killings followed two patterns. First, the young brides were either murdered or forced to commit suicide (18.4 per cent) when their parents refused to concede to continuing demands for dowry. Second, the murders were committed also on the pretext of 'complex family relations'. Extramarital relationships were alleged in 52.6 per cent cases of death. It was also discovered that the conflicts intensified because of the refusal by young brides to yield to overtures made by father-in-law, uncle-in-law or brother-in-law. There were also cases where wives alleged that the husband was impotent. [. . .]

There is no satisfactory explanation for why the system of dowry is growing and indeed spreading to communities where it earlier did not exist.

Nonetheless, its role in perpetuating violence within the home is substantial. Of particular relevance is the fact that dissatisfaction over dowry payments and subsequent presentations result in abuse of the wife not only by her husband but by other affines as well. Apart from ill-health and stress in a violent home environment, the ill-treatment of married women can lead to a total psychological remoulding such as the internalization of deception, manipulative techniques and feigning. It can also lead to anticipation and provocation, a macabre expectation of the inevitable.

Thus wife abuse, a practice shared with many other cultures, acquires a different connotation in Indian society due to the institution of dowry. Here, the term 'abuse' includes physical as well as non-physical acts. There is enough evidence to suggest that such abuse often receives wider familial sanction. It is institutionalized in various forms that range from inhumanity to long hours of labour, often within and outside the home, food denial, neglect of ailments, and verbal abuses by affines to physical violence by the husband and sometimes other family members. In this context, it is important to note the growing number of cases being registered under section 498 A of the Indian Penal Code (IPC 1983) which indicts a husband or relative of the husband for cruelty against a wife. For instance, all-India police data available under this head from 1989 onwards record a steady increase: from 11,803 cases registered in 1989 to 15, 949 in 1992 (an increase of by 37.5 per cent). As entire families and indeed the state become involved in the ramifications of inter-spousal disputes, the incidence of these events continues to spiral upwards, occasionally with macabre outcomes: personal communications with police officials indicated that the unnatural deaths of wives were on the increase each year. [. . .]

In a detailed discussion of wife abuse, Flavia Agnes (1988) has convincingly rebutted the popular myths which surround the phenomenon of wife beating in India, such as middle class women do not get beaten; the victim of violence is a small, fragile, helpless woman belonging to the working class; and the wife-beater is a man who is frustrated in his job, an alcoholic, or a paranoid person, aggressive in his relationships. Nor is it true that so-called loving husbands do not beat their wives or that women provoke men to beat them. Yet many of these myths seem to pervade the analysis of wife beating and feminine expectations in Indian society.

For instance, based on an analysis of cases which had come to the Delhi-based women's organization Saheli, it was evident that wife beating was common among all social classes as it 'is a reflection of the power relationship between a husband and wife', which mirrors a woman's secondary social status (Saheli 1988, 1). However, the pattern of violence differs from one class to another, with the whole neighbourhood being witness when a slum-dweller beats his wife, while a middle class professional's physical oppression of his spouse is extremely private in nature.

Like child rape within the family, another area about which little is known and which is hardly discussed is that of marital rape—in India. Despite some thinking along these lines by feminists and legal experts, there has yet been no amendment in law to include sexual violence as rape within marriage. The only exception is if the wife is below sixteen years of age. Though figures on marital rape as well as other sexually demeaning and violent acts are difficult to obtain, discussions with counsellors working with abused women indicated that a very large percentage of their clients were forced into sexual intercourse. [. . .]

Conclusion

The ever-present fact of violence, both overt and covert, physical and non-physical, has an overwhelming influence on feminine identity formation. A child's sense of self is greatly dependent on how others think, feel and behave towards her. This fundamental difference in identity formation between the sexes has deep roots in the socialization processes, resource allocation within families, the impact of external influences such as mass media, pornography and the educational system. While identity, notions of self, roles and obligations are worked out fairly early in a woman's life, no stage of her life cycle is without change and questioning of received norms. Thus feminine identity and a woman's position within the family continue to be open to modification, depending on her situation in the life cycle. What is important in this context is that these modifications are often determined by the collectivity: individual self-expression is repressed and subjugated and the anger at being violated is internalized.

There is clearly much more that needs to be understood about the Indian family and its internal dynamics. For instance, to pin all violence against the girl child on the fear of dowry appears a convenient rationalization, shrouding a range of motivations. Is it to be assumed that dowry giving is such a widespread and prevalent practice as to influence every parent who goes in for female foeticide, abortion, or infanticide? While, in the absence of adequate data, it is difficult to be categorical, there is clearly a need to further investigate the family's strategies for survival and mobility as well as how dependency of the young, the housewives and the elderly conditions responses to these conditions. It is clear that far from being a refuge from the outside world, the family is complicit in processes and mechanisms of socialization, many of which are oppressive if not extreme in nature.

References

Agnes, Flavia. 1988. Violence in the family: Wife beating. In *Women and Indian society: A reader*, ed. Rehana Ghadially. New Delhi: Sage Publications, 151–66.

Burra, Neera. 1995. *Born to work: Child labour in India*. New Delhi: Oxford University Press.

Dave, A.B. et al. 1982. Child abuse and neglect (CAN), practices in drug abuse in a district of Madhya Pradesh. *Indian Pediatrics* 19, 905–12.

Kelkar, Govind. 1991. *Violence against women in India: Perspectives and strategies*. Bangkok: Asian Institute of Technology.

Kishwar, Madhu. 1986. Dowry to ensure her happiness or to disinherit her? *Manushi* 34, 2–13.

Litke, Robert. 1992. Violence and power. *International Social Science Journal.*

Mahajan, Amarjit and Madhurima. 1995. *Family violence and abuse in India*. New Delhi: Deep & Deep Publications

Poonacha, Veena, ed. 1999. *Women and violence*. Bombay: SNDT University.

Ranjana Kumari. 1989. *Brides are not for burning: Dowry victims in India,* New Delhi: Radiant.

Saheli. 1988. Wife battering: Creating choices for individual women, the role of government and issues facing the women's movement'. Paper presentation at the national workshop on family violence against females, New Delhi.

Sharma, Ursula. 1984. Dowry in North India: Its consequences for women. In *Woman and property: Women as property*, ed. R.Hirschon. London: Croom Helm, 62–74..

The Pioneer. 29 September 1997.

Uberoi, Patricia, ed. 1995. *Family, marriage and kinship in India*. New Delhi: Oxford University Press.

Vatuk, S.1975. Gifts and affines in North India. *Contributions to Indian Sociology* 9, 155–96.

Verghese, J. 1997. *Her gold and her body*. 2nd edn. Ghaziabad: Vikas Publishing House.

Vyas, Anju, Naheed Mohsini and Madhusree. 1996. *Voices of resistance, silences of pain: A resource guide on violence against women*. New Delhi: Centre for Women's Development Studies.

Wadhwa, S. 16 August 1993. Incest cases pose challenge for authorities. *The Pioneer*.

∾

THE IMPOSSIBLE SUBJECT:
CASTE AND DESIRE IN THE SCENE OF THE FAMILY
Susie Tharu

No reader familiar with the canonical texts of modern Indian literatures needs to be told how large the figure of the Hindu widow looms there and in what unexpected, though by no means insignificant, places it might make its appearance. Indeed—and I discovered this to my surprise while working on *Women Writing in India*—from about the middle of the nineteenth century onwards this figure has held a more-or-less center-stage position in the national imaginary. It could be argued, and I am going to do so, that when a writer features a widow as protagonist he or she is, consciously, making an intervention in a debate centred on this figure, a debate whose history is a history of Indian humanism and its intimate yet troubled relationship with Indian feminism. In fact, only when we frame widow-narratives thus, as engaged in the elaboration-contestation of the modern Indian subject, do other critical dimensions of the genre become apparent. The widow is a figure whose very life is marked by a specific death. She is *vidhave*—without husband—and consequently in need of sympathy and protection, but also of regulation and governance. Widow stories therefore are invariably also historical engagements with questions of political order and citizenship. [. . .]

To what extent has the embodied and agentive self—or a very similar one—also been the body-self unwittingly affirmed and renewed by historical feminism? What does that norming cost the feminist movement? How might it affect possibilities of egalitarian and democratic alliance or initiative? These are chastening questions and ones that we might learn how to ask as we find our way through the text I want to discuss: Baburao Bagul's 1969 story about a dalit widow. [. . .]

The mandatory summary to begin with. This is a difficult task, because unlike a well-made short story which is pared down to a single focus, the plot here is layered like that of a novel and is bustling with character and event. The time-span of the story has a classical brevity (one evening, seven pages), yet the narrative is structured as a series of episodes that cut from location to location, flashback from the immediate present to the recent and the more distant past, and shift focus from the private world of the subject-self to the outer world of power. I think the only possibility might be to risk brutalization of the structuring of time in Bagul's narrative and present a chronology of events. I hope that the scope and texture of the story can be regained, partially at least, in the discussion.

Sometime before he was born, Pandu's mother and father leave their village and come to the city after the father, in a fit of jealous anxiety, 'almost kills his brother with an axe'. Things are only worse in the city. The mother has to work all day at construction sites to feed the family and pay for milk and medicines. Her husband, drunk and tubercular, is too weak and overwrought with resentment and suspicion of his wife to find work himself. The sexual tension between them builds up and spills out into their already tense world in which abuse and attack are the everyday texture of life, not only for them but for everyone. He accuses her of selling herself for favours, tries repeatedly to deface her (quite literally), makes an attempt to brand her body with hot tongs; she turns on his dying body in vengeance demanding her 'conjugal rights', hoping to hasten his death. When he dies, she feels she has killed him. Ten years elapse. She has continued to work, resisting, for her son's sake, the advances of several men, despite desperate need for the material benefit that would accrue. Pandu is at school, but he is miserable. He never smiles, never responds, either to the teacher or to the taunts of other children. His body, Bagul writes, is lead. One evening, back from a usual school day of attack and abuse, sitting alone in his empty hovel waiting for his mother, hungry yet unable to stomach the cold gruel left for him on the hearth, the small changes in their everyday life begin to 'make sense' to him. He reads them, indeed reads himself in them: new Diwali clothes, a new tilt of his mother's head, a new drape to her clothes, a fresh intensity to the taunts at school and on the street. His mother is a whore. He the son of a— When she returns from work, braving that day as everyday the sexual attacks and the moral reprobations of the street through which she must walk to reach the relative safety of her home, Pandu turns on her the full force of his pain and resentment. He shouts at her and runs out of the house. I quote:

> The room now seemed to her like the cremation grounds . . . She heard the sound of the dogs in the distance, and thinking he had come back, joyfully opened the door.
> 'Come son, forgive this old sinner.'

The door opened and the overseer stood in the doorway. His massive frame seemed to dwarf everything else in the room. 'What's happened? Why do you look so scared? You are sweating.' He hugged her, pretended to wipe the sweat off her face, and started caressing her arms and her breasts. She slowly responded, and out of the hunger of the past ten years of widowhood flared an uncontrollable desire. And that is why she failed to hear the timid knock at the door, the faint, hesitant cry, 'Mother!' He saw them, his mother and the towering figure of the overseer in a tight embrace. His last hopes seemed to crash about his head; broken-hearted, he wildly rushed towards the door. She saw him then, strained after him, calling his name, but the overseer, already blinded with lust, refused to let her go; he was pulling her into the room with his strong brown arms. Pandu was running away at great speed; his fast falling tears had almost blinded him, the stray dogs ran at his heels, snapped at him and now he was screaming, shouting with terror, afraid of the dogs . . .

She was trying desperately to escape from the bear-like hug of the overseer. But like a person stuck fast in the quagmire, she found release impossible . . .

A summary of this kind necessarily scants detail and structure. It also excludes from its scope one of the most stunning aspects of the story—what I will call, following Walter Benjamin, a 'linguistic air'. A few comments on this air. For those normed by its procedures, the everyday use of language assumes, indeed can assume, a fit so close between the sign and its referent that the referent saturates the domain of signification. In 'The Task of the Translator', Benjamin refers to this mode in which language is used as the linguistic air, arguing that translation rises to (but also exists in/has the bearing of) a higher and purer task less with the transfer of meaning or information and more with essaying a mode of signification. The linguistic air in Baburao Bagul's story is related to that of a Benjaminian translation, though it is not identical. The linguistic air of a translation draws attention to the signifying system that is another culture. In the nether world of Bagul's story, on the other side of the border in which sign and referent have a natural fit, language does not just thematize another process/mode of signification. In that air, reality is self-evidently an effect of the symbolic whose logic is apparent everywhere. Signification is a full-scale materializing and de-materializing force. Events, bodies, persons, objects and selves are signs that have to be cautiously investigated and deciphered if they are to make sense.

In this linguistic air, which is as much the air of real life as it is of the art work, bodies are so wayward that they must be branded; tuberculosis is a caste-mark, memory an aspect of present time and public location; it rushes in from the world to habilitate a personal past; a body-subject whose 'life' is not affirmed by another spirals rapidly back into insignificance. There can be no leisure in this world that must move to the busy beat of an elsewhere, no time for pause, no occasion for con-solid-ation for reader or story-teller. Nothing holds, nothings stands still, nothing may be taken for granted. It is the symbolic that gives birth to subjects, and tempts their dreams with agency while it watches ceremoniously over their many and rapid deaths. A single death would indeed be a comfort.

In addition, the subject in this nether world is not 'impossible' simply because agency is an effect of discipline, or because it is in-process, or because it is not affirmed in citation-reiteration, or indeed because one plus one can never actually make a One, an integral whole, and there is always a remainder. It is impossible because it is continuously annihilated.

'Mother' could well be read as the drama of life and death in the scene of the untouchable family. The narrative turns us into witnesses as mother, son, husband, wife, lover, suitor, man, woman and child give birth, one to another, and die, kill, desire or imagine the death of the other in a series of overlapping acts of affirmation and denial. Indeed the story opens with a longish account of one such coming-to-life and its death. Normally indifferent and listless, 'backward' children thrill to 'a new joy of being' as they listen to a teacher read out a poem about a mother who is a river of life, a Vatsalya Sindhu. The poem 'transports' them into another realm and their 'muddy faces their unkempt hair.' Enabled by the poem to map those mythic proportions onto memories of his own mother, the young protagonist, Pandu magically comes to life as 'a child'. A body stooped with the load of his living, straightens into normality. It returns to him, rather, it returns him to himself: he wants to shout, to wave his arms about in joy. The new propriety also finds this untouchable housing in a community: 'the hostility he usually felt towards his classmates abated somewhat. He sat watching them at play and a benign smile slowly came to his face'.

Sealing the contract of reconciliation between secured self and habitable world is the high point of Pandu's new-found happiness and vitality: the assertion of his own ability to exclude another. 'Snotnose,' he and Lakhu shout out at another boy in spontaneous consolidation of their exuberant togetherness. The poem he listens to in class literally has the power to inspire Pandu. It breathes him into brief life as son, as child and as 'touchable' member of a community. It gives him a mother. Snuffed out by another more compelling one: 'Don't touch Pandu, any of you. My mother say his mother ...' Kishan's yell and the laughter it elicits from the class drains Pandu of life: he slowly returns to his seat and sits down 'woodenly'.

It is a double murder this—of child and of mother—and one that will be insistently re-enacted, elaborated and related to other dramas of life and death in the story. The domain of the symbolic sustains all life and demands merciless maintenance of its extraditions and death sentences of which there are many kinds. There are those rehearsed in the desperate masquerades that play at and endorse power in the very face of power-lessness (Bhaga, the school-rowdy, Dagdu, his community role model, the jealous husband, the sexually demanding wife). Thus, Bhaga put up his shirt collar . . . like a street rowdy, squared his lips and told Pandu. 'You bloody pimp. Just come out. I'm going to murder you.' He removed a rusty old blade from his note book and threateningly placed it at Pandu's throat.

More characteristic of this world, however, are the real murders, not these make-believe ones. Those involve the actual or desired elimination of a killer(s) and are posthumous acts of self-defence in which a murdered person must kill in order that he or she may live again. Thus, orphaned by Kishan's remarks, Pandu feels a 'demonic, murderous rage rising within him. He could have killed them, murdered them all in cold blood. It was good to think of them lying together in a pool of blood.' Walking back from school that evening Pandu encounters a drunken Dagdu. He is scared, but when Dagdu, jealous and depressed, insults his mother, Pandu loses 'his childlike feelings as the murderous fires continued to haunt him; he felt like hurling a heavy rock at Dagdu's swaying, retreating form and his mind's eye was luridly coloured by the spraying blood that he imagined would gush out of Dagdu's head'.

Structurally analogous to the many deaths, murders, births and re-births that constitute Pandu's life, is the coming-to-life and new death of Pandu's mother, the murder she commits, the ones she dreams of committing, the ones committed on her. For a man in this world, a wife's youth or her beauty are not sources of joy but of anxiety and emasculation. Beauty is the property mark of the world across the border, a branding. A beautiful woman is one who has been picked out by its laws, one whose life is held by its designs and its assumptions. To make a beautiful woman his wife, to hold her in that esteemed position and thereby to affirm his own proper masculinity, his status as husband, a man must erase those marks which are also the marks of his emasculation, his dispossession, the impossibility of personhood. Pandu's father's blows, therefore, were always aimed at destroying [his wife's] full-blown beauty. He hoped she would lose a lot of blood, become lame, deformed, ugly and so, in spite of his ebbing strength, he would aim at her face, nose, head, eyes. Then he threatened to kill her when she was asleep. He blamed her entirely for his disease, his failing strength, his joblessness.

For similar reasons, he would rather 'die, allow this child to die' than let his brother, who looks at his wife with 'lust in his eyes', anywhere near them. For Pandu's father, this brother is the most dreaded of mirrors, one into which he cannot bear to look, for he sees there the image of his own utter degradation/death in one who is his own flesh and blood. To survive he must break that mirror—kill, even his brother.

For the woman who is Pandu's mother, the memories that haunt are those of the 'most degrading act of the day' when her husband would strip her and scrupulously check out her body and its clothing for marks of her infidelity. The break point comes when she wakes up one night to find him heating tongs to brand her body, to mark it indelibly, to burn into it the sign of his possession. It will be a mark of power, indeed of patriarchal power, but it is at the same time a mark of his desperation. It is she now who turns to the kill. She will demand—and like the demands that he makes on her, this too is an excessive, impossible demand for his failing tubercular body—she will demand that he husband her, and in the process push him into death. She will want to murder her son too when she recognizes in his eyes the 'same dark suspicion' she has seen before—in the eyes of his father.

Like Pandu, who momentarily comes alive in the promise of the poem, she too glimmers into brief life in the arms of the overseer at the construction site. With the af-firm-ation he provides she can walk straight, 'secure in her newfound love'. Her mirror now refracts a different light and she grows desirable in her own eyes as much as in his. But for this dalit to find bodily life thus, as woman-self, she must die as mother. 'Whore, I spit on your clothes,' Pandu shouts in a desperate, last-ditch attempt to conserve his ethical identity before he runs out of the house into his death as son-child.

Caste and the feminist scene of desire

For a feminist reader secured in her well-made upper-caste world, the story is epiphanic. It eases open and displays a totally different logic to a violence that has hitherto been described to her only in terms that distance and repudiates it as—and I can think of no better example than the comment by the celebrated playwright Vijay Tendulkar, taken from his foreword to Bagul's book—'uneducated, uncultured, abnormal'. It is a logic that (i) implicates both her and her world anew, since it re-places the mark of this extradited 'other' on the many institutions, familial, psychic, ethical, that ground her personal, and therefore as a feminist also her political, life and (ii) renews her understanding of patriarchy and the subjugations that structure and sustain it.

For the widow-mother protagonist—and for the dalit feminist—nothing comes so easily, yet there is in the story the stirring of a new kind of movement: from the never-ceasing shuttle between the extraditions and deaths that comprise her impossible life, to a struggle to leave, and in that single act to re-notate the world. It is a movement, not so much to demand entry into the many temples of the contemporary world, but to redesignate and rework those institutions. The beginnings of a movement, possibly, from untouchable-harijan to dalit.

But what exactly is untouchability in this dalit story? I think it is significant that Baburao Bagul refers to each of the interpretative frameworks that address the caste question, but takes issue with all of them. Thus, both *varnashramadharma* (and untouchability as it is configured in that brahmanical-colonial-gandhian scheme of scholarship and politics) and sanskritization (Indian sociology's attempt to modernize brahmanism by transforming it into a question of consent and aspiration and not bigotry or exploitation) are noted emblematically. It is easy to provide examples: the Hindu (?) widow is the central figure, the move from the village to the city sets the plot in motion, the narrative opens with the child's desire for a mother who is a Vatsalya Sindhu, 'Don't touch Pandu, any of you,' Kishan yells out. The question of consent—more specifically the question of what exactly constitutes consent for a subject that stands thus, askew, in the grids of citizenship—is thematic in this story which might well be read as an extended discussion of the dynamics of that single issue. However, in the citation-retheorization occasioned by this story, each of these classical objects of political theory is so transformed that it is virtually, yet not totally, unrecognizable. In contrast, the question of political economy is addressed, and its effects insistently documented. We are told that the community is backward and ill-nourished, the family immiserated, the father tuberculous and jobless, the mother slaves at a construction site for the pittance that will put a meal a day into their bellies, lower-caste women live in constant fear of sexual attack, the unemployed hang around the basti, drunk and depressed, or move around in lumpen-rowdy gangs. Here too the objects are emblematic, but they are recognizable as those of a Nehruvian/socialist scheme of things. Structurally however, the narrative accords neither political economy nor history the status of an interpretative horizon. Work, wages, property, expropriation all figure here, as does the aspiration for a wholesome humanity. But they are drawn into a frame that reworks the discursive logic of untouchability as it proposes a theory of caste (i) as extraditions that are revised and renewed by a brahmanism that is constantly updating its patriarchy, (ii) as desire in the scene of the family, (iii) as bodies that are compelled by, but disallowed, contact into the feminine or masculine; bodies, therefore, that shuttle, always deficient, always in excess. In brief, as terror in the domain of the citizen-subject. [. . .]

~

SPEAKING PEACE: AN INTRODUCTION
Urvashi Butalia

For more than a decade now, women in Kashmir have been caught in the grip of a conflict which, from its beginnings as a militant movement fighting for self-determination, has rapidly turned into a battle involving at least a hundred different militant factions and *tazneems* (groups), with the Indian security forces pitted against them. The situation is no longer one of a simple demand for self-determination. Instead, there are groups who believe Kashmir must ally with Pakistan (and who are supported, both financially and in terms of training, by Pakistan, something which has led to a worsening of the already strained relations between the two countries) and others who are committed to an independent state. All 'sides' in this battle use violence, and it is the people of Kashmir whose lives are deeply impacted by this.

There are many interpretations of how this conflict began, and from which point it can be dated. Some go back to 1989, the year in which violence broke out in the valley, while others date the conflict from the accession of Kashmir to the Indian union (itself something which is debated and sometimes disputed) in 1947, and some histories stretch even further back to the beginnings of Dogra rule in Kashmir. Indeed, many of the slogans of the current movement recall similar slogans of many years ago: as the report of the People's Union for Democratic Rights (PUDR 2001) on the current Kashmir situation points out, the Kashmiris' fight for 'azadi' goes much further back than 1947 and stretches into the time of the harsh and repressive rule of the Dogras, and the British. It was in the context of such oppression and exploitation that Sheikh Abdullah emerged as a popular leader who symbolized the hopes and aspirations of the Kashmiris for their homeland and who, while keeping the focus on the majority Muslim population of Kashmir, did not forget to include Hindus and Sikhs in his political speeches and actions.

The aspirations of the people were symbolized in the Naya Kashmir manifesto, adopted in 1944 by the National Conference under Sheikh Abdullah. The document stressed the future of Kashmir as a secular, socialist state committed to the eradication of communalism and the rights of women. This document [. . .] today reads like a tragic travesty and betrayal of the hopes of the people of Kashmir. Shortly afterwards, the Dogra ruler, growing fearful of the gathering momentum of the movement, arrested Sheikh Abdullah. Despite this, the movement continued apace with men and women taking part in it. It was thus that Sheikh Abdullah was in jail when India was partitioned, during which time the movement against the ruler continued, gaining increasing support from outside.

In 1947, the Sheikh was still in prison while the Dogra king, Hari Singh, played India and Pakistan against each other as he weighed his options on Kashmir: to join with Pakistan or India, or to stay independent. In some ways, the Pakistan-backed raiders' attack of October 1947 settled matters: the Raja needed the Indian army's help to protect his kingdom against the raiders; he was worried too that some small sections of the armed forces had raised pro-Pakistan slogans, and therefore he signed the Instrument of Accession by which Kashmir became a part of India. At the time, it was agreed that once law and order had been restored in the state the 'consent' of the people of Jammu and Kashmir would be obtained. This, of course, never happened. It was also at this time that, at Sardar Vallabhai Patel's suggestion, the Maharaja agreed to release the Sheikh.

The post-1947 history of Kashmir is a record of an initial uneasy sharing of power between three key actors, Hari Singh, Sheikh Abdullah (who remained, for long, a popular leader) and the Government of India. Jammu and Kashmir was granted a special status, through Article 370 of the Indian Constitution. It was this, and other provisions that marked Kashmir as different from other Indian states, that became subjects for heated debate in the years to come. Unlike other states, for example, Kashmir was to have a Prime Minister, not a Chief Minister, and it was to have its own Constitution. This process was, however, derailed when the Sheikh was arrested once again in 1953 (partly because Nehru feared his growing popularity and partly also because he continued to balance Pakistan and India against each other) and held in detention for several years, during which time a sort of puppet regime was installed by the centre.

For more than half a century after 1947, Kashmir has remained at the heart of the dispute between India and Pakistan. The dispute—basically one over ownership of a territory—has led to three full-scale wars, several smaller ones, and a number of 'proxy' wars along the Line of Control, with India holding Kashmir to be an integral part of its territory of Kashmir and Pakistan claiming its right place to be with the Muslim majority state of Pakistan. Currently, a small part of the territory of Kashmir lies with Pakistan, and a larger area with India. The situation in Indian Kashmir is further complicated by the fact that while the state has an overall Muslim majority, Jammu has a Hindu majority and Ladakh a Buddhist one.

The current phase of Kashmiri separatist nationalism began at the end of the eighties, with young men and women coming out into the streets in large numbers. Over the years, the nature of the movement, as well as the actors within it, have changed radically. Paid mercenaries and militants trained across the border have entered the picture; the sheen and romance of militancy for many young men in Kashmir has worn off, and militant attacks on ordinary people, in marketplaces, etc. have become commonplace. Repression, and counter-insurgency measures, have been swift to follow and it is estimated that between 60,000 and 70,000 people have died, some 4000 are believed to be missing or in illegal detention, more than a million people have been displaced; the number of widows and half widows is said to be more than 15,000. The presence of the army, paramilitary and police forces is ubiquitous, and fear of violence and arrest has now become part of the daily lives of ordinary people. Kashmir now comes under the Armed Forces Special Powers Act and the Disturbed Areas Act (and more recently the much disputed and draconian Prevention of Terrorism Ordinance) which means that the constitutionally guaranteed freedoms available to all citizens of India. do not obtain here. [. . .]

It is now widely accepted that while women seldom create or initiate conflict, they—along with children and the aged—are often its chief victims and sufferers. Nowhere is this more true than in Kashmir. Yet, despite this, women's suffering has, until recently, barely been acknowledged. The Kashmir conflict, for example, has generated a vast amount of analytical and historical literature; very little of it actually mentions women. Yet today, in Kashmir, there are large numbers of women who are identified as 'half widows' (women whose husbands are assumed dead but there is no proof to show they actually are), widows, mothers who have lost their sons, or those whose daughters have been raped, young women who dare not step out of the house, women who have been pushed out of employment by the fear and uncertainty created by conflict, and those who are suffering from medical and psychological conditions related to stress and trauma.

Nor is this the only reality of women caught in conflict. For there is enough evidence from research and activist work the world over, and specifically in the South Asian region, to show that conflict—whether long-term or sudden—often results in pushing women into the public space, or in their taking the initiative to carve out their own spaces in which to come to terms with the changed reality around them. Many of the widows of the 1984 anti-Sikh riots in Delhi, for example, were forced to go out in search of jobs after their husbands died. At first hesitant and uncertain—for they had never negotiated the public space without their men—the women gradually began to feel comfortable, and to learn how to deal with their new realities. In Nagaland, in India's conflict-ridden northeast region, the year 1984 saw the founding of a unique organization, the Naga Mothers Association, which took up a campaign for peace, and coined the slogan: 'Shed no more blood'. Appealing to militants, the army, security forces and ordinary citizens alike, the Naga Mothers Association has been in the forefront of negotiations for peace. In Kashmir, the setting up of the Association of the Parents of Disappeared Persons (APDP) by Parveena Ahangar, a mother whose son has been missing for more than ten years, is another such initiative. With its largely female membership, the APDP has a single point agenda: tracking down the hundreds, indeed the thousands, of missing persons, so that families can either regain their loved ones, or put a closure on their lives. Similar examples abound, not only within India but also in neighbouring Sri Lanka (as with Tamil Hindu women of the LTTE), Bangladesh (as in the Chittagong Hill Tracts), and others.

In a study of Tamil women in the Sri Lanka conflict, Darini Rajasingham Senanayake points out that 'women's agency or empowerment is rarely unambivalent in war or peace' (Senanayake 2001). While some women may indeed gain in post-conflict situations, the terms of access vary across caste and class and, in some cases, can result in placing a double burden on women. Moreover, and here is something that has received much less attention than it should, how do we understand the sometimes willing participation of women in political conflict, the fact that they are increasingly beginning to form the critical mass of violent cadres, and how, further, do we then understand women's relationship with the nation and nationalism(s), and with the state? Sometimes there is a direct causal link between women taking up violent ideologies—for example, seeking revenge for a sister raped, a mother killed, a son taken away—and at others, it is a matter of wanting to do something for the country. In both cases, interventions for peace need to be sensitive to the importance of these different realities.

When [our] project began in Kashmir, it took a two-pronged approach. The first was to speak to women in different parts of the state and, through detailed interviews, to try to arrive at some understanding of what they had had to live through, and how they saw their present and future. [. . .] The second was to work with locally based groups and to conduct workshops on stress and trauma with affected women, and then to move gradually into collecting more quantitative data, for example on the number of families in a particular place who had lost a family member, the number of children out of school, the number of widows who had received compensation, and so on. Stress, trauma, depression, spontaneous abortions, miscarriages, these are now common problems among the people of Kashmir, and more specifically among its women, children and the ageing. [. . .]

Clearly, conflict has created a situation of tremendous fear and uncertainty in women's lives. Kashmir was a state, one woman told us, where if you wanted to kill a chicken you had to ask the permission of your elders, and, she said, 'look at what it has become today. Violence is a way of life. The gun is like an old familiar—children ask to be given AK47s as birthday presents.' A statement that is heard time and again today relates to another condition created by the conflict, and that is about the lack of trust. 'Our fear is as much from the gun,' we were told, 'as it is from each other. We no longer know whom to trust. Sometimes your closest friend, even your brother, may be an informer, or a militant, sometimes he may be a renegade [the local term used for 'surrendered' militants].' Further, for women, this lack of trust works in other ways. In a dialogue between Kashmiri women and women from the northeast of India, a number of Kashmiri women, widows and half widows, spoke of the suspicion they faced from their own families. Being without an earning member in the family meant that they were forced to go out and seek work, but the moment they stepped out of the home, or stayed away from it, family members would accuse them of being women of 'bad character'— a stigma that is difficult to live down, the more so when it is added to the stigma of widowhood (the latter is largely a Hindu phenomenon, but in Kashmir, is conveniently added on to Muslim women as well).

Statistics are hard to come by in Kashmir. There has been no census there since 1981—by the time the date for next census came round, the trouble had already begun—and much has changed in twenty years. Figures for the number of people killed in the violence, the dead, the missing, women widowed, raped women, children orphaned—all these vary widely depending on where they come from. Government figures are always lower than those calculated by human rights and civil liberties activists. While the lack of 'proper' statistics is a problem that needs to be addressed, one does not need statistics to measure people's grief and suffering, and their desire for peace. If the women of Kashmir, whether Muslim, Hindu, Sikh, or Ladakhi are to be believed, the levels of domestic violence have gone up sharply in the state in the last decade or so. For women, then, the external violence of war or political conflict is not something that is happening 'out there', but has made its way into their homes and hearths. Yet, in the hierarchy of violence set up by such situations, the 'external' violence of conflict somehow comes to acquire much greater significance than the 'internal' violence of domestic strife, no matter that domestic strife may be generated, or exacerbated, by the external violence. Women who become the targets of such violence, have no one to talk to, for to everyone, it is the male who is the hero, whether as an army man, or a mililtant, or simply someone caught in conflict. She does not count.

In this context another question becomes important: that of the nature and meaning of peace. Does the 'return' of peace then mean a going back to the conditions that existed—the status quo—before conflict broke out, no matter how terrible those conditions might be in themselves? For women for whom levels of violence have escalated sharply, what will a return to 'normalcy' mean: the status quo 'then' (i.e. pre-conflict) or the status quo 'now' (i.e. during conflict)? Will 'peace' mean only the end of conflict 'outside' so to speak, or can women expect peace to extend within the four walls of the home as well? These are questions to which we do not, as yet, have any satisfactory answers. But it is clear that just as it is important to look at how conflict changes realities in the outside, public world, so also is it important to see the transformations, both positive and negative, that it creates within the home. [. . .]

There are other questions that need to be posed. While feminist activists have begun to involve themselves in Kashmir, much, if not most, of their work has been limited to the Valley, and more importantly, to women who are victims of the excesses of the security forces, and to a lesser extent of the militants. Similarly, it is only recently that the plight of Kashmiri Pandit women has become part of the agenda of women activists—as the work of Sushobha Barve who has been organizing dialogues between Pandit and Muslim women shows. But there is still considerable reluctance to involve oneself with, say, the wives of men in the army and the security forces who, too, are victims of this conflict, no matter that their husbands may be advancing the agenda of the state. In some ways, the problems of working with all 'groups' of women are not difficult to grasp. If the work is to be done in Kashmir, activists need to have the trust—a rare commodity in these troubled times—of the women they are working with. And yet, working in such a politicized terrain means that when you work with one 'group', the other looks on you with suspicion. In such a situation, you make certain choices, dictated by your politics and your values, and these are inevitably choices that leave out certain possibilities. Building trust, as most women activists know, is a long and slow process and women's groups have only just begun to take the first steps in this direction. In the end, however, this is what is important. Women's groups may have been slow to get involved in Kashmir, but once such involvement is there, it can only grow.

[Our project . . .] does not pretend to be a history of Kashmir, or a comprehensive account of the situation of women in the state. Rather, it aims to mark a moment in the history of the conflict in Kashmir and the involvement of the state and militants in it, a moment when the presence of women, whether as victims, agents or perpetrators can no longer be ignored, a moment which makes it clear that any initiative for peace and resolution of the conflict must take women into account and involve them centrally, a moment at which the women's movement must rethink its involvement with such questions. That there is considerable lack of knowledge of the situation of women in Kashmir, and that the 'mainstream' discourse about women represents them in only one way, do not need reiteration. [. . .]

The desire for peace [. . .] is echoed by Sushobha Barve who [has been . . .] busy organizing a dialogue between Pandit and Muslim women where they can share their thoughts and experiences, a first step in any movement towards peace and reconciliation. This dialogue resonates with a similar one organized by Sahba Hussain and Urvashi Butalia between women from the northeast of India and from Kashmir, where, both 'sides' for the first time, understood that their pain was not only echoed, but also shared, on the other side. For the women from the northeast, the fact that their region has had a long tradition of women's groups—mahila samitis and others—at the village level, and that, in some instances the church and village councils have been supportive of their demands—has meant that they have been able to mobilize in ways that seem impossible for Kashmiri women, who have no tradition of organizing at the village level, and who face the combined wrath of the patriarchal practices of all men surrounding them, whether militants, or security forces, of their own families, or indeed the state. (Indeed, even the few groups that do exist, such as the Dukhtaran-E-Milat and the Muslim Khawateen Markaaz, seem to have faded into the background today. More recently, a Pandit group called Daughters of Vitasta has been set up.) Thus, an impassioned plea from Kashmiri women to their sisters in the northeast was that they come to Kashmir and help them to learn how to set up women's groups on the ground. [. . .]

While the desire for peace cuts across all classes and groups, it does raise other questions. How will peace return to Kashmir? It has become all too easy, these days, for people to voice what are increasingly becoming empty slogans: any peace, we are told, must involve the people of Kashmir. The state says this, ordinary people echo it and everyone accepts it as a given truth. Yet, [. . .] who and where are the people of Kashmir? Would a Kashmiri who lives outside of the state but has a family there, count as a Kashmiri, or would many of the 'plains' Kashmiris who have migrated, or would the Pandits who now live in refugee camps? And where, [. . .] is it possible to find, or to recreate the ideal new community, the ideal new nation? Can a critique of the nation state, a movement away from it, only be answered by the creation of another nation? These are questions that become more and more complex as the violence in Kashmir escalates and the situation grows worse. Perhaps the only way they can be addressed is by an open and sensitive dialogue which takes into account the wishes, feelings, fears and doubts of those who are affected by the conflict. Shabnam Lone, a young lawyer and daughter of the All Party Hurriyat Conference leader Abdul Ghani Lone, has this to say: 'In my opinion the only way out of the impasse is to listen to everyone, even the most extreme militant—listen, with patience and without any preconceived notions. To find a solution, there has to be an understanding of the historical, political, economic and real problems here. It is a complex situation that requires a collective solution. The thought process hasn't even taken off yet. Everyone here wants peace and stability. They realize that the best place to live in is where there is dignity and respect for human rights.' [. . .]

References

Senanayake, Darini Tharasingham. 2001. The tragedy of Tamil women in conflict. In *Women, war and peace in South Asia: Beyond victimhood to agency*, ed. Rita Manchanda. New Delhi: Sage Publications.

6

~

LAW

No one would contest that the law has been a privileged site of struggle and debate in the contemporary women's movement. Diverse campaigns—from those relating to forms of violence to unequal rights in the family, community or the workplace—placed direct and central emphasis on the law if a transformation in women's subordination was to be realized. Once again the 1970s and 80s were watershed years, when the disenchantment with the Nehruvian legacy and the failures of the state found fresh ground in the discovery of fundamental problems with laws relating to women and gender equality. After three decades of reform and genuine changes in legislation, activists, legal experts and scholars are presently poised at a different moment of reflection and action.

Today, when many remark on the loss of optimism of earlier decades, it is vital not to lose sight of the range of the issues that were raised around the law. Thus, for instance, in the context of the movement for changes in rape laws in the late 1970s, awareness was stoked by the shocked realization that existing laws had been put in place during the nineteenth century and never been subjected to scrutiny since, thus revealing continuities in colonial and national patriarchies. Women's organizations went beyond the letter of the law to critique representations of the raped woman in legal texts, in the court room and among the police, not to speak of popular culture and the media. The discussion of the Rameeza Bee case in the section on violence is one example of how the state machinery delegitimized the victim by effectively placing her outside normative ideas of womanhood. In order to capture the force of that moment, the first contribution to this cluster is the Open Letter

to the Chief Justice of India, written by four university teachers in 1979—
Upendra Baxi, Vasudha Dhagamwar, Raghunath Kelkar and Lotika Sarkar.
They discovered the case of Mathura, a young woman labourer who had
come to a police station with her family in 1972, and who was then detained
and raped by one of the policemen. In a series of reversals, the Trial Court
first acquitted the police, a ruling which was then overturned by the High
Court of Maharashtra, only to be dismissed yet again by the Supreme Court.
The open letter goes over the details of the case to show the extent of legal
bias and the double standards at work in legitimizing the acts of the
policemen and claiming consent on the part of Mathura. The letter became
the rallying point for feminist organizations across the country and resulted
in the women's movement's first nation-wide campaign, when they demanded
a retrial and changes in the law against rape. (While the retrial was dismissed,
amendments to the rape law came into force in 1983, which included
defining custodial rape as a particularly serious form of rape, and making the
disclosure of the identity of the victim an offence.) In the context of this
reader, the critical role played by law professors in critiquing the law and the
functioning of the Supreme Court should not be forgotten.

Given the enormous publicity that surrounded agitations within criminal
law (rape- and dowry-related crimes especially), other initiatives of this period
have tended to be forgotten. A parallel demand of the early 1980s concerned
the sphere of 'personal law', which was realized in the Family Courts Act of
1984. In the absence of a uniform civil code (UCC) on matters relating to
marriage, divorce, inheritance, child custody and so on, the special purpose
of separate Family Courts was to simplify procedures for women within the
ambit of the existing rights available to them under their respective personal
laws. However, as Flavia Agnes in this article on the experience of the Family
Courts in Mumbai attests, these courts were more concerned with the
preservation of the institution of the family than in providing justice to
women. In her view, the wide powers given to marriage counsellors who urge
for reconciliation, the elaborate procedural codes, and the absence of lawyers,
quite apart from the need for substantive law reform, have prevented the
Family Courts from fulfilling the function for which they were set up.

The first two pieces in this section address themselves to the legal system,
and are thus indicative of the expectations and demands placed on the law
by feminists and scholars. The next two essays provide glimpses of internal
debate and different positions among feminists on whether and how to look
to the law for justice. The excerpt from Nandita Haksar's essay on human
rights lawyering has as its backdrop the long drawn out—and, at times,
bitterly fought—question of a uniform civil code. Other sections in this
volume also discuss the uniform civil code, especially in the Shah Bano case
and the communalization of women's issues that ensued. (See Radha Kumar's
account in the section on religion and communalism and Brinda Karat's

views on the UCC in the section on the family.) Nandita Haksar argues that Indian feminists have been too reliant on a liberal framework in their approaches to women's rights, which gives primacy to the individual above all other considerations. Such an approach generates conflict if not opposition between women's rights and community rights. The focus of her critique is not on the communalization of the UCC, but on the situation in Adivasi areas and the Northeast where tribal rights have been pitted against women's rights. Rather than resort to the language of rights, which she feels will have destructive consequences in these societies, gender inequalities require alternate approaches that draw from and politicize local traditions.

Ratna Kapur's discussion of the laws on sexual harassment is another example of how, over time, different positions have emerged among feminists over the potential of the law as a tool of emancipatory change. On the one hand, the new 'sexual harassment' law is a definite step forward in its non-trivialization of the harm women experience in public spaces like workplaces or universities, when they are the focus of unwelcome sexual attention, and are unable to complain for fear of retaliation. On the other hand, the issues raised take us back to the arguments of the 'Open Letter' in the Mathura rape case so many years ago, especially the question of 'consent' and the problematic use of the sexual history of the victim. Ratna Kapur believes that in the current moment, when sufficient concern has been given to women's 'sexual wrongs', an exclusive demand for laws to regulate and penalize sexual conduct will be counter-productive and only reinforce dominant sexual norms. Too little interest is being paid to 'sexual rights', except by sexual minorities, and to non-legal strategies to counter sexual harassment.

The official structures and forms of the law, including feminist interventions to change them, are thus continually being subjected to critique. Though there has been some acknowledgement of the diversity of laws in the Indian context, criminal and civil, the possibilities and limits of rights, and so on, 'local' laws and customs remain overwhelmingly on the fringes of scholarship and activism. While Nandita Haksar's essay did allude to their importance, a common assumption is that such laws are only significant among marginalized groups, for those excluded from the 'mainstream'. Prem Chowdhry's discussion opens a window onto the role of local law ways by caste panchayats in India's heartland. The context of her essay is the extreme violence that has been meted out to young couples involved in runaway marriages in the urbanizing regions of Haryana, around Delhi and western Uttar Pradesh. These marriages, both inter-caste and intra-caste, flout existing norms, and have invited the most brutal of reprisals—sometimes from family and kin, but more often than not, by the decision of the local caste panchayat. Not only does the official law in the form of the police completely abdicate from intervening in these lynchings, but Chowdhry suggests that—though ill-understood—such power over the lives and choices of a younger generation is probably quite recent, and represents the desire to control and invoke dubious 'traditions' of caste purity in a context of significant economic change and processes of democratization.

What of laws that are being enacted by the state with a view to furthering its aims of development, but with hugely problematic effects on women? Arguably, just such a set of laws in several states of the country revolve around recent enactments and pressures to have no more than two children. The last essay in this section by Mohan Rao describes the many forms of this two-child norm, and the incentives and disincentives that accompany it, from being disbarred from standing for elections in local panchayats to holding a government job. Overriding concern for population explosion, increasingly held up as the most important impediment to development, is the reason supplied. However, as Mohan Rao demonstrates, not only have large parts of India already entered the stage of demographic transition, but the imposition of this norm only serves to further exclude those already marginalized in society—by poverty, caste and education. Not only that. There is growing evidence today of a direct link between the recent drop in fertility in northwestern states and heightened imbalances in the sex ratio, as small families ensure the birth of at least one son through methods of sex selection.

From demands for legal reform to criticisms among feminist legal scholars, from problems of 'local' concepts of justice to those structuring official policy, the law has become simultaneously the most used and criticized sphere for thinking about justice for women. However, this situation has been productive in at least one respect—today, some of the most important scholarship within the broad ambit of women's studies has been furthering the debate through detailed explorations and book-length critiques of the worlds of the law and the histories of rights. The whole realm of feminist legal education, moreover, that had been relatively neglected in the early headier days of the women's movement, is gaining ground. In the present moment characterized by diverse positions and attitudes, after the pendulum has swung from high reliance on the power of the law to a more nuanced and critical relationship, this small selection of essays leaves us with many questions: Have we in fact recognized the extent and depth of the hold of the law in our everyday lives? If the law was never meant to be taken narrowly, but as inextricably enmeshed in dispositions and institutions, what makes it such an attractive 'tool' or 'lever' of change? How can we deepen feminist engagement with multiple forms of legal subjection? How far down the road of extra-legal strategies have we gone? For women's studies this might be a partial list of questions to take feminist engagements with the law forward.

≈

AN OPEN LETTER TO THE
CHIEF JUSTICE OF INDIA

Your Lordship,

We, as Indian citizens and teachers of law, take the liberty of writing this open letter to focus judicial attention and public debate over a decision rendered by the Supreme Court on September 15, 1978 which has been recently reported. The decision was rendered by Justice Jaswant Singh, Kailasam and Koshal in *Tukaram v. State of Maharashtra*, (1979) 2 SCC 143.

The facts of the case briefly are as follows. Mathura, a young girl of the age 14–16, was an orphan who lived with her brother, Gama, both of them labourers. Mathura developed a relationship with Ashok, the cousin of Nushi at whose house she used to work, and they decided to get married. On March 26, 1972, Gama lodged a report that she was kidnapped by Nushi, her husband and Ashok. They were all brought to the police station at 9 p.m. when their statements were recorded. When everyone started to leave the police station, around 10.30 p.m., Tukaram, the head constable and Ganpat, a constable, directed that Mathura remain at the police station. What happened thereafter is best described in the words of Justice Koshal, who wrote the decision of the Court:

> Immediately thereafter Ganpat . . . took Mathura . . . into latrine at the rear of the main building, loosened her underwear, lit a torch and stared at her private parts. He then dragged her to a chhapri . . . In the chhapri he felled her to the ground and raped her in spite of her protests and stiff resistence on her part. He departed after satisfying his lust and then Tukaram . . . who was seated in the cot nearby, came to the place where Mathura . . . was and fondled her private parts. He also wanted to rape her but was unable to do so for the reason that he was in a highly intoxicated condition.

There was natural anxiety outside the police station as the lights were put off and doors bolted. They shouted for Mathura but to no avail. A crowd collected; shortly after, Tukaram emerged to announce that Mathura had already left. Mathura then emerged and announced that she had been raped by Ganpat. The doctor to whom people approached advised them to file a report with the police. Head Constable Baburao was brought from his home to the station, by the fear of the restive crowd, and first information report was lodged.

Mathura was examined by the doctor on March 27. She had no injury. Her hymen revealed old ruptures. Other aspects of physical examination revealed that she had had intercourses in the past. Presence of semen was detected on her clothes and the pyjama of Ganpat.

The Sessions Judge found this evidence insufficient to convict the accused. The farthest he would go was to hold that Mathura had sexual intercourse with Ganpat! But sexual intercourse cannot be equated with rape; there was 'a world of difference', in law, between the two. He feared that Mathura had cried 'rape' in order to prove herself 'virtuous' before the crowd which included her lover. He was also not sure that the semen on her clothes was from intercourse with Ganpat; and although he was disinclined to accept Ganpat's claim that semen on his trousers was due to habitual nocturnal discharges, he entertained the possibility that the semen stains on his clothes may well be due to the possibility of his having intercourse 'with persons other than Mathura'.

The Bombay High Court (Nagpur Bench) reversed the filing and sentenced Tukaram to rigorous imprisonment for one year and Ganpat for five years. Its grounds for reversal were that since both these 'gentlemen' were perfect strangers to Mathura, it was highly unlikely that 'she would make any overtunes or invite the accused to satisfy her sexual desires'. Nor could she have resisted her assailants. The High Court came to the conclusion that the policemen had 'taken advantage of the fact that Mathura was involved in a complaint filed by her brother, and she was alone in the dead hour of the night' in a police station. This proved that she could not, in any probability, have consented to intercourse.

Your Court, Your Lordship, *reversed* the High Court verdict. The reasons given by Justice Koshal are as follows. First, Justice Koshal held that as there were no injuries shown by the medical report, the story of 'stiff resistance having been put up by the girl is all false' and the 'alleged intercourse was a peaceful affair'. Second, the Court disbelieves the testimony of the girl that she shouted 'immediately after her hand was caught by Ganpat'; that she was not allowed to shout when she was taken to latrine and 'that she had raised the alarm even when the underwear was loosened and Ganpat was looking at her private parts with the aid of a torch'.

The Court holds that the 'cries and alarms are, of course, a concoction on her part'. This is said because when she was leaving the police station with her brother, Ganpat had caught her by the arm and she made no attempt to resist it then. The Court says, 'if that be so, it would be preposterous to suggest that although she was in the company of her brother . . . she would be so overawed by the fact of appellants being persons in authority or the circumstance that she was just emerging from a police station that she would make no attempt at all to resist'. Third, the Court holds that under Section 375 of the Penal Code, only the 'fear of death or hurt' can vitiate consent for sexual intercourse. There was no such finding recorded. The circumstantial evidence must be such also as to lead to 'reasonable evidence of guilt'. While the High Court thought there was such reasonable evidence, the Supreme Court did not. Tukaram too was held not guilty because Mathura had in her deposition attributed far more serious things to him and later attributed these acts to Ganpat instead. The fact that Tukaram was present when the incident took place and that he left soon after the incident, says the Court, is 'not inculpatory and is capable of more explanations than one'. But these other explanations are not all indicated by Justice Koshal in his judgment.

Your Lordship, this is an extraordinary decision sacrificing human rights of women under the law and the Constitution. The Court has provided no cogent analysis as to why the factors which weighed with the High Court were insufficient to justify conviction for rape. She was in the police station in the 'dead hour of night'. The High Court found it impossible to believe that she might have taken initiative for intercourse. The fact remains that she was asked to remain in the police station even after her statement was recorded and her friends and relations were asked to leave. Why? The fact remains that Tukaram did nothing whatsoever to rescue the girl from Ganpat. Why? The Court says in its narration of facts, presumably based on the Trial Court records, that Tukaram was intoxicated. But this is not considered material either. Why? Why were the lights put off and doors shut?

Your Lordship, does the Indian Supreme Court expect a young girl 14–16 years old, when trapped by two policemen inside the police station, to successfully raise alarm for help? Does it seriously expect the girl, a labourer, to put up such stiff resistance against well-built policemen so as to have substantial marks of physical injury? Does the absence of such marks necessarily imply absence of stiff resistance? If anything it is Ganpat's body which would have disclosed marks of such resistance by Mathura, like clawing and biting.

Maybe, the evidence of shouts for help and 'stiff resistance' is all 'a tissue of lies'. But does the absence of shouts justify an easy inference of consensual intercourse in a police station? (Incidentally, what would be the Court's reaction if the victim was dumb or gagged?) In any event, how could the fact of shouting within closed doors of a police station be established in such cases?

In restoring the decision of the Sessions Judge, does the Supreme Court of India really believe with him that Mathura had 'invented' the story of rape, and even the confinement in the police station, in order to sound 'virtuous' before Ashok? Does the court believe that Mathura was so flirtatious that even when her brother, her employer and her lover were waiting outside the police station, she could not let go the opportunity of having fun with two policemen and that too in the area adjoining a police station latrine? Does it believe with the Sessions Judge that Mathura was 'habituated to sexual intercourse' to such an extent? And therefore further think that the semen marks on Mathura's clothing could have come from further sexual activities between the police incident and the next morning when she was medically examined? What about semen marks on Ganpat's trousers? Why these double standards? Ganpat's sexual habits give him the benefit of doubt of having 'raped' Mathura; her sexual habits make the Court disbelieve the story of the rape altogether!

We also find it surprising that the Supreme Court should have only focused on the third component of Section 375 of the Indian Penal Code, which applies when rape is committed with the woman's consent, when 'her consent has been obtained by putting her in fear of death or hurt'. But the second component of Section 375 is when rape occurs without her consent. There is a clear difference in law, and common sense, between 'submission' and 'consent'. Consent involves submission; but the converse is not necessarily true. Nor is absence of resistance necessarily indicative of consent. It appears from the facts as stated by the Court and its holdings that there was submission on the part of Mathura. But where was the finding on the crucial element of consent?

It may be that in strict law Ganpat was charged with rape on the third component of description of rape. In that case, the issue before the Court was simply whether the act was committed with her consent, under fear of death or hurt. But still the question whether there was 'consent' was quite relevant; indeed it was crucial. From the facts of the case, all that is established is *submission,* and not consent. Could not their Lordships have extended their analysis of 'consent' in a manner truly protective of the dignity and rights of Mathura? One suspects that the Court gathered an impression from Mathura's liaison with her lover that she was a person of easy virtue. Is the taboo against pre-marital sex so strong as to provide a licence to Indian police to rape young girls? Or to make them submit to their desires in police station?

My Lord, the ink is hardly dried on the decision in *Nandini Satpathy* (1978) 2 SCC 424 when the Supreme Court, speaking through Justice Krishna Iyer, condemned the practice of calling women to police stations in gross violation of Section 160(1) of the Criminal Procedure Code. Under that provision, a woman shall not be required to attend the police investigation at any other place than her place of residence. The Court stated in *Nandini* that it 'is quite probable that the very act of directing a woman to come to the police station in violation of Section 160(1) CrPC may make for tension and negate "voluntariness"'. This observation was made in the context of the right against self-incrimination; is it any the less relevant to situations of 'rape' or, as the Court wishes to put it, 'intercourse' in a police station?

Certainly, the hope expressed by Justice Krishna Iyer that 'when the big fight forensic battles the small gain by victory' has been belied. The law made for Nandini Satpathy does not, after all, apply to the helpless Mathuras of India.

There is not a single word condemning the very act of calling Mathura, and detaining her at the police station in gross violation of the law of the land made by Parliament and so recently reiterated by the Supreme Court. Nor is there a single word in the judgment condemning the use of the police station as a theatre of rape or submission to sexual intercourse. There is no direction to the administration to follow the law. There are no strictures of any kind.

The Court gives no consideration whatsoever to the socio-economic status, the lack of knowledge of legal rights, the age of the victim, lack of access to legal services, and the fear complex which haunts the poor and the exploited in Indian police stations. May we respectfully suggest that yourself and your distinguished colleagues visit incognito, wearing the visage of poverty, some police stations in villages adjoining Delhi?

My Lord, your distinguished colleagues and yourself have earned a well-merited place in contemporary Indian history for making preservation of democracy and human rights a principal theme of your judicial and extra-judicial utterances, especially after March 1977. But a case like this with its cold-blooded legalism snuffs out all aspirations for the protection of human rights of millions of Mathuras in the Indian countryside. Why so?

No one can seriously suggest that all policemen are rapists. Despite massive evidence of police maltreatment of women in custody which rocked the state of Madhya Pradesh in 1977–78 and Andhra Pradesh in *Rameeza Bee case* not too long ago, we would agree with the Court were it to say it explicitly that the doctrine of judicial notice cannot be used to negate the presumption of innocence, even in such type of cases. But must presumption of innocence be carried so far as to negative all reasonable inference from circumstantial evidence?

Mathura, with all her predicaments, has been fortunate that her problem reached the High Court and your Court. But there are millions of Mathuras in whose situations even the first information reports are not filed, medical investigations are not made in time, who have no access to legal services at any level and who rarely have the privilege of vocal community support for their plight.

The Court, under your leadership, has taken great strides for civil liberties in cases involving affluent urban women (e.g. Mrs. Maneka Gandhi and Mrs. Nandini Satpathy). Must the illiterate, labouring, politically mute Mathuras of India be continually condemned to their pre-constitutional Indian fate?

What more can we say? We can only appeal, in conclusion, to have the case reheard, as an unusual situation, by a larger bench, and if necessary by even the full court. This may appear to your Lordship as a startlingly unconventional, and even a naïve suggestion. But nothing short of protection of human rights and constitutionalism is at stake. Surely, the plight of millions of Mathuras in this country is as important as that of Golak Nath, and his Holiness Keshavananda Bharti challenging the validity of restriction on the right to property as a fundamental right, whose cases were heard by a full court.

Maybe on re-examination Ganpat and Tukaram may stand acquitted for better reasons than those now available. But what matters is a search for liberation from the colonial and male-dominated notions of what may constitute the element of consent, and the burden of proof, for rapes which affect many Mathuras on the Indian countryside.

You will no doubt forgive us for this impertinence of writing an open letter to you. But the future of judicial protection of human rights at grassroots level in India at the turn of the century, a concern we all share as citizens and as lawmen, leaves us with no other and better alternative.

With best regards and greetings, we remain,

Sincerely yours,

Upendra Baxi, Vasudha Dhagamwar, Raghunath Kelkar and Lotika Sarkar

Delhi, 16 September 1979

≈

FAMILY COURTS:
FROM THE FRYING PAN INTO THE FIRE?

Flavia Agnes

Historical background

In 1975, the Committee on the Status of Women recommended that all matters concerning the 'family' should be dealt with separately. Accordingly, a provision for special proceedings in family matters was included in the Code of Civil Procedure by an amendment in 1976. The family was broadly defined to include brothers, sisters, ancestors and lineal descendants. But nothing further was done in this respect till the issue of family courts was raised by the women's movement during the early eighties.

The women's movement raised demands for reforms in laws concerning women. In response to this, the rape law was amended in 1983; the Dowry Prohibition Act was amended in 1984 and again in 1986; cruelty and harassment to wives was made a cognizable offence under Section 498 (A) IPC in 1983 and a special section to deal with dowry deaths was included in the IPC (Section 304 B) in 1986. The Family Courts Act which was passed in 1984 was part of the same trend of legal reforms concerning women.

The women's movement, which had raised these demands, focused attention on the unequal power relationship between men and women at every level and the anti-women bias against women, within the law and in court. A demand was made for laws and procedures which would ensure women's economic rights within marriage and make divorce proceedings speedy, less expensive, less traumatic and more just for women.

The requirement was for matrimonial laws and courts somewhat along the lines of labour laws and labour courts, which recognize the unequal power balance between labour and management. Special statutes and procedures have been enacted so that the balance is tilted in favour of labour. According to legal experts O.P. and K.R. Malhotra, the law governing industrial relations is an attempt to mitigate the disequilibrium inherent in employment relations—moulding contract through legislation. The main object of industrial adjudication is to be a countervailing force to counteract the inequalities in bargaining power which are inherent in the employment relationship. This is achieved by the extension of existing agreements or by making new ones or, in general, by the creation of new obligations or the modification of old ones. The aim of industrial adjudications was to be free from the subconscious pressures of preconceived notions and the tyranny of dogmas to adopt a realistic, rational and pragmatic approach.

Laws and procedures were needed in matrimonial matters which would apply the same principles in order 'to mitigate disequilibrium inherent in marriage relationships by creating new obligations or modifying old ones'. The aim of the family courts ought to have been 'to be free from subconscious pressures the preconceived notions and tyranny of dogmas and adopt a realistic, rational and pragmatic approach'.

The Family Courts Act: Pro-family and anti-women

Since the demand for a uniform, secular and non-sexist code was not conceded, the Family Courts Act was seen as a positive step, at least where procedural law is concerned; because only half the problems women face are located in substantive laws. The other half are located in procedural laws— the hostile and intimidating atmosphere within courts, endless delays, strict technicalities and the sexist and anti-women interpretations of laws by judges.

But the Family Courts Act was not aimed at tilting the balance in favour of women. Instead, the Act was committed to preserving the institution of marriage. This was a regressive approach, as by now it is a historically well-established fact that the institution of marriage can be preserved only at the cost of women—by denying women property rights and the right to divorce. In fact, all recent laws which are considered to be progressive and pro-women have been anti-family. For instance, the Dissolution of Muslim Marriages Act, 1939, and the Hindu Marriage Act, 1955, which gave Muslim and Hindu women the right to divorce, the Hindu Adoption and Maintenance Act, 1956, which recognized the right of Hindu women to reside separately and yet be maintained by their husbands, the amendment to the Hindu Marriage Act in 1976 which included the provision of mutual consent divorce, can all be viewed in a traditional sense as being 'anti-family'. The next logical step was to move further in the same direction by making this right of divorce a practical and feasible reality rather than a nightmare by ensuring that divorce proceedings are speedy, devoid of anti-women bias and economically more fair and just to women.

The judiciary and court officials have to be carefully selected or alternatively oriented towards achieving this end. The object has to be gender justice. But instead, the act stipulated that persons committed to the need to protect and preserve the institution of marriage should be appointed as judges. Ironically, by this very definition, women activists and lawyers whose sustained campaign for legal reforms had in the first place raised the demand for family courts, would be disqualified from being appointed as judges or counsellors in the family courts, by the very nature of their activities, which can be labelled as 'feminist' and hence 'anti-family'.

The (Family Courts) Act also makes a presumption that children's welfare lies within the 'family', with both the parents living under one roof. Anyone who has any grassroots experience of working on women's issues will realize that this is a baseless presumption. In a broken marriage, it is far better for the children who are daily exposed to verbal abuse, physical battering, humiliation and degradation of their mother to be brought up by a single parent, inspite of the lowering of their economic standards. Many a time it is the children who advise their parents to separate rather than stay on in a bad marriage. But the woman is often advised to stay on in a bad marriage only because society does not offer any alternatives. Instead of creating an environment where women can live in dignity with their children by strictly enforcing women's economic rights, by allowing women and children the use of the matrimonial home even after divorce and generally creating the social space by making houses and jobs available to single mothers, the Act just presumes that the institution of marriage should be preserved in the interest and well being of the children.

Unfortunately, women's groups at this juncture did not raise a strong objection to the Act and were under the illusion that the actual functioning of the courts would work in favour of women.

The Act also did not define 'family'. Matters of serious economic consequence which affect the family, like testamentary matters are not within the purview of the family courts. What is within the purview of family courts are matters concerning women and children (divorce, maintenance, adoption, etc)—issues which the courts were supposed to deal with on an emotional plane rather than on a legal one. Also, the Act is indifferent to issues concerning minority marriages (Parsi and Christian) which are within the jurisdiction of the High Courts. No statement has been made whether the jurisdiction will continue with the High Court or will now be transferred to the family court.

The Act also brought civil and criminal jurisdiction under one roof. This was seen as a positive measure which would centralize all litigation concerning women. But the maintenance under Chapter IX of the Criminal Procedure Code had served a specific purpose. Since there are magistrates' courts in every area, a woman could file an application at a place close to her residence.

Secondly, the very nature of criminal courts facilitated quicker disposal of applications than a civil court. Thirdly, there was a seriousness and a sense of intimidation which is associated with a criminal court, which would act in a woman's favour. Also the Act brought under one roof matters which were handled by forty odd magistrates and at least two courts in the city civil court into five court rooms in the city of Bombay.

Alternative provided

While the Act laid down the broad guidelines, it was left to the state government to frame the rules of procedure. But the state governments failed miserably to create an alternative. Most state governments did not bother to frame the Rules and set up family courts. Rajasthan and Karnataka were the first two states to set up family courts. But soon women litigants as well as activists were disillusioned with the functioning of the courts. The situation has become even worse for women within the family courts. The discussion here is limited to the situation in Maharashtra and more specifically, Bombay. But the overall situation is the same everywhere, with minor differences. For instance, in Karnataka the tenure of the judges is fixed for five years, so that, in the absence of a judge selected specially for his commitment to safeguard women's rights, some feel that they are saddled with an anti-woman judge with no hopes of his transfer in the near future. In contrast, in Tamil Nadu, the marriage counsellors keep changing every three months and each time the woman meets a new counsellor to whom she has to explain her problems all over again, with no continuity in the discussion.

The Maharashtra Family Courts Rules framed in 1987 deal elaborately with the function and role of marriage counsellors in family courts. In fact, twenty-seven out of the thirty-seven sections deal with this aspect. Wide powers have been given to the marriage counsellors—i.e. to make home visits, to ascertain the standard of living of the spouses and the relationship with children, seek information from the employer, etc. While a rare and sensitive marriage counsellor can and may use this power in the interests of women, more often than not, these powers are used against women—in the interest of the family—since the primary commitment of the marriage counsellor is to 'preserving the institution'.

Further, and even more strange, after all the elaborate provisions in the Rules regarding marriage counsellors, their report is not even binding on the judges. The report of the marriage counsellor is kept confidential and they cannot be cross-examined.

The marriage counsellors state that their duty is only to ascertain whether reconciliation is possible. While the marriage counsellors might make a useful intervention during the initial stage of conflict, where the marriage has broken down irretrievably this would only delay the proceedings for the enforcement of economic and other rights of women and children.

After the preliminary meeting with the marriage counsellor, the case would proceed as per the Rules of the Code of Civil Procedure. Thus ironically, those litigants who are expected to present their case in person, and are not expected to have any expert knowledge, face the maximum procedural problems. While the Rules laid down by the state government (in Maharashtra) have dealt elaborately on irrelevant issues, no attention is paid to creating alternate rules of procedure. This has resulted in total chaos in the functioning of the family courts. The Rules did not simplify procedures but have merely reproduced the Code of Civil Procedure with the minor addition that parties should be present in person. While lawyers are excluded from representing their clients, litigants can ask legal advice at any stage of the proceedings. Even simple things like service by advocates on behalf of their clients has not been changed, but an additional provision that it can also be served on the parties concerned, but an additional provision that it can also be served on the parties concerned, has been added. [. . .]

Absence of lawyers

It is a myth that the Act does away with the need for lawyers. The family counsellors themselves state that litigants are exploited by lawyers who charge exorbitant fees just to give legal advice and do simple drafting of the petition. All the technicalities of a civil court are strictly followed by the family courts. So long as the substantive law (in this case the personal laws based on religion which are diverse, complex and confusing) and the technicalities of the Code of Civil Procedure are strictly followed, the need for lawyers cannot be eliminated.

The Civil Procedure Code lays down the procedure which ought to be and can be followed in court, which is meant for lawyers to understand and follow. For a lay person who is not familiar with legal jargon, it is extremely difficult to follow this Code. The Act and the Rules exclude representation by lawyers, without creating any alternate and simplified rules. Merely stating that the proceedings are conciliatory, and not adversarial, does not actually make it so. The situation has worsened, because in the absence of lawyers, litigants are left to the mercy of court clerks and peons to help them follow the complicated Rules. Women are not even aware of the consequences of the suggestions made by court officials. For instance, when a woman files for divorce and maintenance, the husbands turn around and press for reconciliation only to avoid paying maintenance. It is crucial to the woman that people who are mediating are aware of these strategies. But if a judge or a counsellor feels that a woman should go back to the husband only because he is making the offer and as a wife it is her duty to obey him, it will be detrimental to the woman's interests. Reconciliation can be brought about only by persons committed to protecting women's rights.

Substantive rights lacking

In addition to procedural lacunae, older problems connected with substantive law persist. Family courts have been set up to deal with problems which arise on the breakdown of a marriage—divorce, restitution of conjugal rights, claims for alimony, and maintenance and custody of children. The setting up of family courts does not in any way alter the substantive law relating to marriage.

Marriage by itself does not confer any rights on women except the right to live in the matrimonial home during the subsistence of the marriage and the right to be maintained. Divorce disentitles a woman to the matrimonial home. Whether or not she gets maintenance during a separation or after divorce, will depend on her ability to prove her husband's means. In a situation in which women are often unaware of their husband's business dealings and sources of income, it is difficult, if not impossible, to prove his income. To make matters worse, the existence of a parallel black economy makes it impossible to identify the legal source of income.

In such a situation—unless the law changes radically conferring rights on women and creating new rights in their favour—the setting up of family courts will not help alter their position. The right to matrimonial property would be the first step in ensuring security for women. This would mean that all property acquired after the marriage, and any assets used jointly, such as the matrimonial home will belong equally to the husband and wife. Based on such a law, family courts would be able to provide effective relief to women on the breakdown of a marriage. Even otherwise, courts must be empowered by law to transfer the assets or income of a husband to his wife and children or to create a trust to protect the future of the children of a broken marriage. As the law stands today, courts have no power to create obligations binding on the husband for the benefit of the wife or children. The other much neglected area of law for women is domestic violence. Wife beating is prevalent in all classes and yet there is no effective law to prevent it or protect a woman against a violent husband.

With these substantive changes, family courts will be empowered to protect women, but without them, these courts have ended up being poor substitutes for civil courts.

The adversarial system is unsuited to the needs of women who are in any case disadvantaged and have no access to information relating to the husband's assets and income. Family courts must have investigative powers so that they can compel disclosures of income and assets to pass orders of maintenance. Such procedures have not been introduced in the Act, once again making the Act meaningless. There is an overemphasis on criminal redress. Little or no thinking has gone into evolving effective civil remedies. The Family Courts Act does not explicitly empower the court to grant injunctions preventing violence or ouster of violent husbands. As a result the Act has ended up being an ineffective instrument to give justice to women.

The court is seen more as a court doling out maintenance orders which cannot be enforced, rather than as a court deciding crucial legal and economic issues concerning women. The provision that women judges should be appointed and that the judges should have expertise and experience in settling family disputes have remained only on paper. The family court in Bombay does not have a single woman judge. Also, the judges appointed to the family court do not seem to have any special experience or expertise in dealing with family matters, nor any special expertise in settling disputes through conciliation, a requirement prescribed in the Act. In fact, the experience of the family court in Bombay during its brief tenure of ten months indicates that the post of principal judge is a stepping stone and a stop gap arrangement for an elevation to the High Court.

The Act and the Rules provide for legal experts to be appointed as 'amicus curiae' and also a panel of experts in various fields to help the courts to arrive at settlements. The Act also provides for legal aid services for the economically weaker section of litigants. All these positive suggestions have remained only on paper. The Rules provide for tape recorders to be used while recording evidence which could be used at the appeal stage. But this proposal is too far-fetched for the family courts which did not even have adequate provisions for paper and stationery to begin with!

While not denying the fact that family courts are the felt need of the day, merely instituting such courts haphazardly, in a perfunctory manner, will not in any way further the spirit of such courts. While some of the problems are the teething problems of any new institution, others are more inherently built into the Act and the Rules. Unless they are corrected at this juncture, the family courts will be a hindrance rather an aid to a woman's fight for justice.

≈

HUMAN RIGHTS LAWYERING:
A FEMINIST PERSPECTIVE
Nandita Haksar

I am a product of both the feminist and the human rights movements that emerged in our country in the post-Emergency period. These coincided with the international upsurge in democratic consciousness beginning in the 1960s with the civil rights movement in the USA, the student movement in

Europe, and the rise of the ecological and feminist consciousness in the 1970s. It was a time when questions were raised about the meaning and significance of all aspects of our lives.

I joined law after we realized the need for feminist lawyers because of our frustration in trying to make other lawyers understand the need to translate our politics into legal action. However, after the initial years I was a full-time human rights lawyer. Thus I was lucky to be a part of the rich debates in both these movements but often found that the discussions in each took place in ignorance of the discussions in the other movement.

I do not think I will be able to capture the excitement of those heady days when we spent hours discussing each word and trying to redefine the meaning and content of concepts from the point of view of our politics. These debates were invariably and unashamedly linked to questions of ethics and morality. And that is what gave the movements their depth and their reach. Here I will deal with some specific questions that arose in the course of the two movements which touch on the problems of international human rights standard setting. [. . .]

The liberal human rights model is based on the primacy of individual civil liberties over all rights. Indian feminists have often fallen into the trap of accepting this model and articulating their demands in terms of individual civil rights for women. Thus, often women's rights have seemed to be in contradiction with the rights of minorities. The question is whether women's rights are necessarily in conflict with the rights of minority communities.

I shall give an illustration of how this emphasis on individual liberty has created a false dichotomy between women's rights versus tribal peoples' rights. Liberal feminists have been attacking customary laws among the tribal peoples in the Northeast on the grounds that it is patriarchal. It does not treat men and women equally. They by implication look upon the customary law as 'traditional' and compare it to 'modern' legislation. At a purely superficial level this stand is absolutely correct from the tribal women's point of view. And it is also true that some of the tribal women facing anti-women customs which deprive them of their basic rights have also joined in the demand that the customary law must go.

Thus we see that the same women's groups (including some feminists) are asking for a uniform civil code in the Northeast even though they have stopped demanding this for the rest of India ever since the slogan was taken over by the Hindu communal forces. They now see that their dream of a uniform civil code can be imposed on the peoples of the Northeast in the name of upholding women's rights.

Within this perspective the only way a women's organization can intervene is by supporting the demand for the codification of tribal laws, and for the anti-women customs to be declared violative of Article 14. And that is precisely what some of the women's groups have been advocating. All this seems logical and consistent with the slogan that women's rights are human rights.

But international human rights law also recognizes the rights of indigenous people to their way of life and in the case of the Nagas this is protected by Article 371-A of the Indian Constitution. The Article protects Naga social and religious practices and their customary laws and procedures. In addition, just a few years ago the world celebrated the Year of the Indigenous People. How do we see this contradiction?

The Vienna Declaration on Human Rights of 1995 has a special section on indigenous peoples' rights. Article 31 states that the World Conference on Human Rights urges states to ensure the full and free participation of indigenous people in all aspects of society, in particular in matters of concern to them. And customary law would certainly fall in that category.

Thus some activists are inclined to give primacy to the rights of the community and the rights of indigenous people over the rights of the individual tribal woman. This approach comes easily to those sections within the third world who, in the process of attacking the primacy of individual rights within liberal theory, have gone on to give primacy to socio-economic rights. This stand has the effect of sacrificing vital civil and political rights and even justifying their violation in the name of some 'larger' principle, which may be community, nation or state.

Can we think of a third model of human rights? A model which gives equal importance to individual and collective rights? I think we can. But it requires that we build a jurisprudence which would question the premises upon which the present human rights and some kinds of feminist jurisprudence are based. We have to create new human rights.

But contemporary Indian feminists have not (with a few exceptions) really produced a critique of the law, without which it is not possible to evolve a new jurisprudence. In fact they seem to have accepted a premise of liberal theory that rule of law can guarantee human rights and, by extension, women's rights. In a draft on law reforms some feminists state that 'the law has to provide more rights and equality than the society itself . . . the law also has to be forward-looking and progressive'.

The human rights movement in India has, through its work over more than two decades, shown how oppressive the state is. Through its continuous fact-finding efforts, it has built up a systematic critique of the Indian state which leaves no room for doubt that the law is primarily an instrument for the conservation and perpetuation of present social, economic and political inequality, and injustice. Human rights literature all over the world bears testimony to the fact that the law in a liberal state is not at all a neutral and objective arbitrator of rights. In fact, in the guise of protecting rights the law protects power.

Legal ethics, which are supposed to uphold the dignity of the profession, are also meant in fact to mystify the real role of the law and the lawyer in maintaining the status quo. The law is anti-women and casteist. It is not only a question of wrongful implementation but the inherent intent of the statute.

If we understand this we see that the existence of an alternative legal system assumes a very important role in showing us that there are other ways for dispute settlement than the so-called modern legal system. It is in this context that the fight of indigenous peoples all over the world, including in India, against the imposition of the alien legal system on them assumes a special political significance.

In fact, what is derogatively or rather patronizingly called tribal customary law is in fact tribal jurisprudence. I do not mean to either mystify this system or romanticize it, but having studied some aspects of it, I can say that tribal jurisprudence has evolved ways and means of preserving the ecological balance and preventing ecological degradation by evolving complex sets of practices which form a part of their jurisprudence.

Central to their jurisprudence is the concept of collective rights to natural resources and the concept of common property. It also balances the rights of the individual with that of the community in ways that caste-based communities do not. For the purposes of this article, I need not go into the details of the law except to say that tribal societies are based on common property and collective rights. If these are eroded, the whole society would be destroyed.

The Indian state knows this very well. And that is why it has encouraged the slogan for the codification of tribal laws. They say that in order to implement the laws they need to be written down. However, the problem is not only of writing them down but of codification. Once any customary law is codified it will get fossilized and die a natural death because it will not be able to evolve. By defining tribal customary laws as 'traditional', the state makes out that its relevance is historical, and it takes away the rights of the tribal people to evolve their customs in accordance with the times.

In fact, tribal laws have been evolving over the times. In Mizoram, Nagaland and in Meghalaya (I do not know of the other states), I know of many instances when the customary law has been used to solve complex issues, including interventions in student movements or inter-village disputes. It is also true that there are powerful vested interests within their societies who do not want customs to change or misinterpret it in order to serve their narrow personal interests. For instance, the chief minister of Nagaland who said that reservations for women would be against the traditional society.

Women in the Northeast could in fact fight for the right to evolve their own customs in consonance with the times. The student movement and the civil rights movement would support their efforts to a large extent. But this would mean reading and understanding their own society with a new perspective. It is a far more difficult task than filing a petition under Article

14 or getting the support of women who have no stakes in the future of tribal societies.

This path would not lead to a confrontation between women's rights and rights of indigenous peoples as much as the second approach. Unfortunately, women from the middle classes, whether in tribal society or non-tribal, have used the women's movement for either solving their individual problems without any commitment to a larger movement or to get into the same patriarchal structures which are the cause of oppression.

Many of us have seen that the language of the feminist movement has changed from human rights to expediency. Just as upper caste and upper class women began using the movement to get the right to participate in the very system they had said was exploitative and oppressive, tribal elite women are using the movement to get rights to become a part of their own system which they say is patriarchal.

We have already seen how the demand for a uniform civil code has been usurped by the Hindu communal forces. For the women involved in the national movement it was a demand linked to secular, modern and rational politics of nation building. The insensitivity of the feminists to minority rights and feelings of Muslims was an important reason for the success of the Bharatiya Janata Party in communalizing our demand. Some feminists have been equally insensitive to the problems of tribal peoples in the Northeast, and their patronizing attitude can be used by the state to justify the breaking up of the Northeast societies by imposing an alien legal system based on individual liberty and private property.

Such disintegration of those societies is taking place for many other reasons, but the women's movement can be a powerful legitimizer. The government wants to liberate the land from the peoples' control for developmental projects which will lead to further landlessness and impoverishment of the people.

Some years back a similar controversy came up in the context of land rights of the Ho women in the heartland of Jharkhand. A fact-finding team had gone to inquire into a police firing and reports of police atrocities in Singhbhum district of Bihar. The committee was sponsored by the All India People's Union for Civil Liberties and *Manushi*, a women's magazine. The team included Madhu Kishwar of *Manushi* and in the course of the fact-finding she found the Ho women suffered greatly because of the denial of land rights to them. She decided to challenge this discrimination against women under the Chotanagpur Tenancy Act [CNT] 1876. The petition challenged the provision as a violation of Articles 14 and 15 of the Constitution read with Article 46 of the Directive Principles of State Policy.

The petition prayed that in order that these fundamental rights become meaningful in the lives of Ho women, it would be necessary that the provisions of the Succession Act 1925 apply to the Ho people. At a superficial level there is nothing objectionable about the contention that Ho women should not be denied the benefit of the equality clause in the Constitution and be given the right to inherit property. The petition is based on the classical human rights arguments.

When I say classical human rights, I mean the first generation rights which include the right to be treated equally under the law, that the law apply equally to all citizens and that any discrimination must be based on valid classification. Let us examine each of these rights in the context of the petition filed by Madhu Kishwar.

The Constitution and international human rights law also recognize the right of tribal peoples to be given special protection. Thus there are different sets of laws which apply to tribal peoples and to non-tribal peoples. Section 76 which Madhu Kishwar seeks to have deleted is the section which constitutes the major part of the CNT's concern with and defence of the Adivasi land system. Without this section the Act becomes merely an assurance of rent free holding of those few remaining sections of land registered as bhumihari and khuntkatti.

The remainder of the Act, which forms its major portion, consists in a defence of non-Adivasi rights in land, e.g. the rights of superior landlords. Thus the role of the Act in defending the tribes becomes subverted, its power to defend tribal tenancy becomes destroyed, when Section 76 is deleted.

The Adivasi land system is based on a communal land system in which no one has absolute rights to land. In a system of common property the people have mainly a right to use the land rather than private property rights of absolute ownership. This is true for a majority of the land systems in the Northeast. If the Indian Succession Act were introduced, it would mean the government and other vested interests would use it to break common property into private property, since the Succession Act 1925 does not recognize common property or use rights.

Then we come to the question of the discrimination between men and women. There is no question that it exists within Ho and other tribal societies. However, the position of women within tribal societies is far better than the position of women in caste society. There is equal availability of divorce to both men and women, there is a right to remarry, absence of religious taboos concerning menstruation and absence of physical seclusion. The sense of human dignity and self-respect is the basis of tribal societies.

Inviting the Supreme Court's intervention into the affairs of the Ho community and asking the Supreme Court judges to evaluate their society is in many ways similar to what happened in *Shah Bano's case*, when the judges were invited to interpret the Holy Koran.

The destruction of tribal societies means the destruction of ways of life, philosophies and traditions which are a rich source of cultures which teach values based on co-operation, rationality and consensus, in contrast to the capitalist values of competition, elections and conflict. When I say this, it does not mean that I am advocating the 'preservation' of these societies in museums. Nor do I think that we can revive the past. What I am saying is that there are alternatives to filing writ petitions on grounds of violation of human rights or fundamental rights; there are other ways of dealing with the problem of inequality between men and women in tribal societies.

What are these ways? First of all there is a need to build a movement based on tribal socio-cultural traditions. It is not possible to discuss these political strategies within this space. But an alternative to a movement cannot be a petition. I strongly feel we should resort to the law only when the movement is strong enough to carry the law reform forward. In almost all such cases, a legal battle should only supplement the political battle outside the courts. If the legal battle is allowed to take precedence over the political one, the law is easily used by the state to subvert the political battle's objectives.

Having said this, I feel that we do need to build a movement for creating a new jurisprudence which draws on the human rights law and certain feminist legal critiques. But both human rights jurisprudence and liberal and radical feminism place a great deal of stress on individual rights and the primacy of individual liberty over all other kinds of human rights. Already western feminists have found the limitation of this approach. For instance, Carol Smart (1989, 139) writes that while the language of rights was important in challenging the conservative order in the past for women and other oppressed sections, she feels that 'the rhetoric of rights has become exhausted, and may even be detrimental. This is especially the case where women are demanding rights which are not intended (in an abstract sense) to create equal rights with men, but where the demand is for a "special" right (e.g. women's right to choose) for which there has been no masculine equivalent'.

I would add that the rhetoric of rights is also not useful wherever we need greater state protection and regulation. In such situations human rights arguments can be and have been used to deny women's rights. An extreme case is of the United States government's refusal to ratify the Convention on the Elimination of Discrimination Against Women on the grounds that it invites greater state regulation in 'private' areas which is against their Constitution.

The conflict between individual rights and collective rights is inherent in human rights law. And this conflict is specially relevant to the women's movement and also to the other movements concerned with the equality of races and the rights of other oppressed groups. It is also important for those engaged in a struggle for workers' and peasants' rights. In fact, trade unions have forced the international human rights law to recognize the right to collective bargaining. It is a recognition of a modern community right and not a traditional one. Article 29 of the International Bill of Human Rights is not a traditional one. Article 29 of the International Bill of Human Rights also recognizes that '(e)veryone has duties to the community in which alone the free and full development of his personality is possible'.

In this effort to construct a new jurisprudence, we can draw upon the human rights tradition, the feminist critiques of law and on tribal jurisprudence. But we cannot hope to begin this task without a political understanding of our society and economy and without a vision of a future society. If our vision is limited, so will be our legal strategies. It is not an easy task. But then nothing worth doing is or has been easy. There lies the challenge.

Reference

Smart, Carol. 1989. *Feminism and the power of law*. London: Routledge.

∾

SEXCAPADES AND THE LAW
Ratna Kapur

Lurid stares, offensive remarks, sexual innuendos, sexual tones, embarrassing jokes and unsavoury remarks are among the litany of conduct and expression that is being captured in the net of the sexual harassment law and policy as it is emerging in India. While sexual harassment of women (and other groups, including sexual minorities) remains a pervasive and systemic phenomenon, there is considerable scepticism whether cabining and containing sexual conduct and expression is an effective way in which to address the problem.

Do we want the heavy weight of the law to block the lurid stare? Silence the embarrassing joke? Modulate one's sexual tone? Are sex codes on university campuses going to empower women or lead to moral surveillance of sexual conduct? Is the National Commission of Women producing a code of conduct that liberates sex, sexual speech and conduct from the Victorian/ Hindutva closet, or does it penalize sex per se as a negative and contaminating force? These are some of the concerns provoked by the law and policy on sexual harassment which need to be debated and addressed if we are keen to produce an empowering project for women and deal effectively with the problem of sexual harassment. [. . .]

Sexual harassment law in India evolved through a series of cases, which ultimately culminated in the Supreme Court decision in Vishaka v. the State of Rajasthan (August 1997). The Vishaka case was a class action petition brought by a number of social action groups and non-governmental organizations, seeking legal redress for women whose work was obstructed and inhibited because of sexual harassment in the workplace.

The Supreme Court decision accepted that sexual harassment in the workplace violated women's equality rights and that employers were obligated to provide a mechanism for the prevention of sexual harassment and for the resolution, settlement or prosecution of sexual harassment. The court set out guidelines on sexual harassment in the workplace and declared the guidelines as constituting the law of the land until further action was taken by the legislature.

The legal definition of sexual harassment provided by the court is as follows: 'Sexual harassment includes unwelcome sexually determined behaviour (whether directly or by implication) as: physical contact and advances; a demand or request for sexual favours; sexually coloured remarks; showing pornography; and any other unwelcome physical, verbal or non-verbal conduct of a sexual nature where such conduct was humiliating and constituted a health and safety problem.' More specifically, the court held that such conduct would constitute discrimination if a woman has reasonable grounds to believe that objecting to the conduct would disadvantage her in terms of her recruitment or promotion or when it creates a hostile work environment.

The court places an obligation on employers, in both the public and private sectors, to 'take appropriate steps to prevent sexual harassment' and 'provide appropriate penalties' against the offender. The criminal law should be resorted to where the behaviour amounts to a specific offence under the Indian Penal Code. It also recommends that a complaint mechanism be created in the employer's organization to redress the complaint made by the victim and that such a committee should be headed by a woman, and not less than half its members should be women.

The Vishaka judgement is significant at a symbolic level for its validation of the problem of sexual harassment and recognition of the fact that it is an experience many women are almost routinely subjected to in the workplace. As regards the definition, there are no doubt certain clear cases of sexual conduct that constitute sexual harassment—for instance, what has been called quid pro quo sexual harassment in which a threat is made or a benefit offered in order to obtain sex.

The employer who tells his office manager that she will receive a promotion if she has sex with him, or the professor who informs his student that she will not pass the class unless she goes on a date with him, are engaging in this type of sexual harassment. In these situations, certain individuals use their position of relative power to coerce or intimidate others in positions of lesser power to engage in sexual interactions. This type of behaviour clearly constitutes sex discrimination and remedy ought to be made available to the woman who is harmed.

The decision is important in so far as it validates that women do experience sexual harassment in many different areas of their lives. However,

I question the formulation of the sexual harassment guidelines for two primary reasons. The first is that the guidelines impugn a vast breadth and scope of sexual conduct. Second, they reinforce sexual conservatism and Puritanism within our society (the Hindu right is among those who support these guidelines). These issues highlight the core concern that underlines this article, the erosion of the possibility for sexual freedom, which must be addressed if any effective redress is ever to be available to women for sexual wrongs.

The primary ingredient of sexual harassment as defined by the Supreme Court guidelines is that the sexual conduct must be unwelcome. A second requirement appears to be that the conduct must disadvantage a woman, such as affect her recruitment or promotion or create a hostile work environment. Unfortunately, the second leg of the definition seems to have been dispensed with in a subsequent Supreme Court decision, leaving open the possibility that any kind of sexual remark can be impugned under the guidelines. [. . .]

In the first major decision after the Vishaka judgment, the Supreme Court not only broadened the scope of the sexual harassment test, it also delivered a decision that should leave us worried about how the law is being used to reinforce women's sexual conduct along the boundaries of traditional sexual behaviour without necessarily remedying women's claims of sexual harassment (Apparel Export Promotion Council v. A.K. Chopra (1999).

In the APOC (Apparel Export Promotion Council) decision, the complainant was the private secretary to the chairman of the company. The chairman had tried to molest the complainant on several occasions during the course of her work, including trying to sit beside her when she did not desire it and trying to molest her in a hotel elevator. The chairman was dismissed after a departmental inquiry. He challenged the order through the courts, arguing that he had never actually touched the complainant. The High Court held that 'trying' to molest a female employee was not the same as actually molesting her and that the chairman's conduct could not therefore be impugned. The company appealed to the Supreme Court.

Among the several questions considered by the Supreme Court, I want to focus on the following: (*i*) Does the action of a superior against a female employee, which is against moral sanctions and does not withstand the test of decency and morality, amount to sexual harassment? (*ii*) Is physical contact an essential ingredient of the charge?

The court accepted the definition of sexual harassment as laid out in Vishaka. However, it went on to determine the content of the sexual harassment, holding that 'any action or gesture which, whether directly or by implication, aims at or has the tendency to *outrage the modesty of a female employee,* must fall under the general concept of the definition of sexual harassment' (Ibid., 775; emphasis supplied).

The court further held that the 'victim's testimony' must be evaluated against the backdrop of the entire case, thus adopting a test of reasonableness that seems to be based on the victim's perspective. It accepted that sexual harassment violated a number of international conventions including the Convention on the Elimination of All Forms of Discrimination Against Women. Further, that the conduct of the chairman in trying to sit next to the complainant and to touch her, despite her protests, constituted 'unwelcome sexually determined behaviour' on his part and was an attempt to 'outrage her modesty'. His behaviour was against 'moral sanctions' and did not withstand the test of 'decency and modesty' and amounted to unwelcome sexual advances. Together, his actions constituted sexual harassment (ibid., para 23).

The court also considered the evidence of the complainant's colleague who stated that when she inquired into the complainant's distressed state she stated that 'being unmarried, she could not explain what had happened to her'. The court held that the material on record thus clearly established that the unwelcome sexual behaviour on the part of the chairman was also an attempt to outrage her modesty.

'Unwelcome' signs

The core ingredient of the definition is that the sexual conduct must be 'unwelcome', which remains for the complainant to prove. However, this burden is conditioned by dominant sexual norms and the complainant's conduct. More specifically it means that the complainant's sexual past, mode of dress and conduct may be introduced as relevant evidence in determining whether the conduct was 'unwelcome'.

Dress, conduct and even profession, may thus be used to show that the harasser was incited to the conduct and thus constitute sufficient evidence to disqualify her claim of sexual harassment. Bar room dancers, waitresses, performers, are all vulnerable to such claims. Indeed the definition seems to provide scope for reproducing and reinforcing dominant assumptions about sex, women's sexuality and sexual practices.

These concerns are reminiscent of the experience women have had with the operation of rape laws, and the requirement of 'lack of consent'. A rape victim's dress, speech, sexual history, chastity have all been deployed to undermine her claim that she was forced to have sexual intercourse against her will or without her consent. Her conduct invited sex. She asked for it. In rape law, a woman's consent has been contingent on her previous sexual history, her conduct at the time of the encounter (did she reasonably resist or simply submit?)—questions that have not been effectively addressed.

Indeed, even in the legal arena, the constant call for the repeal of the legal provision, that permits the defence to introduce facts about the victim's previous sexual history in court in order to discredit her testimony, has simply been ignored by the government and has not been pursued by women's groups. A woman's conduct will be the key in determining whether or not the sexual behaviour is welcome or unwelcome. Her dress, speech, demeanour, personal history and relationship with the harasser will all be called into question. As long as women's sexual conduct remains constrained, conditional, and subject to moral scrutiny, sexual laws for her benefit will be subject to those very same constraints.

In the APOC decision, the complainants' pristine conduct, including her lack of knowledge about sex (as she was not married) were factors that redeemed her credibility. Had she been knowledgeable, and described in minute detail what happened to her (and it is not in the least bit clear from the reading of the decision what happened to her), then presumably her sexual knowledge would have damaged her credibility. Had she used foul language, or sexual language in her interactions, it could have undermined her claim that the conduct was unwelcome. Had she spoken in a language that is replete with sexual innuendos such as Punjabi, would that also have diminished her claim that the conduct was unwelcome?

I focus on the word 'unwelcome' in the definition of sexual harassment to emphasize the point that it is a qualified term. The requirement of 'unwelcome' will be informed by outdated stereotypes about women's behaviour and sexual conduct. If her speech or dress is found to be sexually provocative, it can be relevant in determining whether she found particular sexual advances unwelcome. The defence could well argue that her dress and manner welcomed sexual attention. How do we determine the distinction between sexual attention and unwelcome sexual conduct?

The court also read the notion of 'outraging the modesty of a woman' into the definition of sexual harassment. This phrase has not been defined in any statute or code, but has been interpreted by the Supreme Court as an action that could be perceived as one which is 'capable of shocking the sense of decency of a woman'. Given that the origin of the 'outraging the modesty of a woman' standard is Victorian and colonial, it represents an understanding about women's sexuality that is chaste, pure, asexual and disinterested in pleasure. There is little connection between this concept, which is being cast as a core 'Indian value', and contemporary understandings of women's sexuality.

This decision is indicative of the way in which sexual harassment law will operate when formulated without sufficient attention to the Indian context— the content of the definition as well as to dominant sexual norms. It suggests that sexual harassment law is not a force for change for women. The APOC decision highlights how sexual harassment is contingent on a woman's sexual status and knowledge. A victim's narrative of the encounter is substantially qualified by the framework of dominant sexual norms. If she has transgressed any of these norms, then her story of sexual victimization can be converted into a narrative of agency, invitation, provocation and 'welcomeness'.

Sex talk under siege

My second concern is over the over-inclusiveness of the definition to the extent that all sexual speech and expression will be curtailed or implicated as sexual harassment. Unfortunately, this line was further extended by the Supreme Court in the APOC decision where it greatly weakened the second leg of the definition of sexual harassment, the requirement that the conduct result in an abusive and hostile working environment. By including the outraging of the modesty of a woman into the sexual harassment standard, the court did not build on the idea that sexual harassment was a violation of women's rights to equality, life and liberty. But rather, that a woman's modesty, a creation of nineteenth-century Victorian and colonial mentality, was sufficient to succeed in a claim of sexual harassment. Indeed the decision represents a step backward in the creation of a workable sexual harassment law.

More broadly, I am concerned about the implications of sexual harassment on the current sexual climate. In the contemporary moment, women have fought hard to create space, public space, for the discussion and legal redress of sexual wrongs—this includes rape, sexual assault, child sexual abuse and other forms of sexual violence. At the public level there is now considerable awareness about these wrongs, though the legal means for redressing such wrongs remain inadequate. However, there has been little simultaneous effort to educate and develop legal strategies for claiming sexual rights.

We operate in an environment where there is increasing room to discuss sexual violence and sexual wrongs—indeed the only way in which people can openly and publicly talk about sex is through the lens of violence, harm and wrongs. There continues to be a lack of space, indeed an erosion of what little space exists for the expression, assertion and enforcement of sexual rights. There has not been a single piece of legislation nor constitutional decision promoting women's sexual rights. Sexual rights have not been read into law in the same way that sexual wrongs have. And yet sexual rights are intrinsic to women's right to equality, to life and liberty, to free speech and expression. [. . .]

This article is not arguing against sexual harassment. It is a serious problem and affects women across the social spectrum. There is a need to ensure that women's rights to equality in the workplace are not secured at the cost of or set up in opposition to their rights to sexual autonomy, freedom of speech or association. The questions being addressed in this article are intended to ensure that sexual harassment concerns are effectively addressed in support of and not at the cost of women's human rights.

I would argue that a combination of legal and non-legal strategies must be deployed. Chastity laws that impugn women's conduct when she fails to conform to sexual norms must be repealed. These would include laws that permit the defence to introduce evidence of a woman's sexual history to discredit her testimony, that make a Hindu woman's right to maintenance contingent on her chastity, eliminate a husband's right to rape his wife, remove criminalization of consensual sexual activity, including sodomy. Antiquated laws such as the outraging of a woman's modesty or eve-teasing, which are informed by nineteenth-century Victorian and colonial lawmakers need to be rethought. Finally, a woman's right to mobility cannot be curtailed because of her sexual identity or conduct.

It is not at all self-evident that the response to sexual harassment should be a legal one. I would argue that the law can be disruptive of dominant sexual norms if used as a political tool rather than as a solution to the problem of sexual harassment, which I have argued the law is incapable of providing. For example, sexual harassment complaints of sexual minorities could be a specific political and legal project. The harassment of sex workers on the street, or gays and lesbians by employers could be a part of the sexual harassment project. The purpose of such a strategy would be to unmask the dominant sexual and conservative norms that are incorporated into law as well as into the public psyche . . .

Two further non-legal strategies would be to give priority to sex-education programmes. Such a strategy is all the more critical in the context of HIV/AIDS. In light of the recent historic special session of the UN General Assembly to consider the HIV/AIDS crisis, we have been alerted to our responsibility in foregrounding this issue. Providing information about safe sex is crucial to any strategy on HIV/AIDS. Yet how would safe sex posters, codes, or ads sit with the sex codes advocated by sexual harassment campaigners?

A second strategy is to promote sexual rights. The only groups in the contemporary moment that are claiming or asserting these rights are sexual minorities—gays, lesbians, sex workers and hijras—the primary movements that have been creating space for the affirmation of sexual difference, sexual rights and consensual sex.

If we fail to pursue a more radical and affirmative strategy on matters related to sex we will fail to adequately address the sexual harms women continue to experience. Sexual harms have never been eradicated through regulation of sexual conduct, muzzling sexual speech, or moral surveillance of women's lives. Such strategies have only perpetuated sexual stereotypes, sexual orthodoxy, and compromised on women's fundamental rights.

≈

ENFORCING CULTURAL CODES:
GENDER AND VIOLENCE IN NORTHERN INDIA

Prem Chowdhry

Most family-related crimes like dowry, bride-burning, rape and incest are well-recognized. They are given enormous publicity and draw social and academic interest, attention and condemnation. One crime which continues to go neglected and underreported relates to the violence inflicted on those who risk inter-caste and intra-caste marriages which infringe on cultural norms and practices. Such marriages are frequently runaway marriages or elopements. Moreover, they are not uncommon, and have shown a tendency to escalate over the years. Most of them result in acts of direct violence inflected by male members of the family on the couple generally and on the girl specially. Although regarded as a private family matter, which must be hushed up and kept confidential, some cases spill over into the wider community domain. It is through this process that they have attracted media attention.

The following analysis of this widespread phenomenon in rural north India throws up aspects of caste, class and gender which are crucially interconnected. As marriage provides the structural link between kinship and caste, marital alliances are coming under closer surveillance. Kinship linkages by marriage, and relations established through marriage, give a caste group its strength, recognition and leverage in the wider society and polity. Any breach in these caste linkages brings down the status not only of the immediate family but also that of the clan and finally of the entire caste group. This factor was and remains a potent consideration in the enforcement of strict caste and sexual codes.

At the centre of these codes, therefore, lies the control of female sexuality, since its bestowal in marriage is so crucial to patriarchal forces, given their concern with caste purity, status, power and hierarchy. Those who infringe caste and kinship norms in marriage meet with extreme violence. Although the upper caste and lower caste groups differ significantly, resulting in ambiguous responses, any infringement of the prescribed codes commonly evokes a violent response.

A challenge to these codes has come repeatedly both from within the caste and outside it. Processes of democratization and the opening up of economic opportunities have altered the dynamics of power relations, making for complex interaction between members of different caste groups as well as between members of a particular caste. In the former, the growing resentment and assertiveness of subordinate lower castes and classes has often resulted in inter-caste liaisons which breach upper caste norms and sexual codes. In the latter, younger members are challenging the caste/kinship ideology upheld by senior male members by questioning sexual codes and taboos, defying demands of status, hypergamy or village exogamy, and discarding notions of honour. In the face of these challenges, emanating mostly from the rural periphery and semi-urban linked social groups, influenced by the kind of urbanization which such regions have undergone, earlier domains of flexibility are becoming constricted. [. . .]

Some of the most talked about incidents are concentrated in rural north India and belong to western Uttar Pradesh, Haryana and the rural belt of the national capital. Perhaps the most shocking of them all was the Mehrana murder case of March 1991. Roshni, a jat girl of village Mehrana in western UP, ran away with Brijendra, a low caste jatav boy, assisted by his friend. The three of them were caught and the jat panchayat sat in judgment on them. Under its decree, they were tortured the whole night, hanged in the morning and then set on fire, while two of them were still alive. The entire village was witness to this savage and brutal murder.

A month later in April 1991, in village Khedakul of Narela (north Delhi), Poonam, a jat girl, was shot dead by her uncle in broad daylight for having an 'illicit relationship' with another jat boy of the same village. Again, several villagers were witnesses. The father and the uncle declared it a 'heinous crime', with death the only punishment. 'Her action had soiled our honour, our pride,' the father reportedly told the police. In August 1993, in village Khandravali in Muzzafarnagar district, western UP, a low caste girl, Sarita, having made a runway match, was axed to death along with her husband Satish, who belonged to her own caste group but hailed from an adjacent sister village and was also distantly related to her. The families of both the victims were bricklayers; it was at a brick kiln in Haryana that they grew intimate and finally eloped. All attempts to trace them failed. However, when they allegedly returned of their own volition, five months after the elopement, they were beheaded in the village *chaupal* by the girl's uncle. Their 'grave social violation' was compounded by their returning to the village, where, according to local opinion, they 'dared to flaunt' their 'disdain for social norms'. The crime was witnessed by the whole village. This was the third elopement within its low caste community. Nothing is known of the other couples. The elders were concerned about protecting the *izzat* (honour) of the village. The brutal hacking was to be a 'lesson to others', said Om Pal, the village sarpanch (headman). In this incident, the girl was blamed by the villagers for 'luring' the young man. The grandmother of Sarita openly declared: 'Our name is mud. Can I look anyone in the eye now?'

Asha was brutally killed by her kin along with her lover Manoj in March 1994 in village Nayagaon in Haryana. Asha belonged to the numerically and economically strong saini caste in the village, locally considered to be a higher caste in relation to the ahirs—the caste group to which Manoj belonged. The boy was declared to be an 'upstart' by the sainis. According to local accounts,

Asha openly asserted her right to choose her life partner. She reportedly told her family members not to interfere.

In June 1994 in village Hendigara in district Hazaribagh, Mahavir Prasad, a low caste youth, was lynched for marrying Malati, a kurmi girl who was stripped by her own caste men and beaten publicly. The villagers confided to the press reporters that Puran Mahato, Malati's father, who was economically hard up, had personally never objected to his daughter's 'love affair'. He was, however, under great pressure from fellow kurmis to marry his daughter within the caste. The girl resisted this openly, by running away with Mahavir. On discovering this, the kurmis convened a panchayat and imposed a fine of Rs. 5000 each on the families concerned. However, a more drastic punishment awaited the runaway couple.

More recently, in June 1995, in Bahagalpur, Bihar, Bijoy Kumar Bind, a low caste boy, was publicly lynched for his involvement with an upper caste girl. The rest of the story follows a familiar pattern. Such examples could be multiplied many times. [. . .]

In most of these cases, the crimes have been committed in public. Yet, the police is neither willing nor able to prepare the *challan* to document the crime or muster evidence from the villagers. A few cases which reach the stage of a court trial result in the perpetrators being let off for lack of evidence. Ultimately no one gets punished. In a candid remark, the Bahadurgarh police station officer, Risal Singh, opined that the police close their eyes to such incidents, all too many in Haryana, and let them go unreported. [. . .]

Inter-caste alliances were not entirely uncommon in the colonial period. However, more often than not, they were confined to a secondary alliance. In the subsistence level economy of this region, with its highly adverse female–male sex ratio, those agriculturists who were hard pressed economically were known to take recourse to wives from among the lower castes as well. [. . .]

By and large, the agricultural castes did not really look down upon lower caste women who became their wives. This is aptly expressed in a local proverb still quoted extensively in Haryana: *beeranki kai jaat* (women have no caste). Yet it is significant to note that in no way was it considered an upward move for the natal family of the low caste woman. For all purposes, she was not only purchased from her parents, but was also made to terminate all connections with them after this marriage. This was essential to keep the myth of her belonging to a higher caste. [. . .]

Taking wives from lower castes, however, never became a norm as such, nor was it practised on a wide scale. Moreover, this practice did not go unchallenged, specially from the late nineteenth century onward, when attempts were made to move the court in those cases of *karewa* (widow remarriage) where caste endogamy had not been observed. A series of such cases was brought to the courts in the early nineteenth century. In the case of *Sahib Ditta vs. Musammat Bela* in 1900, the reversioners (male heirs of a deceased owner's property) challenged the brahmin widow's *karewa* marriage to a jat and sought to deprive her children of their inheritance on the grounds of illegitimacy. It was made out that 'if a brahmin widow cannot marry a brahmin, how can she marry a jat'. The attempt was clearly to invoke the Hindu law applicable to women to refute customary law which was the operable norm in colonial Punjab. The colonial government, for reasons of its own, was more anxious to enforce *karewa;* the case was judged in favour of jat custom, which recognized such unions.

The same position was held in a series of cases involving lower castes like the chamars. It was acknowledged that any Hindu widow, from a brahmin to a chamar, could be remarried to men of agriculturists castes by *karewa*. The coupling of these two caste groups, high and low, is significant. In this region, norms were dictated by the dominant agriculturist castes—the chief being the jats. Consequently, the higher ritual ranking of the brahmin dropped when confronted with the harsh reality of existence in which the brahmins were an agriculturist rather than a priestly caste. Moreover, in relation to the jats they were numerically and socio-economically far inferior.

New norms, claimed on the basis of caste purity, custom and tradition, sought to invalidate inter-caste marriages, and had opened a way for people to claim certain rights which could not be claimed through the traditional panchayats. Interestingly, the situation is reversed now, as the traditional panchayats are being used to impose a doubtful tradition. [. . .]

In fact, when the parents are unwilling to act in such cases, the caste *biradari* takes over, as in the case of Mehrana, where the jat panchayat took the decision. In the words of Bihan (Roshni's mother): 'The panchayatwalas stepped in . . . they said to me that *ladkiwalas* did not have a say in the matter and that they alone would decide what punishment was to be meted out to the girl. They took her away and hanged her.'

Caste panchayats are indeed intervening frequently to impose justice according to their own definition. Although very little is known about the working of caste panchayats, they remain in active force in rural north India. They have been generally known to award minor punishments which humiliate rather than injure. Punishments include fines, orders to give obligatory village feasts, rubbing one's nose in the dust before the aggrieved party or even the entire gathering or touching their feet, shaving one's head, and drinking or dipping one's nose in the urine of one or more persons.

The more recent exhibition of the power of public stripping, awarding the death penalty and carrying out executions by the panchayat is closely linked to growing urbanization and consumerism. There has been a steady process of urbanization in Haryana within twenty years; between 1961 and 1981, the total number of towns in Haryana has increased from sixty-one to eighty-one. [. . .]

This kind of urbanization is accompanied by the spillover of an urban consumerist culture. The role model is set by the rural affluent classes, and their conspicuous consumption is emulated by others. Their ideology, signified by 'a jeep, a gun and a bottle of rum', is in keeping with the image of a virile martial race with a macho culture. There is no place for women in the 'modern' urban ethos which is imitated. Paradoxically, despite being so influenced by the lifestyle and consumerist culture of the cities, suspicions toward the urban value system, its culture and influence are reinforced in rural areas specially in relation to women. So, on the one hand, the reigning ideology sanctions and even desires urbanization and the consumerism associated with considerations of male status and upward mobility, while on the other hand, it holds the city responsible for the rapidly changing, now idealized 'traditional' cultural norms of rural north India. This contradiction is not uncommonly resolved through violence at an individual/family level, and/or if that fails to materialize, at a collective community level.

The caste panchayats, in other words, seek to counter the failure of the law of the land by protecting an eroded 'traditional value system' as it is perceived to be enshrined in customary practices. For example, except for certain incest taboos, the legal restrictions on marriage under Hindu Marriage Act, 1955 are almost non-existent. But in rural areas, apart from several restrictions on marriages, the category of incest is a very wide and selective one. Incest, when intra-family or intra-*got*, never meets with similar violence, even when made public. Similarly, sexual codes are sought to be enforced only in relation to upper caste women. The purity of lower caste women, even when breached through rape, is not taken into cognizance.

This intervention of caste panchayats is also an assertion of the combined power and domination of upper caste senior male members over younger men and women. In a way, it is a direct effort to retain power in the face of challenges by aspirants from different socio-economic strata as well as from the younger generation. The new legal system based upon different principles has also cut into their power base. The colonial masters, on the other hand, had nurtured the caste leadership and helped to maintain and strengthen their power. Their concept of justice gave recognition to customary laws and to ancient texts and implemented them selectively in the courts. For example, during colonial rule, the runaway match of an unmarried girl was not given legal sanction because the 'consent' of the guardian had not been forthcoming. Colonial official attitude was moulded according to local custom whereby minor or adult women were always under the guardianship of some male member. Legally, the situation is now vastly altered as 'minor' or 'major' categories are legal categories, so that anyone above eighteen years is an adult and free to act independently without the sanction of a guardian. Caste leadership and caste panchayats are ignoring these kinds of legal interventions. Consequently, the ideology of the guardianship of women irrespective of their age and status remains enforceable through caste panchayats on pain of death.

The ideology of female guardianship is essentially an ideology of control. It is closely tied up with the question of the control of female sexuality, particularly in relation to women of upper caste groups. In the high caste brahminical social order this control is intrinsically connected not only to patrilineal succession but also to the maintenance of caste purity and caste hierarchy. Consequently, miscegeny (the mixing of castes) as well as hypogamy (union between women of a higher caste and men of a lower caste) have been severely condemned and given the highest punishment. In Punjab–Haryana, the brahminical model was not so strong and the concept of caste purity and caste hierarchy were not the same. At the same time, caste endogamy sought to affirm and maintain caste status. Thus, even though the rules of caste purity were breached by men from agriculturist castes (mostly in their secondary associations), women were never allowed to break caste rules. [. . .]

~

THE TWO-CHILD NORM AND POPULATION POLICY

Mohan Rao

On the 30th of July 2003, a three-judge bench of the Supreme Court of India upheld a Haryana government law prohibiting a person from contesting or holding the post of a sarpanch or panch in the panchayat raj institutions (PRIs) of the state if he or she had more than two children. The bench observed that 'disqualification on the right to contest an election for having more than two living children does not contravene any fundamental right, nor does it cross the limits of reasonability. Rather, it is a disqualification conceptually devised *in the national interest*' (Venkatesan 2003).

Interestingly, while the Supreme Court spoke about the 'torrential increase of population', earlier the Rajasthan High Court judges, hearing a similar set of petitions, in their ruling argued: 'These provisions have been enacted by the legislature to control the *menace of population explosion* . . . The government is spending large sums of money propagating family planning. One of the agencies to which the project of family planning has been entrusted for implementation is the gram panchayat. The panches and sarpanches are to set the example and maintain the norm of two children. Otherwise what examples can they set before the public?' (Sarkar and Ramanathan 2002, 42). More recently the Supreme Court added salt to festering wounds by issuing notices to the centre and states on the implementation of the two-child norm, stepping, once again, on not-too-sensitive legislative toes.

Haryana is not the only state that has a population policy with such features, which are not only at variance with the National Population Policy (NPP) 2000 but also strike at the heart of the commitments to reproductive health and rights made by the Indian government at the International Conference of Population and Development (ICPD). Other states, such as Andhra Pradesh, Madhya Pradesh, Rajasthan, Chattisgarh and Orissa also carry this policy prescription. All of these states, in enunciating their population policies, also advocate a mind-boggling host of incentives and disincentives: restricting schooling in government schools to two children; restricting employment in public services to those with two children; linking financial assistance to PRIs for development activities and anti-poverty programmes with performance in family planning; linking assessment of public health staff to performance in family planning and so forth. Indeed, service rules for government employees have been altered in several states making a two-child norm mandatory.

Perhaps not coincidentally, many of these policy prescriptions were also contained in an influential 1993 World Bank document. This recommends, ICPD notwithstanding, that 'targets based on micro-level planning be . . . continued'; 'an innovative package of incentives/disincentives . . . be linked to various benefits being made available under different plans of the government'; ' a suitable plan of disincentives . . . for government employees . . . and the organized sector' (World Bank 1993, 50–51). Given the reach and influence of the World Bank in India's policies, it is not surprising that state governments drafting their state population policies carried these policy prescriptions.

In view of these developments, health and women's groups approached the National Human Rights Commission three years back with a memorandum that the two-child norm was discriminatory, anti-democratic and violative of commitments made by the Government of India in several international covenants. The National Human Rights Council (NHRC) issued orders to the concerned state governments, and, at a national colloquium on the 9th and 10th of January 2003, attended by representatives of these state governments, a Declaration was issued.

This NHRC Declaration 'notes with concern that population policies framed by some State Governments reflect in certain respects a coercive approach through use of incentives and disincentives, which in some cases are violative of human rights. This is not consistent with the spirit of the National Population Policy. The violation of human rights affects, in particular the marginalized and vulnerable sections of society, including women' (NHRC 2003, 1). The Declaration also noted that 'the propagation of a two-child norm and coercion or manipulation of individual fertility decisions through the use of incentives and disincentives violate the principle of voluntary informed choice and the human rights of the people, particularly the rights of the child' (ibid).

But the NHRC Declaration, as much as the concerns of health groups and women's groups, apparently fell on deaf ears, as the Supreme Court ruling has come in for widespread middle-class approbation. Indeed, the Supreme Court ruling perhaps renders redundant some of the private members' bills in Parliament that have been tabled to variously increase incentives or disincentives. Two of them, one named the Population Stabilisation Bill 1999, and the other, the Population Control Bill 2000, for instance, moot the idea of a one-child norm along with a number of incentives and disincentives, including disqualification of persons with more than one child from contesting elections. Yet another bill, the Bachelor's Allowance Bill 2000, suggests incentives to those men who remain bachelors. Men, who, taking advantage of the incentives, subsequently get married, are to be fined and imprisoned. Yet another bill, the Population Control Bill 2000, also seeks to punish people who violate the small family norm with rigorous imprisonment for a term of five years and a fine, not less than Rs 50,000. The Population Control and Family Welfare Bill 1999, proposes in addition to incentives and disincentives, the compulsory sterilization of every married couple having two or more living children. These efforts at prescribing a two-child norm seem to be found also in unlikely quarters: the Tamil Nadu agricultural labourers' insurance bill, for instance, stipulates that labourers losing their limbs can only receive insurance compensation if they have no more than two children. Recently, the Maharashtra government passed a law for differential irrigation fees; farmers with more than two children would be required to pay more for irrigation facilities. More creatively, the U.P. government announced a scheme whereby applicants for gun licences had to produce certificates that they had motivated five cases for sterilization. More recently still, a delegation from the Indian Medical Association has urged the government to, following China, implement a one-child norm. In yet another move, recalling the days of the Emergency, in Rajasthan, school teachers have been given sterilization targets to achieve. And the Election Commission of the state of Uttar Pradesh has suggested a two-child norm for contestants to all elective posts.

Not to be left behind, the Government of India, led by the BJP, announced in April 2003 its plans to introduce in the Lok Sabha the Constitutional (79th Amendment) Bill seeking to restrict persons with more than two children from contesting elections. This Bill, introduced in the Rajya Sabha in 1992, by the Congress, would first have to pass the lower house. The Health Minister, Sushma Swaraj, speaking in the Lok Sabha, announced that should there be consensus on the Bill, the government was prepared to introduce it in the then ongoing session of Parliament. Fortunately elections intervened.

In short then, the Cairo consensus and the Natinal Population Policy notwithstanding, there is widespread consensus among our policy makers and elites, and indeed our middle classes, that something more drastic needs to be done on the population front, that all the social ills in our country have their roots primarily in population. This call for 'giving teeth' to population policy, to 'showing political will', takes the form of disincentives and incentives and the norm for family size.

II

The problem with these punitive approaches is both fundamental and pragmatic. Fundamentally, it represents a profound misunderstanding of the relationship between population and resources. Pragmatically, they are demographically unnecessary, and indeed counterproductive. I would also argue that they are morally compromised since they violate the principle of natural justice, creating two sets of citizenship rights on the basis of fertility. Indeed such policies represent going back to the days before universal suffrage when property rights decided citizenship claims.

What proponents of the two-child norm or disincentives ignore is that there is a substantial demographic transition underway in the country. The Total Fertility Rate (TFR) has declined by almost half a child in the six and half years between National Family Health Survey (NFHS) 1 (1993) and 2 (2000). Replacement level, or close to replacement level fertility, has been reached in Kerala, Tamil Nadu, Karnataka, Goa, Andhra Pradesh, Himachal Pradesh, Delhi and Punjab. It is true that the TFR is high in U.P., Bihar, Madhya Pradesh and Rajasthan. But even in these states it has declined between the two surveys from 4.82 to 3.99 in U.P, 4 to 3.49 in Bihar, and from 3.90 to 3.31 in Madhya Pradesh. Rajasthan is the only large state where the TFR has increased from 3.63 to 3.78. In other words, a substantial and sustained fertility decline is underway in the country. Hastening this, however, requires investments in the social sectors—health, education, employment, food and so on—precisely measures that are being undermined by neo-liberal economic policies.

Interestingly, NFHS 2 also reveals that the fertility rate that is currently sought, 2.13, is lower by 0.72 child (that is by 25 per cent) than the current TFR of 2.85. This is to say, if unwanted births could be reduced, the TFR would drop to the replacement level of fertility. It is estimated that the unmet need for family planning services contributes 24.4 per cent to current population growth. Indeed this is acknowledged in the NPP, which therefore marks as its priority, meeting the unmet need for health and family planning services. There is also the related issue of the high unwanted fertility due to high levels of infant mortality rate (IMR). To propose punitive measures, in this context, is thus clearly absurd.

What is also important to acknowledge is that given the age structure of the population, population growth will continue despite a fall in the birth rate due to what demographers call momentum, i.e. the effect of a young age structure caused by high population growth rates in the recent past. With a large proportion of the population—almost 60 per cent—below the age of 30 years, further growth of population is inevitable, unless of course mortality increases, which cannot be the aim of policy. Population momentum contributes to as much as 69.7 per cent of current population growth.

Above all, it is imperative to bear in mind that demographic transition is not merely a geographical phenomenon, but is deeply imprinted by social inequalities. Thus those sections of the population that have benefited through post-independence development, and are thus assured incomes, child survival, social security, health and education have completed their demographic transition. On the other hand, vast sections of the population—particularly the dalits, the adivasis and the Other Backward Castes (OBC)—who have not so benefited are lagging behind in demographic transition. The NFHS for 1998–99, notes that the IMR among the Scheduled Castes (SC), Scheduled Tribes (ST) and OBCs is 83, 84 and 76 respectively, compared to 62 for Others. Similarly, the Under Five Mortality Rate is 119 among the SCs, 126 among the STs and 103 among the OBCs, compared to 82 among the Others. Not surprisingly, the NFHS also shows that the TFR is 3.15 for SCs, 3.06 for STs, 2.66 among OBCs and 3.47 among illiterate women as a whole. It is, in contrast, 1.99 among women educated beyond the tenth grade and thus more likely to be better off. Imposition of the two-child norm, and the disincentives proposed, would mean that the majority of these deprived populations would bear the brunt of the state's withdrawal of ameliorative measures, pitiably inadequate as they are. With the recent Supreme Court judgement, the majority of these populations are debarred from their right to contest elections in PRIs in one fell stroke.

Laws related to a two-child norm for PRIs were introduced in 1994 in Andhra Pradesh, Haryana, Orissa and Rajasthan, ironically in the very same year that the Government of India was signing the ICPD which called for a new paradigm in population and development, one that was not demographically driven, but emphasized reproductive health and rights. In 2000, these laws were introduced in Madhya Pradesh and Himachal Pradesh, and continued in Chattisgarh. Maharashtra joined this group of states in 2003.

This law of course violates the spirit of the 73rd Amendment to the Constitution. Indeed, one hand of the population policy takes away the space of deprived sections to influence public life that the other hand of the 73rd Amendment provides. A study carried out recently in five states (A.P., Haryana, Orissa, Rajasthan and M.P.) indicated that the fall out of the imposition of the two-child norm on PRIs had been exactly as anticipated.

The largest number of cases of disqualification from contesting elections was with reference to this law. Women formed 41 per cent of those disqualified; the dalits, adivasis and the OBCs formed an overwhelming 80 per cent of those disqualified. The study also found no evidence to support the contention that the law induced the adoption of the small family norm; nor indeed that members of the PRIs were seen as role models. What it did find was evidence of desertion of wives, denial of paternity, neglect of female infants, non-registration of births, non-immunization of daughters to avoid registration. Equally significantly, there was evidence of forced abortions and pre-birth elimination of females (Buch 2005). Another study in five districts of Madhya Pradesh confirms these findings (Sama 2005). In short, the framers of this law utterly ignored how patriarchy and class intersect in India to deny women and the marginalized communities a place in the sun. Indeed, that the law itself serves to further victimize them.

The example of China is frequently cited, although inappropriately, to argue that 'some element of coercion' is necessary in the larger interests of the nation, and to assure economic growth. Comparisons between India and China are inapposite for a large number of reasons, including per-capita incomes, achievements in health, equity and education that India can unfortunately not boast of. Further, China made what can only be called a monumental blunder when it imposed a one-child norm (now officially abandoned). This is because, as Sen has revealed, a long term-secular decline in the fertility rate was already under way and such measures were therefore unnecessary (Sen 1995). Further, they have been counterproductive, contributing to the huge crisis of missing girls, with the 2000 Census giving us a figure of more than six million missing girls in the 0–6 years age group. China currently has a sex ratio at birth of 116.9 males to 100 females, indicating the huge scale of the pre-birth elimination of females, approximately 11 per cent of girls (National Bureau of Statistics of China 2004). The sharply skewed sex ratio has led to the problem of *guang gun-er* or 'bare branches', i.e. young men with no prospects of marriage and family, and contributed to the sharp increase in violence against women. Reports of trafficking of women into sex slavery also occasionally make the news.

The increasing availability of new technologies in our country—from the relatively rare methods of enrichment of male sperm to selection of male embryos for implantation—along with the now ubiquitous ultrasound machines used for sex selection, has provided new and more widespread means to SSA. Indeed, General Electric and WIPRO, the distributors of ultrasounds in India, have sold a disproportionate number in the states of the North and West of the country, precisely the areas that have revealed a precipitous decline of the child sex ratio (CSR) (George 2002). These technologies are often marketed to doctors with loans from GE Capital.

A great deal of concern, even in official circles, has been expressed about the sharply deteriorating juvenile sex ratios in the country, largely due to pre-birth elimination of females. Data on the masculinization of sex ratios at birth is yet another indicator of this phenomenon. What is equally worrying is that the practice has spread to regions and communities where it did not exist. What is not however equally recognized is how population policies, as we have seen, contribute to this phenomenon. It is now abundantly clear that given the strong patriarchy in the country and thus the ideology of son-preference, particularly marked in the high fertility areas of the country, a vigorous pursuit of the two-child norm is an invitation to female sex selective abortion. Indeed, it was the explicit recognition of this link that compelled the Chinese government to officially abandon its one-child per family norm. In India, between 1991 and 2001, in urban areas, the CSR has declined from 935 to 903 and in rural areas from 948 to 934. More ominously, between January and June this year, in Delhi the sex ratio at birth indicates 819 females being born for every 1000 males; in the prosperous and educated South Delhi zone, where demographic transition has by and large been completed, only 762 females were born for every 1000 males. In other words, population stabilization was indeed being achieved, but at the cost of population balance. Interestingly, confirming many of our fears, doctors in a recent study of abortion in Maharashtra, found to be performing SSA even though they knew it had been banned, revealed that they did it for many reasons. One was that that it was for the woman's sake—to save her from illegal abortions. The second reason cited was that if they did not do it, other doctors would. Above all, that it was for the good of the family and for that of the nation—since they were helping bring down population growth (Bandewar 2003).

References

Bandewar, Sunita. May 2003. Abortion services and providers' perceptions: Gender dimensions. *Economic and Political Weekly* 38, no. 21.

Buch, Nirmala. 11 June 2005. Law of two-child norm in panchayats: Implications, consequences and experiences. *Economic and Political Weekly*, vol. XL, no.24.

George, Sabu. 2002. Sex selection/determination in India: Contemporary developments. *Reproductive Health Matters* 10, no. 19.

International Institute for Population Sciences. 2002. *National family health survey (NFHS-2)*, Mumbai, 2000.

National Bureau of Statistics of China. 2004. *Women and men in China: Facts and figures.* N.p.

National Human Rights Commision. 2003. *Declaration.* National Colloquium on Population Policies, New Delhi.

Sama. 2005. *Beyond numbers: Implications of the two-child norm.* New Delhi.

Sarkar, Lotika and Usha Ramanathan. 2002. Collateral Concerns. *Seminar* 511.

Sen, Amartya. 1995. Population policy: Authoritarianism versus cooperation. International Lecture Series on Population Issues, The John and Catherine T. MacArthur Foundation, New Delhi.

Sen, Gita and Aditi Iyer. 2002. Incentives and disincentives: Necessary, effective, just? *Seminar* 511.

Venkatesan, J. 31 July 2003. Two Child Norm Upheld. *The Hindu.*

World Bank, The. 1993. *India's family welfare programme: Towards a reproductive and child health approach.* New Delhi.

7

≈

EDUCATION

The general introduction to this volume has already discussed the central, yet not always reflected on, context of education for women's studies and the women's movement. We saw in particular how the first establishment of women's studies produced a break of sorts from the agendas of an earlier period, and the relative lack of interest paid to education in the early agendas of the women's movement. This makes education at once a very old and relatively new question.

Many historical accounts of the nineteenth-century period of social reform have privileged issues like sati and widowhood, polygamy and child marriage, but without giving the battles over education their due. Or at least, compared to the complex maneuvrings of Raja Ram Mohan Roy, Chandraprasad Vidyasagar or Behram Malabari, the question of education has been rather flat and without controversy. Only recently has the larger significance of multiple struggles over education, including their frequent initiation by women and 'lower' castes themselves, become more widely recognised in the debates on women's rights. A pioneer here was the shudra leader Mahatma Jyotiba Phule who, with his wife Savitribai in 1848, opened the first school for shudra and atishudra girls in western India and was thrown out of his parental home as a consequence. In the eastern region of Bengal, scholars have discovered the wealth of women's writings that burst forth during the latter nineteenth and early twentieth centuries, and the conditions that made them possible. The first two essays of this section offer different perspectives on this development, focussing in particular on the first autobiography of its kind—*Amar Jiban* or *My Life* by Rashundari Debi (1809–1900).

In the present excerpt from his longer study, Partha Chatterjee locates the significance of women's early writings against the backdrop of the changing responses to colonization by male nationalist writers like Bankimchandra Chattopadhyaya. (We have already been introduced to this figure in Jasodhara Bagchi's essay in the section on history.) Partha Chatterjee's larger argument, in the context of the field of power constituted by colonialism and nationalist responses to it, is that a new modernity was first fashioned—not in the public world of political conflict—but in the 'inner' world of the middle class home, with women at the centre. Women's writings, in particular, took the prominent form of the autobiography, and were preoccupied with informing women readers on how to cultivate the right 'self' to cope with the enormous changes taking place around them. Rashundari Debi, the uneducated wife of a rural landlord, managed the extraordinary feat of learning how to read and write on her own and in utmost secrecy. Subsequently describing her lifelong struggle in *Amar Jiban*, Rashundari is interpreted by Chatterjee to have been a pre-modern figure: This is because she attributes to a divine power alone the course of her life and her cherished ability to read.

Tanika Sarkar translated the first part of *Amar Jiban* into English, and the second essay in this section has been excerpted from her introduction to the translated autobiography titled *Words to Win: The Making of 'Amar Jiban', A Modern Autobiography*. Sarkar contextualizes this work within the debates of the time on *strishiksha* or women's education. In spite of there being no references to any public debates in the text, Sarkar discusses how close Rashundari's writing was to the reformism of those years in its style and mode of argument. She goes on to describe the kinds of anxieties and arguments against women's education that circulated in order to emphasize the significance of the articulation of women's equal rights in this sphere, especially given Indian social conditions. Further on in her introduction (not reproduced here), she analyzes aspects of the prose of *Amar Jiban* more closely in order to argue that it is, in her view, a modern text centred around a new notion of selfhood.

By the end of the nineteenth century, certain forms of education had become more available to elite if not middle class women, and in the first decades of the twentieth century these very women took the lead in the emergence of the first major women's organizations. We still do not have a good picture of how reform agendas and demands to broaden education for women changed or receded with the onset of political nationalism, especially in different regions of the country. Scholars like Neera Desai and Vina Mazumdar have critically assessed both pre-independence and early post-independence policies to show that a 'persistent ambivalence' rested on the education of women. While commissions and committees failed to make a link between women's equality and patterns of education, the rapid increase in middle class women's entry into higher education hid many of the contradictions subsequently uncovered by the *Towards Equality* report. Education may not have been on the agenda of the larger women's movement in the 1980s, but lobbying efforts by this generation of women's studies scholars helped in framing the New Education Policy of 1986. The excerpt from this policy document reproduced here speaks of the role women's studies was to play in promoting women's equality.

In the next essay Karuna Chanana provides readers with an overview of the gender discrimination prevalent in primary school education in the country as recently as the 1990s. By this time both education and gender had made a re-entry into wider debates and concerns, but within a different framework from that of the nineteenth century, namely through the dominant discourses of development. Feminists joined others in revealing that the most basic rights of literacy and primary education were far from universal, with the 'gender gap' between men and women of particular groups remaining largely constant over the post-independence period. Chanana's account demonstrates how national statistics provide a revealing picture of gender disparities in different regions, and among the Scheduled Castes and Tribes, the most excluded groups from education today.

A different voice speaks to us in the next piece, 'The Story of My Sanskrit.' Taken from the autobiography *Antasphot (Implosion)* by the Dalit writer and feminist Kumud Pawde written in the 1960s, and translated from Marathi into English in 1992, this extract demonstrates the ongoing power of the autobiographical medium. Other essays in this volume (especially in the section on caste) reveal how invisible the deep structures of caste have been in contemporary India, including radical fields like women's studies. Kumud Pawde jolts the reader at every step as she recounts with pain the casteism she experienced—among classmates and neighbours, in government departments and within the university, as she unswervingly pursued her desire to study that most brahmanical of subjects—Sanskrit. But this is not simply a story of fighting discrimination or tradition. She recalls the admiration of her students, and remembers the orthodox Gokhale Guruji, her most beloved teacher, whom she compares to another, more renowned figure. Exposed to modernity, the head of department at the university was nonetheless completely opposed to her desire to do an M.A. in Sanskrit, and lost no opportunity of telling her so. Pawde was ultimately to become a Professor of Sanskrit in the very college where she studied.

At the time of preparing this section, the difficult relationships between caste and education have once again re-emerged in the public realm in the form of 'Mandal II'. Sixteen years after the proclamation in 1990 to implement reservations for the Other Backward Classes in government services and higher education, we are still largely unaware of the over-representation of certain groups—Hindu upper caste men in particular—in significant spheres of influence and advancement like higher education, or how reservations have been implemented within the educational system. Apart from caste-based exclusion and under-representation, the social situation of Muslims in post-independence India has also only just achieved some belated national attention through the Report of the Sachar Committee. In the next essay, an excerpt from their recent study of Muslim girls and education in five cities, Zoya Hasan and Ritu Menon explore the many factors and processes that work against the ability of Muslim girls to sustain an education. Popular stereotypes would simply blame Islamic religion and backwardness. Instead, Hasan and Menon examine the effects on girls' educational aspirations when the most common forms of employment among Muslim men only require low levels of schooling. Amongst the many factors they examine are perceptions of discrimination and the deep insecurity that followed the demolition of the Babri Masjid. Nonetheless, wherever conditions have been favourable, Muslims are now invested in schooling, with mothers expressing a strong desire to have their daughters educated.

The many dimensions of discrimination that structure access to education and the need to gender this analysis are therefore beginning to be addressed in women's studies scholarship. More than ever before, education is sought after as an avenue for a different future, for a better, if not empowered, life. But in all the current focus on access, how much attention has been given to what is being learnt?

An unexpected crisis, not just for the women's movement and women's studies, but for all progressive intellectuals, came in the late 1990s when the Hindu right, with the BJP in power at the centre, identified education as a major sphere of intervention and ideological transformation. Within apex state bodies such as the University Grants Commission and the National Council of Educational Research and Training, disturbing notions of Indian tradition, value education and the special role of religion were disseminated. In our final contribution to this theme, Dipta Bhog focuses on the National Curriculum Framework or NCF of 2000, meant to provide the basis for new social science textbooks in all government schools, which contained the most explicit formulations of this trend. She begins by pointing out how existing critiques of the NCF's communal and brahmanical distortions and biases have not noticed how gender issues are regressively impacted by the equation of tradition and value with religion. But there is more. How different are these views compared to those put forward in the nineteenth century? Dipta Bhog argues that the NCF echoes many of the anxieties about women voiced a century ago. On the other hand, it is quite true that the NCF represents a clear break from the lauded National Policy of Education of 1986. The less examined question is how or whether the progressive rhetoric of the NPE translated into a corresponding vision in the school textbooks produced in the following years. Bhog's analysis of a selection of language textbooks from this period reveals, however, that little found its way into these books.

Today, in the wake of a very different NCF (2004) and a much wider involvement in the politics of the school curriculum, a hitherto neglected sphere within education has been opened up. How one can productively bring a critical awareness of gender discrimination into the world of children through school textbooks is a deeply challenging project. Women's studies scholars located in diverse institutions—universities and colleges, research centres and NGOs—are revisiting the history of education, the role of the state, trends of privatization, the involvements of rightwing organizations, patterns of exclusion and the responsibilities of women's studies within all these.

∾

WOMEN AND THE NATION: THE TROUBLE WITH THEIR VOICES
Partha Chatterjee

If there is one theme that dominates the new literature which emerged in Bengal in the nineteenth century, it is the theme of change. Everything was changing; nothing was likely to remain the same. Prolonged and bitter debates ensued about how best to cope with all this change. But at bottom the assumption was shared that the force working to alter the very foundation of society was both overwhelming and alien: the source of change itself lay outside and beyond control. It is important to remember this when considering the emergence of a 'modern' consciousness of the self under colonial conditions.

The question of the 'new woman' was, like other contemporary social issues, formulated, as we have just seen, as a question of coping with change. But who was to do the coping? Bankimchandra, the most eminent literary figure in Bengal in the late nineteenth century, wrote in the early 1870s an essay comparing the virtues and faults of women of an older age with those of women of modern times. Bankim began the essay by declaring that in all societies it was men who always laid down the ways in which women must behave. 'Self-interested men are mindful of the improvement of women only to the extent that it furthers their self-interest, not for any other reason.' There was, consequently, no confusion in Bankim's mind about the social agency in question when considering the character of women. If the modern woman differed from her predecessors, she did so as the result of social policies pursued by men; men's attitudes and actions were on trial here.

Bankim then goes on to list the virtues and defects of the 'new' woman compared with those of the 'traditional'. It is a familiar list, reproduced, embellished and canonized in succeeding decades in the prodigious nationalist literature on women. In the past, women were uneducated, and therefore coarse, vulgar and quarrelsome. By comparison, modern women have more refined tastes. On the other hand, whereas women were once hardworking and strong, they were now lazy and fond of luxury, unmindful of housework and prone to all sorts of illness. Further, in the olden days women were religious. They were faithful to their husbands, hospitable to guests and charitable to the needy. They genuinely believed in the norms of right conduct. Today, if women do these things, they do so more because of fear of criticism than because they have faith in dharma.

Bankim may have felt that despite his initial remarks about the responsibility of men as lawmakers of society, the essay was likely to be read as a criticism of women themselves, whether traditional or modern. In the subsequent issue of the journal in which the essay appeared, Bankim appended three letters, supposedly written by women in response to the article. All three complained that women had been treated unfairly by the author. The first retaliated with a list of accusations against the educated male.

Alright, we are lazy. But what about you? . . . You work only because the English have tied you to the millstone . . . We have no bonds of religion, you say. And you? You are ever fearful of religion because it is like a noose around your neck: one end of the rope is held by the owner of the liquor store and the other by the prostitute.

The second argued that the defects of the modern woman had been produced only by the 'virtues' of the modern man. [. . .]

The third correspondent offered to exchange places with the modern male. 'Come indoors and take charge of the house. Let us go out to work. Slaves for seven hundred years, and still you pride yourselves on your masculinity! Aren't you ashamed?'

I mention this essay by Bankim at the very beginning of my discussion of women's writings about themselves not only to remind us that the hegemonic discourse which framed these writings—the discourse of anti-colonial nationalism—was in its core a male discourse, but also to point out the capacity of this discourse to appropriate discordant, marginal and critical voices. In Bankim's case, the device was self-irony. The strand of nationalist thinking Bankim represented sought to create a national leadership in the image of ideal masculinity—strong, proud, just, wise, a protector of the righteous and a terror to the mischievous. Relentlessly, he poured scorn and ridicule on an educated elite that, he thought, was failing to live up to this ideal. Self-irony was the mode by which he could, as a member of this inadequate elite, expose to itself its own weaknesses, even by assuming the voices of its 'other'—those of the illiterate, the poor and the 'mad', and also those of women. The form was used widely. Indeed, fiction and drama in late nineteenth century Bengal are full of instances of women, from 'respectable' families as well as from the urban, using the rhetorical skills of 'common' speech and the moral precepts of 'common' sense to show up the pretentiousness and hypocrisy of the educated male. We must not overlook the hegemonic possibilities of this internalized critique: it could, up to a point, retain its own legitimacy and appropriate both feminine and popular ridicule simply by owning up to them.

The question is: up to what point? Or rather, in which discursive field? Within what sort of boundaries? We cannot find a historically nuanced answer to this question unless we think of the field of discourse as one of contention, peopled by several subjects, several consciousnesses. We must think of discourse as situated within fields of power, not only constituting that field but also constituted by it. Dominance here cannot exhaust the claims to subjectivity, for even the dominated must always retain an aspect of autonomy. Otherwise, power would cease to be a relation; it would no longer be constituted by struggle.

If nationalist ideology in the late nineteenth-century Bengal legitimized the subjection of women under a new patriarchy, its history must be a history of struggle. The difficulty which faces historians here is that by working from the conventional archives of political history, women appear in the history of nationalism only in a 'contributive' role. All one can assert here is that women *also* took active part in nationalist struggle, but one cannot identify any autonomous subjectivity of women and from that standpoint question the manner in which the hegemonic claims of nationalist culture were themselves fashioned.

My argument is that because of the specific conditions of colonial society, this history is to be found less in the external domain of political conflict and more in the 'inner' space of the middle class home. Fortunately, there exists something of an archive for us to delve into: a series of autobiographies by educated women who wrote about their lives and their struggles in this eventful period of modern Indian history.

The autobiography would seem to be obvious material for studying the emergence of 'modern' forms of self-representation. Unfortunately, here too the colonial condition works to displace the points of application of the usual critical apparatus. Historians of Bengali literature conventionally agree that the modern forms of the biography and the autobiography made their appearance in Bengal sometime in the middle of the nineteenth century because of the emergence of a new concept of the 'individual' among the English-educated elite. Yet, despite the continued popularity of the genre, it is difficult to explain why the facts of social history and the development of new cultural norms for the collective life of the nation, rather than the exploration of individuality and the inner workings of the personality, constitute the overwhelming bulk of the material of these life stories.

Not unexpectedly, autobiographies of women have characteristics rather different from those of men. It is not simply that women's life stories are concerned more with the domestic than with the public sphere, a feature often noticed in women's autobiographies of the modern period in all countries. Nor is it a particular characteristic that the self-discovery of female identity acknowledges 'the real presence and recognition of another consciousness' and that 'the disclosure of the female self is linked to the identification of some "other"'. In a fundamental sense, all identity has to be disclosed by establishing an alterity. Men's autobiographies, it seems to me, do the same: the difference lies in the textual strategies employed. In the case of the women's autobiographies discussed here, the most striking feature is the way in which the very theme of disclosure of self remains suppressed under a narrative of changing times, changing manners and customs, and changing values.

What made the narrative history of domestic life particularly suitable as a 'feminine' literary genre was the belief, inculcated, needless to say, by male guardians of literary conventions, that this required little more than the retelling from memory of impressions left by direct personal experience. The genre, in short, did not require the author to express her 'self' or examine the development of her personality. It was not the telling of an exemplary life, not even of a life of any importance. To this day, it is useful to remember, there are fewer biographies of Bengali women written by others than there are autobiographies. The genre required the writer only to tell her readers, mainly women from a younger generation, how the everyday lives of women had changed. This allowed the questions to be raised: How are we to cope with this change? These were, of course, the central questions of nationalist discourse. However, in this particular case, the discourse enabled a more specific question to be asked—and answered: How must women behave in these changing times?

To discover how educated women of the nineteenth century answered this question, we will now look at some of their own writings. We will listen to their own words, but we will also do well to remember that sovereignty over language, a tricky business under the best of circumstances, is doubly vitiated for those who were subordinated, at one and the same time, to colonialism as well as to a nationalist patriarchy.

Before enlightenment

Shanta Nag, who came from a generation of middle-class women whose mothers were already educated, tells the story of how she learned to read the alphabet. It was sometime around the turn of the century. Her mother would sit across the table teaching her elder brother and she would stand beside her, silently watching the proceedings. In a few months, without anybody suspecting it, she had learned to read the first two books of the Bengali primer. The only difficulty was that in order to read, she had to hold the book upside down. Of course, by her time the education of women had become normal practice in middle class homes in Bengal, and she herself would have learned the alphabet and gone to school as a matter of routine. But the sense of acquiring a skill that was really meant for somebody else seems to have stayed with these early generations of educated women.

Nowhere is this more poignant than in the story of Rassundari Debi (1809–1900). For her, learning to read and write was nothing less than a lifelong struggle. She had been born in a wealthy, landed family and the village school was located in one of the buildings on the estate. When she was eight, her uncle sent her to this school, where, for the next two years, she sat everyday on the floor, the only girl in a roomful of boys, and was taught the Bengali alphabet, some arithmetic, and some Persian (which had still not been replaced by English as the language of bureaucracy). The teacher was an Englishwoman. Rassundari does not tell us this, but we know from other sources that during this brief spell in the early nineteenth century, Christian missionary women attempted to educate Indian girls, first in schools and then in their homes. The attempt had to be given up rather quickly because the idea of women being exposed to Christian influences seemed far too threatening to the men of their families, and it was only in the latter half of the century, when Indians themselves began to open schools for women and to produce what was considered a suitable modern educational literature in Bengali, that the practice of middle class girls going to school would become legitimate.

In the meantime, Rassundari's education came to an abrupt halt when she was ten because the building in which her school was housed was destroyed in a fire. It is doubtful how far her education would have progressed in any case, because at the age of twelve, in accordance with the prevailing custom, she was given in marriage.

From then on, her life was enclosed by the daily performance of her household duties. After the death of her mother-in-law a few years later, she had to take on the entire burden of running the house. She cooked three times a day for about thirty members of the household. She gave birth to twelve children, of whom seven died in her lifetime. Her responsibilities in the family would not allow her to go anywhere. Even when she did, to visit her husband's relatives on weddings and other ritual occasions, she would be accompanied on the boat by two guards, two maids, and ten or fifteen other people, and, 'like a prisoner on parole', would have to return in a couple of days. Rassundari particularly lamented her failure to visit her mother before she died.

> I tried so many ways to go and see my mother, but I was not fated to do
> so. This is not a matter of small regret to me. Oh lord, why did you give

birth to me as a human being? Compared to all the birds and beasts and other inferior creatures in this world, it is a rare privilege to be granted a human birth. And yet, despite this privilege, I have failed grievously in my duty. Why was I born a woman? Shame on my life! . . . If I had been my mother's son and known of her imminent death, no matter where I happened to be, I would have flown to her side like a bird. Alas, I am only a bird in a cage.

Had this been all there was to Rassundari's life, it would have been no different from those of thousands of other women in upper caste landed families in early nineteenth-century Bengal, and we would have had no opportunity to read about it in her own words. Fortunately, she nursed a secret dream. She was always a devout woman, and sometime in her late youth she had a longing to read the religious epics and the lives of the great saints. She did not so much as dare look at even a piece of paper that had been written on, for fear of adverse comments, but every day, she tells us, she would pray to her god: 'Oh Lord, give me learning, so that I can read books . . . If you do not teach me, who will?' And yet, she did not know how this impossible feat would be accomplished.

The way was shown to her in a dream.

One day, in my sleep, I dreamt I had opened a copy of the *Caitanya-bhagavat* and was reading it. As soon as I woke up, my body and mind were filled with delight. I closed my eyes and again thought of the dream, and realized what a precious gift I had received . . . I said to myself, 'How remarkable! I have never seen a copy of the *Caitanya-bhagavat* and would not recognize it even if I saw one. And yet, there I was reading it in a dream.' . . . Every day I had asked the Almighty, 'Teach me to read. I want to read books.' The Almighty had not taught me to read, but had now given me the power to read books in my dream. I was delighted and thanked the Almighty.

Rassundari, however, was to be blessed even more generously. That very day, while she was busy in the kitchen, her husband came in looking for their eldest son and said to him, 'This is my *Caitanya-bhagavat*. Keep it here somewhere. I'll send for it later.' Rassundari waited until no one was around, removed a page of the unbound manuscript, and hid it in her room. Later, she tried to read it and discovered that so many years after her brief period of schooling, she could not recognize most of the letters. She then stole a page on which her son had practised his alphabet, and for months thereafter, whenever she was alone, she would compare the two pieces of paper and, painfully and in absolute secrecy, teach herself to read.

Over the next couple of years, she worked her way through the *Caitanya-bhagavat*. No one in the household, except a few trusted maids, knew of her accomplishment. But Rassundari had perceived the existence of a whole new world that still seemed out of her reach.

My mind seemed to have acquired six hands. With two of them, it wanted to do all the work of the household so that no one, young or old, could find fault with me. With two others, it sought to draw my children close to my heart. And with the last two, it reached out for the moon ... Has anyone held the moon in her hands? ... And yet, my mind would not be convinced; it yearned to read the *puranas*.

Rassundari gathered up courage and shared her secret with her widowed sisters-in-law. To her surprise, not only did they not reprimand her, but in fact eagerly conspired to start a secret reading circle, arranging to procure books from the outer quarters of the house and setting up an elaborate warning system to prevent discovery.

In time, when the sons were grown, it was no longer necessary to keep up the secrecy. In any case, the times had also changed, and men of her son's generation looked upon the education of women as a virtue. It was with the assistance of her sons that Rassundari learned to read the printed book and later on to write.

Rassundari thought of her achievement as a divine gift. In fact, her testimony is quite unique in the collection we are looking at for the utterly sincere way in which it tells the story of a life shaped entirely by the inscrutable whims and fancies of a divine power, including the dreams and miraculous coincidences in which that power revealed its presence. It could well be a fragment, paraphrased in the prose of the nineteenth century, from the devotional literature of an earlier era. All subjectivity is attributed here to a divine agency, and Rassundari recounts her toil and sorrow—'the burden of three lives thrust into one'—only as the story of a fate assigned to her. I should also mention that she notes with great satisfaction the good fortune of women younger than her, for 'the Lord of the Universe has now new rules for everything. Women today do not have to suffer ... Nowadays parents take great care to educate their daughters. I feel very pleased when I see this'. [...]

Nationalists of the twentieth century saw in Rassundari's story only a confirmation of their construction of the true essence of Indian womanhood; self-sacrificing, compassionate, spiritual, and possessing great resources of emotional strength drawn from personal faith and devotion. This essence, they thought, needed to be recovered from the morass of bigotry and superstition into which tradition had fallen, and reform and education could accomplish this. What they did not recognize was that Rassundari's struggle emanated from a consciousness that was yet uncolonized by the Enlightenment. She submitted to as well as resisted a patriarchy that was pre-modern; her strategies of resistance also sprang out of traditions that far predated the advent of 'women's education' as an agenda of nationalist reform. Above all, the intervention of nationalist male reformers was not required to set Rassundari's consciousness into motion. Indeed, in her time, the nationalist project had not even begun. Only later did nationalism appropriate her story into its own pre-history. [. . .]

~

STRISHIKSHA OR EDUCATION FOR WOMEN
Tanika Sarkar

[. . .]

'Must we live in chains'?

In her own way, Rashsundari had a great deal to say about what had emerged as a central theme in nineteenth-century reform in Bengal: on women's education, on the strictures against it in orthodox families, on its growing availability in her later years. She does not, however, refer to the debates among reformists and the orthodoxy as such, even when her own observations come close to the reformist position. Here she stands apart from the nineteenth-century Maharashtrian widow Tarabai, who declares her differences from the reformist agenda even when she wants education for women (O' Hanlon 1994). She also stands apart from the polemical writings of a Bengali predecessor, Kailashbashini Debi, who wrote a whole book on the educational deprivation of Hindu women. Rashsundari refuses to insert herself openly within an ongoing debate on reform, although she was undoubtedly a partisan.

The refusal could not have flowed from her ignorance of the issues. In 1865, a little while before her book was finished; as many as seven schools had been set up for girls in the district of Pabna, her birthplace. [. . .]

At the time of the publication of her book, she was no longer a timid young wife, insulated from information about public events and debates, but had become an elderly matron whose learning was known and welcomed within her family. Rashsundari could not have failed to understand that what she had to say on women's education plugged into a lively, even acrimonious public debate. In fact, Jyotirindranath's preface to her book dwells on the controversies. With Rashsundari, however, all reflections needed to be shown as entirely rooted in her own experiences and understanding: that understanding, moreover, must be stripped bare of all external influence except divine interventions.

Yet, she does approximate a tone of polemical anger and zeal on this question that is surprisingly close to the more explicit reformist advocacies. The nineteenth-century debate on *strishiksha* or women's education was something whose terms included far wider social problems and perspectives than the matter of education alone. Rammohan Roy, in an early writing against widow immolation, was one of the first people to question some of the fundamental grounds and implications of the norm that prohibited education for women. He linked it up with an entire structure of regulations that had actively denied moral and intellectual facilities to women and had then naturalized the results of the deprivation by describing the results as the cause: women's minds were too inferior—so said the conservative opponents of reform—to accommodate serious thinking. Rammohan separated and reversed cause and effect. It is interesting that Mary Wollstonecraft had similarly related differences in women's intellectual achievements to a difference in opportunities and not to innate nature. Rammohan might not have read her book, but he could have been conversant with the controversies that it had provoked. Later Bengali women, however, made the same point on their own, although in their case, there could be no direct influence at all (Baker 1992).

Rammohan wrote in 1818: 'When did you ever test the intelligence of women that you can so easily designate them as foolish creatures? . . . You withheld education and knowledge from them, so how do you decide that they are incapable of learning?' This was written at a time when the first moves were afoot to provide for women's education. In each subsequent decade, with the inauguration of new suggestions for *strishiksha*—whether by missionaries in the 1820s, by the iconoclastic Young Bengal reformers in the 1830s, or by Vidyasagar and sober Brahmo reformers in the 1840s and 50s—the debate gathered new strength and new bitterness. Invariably, the arguments would roll into and interrogate—or defend—the fundamentals of an entire order of upper caste patriarchal injunctions. We find, therefore, yet another relationship with the world of *vidhi-nishedha* that would, through concrete and partial demands of reform, set up some cracks within the ruling social order. Actually, in the historical context of the early nineteenth century, the most minimalist plans for education would open up quite a considerable excess beyond *sansar* and its demands—a potential that would steadily diminish for middle class women as, very gradually, *strishiksha* became normalized. Its transformative implications for poor people and poor women, however, still retains some of the older valencies in a country where bare literacy remains a scarce resource.

Reformers rarely claimed to do more than loosen up older disciplines a little; they would, in fact, flaunt their limited charter as highly controlled and soberly responsible measures. The orthodoxy, however, saw in each venture a definitive beginning of the end. Through the fiery contentions over *strishiksha*, we shall probe the nature of the fears, as a way of measuring exactly what the reforms could challenge and change.

Around the time that Rashsundari's book went to press, a vital and new dimension had been added to the debate. Women themselves had started writing about the question of their education, and the print medium had incorporated these in the public sphere of debates and arguments. One of the first printed pieces on the matter came from a girl of nine. Proponents of *strishiksha*, connected with the reformist newspaper *Sambad Prabhakar*, published a news item on 26 Baisakh 1256 (May 1849). They had visited the young girl at her home and had set a test for her. They also vouched for the fact that she had composed the answer in front of them. She was asked to write a poem on the theme:

'Girls of this land are not educated. How are they inferior to men?'

The little girl composed a poem in reply within an hour. It was a highly finished piece, written in a rather erudite style, and the verses rhymed perfectly (Ghosh 1987).

Women are kept like animals since they do not get education
People call them the weaker sex and they are not respected
Since men cannot be born without women
Why are women not cared for?
Men treat them with contempt just because they are women
They do not accept that women, too, have inner qualities.

The paper reported this at considerable length, for it was a major event. It was proof positive—and proof, badly needed—in a debate where they had tried to argue that education, if impartially distributed, would fetch the same results from a girl as from a boy. [. . .]

Shrimati Soudamini Debi from Bakarganj wrote in 1865: 'Why have men kept us in such a low state? Are we not the children of the Great Father? . . . How much longer do we stay chained to our homes?' Shrimati Kamini Debi wrote from Khaipara in 1867: 'It is no exaggeration to say that our women live lives that are no better than that of animals.' An anonymous woman wrote in 1868 from Konnagar: 'Our father! Must we live in chains all our lives, even though we are your daughters? Alas! Were we born in this land only to perform low tasks? . . . Why must we live all our lives like caged birds within the home?'

The words, sentiments and particularly the motif of the caged bird and the prison-like home, are familiar themes in *Amar Jiban (AJ)* [Rashundari's autobiography]. We might infer two things from the similarity, and both could be partly true. Rashundari could have read some of this before she finalized her autobiography. She does not refer to any modern reading matter at all, but the fact that she claims to have read only some sacred texts might have been a tactical move to underline her general obedience and traditional virtue. In any case, she probably would have read some new prose in order to compose a prose text, inspiration for which could not have come from the sacred verses alone. By the 1860s, when the first version of *AJ* was being composed, Bengali journalism had already come of age, and the new postal system had developed well enough to carry newspapers and periodicals into even remote village homes.

At the same time, the availability of the new journal for women and women's writing at just about the time when she wrote her book might indicate something else. It might take us toward an emergent structure of feeling among upper caste, rigidly secluded women whose families would be well-off enough to educate them if they had wanted to do so. It would be a desire for a new form of female identity that would reorient domesticity as well as disalign women somewhat from the domestic confines that they insistently described as a prison and a cage. Of course, a lot of these letters might actually have been penned by men, writing under a feminine pseudonym to carry credibility for their suggestions at a time when few women could come up with written and printable matter. But when we compare them with the few pieces of actual women's writings, we find little discrepancy.

AJ, as an authentic piece of a woman's writing, not only intervenes in the debate at its initial stage although without seeming to do so. The fact that its author was someone who was not connected with reformist circles at all went a long way to give it status as an autonomous female argument that could not have been mimicking male reformism. Historically, its appearance coincided with a stage in the debate when, for the first time, women could express their opinion within the public sphere of the press and print culture. Rashsundari's very distance from the centre of that sphere—reformist circles in Calcutta—and her silence and implied ignorance of the public nature and import of the issue, made her book appear as even more authentic than the spontaneously, even innocently, produced article.

What men feared about Strishiksha

Whereas on her loss of the natal home, she uses the first person singular consistently, on the subject of education Rashundari generalizes, talking about all Bengali women in past and present times—a rare departure for her. She does not usually write in the discursive mode on social matters but translates her general concerns into deeply personal experiences of pain. While talking about women and education, she refers to two distinct phases: the first covers the early years of her childhood and the first years in her new home when she had to keep her thirst for knowledge a secret, the second was a somewhat altered context in the late sixties, when the first part of her book was nearing an end.

Even in her mother's home, where she had picked up some letters from listening to her brothers' reading, no one was told about it. After her marriage, when she was fourteen—around the mid 1820s—she began to long to read, but her fears were great about letting anyone know of this desire. Already, male guardians were complaining about 'the Queen's rule' and about how that had encouraged a subversive spread of education among women. Both her desire and the male fears were obviously produced by some beginnings that had already been made to educate women by the early twenties. [. . .]

Women's literacy was virtually an unknown quantity when the nineteenth century opened. Ward's Report of 1803 mentioned that nearly all Bengali villages had primary schools or *pathshalas* but they seemed to have catered to boys alone (Mitra 1967). Adam's Report described a roughly similar picture in the mid-1830s but, again, precolonial educational facilities—well organized as they were for those times—seemed to have offered nothing to girls. It was not simply a question of omission. Girls were expressly forbidden to read in literate, even well-educated, households.

In this report, Adam refers to two separate orders of fear that choked off women's education. One was the fear of sexual intrigues, since a literate woman could write and make secret assignations of an illicit nature. In the early part of the century, Shibnath Shastri, the Brahmo reformer, was taught at home by an exceptional mother who was fairly well-educated. When he went to attend the village school and told his teacher that he was being supervised by his mother, the teacher sent a letter of assignation to this entirely unfamiliar woman through her unsuspecting son, secure in the certain conviction of her immorality (Shastri 1952).

The other kind of fear was about the impending threat of widowhood for the educated woman.

Education, then, is a double repudiation of the husband. It is, therefore, both immorality and non-conjugality. If we extend the connection a little further, beyond the figure of the husband, we find that the new educated woman is meant to be the opposite term of the domesticated/chaste good wife of old times. If the signification is widened out a little more, then education equals the end of the patriarchal marriage system. We thus have here a fundamental kind of binary opposite between two entire ways of being, two gender systems. This puts a weight on the meaning of women's education—and on social reform in this sphere—that is significantly in excess of the strict programmatic content of nineteenth-century *strishiksha*. There is a continual over-production and leakage of meaning that inexorably encompasses the future of Hindu domesticity. Reform, therefore, may appear partial and limited in intent, but to its adversaries—as we shall see—it was necessarily laden with momentous consequences.

On the educated woman

Very often, Indian reforms, especially those related to education for women, are seen as a simple function of mimicry, of aspirations towards Victorian gentility, for an emulation of companionate marriage (Vaid and Sangari 1989). This argument shoves the reformed and the educated woman under a doubled servitude—to her husband's new needs for a more sympathetic wife, and to western, Victorian standards of patriarchy. I think we need to emphasize very strongly, however, that the normative and moral horizons between the two cultural systems were so very different and distant that plain mimicry was plainly out of the question. Even if the basic digits of self-fashioning look superficially similar—a little education, closeness to the husband's interests, intelligent housekeeping, educating infants—the processes through which all this would be achieved were so vastly divergent that seemingly similar conclusions would lead up to entirely different experiences and norms. The Victorian lady did not have to hide her literacy, she was not married off in her infancy, her husband could not be formally polygamous and the widow was not customarily barred from remarriage. Nor did she live in virtual seclusion. The reforms that Victorian feminists struggled for were not basic education, end to widow immolation, legalizing widow remarriage, de-legalizing infant marriage. For the nineteenth-century Bengali Hindu woman, moreover, even the minimalist idea of these reforms would be possible to conceive of only after a very hard struggle against ruling *vidhi-nishedha*, after a radical break with her own inherited sensibilities. It would come about through a process that was inevitably painful and crisis ridden. It is a historical fact of immense significance that women articulated an early yet strong sense about non-gendered, inalienable, equal human rights, first of all in the sphere of education; in contrast, abolition of widow immolation, legalizing widow remarriage, a higher age of consent and marriage were rights that male reformers initiated. I think that such misrecognition of historical developments arises when we confine ourselves to assessments of finished literary products as the sole gauge for sensibilities of the day: we need to look closely at the concrete historical processes that went into their making to uncover more hidden breaks, ruptures and challenges that the formal texts do not make evident.

It was to cancel out the association between education on the one hand, and widowhood and immorality on the other, that the first women writers carefully underlined the fact that their education was initiated by the husbands.

The only exceptions to the prohibition seemed to have been the rich landlord families. According to Adam, girls of many such families were educated since, in case of widowhood, they were expected to manage the family properties. Yet, not all landlords' daughters could have been educated since Rashsundari herself belonged to such a household and nobody tried to teach her anything.

The other known category of women who were literate were those from mendicant Vaishnav orders—the *boshtomis* from popular, often low class and caste devotional sects, who made an income from teaching women from upper caste households. The subject matter, obviously, would relate to the illicit love between Krishna and Radha. Perhaps, for that reason, not every affluent household would use them to teach their girls. For most respectable upper caste families, the association between *boshtomis* and literacy itself would act as a counter model and inhibit the extension of education among their women, since *boshtom* orders were looked down upon and were suspected of all kinds of sexual peccadillos. Rashsundari's families were devout Vaishnava as well as highly educated, but they were strict about withholding education from women. [. . .]

References

O' Hanlon, Rosalind. *A comparison between women and men: Tarabai Shinde and the critique of gender relations in colonial India.* Madras: Oxford University Press 1994.

Baker, Keith Michael. Defining the public sphere in 18th century France: Variations on a theme by Habermas. In *Habermas and the public sphere*, ed. Craig and Calhoun. MPP Press: Cambridge, 1992. 203–08.

Ghosh, Benoy, ed. *Samayikpatre banglar samajchitra.* Vol. 2. Papyrus: Calcutta, 1978. 27–28.

Sangari, Kumkum and Sudesh Vaid, ed., *Recasting women: Essays on colonial history.* New Delhi: Kali for Women, 1989.

Mitra, Ramesh Chandra. *Education, 1833–1905.* In *History of Bengal, 1757–1905,* ed. N.K. Sinha. Calcutta: n.p., 1967.

~

EDUCATION FOR WOMEN'S EQUALITY: NATIONAL POLICY ON EDUCATION, 1986

Department of Education

The present situation

1. Provision of educational opportunities to women has been an important programme in the education sector since independence. Between 1951 and 1981, the percentage of literacy amongst women improved from 7.93 per cent to 24.82 per cent. However, in absolute numbers, illiterate women have increased during this period from 158.7 million to 241.7 million (excluding Assam). Women comprise 57 per cent of the illiterate population, and 70 per cent of the non-enrolled children of school stage are girls. In spite of the efforts made so far, the education system has not been able to make sufficient contribution towards women's equality.

Targets

2. (a) A phased time-bound programme of elementary education for girls, particularly up to the primary stage by 1990, and up to the elementary stage by 1995.

(b) A phased time-bound programme of adult education for women in the age group 15–35 (whose number is estimated to be 6.8 crores) by 1995.

(c) Increased women's access to vocational, technical, professional education and to existing and emergent technologies.

(d) Review and reorganization of the educational activities to ensure that it makes a substantial contribution towards women's equality, and creation of appropriate cells/units therefore.

Policy parameters and strategies

3. The National Policy on Education (NPE) envisages that education would be used as a strategy for achieving a basic change in the status of women. The national education system would (i) play a positive interventionist role in the empowerment of women, (ii) contribute towards development of new values through redesigned curricula and text books, and (iii) women's studies will be promoted as part of various courses. The main features of the targets and implementation strategy will consist of the following:

   i.   to gear the entire education system to play a positive interventionist role in the empowerment of women;

   ii. to promote women's studies as a part of various courses and encouragement to educational institutions to take up active programme to further women's development

   iii. to widen the access of women to programmes of vocational, technical and professional education;

   iv. to create dynamic managerial structure to cope with the targets envisaged.

Empowerment of women

4. Women become empowered through collective reflection and decision making. The parameters of empowerment are:

   — building a positive self-image and self-confidence;
   — developing ability to think critically;
   — building up group cohesion and fostering decision-making and action;
   — ensuring equal participation in the process of bringing about social change;
   — encouraging group action in order to bring about change in the society;
   — providing the wherewithal for economic independence.

5. The following measures will be taken for the achievement of the above parameters;

   a. Every educational institution should, by 1995, take up active programmes of women's development built around a study and awareness of the women's predicament and for promotion of communication and organization among women.

   b. All teachers and Non-Formal Education/Adult Education (NFE/AE) instructors should be trained as agents of women's empowerment. Special training programmes will be developed by NCERT, NIEPA, Directorate of Adult Education (DAE), SCERTs, State Resource Centres (SRCs) and UGC to incorporate in all training programmes of teachers and NFE/AE instructors elements which would motivate them to work for women's empowerment. Voluntary agencies and activist groups for women's development will be involved in these training programmes.

   c. Women teachers and women instructors in adult/non-formal education programmes should receive special orientation to enable them to play on activist role towards women's equality.

   d. Special programmes should be developed by research institutions, voluntary institutions and professional groups of artists to promote general awareness and self-image amongst women through a variety of programmes like discussions, street plays, skits, wall papers, puppet shows, etc.

   e. An environment should be created in which practically all sections of the society will commit themselves and work for achieving this objective enunciated in the National Policy on Education. Keeping in view the important role played by media in this sphere, clear policy guidelines should be developed by radio and TV in 1986–87 and measures taken to persuade films and other media on these lines.

   f. Preference in recruitment of teachers upto school level should be for women. This will create a greater confidence in the rural areas and motivate the parents to send girls to the school.

   g. The common core curriculum is a powerful instrument for the empowerment of women through the incorporation of values commensurate with the new status of women. The Women's Cell in the NCERT will be reviewed and given the responsibility for preparing the component of the core curriculum relating to women's equality. The Cell should also accelerate its work of eliminating existing bias and sex stereotypes from school text books. The Women's Cell of NCERT should take the active help of all persons on playing its assigned role.

h. Sensitization of teachers, trainers, planners and administrators to women's issue, will be taken up as a major programme by NIEPA and appropriate state level agencies, through initial training, in-service training and refresher courses. NIEPA should also have a strong cell for planning and execution of these programmes.

Women's studies

6. Women's studies programme has four dimensions—teaching, research, training and extension. In teaching, the following activities will be taken up:

   (i) Incorporation of issues relating to women's status and role in the foundation course proposed to be introduced by University Grants Commission for all undergraduate students;
   (ii) Incorporation of the women's dimension into courses in different disciplines;
   (iii) Elimination of sexist bias and sex stereotypes from textbooks.

7. Under research, the following steps will be taken

   (i) Encouraging research in identified areas and subjects which are crucial in advancing knowledge in this area and to expand the information base;
   (ii) Critical appraisal of existing tools and techniques which have been responsible for the disadvantages suffered by them, and where necessary reformation of research methodology.

8. The following measures will be taken under training:

   (i) Dissemination of information and interaction through seminars/workshops on the need for women's studies and its role in university education;
   (ii) Orientation of teachers and researchers to handle women-related topics and to incorporate women's dimension into general topics;
   (iii) Workshops for restructuring the curriculum.

9. Under extension, it is proposed to encourage educational institutions to take up Programmes which directly benefit the community and bring about the empowerment of women.

10. These would include actual implementation of development programmes directly aimed at women's empowerment such as adult education, awareness building, legal literacy, informational and training support for socioeconomic programmes of women's development, media, etc.

Universalization of elementary education and adult education

11. The present programme of non-formal centres for girls on 90:10 pattern will be extended to all educationally backward pockets of the country. NFE Centres should be community based. Responsibility of planning, selection of instructors and monitoring should be with the community, including parents. Increased assistance to voluntary agencies to run non-formal education centres for girls should be given.

12. In the rural areas, girls are kept busy at home in sibling and household care, in fetching fuel, fodder and water, or in earning a day's wage. Therefore, special support services referred to in the Policy need to cover all these areas up to 1995. Early childhood education centres are an important support service in increasing enrolment and retention of girls in schools. Programmes of social forestry, drinking water supply, mid-day meals, and other nutrition programmes, smokeless chullahs and other devices aimed at eliminating drudgery from women's lives should be formulated by the Ministry and organization concerned up to 1990 to coverage with the objective of universalization of education.

13. Skill development linked to employment or work opportunities in the villages or local areas are required to be given overriding priority so that there is an incentive on the part of the parents to educate the girls.

14. Mass scale adult education programmes for women in the age group 15–35 should be developed to eradicate illiteracy amongst women by 1995. As a majority of women in this age group are workers, literacy per se may not have any relevance for them. It is, therefore, necessary to develop adult education programmes for women linked with upgradation of their skills and income generating activities.

15. Skill development for girls and women should be a continuous process of learning starting from the NFE centres and AE centres. Continuing Education Centres should be set up in a phased manner which should organize vocational training, provide opportunities for retention of literacy skills and application of this learning for improving their living conditions.

16. The skill development given by the Continuing Education Centres will be supported by other programmes of non-formal, vocational training and skill development to be administered by a variety of organizations and institutions, such as Polytechnics, Community Polytechnics, ITIs, Shramik Vidyapeeths, Central Social Welfare Board, State Social Welfare Advisory Boards, Voluntary agencies, Krishi Vijgyan Kendras, Women's Centres in Agricultural and Home

Science Colleges as part of their extension activities. Besides, industries which employ women should themselves run non-formal vocational training courses. For effective learning and monitoring, a Women's Bureau is to be set up in the Department of Education.

Women's access to vocational, technical and professional education and to existing and emergent technologies

17. At each stage in school education, or a part of work experience or vocationalization, girls should be exposed to a variety of vocational training activities. The method of vocational training should be both through the formal and non-formal courses. The choice of skills to be taught will depend on the natural resources, traditional occupations and new activities being taken up through government and private investment.

18. There are 104 ITIs functioning exclusively for women and 97 wings in general ITIs reserved for women. It is proposed that these institutions be revamped during the period 1987–90 on the following lines:

(i) Diversification of trades and courses, will be done, keeping the job potential of the area in mind. There will be an efficient placement system which will enable the institutions to have continuous dialogue with employers. The idea behind this diversification is that while girls will continue to receive preferential treatment in trades/occupations, for which they are particularly well suited (e.g. teaching and nursing), this will not become a barrier for their participation in technical and professional courses of higher level, and equal opportunities will be provided for them in all vocational, technical and professional courses.

(ii) There will be a strong element of vocational counselling in each ITI/RVTI/NVTI, polytechnics, suitable orientation should also be provided in the schools as preparation for motivating the girls to choose non-traditional courses.

(iii) Information about credit, banking, entrepreneurial development, etc. will be provided by the ITI/RVTI/NVTI, polytechnics and community polytechnics along with practical on-the-job training. The implementation of the apprenticeship scheme will be strengthened to increase the coverage of women.

(iv) In order to substantially enlarge the opportunities to women for craftsmen's training, shift system will be introduced in existing ITIs, one in the morning and the other in the afternoon.

(v)   DGE&T office should have a separate Directorate of Women's Vocational Training.

(vi)   Women's access to technical education will be improved qualitatively and quantitatively. The choice of trades/disciplines offered to women at Certificate/Diploma/Degree levels in all types of technical education institutions will be made keeping in view the objective of bringing about women's equality. Necessary incentives, as spelt out in the section of Technical Education, will be provided.

Management structure at centre and state level

19.   The interventions and programmes referred to above will be planned, coordinated, monitored and evaluated continuously both at the national and state level. Each of the organisations responsible for the programme will have to be strengthened. The Women's Cell in the NCERT will be revived and strengthened. NIEPA and Directorate of Adult Education will have strong cells to plan and administer women's training programmes. The Women's Cell in the UGC will be strengthened in order to monitor the implementation of various programmes at higher education level.

20.   At the state level, Women's Cells should be set up in all the states with adequate supporting staff to be headed by an officer of at least joint director's status.

≈

THE STORY OF MY SANSKRIT
Kumud Pawde

A lot of things are often said about me to my face. I've grown used to listening to them quietly; it's become a habit. What I have to listen to is praise. Actually, I don't at all like listening to praise. You may say that this itself is a form of self-indulgence. But that isn't so. I mean it sincerely. When I hear myself praised, it's like being stung by a lot of gadflies. As a result, I look askance at the person praising me. This expression must look like annoyance at being praised, for many misunderstandings have arisen about me in this connection. But it can't be helped. My acquaintances get angry with me because I am unable to accept compliments gracefully. I appear ill-mannered to them, because there isn't in me the courtesy they are expecting.

Now if you want to know why I am praised—well, it's for my knowledge of Sanskrit, my ability to learn it and to teach it. Doesn't anyone ever learn

Sanskrit? That's not the point. The point is that Sanskrit and the social group I come from don't go together in the Indian mind. Against the background of my caste, the Sanskrit I have learned appears shockingly strange.

That a woman from a caste that is the lowest of the low should learn Sanskrit, and not only that, also teach it—is a dreadful anomaly to a traditional mind. And an individual in whose personality these anomalies are accumulated becomes an object of attraction—an attraction blended of mixed acceptance and rejection. The attraction based on acceptance comes from my caste-fellows, in the admiration of whose glance is pride in an impossible ahcievement. That which for so many centuries was not to be touched by us, is now within our grasp. That which remained encased in the shell of difficulty, is now accessible. Seeing this knowledge hidden in the esoteric inner sanctum come within the embrace, not just of any person, but one whom religion has considered to be vermin—that is their victory.

The other attraction—based on rejection—is devastating. It pricks holes in one's mind—turning a sensitive heart into a sieve. Words of praise of this kind, for someone who is aware, are like hot spears. It is fulsome praise. Words that come out from lips' edge as filthy as betel-stained spit. Each word gleaming smooth as cream. Made up of the fragility of a honey-filled shirish-blossom. Polished as marble. The sensation is that of walking on a soft velvety carpet—but being burnt by the hot embers hidden in someone's breast, and feeling the scorching pain in one's soul. The one who's speaking thinks the listener can't understand—for surely a low caste person hasn't the ability to comprehend. But some people intend to be understood, so that I'll be crushed by the words. 'Well, isn't that amazing! So you're teaching Sanksrit at the Government College, are you? That's very gratifying, I must say.' The words are quite ordinary; their literal meaning is straightforward. But the meaning conveyed by the tone in which they are said torments me in many different ways! 'In what former life have I committed a sin that I should have to learn Sanskrit even from you? All our sacred scriptures have been polluted.' Some despair is also conveyed by their facial expressions. 'It's all over! Kaliyug has dawned. After all, they're the government's favourite sons-in-law! We have to accept it all.'

There are some other people I know, who have a genuine regard for me. They are honestly amazed by how I talk, by my clean, clear pronunciation. They speak with affectionate admiration about my mode of living. The food I cook is equated with ambrosia. They detect a brahminical standard of culture in my every thought and action—enough to surprise them. They constantly try to reconcile the contradiction. It's my good luck that I'm not always being asked to account for my antecedents. The main point is that they are trying to understand my evident good breeding in the context of my caste, and that is what makes everything so novel for them.

The result is that although I try to forget my caste, it is impossible to forget. And then I remember an expression I heard somewhere: 'What comes by birth, but can't be cast off by dying—that is caste.'

Beyond the accepters and the rejecters lies yet another group. In wholeheartedly welcoming the admiration of this group, every corner of my being is filled with pleasure. This group consists of my students. Far removed from hostile feelings. Without even an iota of caste consciousness. Away from the prejudices of their elders. Pure, innocent admiration, prompted by the boundless respect they feel, fills their eyes. Actually these girls have reached the age of understanding. The opinions they hear around them should by rights have made an impression on their minds. But these precious girls are full to the brim with the ability to discriminate impartially. And they keep their admiration within the limits of their gaze; they do not allow it to reach their lips. And that's why I yearn for that admiration. The occasional forward girl who has suppressed her timidity makes bold to express her feelings. 'Madam, I wish your lesson would never end!' And I answer her woodenly, 'But the college doesn't feel that way.' She feels snubbed, but I don't wish to encourage her admiration, in case it becomes a habit.

If the admiration had stayed limited to this individual level, I would tolerate it, but it goes beyond the prescribed boundaries. In other words, it starts to be blazoned even at the official level. As usual they start beating the drum of my caste, and tunes of praise of my knowledge of Sanskrit begin to mingle with the drumbeat. In 1971, the Maharashtra state government arranged, at Nagpur, a felicitation meeting to honour scholars of the Vedas. According to the wishes of the honourable ex-minister of education, Shri Madhukarrao Chaudhary, I was to introduce these honoured scholars. The introduction was to be made in Sanskrit. 'In the time of the Aryans it was noted down, and moreover impressed on the minds of the common Indian people, from the Himalayas to the tip of the peninsula, that my ancestors should consider themselves guilty of a crime if they even heard the sound of this language. And that is the language in which I have to speak.'

My God! How I was I going to manage? My heart began to beat rapidly. My mind was dark with anxiety, and I was drowned in feelings of inferiority. A conflict of emotions—and once again a confrontation with public praise. 'Whereas our traditional books have forbidden the study of Sanskrit by women and Shudras, a woman from those very Shudras, from the lowest caste among them, will today, in Sanskrit, introduce these scholars. This is the beginning of a progressive way of thinking in independent India.' A thunder of applause. I look towards the sound of the applause. Most of the people here are from government offices. Looking at them through an artist's eyes, I see what looks like a wild disco dance of different emotions. The frustration of the defeated, the fury of the traditionalists, the respect of some acquaintances, the hostility and disgust of others, are obvious to my experienced eye. Some gazes ask me, 'Why did you need to make the introductions in this manner? To humiliate us?'

In response to these hissings of wounded pride, I experience a mixture of emotions. Seeing this hostility and disgust, I slip into the past. This disgust is extremely familiar to me. In fact, that is what I have grown accustomed to, ever since I was old enough to understand. Actually, I shouldn't have any feelings about this disgust, and if I do have any feelings at all, they should be of gratitude. For it was this disgust that inclined me towards Sanskrit. It so happened that the ghetto in which there stood my place of birth, the house where I was welcome, was encircled on all sides by the houses of caste Hindus. The people in our ghetto referred to them as the Splendid People. A small girl like me, seven or eight years old, could not understand why they called them 'Splendid'. And even as today's mature female with learning from innumerable books, I still cannot understand it. That is, I have understood the literal meaning of the word 'splendid', but not why it should be applied to them,whether they deserve to have it applied. The girls who studied along with me were brahmins or from other higher castes. I had to pass their houses. I paused, waiting casually for their company. Right in front of me, the mothers would warn their daughters, 'Be careful! Don't touch her. Stay away from her. And don't play with her. Or I won't let you into the house again.' Those so-called educated, civilized mothers were probably unconscious of the effect of this on my young mind. It wasn't as if I could not understand them.

Every day, I bathed myself clean with Pears soap. My mother rubbed Kaminia oil on my hair, and plaited it neatly. My clothes were well-washed and sparkling clean. The girls of my own caste liked to play with me because it enabled them to smell some fragrance. For my father himself was fond of toiletries. So there was always a variety of oils, soaps and perfumes in the house. The other girls in my class (except for those who lived near my ghetto) also liked to sit next to me. So why should these women have talked like that?

What's more, if one were to compare houses, our house was cleaner than theirs. My mother daily smeared the floor with fresh cowdung. The white-powder borders were delicately drawn. The courtyard was well-sprinkled, and decorated with rangoli designs. Almost every fortnight, on the occasion of a festival, the house was whitewashed from top to bottom. Every scrap of cloth was boiled in a solution of soda bicarb before it was washed. The metal vessels were scrubbed to gleaming. On the other hand, one could see water stains and a greasy film on even the drinking-vessels those girls had. In fact, it was I who didn't like to sit next to those girls. For, from my childhood, my sense of smell, in particular, had sharpened beyond limit. Though, of course, the nose that conveyed it was broad and misshapen. The sour smell, like buttermilk, that rose from the bodies of those girls! I couldn't bear the smell of shikakai mixed with the smell of their hair. Their bad breath, too, was unbearable. And, in spite of all this, they found me disgusting? So, even at that young age, this emotion of disgust taught me to think. It inspired me to be introspective. At an age which was meant for playing and skipping around, these thoughts would rouse me to fury.

One event outraged my self-respect. There was to be a thread-ceremony for the brother of one of my classmates. I had not actually been invited but my restless curiosity would not let me sit quiet. I stood outside the pandal looking in at the ceremony going on inside. The sacrificial fire was lit; the air all around was filled with the smoke and fragrance of incense and the grain burnt-offering. The reverberations of the Vedic chants threatened to burst through the cloth walls of the pandal. I was lost in watching the head movements that accompanied the chant of 'Svaha!' each time a libation was poured. All this was extremely new, unknown, never seen before. I was totally engrossed, at one with the chants and the incense.

My concentration was suddenly broken. One voice: 'Hey, girl! What are you staring at? Can you make head or tail of it? Here, take a sweet—and be off!' A decked-up woman past her prime, dripping with gold and pearls, stood in front of me, adjusting her heavily brocaded sari. Her nose was wrinkled in disgust, like a shrivelled fig. 'What do you take me for—a beggar? Giving me a sweet! Can you see injuries on anyone just because I watched them?' I retorted, and briskly walked away.

Words followed me: 'These Mahars have really got above themselves.' The intonation was the typical superior nasal tone of the Pune brahmin.

My young mind thought, 'Why was I so wrapped up in watching? What had that ceremony to do with me? And why should that woman behave so bitchily with me?' There was definitely some intimate connection between me and those Vedic mantras. Otherwise why should that woman have noticed my innocent absorption? Why should she have taunted me disgustedly? She must have been unwilling to let those chants enter my ears. I used to ask my father, 'What language are the Vedic mantras composed in?' He used to say, 'They're in Sanskrit, my girl.' 'Is Sanskrit very difficult? Can't we learn it?' My father used to answer, 'Why shouldn't we? After all, we're independent now. Those days are gone. Learn Sanskrit. Don't I too know the Gayatri Mantra?' And he used to say 'Om' and begin to recite the Gayatri mantra. In simple delight, I used to tell my neighbours, 'I'm going to learn Sanskrit.' The educated people next door used to poke fun at me. 'Is Sanskrit such an easy language? It's very difficult. Did our forefathers ever learn it?' Hearing this, I would be discouraged. Seeing my crestfallen face, my father would start cursing those people, sometimes obscenely, sometimes more elegantly. He used to encourage me, and the encouragement would make me glow with confidence once again.

After I entered high school, I took Sanskrit as an elective subject in class nine. The school where I went supported brahminical prejudices. All sorts of indirect efforts were systematically made to prevent me from learning Sanskrit. 'You won't be able to manage. There will be no one at home to help you. Sanskrit is very difficult,' etc., etc. But I was as firm as a rock. Seeing that no form of persuasion had any effect on me, the persuaders stopped persuading. But how to remove the prejudice in their minds? I did not want to pay heed to every single opinion. I just wanted to keep my teacher, Hatekar, happy. He had been full of praise of me since I was in class six. 'How can this little slip of a girl give answers so fast in every subject?' I asked him, 'Sir, I should take Sanskrit, shouldn't I?' 'Do take it. But you've taken all the Arts subjects, though you're good at maths. Take science and maths, along with Sanskrit.' 'But sir, I don't enjoy maths.'

'But you can become a doctor, can't you?' 'I don't want to be a doctor. I can't bear suffering.' He laughed and said, 'On the contrary, it is precisely those who can't bear suffering, who are fit to become doctors. Won't you be able to help the afflicted? That's what's needed among your people. But it's your decision.'

With great eagerness and interest, I began my study of Sanskrit. As I learnt the first-declension masculine form of the word 'deva', I picked up the rhythm of the chant. I must make special mention of the person who helped me to learn by rote the first lesson about aspirates—my teacher Gokhale. If I omit to do so, I shall feel a twinge of disloyalty in every drop of my blood. Gokhale Guruji. Dhoti, long-sleeved shirt, black cap, a sandalwood-paste mark on his forehead. The typical robust and clear pronunciation of the Vedic school. And an incredible concern for getting his students to learn Sanskrit. At first I was afraid. But this proved groundless. What actually happened was the very opposite of what I had expected.

But there were many obstacles. Against them all, I at last matriculated. On seeing the marks I got for Sanskrit, I announced, 'I shall do an M.A. in Sanskrit.' Our enlightened neighbours laughed as they had before. Some college lecturers and lawyers also joined in the joke. 'How can that be possible? You may have got good marks at Matric. But it isn't so easy to do an M.A. in Sanskrit. You shouldn't make meaningless boasts; you should know your limitations.' The discouragers said what they usually do. The point was that the people who discouraged me were all of my caste. But their words could not turn me from my purpose. I didn't reply—I wanted to answer them by action. For that, I needed to study very hard. In order to take an M.A. in Sanskrit, I would have to go to the famous Morris College. I had heard so many things about the college from my friend's sister. About the learned professors with their cultivated tastes, about the mischievous male students, the beautiful girls, and the huge library. My interest was limited to the professors who would teach me, and to the library. And I joined the college.

The Hindus from the high-caste areas used to taunt me. 'Even these wretched outcastes are giving themselves airs these days—studying in colleges.' I pretended to be deaf. I had begun to have some idea of what Savitribai

Phule must have had to endure on account of her husband Mahatma Jhotiba Phule's zeal for women's education.

I went through some mixed experiences while I studied. I would call my lecturers' even-handed fairness a very remarkable thing. I was never scared by the prejudice of which repute and rumour had told me. What is more, praise and encouragement were given according to merit. Some people may have felt dislike in their heart of hearts, but they never displayed it. One thing alone irked me—the ironical comments about the scholarship I got. 'She's having fun and games at the expense of a scholarship. Just bloated with government money!' From the peons themselves to the senior officials, there was the same attitude. I couldn't understand. Was it charity they were dispensing from their personal coffers? They were giving me government money, and if that money was going from them to the government in the form of taxes, then equally, a tax was being levied on the public to pay their salaries. And that tax was collected in indirect forms even from the parents of the scholarship holders. So who paid whom? When the Dakshina Prize Committee used to give stipends, there was no complaint of any kind from any level of society. Then why now? Oh, well . . . So now, the story of my M.A.

In the second year of our M.A., we went to the postgraduate department in the university. Very well-known scholars taught us there. The head of the department was a scholar of all-India repute. He didn't like my learning Sanskrit, and would make it clear that he didn't. And he took a malicious delight in doing so. The sharp claws of his taunts left my mind wounded and bleeding. In a way, I had developed a terror of this great pandit. His manner of speaking was honeyed and reasonable, but filled with venom. I would unconsciously compare him with Gokhale Guruji. I couldn't understand why this great man with a doctorate, so renowned all over India, this man in his modern dress, who did not wear the traditional cap, who could so eloquently delineate the philosophy of the Universal Being, and with such ease explain difficult concepts in simple terms, could not practise in real life the philosophy in the books he taught. This man had been exposed to modernity; Gokhale Guruji was orthodox. Yet one had been shrivelled by tradition, the other enriched by it, like a tree weighed down with fruit. Days go by; you survive calamities; but the memory of them sets up its permanent abode in you. In the inmost recesses of your inner being. I survived even through such a difficult ordeal. I got my M.A. with distinction . . .

And now I would be a lecturer in Sanskrit! My dreams were tinted with turquoise and edged in gold. The images I nursed about myself were taking strange shapes in my mind. A high-paid job would come to me on a platter from the government. For I must have been the first woman from a scheduled caste to pass with distinction in Sanskrit. Every nook and cranny of my mind was filled with such hopes and expectations. But those ideas were shattered. My illusions proved as worthless as chaff. I became despondent about the efficiency of the government. I started attending interviews in private colleges. And that was a complete farce. Some said, 'But how will you stay on with us, when you've passed so well?' (In other words, they must have wanted to say, 'How will you work for less pay?') In other places, the moment I had been interviewed and stepped out of the room, there would be a burst of derisive laughter. I would hear words like sharp needles. 'So now even these people are to teach Sanskrit! Government brahmins, aren't they?' And the ones who said this weren't even brahmins, but so-called reformers from the lower castes, who considered themselves anti-brahmin, and talked of the heritage of Jyotiba Phule, and flogged the mass of the lower castes for their narrow caste consciousness. And yet they found it distasteful that a girl from the mahar caste, which was one of the lower castes, should teach Sanskrit. When people like these, wearing hypocritical masks, are in responsible positions in society, it does not take even a minute for that society to fall.

Two years after my M.A., I was still unemployed. There must be many whose position is the same as mine. In my frustration I took a bold step to get out of the trap. I presented my case in writing to the Honourable Shri Jagjivan Ram, the noted minister in the central cabinet. I condemned the flimsy pretence of the state government and the administration that flouted the Constitution. My words had all the power of a sharp sword. For they were a cry from the heart of a person being crushed to death under the wheels of circumstance.

The Honourable Minister Jagjivan Ram placed the letter before Pandit Nehru, who was astonished by it, and sent me an award of Rs. 250/-, telling me to meet the chief minister of Maharashtra. Accordingly the chief minister of that time, Yeshwantrao Chavan, sent me a telegram asking me to meet him. Within a day or two, one wire after another had electrified me into wondering who I'd suddenly become. Getting past the ranks of spearmen and macebearers at the government office was quite an ordeal. But finally I got to see the 'Saheb'. Now, I thought, I would get a job at once—as a clerk in the government office, at least. A naive expectation. The chief minister made me fulsome promises in his own style. 'We'll definitely make efforts for you— but you won't get a job in minutes; it'll take us some time. We'll have to give thought to it; have to hunt out something.' And with this assurance came a fine speech that qualified as an example of literature. 'A student of Sanskrit is intoxicated with idealism. It is a deeply felt personal desire. You shouldn't run after a job. Involve yourself in research. Pursue your studies.' Now the controls of endurance that restrained me started to break rapidly, and the words that had been bound within me broke out. 'Saheb, if you can't give me a job, tell me so, clearly. I don't want promises. Promises keep false hopes alive. Research is the fruit of mental peace. How do you expect me to have mental peace, when I am starving? And I'm tired of speeches.' I was fed up with life. Otherwise in AD 1960 it would have been impossible for a wretch like me even to stand before a dignitary like this, with all the power of *kartumakartumanyathankartum*, (to do, omit to do, or do in another way), let alone speak out to him.

Waiting for a job, I passed the first year of an M.A. in English Literature. It was just an excuse to keep myself occupied. That year I got married—an inter-caste marriage. That is a story by itself—a different glimpse of the nature of Indian society. Let that be the subject of another story. The surprising thing is that two months after my marriage, I got an assistant lecturership in a government college. The deputy director who was on the interview board was amazed. 'How did this girl remain unemployed for two years?' Today, I am a professor in the famous college where I studied, whose very walls are imbued with the respect I felt for that institution. But one thought still pricks me: the credit for Kumud Somkuwar's job is not hers, but that of the name Kumud Pawde. I hear that a woman's surname changes to match her husband's—and so does her caste. That's why I say that the credit of being a professor of Sanskrit is that of the presumed higher caste status of Mrs Kumud Pawde. The caste of her maiden status remains deprived.

~

GENDER INEQUALITY IN PRIMARY SCHOOLING IN INDIA: THE HUMAN RIGHTS PERSPECTIVE

Karuna Chanana

Introduction

In recent times, gender as a principle underlying the distribution of resources and entitlements within the household and society, namely, education, economic rights, health care, and political participation, has become crucial in educational discourse due to the linkages of education with indicators of development.

It is now generally accepted that education, as a source of social mobility, equality and empowerment, both at the individual and at the collective level, is imperative for women, who constitute half of human kind, if societies have to develop in any meaningful way.

It is a widely known fact that, compared to men, Indian women have lower literacy rates, lower enrolment rates and higher non-enrolment and drop-out rates. Although the education system has expanded rapidly since India achieved independence in 1947, the gender gap continues to be substantial. In other words, women who constitute less than half the Indian population are deprived of the right to education, information, knowledge, skills and thinking associated with formal education.

This chapter presents an analysis of some of the parameters at aggregate and disaggregate levels to highlight the disparities among the states as well as those between castes, tribes and residence in rural–urban areas. Gender provides the overall framework of analysis.

Literacy

The literacy rate as per the 1991 census is 39.29 per cent for females and 64.14 per cent for males. Although it has increased from 15.33 per cent in 1961, the gap between male and female literacy remains almost constant during 1961–1991. It was 25.06 per cent in 1961 and 24.84 per cent in 1991. Moreover, interstate disparities reveal even more imbalances. For example, it varies from 38.48 per cent in Bihar to 89.81 per cent in Kerala, which has the highest literacy rate. Again, the difference between rural and urban literacy is high and affects women adversely. For example, rural female literacy varies from 30.37 per cent in Rajasthan to 88.92 per cent in Kerala.

The female literacy among the Scheduled Castes (SC) is 23.76 as compared to 49.91 per cent among the males. The corresponding percentage among the Scheduled Tribes (ST) females is 18.19 per cent compared to 40.65 among the males.

If the macro data are further disaggregated by rural–urban residence, literacy among both ST males and females is much lower than the non-tribal population. For instance, the overall rural literacy rate is 48 per cent (60 per cent male and 36 per cent female). The corresponding figures for ST males and females are 37 and 15 per cent respectively and the overall tribal literacy rate in the rural areas is 26 per cent. Inter-state disparities are equally glaring. For instance, the literacy rate among SC females is as low as 7.07 per cent in Bihar to a high of 81.25 per cent in Mizoram. The corresponding percentage for ST women is 4.42 per cent in Rajasthan to 78.70 per cent in Mizoram.

The gender gap in literacy is very high in educationally backward states like Rajasthan (35 per cent male and 4 per cent tribal females). The five states of Madhya Pradesh (10.73); Bihar (14.75); Orissa (10.21); Andhra Pradesh (8.68); and Rajasthan (4.42) which have 51.69 per cent of female ST population were below the national average for ST female literacy during 1981–1991 (NCW 1994, 95).

Further disaggregation of data shows that there are some geographical areas and certain tribes which are very backward. Since the 1991 census data are not yet published tribe wise, the 1981 census data are used here. In 1981, ten ST communities living in rural areas in different states had a female literacy rate below 5 per cent, e.g. 0.72 per cent among the Bhils and Bhil Garasiua tribes in Rajasthan; and 1.12 among the same tribes in Madhya Pradesh (NCW 1994, 54).

Thus, a large proportion of Indian women reach adulthood without access to even basic literacy skills. The situation of women who live in the rural areas and who belong to the deprived sections is the worst. If this is the situation regarding adult women, what is the situation of young girls in the 6–11 age group? Are we taking steps to prevent girls from being brought up as non-literates? In other words, do they have access to primary education?

Primary education

The last four decades have seen a phenomenal expansion of primary schools (Class I–V) which increased from 209,671 in 1950–51 to 572,923 in 1993–94 (MHRD 1995, 8). Yet it is estimated that about 20 per cent of the rural population are without a primary school or section. Nearly 108 million children were enrolled in 1993–94 as compared to 19.2 million in 1950–51. The proportion of girls has increased from 5.4 per cent to about 40.0 per cent. ST students constituted 7.91 per cent of primary school enrolment (8.36 per cent boys and 7.28 per cent girls) in 1991–92.

Enrolment at Elementary Stage (in millions)

Stage	1950–51		1993–94	
	Total	Girls	Total	Girls
Primary upper	19.2	5.4	108.0	46.4
Primary	03.1	0.5	39.9	15.7

Source: MHRD 1995, 16

The increase in enrolment compares well with the gross enrolment ratio (GER) in the 6–11 age group. It has increased from 24.9 per cent in 1950–51 to 85.02 per cent for girls and from 60.8 per cent to 106.20 per cent for boys in 1993–94. It is much less for rural children, i.e. 87 per cent for boys and 61 per cent for girls. On the other hand, 86 per cent urban girls and 92 per cent urban boys are enrolled.

Gross Enrolment Ratios in Primary Education

Demo	1950–51	1993–94
Total	42.6	95.0
Boys	60.8	106.2
Girls	24.9	85.0

Source: MHRD 1993 and NCERT 1995

There are tremendous inter-state differences in the GER of girls. Here, data are given for ST girls. It is 54.34 per cent in Madhya Pradesh (84.82 for boys), 58.09 in Orissa (125.22 for boys); 122.59 in Kerala (123.01 for boys); and 173.03 for girls (198.24 for boys) in Assam. High GERs, especially above 100 per cent, indicate not only that average and underage children are included; it is also an indication that there is pressure to enrol the boys or to declare them as being enrolled, which is the first step, howsoever tentative, towards looking at education as being socially desirable. It may be reasonable to infer that this pressure does not seem to exist for girls, especially in those states where it is as low as 55 or 58 per cent.

Even though enrolment has expanded phenomenally and even if one were to accept that the statistics reflect the reality, vast numbers of children are currently not enrolled or have never been enrolled. In addition, there are those who drop out of the educational system, thereby making the situation more complex.

Nearly half the children who join Class I drop out before reaching Class V, as the percentage of Class I enrolments stood at 54.59 per cent: 49.10 per cent for rural and 74.66 per cent for urban schools. Inter-state variations range from 16.17 per cent in Kerala to 79.23 per cent in Arunachal Pradesh. (Gender wise differences in drop-out rates between Class I and V were 35.1 per cent for boys and 38.6 for girls in 1993–94 (Tilak 1996).) The drop-out rate for ST girls in 1988–89 was 68.73 per cent, 61.94 among ST boys and 47.93 per cent for all communities (NCW 1994, 57, 107).

Besides those who enrol and then drop out, there are those who never enrol and are currently not enrolled. The 1991 census and the MHRD do not provide these data but according to the National Sample Survey Organization data, as many as 73 million were currently not enrolled in schools. The percentage of boys never enrolled in the 6–11 age group was 18.4 and 25.2 per cent respectively in 1986–87 (Tilak 1996: 279). The difference in the rural and urban areas is quite glaring, i.e., 22.7 per cent of girls in the rural and 2.5 per cent in the urban areas were never enrolled.

Inter-state variations for the 6–14 age group ranged from 2.7 per cent for girls in rural Kerala to 74.7 per cent for girls in rural Bihar and from 1.3 per cent in urban Kerala to 46.7 per cent in urban Bihar.

Barriers to gender equality

In spite of policy pronouncements, gender disparities persist in primary education. Are the incentives offered to attract students to schools and to keep them there working any better?

State supported primary education is generally expected to be free in most provinces. In addition, there are several state-supported schemes which offer incentives such as mid-day meals, textbooks, uniforms, attendance scholarships, etc. All the schemes are meant for the poor and the deprived.

The incentive schemes are funded by the centre, the state, or by both. The number of benefits and the amount tend to vary from state to state. The all-India average amount of scholarship varies from Rs. 67 for girls to Rs. 103 for boys in the rural areas. In addition, fewer girls than boys receive scholarships. Also, most states discriminate between boys and girls in that girls receive a lower amount than the boys, with some exceptions such as rural Assam (Rs 347 for the girls and Rs 15 for boys), rural Maharashtra (Rs 220 for girls and Rs 8 for boys), urban Gujarat (Rs 197 for girls and Rs 131 for boys); and urban Tamil Nadu (Rs 429 for girls and Rs 147 for boys). Otherwise, the differences are in the reverse, e.g. Rs 1 in urban Jammu & Kashmir for girls to Rs 70 for boys; Rs 75 for girls in rural West Bengal to Rs 146 for boys; Rs 26 for rural girls in Rajasthan to Rs 127 for boys, etc (Tilak 1996, 360).

Apart from the gender gap in the amount of the scholarship, there are general problems with most incentive schemes. For example, they cover only a small proportion of students (e.g. in urban Tamil Nadu 0.21 per cent boys and 0.66 per cent girls receive scholarships). The highest average is 7 per cent (boys and girls) in rural Rajasthan and 6.07 per cent (boys and girls) in urban Kerala. Secondly, the disbursement is faulty, the amounts remain unutilized, students receive the benefits late, or a lesser amount is earmarked for them.

Moreover, even though education is free, there is enough evidence to show that tuition fee is a source, however small, of educational revenue which proves that primary education is not really free. The point to be noted, however, is that official programmes discriminate against girls.

In addition, households spend less on girls than on boys. The National Sample Survey Organization (NSSO) 42nd Round provides detailed data on household expenditure on primary education of boys and girls in government and private schools. The average per capita household expenditure in government schools in rural areas is Rs 87 for boys and Rs 80 for girls. The corresponding figures for urban schools are Rs 183 and Rs 169 respectively. In private schools in the rural areas, it is Rs 232 for boys and Rs 194 for girls while it is Rs 493 for boys and Rs 396 for girls in the urban schools (Tilak 1996, 362). State-wise disaggregated data show that this discrimination against girls is common to most states.

Again, households generally spend less on girl students in government as well as in private schools than on boys. This difference is more in private schools than in the government schools as, for example, in rural Bihar (Rs 350 for boys and Rs 175 for girls), rural Rajasthan (Rs 334 for boys and Rs 262 for girls), urban Orissa (Rs 1028 for boys and Rs 571 for girls). Exceptions are urban Assam and rural Jammu and Kashmir, etc. The implications of this have to be seen in the context of the socioeconomic status of children in private schools. Generally, parents spend more on the education of their children in private than in government schools. These children also come from better-off homes. But even in these homes, gender discrimination is practised. Principals of private unaided schools tend to confirm this trend when they mention that, in their expensive co-educational schools, it is not surprising to find that while the son is enrolled, the sister is being sent to a cheaper school.

Number of (6–11 Age Group) Never Enrolled Children in Primary Schools

	Boys	Girls	Total (in millions)
Rural	16.4	22.7	39.1
Urban	02.0	02.5	04.5
Total	18.4	25.2	43.5

Source: NSSO 42nd Round Data, as given in Tilak 1996, tables 6 and 7

In addition to the discrimination in terms of state and household expenditure on girls, families reinforce this discrimination by using girls as domestic help, thereby preventing them from enrolling in schools. For example, according to the 1986–87 NSSO data, 43.6 million children in the 6–11 age group were never enrolled. Of these, 39.1 million were in rural areas and 4.5 in urban areas. Again, out of 43.6 million children, 18.4 million were boys and 25.2 million girls. In other words, 42.3 per cent of the children in rural areas (32.5 per cent boys and 53.5 per cent girls) were never enrolled. The corresponding figures in urban areas were 14.2 per cent boys and 21.6 per cent girls.

Moreover, among the currently not enrolled children, 10.4 per cent of the rural children (14.3 per cent boys and 7.5 per cent girls) in the same group were economically active. The corresponding figures for urban areas were 8.9 per cent (13.4 per cent boys, 5.7 per cent girls). However, the largest category is of those who are engaged in domestic chores: 16.8 per cent in rural areas (8.1 per cent boys and 23.4 per cent girls), and 15.1 per cent in urban areas (5.7 per cent boys and 23.3 per cent girls).

This large category is in addition to those who are prevented from access to schooling because they are 'economically active' and poor. This observation is also supported by qualitative case studies. For example, some girls do join school but most leave soon after. Nishtha started a school with forty-five students, of whom twenty-five were girls. After six months, there were only four girls left. The girls were so busy with household chores that they had no time to come to school. They had to look after siblings, collect firewood, organize food for domestic animals, fetch water, etc. Then they also had to help in the fields, and at home they lent a hand with the parboiling of rice and cutting of beedi leaves. Most feel that daughters must stay home and help with 'women's work' and so do not ask their daughters to go to school.

There is far greater parental pressure on boys to attend school (Das 1988, 33).

Another study of beedi workers in Andhra Pradesh reported that while it was customary even for the poorest to enrol their children in school (even if they were sent only because there was no work at home), yet not a single female child of the beedi workers attended school. Instead, they stayed at home to do the work their mothers could not do (Burra 1987, 8). According to another study, 'Five year old Mangala comes to school with her nine-month old brother in her arms. None of our male students ever brought their younger siblings to school with them while most of our female students do so' (Das 1988, 32). Domestic chores undertaken by young girls release their mothers for work. Therefore, they are making an economic contribution to the household. Thus, domestic work is a major barrier to girls' schooling, followed by economic costs at the household level and negative discrimination by the state.

At the micro level too, factors which create gender disparities in education have been identified by researchers. There are several, such as early marriage, household responsibilities, parental apathy, dissonance between social role and perceived function of education, social practices such as purdah; instruction in a language other than the mother tongue, the indifference of the teachers, and so on.

Even though Indian girls are denied access to education, yet once they enter school they do better than the boys. In fact, their performance is better at all levels of education and across different subjects, as becomes evident every year when the results of school board examinations are declared. Even then, gender stereotyping of roles is reinforced within the schools. For example, according to the content analysis of school textbooks, the projection of masculine and feminine images is along traditional lines. Secondly, it is achieved through the organization of subjects and extra-curricular activities. For example, science subjects are not taught at plus two stage in girls' schools. Again, informal counselling at school and at home discourage girls from taking up science subjects. Girls are not allowed to play football even in co-educational schools. Instead, they play on the swings. Again, boys are encouraged to take craftwork while girls have to take up home science. This division gets more subtle in music. Girls are encouraged to take up vocal music while boys are directed to play the drums and harmonium. The informal views and comments of the teachers are also very crucial in the gender division of school activities and in directing boys and girls towards gender-typed subject choices and extra-curricular activities.

Concluding observations

Even though there are striking inter-state and inter-group differences, poverty (over-lapping with caste, tribe and rural residence) and gender are the main parameters of denial of education. Again, sociocultural biases and the emphasis on domestic role are almost universal, yet their combination with poverty has an extremely detrimental effect on the participation of girls in education.

Therefore, a great deal has to be done before the human rights of women in education in India becomes a reality. Inasmuch as education is a crucial indicator of status, the provision of primary education and raising the status of women must be a priority.

References

Burra, Neera. 1987. Sight unseen: Reflections on the female working child. Mimeo.

Das, Mina. 1988. Nishtha: Our experience in organizing women. In the report on state level workshop on the girl child, UNICEF. Mimeo.

Ministry of Human Resource Development (MHRD). 1993 *Selected educational statistics.* New Delhi: Department of Education, Government of India.

Ministry of Human Resource Development (MHRD). 1995. *Towards meeting a commitment: Achievements under education for all.* New Delhi: Department of Education, Government of India.

National Council of Educational Research and Training (NCERT). 1995. *Sixth all India educational survey.* New Delhi.

National Commission for Women (NCW). 1994. *Report on development of female education among tribal communities.* New Delhi.

Tilak, J.B.G. 1996. How free is 'free' primary education in India? *Economic and Political Weekly* 31 (5), 275–282; 31 (6), 355–366.

~

CREATING AN ENABLING ENVIRONMENT
Zoya Hasan and Ritu Menon

The urge to educate girls

In the last two decades of the twentieth century, winds of change began to affect Muslims and became apparent in, for instance, a strong urge towards school education for girls and boys, an urge which members—especially female members—of the community are striving to meet. It was the consequence of two impulses: Muslim organizations campaigning for more education and Muslim women recognizing the importance of education for their daughters. One indication of this change is the increase in school enrolment. School enrolment figures indicate that, up to the primary level, although poor and illiterate, Muslim girls are enrolled in more or less the same proportions as Hindus. This is an indication, both, of a *desire* for change, especially among mothers, for their daughters; and the availability of some variety of schooling for most people, albeit often unsatisfactory in one respect or another.

Educationalists whom we interviewed put this attitudinal change down to the impact of television and other media, others to a strong desire for betterment. 'Even the *telis* and *kasais* (oil pressers and butchers) want their girls to be educated,' said Khubroo Khanum, a teacher at Bulbul-e-Khana in Old Delhi. In fact, the demand for schooling is outstripping supply as more and more Muslims perceive education to be their main chance for upward mobility. [. . .]

The story of education in the five cities studied, however, presents a regionally varied and differentiated picture of schooling and prospects for its improvement. Our case studies suggest a complex interplay of the social forces of gender, class and region across time and space. This broader consideration of the matrix of social processes is important because it frames the responses of women, men and communities to educational interventions and their relative success or failure; and it also cautions us against explaining away these differences by referring to the essential or doctrinal features of religion.

Historically, educational development is the product of social and economic ferment in different regions—education and literacy are the products of economic growth, rather than its precursors. Its rub-off effect and developmental changes in economy and society itself create the demand for literacy and education. This is reflected in the growth of education in states with higher school participation rates such as Tamil Nadu, Maharashtra and Karnataka with their high economic and commercial growth, or Kerala with higher levels of social development. All groups, including minorities, benefit from the overall development of the region. However, even in the absence of such favourable socioeconomic conditions, educational development can be boosted through state initiatives. Andhra Pradesh is an example of how they can help, especially in advancing girls' education, through innovations such as the mid-day meal and three-kilo rice schemes for low-income families, and 33 per cent reservations for girls in professional colleges. Furthermore, support has also come from the establishment of Urdu-medium schools, and of minority coaching for classes VIII, IX and X. Malika Qizilbash lamented that coaching for Muslim girls was necessary yet unavailable, because of the expense entailed. This is particularly marked when it comes to clearing mathematics and science at class X—many girls discontinue their school education because they fail these subjects and cannot progress to plus two.

The easy availability of public transport, including free travel for children up to age twelve has also made an enormous difference—indeed, the significant improvements in girls' schooling in the southern states is directly linked to the greater availability of government, government-aided schools and girls' schools in minority concentration areas, and transport to go to school. The considerably better educational performance of states like Kerala underscores the importance of state support but, though necessary and important, this support alone cannot guarantee high levels of attainment. One dramatic illustration of this is in the drop-out rates reported by the four southern states. Kerala records zero drop-outs for classes I–VIII, but a sharp gender difference in high school, with the rate for boys at 20.67 per cent, and for girls, 12.47 per cent. Overall, the figure is 16.6 per cent. Andhra Pradesh's figure is a high 70.12 per cent; Karnataka 61.65 per cent; and Tamil Nadu, 57.66. West Bengal is a surprisingly high at 78.52 per cent. The greatest gender disparity in all states (bar Kerala) occurs at middle school (Hasan 2004).

Overall, however, as far as Muslim girls are concerned, educational progress is reasonably good in regions where Muslims have enjoyed the benefits of state support in the form of accessible schools, which simply means schools in minority concentration areas and scholarship or mid-day meal schemes for underprivileged children. The scarcity of Urdu books, inadequate provision of Urdu-medium and single-sex schools are additional factors; not only are there too few Urdu-medium schools in places where they are most needed, they are also ineffective and starved of funds.

Besides state policy, community initiative, diverse community inputs and voluntary effort have played an important part in the growth of Muslim education in south India. Flourishing commerce and trade among Muslims in this region have resulted in the building of educational institutions and infrastructure. Thus the Muslim Educational Society in Kerala, Al-Ameen Educational Society in Bangalore and the Islamic Foundation in Chennai have been involved in launching major educational schemes for Muslim girls, and have taken the lead in setting up medical, technical, engineering and women's colleges. In the Malabar region, Farooq College is an excellent example of community initiative, which has enjoyed the backing of successive Congress and CPI (M) governments. Likewise, community initiative in Andhra Pradesh has resulted in the establishment of a number of private, aided and non-aided schools for Muslims with Urdu-medium instructions. The presence of a sizable middle class in these regions has meant that financial support for unaided schools is available, and this has contributed to the expansion of Muslim girls' education. [. . .]

Institutional and cost factors

An extremely important reason for low levels of enrolment among Muslims is financial constraints, when even government schools are beyond the financial capability of most low-income families. Several school teachers we spoke to pointed out that low school enrolment and gender disparity were manifestations of poverty and the inaccessibility of the school system. The high cost of education, especially that of tuition and coaching centres, is a major consideration in decisions made on schooling, especially for girls (Tilak 1995).

A second reason is that poorer households are more dependent upon the labour of their children to supplement household income. The work that children do can be waged in the marketplace, or in the family farm/household enterprise; or it could be indirect, by taking up household chores which liberates adult labour for other remunerative work. Shahnaz Begum of Anjuman Girls' School in Calcutta says girls can earn Rs 20–25 for washing clothes, and if they do this in four or five houses they can bring in Rs 100 per month. The probability that a girl will drop out of school is also determined by the social and economic characteristics of the household. Rural girls are less likely to attend school if the head of household is non-literate, or if the dominant activity of working people in the household is self-employment. Again, if lack of financial resources is the main constraint, then girls are more likely to be withdrawn than boys, sisters sooner than their brothers. School enrolment improves as household income increases, and this improvement is particularly marked among females.

However, it is not always low income levels that are responsible for discontinuation or non-enrolment among girls; rather, social norms that insist on early marriage, unwillingness to accept school discipline and general dissatisfaction with the educational infrastructure are also responsible. Children go to school wherever education is perceived to be a means of social mobility. Low educational attainment is also due to the low quality of educational institutions—unsuitable school timings, irregular attendance by teachers, lack of toilets for girls and poor teaching. A willingness to bear the cost of children's education, despite poverty, may be high if the quality of schooling is high. More generally, the inflexibility of the schooling system and textbook teaching which do not take into account the work patterns of households, particularly in rural areas, often result in absenteeism and dropping out.

School location is clearly another important issue that determines the decision about whether to send girls to school or not. Very few girls continue schooling beyond the fifth class if it involves travelling outside the village; it is then contingent upon relatives living in the town to provide social respectability, or on the ability to study privately. The location of the schools is such that they are often far from Muslim residential areas, making it even more difficult for Muslim girls to travel. Several studies of girls' schooling have underlined this aspect. In Maharashtra, 85 per cent students in the Greater Bombay area had no problem getting to school, but in rural Maharashtra, where accessibility is much lower, girls were not sent to school.

It is the same story in Uttar Pradesh: a state with low female and Muslim female literacy rates, accessibility to high schools is below the national average. Nearly half of all school-going girls went to school outside their village or locality.

One of the major grievances reported to the Group on Minorities in Uttar Pradesh, Bihar and Delhi (1994) was the status of Urdu: the non-availability of Urdu textbooks, vacant posts for Urdu teachers and an inadequate number of Urdu-medium schools. In this context, it is worth noting that states that have recognized Urdu as a second language have also been more successful in promoting Muslim education. Government support for Urdu in Andhra Pradesh, Maharashtra and Karnataka through special measures to promote the language has given Muslim education a fillip (Chanana 1993). Kerala is the exception in the south, where the community is well enough integrated socially for Malayalam to be completely accepted as the medium of instruction; but in West Bengal, Bengali has precedence despite a substantial Muslim population.

Our interviews, however, draw attention to the dilemma confronting Muslims in the north with regard to Urdu and Hindi. There is a strong desire for Urdu to be recognized and made available, but at the same time it is obvious that schooling in Urdu-medium schools limits opportunities for higher education and white-collar employment. Schools that allow instruction in Urdu therefore face problems of bilingual instruction (in Urdu and Hindi) at the higher secondary level. All science subjects are taught in Hindi, with only social sciences taught in Urdu. Bilingualism has suffered an overall decline because it is not a passport to well-paid employment, with the result that more and more Muslim families, both elite and non-elite, are abandoning Urdu in favour of Hindi and English for their children's education.

Gender biases in schooling

Low levels of educational attainment by Muslim girls are not, however, entirely due to institutional constraints. Controlling for institutional and economic factors, Muslim girls are still less educated than their counterparts in other religious communities. Indeed, interviews and secondary literature show that, even when educational opportunities are available, Muslim girls' participation in schooling is usually lower than that of girls from other communities. Although their enrolment in, and completion of, primary level schooling is equal to that of Hindu girls, drop out rates in middle school for Muslim girls are higher, and this is linked to community-specific factors, among them gender relations.

Rather than conservatism or obscurantism, economic and political interests of the Muslim community determine school participation rates. The occupational structure of the majority of Muslims does not require high levels of education because they are predominantly true of artisans, skilled workers, craftsmen and small business families make up the bulk of the community. Formal schooling is not likely to enhance either their skills or those of their children, nor does it improve their job prospects. Furthermore, most such families need extra hands for earning an income and some of them are too poor to be able to forego this resource (Ahmad 1981). Education is likely to be utilized by those social strata that are oriented to employment in the professions and government services; among Muslims this strata was greatly reduced following the Partition of India. In the immediate aftermath of Partition, Muslims suffered a general decline in their economic and political position because urban and rural elites migrated to Pakistan; those who remained in India were economically marginalized, engaged in occupations that are traditionally structured and require skilled manual labour. They also suffered from substantially greater deprivation than other religious minorities, and the disparity is greater in urban India where the majority of Muslims live. For the majority of self-employed Muslims, economic transactions take place within the community rather than with the state, and most trade and business are conducted on traditional family lines. For example, when they need loans they are more likely to rely on their families than on the government or banks. Over the past few decades, some sectors of this population have benefited from developments in agriculture and the growth of small-scale business and the handicrafts sector; through this process the Muslim middle class has grown, but slowly, as it is largely dependent on the lower middle class for recruitment.

The key question is the extent to which schooling leads to jobs. We were repeatedly told in interviews that most Muslims do not believe they will get jobs, no matter what their educational qualifications, whereas the chances for other communities are better. As the principal of a girls' school in Aligarh put it:

> Boys don't continue their education because there are no real employment prospects; therefore, there is little value for education. Muslims don't even get jobs as peons. If there were vocational training schools they could acquire useful skills. Failing this they fall into family trades and occupations. (Saxena 1983)

At the heart of this perception lies the inability of educated Muslim men and women to enter the paid workforce, in both the public and private sectors. There may not be any firm evidence on this but the fact that Muslims believe it to be the case is a significant element in their calculations and decision-making about the costs and opportunities of schooling. Some commentators have argued that Muslims overstate the problem of under-representation in government jobs to emphasize that they suffer from discrimination; they argue, moreover, that this is a problem concerning the Muslim middle class and therefore should not be taken as the only economic problem of the community. Nevertheless, the under-representation of Muslims in state services is undeniable; in 1996, the Planning Commission's sub-group on minorities found Muslims to be poorly represented in the police force, the railways and state and all-India services.

This presents a peculiar predicament for girls. As one educationalist put it,

> Even if girls don't work, education is perceived to be an advantage. The problem is that highly educated girls may find it difficult to get married. But they are economically independent and this is very healthy. Still, tensions persist especially if the husband is less educated or capable.

Ironically, every now and then girls are able to complete school because girls' education is not linked to employment the way that boys' is, but for the majority, there is little sense in letting the girl complete her school education and disqualify her for marriage by being more highly educated than her prospective husband. Muslim boys drop out because the opportunity costs of education in terms of monetary loss are greater than the gains from employment; Muslim girls drop out because the boys discontinue their education. Moreover, Muslim business families (like other business families, it should be noted) discourage higher education because of their business background which places a low value on education generally, and even less on girls' education.

A second major problem for girls' education is the social norm of early marriage. Most girls are engaged by the time they are in the eighth or ninth class, and there is no question of continuing their education after marriage. As one of our informants puts it: the main problem in a woman's career is marriage and a family. The ideology of hypergamous marriage, influential in many parts of India, under which it is desirable that a woman marries 'up' in the social scale, turns female education into a liability. If an educated girl can only marry a more educated boy then, other things being equal, she is likely to be more difficult to marry off. This ideology is widespread. Among Hindus, it means dowry payment increases with the education of the groom; among Muslims, several people we interviewed pointed out that Muslim girls downscale their education in order to upscale their 'eligibility' for marriage to comparably less educated boys. In other words, many of our informants were clearly apprehensive about the adverse impact of girl's marriage prospects if she were highly educated. [. . .]

Cultural factors

Purdah, or the seclusion of women, was a cultural norm for both Hindus and Muslims especially in north India. Purdah is of two kinds: one which confines women within the house and limits male–female interaction to the immediate family; and the second, which allows them to move out of the house and interact with men, but only if they adhere to a dress code and wear a burqa or hijab. The second is practised in parts of India, but observance differs from class to class, from urban to rural, and from region to region. It has also changed over time, and today it is the exception rather than the norm: even when it is observed it is far more relaxed than in the past. The migration of Muslims to the Gulf and Saudi Arabia since the early 1970s has seen its revival in regions which have seen the maximum migration; but a notable feature of contemporary purdah is that it does not entail seclusion, and thus it does not always curb mobility. Rather, the idea of the veil affording anonymity and protection seems to be at work here. However, we cannot discount the fact that sex segregation in educational establishments has ramifications that cannot ignore the long-term impact of veiling.

Most of our interviews suggest that purdah is not a major issue, at least as far as the retention and completion of girls' education is concerned. Very few of the women we spoke to even mentioned it as a problem, whereas they did mention other obstacles, such as the social norm of early marriage. [. . .]

Quite a few school teachers in Hyderabad and Aligarh, however, spoke about a growing feeling of insecurity in the community following the demolition of the Babri mosque in Ayodhya in December 1992, the growth of communal politics and the communal violence that broke out in several cities. This, they believe, has created anxiety and uncertainty in the community, making them feel vulnerable and anxious about women when they venture out. In Hyderabad, several activists found that families are more disposed towards female seclusion as a result. In addition, owing to the influence of Saudi Arabia, exposure to the Gulf countries, the rise of Hindutva and identity politics, *hijab* is on the rise in Hyderabad. Jameela Nishat, an activist in the old city of Hyderabad, notes that burqa has become a symbol of Muslim identity and some schools have even made *hijab* compulsory.

We found that the popular perception that Muslims opt for a religious rather than a secular education, and that this preference is responsible for their backwardness, is quite misplaced. Some Muslims may indeed prefer religious education, especially those families that have come under the influence of the Tablighi Jamaat, but for most of them religious education is no alternative to a secular one. (Our survey findings indicated that less than two per cent girls attended a madrasa: ninety-eight per cent went to government schools.) Nevertheless, those who want the latter face several constraints. One is the lack of Muslim institutions that impart secular education but function within a Muslim ethos, which is why those who can afford them prefer to send their daughters there. Even among upwardly mobile groups, girls are often withdrawn from higher education at the age of fifteen or sixteen, because exposure to the outside world may be prohibited once they reach a marriageable age.

In this context, one community-specific factor is the late entry of Muslim girls into school which impinges on the drop-out rate after middle school. Unlike girls of other communities, many Muslim girls undergo a course of religious education before entering school; this delay means that while other girls have finished matriculation before they get married, Muslim girls will barely have managed to complete middle school. This is a particularly serious problem for the poor who go in for religious education because they cannot afford formal schools, even when they are free. For the rest, however, religious and secular education is not mutually exclusive.

One of the standard assumptions about Muslims is that their religion prevents them from having equal access to education. It is certainly true that Muslim women are less likely to have a full school education; however, conversations with educationists and activists have indicated that material reality in many ways impinges much more directly on their educational status than birth-bound religious identity. Significant differences in educational attainment between communities are a consequence not so much of religious or community difference, as social and economic class, urban or rural residence and regional location. This means that Muslim women are educationally backward not because of religious conservatism but because they are poor, women and Muslim, which together aggravate the particular disadvantages of any one of these identities. Moreover, religious conservatism cannot account for the educational backwardness of the community as a whole, a point that is often glossed over in debates on Muslim women's education.

In sum, low income, widespread poverty, social norms that inhibit girls' education, a patriarchal ideology that prioritizes marriage and domesticity for women, and gender inequality on the one hand; and perceptions of discrimination, limited job opportunities and slow upward mobility are constraints that Muslims experience as a community. On the other hand, however, are objective factors such as the inaccessibility of schools, poor instruction, lack of teaching in the mother tongue, and so on. In the ultimate analysis the progress of Muslim female education—as indeed, female education generally—has been particularly slow in north India where the gender division of labour, hypergamous marriage and related patriarchal norms tend to be more prevalent. Additionally, for Muslim women, the failure to utilize educational opportunities is often due to the lack of provision for Islamiyat, fear of the imposition of a majoritarian culture through educational programmes, bias against Urdu and the high cost of schooling.

References

Hasan, Mushirul. 2004. Muslims in secular India: Problems and prospects in education. In *Will secular India survive?* ed. Mushirul Hasan. New Delhi: Imprint One, 291–305.

Tilak, Jandhyala B.G. 1995. How free is free primary education in India? NIEPA Occasional Paper no. 21. New Delhi.

Chanana, Karuna. 1993. Accessing higher education: The dilemma of schooling: Women, minorities, scheduled castes and scheduled tribes in contemporary India. In *Higher education reform in India: Experience and perspectives,* ed. Suma Chitnis and Philip G. Altbach. New Delhi: Sage Publications. 148.

Ahmed, Imtiaz, ed. 1981. *Family, kinship and marriage among the Muslims in India.* New Delhi: Manohar Publishers.

Saxena, N.C. April–September 1983. Public employment and educational backwardness among Muslims in India. *Political Science Review.*

∾

GENDER AND CURRICULUM
Dipta Bhog

The National Curriculum Framework (NCF) introduced by the government on 14 November 2000 has raised considerable debate and controversy regarding the content of social science textbooks. More specifically, the NCF has been accused of adopting a communal and brahmanical view of history and of seriously undermining the historical method of inquiry through bureaucratic and political interference. While the primary focus has been on the question of history and deletions that have been mandated by the National Council of Education, Research and Training (NCERT), what has not been put under scrutiny is how the NCF jeopardizes the government's own commitment to providing gender-just education. Despite its reiterations regarding equality, fundamental rights and quality education for all, a closer reading of the document points to a move towards ensuring that women learn to play out their 'traditional' social roles as good mothers, wives and daughters within the family and the nation.

This article is divided into two sections. The first one looks at how the core thrust of the NCF might impact on the likely content of future education. It argues that the emphasis on Indian tradition and the collapsing of value education with religious education puts on hold the possibility of education emerging as an enabling tool for women's empowerment. Comparing the NCF with nineteenth-century debates in colonial India about women's education reveals that the new discourse is, in a substantial measure, no more than a restatement of old anxieties and equally antiquated solutions. As a counter point of these debates, the second section revisits, albeit briefly, the vision and policy framework of the New Education Policy (NEP) of 1986 with regard to women's education. More concretely, it will analyze the 'trickle down' effect of progressive policy rhetoric on the actual writing of school textbooks, particularly those relating to language teaching. As the review points out, the decade following the 1986 policy refinements did not result in any significant positive yield in the manner in which gender was dealt with in the texts. The uptake of this analysis is clear: even as one must critique the NFC for its regressive views on women, there is no reason to believe that progressive rhetoric alone can change the entrenched gender stereotypes in school curricula. Unless the policy framework can deal with issues of actualization of alternative images and representation for women, no real progress can be made.

Burden of tradition

As is well known, the nineteenth century saw the emergence of women's education as a significant issue in colonial India. It witnessed the setting up of institutions of learning for women and girls by social reformers and the British government. Throughout the century, but particularly in the latter half, questions regarding the nature and content of women's education became a subject of heated debate—within the broad parameters of a nationalist consciousness—between the so-called liberal progressive elements, on the one hand, and conservative revivalists, on the other. Transcending the differences between the two camps were some common points of agreement. First, both sides concurred that the contemporary absence of education amongst women—regardless of what might have historically contributed to such a situation—was a sign of India's lack of civilization, an indicator of its low position in the evolutionary spiral that was history. The corollary was straightforward: If India had to catch up with the west in terms of its material achievements, then the nation's women had to be urgently educated. At the same time, this education could not be left to the alien colonial state or the missionaries. [. . .]

The anxiety about the content of education was not just in terms of threat to native identity. It was also powered by fears of a modernist onslaught, based on the rationalist-humanist message of enlightenment on the existing social order, overturning hierarchies of power—relating to caste, ethnicity or gender—and leading to a state of anomie. Not surprisingly, there was an increasing preoccupation with defining the kind of education that would be suitable for Indian women.

The most celebrated 'progressive' face of Indian nationalism in the late nineteenth century, Dadabhai Naoroji, voiced these anxieties in a more sophisticated garb: 'The time will come when natives generally will see the benefit of female education as a great social necessity to rise in civilization and to advance social happiness and progress; and will understand that women had as much right to exercise and enjoy all the rights, privileges and duties of this world as man, each working towards the common good in her or his respective sphere. *But that time has not come yet . . . Good and educated mothers only will raise good and educated sons.'* [. . .]

The intent is unambiguous: women's education was not so much an end as it was a mean to an end—the betterment of the family and the nation. While Naoroji does mention that women have the rights available to men, there is no mistaking the familiar note of women raising sons for the nation. Elsewhere he has expressed his fear about 'anglicized' Indian women discarding their own culture and tradition and moving towards acquiring 'tastes' that Indian men will be unable to fulfil.

Intrinsic to this creation of a new nationalist patriarchy was the intellectual labour which went into distinguishing oriental from western women. As Ram Mohan Roy had put it nearly half a century earlier: Hindu women were 'infinitely more self-sacrificing than men', and their 'exemplifying wifely devotion and spiritual strength' was their distinguishing feature as oriental women.

The NCF harks back to the nineteenth century. Its overarching concern, too, is to locate the curriculum within a self-evident and unproblematized Indian tradition. In an embarrassingly faithful echo of the earlier debate, the refrain of 'Indianizing' the curriculum, so as to maintain the best qualities of Indian womanhood and prevent Anglicization in the face of technological modernity—runs through the framework document.

Predictably, there is a deep anxiety about contemporary Indian society distancing itself from its 'religio-philosophical ethos':

> However a sizable segment of the contemporary Indian society, seem to have distanced itself from the religio-philosophical ethos, the awareness of the social design and the understanding of the heritage of the past. Influenced by the alien technological ethos, the parents and the educational institutions emphasize the acquisition of high grade techno-informative knowledge alone. However, the impact of westernization has been limited to only the elite members of the society, leaving the masses unaware of these developments. This has brought into sharp focus the rural–urban, the agrarian–industrial, the affluent–destitute, and the literate–illiterate divide. In this way the structure of the authority of the Indian agrarian society has been disturbed. An individual in the formal work system could exercise authority over those who where otherwise superior in age and societal structure. In the agrarian society, successive generations followed the occupation as well as the goals set by the family or the caste at large. (NCF, Context and Concerns, 3)

In other words, the trope of tradition is invoked to contain the potentially destabilizing influence of education. The NCF desires to relocate education where it traditionally belonged—in maintaining and reproducing power relations within traditional caste society. It views contact with western civilization as a source of undesirable social conflict and turmoil and singles out westernization, defined simply as a challenge to establish authority, whether at the level of the family or the community, as a grave danger. This forms the crux of the fear that pervades the NCF—how to embrace the fruits of 'an alien technological ethos' without abandoning the 'high principles of ancient Aryan religious morality' as desired by the Mahratta.

Needless to say, forgotten in this anxiety is the definition of education as a force for change or liberation. Nowhere in the document does the NCF envision education as a tool for empowerment or as a means to achieving social mobility or an egalitarian society.

Interestingly, the section on 'Education of Girls' comes under the broad heading of 'Education for Social Cohesion' (rather than, say, change or progress) in the framework document. The dilemma presented is remarkably similar to the one emphasized by Naoroji's statement on women's education. And so is the form; it begins with a large and abstract statement of gender equality and then quickly reduces itself to emphasizing gender specific roles.

Equality among sexes is a fundamental right under the Constitution of India. Besides making education accessible to more and more girls especially rural girls, removing all gender-discrimination and gender-bias in school curriculum is absolutely necessary. Moreover it will be most appropriate thing to recognize and nurture the best features of each gender in the best Indian tradition.

After all, India gave her women the right to vote without any prolonged battle for it, unlike in the west. There is a need to develop and implement gender inclusive and gender sensitive curricular strategies to nurture a generation of girls and boys who are equally competent and are sensitive to one another, and grow up in a caring and sharing mode as equals and not as adversaries. (NCF, Contexts and Concerns, 9)

Where it differs from Naoroji is in its acute awareness of the potential social conflict that education and notions of gender equality can engender. Hence, the conceptual positioning of education for girls under the rubric of social cohesion. And the idealized strategic roadmap which would ostensibly lead to women's equality begins with a massive negation of the relevance of agitational politics. Unlike the west where the demand for women's rights has resulted in the breakdown of the family, women in India need not protest for their rights because, as in the case of the right to vote, they would be granted their legitimate dues in the natural course by the ever-generous Indian patriarchs. The NCF resonates with facile dichotomies between western civilization and the Indian tradition, mistaking secular social trends as a marker of essential cultural difference. Witness, for instance, the following lament: 'In contrast to the joint family and the extended family, the society is now witnessing the phenomenon of nuclear families, single parents, unmarried relationships and so on . . .'

The irony is as pathetic as it is profound: Even as the Indian state proclaims its progressive credentials by legislating against domestic violence and sex-selection technologies, it shuts the door on any critique of the family as an institution— something that the women's movement in India has been fighting for long to legitimize.

Religious instruction as value education

In collapsing the distinction between value education and religious education, the document raises new questions regarding the objectives of educating women and girls in our society. Value education and education about religions would not form a separate subject of study or examination at any stage. These would be so judiciously integrated with all the subjects of study in the scholastic areas and all the activities and the programmes in the co-scholastic areas, that the objectives thereof would be directly and indirectly achieved in the classroom, at the school assembly places, play grounds and other such places (NCF, Chapter 2, 35).

In a society where women have carried the exclusive historical burden of upholding tradition and religious identity, the NCF aims at accentuating the bias. It ignores the subordinate position that women occupy in different religions. Contrast this with the National Education Policy of 1986: 'Education will neutralize the accumulated distortions of the past.' In actual fact, the NCF does worse than going back on the bland promise of its policy predecessor: it expands the agenda of reaffirming religious identities from the confines of the classroom to the very fabric of social interaction.

What's more, it introduces a vague and ill-defined concept, that of spiritual quotient or SQ, as an indicator of educational achievement. Not surprisingly, the document remains unconcerned about how this new-fangled intellectual sophistry might be given practical shape. It remains silent on how SQ, even assuming it has a determinate, objective content, will be evaluated and by whom. Could it be that women would have to prove their selfless, sacrificing and devotional qualities in order to score high marks? Alternatively, how will those who break with tradition be judged?

II

The NCF is without doubt a huge step backwards from the National Education Policy (1986). The latter saw education as, 'an agent of basic change in the status of women'. 'The National Education System,' it argued, 'will play a positive, interventionist role in the empowerment of women.' But we need to assess the impact of its progressive policy rhetoric on the actual making of the textbooks. Did it really 'neutralize the accumulated distortions of the past'? Did gender get portrayed in a manner that was significantly different from past representations of women and girls?

The following is a brief look at the NCERT's language textbooks for classes III, V and VIII, in the decade following the formulation of NEP. The rationale for focusing on language textbooks is that language is a key issue in feminist pedagogical practice. It is a powerful site for the construction and communication of gender identities and for reinforcing power relations.

In the preface to the language textbooks, it is claimed that the objective is to expand the horizons of the child, to increase her ability to think and to inculcate values within her. The values that are described in the preface are: discipline, timeliness, the importance of hard work, social service and love for the nation.

The preface suggests that the teacher tackle language teaching through methods that facilitate discussion and interaction in the class as a whole. By encouraging children to undertake role-plays, for instance, it is possible not just to elicit the active participation of the students but also to raise their confidence to communicate. However the content and the presentation of the lessons leaves one with serious doubt as to whether the teacher would be able to achieve these aims, particularly with regard to the girls in her class. Consider the following statistics based on a review of seventy-five lessons from the textbooks:

— In as many as thirty-four lessons, that is nearly fifty per cent of the aggregate, men and boys were the only actors in the texts. There were no female characters in the narratives.
— In ten lessons, the presence of women was either mentioned in passing or confined to traditional roles—i.e. as mothers, sisters and so on.
— No fewer than twenty-three lessons were in the category of information dissemination: didactic pieces on 'the exploding population', the virtues of healthy eating, and such like. In this category were also lessons comprising 'dohas' (couplets) and other poetic forms which might be, prima facie, seen as having no gender bias.
— About one in ten lessons—eight to be precise—sought to represent women and girls 'in a different light'. Among them there is one chapter on swimming, which includes references to women who have achieved excellence in that sport. In another such lesson, a girl writes to a friend about her visit to the zoo. A third describes a sports day celebration which has girls as active participations. In addition, there are three others which make a genuine attempt to represent women in a different light—but even these scanty offerings are not without their own problems. Of the three, two are biographic accounts of Rani Laxmibai and Madame Curie while the third is an account featuring the discrimination experienced by a girl in the village.

They were born great men!

For the purposes of critique, it is important to look at how men of honour and achievement are represented in these narratives. The texts in question comprise biographical profiles, childhood experiences, letters or anecdotes from the lives of great men. They cover, largely, 'the usual suspects'— Mahatma Gandhi, Lal Bahadur Shashtri, Rajendra Prasad, Ishwarchandra Vidyasagar, Edison, Chandrashekhar Azad, Vikram Sarabhai, Veer Abhimanyu, Jagdishchandra Basu, Baba Amte and Arjun.

The narratives of their lives and achievements are very much in the public realm. No details are given of their family life or their home. There is in Baba Amte's life history a mention of the impact that his mother had on him but this is an aspect of the customary supporting role that women have to play in the lives of great men.

Minor events in the lives of the men are imbued with great meaning— for example, in the case of Lal Bahadur Shashtri, his stealing a rose from a garden and the consequent words of admonition from the 'mali' are supposed to change his life, motivating him to become a great leader of the future. Apart from the careless mythmaking of it, there is something of interest in what the mali actually tells the little Lal Bahadur: 'You don't have a father! Your behaviour ought to be unimpeachable. You should try and please everyone—just like this rose.'

Not having the presence of a father in his life would no doubt have serious implications for the life of a boy. But does that mean that he has to please everyone? Only if the absence of a father is also understood as an absence of moral authority, not to mention the absence of a credible figure who might protect the boy against the temptations of the world. Equally, the boy is also expected, in time, to take over the role that his father has prematurely given up. In other words, to assume the mantle of responsible male leadership in the family.

In the minutiae of men's everyday lives—preferably the early years, since the presumption seems to be that you are either born great or achieve greatness first thing in the childhood—lie grand moments of revelation, of courage, strength, determination and struggle.

That's what girls are for!

Contrast this seamless valorization with the somewhat muted accounts of the two valiant women who are mentioned in the texts.

Rani of Jhansi is no doubt a great rider and fighter but she is vulnerable too—prone to depression (at the death of her son and husband) and doubt, the Rani often finds refuge in prayer and withdrawal from the world. Even when she comes back to fight the British, she has to take recourse to spiritual fortifications—she is said to pray every morning—before commencing on worldly matters. No such doubts plague great men in their lives; they face all challenges with calm assurance and self-certainty.

If it is not doubts that assail women, then there are other equally important 'distractions'. In the case of Madame Curie, for instance—even as she busies herself in the laboratory, surrounded by chemical fluids, test tubes and complicated experimental equipment, not to mention her scientist husband—we are informed, 'Maria used to do all the housework herself. She would clean the house, wash clothes, cook food and wash dishes. After two years of marriage Maria gave birth to a girl child. This increased the work load on her but did not affect the quality of her work.' Fine words to describe the double burden of women! Apart from making a not-so-subtle case for how it is eminently possible for women, if they so choose, to both work at home and make a 'contribution' to the larger cause of humanity. Ultimately, however, these digressions into the domestic duties of eminent women have a different meaning and purpose. They are meant to be narrative devices which render these women 'normal' for the average reader. In other words, the idea is to 'tame' them, to contain the 'dangers' they pose to the existing order as different women. This provides a stark counterpoint to the lives of great men, where the emphasis is on larger-than-life mythmaking and deification, to render the subjects as distant and towering as possible. The concluding line from the Rani Jhansi story is instructive: 'By her *sacrifice* the Rani proved that *if called upon* [in the rather extraordinary circumstances no doubt], the Indian woman too could give the enemy a tough time.'

Of boys and men

This raises questions about the role models that these texts place before the girl child. Her exclusion becomes all the more evident from the way young boys dominate other narratives. Boys are invariably shown as striving for the higher virtues of morality and character—of courage, hard work, grit and determination in the face of all odds (like being blind, parentless) and limitless intellectual inquiry. (But what is the meaning of learning for girls?)

Equally, boys in all three textbooks exhibit greater mobility, travel to various places on their own, and, crucially, possess the ability to comment on and describe new experiences. Where women feature in these travels, they are shown to lack in understanding or knowledge. For example in the lesson 'Tamil Nadu ki Yatra', Dinesh is visiting Chennai for the first time. His friend goes to pick him up from the station. Even before they leave the station Dinesh begins to tell his friend about the geographical details of the state. His friend's wife, Maya, who has lived in Chennai all her life comments: 'Bhai Sahab, I am hearing these special facts about my state for the first time. How do you know so much?'

We move on further in the travel and Dinesh's wife is shocked at the amount of fish the fishermen have caught in their nets. She exclaims: 'Chi! Chi! O god, how heartless! These fishermen are killing all these fish. What wrong have these fish done to these fishermen! . . . These mean fishermen catch the fish (at night) while they are asleep.' On hearing her comment, says the narrator, 'We all collapsed with laughter, holding our stomachs.'

The question is: Who gets to tell the narrative and to whom? How are women positioned within these narratives in relation to others?

Despite being a grown woman, Maya is lacking in information about a place where she has lived all her life, and her responses are typically naïve and innocent—not to be taken seriously. Throughout the lesson the voice of the male narrator dominates to give us all the description about what is worth knowing about Tamil Nadu.

Women as they are?

Women come in predominantly in their role as mothers—maternal love flows unquestioningly in her in the poem 'Kadamb ka Pedh'. At other places, they inspire their sons to grow up in the service of the nation, much like the idealized women of the freedom struggle, the mothers of the nation's current and future generations.

But what constitutes the feminine and masculine emerges most significantly through stories and poems. The feminine is what is close to nature, a matter of habit, while the masculine is cultural, a matter of struggle and accomplishment. For instance, birds are the embodiment of the feminine, when they sing their sweet song and dance with the fairies and buzz around flowers that dance in the garden: soft, tender and vulnerable. [. . .]

Conclusion

It is quite clear from the analysis of language texts that despite an explicit policy commitment from earlier governments to provide an empowering education for women and girls, the situation on the ground did not improve a great deal. Traditional meanings of the masculine and the feminine continued to persist along with the oppositional, dichotomous categories of active–passive, emotional–rational, nature–culture and dependent–autonomous.

Clearly, gender-sensitive material at the primary and secondary levels require inputs from those who have struggled to bring women's voices, narratives, experiences and worldviews into the academic mainstream. Without this knowledge base, those charged with rewriting texts will restrict themselves to superficial tinkering: either by increasing the number of times girls are visually or verbally represented in the books or by facile role reversals.

The fact that those who have contributed to the creation of knowledge regarding women have had little to do with the writing of text books might be, in the end, an extremely important reason why we have not, despite a decade-and-a-half of rhetoric, moved beyond the stage of pious policy pronouncements.

Indeed, why instead of moving ahead, we might be in the midst of a severe regression.

8

≈

HEALTH

Often operating in tandem with debates on development, the field of health has witnessed a growing involvement by Indian feminists and women's studies scholars. The earliest interventions in this domain can be traced to the debates of the 1970s and 80s, when the limits of the medico-scientific worldview—especially in relation to women's health problems—were first recognized. Women's complaints of tiredness, giddiness, feverishness or backpain were usually dismissed by doctors and labelled either as psychological or as 'non-specific'. Even complaints of menstrual pain, cramps, vaginal discharge or painful intercourse were often described as purely 'subjective' symptoms by health personnel. Some medical textbooks went so far as to suggest that such symptoms could be traced to women's excessive preoccupation with their bodies in the absence of any gainful employment.

It is, therefore, fitting that we begin this cluster on health with a study undertaken during the 1980s that was part of a national effort by feminists to look into the health hazards of working women, which was incorporated in the report *Shramshakti*, (under the leadership of Ela Bhatt, SEWA). Veena Shatrugna and her colleagues at the National Institute of Nutrition pioneered an investigation into backpain, that most common—and most disregarded—of 'feminine afflictions'. Tracing the problem of chronic backpain to the weakening—and ultimately the snapping—of bones, they investigated medical records and interviewed patients of Osmania General Hospital in Hyderabad, to unearth the extent of women's proneness to specific fractures. In the course of their study, they discovered that a large number of women were recorded as 'absconders' and 'late reporters', unable to complete the specified treatment. On the one hand, it became clear how little the existing medical system was able to respond to women's problems; but equally fundamental was the crisis that hits families when it is women that require hospitalization.

The health profession's overwhelming concern with the population 'problem' has also been a shock to many. The 1970s and especially the Emergency years are still remembered for their criminal excesses in the field of 'family planning'—during 1975–77 in the city of Delhi alone, forced sterilization camps resulted in the deaths of at least 2000 men, and these are official estimates. It should come as no surprise, then, that the post-Emergency decades have witnessed two developments—the growing concentration on women as targets of contraception and the dwarfing of the overall health care system by family planning. The intrauterine device, the pill and tubectomy are the typical services offered to a woman visiting a government hospital. Other problems tend to get ignored or marginalized. Contraceptive side-effects, however serious, have been largely disregarded as family planning targets for contraceptive services replace the rest of the government health programme. The next two essays address themselves to these concerns. Vineeta Bal and her colleagues in the women's organization Saheli have undertaken a special study looking at worldwide research in the fields of reproduction and contraception. Their findings show a definite quantitative bias in scientific and technological research in favour of the female and against the male reproductive system, which increases substantially when the focus shifts from fundamental research to technological research on contraception, and more specifically to studies of clinical trials. Their basic argument is that—contrary to general perception—this bias has no biological basis whatsoever. In her contribution to these issues, Imrana Qadeer questions the recent agenda of 'reproductive health' being pushed by the state and international agencies, with its narrowly technical and biological focus on fertility control, at the cost of women's general health problems. In a detailed analysis of national mortality data, she emphasizes the extent to which communicable diseases, anaemias and malnutrition are the biggest killers in all age groups of women, with maternal mortality constituting just 2–3% of all deaths. This is not to belittle the significance of maternal deaths, which, however, fail to gain the requisite attention in the reproductive health regime.

So far, the medical system under scrutiny has been the dominant model of western allopathic medicine, and the demands have been to reconceptualize and restructure public health care for women and men. But this has not been the only approach or mode of critique. The next essay is taken from a book-length monograph by the group Shodhini, whose members have been devoting their attention to the potential of alternative, local knowledges in curing women's diseases. The remarkable effort of this group lies in going beyond romantic searches of vanishing practices; instead, their investigations were effectively located at the intersections of three broad systems of medicine—local or 'folk' knowledges of specific plants in different regions, classical Indian systems, and, finally, western medical conceptions of 'validity' involving field testing and cross-checking their findings. Though undeniably modest in scope, this project involved a complex mix of individuals, organizations and village women in different locations over a number of phases.

The next article in this section by Bhargavi Davar offers a glimpse into the massively neglected domain of mental health. It might go without saying that physical conceptions of ill health have been hegemonic even among feminists, and that the world of mental distress, though so familiar to women, has not figured on movement or women's studies' agendas, compounding the lack of a gendered understanding among mental health professionals. If, indeed, mental illness were 'gender neutral', this glaring omission might be less significant, but as Bhargavi Davar's overview demonstrates, this is not the case. By exploring the available secondary literature she discovered not only that women appear to be more prone to mental disorders than men, but that the distinctions drawn between 'severe' and 'common' illnesses are gendered as well. In contrast to those explanations that look for biological causes in women's reproductive and hormonal cycles, Davar suggests that it is precisely in those forms of mental illness where social and psychological dimensions are recognizably involved that women are the most affected. Such preliminary findings constitute a powerful appeal to the fields of medicine, psychiatry, psychology and women's studies, surely amongst the most poorly connected within the broad field of health.

The final essay in this cluster comes from a movement that is just emerging in our context—that of disability. To what extent have both feminists and health activists depended on normative ideals of able-bodiedness? The arrival of the disability movement is challenging the very idea that a minority of people suffer from personal physical impairment. As Anita Ghai argues, it is only when disability is recognized as a form of social oppression which society must change that feminism will become truly more inclusive. This demands going beyond 'additive' approaches to women's oppression, reconceptualizing the feminist politics of care, and, indeed, recognizing that even the healthy individual herself is only temporarily able-bodied (what Ghai calls TAB). Undergirding this essay is therefore the promise of the transformative potential—both politically and theoretically—that perspectives of disability can have on the agendas of women's studies and the women's movement.

Among the sciences as a whole, health stands alone in having responded to feminist concerns, however inadequately. While the agendas of the state and funding agencies in controlling women's fertility have been amply exposed, positive redefinitions of the parameters of health and well-being, from the psycho-social contexts of women's embodied lives to the forms of health care and social support available, are constantly being expanded and rethought. No other field is more volatile, as structural changes visibly alter the landscape of public and private health systems, and as new stresses and destructive experiences make it harder to stay physically and mentally healthy. Norms of the healthy body as well as of the able body are marginalizing the vast majority of our women and men. More than ever, interventions at the interface of women's studies, health and disability will be needed to build on the kinds of efforts that have gone before.

∼

BACKPAIN, THE FEMININE AFFLICTION

Veena Shatrugna, Nirmala Soundarajan,
P. Sundaraiah and Leela Raman

A complaint like backpain may accompany almost every illness in women. It is especially common around the age of thirty in those who work long hours as beedi makers, maid servants, stone breakers, vegetable vendors, agricultural labourers, cobblers, construction workers etc. Even typists, clerks, teachers, nurses and 'housewives' do not escape this affliction. Most women's experiences with health specialists have been frustrating—though women constantly complain of backpain, doctors prefer to administer drugs for 'clinically well diagnosed diseases' and place backpain in the 'nonspecific' category. After a few years of practice this complaint ceases to register in the minds of the doctors. But when women persist in their demand for treatment, they are usually dismissed with pain killers that usually work for four to six hours. Other sympathetic professionals might want to rule out a gynecological problem or even an orthopedic one. But most doctors scold the women, blaming them for their bad posture (without suggesting alternative postures for work such as beedi making, housework) and for neglecting the problem. This is so because most doctors find backpain an embarrassing reminder of their inadequacy. Medicine/medical practice does not find women's diseases exciting—but if in addition women's illnesses do not fall into given categories and expectations of the modern health care system then the illness must be delegitimized, not the science.

What is backpain? The back bone is made up of small pieces of bones (vertebrae) balanced vertically one over the other by the attachments of numerous muscles and other fibrous ligaments. The bones are kept in position by the tone and coordination of these opposing muscles. Another factor that helps to keep the bone in position is the integrity of the bone itself. A very thin fragile bone cannot be held in place even if the muscles were theoretically strong and well-toned; the bone would in fact crack with muscle pulls. Whenever the critical balance between the small bones and the balancing muscle is upset, it alters the architecture of the back resulting in pain. The nerves coming out of the spinal cord are caught between the badly balanced vertebrae resulting in excruciating pain. As these nerves originate in the spine and go a long way to the distant muscles of the arms, legs and other regions, the pressure on the nerves near the spine causes radiation of pain from the back to the groups of muscles supplied by the nerves. These muscles then tend to become stiff due to pain, further upsetting the architecture of the back.

The factors that affect the proper alignment of the vertebrae are: (1) Tautness of muscles holding up the bones of the back; (2) Integrity of the bony vertebrae; (3) Diseases of the vertebrae (like prolapsed disc cancers or any other infection, these do not come within the purview of this study).

Tautness of muscles may be achieved by proper exercising of all the groups of muscles responsible for the architecture of the back bone. [. . .] Apart from muscles action (exercise), there are other factors that determine the integrity of the bone. These are:

(i) Calcium is an important mineral contributing to the integrity of any bone. Any deficient intake results in the depletion of bone for supplying calcium to the rest of the body since bone acts as an important reserve of calcium. Calcium is also needed in small quantities by all the other organs, for the numerous functions, and all these needs are met by bone calcium. Once the bone reserves of calcium are depleted, the bone becomes thin and porous. This is the beginning of osteoporosis. Prolonged deficiency of food calcium results in severe bone thinning and such a bone can snap or fracture without any injury. [. . .]

(ii) Anaemia and protein/energy deficiency can complicate calcium deficiency and affect bone integrity.

(iii) It has been observed that thin-structured, lean, emaciated women are more prone to thinning of bones because of the absence of fat in the body. Fat is needed for storing the small amount of estrogens in the menopausal period.

The story of calcium depletion and pain is not dramatic but goes on throughout life unrecognized, till the bones snap after the age of forty. Most fractures at this age represent the culmination of events leading to osteoporosis, leaving women crippled for the rest of their lives, dependent on the family and the expensive health care system.

Diagnosis of calcium deficiency

An 'objective' study of calcium deficiency and back pain is difficult to conduct in a population of women traditionally labelled 'unreliable', 'hysterical' and 'malingering'. In addition, the laboratory tests to identify calcium deficiency are very difficult. [. . .]

It was, therefore, decided that a study of the incidence of various kinds of osteoporotic fractures in women would be taken up and this could be easily identified for the purposes of the study. Osteoporotic fractures occur in the older age groups without any external injury or with very minimal trauma. In fact, women usually recall that the fall while walking occurs without any provocation. It is felt that the snapping of the thin bone causes the fractures and the fall, and not vice versa. The fractures listed below are typically osteoporotic, unless there is a history of accidents and external violence (a) thigh (fracture at neck of femur); (b) pelvis (hip); (c) vertebrae (back); (d) humerus (upper arm); (e) arm (end of radius called colles fracture).

This study was carried out in two parts: (i) retrospective and (ii) study of currently admitted women in the orthopaedic ward of the Osmania General Hospital, Hyderabad.

The retrospective study was designed to look into the incidence of various fractures in women who were admitted in the hospital during ten months between January and October 1987. Out of the 297 women admitted between January and October 1987, 289 case-sheets were retrieved, eight records could not be traced. For the sake of comparison, a 10 per cent systematic sample of all the men admitted during the same period was used to study the incidence of these fractures in the men's wards. The total admissions in the men's wards were 1112 for the ten months but only 107 records could be traced for comparison.

For the qualitative study of women currently admitted in the ward, thirty-seven adult women admitted in the orthopaedic ward during the period of study (September–October 1987) were interviewed. The interviews were conducted in two or more sittings. Very often women themselves refused to participate in the discussion. Since we wanted to record their experiences, attempts were made to get as much information as possible from the women attending on the patient. The hospital conditions were such that the attendant (invariably a close relative of the sick person) suffered all the travails that the ill person did. Sometimes, the attendant faced many more problems as she had to take care of all the needs of the sick person, and also fend for herself, for food, baths, etc. During the course of the study we realized that the problems of the attendant are not even recognized by the health care system where nursing care is minimal or absent.

Apart from the usual demographic details the patients were involved in discussion to elicit the following: (i) the person supporting her at the time of fracture, (ii) work during pregnancies, place of deliveries, breast feeding pattern, (iii) food intake (a qualitative diet survey to indicate calcium intake), (iv) problems of food in the hospital, and (v) other problems in the hospital.

Of the 289 case records scrutinized, 209 belonged to women who were 40 years or older while eighty women were between 18–39 years. In the older age groups most of the fractures resulted from either minimal trauma or while walking. Of these women 145 above the age of forty had been admitted for fracture of the neck or the femur, which is typical of osteoporosis. They formed around 70 per cent of all women above the age of forty. Another fourteen per cent of women in the over-40 age group had other fractures also suggestive of osteoporosis, while the rest (15.9 per cent) of them had fractures due to external injury (due to accidents at worksite or violence). The younger women (below forty years) comprised 27.7 per cent of the total admitted. They had been admitted with fractures related to work in agriculture, construction etc. A large number of accidents at the worksite were labelled medico-legal and it would be interesting to see if these women ever received any compensation from their employers. Medico-legal cases are rarely pursued by the women because they are understandably dubious about the results. What was important was their desire to get well and get back home.

Though osteoporotic fractures were the most common types in all ages after forty years, what was surprising and definitely alarming was that after sixty years of age, only these types of fractures were seen in women to the exclusion of all the others. It has been recognized that once an osteoporotic fracture occurs, then these women become prone to repeat fractures. In the case of men, it was obvious that trauma due to vehicle accidents and occupational injuries were largely responsible for the fracture incidence. They were, therefore, much younger on admission (57 per cent were less than forty years).

Though 31 out of 107 men had fractures at the sites that are typically seen in osteoporotic bones—a look at the ages and history of accidents showed that most of the men (18 out of 31) had sustained fractures at these sites due to an impact received during the accident and only thirteen men could be classified under the osteoporotic category. None of these men had left the hospital before the completion of the course of treatment.

Of the 176 women with osteoporotic fractures who were required to stay between 15 and 45 days in the hospital (depending on a host of factors such as type of fracture, need for operation, associated complications and progress of the patient) what was surprising was that fifty-five (31 per cent) women left the hospital without undergoing the full course of treatment such as traction and operation, and were labelled 'absconders', while about forty-nine (28 per cent) women had arrived at the hospital many days or weeks after the fracture had occurred. It is possible that this group of women—both 'absconders' and 'late reporters' (59 per cent)—visited traditional bone setters or doctors who did not insist on hospitalization. There is an urgent need to acknowledge and understand the services offered by these practitioners. They could be supported by the modern health care system, so that treatment offered by them becomes more significant for the speedy recovery of fractures in women.

The case-sheets did not have comprehensive details of the general health of the patient. Only 30–50 per cent of the patients were investigated for hypertension, heart diseases, diabetes or anaemia. In fact such associated diseases result in the postponement of operations for the patients and delay recovery due to complications.

It was not surprising that certain kinds of information did not find any place in medical records. A system that concentrates its energies on treatment and operative intervention buffers itself from the sociocultural background of the patient. This has been the only way that men and women, working round the clock in the orthopaedic ward, ensure 'efficiency'. Any involvement with the patients' problems, such as the understanding of the socioeconomic determinants of women's illness, and the long years of neglect, would need a different kind of a hospital, an altogether new set-up. The understaffed and overworked medical department has been required to deal with only 'diseases' or 'problems'. Therefore, it was not surprising that the following information was not found in the case-sheets: (1) occupations and incomes; (2) number of pregnancies, abortions, still births and live children; (3) periods of breast feeding; (4) age of menopause; (5) previous drug use, if any; (6) dietary history, to reflect calcium intake, etc.

Thirty-seven women aged eighteen and above admitted to the wards in September and part of October were interviewed. The stress was on obtaining information about their lives, occupations, families, children and associated problems in the hospital. This task was not easy. Women could not recall a number of details while some information was very difficult to discuss, such as history and duration of breast feeding, number of abortions and age of menopause. The women were not willing to recall some of these details as it was obviously irrelevant to their present conditions. The attempts at eliciting dietary intakes were also frustrating (to them) because it made the monotony of their diets more obvious, resulting in a lot of bitterness and even anger with the family which did not seem to care for them while the women had laboured hard all their life.

Out of thirty-seven women interviewed in the ward, twenty-four had osteoporotic fractures and their ages ranged from 40–80 years. Their age at menopause was between 35–45 years. There was no event in their life that made menopause significant and therefore ages had to be rounded off in multiples of five years. Most of them were married when young and had given birth to a large number of children. What was significant was that they had all lost at least half the number of children at different age groups.

Thirty-three of the women were in some occupation or the other, while four were 'housewives', but even they had worked long hours in large families all their years with very little money reserves. The working women had worked mostly as agricultural labourers, weavers, cobblers, construction workers and domestic workers. They had worked throughout pregnancy, and had breast-fed each child for two or three years. None of them had any antenatal care during pregnancy and had delivered at home. They had worked till the day of the fracture—cooking, sweeping, minding grandchildren and even filling water. It was really difficult to get them to remember a time in their lives when they had not worked. Except one, all of them had borne children (two to twelve). There was nothing that marked them from the other women of their age and class (in terms of pregnancies and lactation) or any other event that made them more prone to fractures.

Except for two of them, who lived alone, all the others lived in a 'family' with sons, daughters-in-law and grandchildren. A few lived with brothers, daughters or sisters, and the number of members living under the same roof varied from three to ten. In spite of the family, they faced many problems in the hospital, which can only be solved with increased and sympathetic human power. Only daughters and sisters were willing to take care of them in the hospital and this had resulted in the need to appease the sons-in-law or brothers-in-law who seemed to have exclusive right over the services of these women. Some of the sick women had no fixed person taking care of them in hospital, they were strapped to the bed in plaster, immobile, lying there, waiting the whole day for someone to arrive. They were entirely at the mercy of the hospital staff, the attendants of neighbours and the overworked, harassed nurses. They could not get up to answer the calls of nature because of the plaster and were even seen pleading with passers-by for bed pans.

Women have always cared and nursed the sick at home, borrowing money, working hard and staying up nights. But when women themselves are sick, the family comes to a standstill and only a female substitute is expected to step in, depriving her own family of her 'services'. The men are not expected to take on nursing care and they watch on helplessly. [. . .]

Diet histories of the patients were taken with the intention of getting details of frequency of intake of certain foods rich in calcium. It revealed that the daily foods were monotonous and cereal based (such as rice, jowar or wheat) and it was eaten twice or thrice a day with a chilli hot dal. One of the cheap vegetables was made on the day when dal was not cooked. Green leafy vegetables were consumed seasonally, with absolutely no intake of milk or curds. Some patients consumed weak tea once or twice a day and rarely buttermilk. Seven out of the thirty-seven women were paan chewers. Eggs and meats were virtually unknown in their diets because ¼ or ½ kg of meat was bought once or twice a month for a family of six to ten members and stretched the whole day. The hospital environment does not allow a detailed study of other socioeconomic determinants of food intakes. The presence of attendants also precluded any kind of probing discussions.

Conclusion

This study does not lend itself to producing simple solutions or recommendations and therefore no such attempt will be made.

So far, osteoporosis has been understood to be linked to menopause and as such is labelled physiological (even though its incidence is much higher than cardiovascular problems and diabetes). Such a description has helped blame the victim by invoking pet assumptions about women's ageing bodies and (?) minds. These 'findings' have also helped absolve everyone of responsibility and have placed the problem of osteoporosis outside the purview of medical research. At best, the medical establishment has offered hormones to reverse the 'degenerating' process, and perhaps psychiatric help for coping with 'menopause'.

More recently, other solutions have been offered by medical scientists (since the discipline is structured to offer solutions to a deranged human body). Towards this the problem had to be so defined that the cause of osteoporosis could be located precisely in 'chronic calcium deficiency' and could at best be partially true. But it opens up new horizons and problems for research, these being the various interactions between calcium supplementation and other nutrients, such as (a) vitamin D, (b) proteins, (c) iron, (d) fats, (e) phosphorus, etc. and each of the above in combination or alone in relation to hormone replacement therapy. In addition, side effects of toxicity (such as renal stone formation etc.) and carcinogenicity with the various regimens would need to be researched in detail.

Such a scientific mode of enquiry definitely serves to deflect the whole question of osteoporosis into areas that have no relationship to women's day-to-day lives. It becomes important that the complexity of the problem is recognized, and what follows is not necessarily exhaustive.

(i) The impact on the bodies and bones of women brought about by the rigid practices of upbringing of young girls to perform the primary function of wives and mothers—highlighting 'femininity'—requires the forceful adoption of postures detrimental to bone integrity. What occurred due to foot-binding in China is an obvious example, but the unresearched consequences of the veil in parts of India, involving bowing and covering the head for most of the day, the use of tight corsets in Europe, the current popularity of shoes on stilts all over the world; the strain induced by bust/hip emphases encouraged by a culture, the hunched backs adolescents develop, are part of the same problem. In the name of femininity, a whole array of disciplining methods is used for girls when sitting, standing, walking or working, resulting in the moulding of both bodies and brains. Consider the impact of the long hours of monotonous work in fixed postures, that women are said to do better than men and at much lower wages (electronics, transplanting, homebased industry)!

(ii) The impact of being a school dropout or non-literate, and coercion into early marriage, pregnancy and nursing ensures the making of a wife and mother. It is, therefore, not surprising that women who have been disciplined into living for 'others' start denying themselves whatever little protective foods are available for the family.

(iii) The macro policies of a system, be it the green revolution or the white one, and its impact on village economics—the food and milk surpluses in the urban areas created by the market mechanism, resulting in the marginalization of the poor and especially women.

(iv) The feeble attempts made by women to compensate for the deficiency of nutrients like calcium and iron by resorting to paan chewing or 'pica' (a practice involving the consumption of non-food items such as sand and clay, very common during pregnancy).

(v) The inadequate role of the health set-up, equipped as it is to treat fractures with tractions, pins and other operative procedures. It can at best put on a brave front and systematically evolve more 'effective' and 'sophisticated' procedures to put women back on their feet, but in the case of recurring, even chronic fractures that result from osteoporosis, it is hardly an adequate response.

(vi) The urgent need to understand why women find it so difficult and sometimes impossible to get access to and effectively use hospital facilities—what in fact lurks hidden behind the convenient term 'absconders'.

It would appear that it takes around forty years or more before women break down, for either their bones or their minds to give way in more ways than we know, and there obviously are no simple technical solutions.

∼

CONTRACEPTIVE RESEARCH: IS THERE A GENDER-NEUTRAL APPROACH?

Vineeta Bal, Vani Subramanian and
Laxmi Murthy, Saheli

Background

The year 2000 has come and gone and the status of primary healthcare facilities has only deteriorated over the years in India. The universal goal of 'Health for All by 2000', declared at the international conference held in 1978 at Alma-Ata, is far from being realized. Access to healthcare for people below the poverty line (BPL) is minimal, and for women in the BPL group it is even worse than that. In post-independence India, many health programmes concerning women have been initiated, renamed and their aims modified over the years. Soon after independence, a Maternal and Child Health (MCH) Programme was initiated in association with the Family Planning Programme (FPP); the Integrated Child Development Scheme (ICDS) of 1975 was proposed to integrate FPP, MCH and Nutrition Services.

Following the International Conference on Population and Development (ICPD) in Cairo in 1994, national governments were forced to acknowledge that population growth is related to many complex factors, and cannot be focused on one variable alone, i.e. contraception. The subsequent paradigm shift resulted in the focus on a Reproductive and Child Health (RCH) strategy and a target free approach in order to do away with incentives and disincentives for contraceptive use. Yet, despite this stated shift, over the years women's health is being more rigidly equated with reproductive health.

While the effective implementation of developmental programmes would reduce overall poverty, and targeted schemes to address malnutrition would reduce morbidity and mortality, the lopsided emphasis on maternal mortality alone results in an undue emphasis on contraceptive methods as the 'cure'. The state thus pursues a population policy which talks of meeting the unmet needs for contraception as its first priority over and above healthcare infrastructure. Such a policy has come back full circle, despite public avowals to the contrary, to the population policy of old, with incentives and disincentives and target orientation at all levels.

Against this background, it is instructive to look at the social context involved in deciding priorities in contraceptive research, both at the level of biological research underlying the development of contraceptives, and in the actual development and marketing of successful contraceptive methods.

Research in reproduction and contraception

Research in any field of the biological sciences can fall into one of two categories: research undertaken to improve understanding of the biological mechanisms involved; and, secondly, research undertaken with the express intention of developing products. The first category can broadly be called scientific research and the latter technological research. Priorities for technological research are more obviously decided by social forces such as 'national priorities', the aims of funding agencies and so on. For scientific research, there may not be such clear prioritization, although the social context of individual researchers undoubtedly plays a part.

The primary attempt in scientific research is to make a model of the mechanisms involved, based on the current state of understanding, and to continue refining it to increase the predictive value and hence 'reliability' of the model. With every new result obtained, there may or may not be forward movement in terms of improvement of this model. Frequently, lateral connections may be discovered, and a pathway and model quite unrelated to the earlier one are pursued. Individual scientific researchers working in the same broad field thus work as if they are separately trying to solve the same jigsaw puzzle. However, there is no clear idea what the ultimate puzzle picture looks like, and by the time a fit is achieved between two adjoining pieces, the size of the puzzle might have increased several fold, thus increasing complexity almost endlessly. In contrast, the development of products, or technological research, is undertaken on a relatively less complex, better defined path with a clearer understanding of tangible 'success' and 'progress'.

Research in the field of reproduction and contraception can be separated to some degree into 'science' and 'technology' as well. Scientific research in the broad field of reproduction would include many areas of pursuit which are likely to add to the understanding of the development, structure and functioning of the processes of reproduction. The information gathered during these efforts may or may not be useful for developing products. Most contraceptive research is technological, focusing on a specific aspect of reproduction with the explicit aim of producing contraceptives for the market. The impact of the social context is likely to be much greater in the sphere of product development than that of mechanistic model-building.

Rationale and methodology: Survey of published literature

In order to examine any gender-linked bias in terms of scientific and technological developments in the field of reproduction and contraception, a MEDLINE search for papers published from the initiation of the database in the mid 1960s until May 2002 was undertaken. The keywords used primarily consisted of male and female reproduction-specific organs and hormones as listed in Table 1 and 2.

Table 1. Organs Involved in the Process of Reproduction

In Males	In Females
• hypothalamus	• hypothalamus
• pituitary	• pituitary
• testis	• uterus
• prostate	• ovary
• seminal vesicle	• cervix
• penis	• vagina
• epididymis	• vulva

Table 2. Hormones Involved in the Process of Reproduction

In Males	In Females
• FSH	• FSH
• LH	• LH
• GnRH	• GnRH
• testosterone	• oestrogen
• oestrogen	• progesterone
• inhibin	• hCG
	• prolactin

In addition to these, the following keywords were used to widen the search for publications on male reproduction: clinical trial, contraception, sperm, Leydig cell and Sertoli cell (two types of cells exclusively found in the testis), vas deferens (the tube which is tied during vasectomy) and vasectomy. Similarly, additional keywords for publications on female reproduction were clinical trial, contraception, zona pellucida (the outer layer of the egg during and after fertilization), fallopian tube (which is tied during tubectomy) and endometrium (the inner lining of the uterus which gets shed during menstruation). The keywords used were selected to give some idea about research publications dealing with the structure, functioning and development of the reproductive system from human and non-human mammals in which these organs and hormones are present. The search thus had the advantage of including publications using both experimental models and dealing with contraceptives tested in clinical trials.

Gender bias in scientific and technological research on reproduction

A keyword based search gives an idea of the quantity of research work done on the given subject; however, it does not give any idea about the quality of the research work. Database searches screen for the presence or absence of a keyword in the title and the abstract or the summary of the article and not the whole article. The search is, thus, representative of the contents of the article with an assumption that almost all the relevant observations of a given article will find a mention in the abstract. Within the constraints of such a search, interesting findings emerged. As expected, a large number of papers have been published which are concerned with male or female reproductive tract research including contraception—407,600 publications on female reproductive tract research (including contraception) and 252,702 for men, thus providing a large sample size for the survey. The proportion of papers on female reproduction thus exceeds that on the male reproduction, with a female-to-male ratio of 1.61.

The approaches used in these papers could be considered a reflection of how scientific and technological pursuits are conducted. The next aim was to look at specific publications on contraceptives for men and women which are more indicative of directed, technology-oriented research. The search now brought up a reduced numbers of publications (24,631 for women and just 7276 for men). The strong bias towards working on female contraceptives is visible in the increased female-to-male ratio of 3.38.

The next aim was to get an estimate of publications directly involved in contraceptive technology development efforts. Only a proportion of publications involving contraception can be expected to be about the development of new contraceptives and/or improvements in existing contraceptives. Publications reporting clinical trials (from Phase I to Phase

III/IV with post-marketing surveillance, if indicated) are tangible indicators of the development of a 'product'. The number of such papers is obviously smaller, and notably, very few trials are reported on male contraception (just 305) in contrast to female contraception (1882), with a female-to-male ratio of 6.17.

Taken together, these figures show that, as one progresses from looking at the large effort of mechanistic investigations into reproductive biology to research focused around contraception, and then to the specific area of information on clinical trials of contraceptives, there is a steady increase in the emphasis on the female rather than the male. Even when the two are considered separately, there is a greater proportion of papers dealing with females concerning contraception and contraceptives. Thus, Table 3 shows that, out of all the publications on male reproduction, only 2.88% address the issue of contraception, and only 4.19% of those studies reach the stage of clinical trials. Thus, only 0.12% of all papers on male reproduction report on clinical trials for male contraceptives. In contrast, 6.04% of the papers on female reproduction talk about contraception. Many more of these (7.60%) report on clinical trials, and the clinical trials *per se* form a larger proportion (0.46%) of the total research carried out on female reproduction.

Table 3. Increasing Bias

Parameter	For Males	For Females
Papers on contraception as a proportion of total publications	2.88%	6.04%
Papers on clinical trials as a proportion of publications on contraception	4.19%	7.60%
Papers on clinical trials as a proportion of total publications	0.12%	0.46%

Thus, there is considerably less original scientific input in understanding the physiology and pathology of male reproduction to begin with. Efforts to work on male contraceptives are only half of that spent on female contraception. Further, what little work gets done on male contraception is less geared to the development of usable contraceptives as evidenced by the proportion of efforts spent on clinical trials. As a result there are proportionately four times more, and in absolute numbers six times more, clinical trials conducted on women to develop usable contraceptives.

A reflection of the efforts that have gone into the development of contraceptives over the past many decades with this bias can be seen in the outcome. There are many more methods for spacing of children available for a woman to use. The same is true for terminal methods too.

Table 4. Common Methods of Contraception Available Today

For Men	For Women
Reversible method—condom	*Reversible methods*—IUD (Copper T), oral pills, hormonal injectable contraceptives, hormonal implant, morning after pill, abortion
Permanent method—vasectomy	Permanent methods—tubal occlusion or ligation, hysterectomy

Does biology and physiology explain the observed bias?

It could be argued by people not familiar with the biology of reproduction that differences between the male and the female reproductive systems contribute to the bias observed. However, the list of keywords used for this search already shows otherwise. The number of reproduction associated organs present in the two sexes (Table 1) and the list of hormones (Table 2) involved in the process of reproduction in males and females suggest no significant differences at a gross level in the complexity of the biological systems of the two sexes. Admittedly, females carry the additional burden of pregnancy. No exclusive reference to pregnancy was included in the search to avoid this bias, nor research publications related to female breasts *per se*. Had they been included, the complexity of the female reproductive system would have been further compounded and the gender bias correspondingly worsened.

Another argument could be that since millions of sperms are produced and ejected during each intercourse, whereas only one mature egg is produced per month by the woman's body, in the search for contraceptive targets it might be easier to work on the woman's body. But if one looks at potential approaches listed for intervention in fertilization in Table 5, there are theoretically as many approaches for male as for female contraception. Other non-biological factors are contributing to the final basket of choices available for contraception.

Table 5. Potential Approaches for Contraception

In Males	In Females
• prevent sperm production	• prevent egg production
• decrease sperm production	• prevent egg maturation
• decrease/inhibit sperm maturation	• prevent egg fertilization
• prevent transport of sperms	• prevent egg implantation
• prevent ejaculation of sperms	• prevent egg transport to uterus

In Males	In Females
• decrease motility of sperms	• increase motility of the uterus to cause expulsion of the fertilized egg
• inhibit egg penetrating properties of sperms	• prevent deposition of sperms
• make essential sperm nutrients unavailable	• destroy deposited sperms

Sociological factors and biological research

Finally, the question comes down to societal attitudes towards women as well as the social upbringing of researchers. Though the science they practise may be more indirect (and hence more 'neutral') in its impact on society than is the development and use of technology, both are practised by men and women whose mindsets belong to the same society, which is patriarchal and discriminatory. Representations of womanhood as sacrificing and loving mothers, or obedient and tolerant wives, are repeatedly projected. As a reality, the subjugation of women forms a part of the social context of the researchers.

One outcome of this attitude can be observed in the number of women in the research profession. While more and more women are entering the field of the natural sciences for their training, their progress to senior levels is not proportionate to the number of women entering the field. Generally, women are found in larger numbers in the field of the biological sciences as compared to the other fields of the natural sciences. Data collected from the Massachusetts Institute of Technology have been presented in Table 6 as an example, and the trends in India are likely to be similar. Many more women researchers disappear soon after completing their doctoral studies. There are very few women researchers at senior and/or permanent faculty positions. More often than not senior scientists are chosen as technocrats (or 'scientocrats') and policy makers, and hence even fewer women seem to attain such a status.

Because of women's status as secondary citizens and because of their marginal presence or complete absence in policy making bodies, women's voices are only rarely heard in such fora. Research policies are thus rarely influenced by women. This in itself might be one of the reasons behind the major bias in the development of women-directed approaches, although, of course, the presence of women in policy making does not necessarily mean that policy making will be more pro-women.

Table 6. Disparity in Sexes at Higher Echelons in Academia

	Biology		Chemistry		Physics		Mathematics	
	F	M	F	M	F	M	F	M
Undergraduates	147	142	59	53	40	160	53	123
Graduates	101	118	73	176	30	267	17	95
Postdocs	25	57	20	71	3	12	2	5
Faculty	7	42	2	30	4	77	1	47

(Number of women (F) vs men (M)—undergraduate to faculty in the School of Science, MIT 1994.)

Impact of gender bias in contraceptive research

The undue emphasis on women in contraceptive research is an outcome of a mindset that holds women solely responsible for childbearing. Male responsibility in reproduction, while it has become a buzzword of late, finds relatively little reflection in the direction of contraceptive development efforts. Some examples will serve to illustrate the point.

Over the past two decades, major efforts are directed at popularizing the use of injectable hormonal contraceptives in developing countries where there is a perceived population problem. India and Bangladesh are looked upon as 'natural choices' for clinical trials. Most of these trials are conducted on women from the relatively poorer sections of the society who use public hospitals for their healthcare. Notions of informed consent normally remain on paper with a possible thumb impression as proof of consent. In the case of injectable hormonal contraceptives which act as slow-release depot preparations of the hormone, providing contraceptive effect ranging from 2–3 months to five years, women participants of clinical trials have complained about menstrual disturbances, body ache, headache and depression as frequent problems. These are considered minor side effects by the people conducting and/or evaluating trials. Women who can easily afford to pay for health services do not opt for injectable contraceptives, indicating that neither private practitioners nor their patients consider these problems to be 'minor' as shown by a survey conducted on private practitioners of gynaecology and obstetrics.

Another example is that of quinacrine, an anti-malarial drug, which is used illegally for the chemical sterilization of women in developing countries including India, Vietnam, Bangladesh, etc. Some 'trials' to gauge the efficacy of quinacrine took place near Calcutta, Bangalore and other places in India, without clearance from the Indian Council of Medical Research (ICMR), the body which is supposed to supervise such procedures. The women undergoing sterilization were provided no follow-up or help and many of them suffered severe side effects. These also are described as 'minor' in nature, when they are acknowledged at all. Far from being 'minor', the use of quinacrine for female sterilization has also been associated with serious complications like cervical stenosis (closure of the aperture of the cervix), ectopic pregnancy, perforation of uterus and the possible development of cancer of the uterus.

Over the years, voices repeatedly raised by health and feminist activists about these malpractices have fallen on deaf years. After having failed to report success in clinical trials with Net-En, a progesterone-based injectable contraceptive for women, ICMR is going ahead with another proposal of Phase IV trials in a few centres in India with a view to introduce it in the government's family welfare programme.

In sharp contrast, safe spacing and sterilization methods for men are getting less attention and are being pushed reluctantly, if at all. Though the coercion experienced during the vasectomy drive in the Emergency period in the 1970s is condemnable, the reasons for the failure of vasectomies were never analyzed and publicized. Any surgical method tried in a camp on a large scale is more prone to failure than the non-camp approach. Not only men but even women undergoing tubectomies in camps have suffered immensely. However, after more than twenty-five years of the criminal excesses of vasectomy camps during the Emergency, no serious efforts are being made to popularize vasectomy, dispel the myth that it compromises a man's sexual performance, and gain the confidence of men. Instead, the strategy adopted by international funding agencies, in connivance with the state machinery, is to push the burden of provider controlled spacing methods as well as permanent methods like sterilization on to women. The only newer spacing methods in early phases of clinical trials for men in recent years are the ones using injectable hormonal contraceptives, a trend which is not healthy for reasons similar to the ones applicable for poor, underprivileged women.

Thus, in the context of contraceptive research, male-centred processes dominate the scene. Despite not having biological or scientific reasons to offer a larger basket of contraceptive choices to women, gender bias creates a situation in which this appears inevitable. As shown above, even in the relatively isolated area of investigations into biological mechanisms, gender bias operates, probably as a result of the socially conditioned cultural baggage researchers bring, leading to greater focus on the reproductive functions of women's bodies. This same sociocultural upbringing also moulds the psyche of the policy makers who give directions for technology development, technologists implement them to deliver the products and pharmaceutical companies reap the benefit.

References

Government of India, National Population Policy 2000.

MEDLINE <http://www.ncbi.nih.gov/entrez/query.fcgi>.

The MIT faculty newsletter 9, no. 4, March 1999.

<http://web.mit.edu/fnl/women/women/html>.

Saheli. 1999. Enough is enough: Injectable contraceptive Net-En, a chronicle of health hazards foretold. Saheli: New Delhi.

Saheli. 2000. Quinacrine: A sordid story of chemical sterilizations of women. Saheli: New Delhi.

〜

REPRODUCTIVE HEALTH:
A PUBLIC HEALTH PERSPECTIVE

Imrana Qadeer

The replacement of the concept of 'women's health' by 'reproductive health' is yet another key contribution of the advocates of human development. Instead of visualizing health issues as women of different regions see it for themselves, they merge them into universal reproductive health and rights issues. As a consequence of their own priorities, they never really examined either the epidemiological basis of reproductive health or the reasons behind some women's silence vis-à-vis reproductive health problems. Had they done so, the immensity of women's health problems and the social constraints on women's lives would have revealed the inadequacy of their isolated strategy in the context of the expressed needs of women for land rights, freedom from atrocities, food, security systems, minimum wages and communal harmony along with the need for health services. We will explore in a later section patterns of women's illness and its implications for planning health care services.

Given the complexity of the environment we live in, the causality of reproductive health is no more confined to the conventional medical domain of infections, sexual or reproductive processes. At times, the causes of reproductive ill health lie outside conventional medical boundaries and even when they severely affect reproductive health, they may not be amenable to cure through reproductive health strategies. Yet, once reproductive health is placed centre stage, strategies are evolved for direct intervention in a wide range of reproductive problems, including those not actually rooted in the medical domain, but where reproductive damage is merely a spin-off. [. . .]

Despite all the emphasis on 'empowerment' and 'enabling conditions', the concept of reproductive health has derived heavily from the notion of the 'biological vulnerability' of women (who, in fact, are biologically the stronger sex!), and the concept of 'life cycle'. This has brought about a subtle shift and transformed the social process of bearing and rearing children into an essentially biological event. The notion of 'life cycle' compartmentalizes women's lives, creates artificial disjunctures and places bio-demographic aspects above class and gender influences on health.

Having thus marginalized the role of socioeconomic and political factors on the lives of women, the life-cycle approach opens intimate spaces for intervention at two levels—individual and family health. This compartmentalized perception of family and reproduction performs an important theoretical function. One, isolated activism, where empowerment can be granted through reproductive health activities alone. Two, ignoring the necessity of creating a sense of security at the social level, while intervening with alacrity at the family level. The family as an institution in a patriarchal capitalist society is structured to absorb economic and social pressures generated outside it. The most important absorbent is the woman herself.

Population council experts, for instance, define reproductive health as 'prevention and management of unwanted pregnancies, services to promote safe motherhood and child survival, nutrition services for vulnerable groups, prevention of reproductive tract infections (RTIs) and sexually transmitted infections (STIs), reproductive health services for adolescents, health, sexuality and gender information, education and counselling, establishment of an effective referral system' (Pachauri 1995). They thus transform reproductive health into a gamut of services all based on technology. It is inevitable, therefore, that the actual operationalization further narrows the scope to contraception, maternal and child health, nutrition, services for RTIs and STDs, AIDS, abortions and sterility. [. . .]

A public health perspective

Reproductive health is a part of primary health care and therefore the responsibility of the state. The concept of reproductive health, as advanced by the state and the aid agencies, focuses on fertility regulation irrespective of health and developmental strategies. Its operationalization into technocentric strategies, rather than into social, structural and legislative alternatives, its neglect of eminent general health problems, and its inability to confront the detrimental impact of structural adjustment policies on women, make it amenable to appropriation by the technologically oriented population control lobby. The official concept of 'reproductive health', then, is not necessarily pro-women, it is only women-centred. There is, therefore, a need to grasp the full complexity of the term 'reproductive health' and to put it in a public health perspective.

There is no denying the fact that reproductive health constitutes an important aspect of women's health. However, the challenge is to define priorities within it according to the objective and subjective definitions of women's needs, and to make it a part of a larger developmental programme, based not only on equity of distribution but also on access and control of productive resources.

The subjective definition of reproductive health depends upon women's life experiences and is reflected in their perceptions and what they themselves say. Deeply rooted in the social matrix of each society, the actual expression of reproductive health needs depends upon the status and social position of women in it. Thus, it is not necessary that women would be in a position to articulate these needs in their entirety, especially in the third world. This does not mean that till women start articulating their needs no interventions can be made. On the contrary, it calls for identifying the possible levels of intervention as well as evolving strategies for intervention.

Instead of looking at inter- and intra-household relationships as two distinct sets of relationships, we need to understand power relationships between the sexes within the socioeconomic context which constantly impinges on and alters power relations within families. This social level of intervention is one which calls for social and political mobilization to create conditions that make women's assertion of needs within families easier. It also calls for sensitive and perceptive policies based on women's needs and priorities. To this extent the proposed activation of panchayats (local bodies) to implement socio-demographic agendas at village and community levels are a welcome step. Whether they will actually be effective will depend on the degree to which the new panchayats are able to change power structures, and the kind of support they get from the government and the civil society.

In a milieu where privatization, cutbacks in allocation to the social sector, shrinking wage structures and work opportunities, and dwindling food security systems are hitting women the hardest, their basic survival needs cannot be given a secondary status. The fact that women are being pushed back into the unorganized sector or the boundaries of their homes to help families absorb the shock generated by a receding state makes them even more vulnerable. At the family and community level, therefore, the only way to tackle reproductive health issues is to locate them within the broader spectrum of needs as experienced and perceived by women. To do otherwise would mean rejecting women's context, their perceptions and their strategies for survival. [. . .]

Over the past few years there has been a spurt of literature on reproductive health. The field studies are either clinical or exclusively focus on women's reproductive health problems. Though important, these reproductive diseases are not the only health problems of women. We examine here the mortality data from the Model Registration Scheme of the government of India to get an idea of the reality. Two things need to be stated:

(a) The Model Registration Scheme has its limitations, as it is conducted by non-medical investigators, uses symptom complexes for a retrospective diagnosis, and samples only PHC villages. Yet, it provides systematic information on causes for seven to ten thousand deaths annually.

(b) It has become a common argument that looking at deaths is not sufficient and that reproductive morbidities constitute a major indicator. Within a comprehensive public health perspective, however, the link between morbidity and mortality should not be lost. Preventing deaths at times leads to higher morbidity, but lower morbidity with high death rates is not necessarily indicative of good health. Therefore, when resources are limited, a judicious handling of the two with a focus on handling those problems first which lead to mortality is an accepted principle. Our assessment of data therefore will be within this perspective.

Table 1 shows the age specific and total female deaths in India over the decade 1982–93. It highlights the very high proportion of mortality in 0–four years of age (22–28 per cent) as compared to the 5–14 year age group (4.7–5.4 per cent). While the highest mortality proportions of age group 45 years and above are expected, the proportions of death among 15–44 years over the decade (16–19 per cent) is a matter of concern. It is also worth noting that while in the 0–4 year age group the lowest proportion of death was achieved in 1990, a reversal began in 1991. For the 15–45 year age group there has been a slow and consistent increase from 16.36 to 19.13 per cent over 1982–93. The proportion of death in the more than 45 year age group shows an increase over 1988–91 and then again comes back to the initial levels in the early 1990s. But in the 5–14 year age group there is very little change over the 11-year period.

An examination of the main causes of death (from other data sources) reveals that deaths due to childbirth constitute 2.1 to 2.9 per cent of total female deaths. The main causes of death among women remain respiratory diseases, causes peculiar to infancy, diseases of the circulatory system (which includes anaemia), fevers and digestive disorders. Time trends show very little decline in these proportions. The proportion of death due to injuries actually increases slightly and those due to fevers decline over the entire period. For causes falling within the purview of maternal and child health (child birth and pregnancy, causes peculiar to infancy and diseases of the circulatory system including anaemia), there is an initial decline in proportions till 1988–89. Then a slight but consistent reversal of this trend sets in.

To acquire a better idea of the distribution of causes we have identified from each group specific communicable diseases. Deaths due to gastroenteritis, cholera, dysentery, tuberculosis, pneumonia, whooping cough, meningitis, jaundice, tetanus, chicken pox, measles and poliomyelitis have been clubbed together to look at three specific groups of causes of death—communicable diseases, maternal deaths (deaths related to pregnancy and child birth) and anaemias. The important features are that in all age groups communicable diseases cause the highest proportion of deaths. In the 15–44 age group these deaths are more than double those caused by maternity. Of all communicable disease deaths, 47–53 per cent occur in young girls and 21–24 per cent in the 15–44 year age group. The proportion of deaths due to communicable diseases in the reproductive age group increases after 1991.

Over the entire period of 1982–93, communicable disease deaths remain the most eminent, and emphasize the fact that isolating the reproductive age group performs the function of ignoring the heavy mortality caused by communicable diseases in the age groups fifteen years and under and forty-five years and above.

Table 1

Age Group in years	1982	1983	1984	1985	1986	1988	1989	1990	1991	1992	1993
0-4	2000 (28.05)	2065 (26.62)	2113 (26.74)	2080 (27.01)	2155 (26.32)	2546 (24.76)	2309 (24.32)	2055 (22.32)	2274 (22.68)	2680 (23.56)	3258 (24.51)
5-14	368	392	412	391	426	510	452	472	(5.43)	551	654
15-44	(5.16) 1168	(5.05) 1340	(5.21) 1300	(5.08) 1319	(5.20) 1414	(4.96) 1603	(4.76) 1724	(5.14) 1661	1770 (17.66)	(4.84) 2144	(4.92) 2543
>45	(16.38)	(17.27)	(16.45)	(17.12)	(17.27)	(15.9) 5624	(18.16)	(18.09)	5437 (52.23)	(18.89)	(19.13)
>15	3593 (50.40)	3961 (51.06)	4077 (51.59)	3912 (50.79)	4192 (51.20)	(54.69) 7223	5009 52.76	4992 54.38	7207 (7189)	5998 (52.74)	6836 (51.43)
Total									10025		
Deaths	4761 (66.78)	5301 (68.33)	5377 (68.04)	5231 (67.91)	5606 (68.47)	(70.28) 10283	6733 (70.92)	6653 (72.47)		8142 (71.59)	9379 (70.56)
	7129	7758	7902	7702	8187		9494	9180		11373	13291

When we look at deaths due to anaemia in the 15–44 age group, we find that as a complication of pregnancy it has certainly not declined, as its share has come down from 3.4 per cent to 1.93 per cent in 1988 and then again risen to 3.07 per cent in 1993. General anaemia (without pregnancy) is an equally serious threat to women's lives. Even if the 1993 figures are treated with caution, the rising contribution of general anaemia to deaths cannot be denied.

If we add to this the low levels of average calorie intake, as shown by the National Monitoring Bureau (1980) data, the picture of general health becomes very poor. For example, in nine major states, for 1975–78, the women who were sedentary workers (requiring 1900 calories) showed a mean calorie intake of 1307–1816 in all states except one. For moderate female workers too, all except one of the nine states had values less than the required 2200 calories and here too the range of mean intakes was 1141–1976. This reflects the severe deprivation of adult women in Kerala, Tamil Nadu, Andhra Pradesh, Maharashtra, Gujarat, Madhya Pradesh, West Bengal and Uttar Pradesh. In 1996 among sedentary workers, the mean calorie intake went above the recommended levels in two out of eight states, and for moderate women workers four states had values above those required. In the 1996 data, however, Uttar Pradesh and West Bengal were replaced by Karnataka and Orissa!

The Model Registration data emphasize the following:

(1) The importance of dealing with the health problems of under 15 year old girls, who bear a high load of mortality and who enter reproductive age with a disadvantage.
(2) The importance of communicable diseases which not only kill the young but remain the second major killers of women in the 15–45 years age group.
(3) The inappropriateness of exclusive reproductive health interventions for women in the reproductive age group when communicable diseases, anaemias and malnutrition are their major killers across all age groups.
(4) The need to retain the focus on maternal mortality, before opting for broadening the base of maternal and child health services in the face of severe cuts in health sector investment. This broadening into peripheral areas of reproductive health will dilute the efforts of the public sector which through the Famly Planning Programme is already concentrating investment in contraceptive services.
(5) The need to recognize the impact of general illness on maternal health as the complications caused add to maternal mortality.

This data gives a clear basis for policy level interventions in the area of public health. It also explains partly the 'silence' of poor Indian women on the issue of reproductive health and rights other than basic maternity services.

From a public health perspective two things are clearly needed. Firstly, within reproductive health, priorities should be clearly articulated and reflected in the budgetary allocations. Secondly, maternal and child health, nutrition, contraceptive services and communicable disease control must be integrated. Within the sphere of the health service system this will provide a solid foundation for women's health including their reproductive health. Handling reproductive health in isolation is not only an inefficient way of dealing with the problem of women's reproductive health but it also robs them of their dignity. An integrated approach alone can give optimal results by handling women's health as an entirety. To achieve the best results the health service system needs supportive social, economic and legislative action favouring women.

The issues of women's health (including reproductive health) thus go well beyond the domain of the public sector in health. Woven into the fabric of society, it is open to intervention at different levels. Policy, welfare programmes, training health activists and community level mobilization can influence it deeply. It is therefore incumbent upon those who choose to intervene that they should grasp the limits of the levels at which they intervene and the complexity of women's health. It requires an effort to link up these levels and create a multi-pronged strategy for intervention. The blurring of this matrix and isolated interventions can create an illusion of achievement where little exists.

References

Pachauri, Saroj. 1995. Defining a reproductive health package for India: A proposed framework. Regional working paper no.4, Population council South and East Asia, New Delhi.

≈

OUR HEALTH OUR HERITAGE
Shodhini

As the saying goes in Kannada, hitalla gida maddalla (my backyard plant is not medicine). For most of the diseases we suffer from, we can find out medicines from the plants available in our own back yard; even if we have knowledge of it, we do not try to utilize it, but we use instead expensive tablets and drugs.

—Savitri, Aikya

Savitri's words capture the essence of Shodhini.

The idea of Shodhini emerged during a national level consultation of women's groups organized by SRED and SHAKTI in Tamil Nadu in 1987.

This consultation was attended by around fifty women's health activists, both rural and urban.

The women articulated their concerns and their experiences in relation to women's health. They talked of the failure of the modern health care system to meet women's health needs. They spoke of their fear and humiliation at being treated like objects and targeted by the service providers. On the other hand, they mentioned that traditionally women have been care providers. Some older women in the villages, it was expressed, continue to be treasure houses of traditional remedies for common problems among women. Concern was also expressed that this kind of knowledge is rapidly dying out.

While the urban women present at the consultation wanted to know about the traditional remedies and plants for women's health, the rural women wanted to learn about modern developments in health. The discussion during this consultation led in time to a small group of women coming together under the banner of 'Action Research on Alternative Medicines and Women's Health'. (This group later took on the name of Shodhini.) Over a period of about one year, the members of the group met and discussed and arrived at some clarity with regards to their vision. They expressed that they wanted to work collectively to create an alternative for women's health, an alternative that sought to:

— empower women by validating their traditional knowledge and enhancing its status;
— increase women's control over their own bodies and their own health by training local women in simple gynaecology; and
— increase women's control over technology and over resources by growing medicinal plants.

Shodhini's work moved through four distinct phases:

Phase I   collection of information on plants and natural elements commonly used for women's health problems.
Phase II   training local women health workers/ healers in herbal medicine, using self-help and a holistic approach.
Phase III field testing and validating the use of common herbs in a systematic way at the community level.
Phase IV   in the process of working on the above three phases, developing a team of concerned women with bare-foot gynaecological skills to continue and sustain the work of developing alternatives in women's health care.

Data was gathered from nine field locations from six states across India. Through discussions and meetings with different groups of women, the group attempted to find out about the common, yet neglected, health problems of women. Field interactions with women revealed that they suffered from a range of complaints like vaginal infections, problems linked to the menstrual cycle and so on. Thus, through a series of meetings, discussions and dialogue with various regional women's groups, we arrived at the following areas for our action research:

— problems of the menstrual cycle
— urinary tract and vaginal infections
— uterine and cervical tumours, benign and malignant
— problems during and after pregnancy: anaemia, nausea, lactation failure, weaknesses, etc.
— other neglected aspects of women's health—back pain, joint pain, weakness, genital prolapse (vaginal, uterine), fatigue and depression.

Methodology for research on plants

Information sheet and herbariums

To carry out the action research, an information sheet was made covering all essential information with regard to herbal remedies for women's health. Supplementing each information sheet, herbariums were also made to ensure that names of species could be identified and verified by Shodhini members taking the help of botanists and vaidyas. The data collected by women was translated into English, crosschecked and verified through field visits to the forests and fields along with the women who shared this knowledge with us. They showed us the plants and trees which were of medicinal value and educated us in the process. Along with this, we also collected information from other sources, including literature on medicinal plants, data from health professionals and others who were working with herbs for women's health.

At the end of this period of data collection, all these information sheets and herbariums were scrutinized by Dr. Indira Balachandran of Kottakal Arya Vaidya Sala, Kerala, who is a botanist and a member of Shodhini. She confirmed and verified their medicinal properties with regard to the symptoms and uses for which the women had cited them.

In all, 411 sheets were prepared including 176 information sheets from secondary sources (that is, not from field data). We found that a total of seventy plants were recommended more than once for the same complaint from different regions, and some of them were cited in the same regions twice or thrice by different healers, thus reinforcing the field data. For example, herbs like neem (*Azadirachta indica*), castor (*Ricinus communis*), and shatavaru (*Asoaragys racemous*) are being used in Uttar Pradesh, Andhra Pradesh, Karnataka and Tamil Nadu for vaginal infections and menstrual problems.

Categorization of plants

Our final list of 252 herbs consisted of different plants growing across Andhra, Karnataka, Tamil Nadu, Uttar Pradesh, Madhya Pradesh and

Gujarat. This field information was checked systematically against the standard literature on medicinal plants. Herbs were categorized as A, B and C which we defined as follows:

A: herbs mentioned in the standard existing literature for the same symptoms and properties as the healers were using them for

B: herbs mentioned in the standard literature but not for the symptoms that the healers used them for, but with properties which indicated they could be used for particular women's problems

C: herbs for recipes which seemed to be toxic and dangerous.

First round of field testing

By the end of 1990, we were ready to review the information collected and to apply it in the field. This process gained momentum by January 1991 with a selection of thirty-five plants for the first round of field testing. This list included many plants from the A category and a few from B category selected from all the regions. The criteria of selection of the plants for the first round were that they be safe, proven through literature and in 'common' knowledge (for instance, neem, garlic, turmeric, etc.). Subsequently in each area, namely, Andhra, Karnataka, Gujarat and Delhi, the field testing began from early 1991. This phase covered mainly common complaints like vaginal infections, urinary infections, constipation, painful periods. The plants that each field area selected from the list were: traditionally locally used, currently locally available, made from a single ingredient and prepared by a simple process. To assist the healers to record their diagnosis and herbal treatment easily, pictorial case sheets were designed. These case sheets were explained to the health workers and made easy to understand by using role plays.

Second round

After a period of six to seven months of field testing of the first list of thirty-five plants, we moved ahead to the second list. We found that our gradual and phased approach of testing a few selected categories of herbs and training the women in basic diagnosis paved the way for testing the next list of herbs. The second list consisted of many B type herbs. This time, the field covered was not only simple complaints like vaginal problems and heavy bleeding, but also complaints like uterine problems, hormonal imbalances, tumours, etc. By now, we felt that the health workers and healers had gained enough experience to look at new problems like fibroids, prolapse, hormonal imbalances, etc.

Results

On the whole, we found that many of the herbs tested worked well, be it for simple vaginal complaints or for difficult uterine problems. For instance, we found that across different regions *Asoaragys racenisys* (shatavaru) was useful in dealing with non-specific vaginal infections. In Pastapur, Andhra Pradesh, two herbs that gave good results when used for vaginal problems were *Abutilon indicum* (atibala) and garlic. Also neem proved to be very effective for vaginal infections of different types.

Another common herb which we found was very useful in healing a variety of complaints was *Mimosa pudica* (touch-me-not) that healed not only vaginal and menstrual problems but also fever, body pain and allergies.

Tinospora cordifolia (amruthavalli) and *Hemidesmus indicus* (sarsaparilla) were found to be two other excellent herbs, that worked as hormonal regulators, as well as tonics besides providing relief in different uterine problems.

Issues emerging from the action research

Interfacing of different healing systems

The Shodhini experience brought together at least three different systems with their different frameworks of knowledge and reality: popular practice of herbal medicines ('folk medicine'); knowledge acquired and handed through practitioners of Ayurveda, Siddha, Unani and related systems (classical, traditional systems); and some suitably demystified practices and precepts of modern (or 'western', dominant science) medicine.

At the first level of inquiry, we tried to find out whether the herbal medicines used by 'folk' or popular practitioners had any Ayurvedic references. We then called these medicines by the somewhat loaded term 'valid' or suitable for further 'shodh' or inquiry. At another level, we trained healers to diagnose women's gynaecological problems based on the modern western system of health care and treat these problems with the 'valid' remedies. Working through these three interfaces was a very complex process. Decision-making criteria had to be evolved, so that we could recognize the contradictions and complexities and yet move forward.

Initially, we as facilitators used the 'modern' paradigm and the feminist perspective to evolve yardsticks for good and bad. But when all of us women participants evolved the decision criteria, the only common criteria was what is empowering, according to the subjective experiences of the women involved.

Thus, on reflecting on the process, one point which stands out very clearly is that the bottomline of the decision-making criteria was the empowerment of the women concerned. We understood empowerment both as a goal and as a process. Empowerment would enable greater control for women (and men) over sources of power in society. In practice, this would mean that women would be able to assert themselves in their daily lives, not buckle under oppressive conditions, and, in general, lead relatively free and autonomous lives as human beings.

'Validity', field testing and the shodhini approach

How did we judge the 'validity' of traditional medicines? How did we know a particular herbal remedy works? Modern medicine is very categorical about the procedures of judging the validity: the desirable route of determining the worthwhileness of a treatment or procedure usually involves some combination of double-blind clinical trials, *in vitro* and *in vivo* testing, and community-based epidemiological studies. Application of these methods for testing the efficacy of traditional medicines has been discussed in the literature. This usually means standardization of plant remedies and extraction of the so-called active principle in each plant.

However, almost all traditional system practitioners feel that the full therapeutic effect of a plant is decreased and can even vanish completely if extraction and fractionation is carried out. Standardization of the parts of the plants to be used and quantities to be used is also difficult, particularly so, as the same plant can have varying alkaloid contents depending on environmental and climatic factors, geographical location, and even the time and the year of plant collection.

Therefore, as a methodology, modern clinical trials do not lend themselves to testing the validity of traditional medicines. Double-blind trials also have procedural and ethical problems. How do we 'disguise' a plant during a double-blind clinical trial when the entire plant or substantive parts of it are supposed to be used? Even if we could disguise the plant, why should a feminist research group, seeking humane alternatives, resort to deceiving the patient?

Traditional medicine practitioners, and advocates of traditional medicine like us, do not want to throw out the baby with the bathwater. We realize that other forms of inquiry, with all their limitations, have their uses in the realm of traditional medicine. These other forms can possibly add to the utility of traditional medicines in the long run. However, in the short run, modern pharmacological research, aided by drug companies, tends to exploit traditional knowledge of plant-based medicines through a free market economy. Also, at the level of sociopolitical relationships, such 'validation' by modern medicine adds to the bargaining power and status of those who practise and advocate traditional medicines.

It was thus encouraging for us to discover that several of the plants that we are working with and considered valuable are also undergoing scientific trials and experimentation elsewhere. For instance, *Tinospora cordifolia* which gave us promising results against heavy bleeding appears to be a particular focus of research in more than one medical establishment for carcinoma of the cervix. [. . .]

Confirmation of remedies

What works or does not work can be judged only if the data can be verified or confirmed. Attempts were made to introduce checks and balances in the field trials of the traditional remedies. For example, the women health workers were trained to differentiate between various types of white discharge and to record these differences with accuracy. The case sheets included diagrams, on which the women health workers were supposed to locate the various symptoms of their clients. Secondly, the treatments and dosages were standardized to the best of our ability. Using finger and hand measurements, the amount of the bark, root or stem of the plants to be taken were standardized. The method of preparation of the medicines, for example, tinctures, powders or decoctions were also standardized. In some of the field areas, these attempts at building uniformity and standards succeeded, while in others, it was just not possible to ensure that the standards are followed. The culture and practice of traditional medicines are just not compatible with 'rigorous', uniform standards.

A second way of confirming the efficacy of the treatment was doing a second examination of the clients after at least a month's treatment to ensure that the symptoms had receded. Again, while this was possible in some field areas, in others we could not establish this as a firm practice. The women would say, 'We have told you that our symptoms have gone away, we won't let you examine us now.' At this stage, after about two years of practice in the field, Shodhini has at least 200 case sheets of women who have been treated successfully, with a physical evaluation and follow-up of these women to verify the matter contained in the case sheets.

Patenting and traditional medicines

Shodhini has been accused of making it easy for drug companies and other commercial interests, by publishing the findings of the plant-based remedies. We, however, see it in a different light. Firstly, we do not see any resource efficient way of propagating this traditional knowledge other than by putting it in book form and in several language translations. Secondly, if we and others like us do not do even this, whatever useful knowledge that exists in local health traditions is likely to go into an even more rapid extinction. Thirdly, the information we have documented is considered the inherited property of humankind, which it is, and is therefore not patentable. Only chemical modifications of the active principles of plant-based medicines, and their derivatives, can be patented. Therefore, what we are doing is to provide, or rather reconfirm, hints for research for the modern drug industry and scientific laboratories. Such hints exist by the thousands in traditional pharmacoepias and materia medicas, which are all easily available in printed form.

But all the above discussion bypasses the basic question of agreeing to a patent regime, whether those who believe in the free use of intellectual properties for the benefit of humankind should play the patent game at all, even if they could? Shodhini is hesitant to play the patent game, and we suspect patenting is a wrong strategy in the long term to battle those who believe in collecting royalties for their 'discoveries' and 'inventions'. Organizing local communities to protect their traditions, resources and biodiversity is probably a more sustainable strategy.

Limitations of the study

Shodhini was a complicated venture involving a number of individuals, organizations and village level women from all over India. The pace and the time schedule that was set by the network members was unrealistic, as far as village level processes were concerned. For example, it took the healers longer to learn the basics of gynaecology than has been estimated by network members. Also, the time it took the healers to win the rural women's confidence and begin examining them was longer than estimated.

Although Shodhini as an idea has immense political significance, the scale at which it could be tried out was very tiny. Ultimately, only three field-based groups participated in the community testing phase of the herbs. The range of symptoms or problems that could be taken up in the three years was very limited. In fact, two very crucial areas which could not be included in this study were women's traditional contraceptives and abortifacients. In a country like India, where the state has placed such an emphasis on the family planning programme, finding an alternative to the invasive technologies being pushed by western forces becomes an imperative need.

Another aspect of the limited scale of this experiment that needs to be mentioned is the backward and forward linkages. Report from all our field areas indicate that the medicinal plants and trees are becoming more scarce. Regeneration of these resources, as a backward linkage, and the processing of these into simple formulations as a forward linkage, also need to be done. Perhaps, the next phase of Shodhini should include these aspects.

Most importantly, the Shodhini experience is most relevant at the primary level of gynaecological health care. At present, we, that is the Shodhini group, do not have any answers, meaning herbal remedies, for more complicated problems requiring secondary and tertiary levels of care.

OUR MIND OUR MADNESS
Bhargavi V. Davar

A brief synopsis

The mental health of Indian women has so far received scant attention from mental health professionals and women's organizations alike. As information is wanting in the area, we did a brief study on the psycho-social aspects of the mental well-being of Indian women.

The aim of the study was to provide an overview of the mental health status of Indian women. Three important issues were identified as being crucial: i) to harness information on the prevalence of mental disorders among Indian women, ii) to review information on the psycho-social causes of mental disorders that women are particularly prone to, and iii) to expose the gender politics in mental health care in the country by reviewing information on the utility of mental health facilities; institutional, professional and social attitudes towards mentally ill women; and finally, mental health law.

The study is not an empirical survey, but rather a secondary analysis. It is an interpretative review, perspectivizing available data, particularly from epidemiological studies and other psychiatric research in the country, from the viewpoint of gender.

Main suggestion of the study

The 1970s and 80s saw a spurt of interest in epidemiological studies of the prevalence of mental illness in different parts of the country. It is now accepted that the general prevalence of mental disorder in the community is around 11 per cent, of which 3 per cent require active intervention and 1 per cent require hospitalization. Using the primary data from these studies, we found that mental illness is far more frequent in women than in men, with the frequency of occurrence being as high as 15 per cent, as compared to 11 per cent among men.

Gender difference exists also in the type of mental illness exhibited. Mental disorders may generally be classified as 'severe' and 'common'. Disorders such as schizophrenia, manic depressive disorder and other organic forms of psychoses, epilepsy and mental retardation, are usually classified as severe mental disorders. They cause great psychological, personal and social breakdown. Neurotic disorders such as anxieties, phobias, hysterias, obsessive-compulsive disorders and major depression may be classified as common mental disorders. Even though there is no fundamental impairment at the cognitive level, such as thought disturbances, loss of reality, etc. great personal distress and social breakdown may be experienced.

One of the significant suggestions of our study is that there is no gender difference in the prevalence of severe mental disorders, whereas women are at least twice as frequently ill as men in the case of common mental disorders. Data showed that up to 11 per cent of women in the community may be suffering from common mental disorders.

This particular pattern of prevalence is quite telling. International research in the etiology of mental illnesses suggests that bio-genetic factors may lie at the root of severe mental disorders, whereas common mental disorders, especially major depression which is very frequent among women, may have psycho-social origins. On the basis of the data on prevalence and etiology available to us, we have found it reasonable to infer, therefore, that where mental illness has a purely biological basis, frequency of illness is the same across gender; and where mental illness has a psycho-social basis, women are far more frequently ill than men.

It has often been argued that the greater frequency of mental illnesses in women is due to hormonal changes co-occurring with the reproductive cycle. The 'menopausal' theory of mental illness is a particularly popular explanation. However, there is no conclusive evidence relating hormonal change with psychiatric disturbance. Postnatal psychoses could be caused by infections, malnutrition, anemia, etc. However, pregnancy related depression has a strong psycho-social basis, with marital and family discord, lack of parental support, stresses relating to added responsibilities of child care, long-term breast feeding, fear of outcome of pregnancy, etc. being some known contributing factors. Depression cannot be conclusively linked with menopause, and mid-life changes may play an important role in the onset of the disorder. The explanation of greater incidence of mental illness in women by referring to hormonal changes is therefore pseudo-scientific. It is offered by mental health professionals only to maintain a distance from the social reality of women, whose attitude, in turn, encourages and perpetrates the ruling paradigm of patriarchy.

Our analysis of epidemiological data, relating mental illness with age, marital status, education and occupation helped us outline the profile of mentally ill women. Frequency of illness in women is highest in the reproductive years of a women's development, that is, between 16 to 40 years, falling off steeply after this. In men, illness shows no particular pattern of frequency of prevalence with respect to age until fifty years or so, after which it increases sharply. Added to this, marital status is an important predictor of mental illness in women, but not so in the case of men. Married women are more frequently ill than single women, though divorced/separated/widowed women are most frequently ill. As an occupational category, housewives exhibit a very high frequency of mental illness, comparable only to unemployed persons and unskilled labourers. Unclassified categories of occupations, such as prostitutes, beggars, household maids, women-headed households, etc. show the highest frequency of illness.

All our analyses point to the fact that marriage and the family are necessary stressors in the cause of mental illness among Indian women. We have detailed the probable stress factors in marriage and family from both the developmental viewpoint and the psycho-social viewpoint. This approach is in keeping with current thinking on the etiology of common mental disorders, according to which developmental, social as well as psychological factors have been identified as important causes. Empirical research shows that depression has a strong psycho-social basis. Contributing factors may be family and marital problems, lack of confiding relationships, particularly with the husband, having more than three young children to care for; long-term social or economic adversity; role-strain or overload of role-related functions; domestic and other kinds of violence against women, particularly rape and childhood sexual abuse.

In the Indian context, many of these factors appear to be relevant, as is clear from studies in sociology. The discriminatory socialization of children on the basis of gender plays a special role in preparing the female psyche for subservience and the male psyche for dominance. The denial of material resources, such as food and education, and the early weaning away of psychological support from female children, the pressure on them to adopt care-giving functions quite early, the sex-typing strategies used by parents in work and play activities, all these result in the early maturation of girl children. Early maturation, while it helps in the spontaneous remission of childhood related disorders in girl children, however, results in a rigid conscience and allows for greater possibility of conflict, guilt and consequently, adult depression. Thus, the social role that girl children are taught to play is conducive for expressions of mental illnesses that women, in their adult life, are generally prone to.

Stresses related to marriage, particularly the painful and often traumatic process of initiation into the world view of the marital family; lack of intimacy with the husband and lack of privacy; rigid moral conformity according to cultural imperatives rather than the inner call of conscience; control on sexuality and the strongly communal basis of personal experiences, such as pregnancy, childbirth and upbringing; and finally, domestic violence, have been detailed as important psycho-social stressors in Indian women.

What is strikingly evident from our discussion on the development and socialization of Indian women is the sheer exteriority of her life; the fact that her values, her goals and her actions are decided, not from within, but from without, by our socio-cultural imperatives. The inner voice of Indian women is silenced during the process of becoming a socially useful and acceptable being. If self-identity may be described as a spiritual experience of one's inner being and existence, of one's ability to make choices, this is not allowed to develop in the average Indian woman, even in her most intimate experiences and relationships.

Instead, the social goal of subservience, inculcated in them from infancy, results in feelings of moral inferiority, guilt and worthlessness. These characterize the cultural unconscious of Indian women. Our social and religious practices nurture and sustain these facets of the female psyche in our culture. Projection of guilt and mental illness in Indian women often takes a religious form, evident from the preponderance of mentally afflicted women in allegedly curative temples. Indian communities encourage this dependence of women on magico-religious cures and promote the practice by attributing fatalistic concepts of '*karma*' and '*pida*' as the causes of mental illness.

Their low self-esteem is the pathological result of a logical process of socialization, the main goal of which is the sustenance of patriarchy. As no cultural routes of expression of aggression are allowed in women, they redirect their aggression against themselves and against other women, so that a unionization of women and their participation in a collective feminine identity cannot be realized. This maintains the system, with all its power equations and injustices.

Data on utility of services and sociological studies show that women in Indian communities are less likely to get mental health care. Even though women are more frequently ill than men, admission by women at various professional service outlets numbers half or less than that of men. Availability of hospital care for women is restricted because not as many beds are available for them, as for men. However, at non-professional treatment centres, such as healing temples, faith healers, native healers, exorcists, etc. women outnumber the men. In mental hospitals, even though only a small proportion of the patients admitted are women, a large proportion of these are condemned to spend the rest of their lives as long-stay patients as they are not claimed by their families. Afflicted women are not only a threat to domesticity and its routines, but also, they are a threat to its valour and honour. Married mentally ill women are more likely to be sent back to their natal homes than abandoned, deserted or divorced women. Greater social losses, such as loss of spouse, family, children, property and employment befall mentally afflicted women.

If large-scale neglect characterizes our social attitudes towards the mental health needs of women, our National Mental Health Program (NMHP) only reflects and reinforces this social attitude. The NMHP prioritizes epilepsy and psychoses, the severe mental disorders. This prioritization pays no heed at all to the frequent occurrence of common mental disorders in the community in general, and among women, in particular. Even though the NMHP is heralded as a landmark in mental health policy, it is only a footnote to the general health policy, and ignores the psycho-social bases of mental disorders. Thereby, it grants implicit sanction to the widespread use of invasive treatment methods, such as drugs and ECT.

The study also highlights some aspects of institutional and professional biases that colour their approach towards explaining and treating mental disorders among women. The inadequacies of the currently operative mental health law have also been discussed.

Thoughts on action

An adequate response to the mental health problems of women in our country must be in terms of their psychological empowerment.

Women must be given back their capacity to experience their spirituality: their inner sense of being and acting. Any mental health policy or programme for women must cease to take the culture and its values for granted. Instead, it must self-consciously evaluate the benefits and liabilities that our culture brings about, the power equations it promotes and the impact these have on the social and psychological behavior of individuals in general, and women, in particular. A social commitment, rather than the hitherto practised clinical commitment, must be the ethical goal of the mental health professions and other interested institutions and organizations.

Women's organizations, mental health organizations and other institutions working in the area of health can contribute to the understanding and mitigation of the problem of mental health of women by:

(i) Including 'mental health' on their health agenda.

(ii) Promoting research in the area: data is wanting on a wide number of issues, such as parenting, socialization, coping and conflict resolution strategies in Indian families; data on homeless, destitute and chronically mentally ill women; information on the comparable merits and demerits of treatment options for women; health rights issues; policy and legal issues. We must begin to think aloud about these issues from a gender perspective.

(iii) Organize discussions, seminars, etc. on the issue.

(iv) Organize self-help groups to help disseminate information and guide women in distress to make informed choices about their psychological problems.

(v) Team up with professionals and learn simple diagnostic and illness management skills. Training for interested organizations and individuals can be obtained from premier mental health institutions, such as NIMHANS.

(vi) Form support and activist groups to take up social issues relating to mentally ill women.

A DISABLED FEMINISM?

Anita Ghai

Women with disabilities in India and elsewhere encounter discrimination on several levels, each of which restricts their options and opportunities for equal participation in the economic, social and political life of society. They are disadvantaged attitudinally, economically, politically, psychologically and socially. Aside from ableism, disabled women also face the same pressures as other women. Over a decade ago, Marian Blackwell-Stratton and her colleagues argued that, 'For the disabled feminist, neither the disability movement nor the women's movement fully addresses her concerns ... we must educate both movements in the issues specifically affecting disabled women, especially since the women's movement has shown a willingness to learn about the issues affecting women of dual identities ...' (Blackwell-Stratton et al 1997).

Why do such statements remain as critically important in the twenty-first century as they did nearly over a decade ago? Social movements are well recognized as characteristic phenomena of the contemporary era, yet neither social movement analysts in general nor feminist scholars in particular have paid serious attention to the disability movement, and drawing the two movements together remains a crucial issue. It is clear that a gendered account of this engagement can offer a meaningful analysis of social change. Examining the complex relationship between identity formation as a social process and collective action is crucial to understanding the newly emerging political activism of, and theory building by, disabled women. The last thirty years have seen disabled people organizing themselves across impairment categories to demand changes to social structures. Instrumental has been the fight to redefine disability as a form of oppression, not a biological medical condition. What is now popularly known as the social interpretation of disability made a crucial distinction between impairment as the functional limitation within the individual, and disability as the loss of opportunities due to physical and social barriers. The commonality between the disability and women's movement has been the assertion that both disability and gender then are social constructs predicated upon physical characteristics. Hence, both the disability movement and the women's movement have argued that society should be changed in order to include all its citizens irrespective of their biology. Notwithstanding the similarities, disabled people often confront a normative culture both in India and the world over that carries existential and aesthetic anxieties about difference which gets constructed as a deficit and a lack. They have thus experienced acute marginalization, discrimination and stigmatization. As is always the case, disability is much harder for women as the internalizations that disabled women carry in such a cultural milieu make disability a personal tragedy to be borne alone. As a fellow disabled Ayesha Vernon puts it, 'Social relations of domination shape our lives according to the number of privileges or penalties scored depending on the number of norms an individual conforms to or deviates from respectively' (Vernon 1998). It is true though that disabled women, in general, do not deal with the same oppressions that non-disabled women do primarily because disabled women are not seen as women in an able-bodied society. For example, women with disabilities have not been 'ensnared' by many of the social expectations that feminists have challenged. However, this confinement is actually indicative of a negative rendering of their lives as the usual roles such as marriage and motherhood are out of bounds for them. While it is true that the specific issues for women with disabilities may vary from those of non-disabled women, the reality of womanhood which includes the usual experiences and fears of a patriarchal society are bound to be similar. However, with a body that does not 'measure up' to the societal norm, the situation becomes precariously unbalanced. Janet Price and Margrit Shildrick suggest that, 'Given that all women are positioned in relation to and measured against an inaccessible body ideal, in part determined by a universalized male body, the experience of female disablement as such may be seen as the further marginalization of the already marginal' (Price and Shildrick 1999, 434).

The reality however is that disability is represented as a deficiency that becomes the defining characteristic of the person and is accounted for mostly in terms of a medicalized biography. Constituted as being profoundly 'Other', disability symbolically represents lack, tragic loss, dependency and abnormality. Such understandings do not take into account the fact that human minds and bodies are always in transition, moving from an incomplete, imperfect and vulnerable existence to a relatively autonomous existence. The possibility of this movement, however, has not been accorded to the disabled, as it is believed that she/he does not have to deal with the vulnerabilities or lack, unlike the whole person who has to come to terms with it and therefore suffers the experience of marginalization by what disabled women would consider their own fraternity and natural ally. A closer analysis reveals that this exclusion of disabled women was a consequence of theoretical and activist orientations which presumed that the general rubric of 'woman' is all inclusive. However, the universalism was problematized by passing through a progression which goes through a patronizing tokenism, by arguing that though the exclusion of disability was real, the system was helpless to challenge the perfectionist norms of a biased society. The rationalization has been that there are too many issues to be confronted, a resource crunch, and possibly the anxieties associated with bodily disintegration. If at all the gender dimension has been considered, it has been through a 'double disadvantage' hypothesis. The feminist discourse in the west attempted to connect disability theory and feminism by arguing that disabled women must deal with the twofold but separate oppressions of being a woman in a sexist society and being disabled in an able-normative society. Once each oppression has been charted out, one can then 'add' the two together to understand the disabled women's oppression. In other words a disabled woman faces dual oppressions, one on the level of 'disability', the other on the level of 'gender'. Both the identities are similar in that neither impairment nor sex in and of themselves is problematic or difficult—that is, they become a problem only when placed in a social context that is designed to be unwelcoming to those biological characteristics.

So, if the reality of disabled women's lives is to be comprehended, the negativity associated with both sex and impairment needs to be visualized. Further, their interaction in formulating a 'dual oppression' for disabled women has to be understood. Many feminist thinkers in the field of disability have objected to this double disadvantage, as such writings, they believe, do not empower. In fact, the rendering of disabled women's lives in terms of compound and unique kinds of oppression is burdensome. While we have to find a way of making our experiences visible, sharing with non-disabled people, both men and women, we do not have to do it in a way which undermines our wish to assert our self worth. An 'additive' framework in which the attempt is to understand separate oppressions and then add them back together as if that would explain the whole experience marks this kind of thinking. An implicit assumption of this model is that gender, disability, impairment, and sex are binaries. As a result, disabled women are theorized by adding the two 'biological foundations' of sex and impairment together to conclude that disabled women are oppressed along the twin axes of gender and disability. The approach very clearly rests on biological determinism. From a feminist perspective, this demands the acceptance of the position that such social constancies cannot be transformed.

Another challenge was/is that disability within women studies is used almost synonymously with the identity of being a 'woman' such that its specific character does not receive its due and is lost in the concern for women's rights in general. It is true that in a country like India, where there are innumerable problematic issues, some prioritization does take place. However, for the disabled women the resulting scenario becomes a replication of the patriarchal order where the male order decides on what the agenda and priorities of human life should be. However, it is not uncommon to hear that 'Being a woman is the biggest form of disability' or that we are all disabled or that disability is like belonging to the lowest caste possible. There are several ways of understanding these analogies. One option is to look at the socio-cultural meanings ascribed to female bodies and those assigned to disabled bodies. Both the female and the disabled body are excluded from full participation in public and economic spheres; both are conceived in opposition to a norm that is assumed to possess natural superiority. Such comparisons can be both emancipatory and oppressive. If the objective of invoking such comparisons is to understand different people's lived experience and grasp their authenticity, the potential is immense. However, if the underlying realities of the categories serve only at a metaphorical level, it can lead to a total erasure of the category which is being invoked. It is true that analogy is a theoretical device that is meant to enable the move from more familiar to relatively unknown terrain in order to understand how a set of relations evident in one sphere might illuminate the other. However, if a comparison or the parallel pits one set of relations against the other, as is the case of women against disability, the strategic advantage of the analogy gets lost.

I want to problematize such metaphorical moves, as there is a lot that gets 'suppressed' in the process. The harsh reality of disabled women's lives is limited by conditions that are much more difficult to transcend. A shift from the metaphorical to the material is essential to render visible the 'culture constructions' that have supported the currently flawed conceptualizations of disability and womanhood. In fact, a careful analysis of such metaphors is required to unearth their meanings and functions, so that their power can be subverted. Till the popular refrain that being a woman is the biggest form of disability operates, the road to emancipation/empowerment is going to be a difficult one. It forecloses the possibilities of a meaningful dialogue of the category that is being used as a symbol. Consequently the emancipatory possibilities are lost, as attention is focused on the main object, women in this case, leading to the marginalization of the disabled voices, which for cultural reasons have anyway never been heard. It would perhaps be wiser to recall Trinh Minh-ha's caution, 'Theory is no longer theoretical when it loses sight of its own conditional nature, takes no risks in speculation and circulates as a form of administrative inquisition. Theory oppresses when it wills or perpetuates existing power relations, when it presents itself as a means to exert authority—the voice of knowledge' (Trinh Minh-ha 1989, 42). I hope the present endeavour will underscore the reality that for the Indian feminist— to borrow Jane Flax's terminology—'the model person in feminist theory still appears to be a self sufficient individual adult' (Flax 1987, 640).

I am also weary of establishing hierarchies of oppression. In recognizing the pitfalls of identity politics, Pratibha Parmar cautions us of the ways in which identity politics employs a language of authentic subjective experience. As Parmar explains, identity politics has 'given rise to a self-righteous assertion that if one inhabits a certain identity, this gives one the legitimate and moral right to guilt-trip others into particular ways of behaving' (Parmar 1990, 107). Parmar illustrates this by taking the example of the women's movement, which has experienced problems because of such tendencies. Parmar adds, 'There has been an emphasis on accumulating a collection of oppressed identities which in turn have given rise to a hierarchy of oppression.

Such scaling has not only been destructive, but divisive and immobilizing' (Ibid.). As is clearly evident from Parmar's thesis, the danger vested in such identity politics is that both difference and identity get organized into hierarchies. The right to speak therefore becomes a matter of collecting oppression indicators. If one can establish the authenticity of one's victimization, one will have both moral and political rights.

Another area in which I sense challenges is in the contested meaning of care. It is possible to identify many different approaches to care. Nowhere is this difference clearer than in the contrasting ways in which caring is described by feminist scholars and disability activists. This difference is, in part, one of emphasis. Generally, for feminist scholars, the emphasis is on the giver of care (usually female); whilst in disability studies the recipient of care (male or female) is the locus of interest. Given the political agenda and standpoint of these two social movements, the contrast in focus is understandable. However, whilst these groups have a different agenda, both regard the parties involved in the caring relationship as constituted and colonized by its dynamic. Yet this dynamic is envisaged in different ways. As Bill Hughes, Linda McKie, Debra Hopkins and Nick Watson put it, 'Despite its empirical vicissitudes and even the violence that sometimes accompany it, there is a tendency in feminist thought to valorize the caring relationship for its potential to symbolize and be the very embodiment of genuine intimacy and reciprocity that cannot find expression in a society dominated by the male imaginary. For disabled people especially care is often demonized and its organization is regularly represented as a significant barrier to the emancipation and independence of disabled people' (Hughes et al 2005, 260). My contention is that the feminization of care in a phallocentric culture makes participants in the caring relationship—regardless of gender identity—necessarily subordinate.

This assumption by feminist researchers, that a split exists between women who care and 'dependent' people (whose gender is irrelevant), denies the reality that most people being cared for are women, too. It also obscures the fact that many people who need help with daily living tasks are also looking after others. By redefining independence as having choice and control over the assistance required rather than doing everything yourself, disabled people do not want or need 'care' but instead want their rights as citizens recognized. Even if dependency is recognized as an essential part of the human condition this should not obscure the fact that some people's experience of some bodies (their impairment) places them at much greater risk of losing their human (and civil) rights than the majority of the population. Someone who, for example, does not use speech to communicate, has a high level of cognitive impairment, and/or relies on others for help with all their bodily functions. While it may help to recognize the way we are all— as social beings—dependent on one another, I would argue that limitations can be qualitatively different. To depend on others for assistance in intimate tasks is not the same as depending on a mechanic to service your car. In each situation, we want the assistance to be reliable and competent, and we want to be treated with respect, but there are qualitative differences in the experiences which are rooted in the experience of impairment. There is research by Julia Twigg on older people's experiences of being given a bath: 'One person, strong and able, stands above and over another who is frail and physically vulnerable, forced to rely on their strength and goodwill. Being naked in the face of someone who is not, contains a powerful dynamic of domination and vulnerability, and it is often used in situations of interrogation and torture as a means of subjugating the individual' (2000, 21).

The ethics of care therefore has to begin from the position that everyone has the same human rights, also recognizing the additional requirements that some people have in order to access those human rights. The recognition of our difference (including our dependence), because of our impairments is critical. Within this context, I think the state definitely has to be involved in providing support so that both women as well as the disabled woman do not get the sole responsibility.

One apparent solution is to remove disabled people from being born and this brings me to abortion rights. Abortion is a central issue for both the disability movement and feminism. Disabled people have been highly critical of prenatal screening and selective abortion, seeing them as a new strategy of eugenics. Non-disabled feminists, however, have largely welcomed prenatal testing, seeing it as another means through which women can gain control over their own reproduction. There seems then to be a conflict between this feminist perspective on abortion, and a disability rights perspective. The new reproductive techniques reinforce the notion that there is an ideal that humanity must aspire for. Such a position looks at disability as deficit. However, this approach is like a slippery slope to other forms of selection, and thus eventually to a world of new 'designer baby' eugenics. If new technologies make it possible to fulfil desires and satisfy preferences, is that reason enough to use them? More precisely: If we can, does that mean we ought? If you are going to be consistent about choice, then why stop at impairment? However this then runs counter to the idea that women can never be conscious agents. Then how are we to make sense of such a scenario? Regretting choices that women are compelled to make is not the same as saying that they are participating in discrimination. Instead it points to the ways in which woman too are delimited by the burden of knowledge. Our fantasy might be that women should avoid selection. However, it is unjust to demand that they should not abort when the problem lies not with their individual choice, but in the context in which choice is taken. What is perhaps required is an analysis of screening that can reflect on the social values and structural inequalities that promote the choice. Therefore if prenatal screening is to be made available, it must be accompanied by efforts to re-educate the public, including prospective parents, about disabled people's lives. It has to be coupled with efforts to improve financial and other support systems for disabled people and their families. To my mind these dangers need to be acknowledged.

Further, I think the challenge is to redefine women studies departments and curricula to include disability issues. It would be helpful to understand how the discourses of critical disability studies deconstruct and transform oppressive ideological and professional practices experienced by disabled people. The persistent assumption that disability is a self-evident condition of physical inadequacy and private misfortune whose politics concern only a minority of women needs to be exposed. It is not possible to re-theorize, rethink and re-imagine disability as a social category till an academic engagement can be created. While deconstruction can assist in breaking down the binary oppositions, the task does not end there. The idea of the temporarily able bodied (TAB) is an indicator of the precariousness of human existence, and is extremely helpful in destabilizing the binaries of health/ill health, non-disabled/disabled. Thus, the boundaries which divide us into categories are tangentially wobbly, such that constant replication is needed to keep them in check. In a similar way as we perform our gendered/disabled/sexed/impaired identities, we also need to perform what is expected of a healthy body, so that it is not tainted with bodily breakdown. The negation of binary thought opens up the realm of continual negotiation, within which it might be possible to work towards a truly inclusive society. However, it will be vital to remember that this is not a one time attempt. It has to be conceptualized as a process so that an analytical stance can be generated. A feminist underpinning of disability thus has the potential to question those norms that fail to fully contain or express their ideal standards.

Perhaps it would also help to problematize 'feminist' writings within disability that prioritize subjective experience over more theoretical explanations of disablement. Though experience is the starting point for the production of feminist knowledge, experience alone cannot help in understanding the processes and practices that have to be seen as constituent parts of feminist epistemologies or knowledge frameworks. To repeat and describe what women might have to say, while important, can lead to individualization and fragmentation instead of analysis. Feminism has to go beyond the experiential level. As a woman who supports the collective emancipation of both women and disabled people, I think women's studies can evolve frameworks which are completely commensurate with social interpretations of disability. The recognition that the personal is political is shaped by culture with all its prejudices. When individuals who somehow embody difference are asked to share their experiences this may serve to reinforce rather than challenge the objectified otherness of the person who is cast as the other. It is for this reason that it is significant to understand that disabled women embody a complex of interlocking situations. To quote Eli Clare, 'Gender reaches into disability; disability wraps around class; class strains against abuse; abuse snarls into sexuality; sexuality folds on top of race ... Everything finally piling into a single human body' (Clare 1999, 123).

References

Blackwell-Stratton, Marion, et al. 1997. Smashing icons: Disabled women and the disability and women's movements. In *Women transforming politics: An alternative reader,* ed. Cathy Cohen, Kathleen B. Jones and Joan Tronto. New York: New York University Press.

Clare, Eli. 1999. *Exile and pride: Disability, queerness and liberation.* Boston: South End Press.

Flax, Jane. 1987. Postmodernism and gender relations in feminist theory. *Signs* 12, no. 4: 621–43.

Hughes B., et al. 2005. Love's labours lost? Feminism, the disabled people's movement and an Ethic of care. *Sociology* 39, no.2.

Parmar, Pratibha. 1990. Black feminism: The politics of articulation. In *Identity, community, culture, difference,* ed. Jonathan Rutherford. London: Lawrence and Wishart.

Price, Janet and Margrit Shildrick, ed. 1999. *Feminist theory and the body: A reader.* New York: Routledge.

Minh-ha, Trinh T. 1989. *Woman native other: Writing, postcoloniality and feminism,* Bloomington: Indiana University Press.

Twigg, Julia. 2000. *Bathing: The body and community care.* New York: Routledge.

Vernon, Ayesha. 1998. Multiple oppressions and the disability people's movement. In *The disability reader: Social science perspectives,* ed. Tom Shakespeare. London: Cassell, 201–10.

9

≈

HOUSEHOLD AND FAMILY

This theme on the household and family throws up some of the most interesting questions for women's studies and the women's movement. The very fact that this section has not simply been titled 'the family' is indicative of the presence of multiple approaches towards the so-called private or domestic domain. To put it most simply, the sphere of the family has rarely, if ever, been treated as the primary root of patriarchy, as has been more common elsewhere. Moreover, earlier sections have already introduced us to the family—in the context of forms of violence, in relation to the law, in the world of politics and of development. Subsequent sections will continue to show how existing conceptions of the family have had to be revised and rethought.

How, then, has the domestic sphere of gender relations been approached by feminist scholars? The essays in this section offer a few examples. The first two pieces draw attention to the concept of the household (as distinct from that of the family) and from different disciplinary and methodological perspectives. Devaki Jain and Nirmala Banerjee, in this excerpt from their introduction to an early volume on women's work entitled *The Tyranny of the Household*, are particularly keen to address and draw from the discipline of economics to make their arguments. Recognizing that the family has been seen as one of the strongholds of women's oppression the world over, Jain and Banerjee nonetheless privilege the household—defined through residence, labour and the individuals within it—rather than the family, 'worshipped' as the realm of mutual relationships. Opening up the economic world within the household offers a sharper perspective on existing patterns of inequality and the divergent experiences of its members, especially in contexts of poverty where the family falls apart. In the following essay, Rajni Palriwala demonstrates the usefulness of ethnographic description for understanding processes of change in intra-household relations in rural Rajasthan. The special focus in this excerpt is the sphere of consumption in patrilineal households, where women do possess a certain authority, unlike in the sphere of production, which tends to be in the hands of men. Palriwala describes the complex transactions and conflicts over something as seemingly mundane as the serving of food, to show just what spaces are available to different women for exercising control in a situation of dependency.

The next essay introduces a familiar figure in the history of the women's movement, namely the widow. The unprotected wife who has lost her husband was central to the earliest public campaigns of the nineteenth century in regions like Bengal and Maharashtra. In this piece, Jaya Srivastava describes the widows of 1984, those Sikh women whose husbands were brutally and deliberately killed in the anti-Sikh riots that broke out in Delhi in the wake of the assassination of Indira Gandhi. Against the backdrop of the existing trauma of the riots and orchestrated massacre of young able-bodied men, Srivastava's main concern is to question the mechanisms invoked by families and by community panchayats to 'solve' these widows' victimhood. Srivastava alludes to their own work in one of the resettlement colonies, where the effort was to rebuild these women's lives against massive odds. However, for these women the biggest struggle has been to see justice delivered by the state—in spite of all the evidence available, not one perpetrator has been indicted so far.

Marriage, too, is an 'old' question from the colonial period, going back to campaigns to raise the age of marriage. However, while marriage relations have, since the 70s, been the context for agitations against dowry and domestic violence, or again, for legal debates on divorce and the role of family courts, feminist scholarship has not engaged with the contemporary institution of marriage as much as one might have expected. (This is all the more telling when one notices the near universal status of marriage in India, and the extent of its normative hold on society.) The present essay by Amita Tyagi and Patricia Uberoi offers an unusual view into the ideology of romance and marriage, through the lens of popular fiction. Analyzing the short story feature of the hugely popular magazine *Woman's Era* (which has outstripped older and glossier magazines like *Femina*), they make an important comparison with Harlequin (Mills and Boon) romances. While stories of love and courtship are also to be found in the pages of *Woman's Era*, it is life after marriage that is the more interesting subject of many of these tales, not the romance that leads up to it. This body of fiction and its 'adjustments', the advice columns, (and the sociological literature shaping this ideological domain for readers) offer a challenge to feminism that has not been sufficiently engaged with.

The final contribution to this section is a discussion on the uniform civil code by Brinda Karat. The entire set of civil laws pertaining to marriage and divorce, inheritance and succession, custody and adoption, effectively address themselves to women's legal rights within the family. Due to colonial intervention these laws have come under the jurisdiction of state enacted religious laws, and the question of whether this legacy should be changed in favour of a common code governing all citizens has been amongst the most long drawn out and complex battles to have been fought in the women's movement. It would be impossible to provide an overview of this history here. Instead, we offer one of many voices in order to show the range of issues that have come to attach to this debate on gender equality in the family domain. Karat's essay underscores the extent to which many feminists have in fact distanced themselves from an initial position in favour of demanding a common code for all. Her discussions not only contextualize the debate within the heightened communalization and minoritization of Muslims and Christians today, but show how even the desire for a complete overhauling of all laws would need to work step by step, taking each issue at a time. A good indication of the fluidity within the contemporary situation can be gauged from the fact that some of the issues she raises—such as the obstacles encountered in the reform of Christian law on marriage and divorce, and the absence of legislation on domestic violence—have since been overcome, though not without controversy.

Here, then, are glimpses into the interlinked domains of household and family, as these have been identified by activists and scholars. One might venture to say that while certain dimensions, such as the economic and legal aspects of women's domestic lives, have seen considerable engagement, others remain less explored. Questions of marriage, including remaining outside marriage (whether by choice or otherwise) have not been on many agendas; it is perhaps not accidental that the most direct critiques of marriage as an institution have come from queer perspectives, as has been articulated in the section on Sexualities by Rinchin later on this volume. It is also remarkable how little we have had to say about parenting and the entire domain of children, outside of critiques of population policies and the two-child norm, or the state's Integrated Child Development Schemes (ICDS). We live in a media saturated culture that is constantly updating its efforts to resolve the problems of the new woman of the twenty-first century—and here, too, engagement has been few and far between. Essays in the next sections will have more to say about what ongoing and fresh battles, cutting across the private and public spheres, need to be taken further in order to confront the many tyrannies of the 'household–family domain'.

〜

THE TYRANNY OF THE HOUSEHOLD
Devaki Jain and Nirmala Banerjee

A perception which arises out of the studies of family and household, from the point of gender, is the troubled question of the traditional hierarchies associated with these forms of organization. Family with father and mother or husband and wife, the rituals that have gone into marriage, the rules of behaviour, and the role allocations that have been spelt out, sometimes provide an impossible barrier to equality between the sexes. Thus it is a common phenomena all over the world and across history—that, as women begin to feel their way and wish to affirm some autonomy for themselves, some freedom to choose and fulfill their individuality, the first institution that begins to crack is the family. It is understandable that today, women, whether in the first world, the socialist world or the third world, often attack the institution of the family as one of the strongholds of female oppression and want to challenge this concept, and ask for space to create new families.

These new families would try to have the sense of bonding, of responsibility, of social security, of even continuity as the old families had, but they would also provide the individuals choices in coming together, and building a relationship on their own terms, and not on terms handed to them by antiquity, traditions, ideology—most of which stemmed from patriarchy or male attitudes to female capabilities and roles.

It is difficult to demarcate, but it is important to show that the household as a concept does not necessarily come under the same form of attack because it is associated with residence. Yet, since very often the two are taken as one and the same, and since household is the term used more frequently in economic and statistical analysis, a detailed examination of the dynamics of the household is important. It can help not only to examine the types of tyrannies as well as possibilities that exist in the household, but also to see how far the concept of household can be reorganized to provide the kind of organization that women may want to belong to, especially in the developing world.

Family and household are not the same entity either conceptually or in relation to statistical theory and method. Household is usually defined in terms of residence or habitat and family in terms of something more intimate in human terms of relationships. In some ways the word family is used for representing the most primary form of social organization by sociologists whereas the term household is used by economists and statisticians, but again with the same purpose, namely, as the ultimate or primary unit of organization.

We have concepts like household occupation, household enterprise, household type, which are similar but not the same as family occupation, family enterprise or family type. A household may be engaged predominantly in a certain occupation but that may not be the family occupation or the family enterprise. Family occupation and enterprise seem to suggest either ownership by the family or some traditional homogeneous type of skill or activity.

Yet, analytically, especially when we look at age and sex-based inequalities within these two forms of social and economic organizations, we find that the two are not very different whether within the household or within the family. Both in terms of allocation of social powers and in the allocation of physical items, women are always lower in the hierarchy. Further, if sometimes they do have positions of social power within the family due to age or custom or what are called the rules of conduct, this is certainly not associated with economic power, namely control over resources, incomes and their distribution.

Thus, it could be said that it is more often the case that the household more than the family contains or conceals within it gender-based inequalities. It is often also suggested that this inequality strides across the usual barriers of stratification such as class, caste, race and religion. It is even suggested that while in a highly stratified society like India it is difficult to justify gender as a basis of social and political formation, as gender too is riven by class, caste and religion based distances, if conceptually we move away from *inter-household* distances to *intra-household* analysis, it is possible to find the basis for such formations. In other words, whereas clustering by class or caste is done on the basis of *units of household* clusters; clusterings on the basis of gender could be derived form the intra-household characterization, *units of individuals*. By emphasizing individual autonomy, perhaps women would provide a strategy for all, that is women, men and children. In other words, women's choices of alternative paths to progress would establish opportunities for all.

Thus, women from within households have the common experience of facing different forms of intra-household subordination whatever the class or caste, and this common experience within this world of the household could not only provide the basis of organization but also provide perspectives which could be called feminism, or the method and articulation of women.

Today, amongst the poor in rural areas, whether they are scheduled castes or not, poverty and unemployment are so acute that there is a great push towards various types of migration which has also diluted the family. Then there is the economic phenomenon of female-headed household where women are bread-winners and nurturers. Family, therefore, is not a crucial foundation for these classes and castes.

In the Indian context, where the tradition of family, its bonds, its interdependence, its burning loyalty to each other are worshipped, whether they are real or not, the way the scenario is usually painted is to suggest that the family is a homogeneous unit. Individuals work towards the optimization of family well-being. In other words, the interest of all members of the family would naturally coincide, as each of them would be working not for himself, but for the benefit of all the interconnected units. A father would labour to bring home bread for the rest of the family, the women, the children, his parents, perhaps even his brothers and sisters. The women and children in turn would work to look after each other and the rest. If one person in a family is called to represent the family, or given access to development opportunities, the interest of all would be covered, and, further, if information is being gathered for a decision-making purpose, whether it is to design a programme of benefits, whether to collect an opinion on the wider polity, or on local crises, one person from the family, male or female, should be able to reflect that family's needs.

This is perhaps quite all right when the family does have a lifestyle where there is some sharing of information, even if not sharing of tasks, and when there is at least a basic minimum wherewithal which does not require difficult decisions of distribution within the family. In other words, this is a fair presumption in families like yours and mine.

But in a household with a crisis for survival, with insufficient resources, at the lowest levels of poverty, the patterns of family life are different. Man, woman and child are all endeavouring to keep themselves alive through some activity, whether it is to dig for roots, to examine garbage for waste, or to travel long distances for wage work. There is not much time to share each other's lives around a family hearth or sitting room. Lives, by necessity, get acutely segregated both in space and in tasks and to that extent perceptions are limited to personal experience.

Men may know that their women are working hard to fetch water and fuel, to tend children or cattle, but they may not know how hard and at what cost. Women may know that their men are labouring for a wage, that a job may be humiliating and enervating—but they may not know what the men know. Domains of experience become thickly demarcated and so ignorance gets petrified. Individual members of the family are unable to speak for the others and those who have less access to this tool of communication, such as women and children, remain neglected.

Little children do not know family as we know it. What do the little children of construction workers in Delhi know of family, or of any social institution such as a school? They know rubble, they know one parent—or perhaps not even a parent—a sibling. They grow up without a neighbourhood, seeing large numbers of men and women working around them. Similarly, what would a child from Ratnagiri or from Tehri Garhwal know of family? The father may be away in Delhi working as a cook or a driver, if from Tehri Garhwal, or in Bombay, if from Ratnagiri.

Much has been written about the sociological family—the customary formal, non-formal rules and procedures that operate within it. But the sociological family is different from the economic family—and the economic family, especially amongst the poor, has not been studied sufficiently. These households are not institutions with rules and regulations. Their autonomy is a fiction—and the usual argument that any interference with allocation within the household is aggression on the household's autonomy, a convenient and cruel morality or moral blindness. Where there are no choices, what freedoms are we taking away?

The much studied sociological family is often described as the microcosm of the world—or larger society. It may not be sufficiently realized how true this is of the economic family—for this economic household contains in it the economic characteristics of the larger world: namely unequal distribution of economic power; benefits related to ownership, capital, access, responsibility and gender. The less the resources in a family, the greater the inequality within it.

Many societies have attempted to move away from family to new forms of collective organization. The communes of China and Vietnam, the Kibbutz of Israel, the ashrams of Gandhi, and even the new communities in Europe and North America are examples of this thrust.

But while most of them arose out of an interest in reorganizing production and distribution, Gandhi's effort arose out of a recognition of the tyranny of the family on women. He wrote:

Marriage is probably the oldest social institution and the most abused . . .
In this unequal struggle of women against social tyrannies imposed on them, nothing has played so crucial a part as marriage. It is in fact the base from which the continuous attacks on them are made. For men it is a cloak which covers a multitude of their failings, the betrayals of their social obligations.

He saw role allocation, whether between men and women, or between castes and classes, as the source of stigma and subordination. So he made an attempt to make manual work, night-soil lifting, kitchen work and sewing, tasks for all men and women who lived in an ashram. Today, when women find the family tyrannical—in the West or East—they demand an end to role stereotyping. [. . .]

∽

ECONOMICS AND PATRILINY:
CONSUMPTION AND AUTHORITY WITHIN
THE HOUSEHOLD
Rajni Palriwala

In this paper, I make some tentative attempts at tackling . . . the question as to why women seem so concerned with maintaining their 'family', with fostering kinship ties and values, when these evidently are the immediate structures constraining them. [. . .] I examine the effects of the growth of a money economy and a shift away from the household as the unit of production and/or management on the social and economic strategy of households. These in turn are related to the form and notions of patriliny, in which the nature of patrilineal property and patrivirilocal residence are central, defining women's rights and women's place. The dynamics of intra-household consumption are analyzed in this context. [. . .]

The issues raised in this paper are discussed in the context of Panchwas village in Sikar district. [. . .] In early 1981, there were 272 households in the village, and the composition of around 62% was other than simple (or elementary), indicating the significance of complex household living. There were fourteen Hindu and Muslim castes in the village, covering the range of the caste hierarchy. Jats formed 53% of the village population, balais (chamars) and naiks over 14% and Muslims nearly 15%. [. . .]

Intra-household authority and consumption

Normatively, the household head was always the senior-most male. All members were expected to submit to the authority of the head in terms of income pooling, cash expenditures and any actions seen as effecting the social and political relations of the household. He was also the ultimate authority in labour allocation and distribution of consumption. A household head was expected to consult other household members, particularly men and senior women. However, nobody was expected to question the head once he took a decision. The presumption was that the head, having the most complete knowledge regarding household matters, would have taken the decision in the interests of the unit, for the family good.

The women of the household were under the triple authority of the senior women—the wife or the mother of the male head of the household—their own husbands and the head. Rules of avoidance and segregation led to the appearance of two separate but inter-locking lines of authority. In practice, the authority of the male head depended on his age and the kinship composition of the household. Youth and very old age, widow (-er) hood or absence due to migration generally reduced the control of both the male head and the female manager.

The management of various spheres of activities, including maintenance of required tools, etc, rested primarily on that household member who was seen as having the knowledge and responsibility of ensuring that work was done. With regard to many operations there was no real decision to be taken or the decision was not in fact an intra–household one. Cultivation, carpentry, leatherwork were primarily male responsibilities. The senior woman, as long as she was capable, was in charge of housework, day-to-day consumption and livestock production. If there was conflict in agricultural work it could be between men, between women, and/or between men and women. In 'work in the house' it would be between women. Conflict over work was usually expressed in terms of a perceived discrepancy between work performed and access to consumption goods.

The dynamics of food consumption and control were, in a sense, the baseline for intra-household distribution and authority, and are examined to provide an understanding of them. Ideally, there was little inter-household variation. In practice, caste and religion tied in with economic levels and hence migration (which was influenced by access to traditional skills) to introduce some distinctions. Together these aspects mediated intra-household tensions and division of labour and ideals of status and respectability, leading to a modification in absolute levels of consumption, in household composition and formation, and the attainment of seniority and headship by women and men.

Generally, it was held that women controlled the household grain stocks. They took out the daily or weekly requirements as needed. Most households had an estimate of per day and per annum grain requirements. While these tended to be on the high side, and could be upset by sudden and fluctuating changes in the household composition or number of guests, possibilities of manipulating stocks were narrow. Control was limited for both women and men by the fact that 55% households did not grow enough grain for their annual requirements. Even those which did often had to buy items such as cooking oil and vegetables. In a situation of deficiency, any avenues of manipulation open to women were likely to be used to obtain items of daily consumption for household members, particularly children.

Women managed only that grain which was brought to the house and even then could not deny men access. [. . .]

Despite the ideal of prior consultation, men did not always do so. A woman's options were few if a man insisted on his decision. If there was serious depletion of stocks, especially due to profligate spending, she could ask her kin to remonstrate with him, but intra-household and affinal conflict and tension developed. In two cases I knew of, one jat and one balai, men sold grain to buy alcohol and the women resisted until they were beaten. In a manihar household, a young man took grain to pay for a pleasure trip to Sikar, despite his mother's refusal.

Commercialization and a money economy were diversifying men's options but whittling away women's control. Increasingly, they were dependent on male wages and salaries, on men buying and stocking wheat or bajra for household use from 'their' earnings. Earlier constraints on women's management were exacerbated, and their control diminished, both as normative right and in practice.

Serving food, deciding what and how much to serve whom, was a responsibility/right women jealously guarded. The household did not eat together in one sitting. The various items making up the real meal were served to each individual in a large plate (*thali*) by the senior woman, or another woman to whom she had delegated the task. Norms said that a person must accept what they were served, and the server must take into account the former's status in the household. Nobody, including the head, could serve himself, due to reasons of purity maintenance and the etiquette of the division of labour. The earner, the household head, however, could demand. Children protested any perceived favouritism or demanded any extras they knew of. A woman could face the situation, considered 'reprehensible' by villagers, where a young son physically forced her to give *ghee* or some other item.

The possibilities and area of manipulation and discrimination were largely limited to special foods, such as milk products, sweets cooked at festivals or when there was a visitor, tea and vegetables, and through reduction of the woman's own consumption. This depended on the household's subsistence status, giving women in surplus agricultural households more scope for exercising their discretion. In situations of deficit, conflict over suspected discrimination was likely to increase. This was evident in the presence of a larger percentage of simple households among poor peasants and labourers (of which balais were a significant percentage) than among middle and rich peasants.

As a result of their responsibility for serving food, the onus of providing the means of consumption fell on women in many households, reinforcing constraints on their control. Women faced the brunt of men's anger and children's cries if food was not provided, was not to taste, or was not ready on time. Their particular charge was to provide a *lagan* or accompanying dish to the bread. Barter and 'borrowings' from neighbours and friends was one way to ensure a *lagan* at least for the household head. Pathan women used their tie-and-die income, expressed as for their personal expenses, to buy vegetables or tea leaves. *Ghee* money (from sales of butter), notionally women's income, was so used by jat women.

The nature and perception of control over day-to-day consumption is well illustrated by an incident in a purely agricultural jat household, consisting of a couple and their young children. The husband and wife were having an argument—part serious, part mock. They asked their daughter, Kamala, whom she would side with. At first Kamala said her mother, because who would feed her if her mother refused to serve her? A little later, she said, 'But no, I should side with my father, for it is he who earns and brings the grain, and what if he refuses to do so?' Finally, in a quandary, Kamala remained undecided.

A common saying was that a household was made or broken by the skill and thrift of its womenfolk in managing household stocks. If the latter wished, they could barter it away on fripperies for themselves, for their daughters, or to take back to their natal homes. Barter was one way in which households short of cash expected to acquire consumption articles. Women, particularly, had little or no direct access to cash. They obtained tea leaves and sugar from the village shop, or cloth, thread, combs and lace from itinerant traders in barter. These dealings were often a secret from men, especially when there were differences over items of expenditure. However, the generation and age hierarchy, which gave control of household stocks only to the senior woman, denied junior women even these possibilities.

A range of women agreed that 'there are few women who do not wish their marital households to prosper; ultimately we do not gain by frittering away household stocks on only ourselves or on those who are not members of our households'. Women who could and did do so were few and far between. Women continued to be economically and socially dependent on their homes for subsistence. Their personal status also depended on their reputation as skilled housewives. However, while accepting the idea of family needs, they insisted that items classed as useless trifles were often essential in ritual exchange or prestations, necessary for both daughters' well-being and maintenance of the household's status vis-à-vis the affinal household. Men talked of them as wasteful, but would blame women if the household suffered 'face' because these gifts were not given.

Contradictions in norms and women's direct responsibility meant that tension over consumption was likely to get expressed in anger with or conflict between women. This was made more likely as day-to-day consumption was one of the few areas in which women exercised some authority. They used it to strengthen their situation in a social and economic context which defined them as ultimately dependent on men and their personal influence over household members. This was magnified with the increased significance of individual male incomes in the household economy.

[. . .] A woman's hope of achieving status in her marital home was through her sons. The mother–son bond, viewed as especially tender, was succoured by women as their one support and security. Women [. . .] used their control over daily consumption to discipline young children and instil a feeling in them that their mothers exercised power. They used it to play one son off against another, or to give the emigrant special treatment on his return. 'He had been denied good home food, though he had been working hard to earn money for the household.' She also hoped to ensure that he was favourably disposed towards her. The women who gained most influence in their marital homes were those who had been successful in the above and had been able to contain possible tensions. Suspicions were strongest where the woman manager was the mother or the spouse of the emigrant, and brother's wife to the other men.

[. . .] Leach (1962) argues that any descent system, if it is to be viable, must have areas open to individuals for manipulation to their own benefit. Intra-household day-to-day consumption was such an area for women, who in the course of their life cycle hoped to control it. The knowledge and hope of future power, the apparent exercise of autonomy, gave women an interest in the system, adding to its strength. However, on examining women's authority, it can be clearly seen that the agenda and the options had been fixed before the actual decision-making, as Lukes (1974) points out in his discussion of decision-making as power.

The distribution of food was governed by rules and values, internalized from infancy onwards. Kinship status, specifically agnation, contribution to household income and work, and the concrete context of social relationships were the determinants of intra-household access to consumption. These dimensions could either reinforce or contradict each other, resulting in variations in practice. Adult male agnates had first priority, but the male head of household and the person who 'earned' were first among equals, particularly in the case of delicacies and 'nutritive' items such as *ghee*. The 'earner' was the person who ploughed the land, the main worker in the fields, the manager of household lands, the person who earned a regular non-agricultural income—always a man, except when there was no adult male in the household. Conflict in priority could emerge if the head and the main earner were two different persons, and if household income was low and as the head's authority became a formality.

The old and children had a right to food as agnates and/or because of past labour and future labour respectively. Old men and women continued working at some task or the other, even after retiring from cultivation, rhetorically asking who would feed them otherwise. Children were scolded for playing rather than completing a task their mother had asked them to do, and told not to expect to be fed if they did no work. Simultaneously, kinship and family solidarity dictated the support of agnates, the old, the sick and the young. The old had reared, supported and established the present generation, passing on the basis of livelihood, property and a way of life. The young, particularly sons, were the future support, the heirs, and represented familial continuity. For women, their children rather than their aged in-laws were the loved. Together this meant that often the young were given priority over the aged.

Hence, with the old and the sick, there was often bitterness and suspicion on both sides; the old felt they were mistreated; the present generation resented the former's attempts to retain control. With women living longer than men, the older generation was often represented by an old widow. Thus, this conflict was part of the tension-ridden mother-in-law/ daughter-in-law relationship. Even if it was poverty which led to insufficient food for all, or the household head or 'earner' decided that the old be given only the basics, it was the woman responsible for cooking and serving who was blamed. The mother-in-law socialized new brides into their roles as household manager and food distributor. An oft-repeated saying was that an old woman mistreated by her daughter-in-law had so taught the latter by the example of her own behaviour with her aged mother-in-law. I know of only one case, a balai family regarding which it is openly said that the men in the family for the last three generations had mistreated the old parents and, by example, had taught their wives and children to do the same.

Most people denied discriminating against female children. 'Children are children, whether male or female,' they insisted, and cries of hunger from either are painful for the mother who brought them into the world. Some women said that knowing that their daughters would be denied special foods in their marital homes, they made it a point to serve them what delicacies they could in the years before they left. Villagers asked, 'When as children daughters are a greater help than sons why should they be discriminated against? As goatherds they earn for the household and their own right to consumption.' Goatherds were given little extras to persuade them to spend the day in the sun. Many said that daughters cared more for their parents than sons.

Yet sons were the embodiment of the family's future, and were often favoured with the justification that they must quickly grow into young men and work for the whole family. Furthermore, since a large percentage of households were complex, the mother of the girl was in fact often not the person responsible for serving food. Other women in the household seemed to give into demands of nephews or grandsons more quickly than those of nieces and granddaughters.

[. . .] Evidence contrary to the statements regarding lack of discrimination is fairly overwhelming, in terms of the sex ratio of children in the under-ten age group. It was 884 in Panchwas. Sikar is among the districts in the country with the lowest ratio of young girls to young boys, even though the overall sex ratio is above the all-India average. The higher overall sex ratio may be related to male emigration and the lower sex ratio in the under-ten age group to discrimination between baby girls and boys in food and medical care, as well as differences in nutrition of mothers of sons and of daughters. Alternatively, these contrary sex ratios represent a new trend of devaluation of and bias against female children. [. . .]

New mothers, pregnant women and all other men and women were said to follow in priority in the order listed. The person who cooked and the youngest daughter-in-law, usually the same person, ate last. This itself acted against her, even if there was no conscious discrimination. Thus, after feeding unexpected guests, the person who ate last, the cook, could prefer to do without rather than cook again. In middle peasant households, often there could be no vegetables or lentils left and she made do with a pepper paste and/or *raabri*. In a situation of deficit she went hungry when other household members did not have to.

Normatively, new mothers were given special foods, classed as 'non-heating' and milk-producing, for forty days or so after delivery. Not only was childbirth seen as debilitating, it was literally labour. Actual consumption depended on the economic status of the woman's marital and natal home, and the sex and the serial order of the child. The natal home was expected to provide some of the special diet the new mother would consume. This was often the only extra nutrition she obtained. The mother of a boy was fed special foods for longer than the mother of a girl. Her marital household took greater care and her natal family was expected to send more. People would exclaim, 'If a mother of a son is not fed, who will eat!' This was one more articulation of patriliny, the status of mother of sons being crucial in determining women's access to consumption.

The rights to consumption of women in different castes and classes were discussed in terms of the labour they provided the household. Pathan and charan women among whom norms of *purdah* and seclusion operated such that they were not to work in the fields, would say that jat and balai women had a right to eat because they worked, whereas if nobody gave them food they could not protest as they did not work or earn. [. . .]

Generally female work was valued lower than male work, and the requirements of women were presumed to be less than those of men. Women rarely questioned the valuation that tasks such as ploughing and bunding, men's tasks, were heavier than women's agricultural work. However, they did question the valuation of other tasks, as well as of their requirements relative to those of young non-working males or young emigrants who contributed minimally to household income. Dual residence was used to deny a daughter-in-law's labour, with the statement, 'She works elsewhere (her natal home), and eats here.' However, daughters-in-law did insist that with the long hours they worked—grinding flour, fetching water and cutting grass—they also needed extra nutrition. At the risk of furthering intra-household tensions, they could complain to the husband, to be told that this was for his mother to decide.

In these contexts, labour contribution as a demarcator of rights to the products of labour was overridden, though not without strain and conflict, by interpersonal relations, by income contribution and, crucially, by the parameters of agnation and ownership of property. The last encapsulated the ideas of the male household head and the 'good of the family'. It was the core of the household, the coparceners, the male agnates and their representatives, on whose well-being the good of the household depended, and who had first rights to consumption. The women, whether unmarried or agnatic, had secondary rights, in congruence with their peripheral status in the coparcenary and residual rights in land, and linked to their 'contribution' to the 'family'. The *dhanni* (owner) had first rights to the harvest from his land—part of his identity—as against the worker. Similarly, the lineally ascendant male agnate, the *dhanni,* had prior claims to a child, though there was recognition of the 'labour' the mother contributed in bearing and rearing the child. The male child and the male agnate, the *dhann,* were expressions of each other, not to be lightly separated.

Individuation of property and the significance of individual earnings were acting in concert to strengthen men's consumption rights as against women's. These processes stressed individual male control of property and resources, as against that of the 'family' in which women were perceived as necessary dependents, and were relatively devaluing their work. A woman's present dependence on husbands and sons and future dependence on sons, as well as the normative rights of men, of the *malik,* the *dhanni,* to all household products, and the possibility of physical force, limited women's access to and control over food allocation. The power women exercised was primarily over the work and consumption of daughters-in-law and daughters. It was the circumscribed power of a subordinate category. [. . .]

Working for the family good

Gender, age and kinship hierarchies of agnation, seniority and property were the parameters within which authority, consumption rights and the requirements of various members of a household were played out. Work and income contribution were further delineators, themselves based on a sexual division of labour moderated by caste, class and source of income. The emergent patterns of consumption and authority were integral to definitions of household needs. Economic and employment trends were sharpening the disagreements over valuation of labour and income contribution and thence conflict over consumption, unmasking the true nature of intra-household 'sharing'. Junior men and junior women were interested in establishing households in which they would be in charge, escaping the constraints of age hierarchies. Differences over family strategies, the definitions of family well-being and the needs of various household members were magnifying.

The household, in family ideology, was the patriline. If a household and family were to survive and prosper, men and women, young and old, were essential and had to give and receive their due, which were inherently differential. Ultimately family good meant the maintenance and upward mobility of the male agnatic core. Importantly, women were seen to have no legitimate needs outside common household needs. However, as men mediated between the world and the household, they had individual expenses such as tobacco or a cup of tea in the market. As conflicts developed, women saw these as wasteful rather than as status markers, while men would describe as frivolous the prestations women viewed as essential.

Central to the prosperity of the patriline was the fostering of its social network, oft mobilized for economic and social security, besides expressing status. Women were persons via whom social networks were reaffirmed and expanded in marriage, dowry and continuing affinal prestations. Obligations and rights of daughters and sisters continued even after their marriage, to be balanced against those which were part of their being daughters-in-law. However, this very quality undermined their integration into any one agnatic core.

Ideologically, the household as a concrete unit and expression of family was an individual's primary responsibility, and not any single person who was a member of the unit. It was accepted that persons did develop greater commitment to some members, such as their own children and spouses. However, women's ambiguous membership made their strategies to attach individual men to themselves suspect, especially as obligations to wife, sister, daughter were increasingly cast as fulfilling an individual's needs.

Conflicting pulls over investment in one's social network and fulfillment of obligations to kin versus restriction of the latter to immediate household members or even oneself were continuous. Dowry and gifts to a daughter lessened the immediate economic viability and wealth of her natal household and its agnatic core. The diffusion of dowry practices and inflation in prestations, both at the wedding and after, accentuated the contradiction between retaining wealth and income in the household and giving it away to affines. This was ever more a contradiction between social gain and economic loss, a contradiction between gifts to and desires for an individual's, a daughter's, 'happiness' and the long run economic advancement of the giver's household.

The daughter and sister were cast as liabilities rather than a strategic resource, even among the jats where their labour was recognized, and dowry had been minimal. Similarly daughters-in-law were valued for the goods they brought in. Women's labour was seen to defray the expenses incurred in providing them with prestations rather than contributing to household subsistence, continuity and mobility. Thus, a vicious cycle was established— the devaluation of women's labour and significance for the 'family' and thence her rights to consumption, the justification of dowry in terms of a woman being an economic burden, and demands for prestations feeding into each other.

The shifts in landownership and the pattern of access to new economic opportunities had not seriously upset caste hierarchies or 'traditional' forms of symbolic capital. Behavioural norms for women as well as the normative gender division of labour were reinforced rather than questioned. Developmental processes and the paucity of employment, on the one hand, were resuscitating the need for social networks, collective household strategies and occupational multiplicity. On the other hand, they were demarcating and valourizing individual earners, almost entirely men, and individuating and objectifying patrilineal property, creating the basis for individual rights.

This was reflected in the aspirations of younger men and conflict over the definition of the 'good of the family' and justified expenditure.

Women's economic dependence on husbands and kin had intensified, with crucial implications for their consumption rights, the form in which obligations to them were to be fulfilled and the readiness to do so. Critically, this would intensify the vulnerability of some categories of persons—the landless, widows, divorced and abandoned wives—as their links to networks of support were individualized and lost. As women became increasingly dependent on individual males, tensions between women—between mother-in-law and daughter-in-law or between sisters-in-law—and the control they exercised on each other were exacerbated.

Women's concern to ensure that obligations to daughters and sisters, to affines and other members of the household network were met, that 'family relationships' were kept alive, was central not only to household strategy and deeply embedded moralities, but also to their own personal strategies. Their 'family conservatism' and reassertion of kinship values and sanctions were fuelled by their need to widen their support base, their security net, to resocialize individualized ties, even if these meant a revitalization of those very structures which controlled them.

References

Leach E. 1962. On uncertain unconsidered aspects of double descent systems. *Man* 62, 214.

Lukes, S. 1974. *Power: A radical view.* London: Macmillan.

∿

THE WIDOWS OF NOVEMBER 1984

Jaya Srivastava

Rehabilitation—the word in itself carries connotations of abnormal situations—displacement or evacuation of peoples in the wake of flood, famine, earthquake and drought, or following riots and carnage. The rehabilitation of uprooted peoples must move beyond providing them with the bare physical necessities of a roof and two square meals a day. These people have not only been physically driven out of their habitations, they have had to relinquish their security, culture and an entire way of life, and adapt themselves to completely alien circumstances. In a riot situation, their kith and kin have been wiped out and the entire fabric of their sociocultural existence torn asunder. This is as disastrous as the wanton destruction of life.

It is in this context that the tragedy of women, whether they be war widows or widows of riot killings has to be seen. The added burden of such women in India today is that by virtue of being the second sex, they are already in an inferior position, dominated and ruled by the prevalent 'norms' of Indian society.

Most of the women affected by the carnage of November 1984 have had to bear the multiple trauma of being uprooted at least twice. Some of them came from families driven by the India–Pakistan division of 1947, fled from Sindh and west Punjab. Some of these, mainly the Labhanas of Sindh, first came to Alwar and Bharatpur in Rajasthan, and then to the Sultanpuri–Trilokpuri region of Delhi in search of a livelihood. Most of them had just about managed to settle down to a better life. They talk of how their men folk had finally 'made it' and had begun to fend for their young sons, had just started bringing in a substantial income through rickshaw pulling, *charpoy* weaving, hawking goods or from small repair shops they had set up. This was when tragedy struck again, leaving mothers and housewives helpless witnesses of unimaginable carnage. The scars left on their psyche and on those of their young children and old parents are indelible. A mother watches with glazed eyes by the side of her three-year-old child as she screams through a recurring nightmare. The little one has seen her father's eyes gouged out before he was burnt alive. The average age of these bereft women ranges from 25 to 30 years. Most of them are unskilled. Their families comprise six to seven children and old parents, almost all of whom have seen their dear ones cruelly done to death.

The theory that there was a deliberate design behind these killings gains credence when one notes that it was the young and the able-bodied males that were mowed down, leaving behind 1200 helpless widows unable to fend for themselves, hundreds of aged parents and thousands of fatherless children.

These young widows have not only had to learn to live through it all, but also to make their families survive as well. Most of the women have the inbuilt courage and fortitude to face life. They try to pick up the old threads, if only for the mere survival of their brood, and here comes the rub. The moment they begin to feel life coursing faintly through their veins again, the stringent codes of conduct Indian society lays down for a widow crushes them again into keeping the family's interest and name above their own and their children's hope for a better life.

There were sixty such widows at our centre at Tilak Vihar for the production of garments, west Delhi. In the first few months, apart from liaising with the government for them, all we could offer were our shoulders to cry on and our hearts to share their grief. Our constant attempts at bringing a smile to their faces were like a full-sized battle against an impenetrable cloud of grief. Even a minor victory in this battle brought a silver lining. We organized singing and dancing sessions. It did not matter to us that Satwant Kaur, a young victim of mass rape, and Sarabjit Kaur whose husband had been hacked to pieces, did not put their fingers to a single stitch of sewing. It seemed to us reward enough if we could elicit one smile from them, or have them join in the singing and dancing. Society's expected response would invariably be a reprimand for them and for others who dared to smile when their husbands were dead.

'Settling the widows down', whether they like it or not, with their brothers-in-law, even if they have to wait for these boys to grow to manhood, is a typical practice being followed by the elders who govern their lives. Several years of their youth may be wasted, and the young bridegroom-to-be may not want an elderly sister-in-law as his bride. Jaswant and others like her feel there is no problem. Her twelve-year-old son will be a man in eight to ten years. Her widowed daughter-in-law Sarabjeet Kaur can easily wait for him. Sarabjeet is between fourteen and sixteen, and seems the youngest widow in the area. There is no answer to her suppressed pain except the oft repeated sentence, 'The honour of the family must remain in the family.' Twenty-two year old Kuldip has found the strength to refuse to be bound to her fourteen-year-old brother-in-law who is slightly demented. There are often others like Satwant, Surendar and Bhupinder, who have had to 'settle down' with brothers-in-law who are much older than them, as second, third, or even fourth wives. Very few have been able to resist the onslaught of these cruel societal 'norms', and of these few, the majority often have to face not only ostracism at the hands of their families and society, but drunken beating and exploitation or worse at the hands of their men. Satinder, who defied the panchayat to marry a man outside her community, who promised to care for her five daughters, has lived to regret her decision. The man, who promised her the earth, was jailed at Satinder's own instance, for molestation and rape of her teenaged daughter. Eventually she relented, and the man was set free. The daughter was sent back to the village. The tragedy of Satinder is the tragedy of a spirited woman beaten down by multiple traumas.

The whole area of sexual exploitation of these women is very grey, as it is difficult to understand the exact position in the privacy of family life. However, we are in the know of several cases where the male members of the family have used these women for direct payment even as they are trying to recover from their recent trauma in the relief camps, and our workers have confirmed that prostitution is encouraged by their own men folk. Hand-in-glove in this business are society leaders and police functionaries. Some community leaders reportedly have four wives and two to three flats.

One of our first priorities in trying to help these women has been to try and alleviate their economic exploitation. Since these young widows have become 'sources' of 'charity', doles and government patronage, it is in the interest of the members of their families who can get funds and facilities in their names, to keep them as they are—dependent and without hope. The women have become wiser, and most of them know how to manage their finances.

The hold of the system on their lives is eloquently borne out by the institution of the so-called panchayat—an amalgam of 'respected males' who are invited from places as distant as Bombay and Alwar to pronounce judgment on these women. Women are debarred from the panchayat meetings. A woman is left alone only if she is ready to bribe or feast these men; if not, she should be prepared to bear the brunt of their 'righteous indignation'. Interestingly, every sub-community has its own 'panchayat'. The Sikligars and the Peshwaris have nothing to do with each other. The admonitions of a Labhana 'panchayat' will not bother a Punjabi and vice versa. The entire gamut of caste and class can be seen at work here. The majority of the women prefer to follow the 'diktat' of these groups, rather than risk ostracism and insecurity.

Apart from these societal barriers faced by the women, the role of the administration and government needs to be looked at. The decision taken to resettle about nine hundred families headed by widows and two hundred male-headed families who had lived through the same trauma in a single project in Tilak Vihar, west Delhi, was extremely ill-conceived. Grief feeding on itself creates a most unhealthy mental environment. It also provides a readymade breeding ground for religious fundamentalists, greedy male family members and other interested parties to thrive on and exploit the already exploited in a ghetto-like situation. The Tilak Vihar region has also undergone a process of politicization, whereas this element is fortunately missing in Garhi where seventy-five families headed by widows were settled. In the early days of resettlement, we definitely found that it was easier for the Garhi widows than the Tilak Vihar settlers to pick up their life threads again. More thought, understanding and planning need to be put into resettlement if it is to be a healthy process.

On the economic front, the Sikh widow's position is better. She gets some monetary assistance from the gurudwara from which small amount she tries to save a little money in case she is not able to find a job. Some women are running small shops, and about seven hundred have by now been accommodated in government jobs. Even though all these benefits may not ultimately reach them, it is good to know that this is the first time in the history of riots in this country that such a precedent of creating interest has been taken in the economic plight of the riot widow.

A discussion on the rehabilitation of these Sikh widows would be incomplete if the communal element is not included in our thinking. This is especially the case in Tilak Vihar, where a twenty-five to thirty year old harijan basti lies cheek by jowl with the resettled Sikh colony. This basti has been existing in the hope that the false promises made to them by government after government will be implemented. Left to themselves, the two communities lead peaceful lives, but there is no dearth of extraneous elements like the Shiv Sena, who are interested in creating explosive situations like the minor riots of July 1986, where two Sikh youths were killed, and seventeen harijan homes burnt down. Our on-going commitment in this area is to work towards communal harmony, hoping for a harmonious relationship between the communities. We try to understand the dynamics of the situation within our own framework of activities like adult education and awareness raising programmes. Our reward is in seeing harijan and Sikh girls relaxed and happily involved in working, studying and playing together.

Last but not least is the weighty issue of the denial of justice which continues to elude these tragic women. This effectively blocks successful rehabilitation work. Many of them have identified culprits in court, in affidavits and before the Mishra Commission. Six persons have been convicted lately in cases filed by private citizens, but to date there has not been one single indictment through government initiative. Almost 3000 people were butchered in one day in the capital of India, and we have not been able to do anything except hang our heads in shame. As Rupinder put it succinctly, 'Even if the government had hung one man, it would have given some solace to our burning hearts.'

Most displacements of our time are traceable to human folly or deliberate design, and as such are avoidable. Hence the greater poignancy of the disaster. Rehabilitation in any situation is an extremely difficult process, and in the case of the Sikh widows, whose wonderful spirit and grit rose above the complexities of the historical and political context of the riots of 1984, the sensitive situation and problems are multiplied a hundredfold.

(All names mentioned above are fictitious.)

≈

LEARNING TO 'ADJUST':
CONJUGAL RELATIONS IN INDIAN POPULAR FICTION
Amita Tyagi Singh and Patricia Uberoi

This paper looks at the way in which the problem of love between the sexes is constituted in a particular genre of contemporary Indian popular culture. Our data comprise primarily a set of twenty romantic short stories published over the course of the year 1988–89 in the English-language women's magazine *Woman's Era* reported at length in Tyagi (1989) [. . .] In general, our analysis suggests that these tales serve important instructional and cautionary functions. As contemporary 'fables', they socialize women readers to appreciate the hazards of courtship on the one hand, and on the other to accept the inevitable asymmetry of the conjugal bond through the promise of a fairy-tale 'happy ending' to problems of marital adjustment. Here we address ourselves primarily to the representation of conjugal relations. [. . .]

Woman's Era is known among connoisseurs of Indian women's magazines for its regular featuring of short stories, especially romance fiction. Produced fortnightly and published in Delhi, it is one of a chain of women, children and family-oriented magazines in English and some Indian vernaculars— Hindi, Gujarati and Marathi. (Interestingly, the chain also produces, in Hindi, 'India's only fortnightly magazine for young men'!). According to its publicity material, *Woman's Era* 'carries women-oriented fiction, articles of general interest as well as on family affairs, exotic food recipes [and] latest trends in fashions and films.' It also has a regular personal column which deals especially with problems of mate selection, marital adjustment, intra-family relations, pre- and post-marital affairs, problems of tobacco, alcohol and drug addiction, etc; a regular write-in health and advice column, featuring many queries on female disorders and sexual matters; and a write-in beauty advice column. 'Sagging breasts' is a complaint that spans several categories and seems to worry a number of readers (and their husbands). Unfortunately it seems that there is nothing much to be done about it.

Like Harlequin romances, *Woman's Era* is reckoned to have had phenomenal success in the very competitive world of Indian women's magazines. Starting in 1973 as a sister to the popular Hindi magazine, *Sarita,* it soon became India's largest selling English-language women's magazine, effectively polarizing the market between itself and the more recent, and much more sophisticated, *Savvy,* and pushing aside long-established and reputable competitors, *Femina* and *Eve's Weekly*. [. . .]

Twenty tales of true romance

The stories we examined fall almost evenly into two distinct categories, each with a characteristic pattern of narrative development. On the one hand are tales of courtship, that is, of romance *before* marriage; on the other, tales of conjugal relations, that is, of romance *after* marriage. It is here that one senses an important quantitative and qualitative difference from the western romance fiction which these tales superficially resemble, where the heroine's quest for mature selfhood usually coincides with a narrative sequence of events from boy-meets-girl to marriage-and-living-happily-ever-after. The sheer volume of stories of conjugal relations not only affirms the vulnerability of boy–girl romantic encounters outside the context of marriage, but, more positively, confirms that romance *after* marriage is a major preoccupation for Indian women. In fact, one is tempted to suggest that stories of post-marital romance may be a subcontinental contribution to the international genre of women's romance fiction! [. . .]

Tales of conjugal relations

There is a lot that could be said about the tales of courtship and their structure, content and message (ideology). Our chief interest here, however, is the other type of story, i.e., the tales of conjugal relations, of the vicissitudes of love *after* marriage, of the thorny path to the ultimate 'happy ending': marital bliss.

In the analysis that follows, we seek to identify (a) the substantive problems that are seen to threaten marital happiness; (b) the agency or agencies through which these problems are resolved or mediated; and (c) the nature of the solutions offered as the narrative proceeds from the initial situation of marital crisis through to a final resolution of the crisis. In other words, we have here a fictional or fantasized reflection on the dynamics of 'marital adjustment' which may be placed in the context of the explicit advice that the magazine offers on problems of matchmaking and conjugal relations, and interpreted in the light of the sociological literature on family and marriage in India. [. . .]

To anticipate what is to follow here, the reconciliation between love and marriage in this romance fiction is not a question of reconciling a woman to her mother-in-law, but rather of reconciling a woman to her loss of autonomy, individuality and selfhood in relation to her husband. Where the Harlequin-style romances narrate the steps in a woman's quest for selfhood in relation to a chosen man, these stories seem to chronicle her loss of selfhood, construed ironically as happy ending to a developing conflict situation. Specifically, contradiction is located in the woman's assertion of her individuality and personality, and/ or in her failure to compromise when marital problems become manifest. This is what threatens the stability and endurance of a marriage and, if not corrected in time, it can lead to marital breakdown—the ultimate disaster for a woman. [. . .]

Let us look at the stories of marital relations in greater detail. The plot outlines are very simple. The story begins with a married couple facing problems in their relationship. An event occurs or a mediator is involved to give the story a new turn. If mediation is successful, the couple are reconciled (presumably to live happily ever after). This is a paradigmatic situation. However, occasionally—and this amounts to a warning—the mediation fails, and the marriage breaks down. Very occasionally, the story is left tantalizingly open-ended. [. . .] Substantively speaking, a strained relationship between husband and wife can be manifested in open conflict—the wife does or wants to do something of which the husband does not approve—or it may be the outcome of a feeling of anxiety or insecurity on the part of one partner (usually the wife, in fact).

Sources of marital tension

Open conflict can occur over a number of issues. For instance, to cite some specific examples that came up in our texts:

— the husband may disapprove of the wife's friends, and try to forbid her from meeting them;

— the wife may wish to continue in her job after marriage, even if it entails living in a different city, whereas her husband may expect her to resign and join him;

— a wife may be unwilling to accompany her husband when he is transferred to a distant and insalubrious place;

— a wife may feel offended when her husband, without consulting her, withdraws a large sum of money from their joint account to buy a car.

And so on. There is a conflict of will or interest between husband and wife. Either may be self-evidently in the right, or each of them may have a point. It doesn't really matter. The crucial factor in turning a mere difference of opinion into a marital crisis is what is called in popular parlance an 'ego hassle'.

Anxiety arises from a number of sources, including, of course, the wife's feeling that her husband cares for his mother and sisters more than for her. Childlessness is a major source of feelings of insecurity, vulnerability and worthlessness. So, too, is a husband's real or imagined attraction for another woman. A woman may also feel vulnerable on account of a past indiscretion, fearing that her husband will reject her if he finds out about it. Incidentally, this latter is a problem that regularly crops up in the personal columns, too. The wife feels anxious and wonders if she should confess to her husband about some past relationship. She is usually advised against this, that is, *unless* the husband is likely to find out about it otherwise. Significantly, a husband's pre-marital indiscretions do not make him feel anxious. Rather, once again, they make the wife feel vulnerable, suspecting that he must still be in love with his former girl friend!

Having set up a situation of husband–wife conflict, the narrative then sets about its resolution. Sometimes the mediation is almost effortless: for instance, a very minor incident or gesture persuades an anxious wife that her suspicions are unfounded and that her husband loves her best (and not his mother and sisters) after all. Or a supposed 'affair' is revealed as a perfectly innocent relationship. But usually it requires the mediation of a third person, or a dramatic (indeed, melodramatic) event, accidental or contrived, to set the relationship back on course. Occasionally, the mediation fails and the story concludes unhappily (perhaps unsatisfactorily, also, for the readers). Sometimes the story is left open-ended. [. . .]

In one case of a failed mediation, the mediator was a child. Perhaps this was the reason why the distressed wife could not accept the advice proffered. (Instead, the poor child had his ear boxed!) Or, alternatively, the wife was too set in her ways to make the necessary adjustments in her lifestyle. This was the case with Sunanda, who ultimately died of a 'broken heart':

Sunanda was exquisitely beautiful—vain and self-confident in her good looks which she took enormous pains to preserve. She was therefore dismayed to discover, after many years of (childless) marriage, that her husband had become attracted to a widow, mother of two boys whom he used to tutor in the evenings. One day she sent a favourite nephew to report on the other woman. 'No, she's not at all beautiful,' reported the nephew. 'But she looks so nice even in her faded sari and with hair flying all over her face ... And ... uncle sort of came alive there ... He looked so different ... happy ... If perhaps you tried to become more like that lady, uncle will talk and laugh with you as well ...' As the aunt slapped the boy for his frankness, he repressed a final comment. 'Dear aunt. You have spent a lifetime not tending your mind and spirit. You beautified your body and neglected your soul. It is the latter which lasts and lasts and the former is as short-lived as the morning dew or a blade of summer grass ...' (Anon. 1990, 395)

Shortly afterwards, the aunt died—in the little boy's opinion, of 'a broken heart'. Clearly, then, it is not enough for an example to be set or advice offered: the lesson has to be internalized and acted upon. [...]

Resolution

The wives were not always shown up in such poor light in these stories. On the contrary, the husbands were very often shown at fault. They were either too weak—and thus dominated by their mothers—or too authoritarian, for instance, vetting all the wife's social contracts. Quite often the husband's grievances appear inequitable and unreasonable: the 'expectation' that a wife should automatically resign from her job after marriage, or that he could withdraw money the wife had earned from their joint account without consulting her; or that his extra-marital escapades would not adversely affect his family life.

But wherever the fault resided—with the husband, with the wife, with both or with neither—the reconciliation was brought about in the overwhelming number of cases of marital tension by the *wife* making compromises, 'adjusting', as the very useful Indian English expression has it. In reverse, marital breakdown was the outcome of the wife's failure to make the requisite compromises. Occasionally, the husband was the one to make the compromise. But on the whole the 'adjustment' was asymmetrical on the part of the wife.

The overall consistency of this solution to a marital crisis suggests that a wife's assertion of her will, autonomy and personality, right or wrong, against her husband is the primary source of marital tension which, if not corrected in time, would lead to marital breakdown. Problems with 'in-laws' are merely secondary, or are encompassed within/ adjuncts to the other problems.

How is resolution effected? In cases where the wife has left her husband (usually to live with her parents), she unconditionally returns to him. [...]

If a woman cannot have her own natural children, the tales tell us, she would be wise to agree to adoption—it is, after all, better than rejection. A wife can learn to overlook or rationalize her husband's faults, including infidelity—she has to accept that she would be infinitely worse off without him. She is also often expected to curb her career ambitions in the higher interests of domestic accord, especially when that ambition requires separation from her spouse. She should not seek to compete professionally, directly or indirectly, with her husband. Working wives are not necessarily disapproved of, but clinging to economic independence for its own sake can be construed as an act of defiance—as a reflection on the husband's manhood and capacity to provide. [. . .]

Prescription for a happy marriage

Quite coincidentally, a recent article in *Woman's Era*, entitled 'What makes a Happy Marriage?' (Anon. 1990, 389), corroborates some of the points that emerged from our analysis of the narrative structure of the fictional tales of conjugal relations. Focusing on the first step towards marriage, matchmaking, the author discounts the usual criteria that feature in matrimonial advertisements in India: caste, beauty, colour of skin, age, height, weight, convent education, language, nationality and religion. These should be merely secondary considerations. The really important ones are of the kind that a sociologist would call 'social structure', many of which would place the husband in a position of superior status, authority or power over the wife: (i) that the girl should be of the same social (i.e., class) status as the boy, or of a slightly lower status, but not the reverse, (ii) that the woman should preferably be less educated than the man: 'If the man is less educated than the woman, they will be sitting on the top of a volcano,' and (iii) that the husband should earn more and also have better career prospects: 'The groom is the provider and breadwinner'. Hence, 'if the man wishes to live on the wife's earnings or wealth, a positively mismatched condition will come about,' moreover, significantly: 'if both are earning members before marriage, the groom's income should be greater than the bride's'. If the earnings are more or less equal and if the woman holds a position with rapid promotion prospects, an alliance between the two persons had better be avoided. Additionally, the couple should share the same food preferences, and they should have the same religion or one of them should be 'neutral' in respect to religion. Almost as an afterthought, the author adds that the couple should feel attraction for each other. It is obviously a question to be considered only after other desiderata are met.

If all criteria are fulfilled, this instructive article then goes on to tell us, one has a round peg and a round hole, but a further process of grooving is required before the husband and wife become 'one body'. This is what the author calls 'mutual adjustment' i.e., a process of 'give and take' or, more accurately, 'giving in': 'keep on giving in and giving in until there is nothing left for the other to ask for any more give-ins' [sic]. What the article does not explain in so many words—in fact, the term 'mutual adjustment' disguises the true situation—is the social expectation, so blatantly revealed in the fictional accounts of marital crises and implicit in the fact that women are addresses of this well-meaning advice, that it is the wife, not the husband, who will most often be required to give in. Structural asymmetry—of socioeconomic status, education and career prospects, and of course, of age, which is assumed as self-evident—is built into the ideal match, but satisfactory marital adjustment demands, even beyond this, that a wife learn to give in gracefully whenever a conflict situation develops, and regardless of the rights or wrongs of the issue at hand.

Leaving aside considerations of gender equity, this would appear to be quite sound and practical advice, given that a woman has much more at stake in a successful marriage than a man. In her empirical study of middle class employed women of comparable background to typical *Woman's Era* readers, sociologist Promilla Kapur concluded 'that wives had to make more adjustments in their marriage than husbands had to. Wherever there were disagreements between husband and wife, the wife gave in two and a half times more frequently than the husband did. [O]f the well-adjusted wives 63 per cent were found to be making more efforts to bring about harmony in married life' (1970, 413). She added wryly that a 'wife's being too individualized proves particularly detrimental to marital harmony because men still like to marry less individualized women' (419).

Kapur identified several typical 'patterns' of marital adjustment in which adjustment was mostly from the wife's side. In the first, 'the wife carries out all the household responsibilities herself without even feeling the pinch of sacrifice . . . because she is brought up in an atmosphere where [the] husband is supposed to be a god and [the] wife is supposed to serve him in every way' (432). In the second pattern, ' as her husband does not make the required contribution towards marital adjustment, she does most of it herself to compensate . . . .and bring about harmony in marital relations'(432). As an informant reported on her own relationship with her husband:

> Once she came to realize that obstinacy was a weakness of her husband, she took care not to give him any occasion to get into an obstinate frame of mind. She made it her practice to agree to whatever he said whenever he was in an obstinate mood and thus she avoided hot arguments and unpleasant quarrels . . . her husband appreciated her giving in and agreeing to whatever he said even when he was unreasonable and wanted to do a certain thing only because he liked to assert his superiority. (124)

Of course the couple lived happily ever after. In the third pattern, whose narrative structure is homologous with many of our fictional tales, initial tensions are solved when the wife ultimately learns to 'adjust'.

Conclusion

This paper aimed at exploring the representation of marital relations in a small sample of Indian popular fiction from a well-known English-language women's magazine. [. . .]

The stories begin by arousing the female reader's anxiety in a conspicuously mimetic fashion. Unlike the 'Harlequin' or 'Mills and Boon' romances, which tend to portray exotic or historical locales and glamorous lifestyles, these tales are located in very ordinary middle class Indian families engaged in ordinary, everyday tasks. The issues that precipitate marital tension are, if not part of the personal experience of readers, at least part of their personal knowledge and environment. 'Compromise' or 'adjustment', the stories then go on to tell us, is the key to marital happiness. [. . .]

References

Anonymous. 1990. That summer of '56. *Women's Era* 17, 395.

Kapur, Promilla.1970. *Marriage and the working women in India.* New Delhi: Vikas.

Tyagi, Amita. 1989. Courtship and conjugality: A sociological analysis of the man–woman relationship in Indian popular fiction. M.Phil. dissertation, Centre for the Study of Social Systems, Jawaharlal Nehru University, New Delhi.

∾

ON THE UNIFORM CIVIL CODE: UNIFORMITY VS EQUALITY

Brinda Karat

An important issue concerning Indian women today is that of the uniform civil code (UCC). The secular principle that women of all communities should be governed by a uniform law free from discrimination on the basis of caste or religion was first asserted by Indian women during the freedom struggle. That principle is no less valid today. But how is this to be achieved? Is the slogan for an immediate common civil code in the interests of Indian women today? What Indian women need are gender just laws in areas of crucial concern to them which go beyond the framework determined either by laws based on religious belief or even existing secular laws in the country. Gender justice and the fulfillment of constitutional guarantees of equality need not necessarily be linked to an umbrella legislation. In fact within the *present legal framework* an umbrella legislation could well be counter-productive. Raising the issue itself could also be a diversion from what is immediately achievable in the field of legal reform.

The concept of a uniform civil code has two aspects: uniformity *between* communities (Hindus, Muslims, Sikhs, Christians and Scheduled Tribes etc. all being governed by one law) as well as uniformity *within* communities (between men and women). A gender just secular code would have to take into account *both* aspects or it could end up as a code for the uniformity of male privilege. It is no coincidence that although the fundamentalists of the majority and minority communities are sharply divided on the issue of the UCC and the relevance or otherwise of Section 44 of the Constitution, the arguments both for and against the UCC are limited to the single aspect of uniformity *between* communities.

Take for instance the arguments of the main protagonists for an immediate common civil code, namely the BJP-led communal platform. The basis of their lopsided and motivated approach is that since Hindu laws have been reformed there is already equality *within* the community. The target, so to speak, of a uniform civil code is therefore the personal laws of minority communities. Unfortunately this untruth has been strengthened by the misplaced assertion of the recent Supreme Court judgement that Hindu laws have been adequately reformed. This is a great disservice to Hindu women who are victims of unequal laws in matters pertaining to marriage, inheritance, guardianship, adoption. Those who claim to best represent the interests of Hindu women have not amended a single one of these legal inequalities in any of the states where they rule. On the contrary, in a revealing legislation which was *unanimously* passed by the Haryana Assembly in 1987 (including assent by both the BJP and the Congress), *the equal rights of Hindu women granted to them in non-ancestral property were actually cancelled. It was also specifically mentioned that women would not have equal rights to agricultural land as it would divide and fragment families.* It is another matter that political developments, including elections, prevented the confirmation of the Bill. In practice also it is women of the majority community who are the worst victims of atrocities and discrimination, including in those areas which the reformed Hindu laws were supposed to have liberated them from. This includes the question of bigamy. As has been argued by many commentators quoting from census statistics, the incidence of bigamy is most among Scheduled Tribes, followed by Buddhists, then by Hindus. The lowest percentage is of Muslim men. Thus neither in practice nor in the example of laws can Hindu laws form the basis for a uniform civil code.

The Bharatiya Janata Party, which has been committed to a UCC based on Hindu laws, has now shifted ground to declare that the UCC proposed by it will not be based on Hindu laws alone but on the 'best in all laws'. It has been good enough to include Muslim laws in its scope although without specifying what it exactly means. But is this argument any different or any better? It is still based on the aspect of uniformity *between* communities. In fact, in so far as women's rights are concerned, this is a deception since there are no existing laws which are the 'best laws'. There may be laws which are *comparatively* better but these are still based on inequality between men and women and cannot form the basis for an umbrella legislation.

For instance, which existing law of any community, or even from secular law, can form the basis for equal laws on inheritance? Muslim women may have enhanced rights in this area compared to Hindu women under the Mitakshara system, but they are still not equal with men. No existing law deals with the problem of disinheritance of the female heir through a will, which is an extremely common occurrence. This is one important aspect of equal rights in property which has been willfully ignored precisely because it attacks the common denominator uniting men of all communities: the male control of family and property. In 1976 the Special Marriage Act was amended to ensure that couples who chose to get married under this act, would, in matters of property, if they were Hindu, still come under the discriminatory Hindu Succession Act. Under it, if a Hindu marries a non-Hindu, the former ceases to be a member of the Hindu joint family. By this retrograde amendment, in a supposedly secular law, anyone who marries outside the community is automatically disinherited.

Again, which law could form the basis for a law against bigamy? At present the law in all cases is so weak that it is virtually impossible to prove bigamy, which is why there are so few convictions in spite of the increase in bigamous marriages. In so far as divorce rights are concerned, the related issues of maintenance and custody of children are extremely weak. In this area, Christian women are even worse off since the Indian Divorce Act 1869, applicable to them, discriminates on grounds of divorce. Adultery on its own is not a ground of divorce for women although it is for men. There are many other examples. The point is that even the 'best' in all existing laws will still be a bad law for women.

Another important aspect is that there are some crucial issues of common concern to women of all communities which no personal law deals with. This is also true of the completely inadequate secular laws. Therefore, the very framework of the 'best of laws' for a uniform civil code is severely limited. For example, the incidence of violence within the family against women has increased to a great extent in all communities but there is no comprehensive legislation to deal with this either in personal law or in secular law. The increasing problem of child abuse within the family also needs to be dealt with. Another example is the increasing incidence of desertion. In such cases there is no law to ensure that the property accumulated by the couple after marriage would be in both their names. At present such property is invariably claimed by the male as he is often the earning member. The law for joint matrimonial property requires recognition of the unpaid work being done by women within the household as being equally important for the survival and welfare of the family. There are other such examples available. However, none of these important issues have even been discussed by the fundamentalists of the various communities precisely because none of them even consider the aspect of uniformity *within* communities as relevant.

An umbrella legislation at this stage would therefore amount to building a skyscraper on the weak plinth of a cottage. It would require the complete overhauling of all existing laws to meet the ends of justice. The women's movement has been asking for just such an overhauling, but its experience, even in the sphere of the limited reform it has achieved, has not been very encouraging. One aspect is of course the lack of political will to ensure reforms on even such issues as should be completely non-controversial. For instance, even today there is no specific law against child rape.

The other aspect of the experience is that whenever reform, however inadequate, has been successfully pushed forward it has been on the basis of a single-issue approach, which helped to focus on and fight on different questions raised within a particular issue. This has been the experience in the struggle to amend both the rape and the dowry laws. That is why when the National Commission for Women wanted the abolition of the Dowry Prohibition Act, and proposed instead an omnibus legislation to cover all crimes against women, it was opposed by the national women's organizations. It was felt that in the present context such legislation would not have sufficed to deal with the social aspects of crimes against women, which different laws in specific areas could. What were demanded then were specific amendments in the different laws. This logic is equally, if not more, valid for the argument against the immediate reform of the uniform civil code as it deals with the family, an area sacrosanct for patriarchal domination.

What is also required is the rebuilding of the foundation itself, the expansion of the very concept of social 'uniformity', equal rights between men and women as reflected in the legal framework. This is possible only through a step-by-step approach which will also limit the scope for compromise of women's interests. It means ongoing secular legislation in identified areas. As the area of intervention increases so also the foundation for a gender just family code will strengthen.

Three steps could be taken as the starting point, which are important for women, and are outside the framework of personal law. With the emphasis on decentralization and the importance given to panchayats, it would be appropriate if the panchayats and local bodies could start compulsory registration of all marriages, just as births and deaths are registered. This would not interfere in any way with the nature or rituals of the marriage ceremonies of any community. Secondly, changes in the laws on property could be introduced with a new law applicable to women of all communities giving them equal rights in matrimonial property. Thirdly, the enactment of a comprehensive law against domestic violence to protect the mental and physical well-being of women of all communities within the family should be put through.

The other aspect of equality, i.e. *within* the community, requires a redefinition of the term community itself. At present, at least insofar as the minority communities are concerned, in the popular perception the community means its fundamentalists. This definition does not derive from traditions or cultural patterns but is a conscious part of political practice of dominant parties. The central government, for example, has consciously encouraged this identification as was seen in the Shah Bano case. Recognition and acknowledgement of reformists within communities would shake the status quo and would not be in the interests of vote bank politics; therefore they prefer to talk to and take into account only the fundamentalists or the most conservative elements within a community, and generalize on the profile of the community on that basis. The most recent example of this crass political opportunism has been the refusal of the central government to give recognition to the reformed personal laws framed by the Christian community including those framed by important reformist sections of the clergy. The bill has been pending for over a year with the government. Another example in the reverse form comes from Arunachal Pradesh. Here the state government has taken the lead in passing a bill codifying customary law without any prior discussion within the community. Women in Arunachal Pradesh have strongly protested this bill as it sanctions all traditions and customary practices without specifically excluding even polygamy, bride price and unequal property rights. In this case, the challenge to the status quo has come from within the community but the government, far from strengthening the reformists, is ensuring the opposite.

If a similar situation had existed in the nineteen fifties there would have been no reform in Hindu laws. Even the limited reform that was achieved was possible only because of government backing and the fact that the demand for reform came from within the community itself. In fact, in the parliamentary debates at that time, Muslim members were silent on the issue or were on the side of the Hindu orthodoxy, led by the then Jan Sangh and the Hindu Mahasabha in opposing reform. At one state when the issue of monogamy was being discussed, one argument put forward by the Hindu fundamentalists was that if Muslims could have four wives, they too should have that right! The argument of religion being in danger used by the Hindu lobby at that time because of intervention in personal laws, cutting across party lines, was almost exactly the same as that used by Muslim fundamentalists today. Even though the fundamentalists were in a minority, the government of that time brokered a compromise with them at the cost of equal rights for Hindu women. The Hindu women who demanded change in personal laws were reviled, abused and even physically attacked by the followers of the Hindu 'right'.

If women of the majority community had to suffer then, soon after freedom, how much more difficult it is for women of the minority community to raise their voice for reform today. They are in a situation where, firstly, there is a vicious and violent communal polarization threatening the security of the minority communities, particularly women. Secondly, the government today recognizes only the fundamentalists as representing the community. The communal propaganda of the BJP and its sister organizations, which increases as elections draw closer, puts reformists in the community, including women struggling for equality, completely on the defensive. So much so, that they are unable to take advantage of the favourable example of reforms made in Muslim laws in many Muslim countries. Nowhere in the world are divorce or marriage laws as advantageous to Muslim men as they are in India. If Muslim women are to get rid of the unjust and inhuman laws on polygamy and divorce, of which they are victims, it is necessary to build a favourable secular climate. One such essential step would be a law to prevent the misuse of religion for political purposes. Such a ban will lessen communal polarization and help remove the feeling of insecurity among the minority community which disables them in their struggle against the fundamentalists in their own community. It is also necessary for the government to give public recognition to reformers in the community, including women. In a series of meetings, Muslim women have been discussing a charter which they propose to campaign on within the community, highlighting certain immediate issues like a ban on bigamy, end to arbitrary divorce, and so on. This is a significant development and strengthens the struggle of all women, including Hindu women, for change in their personal laws as a step forward for gender just legal foundation.

It is also argued that a single law for all citizens is essential for national integration. For almost a century Indian citizens have been governed by uniform laws in all other areas like transfer, contract, civil and criminal procedure, penal code and so on. In all such respects the law is more uniform in India than even in the United States of America, where each state has its own laws. If this uniformity has not led to national integration why should a uniform civil code be any different? The issue of national integration should transcend uniformity to incorporate equality. If equality becomes the basis of national integration, nationhood will be strengthened. At present, inequalities between communities are clearly illustrated by available figures. For instance, 52.3 per cent of the Muslim population lives below the poverty line as compared to 36 per cent among Hindus; 35 per cent are landless compared to 28 per cent Hindus; only 29 per cent Muslims are in regular or salaried jobs as compared to 47 per cent Hindus; of all those who have high school education, only 4 per cent are Muslims. It is such inequalities which strengthen the forces of division. *They also strengthen one-dimensional community identity in which personal laws are defined as the symbolic expression.*

On the other hand, there are some secularists who argue that the whole concept of a uniform civil code is misplaced in a pluralist society like India, and reform in personal laws is the only strategy for gender justice. Such an argument is contrary to the reality experienced by women, of the highly patriarchal nature, in the main, of laws based on religion. Reform within that framework can therefore only be limited. Also, given the necessary political will, pluralism need not necessarily be a victim of such a code. As an example, even if one looks at the Hindu Marriage Act, all the different traditions of marriage and customary practice are given equal recognition. It is customary practice which forms the basis on which marriages are prohibited, thus allowing for the recognition of marriages between cousins, or between uncle and niece, as in certain parts of south India, which are prohibited in the north. Another argument used against the code is that since even the Hindus do not have a common code how can others. In this context it is important to note that it is not the concept of one law which is misplaced but the present realities, both political and legal, which make such a slogan counterproductive today. In the history of countries it was only the Socialist countries which could evolve gender just civil codes because these codes were part of the restructuring of the entire system towards equality.

Thus the slogan for a uniform civil code should, at the present juncture, be preceded by the slogan of equal rights, equal laws. This platform envisages the taking forward of the legal framework of gender justice, a starting point, in the spheres of matrimonial property, domestic violence, and registration of marriages for women of all communities so as to strengthen the common secular ground. Many more such issues can be identified. At the same time, women and men committed to reform in all communities need to push forward the frontiers of gender justice within their own community and laws. Finally, it needs emphasis, that this struggle will be strengthened by a ban on the misuse of religion for political purposes. Only such a simultaneous combination can help meet the ends of justice and equality both *between* and *within* communities.

10

~

CASTE AND TRIBE

Caste and tribe are among the most difficult of themes before the women's movement and women's studies today. Each of them occupy very different positions in present-day struggles and thinking, and it is therefore with considerable trepidation that they have been brought together here. While caste has, at least since the 1990s, re-entered national debate (and some women's studies class-rooms), 'tribes' continue to be thought of as a world apart, inessential to current concerns. Yet, each of them throws up questions that challenge the foundations of feminist thinking and practice, and, therefore, will be critical in shaping future directions for the movement and for scholarship.

Caste has already made a few explicit appearances in this volume so far—in the discussion over the stalemate in the Women's Reservations Bill, in the historical legacy of Periyar, in Kumud Pawde's conquest of Sanskrit and in Baburao Bagul's literary rendition of violence in the dalit family. Each of these essays index distinct historical moments—the early twentieth century non-brahmin movement in Tamil Nadu, the dalit literary and autobiographical upsurges in Maharashtra during the 1960s, and, finally, the caste and gender configurations of the contemporary conjuncture. The difficult question is how to explain the effective absence of the multifaceted history of anti-caste struggle in the rebirth of the women's movement and women's studies in the 1970s and 80s. Even though many of the most well-known leaders—Phule, Periyar and Ambedkar—articulated a critique of gender in their attack on the caste system, this had little impact on the agendas of the women's movement or the scholarship that initially emerged.

One event in particular has played a profound role in changing the self-understanding of our time—the anti-Mandal agitations of 1990 against the government order to implement reservations in higher education and government services for the backward classes or other backward castes (OBCs). The extreme turn taken by upper caste student protestors, some of whom immolated themselves, and also the general outcry against existing reservations for Scheduled Castes in the name of merit and a caste-less society, forced many to interrogate their own understanding of caste inequality and oppression. The years that followed have not only witnessed a revival in the dalit movement and a better appreciation of the modern forms of caste discrimination, but also extensive explorations into the history of anti-caste movements. Upper caste biases have had to be confronted within the women's movement and women's studies, as well as the fact that dalit women chose to form their own organization—the National Federation of Dalit Women (NFDW)—in 1994.

The pieces that have been selected in this section belong to these years of reawakening and questioning. The first essay is by Ruth Manorama, longtime activist and one of the founders of the NFDW. Her essay attempts in broad strokes to look at dalits, their history, and the 'downtrodden among the downtrodden'—dalit women. However the caste system may have arisen, dalit culture could not remain immune to the larger patriarchal system, which is why dalit women have suffered many times over. However, and this is her critique of the women's movement and women's studies, the lives of dalit women have never figured in their own right, visible at most in the numerous statistics that document women's work. And yet—precisely because dalit women are not passive victims—'the possibility of a rich and ancient revolutionary base' could well be in the making. The second piece by Sharmila Rege, taken from her introduction to her book on dalit women's testimonios, explicitly focuses on the problems of caste in the women's studies class room. Her discussions take on an added urgency considering her regional location in Maharashtra, where one might have expected less ignorance and more engagement across caste and gender. She addresses the need for what she calls an abrahmanical perspective in women's studies, which involves recovering the political histories of caste, and responding to the acute dilemmas among diverse students—subaltern and savarna—in relating their 'personal' experiences and attitudes to current knowledges of caste and gender.

The next two essays are indicative of how thinking on caste and gender has been developing in different domains—within the field of activist scholarship and within social anthropology. In her presentation 'Dalit women: The conflict and the dilemma', Annie Namala makes her arguments at two levels. The analytical part of her essay seeks to reveal the reasons for the 'difference' of dalit women—not because they have a separate identity—but precisely because of the cumulative effects of class, caste and gender in their lives. The second part interrogates the women's and dalit movements for their priorities and the place accorded to dalit women in their struggles and agendas. It is her hope that spaces for dalit women's leadership will develop in both movements.

The sociologist Leela Dube takes on the subject of caste and women by emphasizing women's roles in maintaining or changing caste relations. She points to the many crucial ways in which the family or household, rather than the larger jati or caste unit, becomes the site for reproducing caste-based forms of exclusion, hierarchy and interdependence. Occupation, food and ritual practices, and, finally, marriage and sexuality, are the three distinct if overlapping spheres where caste differences are vital. This excerpt from Dube's longer essay concentrates on the first and last dimensions. Dube's broad analysis of the entanglements of caste and gender as a system is indicative of what a feminist sociology can provide.

Clearly, then, current understandings of caste have been revised, and from overlapping as well as differing perspectives—dalit, abrahmanical, feminist and sociological. Much remains to be done—we have but a rudimentary sense of contemporary brahminism and upper caste practices, and not even that when it comes to thinking about gender in relation to the OBCs. But what, in comparison, has been the status of tribes in relation to gender? The story is only beginning to unfold, if we go by the last two essays included in this section. Virginius Xaxa reviews some of the ways in which questions of gender have been addressed in the existing literature on tribes. Xaxa's special concern is to argue that the situation of tribes and their alienation from Indian society cannot be discussed in abstraction from both colonial processes and national developments. The gender dimensions of tribal societies in regions such as Jharkhand in particular have become highly political and emotive issues due to deepening forms of control by non-tribals over tribal land. One practice, among others, is that non-tribal men have been marrying tribal women, leading to a conflict between community rights and women's rights.

The concluding essay by Tiplut Nongbri covers very similar ground in her examination of the Khasi Custom of Lineage Bill 1997, which concerns the Khasis of Meghalaya, eulogized for their matrilineal social structure and attendant freedom for women. Her paper shows the extent to which Khasis can now be deprived of membership within the community when their actions are seen as 'disloyal'. While apparently gender neutral, it is Khasi women marrying outsiders who have been at the heart of the controversy. The effects of social change and development by the state are thus being selectively thrust upon women, accentuating processes of conflict and tension, and at women's cost.

All of the essays in this section reveal how familiar notions of gender, and the functioning of the family, are transformed when the workings of caste and tribe become visible. If women's studies has begun to acknowledge the dynamics of caste privilege and exclusion among women (and men), the problems of the alienation of tribes from mainstream society, and, by extension, from the women's movement, has yet to gain sustained attention. Given the marginal status of a field like women's studies within the educational system, it is not easy to accept, much less respond positively to, our own perpetuation of invisibility and exclusion. Claiming and reinventing feminism from dalit and 'tribal' perspectives cannot happen without disorienting existing agendas and upsetting inherited knowledges. But the promise of new energies, directions and the chance of deepening the transformative impulse of feminism is surely a risk worth taking.

∾

DALIT WOMEN:
THE DOWNTRODDEN AMONG THE DOWNTRODDEN
Ruth Manorama

The system of caste is a terrific force of stability and against change, a force that stabilizes all manners, dishonour and lies.

—Ram Manohar Lohia

Instead of 'dispersed inequalities' we find in caste a system of 'accumulative inequalities' where social and political power is concentrated into the hands of the same group.

—Andre Beteille

Almost all the Dalit spokesmen (and most, in fact, are men) clearly recognize women to be the most oppressed of their group—the 'Dalit among the Dalit or downtrodden among the downtrodden' as it is sometimes put. They cite Dr B.R. Ambedker to support this view.

—Gail Omvedt

Introduction: Origin, features of caste system

By way of introduction, I thought it relevant to briefly trace the origin and features of the caste system, before I deal with the topic 'dalit women.'

The caste system is probably the longest surviving hierarchical system in existence in the world today; its roots can be traced back to the Manusmriti, a sacred document of the Hindus dating back to the period between 200 BC and 100 BC. Various hypotheses regarding the origin and passage of the untouchables through the ages have been propounded.

Prabhati Mukherjee, in her book entitled *Beyond the Four Varnas*, delves into Rig Vedic times, even pre-vedic society, and writes that the Aryans came to India, inhabited the territory, had brushes with the indigenous population, came to terms with them or even beat them back. The author, in her book, sometimes in tedious and obscure detail, takes readers through the ancient period when the Aryans grabbed land and wealth, their consolidation of Aryan rule, the evolution of a social structure and the establishment of Aryan rapport with the 'natives'. They achieved this through appeasement or intimidation. Apparently, pre-Aryan communities had a culture of their own and the Aryans, by a slow process, included or resisted autochthonous (the original or earliest known inhabitants) groups and hostile peoples.

One plausible and rational theory is that dalits are the descendants of pre-Aryan Indians. As such, they found no place in the *varna* system which was a post-Aryan creation of their ancestry. One can, without any controversy, claim that theirs was an *autonomous* and *egalitarian* culture. The discoveries in the Indus Valley amply justify this claim.

Thus the *varna* system, from its original beginnings in the Rig Vedic phase, was essentially a retention of class differentiation, sustained by the ideology of caste and political domination of the ruling classes. Indian society was stratified into four *varnas*, but shudras were at the bottom. Below them came the panchamas. According to the Purusha myth, god created the four *varnas* thus, the brahmin (the priestly caste) from the head, the kshatriya (warrior caste) from his arms, the vaishya (traders and artisans) from his thighs, and the shudra from his feet. Some of whom are beyond the pale of caste and are known as untouchables, they have been described variously as avarna (coloured), antyaja (low born) hum shudra, panchamas (fifth order).

Dalits are known by various names and terms

Later, the British called them the 'Depressed classes' until the Census Report of India, 1931, which referred to groups outcasted for lack of caste norms as 'Exterior classes'. 'Scheduled castes' was termed by the Simon Commission and incorporated in Section 279 of the Government of India Act, 1935, thus scheduling 22% of the total population of the country (7% tribes, 15% low castes) for socioeconomic uplift under a State Policy of Protective Discrimination, recognizing their backwardness and socioeconomic disabilities which are the result of cumulative domination through the ages, subjugating them to a life of servitude/slavery to the rest of its population.

It was in 1933, during a temple entry campaign, that Mahatma Gandhiji used the term 'harijan', which Dr. Ambedkar characterized as just an attempt to give the untouchable a sweet name.

Dalit is the name the intellectuals of the Dalit Panther Movement gave currency to in 1970 as a constant reminder of their age old oppression—it literally means 'oppressed' or 'broken', describing both the state of deprivation and the people who are deprived. In this context one may quote Ambedkar who mentioned 'Broken Men' as belonging to the group of untouchables (1979, XIV, 99).

Dalit culture and Dalit identity

The untouchables of yore were an important, independent cultural group forced to surrender by the ruling Aryans. With the scope of arboreal economy becoming restricted and encroachment on their land taking place, the chandalas (and others too) had to come out of seclusion. Deprived of their habitat and livelihood, some of them accepted the 'munificence' of their masters but others did not. [. . .] They were uprooted from their harmonious relations between man and matter (which is ecologically sustaining) and between man and man. Since then they inherited a false consciousness, a false psyche, a false world view, all of which closed the doors for their human future. Whatever was done to these people was done as though it is in consonance with the religious dharma of the brahmanical Hindu culture.

Self-image

Dalits are made to accept a new self-understanding. A false image is infused into their very consciousness, which made it impossible for them even to think in human terms. This mark must be removed. In other words, the real image, the real selfhood of dalits must be revealed to them. Dalits have been the victims of systematic indoctrination done by the oppressive culture makers in traditional India.

Brahmanical culture, which became the dominant force in the subcontinent, refused to integrate the dalits religiously and culturally into itself. Brahminical culture assimilated and subordinated in hierarchical fashion the gods, priests, myths and cult practices of the dalit groups into their religion. By its central values of purity and pollution, the dominant castes deliberately prevented the dalits from rising to their level of culture by imposing on them, by force, various disabilities in worship and in mode of life, such as in matters of occupation, skills, dress, ornaments, foods, etc. The main organizational forces of brahminical culture such as purity and pollution, the devaluation of manual work, conceptions of *svadharma*, karma and ancestor worship built a low image of dalits and their culture.

Today, their predicament can be described in terms of a lost humanity, a dispossessed community, an oppressed psyche and a segregated condition. They lost their human standing along with other Indians, deprived of means of production and alienated from sharing political power. The Christian dalits' condition is an integral part of this predicament. The dalits constitute about 200 million people in India today.

Conversion

It is a historically established fact that the most important motivation for the Dalits to embrace in large numbers other religions like Islam, Sikhism, Christianity and Buddhism was their desire to escape from the Hindu culture and their hope to improve their social and ritual status in the new religion.

There have been a number of religious protest movements from among the dalits in the last 150 years. They were mostly led by particular leaders, such as Messianic movements in many parts of Raipur district, the Satnami uprising of the Chamars in Chattisgarh, Swaminarayan movement in Gujarat, Yogi Pothuluri, Virabrahman movements among the Madigas in Andhra, Ayya Vamyhi in Tamilnadu, Narayana Guru movement, Pratyaksha Raksha Daiva Sabha and Subhananda movement in Kerala, Adharam movement in Punjab etc. Characteristics of these movement are:

i. criticism of the brahminical religion,
ii. internal religious reforms within them, and
iii. abolition of polytheism, magical rituals, animal sacrifice, etc.

The future religious renaissance of this country lies with the liberation of dalits.

Dalit women

The second part of this paper outlines the impact of the caste system on women, and the status of dalit women, describing their thrice alienated position in society.

The impact of caste on women

The four features of caste have a significant bearing on gender. Firstly, caste defines a social division of labour thus lending status to one kind of work and status loss to another kind of work. Secondly, it determines sexual intercourse through marriage alliances. Thirdly, it structures groups in hierarchical relations, thus labelling some castes as high and others as low and, finally, the concepts of pollution and purity provide prescriptions and prohibitions about social interaction.

All these features have negative and worsening implications for gender equality and justice. The increased constraints on women are an essential part of a rise in caste hierarchy.

Nur Yalman links the sexual purity of women with the purity of the caste, suggesting that female sexuality presents a threat because of the danger in her introducing impure or low caste blood into the lineage. The belief is that it is through women (and not men) that the 'purity' of caste/community is ensured and preserved. (The) danger of low quality blood entering their caste . . . only exists with women. The male seed they receive should be the best available. Veena Das takes Yalman's analysis a stage further, adding to the notion of purity, the questions of success: 'Women were literally seen as points of entrance, as 'gateways' to the caste system. If men of ritually low status were to get sexual access to women of higher status, then not only the purity of the women but that of the entire group would be endangered. Since the main threat to the purity of the groups came from female sexuality, it becomes vital to guard it.'

Within the patriarchal joint family, women were considered as part of man's property in the same way as a piece of land belonged to the men of the family. Only sons are valued and are inheritors of immovable property, the daughters are not valued and, therefore, taken as dowry in the form of goods to their marital family. Thus, cultural explanations of caste hierarchy had its material basis. Therefore, gender division reinforced the caste division and gender ideology legitimated not only the structure of patriarchy but also the organization of caste. Another crucial dimension of this ideology is that the lower caste (dalit) women are considered inferior and also sexually loose.

The story of women in India in general depicts a continued one of exploitation and discrimination. Society refuses to recognize their potentialities, hard work and contribution to the welfare of society. [. . .] They are called the 'fair sex' and are shown 'unfair treatment'. Anti-women ideas and acts are glorified. (Female) child marriage, forced widowhood and compulsorily burning the wife on the funeral pyre of the husband are all advocated in Hinduism. In cases of individual or communal or national feuds, women are the first casualties.

But a dalit woman, who fortunately had not fallen prey into the net cunningly woven by Hinduism, was more free and less dependent. She was physically strong and could work hard. Anti-women feelings were not to be found in their social life. Child marriage, strict monogamy, widowhood, dowry practices and the heinous practice of 'sati' were all unknown to them. Divorces and remarriages were not resented in their society.

But this commendable status of dalit women was slowly eroded by Hinduism. In their vain attempt to be identified with and approved by the caste Hindus, dalits tried to follow their practices, forcing their women into subjugation, widowhood was thrust on them. They are forbidden to remarry. The freedom that the dalit women was enjoying was mercilessly taken away. So in present-day society a dalit woman is also considered to be unequal to her man. Today, dalit women, who constitute the major working force, are thrice alienated and oppressed on the basis of their class, caste and gender.

Almost all dalit spokesmen (and most, in fact, are men) clearly recognize women to be the most oppressed of their groups, the 'Dalit among the Dalits and the downtrodden among the downtrodden,' as it is sometimes put. They write that Ambedkar supported this view. Dr. Ambedkar, the leader of dalits, described the Hindu caste system as a pyramid of earthen pots set on top of one another. Not only are brahmins and kshatriyas at the top, shudras and the untouchables are at the bottom like crushed and wasted powder. And at the very bottom are the dalit women. Although the dalit poets are mostly men, their sense of the oppression of women comes through powerfully in their poetry. The majority of the dalit poets have tended to see women as *victims rather than victors.*

Dalit women are overwhelmingly found to be less educated and in low paid jobs. Social mobility for a man in the intermediary lower caste may mean withdrawing women from outside work participation. Dr. Kanahare, in her study of women's work and employment among some low status caste communities in a metropolis, observed thus: 'Gola (rice pounders) women continued cleaning grains, Rabari (cowherd) keep cattle, Khala women do rope making while her husband worked at secure blue collar service jobs' (1984, 6). Similarly, Malavika Karlekar in her study of sweeper women in Delhi found that while men in the balmiki caste were able to come out of the defiling caste occupation, women continue to remain in this low paid, unclean work (1982, 130). At the lower end of the job market—menials, gardeners, domestic servants—the slots are filled by those traditionally associated with the tasks. The new municipal corporation, for instance, has 'chuhras' as sweepers, 'bhistis' to carry water. This is done mainly by dalit women. Bina Agarwal's study on agricultural modernization suggests that technological change resulted not only in the displacement of women but increased disproportionately the work burden on poorer farm women.

Dalit women work under the most exploitative, dehumanizing and unhealthy conditions; neither their work, nor wages are regularized. Women have to work to meet the survival needs of their families. They have been denied all basic amenities (even drinking water), proper health care, and constantly have been facing the insecurity of being evicted from their places where they manage their lives and livelihood. The majority of dalit women do not even know the smell of education and schools, because of their impoverished situations.

The attack and threat on the dalit communities and women are on the increase at present. An analysis of forty rape victims by a platform against rape (Balatkaram Virodhi Manch) revealed that more than 80% of the victims belonged to the lower caste dalit and tribal groups and also came from the poor classes of society (Sakre 1984).

Atrocities Against Untouchables (1977–1978)

Category	Number in 1977	Number in 1978	% increase
Murder	334	456	36.52
Violence	1341	1570	17.20
Rape	332	541	66.87
Arson	716	1202	67.88
Other offences	8156	11,284	38.35
Total	10,879	15,053	38.37

The present situation is worse than before and atrocities are on the rise.

The former Chief Justice of India, P.N. Bhagwati, made the followings observation, while inaugurating the 32nd Biennial Conference on the Status of Women in Our Changing Society, organized by the Maharashtra State Women's Council: 'Rape and molestation are the new dimensions of caste war, used as weapons of reprisal and to crush the morale of a section of the people. This is an increasing feature in the rural areas.'

The Chandragutti episode in Karnataka has thrown open a new form of sexual exploitation of dalit women. Bettale Seva (literally nude worship), an atavistic pastoral ritual associated with the Renukamba temple and Mathangi Katte, has been a part of the annual three-day Renukamba Jatra at Chandragutti. By and large these devotees come mainly from the dalit communities. The Dalit Sangharsha Samithi was determined by their struggle to put an end to this unseemly 'sexual exploitation' in the name of religion.

In all the voluminous social science research in India, women from lower class/caste are rarely to be found as the subjects of study, speaking in their own voices, coping with their own lives and difficulties. Up to now the vast majority of published material on Indian women has dealt with middle classes and upper castes; even the numerous studies of 'working women' have, in fact, focused on middle class employees rather than the working class, peasantry and women involved in other unorganized sectors of labour. With few exceptions, the only material available on lower caste agricultural labourers and working class women has been statistical analysis of work participation. These are mostly by journalists or organizers. The lives and views of poor women are rarely studied with the same sensitivity as those of middle class women and research rarely asks such question as: How do lower caste women actually perceive their position in society? How much do they accept it? How do they cope with the daily realities of their lives? How do they engage, if they do, in action to change their situation?

On the whole, the oppression of the dalit women in India echoes issues such as state violence, denial of land rights, social and legal discrimination, infringement of civil liberties, inferior status, dehumanizing living and working conditions, total impoverishment, malnourishment, bad health conditions, the adverse effect of various contraceptives and the newly invented family planning devices that violate their bodies, illiteracy and ignorance, social ostracism and untouchability maintained by the caste Hindus as well as other religions (such as Christianity). The oppression of Dalit women is of a serious nature in terms of the violation of human rights in India.

Conclusion

To conclude, I quote Gail Omvedt: 'The downtrodden among the downtrodden are not simply passive victims of ignorant tradition. In fact, at every basis of Indian society among the downtrodden, the current mood seems to be not one of the mute acceptance of tradition but one of bitterness, anger and sadness, to look to possible action. When Dalit women are awakened to the contradictions that colour their lives of oppression, the possibility arises that perhaps there is after all in India a rich and ancient cultural base for revolution particularly among the low castes, Dalits, Adivasis and women.'

References

Ambedkar, B.R. 1979. The annihilation of caste. In. *Dr. Babasaheb Ambedkar writings and speeches*, ed. Vasant Moon. Mumbai: Education Department, Government of Maharashtra.

Karlekar, Malavika. 1982. *Poverty and women's work: A study of the sweeper community in Delhi*. New Delhi: Vikas Publishing House.

Omvedt, Gail. 1979. The downtrodden among the downtrodden: An interview with the rural agricultural labourer. *Signs* 4, no.4: 763–74.

~

WRITING CASTE, WRITING GENDER: DALIT WOMEN'S TESTIMONIOS

Sharmila Rege

Looking through the long list of recently published translations of dalit writings, mainly life narratives, one is tempted to think that a rupture of kinds may be taking place in our teaching and learning of caste studies. Two decades ago, for many of us studying social sciences in regional universities in India, caste was considered mainly a 'sociological' subject. Undeniably, caste was central to the courses on Indian society, which, however, were then neatly compartmentalized into social structure and social change over two academic terms. The study of caste, too, was therefore compartmentalized into reading studies on the features of the caste system in one term and modernization and sanskritization of caste in the other. Writings on/by Phule, Ambedkar, Periyar were not on the list of readings and most of us remained largely ignorant of the *abrahmani*/non-brahmanical perspectives on caste. The word non-brahmanical used here refers to an English translation of *'abrahmani'* and is different from *'brahmaneter'* literally meaning all except the brahmans, which has been translated as non-brahman. The concept *abrahmani* has been articulated in the voluminous work of comrade Sharad Patil, the founder of the Satyashodhak Communist Party, and continues to be rigorously debated (see especially Patil 1988). Patil argues that the epistemological conflict in Indian philosophy is between *brahmani* and *abrahmani* schools and that these categories have evolved from the history of social conflict in Indian society. He argues that the Sankhya, Lokayata, Buddhist, Kauala, Shaiva, Tantra and in the modern period Phule, Periyar and Ambedkar schools of thought represent the *abrahmani* tradition. The category *abrahmani* suggests perspectives emerging from, and directed towards annihilation of caste, class and oppression of women, and is thus more specific than categories like transformative and progressive. Patil (1988), in discussing the parameters of *abrahmani* and *brahmani* literature clarifies how Ramayana and Mahabharata are *brahmani* literature not because their subjects are kshatriyas and brahmans but because of their justification and propagation of varna-ashrama-dharma. He explains how the *brahmani* school may include *brahmani* non-brahmans and the *abrahmani* may include *abrahmani* brahmans.

The Satyashodhak and Ambedkarite movements were absent in courses on social movements, and the post-independence dalit, tribal and women's movements were often cluttered into one module. Needless to mention, there were no selections from dalit literature and life narratives in our readings or classes and therefore the epistemological challenge posed by the dalit movement and literature to received social science frameworks was lost on us. A decade later, as teachers of sociology, we realized that the assumed Archimedean standpoint for the objective study of caste had persisted and caste in our classrooms continued to be practised much in the same way.

Indian sociology, as Deshpande (2003) has argued, seems to have done little to counter the tendency for caste to vanish from view in those very contexts where it had been most effective. Indian sociology seems to have invited us to see caste in villages, rituals, rites and so on and suggested as if caste had no active role in urban everyday life. Since the 'upper castes' dominated the urban middle class contexts like the universities and research institutions, caste identity was hardly ever an issue for public discussion. As an upper caste, middle class student on campus, I recall being part of groups that thought discussions about caste identities to be retrograde. In the women's movement too, caste identities were rarely discussed as they were assumed to be transcendable for the larger sisterhood among all women. The marginalization of the non-brahmanical perspectives and experience in the institutionalized scholarship on caste has blurred our understanding of the relations between structural continuities and contemporary change in the social institution of caste. Engagement with anti-caste organizations and emergent dalit theoretical perspectives helped throw light on the pernicious divide between the theoretical brahmins and empirical shudras that social science practice in the last fifty years has continued to harbour (Guru 2002), thus ensuring that classical models of caste as a consensual system based on complementarity persisted. Dalitbahujan scholarship, in the last decade and more, has posed challenges to scholarship on caste, underlining the now apparent disjuncture between academic knowledge systems and social practices of caste. An engagement with dalitbahujan challenges initiated reflections both at the personal and political level; calling forth transformative pedagogies that interrogate institutionalized disciplinary and curricular practices related to caste.

One important challenge to the scholarship on caste came in the form of the post-Mandal violence by savarna elite students. It posed a direct challenge to the assumption that caste identities in urban India were personal and private matters. The burden of caste in our universities and classrooms, as in other institutions, has always weighed more heavily on the dalit and bahujan student. The elite savarna students who had decried the reservation policy have claimed that it was the 'lower castes' who reiterated caste identities and that the upper caste student was secular and did not observe practices of caste. The anti-Mandal protests challenged this assumption of/ about the elite savarna students and drew attention to the new modes of reproduction of caste whether it was through the idiom of citizenship or merit. The second important challenge came with the emergence of the dalit feminist assertions and critiques of the dalit and women's movements both at the regional and national levels. In the early 1990s, dalit feminist articulations, especially on the issue of quotas within quotas, challenged the conceptions of 'genderless caste' and 'casteless gender'. The advocacy of dalit human rights in the context of the Durban Convention on the Elimination of Racial Discrimination posed yet another challenge. As Kannabiran (2001) has argued, the inclusion of caste within the definition of racism by rewriting caste as a knowledge system had posed a challenge to sociological categories. Some sociologists like Gupta (2001) responded to these efforts to forge a common platform against caste and race discrimination by underlining caste and race as not only dissimilar but also incomparable. In the debate that followed, sociological categories were set as if against accounts that derived directly from lived experience and the politics of that experience.

These issues of the 1990s had also posed serious challenges to the women's movement and feminist scholarship in India. Elite, savarna girl students protesting against Mandal had, through their placards, displayed their anxiety at finding educated husbands, thus expressing publicly their commitment to caste endogamy. The writings and manifestos of different dalit women's groups underlined that the 1970s unmarked feminism had in fact been in theory and praxis brahmanical feminism. The NGO Declaration on Gender and Racism issued in 2001 by the National Federation of Dalit Women suggested new directions for feminist internationalism. In debates that followed, the absence of feminist comparative work on issues of race and caste became apparent. Over the last two decades, women's studies in India had raised important questions about the invisibility, distortion and marginalization of gender as a category of analysis in the mainstream disciplines and their practices of canonization. Despite the feminist critiques of mainstream social sciences, the classical frameworks of caste had cast their shadow on women's studies too. Dalit feminist critiques of the 1990s posed challenges to feminist canons, curricular protocols and alliances with brahmanical power and privilege. Except for a few notable exceptions, women's studies scholars did not seriously engage with dalit feminist critiques, and reflections on the transcoding of caste in feminist discourse and practices have been rare. Reflections on caste in the curricular protocols of women's studies have been even fewer. This lack of engagement cannot be dismissed easily; either by the savarna feminist justification of being 'frozen in guilt' (what can 'we' say now, let 'them' speak) or by a resigned dalit feminist position that sees a 'fit of caste identities and ideological positions' (brahman and 'upper caste' women will be brahmanical). The former assumes that caste is solely the dalit women's question and bypasses the need for all women to critically interrogate the complex histories of caste and gender oppression. The latter is resigned to assuming the impossibility of transcending caste identities, thereby amounting to a slippage between brahman and brahmanical and non-brahman and non-brahmanical. As John (2000), commenting on the resurgence of caste and minority issues within 'women's issues', argues, 'The revival of reservations for women in the 1990s—after Mandal, Ayodhya and globalization—offers us the chance to conceive of alternate modernities. This is nothing less than an opportunity to link rather than oppose—women's rights to rights based on caste, class or minority status in the broader context of a common democratic struggle' (3829). The recognition of caste as not just a retrograde past but an oppressive past reproduced as forms of inequality in modern society requires, therefore, that we integrate the questions of caste with those of class and gender. For feminist pedagogues and activists who seek to engage with these challenges, it is politically and academically an exciting moment of reflection. It requires thinking out classroom practices in which the social and political heterogeneity of students is articulated and engaged with to search out new dimensions of the battles of our times.

Recognizing differences, power and connections of class, caste and community means transforming subjectivities, politics and pedagogies. At the level of practice, for those of us who have been complicit in the power and privileges of caste, one of the first realizations is about the little knowledge of the cultures that have been violently marginalized. A large part of the feminist discourse of experience has been an autobiography of the upper caste woman, her conflict with tradition and desire to be modern. As Bharucha (2000) has argued, 'whether it is dalit culture or the grass root secular culture of the Mohalla committees of Mumbai, it becomes necessary to open ourselves to their turbulent processes of learning in order to challenge the manufacture of ignorance in which we are complicit through the privileges of class and education' (82). The women's movement and studies have brought forth shifts in our ways of thinking but this does not mean that all prior assumptions have been discarded or even clearly stated. The relative lack of engagement with the non-brahmanical renderings of caste and gender in the mainstream social sciences has been reproduced in women's studies. For some of us involved in developing undergraduate and postgraduate courses in women's studies, curricular transformation was the immediate site for engagement with this ignorance and projects with explicitly stated pedagogical functions were undertaken.

The first involved interviews and workshops with teachers to map 'gender, caste and class inequalities' as they appeared in the undergraduate and postgraduate curricula of seven universities in Maharashtra. Among several other issues, one of the findings of this exercise was the near total absence of the politics of lived experience of caste in the curriculum. The 'Indian women' in the curriculum were unmarked by caste and the presence of minority communities in the syllabus was feminized through the usual topics on 'problem of talaq, divorce etc'. The optional courses on women/gender were most often neatly dichotomized into western feminist theory and issues/problems related to women in India. There was a near complete absence of anti-race/Black/third world centred feminist theory and Black and third world women remained confined to modules on women and development. Most participants responded to observations about this invisibility or distorted representations with suggestions that can best be described as add the absent element and stir. Hence, the 'problem' of the invisibility of dalit women, Black and third world women feminisms, would be 'solved' by suggestions of adding on courses/modules on dalit/black/third world women. The question was therefore one of avoiding the dangers of 'sprinkling a little bit of dalit women's issues/problems' while leaving the courses philosophically and structurally unchallenged. Several questions emerged—how can we interrogate the much practised models that view caste as a social institution that has frozen in time? How can curricular and pedagogical practices move beyond these models that deny the agency of dalit women? In other words, how can 'private' lived experience and the 'public' practices of anti-caste struggles be brought into the analysis of caste and gender? How can the hegemony of White/brahmanical feminisms as default frames of reference in theory courses be challenged? How can these critiques and self-analyses be helpful for subaltern students? For often, despite the radical interrogative stance of the curriculum, as Jawaare (1997) has observed, the subaltern student remains at the receiving end of either neo-colonial condescension (we will help you speak like 'us') or contempt of the dominant ('they' cannot follow theoretical debates). The subaltern student in the women's studies classroom reacts to this situation by speaking (often outside the classroom) of the 'real' (even 'unimaginable' to the dominant in the classroom) victimhood of women in her everyday lived context. This articulation of victimhood by subaltern students can take the form of a claim of their being the more 'authentic subjects' of women's studies than the elite sections in the classroom. The significance of the women's studies classroom as a space where experience can be brought into the academy has been recognized and valued. However, we need to also discuss the dilemmas and frustrations of navigating these discussions in a politically and socially heterogeneous gender studies classroom. We have often found the sharing of experiences getting locked into two positions—the subaltern women students claiming 'authentic victimhood' and the dominant sections articulating what in our classroom parlance gets labelled as 'sensitive' and 'insensitive' responses. The latter, often articulated by upper caste, middle class and more senior women in the classroom, suggests that the situation of subaltern women is better off, since 'they can at least publicly abuse or hit back their drunken husbands'. The younger women, usually pursuing their postgraduate studies in other disciplines and doing gender studies in addition, often label such responses as insensitive. But one finds this 'sensitive' group, for whom the anti-race/third world feminist critiques of the academy are empowering, speaking the language of merit and citizenship during discussions on reservations on the basis of caste and gender. We need to delve further into our failure both as teachers and as students to connect the dimensions of complex lived experience with critiques of disciplinary knowledges and the academy. How can pedagogical strategies address this and help develop critiques that empower subaltern students to represent themselves more positively? How can the more dominant students in the classroom interrogate their complicity in class and caste privileges without freezing in guilt? How can teachers and students address ignorance about dalit and working class cultures? Discussions on these and other conceptual and pedagogical challenges pointed to the need of putting together teaching and learning materials that would promote political and interpretative engagement with issues of caste. [. . .]

References

Bharucha, Rustum. 2000. Thinking through culture. In *India: Another millenium?* ed. Romila Thapar. New Delhi: Penguin Viking.

Deshpande, Satish. 2003. *Contemporary India: A sociological view.* New Delhi: Penguin Viking.

Gupta, Dipankar. December 2001. Caste, race, politics. *Seminar* 508, 33–41.

Guru, Gopal. December 2002. How egalitarian are the social sciences in India? *Economic and Political Weekly*, 5003–10.

Jawaare, Aniket. 1997. The silence of the subaltern student. In *Subject to change: Teaching literature in the nineties*, ed. Susie Tharu. Hyderabad: Orient Longman, 107–125.

John, Mary E. October 2000. Alternate modernities? Reservations and the women's movement in 20th century India. *Economic and Political Weekly* WS22–31.

Kannabiran, Kalpana. 20 June 2001. Caste, the academy and dalit women. *The Hindu.*

Patil, Sharad. 1988. Sampaadakiya. *Satyashodak Marxvaadi* 7, no. 7–8, 3–69.

∼

DALIT WOMEN: THE CONFLICT AND THE DILEMMA
Annie Namala

Dalit women have been referred to as the dalits among the dalits, the thrice alienated and the thrice marginalized. Is, however, the dalit woman an identifiable category? How does the caste–class–gender combine affect her? How is this combine different from its effects on other women? What are the roles and contributions of dalit women to dalit and women's movements? Would these movements bring liberation to dalit women and beyond all these, is there scope in organizing dalit women specifically? These are some of the main questions behind this paper. Most of what I have to say is based on observation and experience. Our experiences and also the experiences of the many working with dalit women are expressed in these paragraphs.

Two literary characterizations

Lakshmi is a temple sweeper, dedicated to the temple since childhood. She lives with her beautiful teenage daughter, seen by all, known by none. Standing before the deity, she quietly drives a knife into her daughter. She prefers her death to sending her to the commissioner who is visiting the temple. She herself has been a victim of society, having loved a man who could not claim her, bearing a fatherless child, used and looked down upon by society. She had educated her daughter, trusting in a new future for her in life. But the commissioner's visit has shattered her dreams. She does not want her daughter to tread the path she herself had to.

Kashi is the heroine in Bhimrao Shirwale's story 'Livelihood'. Kashi, a daughter of the slums, is married to Dharma, who goes to jail for an accidental murder. To stay alive in her twenty-year wait for Dharma's release, she becomes the mistress of Kesu Ghatgir, the one-eyed bootlegger. In her struggle for survival, the hideous looking child of hers through Kesu becomes her source of livelihood, by exhibiting him for alms. A crowd would queue up every day before her door to lease the child out for fifteen to twenty rupees in return for a day of begging. The day Kesu comes to claim his son, Kashi's life and livelihood splinters and falls apart.

The differentness

One is struck by the difference in the characterization of Lakshmi and Kashi. Both are dalit women, but Lakshmi is the heroine of a non-dalit writer, Kashi of a dalit writer. Lakshmi is a heroine we can recognize, one clothed in middle class values and upper caste terminology. Heroines like Kashi are a portrayal of real dalit women, telling us a story of 'pathos, protest and the undefeatable will to survive'. Lakshmi is a victim of circumstance, bearing her burden quietly and at pains to mould her life into the values of the dominant culture. She prefers death to dishonour and when she is not able to cope, she quietly withdraws. Kashi is the undying spirit that rises up and takes new forms every time circumstances try to crush her. She is the surge of life where the culture and value is living and life alone.

It is time we acknowledge the difference in Lakshmi and Kashi. Is it the portrayal that is different, or is Lakshmi different from Kashi, or are we divorcing Lakshmi from her 'self' and portraying her? What might be the relationship of characters like Lakshmi or Kashi to real dalit women? As her figure emerges in literature, are we also able to recognize her at the crossroads of a new awakening, compelling us to see through her eyes?

Empirical studies make it obvious that while Dalit women share many of the same disabilities arising out of their class position with the poor in general, their caste along with dalit men and their gender with all other women, the extent, intensity and depth vary. The cumulative effects of caste, class and gender are qualitatively different from the impact of each of these independent factors. Let us now look at how these three powerful forces act in isolation and in combination on dalit women.

Her class

Being poor she is caught up in the cycle of lack of education or marketable skills with no chance for a reasonable occupation. Poverty again pushes her daughter into the same cycle. Having no assets to fall back upon, she has no economic standing or independence.

She is totally dependent upon wage labour in the informal sector that is hard to come by, laborious, insecure, uncertain, poorly paid and exploited. She carries the double burden of work outside and inside the home, more often than not the sole bread winner of the family, with no help or support. Her illiteracy and lack of organizing power keep her out of available designated welfare measures and claims to resources. Being poor she is abused and exploited by the landlord, the employer, government officials and the general public.

Her caste

Being a dalit she is an untouchable. She is restricted from entering the homes of other caste people, from entering the temple, discriminated at the village water pump, at the local tea shop. She is made to feel inferior and unclean even in places where she is supposedly equal—in schools, colleges and work places. She is the victim of violence, atrocities, oppression and exploitation arising out of caste hierarchy. She finds no support from politicians, the bureaucracy, police, judiciary, or other castes in the struggle for dignity and justice. Her social mobility in any field such as education, employment, clothing, habits, is the butt of jokes or the subject of comment by others.

Her gender

She bears the double burden of outside labour and domestic work. She is subject to the male members of the family. Family violence like wife beating is common among dalits too. In her work she is discriminated against, restricted from certain kinds of work and paid unequal wages. She is vulnerable to sexual abuse from landlords and other dalit men too.

The three forces act not only in isolation but also place specific limitations and produce forms of discrimination in combination. While it is not easy to analyze definite causal and supportive connections from one to another, their interplay and composite nature cannot be negated. This would be a vital area for further study.

Caste—class

Reflection and experience show a direct and causal relationship between caste and class in the case of dalits. The disabilities and limitations placed on dalits in terms of education, occupation, social interaction and social mobility have resulted in their being pushed to the lowest class—so much so that caste and class are synonymous in our society. Some even prefer to call this 'CLASTE'.

It is not an accident or coincidence that (according to recent figures) 49% of the Scheduled Castes (SCs) are agricultural wage workers as against 25% in the general population; that 85% of SCs are landless or near landless owning 0 to 0.50 acres, and that SCs constitute only 16% of our work force. The fact that these are recent figures—together with the agitations against Mandal and the anti-reservation struggle—explodes the myth that there is great social mobility among the SCs through reservations and that caste is no longer relevant. Coming to dalit women, they face the same limitations and marginalizations in a more severe form. With the majority in the community already landless, there is no possibility of her owning land. Even when government land, house sites or any other asset is assigned, it usually is not assigned to women. The restrictions on certain types of employment, the assignment of unclean work, the lack of organizing and networks, lead to further subjugation and poverty. The very direct, causal, supportive and reinforcing role of caste is evident in our class structure. The impact of caste and class on dalit women is more than the mere sum of these and even more than the impact of caste and class on dalit men or non-dalit women.

Patriarchy—class

A direct causal relation is difficult to establish here though their interaction cannot be negated. Her poverty leaves her with scarce resources to keep body and soul together. She eats the last and the least, her needs like health and other facilities are given lowest importance. The less paid and supposedly lighter work is assigned to her. She is not paid equal wage along with dalit men. Certain agricultural operations like ploughing are denied to her.

Patriarchy—caste

The dalit woman faces atrocities, violence, rape and oppression by men of other castes much more than other women. She is considered to be of loose character and easy virtue. In times of caste wars she is used as the tool and means to take revenge. The devadasi system is an extreme form of forced prostitution that dalit women are subjected to.

The purity–pollution concept, women's ritually unclean status for performing certain pujas, learning Sanskrit or listening to the shruti are instances of the strong similarities found in gender and caste oppression. The woman–man division and hierarchy is found in a more systematized, stringently codified, religiously ordained, hierarchical and closed manner in the caste system.

Dalit women in Dalit movements

Dalit women have been part and parcel of many struggles of class, caste and gender. But a study of the literature on these struggles hardly gives us any picture of her participation, role or contribution to these struggles. As it has been rightly said, the presence of a large number of women in a struggle does not make it a women's struggle. The two movements with which dalit women can most clearly identify are the dalit movement and the women's movement. I will attempt to sketch the response of these two movements to the question of dalit women.

The most urgent, immediate and obvious issues faced by dalit women are those arising from caste and untouchability. It is also true to say that dalits, including women, have become more conscious of the oppression of the caste system which plagues them from before birth and continues after death. Struggles against caste hierarchy, oppression and atrocities; struggles for self-dignity, rights, justice and the claiming of their roots have become the guiding lights of dalit movements. These are also undoubtedly the most serious issues faced by dalit women. The dalit movement is thus inclusive of dalit women's issues.

It cannot be denied that the dalit issue is one of the most burning issues in our country. In its relationships to the Buraku community in Japan, apartheid in South Africa, the Blacks and the native Americans in the United States, in the struggles of all indigenous people, it is also an international issue. In the political arena, too, dalits have become a very potential force. The dalit movement is thus at a phase of trying to consolidate itself as an identity, a community and is also working out its equations with other marginalized sections as a political force. This is what is now termed as Dalit Assertion and the time is pregnant with possibilities.

At this point, any raising of the dalit women's question within the dalit movement as an issue is considered a weapon to divide, undermine and weaken the dalit movement by the leaders of the movement. It is seen as pitching dalit women against Dalit men, and the sidetracking of caste by gender.

Another position is that brahminism is the root cause of all the oppressive and hierarchical orders within Indian society, of both caste and gender. Pre-Aryan society is sometimes eulogized as a society of equals. It is thus argued that the fight against brahminism is the crux of the matter and will lead to a breakdown of caste and gender inequality and oppression. The dalit movement claims that dalit women enjoy more liberty and freedom when compared to other women, which is a fact. Her role and contribution to the economy of the family, her freedom through working outside the family along with other dalit women and men, the relative freedom and acceptance of man–woman sexual relations, sociocultural patterns, and the severe deprivation faced by the community on the whole has led to a more balanced and equal relationship between dalit women and men.

But this is not to deny gender inequality within the dalit communities, or that the male image dalit men develop is similar to that of society around them. Hence we find that male children are preferred; that girl children get marginalized with respect to food intake, education, extra household chores and in socialization; that married women face harassment, wife beating, oppression and desertion; that women do not participate in panchayats. The patriarchal system is the order in dalit communities too.

A look into the dalit movement shows men almost exclusively in leadership positions. Women are the mass, the crowd in these movements. It is even considered strategic to have women in the forefront. The agendas of the movements are to fight for land, but not for entitlements for women; for minimum wages, but not for equal wages.

One cannot deny the patriarchal nature of dalit communities, despite relatively more freedom for the women within the community. Demands and restrictions on women increase as the family climbs up the economic ladder. Dalit families in the middle class in urban areas, or those that have sufficient land for themselves, follow the patterns typical of the middle class and upper castes. The dominant values are favoured and this leads to a new zeal in protecting and controlling women, who are now the keepers of virtue and family esteem. Similar values are exhibited in the dalit movements too, though it is coming to be questioned more and more.

Dalit women in women's movements

The last two decades have seen the growth of consciousness and the articulation of women's issues especially among educated, urban, middle class women. The issues raised by this movement have been mostly on price rise, dowry, rape, reproductive rights, fertility drugs, uniform civil code, man–woman relationship and the like. By and large the women's movement has remained distant from the lives of dalit women, even though they have at times tried to articulate their issues.

The issues of dalit women such as those of untouchability, caste discrimination, sexual violence by upper caste men, the very skewed pattern of land distribution, lack of assets and resources, inaccessibility to government and other welfare and administrative measures, the devadasi system, all of which have cornered dalit women and maintained their status quo, has not found a resonant vibration in the women's movement.

The practice has been to club dalit women's issues under the caption of women's issues and discuss them in general terms. They are analyzed under the headings women in higher education; dropout rates of girl children; employment pattern of women; resource allocation to women; assets and landownership for women; rape and atrocities against women; man–woman relationship; and so on. In this, the movement has not been able to identify that the face behind these issues is that of dalit women. While the factors are analyzed, dalit women have not been integrated into this analysis and focused upon. It is thus not a surprise that the National Women's Conference initiated in 1982 did not take up dalit women as a sub-theme till the fifth conference in 1994 in Tirupathi.

The women's movement too, like the dalit movement, sees it as dangerous to divide women into dalit and non-dalit sections and for similar reasons. Further, it has been argued that 'All women are dalits' and no further division should be 'created'.

It is true that in patriarchal society women are marginalized, but it is also true that the marginalization, exploitation and oppression faced by dalit women is not equal to that faced by other women. Understanding oppression and marginalization is like the pealing of an onion. We start with the most immediate and obvious, because that alone is within our grasp at that moment in time. It is possible to start only from there. As we try to delve more, other deeper forms of oppression face us.

A major handicap here is in understanding the women's movement. Autonomous women's groups are moving towards a position where participation and decision making is solely by women in women's movements. Along with this, women's movements are counted as those that question the inequality between the two genders. Hence the struggles of dalit women against untouchability, atrocities, liquor, land alienation and low wages are not looked upon as being strictly within the purview of a women's movement, since the composition and decision making within these movements is not only by women.

Dalit women—her space within the struggle

The disabilities shared by dalit women with dalit men and women in general cannot be negated. However the presence of agricultural workers in the Telangana movement, or dalits and women in class movements did not automatically bring liberation, freedom or equality for dalits or for women. While there are marginal and proportional changes, it did not question or change the inherent and basic injustice and bias in the society. It did not change caste hierarchy or gender inequality. Along the way, much later, these have been recognized and movements are now afoot to change these deeper inequalities. Similarly, dalit women would find that there is no automatic liberation for her in the dalit movement or women's movements, though changes are wont to occur. Along the way she needs to raise the question of her participation and relationship in these movements. This is not to say that the dalit women's struggle is an isolated anti-dalit, anti-women struggle. There are many battles she needs to fight hand in hand with these two movements. The question of her role and contribution in them should be raised—her space within the struggle.

Micro-experiences in different pockets is a testimony to the relevance of the dalit women's question. The experiences of most action groups is one of a consistent and very potent involvement of dalit women in struggles. The role of dalit women in the struggles in Karamchedu and Tsundur which took on a dalit movement form also indicate their role and contribution. The mainstay of these struggles were women. The anti-arrack movement in Andhra Pradesh was also largely by dalit women. The problem of arrack had in a short span become so crucial that there was a spontaneous movement against it. Middle class and other caste women hardly joined the struggle, though support was extended in terms of publicity, sympathy, seminars and moral support. The experiences here show that dalit women are able to take up issues at wider levels and pursue them consistently. The issue has to be of vibrant importance to them, of an urgent and immediate nature, having very obvious effects on their day-to-day lives. Their battles are not of the abstract kind, with philosophies and ideologies that are distant from their day-to-day experiences.

The women's movement has not recognized the inherent strengths and historically created weakness of dalit women. This has resulted in an exclusion in the analysis and taking up of issues between dalit women and the women's movement. More serious work needs to be done to look into these so that the women's movement can focus on the disabilities of dalit women that are specific and most particular to our society.

Dalit women—more in resonance with Dalit movements

Dalit women have emerged as an identifiable entity. Their participation in all struggles is a historical fact, though scarcely acknowledged. Struggles have failed to recognize dalit women's faces behind their facts and figures.

Dalit women share a lot with the dalit movements and the women's movements. Many aspects are common and overlapping. At present, of the two movements, the dalit movement has addressed very crucial and deep rooted issues of caste hierarchy, untouchability, atrocities and oppression, while also focusing on self dignity and justice. Since these are the everyday, immediate and urgent issues faced by dalit women, they have a better chance to work for their caste liberation from within the dalit movement. Today the dalit movement is an emergent force; the possibilities of a better equation in society are becoming realizable.

The women's movement, on the other hand, has not been able to identify the issues of dalit women as those of a distinct group within women's movements. Questions of men–women relationships and gender discrimination do not have the same immediate or urgent place in dalit women's every day lives that caste discriminations do.

What, then, is their role in the dalit movement? Educated cadre and volunteers among dalit women are voicing the need to recognize the role and contributions of dalit women in dalit movements. This can be done only by the inclusion of dalit women in leadership positions within the movement, analyzing the issues from a gender perspective, looking into the possibilities and constraints placed on dalit women by any issue, making strategies and plans such that she can guide, control and participate totally. It is also essential that the movement not shy away from addressing the gender issue within the movement and the dalit community, administer justice to victims, even if the perpetrators are dalit men, with the full realization that it will strengthen the movement rather than weaken it. Dalit women must claim the space within the dalit struggle.

Dalit women also need to recognize the gender bias not just within their community but in the whole of society. It is a struggle all women go through, though in different degrees and forms. From an identifiable, strong position within the dalit movement, dalit women should extend support and cooperate with the women's movement. They should be able to network with the women's movement. It is not desirable that they subsume their identity under the women's movement at this juncture. As a force from outside they need to support and work together. I feel this is a very sensitive and important area. If the women's movement in India is to reach the most oppressed among our women, address the limitations specific to our culture, and envisage a humane, just society, it cannot do so while excluding the dalit women's question. Women's movements need to take up the cause of dalit women in our society, reach the most un-reached of our women and question basic inequality patterns. It is only if we can question the twin aspects of caste and gender that we can work towards a society based on equality and justice.

~

CASTE AND WOMEN
Leela Dube

This essay explores the relationship between caste and gender: it examines the way caste impinges on women's lives and explores the role of women in maintaining and, to some extent, changing caste. The exercise requires us to situate women as conscious acting subjects of social relationships and processes that constitute, reproduce and modify the social system characterized by the institution of caste. Equally, we need to consider the determinate ways in which women are objectified and become instruments in—even as they introduce flexibility to—the structures and processes implicated in the reproduction of caste. The discussion focuses on (the first and last of the following) three interrelated, indeed overlapping, themes—occupational continuity and the reproduction of caste, food and rituals, and finally, marriage and sexuality.

The three basic characteristics of caste, typified as jati, a birth status group, are exclusion or separation (rules governing marriage and contact, which maintain distinctions of caste), hierarchy (the principle of order and rank according to status), and interdependence (the division of labour which is closely tied to hierarchy and separation). These three analytically separable principles of the caste system operate not so much through individuals as through units based on kinship. The maintenance of rules of behaviour and actions specific to one's jati and the patterns of interaction with other birth-status groups, for instance, critically centre on kinship units, particularly the family and the household. We find then that the punishment for transgression of rules and norms of caste leads to the ostracism of the domestic group of the offender unless s/he is disowned by the household. Women's lives are largely lived within familial parameters. The centrality of the family and the household in their lives cannot therefore be overemphasized.

Similarly, when we turn to the material bases of caste, the most important form of inequality in the caste system, the unequal distribution of resources and exploitative relations of production, can be understood only through an enquiry into the principles of kinship governing the allocation of resources, devolution of rights to property, rights to services and entitlements. A jati or caste group then functions through its constituent familial units or large-scale kinship units. It is not the jati as a whole but the lineages or familial units which hold material resources. This has crucial implications for gender since within these units there are clear distinctions in respect of the rights and entitlements of their male and female members. Thus, if endogamy has the potential for raising one's family status through the forging of appropriate marital links, it can also initiate a tight squeeze by restricting marital choices and putting pressures for material resources for a daughter's wedding.

Occupational continuity

Women's work contributes substantially to the occupational continuity of a caste group. It is, of course, true that the growth of new professions and open recruitment to occupations have been important aspects of social change in Indian society. The picture of inalienable unchanging links between traditional occupation and caste was, in any case, vastly overdrawn. At the same time, there are significant continuities in the link between caste and occupation. Agriculture—although now open to all castes—still gives a distinct identity to a large number of castes of 'traditional' cultivators. Equally some other occupations remain the exclusive privilege of particular castes. A brahmin, for instance, still performs the functions of the purohit (priest), for upper and middle level castes. Among artisan castes of goldsmiths, blacksmiths, potters and weavers, a few members of the group at the very least are imparted the necessary skills, and make a living by the traditional craft. Finally, most ritually polluting occupations—the curing and tanning of hides, the removal of dead animals, scavenging, and the activities of the barber, the washerman and the midwife—retain their association with specific castes.

In these occupations, closely tied to caste, the work of women, carried out as members of households—the basic units of production—is indispensable. It is difficult for weavers and potters to carry on the complex processes of their craft without the continuous help of the women and children of the household, who in turn have well-defined tasks. Women can also take on aspects of men's work: it is not unusual for women from a potter's family to establish contacts with clients and go to the market to assist with the selling of goods. Similarly, basket weaving is a joint activity of men and women. In horticulture, women often carry the major burden of work. In rural areas and small towns it is common for women from households of petty traders and shopkeepers to grind spices and prepare fries, fritters and preserves for sale in the family shop. Despite regional variations, these illustrations underscore the fact that occupational continuity in large measure depends on women. It is telling that a man who runs away with another man's wife is censured for both 'breaking another man's cooking pot' and 'breaking a household'. The forsaken husband, after all, is left without help to carry out the business of living.

Jajmani relations, short-term contractual affiliations between artisans and service castes and landowners, cultivators and traders, and relations of exchange among occupational castes, a feature of many rural and semi-urban areas, function once again at the level of the family. Both men and women render services and receive remuneration—in cash and kind—for their work. Among service castes such as barbers and washermen, women's work in relation to the jajman's family is, indeed, well defined. To the north of the Vindhyas a barber woman renders personal services to the women of the jajman's family—or a family which engages the barber woman on cash payment—which include the cutting of nails, the decoration of feet (with special coloured solutions), a special oil massage and a bath for a new-born baby and its mother, the supplying of leaf cups and leaf plates for feasts, and the role of companion to the bride during the wedding ceremony. In Chhattisgarh, a Raot (grazier and water-carrier) woman has an important supportive role to play during feasts and ceremonies, bringing water, washing utensils, and grinding spices and soaked pulses for preparing fries and fritters. The castes of both the barber and the water-carrier help in preparing pakka food on ceremonial occasions. In the south, a washer-woman's ritual functions are indispensable for the washing of soiled clothes during the ceremony that goes with the first menstruation. In every region there are specific 'untouchable' castes whose women work as midwives: these women, along with the men of their caste, share the essential task of removing the pollution of the upper and clean castes. Finally, in many parts of the country, the bond or contract which ties labourers to their masters is understood to include the services of both the husband and the wife.

The cultural recognition of the significance of women's work in the continuity of caste-linked occupations is clear. At the same time, in order that women pursue these traditional occupations, they have to be trained in them from childhood and have to be socialized into accepting them as proper work which, within limits, is 'destiny'. It has been found that parents may restrict the education of girls to avoid a potentially uncomfortable situation in which the daughter develops a distaste for the traditional occupation of her caste. It then becomes difficult to get her married into an appropriate family. Not formal education, but the capacity and willingness to do traditional work tends to make a girl useful in the husband's family. The necessity of continuing with occupational work is an important basis for marrying within the caste. It is understandable then that a landowning cultivator family of the kunbi caste in rural Maharashtra should be unhappy when one of its sons, after acquiring education, decides to marry an educated brahmin girl. What use would she be in an agriculturist's family? Would she be able to call her husband's home her own? Even home-based work linked to cultivation is seen as outside the arena of her experience and below her status.

In situations of change, women often have to take on the responsibility for continuing caste-based occupations and maintaining the household. When men give up their traditional occupation on account of its low ritual status or inadequate returns, the entire burden of occupational work often falls on the women. Many men migrate to towns leaving behind their families. Women continue their contribution in terms of services or craft, but for want of male help they face the choice of losing their clientele or coping with a doubled work burden. Middlemen intervene. Wives of migrant men often have to work under the authority of their husband's kin who surround them within the neighbourhood and locality. Thus, women's contribution to occupational continuity is carried out within patrilineal limits and under the impositions and controls of caste.

In a study of scavenger women conducted in Delhi, Karlekar (1982) found that while men were increasingly leaving the ritually 'defiling' occupation of their caste, women remained in the same traditional field. These women had to support the males of the household who were trying to acquire skills from entering new occupations, or explore independent sources of income. The men, even when unemployed, were loath to touch their traditional work. Boys were being sent to school while girls joined their mothers at work at an early age. Similarly, the padyachi and nadar families from Tamil Nadu who come to Delhi in search of employment have their women take up work as domestic help in private homes for washing clothes and utensils, and cleaning the house. It is held that in difficult times, women, since they are used to doing domestic work for their own household, can do similar kind of work for others. The men, on the other hand, generally consider it below their dignity to do such jobs. In the absence of regular employment, even odd jobs are preferred to domestic work. Among these migrant groups women are often the principal supporters of the family: women's experience of multifaceted housework becomes the basis for maintaining the household. The controls are retained. Social and ritual matters are discussed and decided upon by the males of the caste within the neighbourhood. [. . .]

Marriage and sexuality

This brings us to the key area of marriage and sexuality. The caste system is premised upon the cultural perception of a fundamental difference in male and female sexuality. First, periodical pollution through menstruation and parturition renders women intrinsically less pure than men. There is, within a caste, a hierarchy between the sexes. At the same time, the difference in the levels of purity/impurity between men and women is much less among the lower castes than among the high castes. Low caste women, apart from self-pollution, also deal with others' pollution through occupational activities such as midwifery, disposal of dirt, the washing of dirty clothes and many other services. But their men, too, have to undertake polluting craftwork and service for others. Among these castes women's substantial contribution to the process of earning a livelihood along with the sharing of impure tasks by both men and women makes the gender division less unequal. It is, of course, true that among these castes menstrual pollution does impose certain disabilities on women in respect of food, worship of deities and ancestors. At the same time, brahmin and other higher caste men neither incur self-pollution of the kind their women do nor do they have to perform the polluting work for other castes. Their women, on the contrary, are involved in pollution incurred through bodily processes, mainly menstruation and childbirth. They are also responsible for doing some of the polluting tasks within the family, although this, perhaps, does not render them permanently less pure than men. There is a pervasive notion that women never attain the level of purity of men of their own caste. It is well known that traditionally women of twice-born castes have been equated with shudras who could not be initiated into the learning of the Vedas.

The other source of impurity for women is widowhood. Widows are not supposed to perform the puja of family deities; they do not cook the pure food offered to these deities. A man, on the other hand, is not similarly affected if he becomes a widower. Such hierarchy between the sexes is more a feature of brahmin and other 'clean' castes. While some of the disabilities imposed on widows are prevalent among all castes, it can be argued that concerns of purity/impurity along the gender divide have an inverse relationship with the ritual status of castes.

Moreover, the cultural schemes which underlie the caste system are based upon a fundamental difference between male and female bodies in respect of their vulnerability to incur impurity through sexual intercourse. Sexual involvement is a much more serious matter for a woman since the act affects her internally while it affects a man only externally. In the case of inter-caste sexual relations a man incurs external pollution which can be washed off easily, but a woman incurs internal pollution, which pollutes her permanently. The contrast is expressed culturally by likening a woman to an earthen pot which is easily and permanently defiled if used by a polluted person within the caste or by a lower caste person or one of a different religion, and a man, on the other hand, to a brass pot which is not easily polluted and, in any case, can be restored to its original state by scrubbing, washing, and if necessary, by putting it through fire, a purifier par excellence. This metaphor—which distinguishes between men and women in terms of their respective vulnerability to pollution through sexual intercourse—is used extensively in caste and village councils when cases of sexual entanglements come up for adjudication. Indeed, it dwells in popular consciousness while judging men and women. It should be clear that upper caste women are much more vulnerable to permanent pollution than lower caste women. Indeed, sexual transgressions within the caste are treated much more leniently, particularly among those castes which allow secondary unions. Equally, it is entanglements with men of castes lower than that of the woman which are taken very seriously. Pollution incurred through food affects both women and men internally, but pollution incurred through sexual intercourse is radically different in character for the two sexes. This is closely linked to the dictum that sanctions hypergamy although within well-defined limits: 'Superior seed can fall on an inferior field but inferior seed cannot fall on a superior field.' [. . .]

The cultural apprehension of the vulnerability of women and the emphasis on their purity and restrained behaviour, which entail limited interaction with the opposite sex, are important components of the management of female sexuality in a caste society. The emphasis on arranged or negotiated marriages and the proper organization of space and time for young girls after puberty derive their justification from this concern with boundary maintenance, which means the maintenance of the ritual purity of caste. All these are implicated in the mechanisms and processes of socialization and in the opportunities for education and employment open to women. Caste thus imparts a special character to the process of growing up as a female. All this does not end with marriage. Women need to be controlled, their sexuality contained, at all times. This is sought to be achieved through mechanisms of proper social control, idealization of familial roles, and an emphasis on female modesty. The importance of the purity of caste affects a woman in all life-stages.

The beliefs and practices which negotiate and contain the threat posed by female sexuality are not uniform across the caste hierarchy and are also marked by regional variations. At the same time, there does exist a shared ideological framework that informs this arena. This framework rests upon a clear demarcation of phases of life with respect to female sexuality—a special ritual value accorded to virginity, the ritualization of puberty and special care accorded to pubescent girls, a glorification of the married state and motherhood, and a clear distinction between primary and secondary marriage—which in turn constitute the institutionalized mechanisms for the containment of female sexuality.

The value attached to virginity is directly linked to the concern with female purity. The pre-pubertal phase is looked upon as a stage of intrinsic purity and is celebrated in a number of ways. The custom of worshipping and feeding virgin girls on specific days such as the eight days of Navaratri is widespread in India. Equally, pre-pubertal girls are given special recognition in life-cycle rituals. A pre-pubertal girl is looked upon as a manifestation of Devi or the mother goddess and is believed to drive away the lurking presence of an evil spirit and an evil eye. The purity and the consequent privileged status of a girl in the pre-pubertal stage contrasts sharply with, and brings into clear relief, the next phase, the onset of puberty.

In south India, this change in a girl's status is dramatized through rituals. The rituals and special prescriptions of diet vary across castes. The core, and the underlying message, does not change. Similarly, in Orissa and Maharashtra, several castes observe the essential features of puberty rituals although they conduct them on a modest scale. The message of these rituals is clear. The girl has become a sexual being: this calls for restrained behaviour on her part and emphasizes the need for protection and vigilance. The occasion is at once auspicious and calls for a guard against the evil eye. The regulations regarding diet and movement are directed towards future fertility: they make the process of childbearing smooth and control the girl's sexuality. Restrained and controlled sexuality is a prerequisite for socially sanctioned motherhood. The puberty ceremony informs the people within the kin group and the jati that the girl has come of age and her marriage is open to negotiation. The mechanisms which set limits and restraints also sacralize and sanctify sexuality. In the rest of India the first menstruation is not marked by any rituals. The event is taken care of more or less unobtrusively. At the same time, restrictions relating to pollution, food, and behaviour do come into play. The onset of puberty then is a definite departure in the life of a girl. She becomes conscious of her fragile purity.

It is, in fact, this preoccupation with female purity and its fragility that helps explain certain aspects of marriage in caste society. In traditional terms it is the marriage of a virgin with full rites within the acceptable limits of connubiality which sacralizes and sanctifies the girl's sexuality. It makes her a full member of her caste, and thus a complete person. In north and central India the matrix of an early marriage of a girl, a long waiting period when she continues to stay in her natal home, and gauna or mukhlawa, the ritual of sending off the girl to her husband's house after puberty, is very common. If the family is not in a position to bear the double expenditure, the two ceremonies may be collapsed into one: the girl is formally sent to her husband's home for two or three days after marriage and is then brought back only to be sent after the onset of puberty. Similarly, the objective of early marriage, namely, to preserve the virginity and purity of the girl until marriage, becomes clear if we look at Rajasthan where in some areas a number of baby brides are formally married to baby grooms in a specially held marriage fair on an auspicious day. It is also customary to marry off all the girls in a family from the age of two to thirteen or fifteen together on a special auspicious day. The logic of an early marriage is clear: such child marriages ensure that a girl is married with full rites while still a virgin, and consummation of marriage can wait until she has come of age. It is significant that while castes and families who can afford to keep their girls secluded and protected tend to marry them off after puberty, other castes who require that their daughters work in the fields or away from home prefer to marry them before puberty. In a village in Sikar district in Rajasthan, where the normal age of marriage of girls ranged between seven to sixteen years, most post-pubertal marriages were among the charans and brahmins whose daughters did not work outside the home and could be segregated and secluded. In Uttar Pradesh, once again, the poorer castes whose women and children have to work outside, away from home and without protection, find safety in pre-pubertal marriage. [. . .]

A strong patrilineal ideology in which male blood is the real determining element in the placement of offspring—unless the mother is of a fairly low caste—is more characteristic of north than of south India. In the case of the jats of Haryana, who represent an extreme case, even the ritual distance between castes was not of much significance. The relative freedom from brahminical injunctions and the weak hold of norms of ritual purity and pollution meant that during the colonial period jat men freely entered into sexual unions with women belonging to very low castes such as the chamar and the chuhra (scavenger). The children born of these women were absorbed into the jat community. In jat self-perception their community is like the sea: whatever falls into it becomes jat.

The rajputs or kshatriyas, once again, have been open to hypergamous unions with women of different castes, often much below them in status. The ruling classes used their privileged status to ritually sanction their marriages with virgin girls of different clean castes. The offspring born of such unions adopted the father's identity; they were known as Rajputs, but had a lower status than their father. Women of secondary unions, of course, were and are looked upon as concubines.

Men have institutionalized mechanisms to escape the incurrence of pollution through sexual intercourse with a low caste woman. This often takes the form of a purificatory bath and the ritual expiation of the offence. Orthodox brahmins in Karnataka and Tamil Nadu, for instance, after sleeping with a low caste woman discard the old scared thread, have a purificatory bath and don a new sacred thread. On the other hand, if a woman from these communities goes 'astray' and the matter becomes public knowledge she is banished, declared dead to the family and a 'mock' shraddha (funeral rites) is performed for her. The fate of the paramour of a high caste woman, if he belongs to a low caste, is severe punishment at the hands of the holders of power—jats, rajputs, brahmins, kammas—loss of sources of livelihood, a good beating, and sometimes, even death.

Dominance predicated upon ownership of resources is intertwined with notions of the ritual status of different castes and the associated idea of graded qualities of blood. Low caste women are sexually exploited by powerful upper caste men owning land. It is not only difficult for low caste men to protect their women against the lust and desire of their upper caste masters and superordinates in the agrarian hierarchy, but there is also a tacit acceptance of upper caste 'seed'. Only if an upper or middle level caste man is excommunicated by his own community for having a sustained relationship with a low caste woman is he identified with her caste; their children grow up in the mother's caste. But things do not often come to such a pass. Fleeting liaisons and acts of sexual aggression by upper caste men are much more familiar. The low caste opposition to these—and other upper caste practices—result in sexual assaults on their women which attack the dignity and honour of the male kin and the community. Rape, as elsewhere, is an act of power through sexual violence. The assertion of dominance is claimed as a right by upper castes. In Utter Pradesh, for instance, it is said that just as a she-goat may be milked at any time at one's own will, so can a chamar woman be enjoyed any time at one's discretion. In Vidarbha, kunbi landowners who are on the lookout for mahar women working in their fields say with contempt, 'Give her a few measures of grain and she will be quiet.' The control of resources and ritual status—together integrally informed by and constitutive of relations of power—reinforce each other and underlie the sexual exploitation of lower caste women by upper caste men.

Conclusion

I will, in conclusion, briefly consider whether apparently inexorable and inevitable processes of change, invoked by myopic mouthpieces of modernization, have led to transformations in the relationship between caste and gender. There has certainly been a considerable loosening of the rules and norms governing commensality and a weakening of the attendant mechanisms of ostracism and excommunication: but the relational idiom of food and the play of rituals, articulated by the mutual intermeshing of caste and gender, continues to be critical for the functioning of families. Similarly, transformation in the nature and magnitude of social interaction characterized by the near-absence of commensal inhibitions, particularly in metropolitan and urban areas, the enactment of state laws which recognize inter-caste marriages, divorce and widow remarriage within the framework of the Hindu legal system, and a greater familiarity with the institution of the civil marriage, have opened up possibilities of marriages outside the bounds of caste. At the same time, negotiated and arranged marriages within the recognized limits of connubiality are the dominant and overwhelming norm. Finally, the increased emphasis on caste identities in the wider context of institutionalized politics centring on the policies and practices of the state, has led to the reworking, refurbishment and reinforcement of 'caste traditions'. Caste is not dead. Gender is a live issue. The principles of caste inform the specific nature of sexual asymmetry in Hindu society; the boundaries and hierarchies of caste are articulated by gender.

References

Karlekar, Malavika. 1982. *Poverty and women's work: A study of sweeper women in Delhi*. New Delhi: Vikas Publishing House.

≈

WOMEN AND GENDER IN THE STUDY OF TRIBES IN INDIA

Virginius Xaxa

In recent years, there has been more analytical discussion on the status of women in tribal societies. Earlier, they were portrayed as having a better status than women in caste societies, with physical mobility, choice in marriage, divorce and remarriage, access to property and resources. Such assumptions were based on an examination of the literature available in monographs with reference to rules of inheritance, right to property, share in the decision-making process, etc. In short, these hinge on the one hand on rights and privileges these women enjoy and on the other, on the kind of role assigned to them by virtue of belonging to a particular gender. Consequently, tribal women were invariably depicted as having higher social status than their counterparts in caste society. However, the economic burden and workload of tribal women as well as their access to education, food and nutrition, modern occupation and political participation, especially in the modern context, have not been given the kind of attention they deserve. [. . .]

Stages of social formations

One of the dominant ways of looking at change in tribal society is to show change in the mode of making a living; this is most glaringly reflected in the change from food gathering to food producing or from swidden (slash and burn cultivation) to settled agriculture. Such transformation is also evident in a shift from communal and collective ownership of land and use of labour to private ownership. Developments such as these have led to a critical examination of the idea of tribal society as an egalitarian one. Forms of inequality in tribal society in its traditional setting have been analyzed. Of these, gender inequality has been highlighted as the most pervasive, irrespective of the stage of social formation. A dimension that has been highlighted in this context has been the relative position of women and men under different types of social formations such as food gathering and hunting, swidden agriculture, settled agriculture and state formation. The position of men and women in different tribal groups has also been studied without treating social formation as the reference point. Such analyses have been done with respect to division of labour, forms of property, religious institutions, family and state. Through an examination of the former, an attempt has been made to show how the establishment of patriarchy took shape in these societies. In social formations such as food gathering and swidden agriculture, rigid division of labour was either absent or gender inequality in one sphere was offset by equality in another. For example, citing the case of Birhors in Jharkhand, Nathan (1997) shows how the greater importance of men due to their involvement in the public domain—in this case distribution of meat (a prestige food)—is neutralized by a similar kind of engagement in women's market exchange and transaction activities. Similarly, among the Khasis, the higher social status of women due to rights of ownership held by them over ancestral property is neutralized by men's hold over the decision-making process.

It is however not clear if this inequality that Nathan explicates is more to do with shifting cultivation or the institution of matriliny and settled habitation of the population as is the case with the Khasis. Again, he traces the monopolization of hierarchy by men primarily to the formation of the state and the establishment of individual property. Men's control over the ritual and public/political sphere is seen to be a crucial factor in the struggle to exclude women from ownership of land. Yet the case of the Khasis with state-like institutions or the Jaintias with full-fledged state institutions does not seem to corroborate such an argument (Sen 1985). Women continue to hold ownership over land and the monopolization of hierarchy by men is as yet absent among them.

Some scholars have traced witch-hunting to the pattern of land ownership in tribal societies. Kelkar and Nathan (1993, 109–18), for example, argue that it is the life interest of a widow in the entire land of her husband that is a major fetter on the property rights of the husband's male agnates. Following this, they argue that victims of witch-hunting are in particular widows who have such a life interest in their husband's land. Such an interest restricts the property rights of male agnates of the deceased husband, who have to wait till after the death of the woman to use the land for accumulation or for consumption. A widow without children is therefore more vulnerable to attack on the pretext of being a witch (ibid., 263). While there may be an association between the two in some cases, it is difficult to generalize that witch-hunting has primarily to do with ownership of land. Anyone who has studied witchcraft is familiar with the fact that it is much more complex than a practice associated only with property rights. In fact, a number of witch-hunting cases have been reported from time to time from the tea gardens of Jalpaiguri district in West Bengal, where access to property was hardly of consequence (Gupta 1979).

The myth of gender equality or higher status of women in tribal societies has also been critically viewed through an examination of customary law in respect of property, marriage, inheritance and so on. It has been shown that women in tribal societies are at a disadvantage vis-à-vis men in their respective societies (Nongbri 1998). It is interesting to note that the very practices that are regarded as indicative of higher social status in one kind of setting turn out to be in-built depressors in other settings. This is brought out by Tiplut Nongbri in her discussion of bride price. Referring to several tribes in Arunachal Pradesh, she points out how women among them are treated as mere commodities to be easily procured by men through bride price. A custom that was originally intended to compensate the girl's family for the loss of an economically active member, bride price has thus become a convenient justification for men to abuse their wives and treat them as disposable commodities. She writes, 'the system of bride price has proved to be the bane for women and lies at the root of proliferation of polygamous unions as wealthy men can take on a number of wives simply by paying an agreed sum to the girl's family' (Nongbri 1998, 33–34). In her study of Taivar Girasia, a tribal group of Rajasthan, Unnithan-Kumar points out how bride price is viewed not so much as a recognition of a woman's contribution to the household or as a payment for the loss of a productive member, but a compensation to the father of the bride and his agnatic group for the past expenditure on her maintenance, particularly consumption and food. Drawing on this, Unnithan-Kumar argues that bride price (valued in practical terms), is regarded as an important contribution that women make. The lack of ownership of property by women is legitimized by the Girasias on the ground that women move on marriage from their affinal villages (Unnithan-Kumar 1997, 205–06).

In this context, I would like to point out that it is an established fact that the division of labour in tribal society is based more on gender and age than on hierarchy and occupation. Division of labour has been both fluid and rigid. It is however not clear as to at what stage and on what principle the division of labour could be said to have assumed the form of inequality of rank or status between sexes in tribal societies. There is little discussion on how and on what basis the differences, especially between the sexes, came to be graded. For instance, whether divisions were mere division of work and labour and therefore devoid of evaluation and gradation, which is intrinsic to the consideration of being of high or low social status. Hence the study of the status of women does pose problems. It is difficult to study them from the perspective of the values inherent in those societies, especially since such values in those societies invariably project the idea of a collectivity. Equality and sharing therefore turn out to be the overarching value in those societies. Hence, rather than talking of high or low social status, it is more pertinent to talk of the inequality of gender. In the latter case, one can examine the relative position of women and men in relation to their access to equal opportunity, both formal and substantive.

Second, the taboo on women touching and using the plough in tribal societies has been seen as a way of denying women control over the means of production viz. land (Kishwar 1987, 96; Nathan 1997). This lack of access and control over land is however already denied in these societies by existing customary laws. For instance, Oraon and Ho women, who are forbidden to hold the plough, are denied access to land by customary laws existing in their societies. The explanation of the denial of women's access to land in terms of taboo thus seems far from adequate. After all, even the brahmins are prohibited from ploughing. That does not mean denial of access to land. Even in swidden agriculture, which Esther Boserup describes as a women's farming system, the allocation of plots is made to men in their capacity as the heads of the household though women exercise greater control over the plots after these have been allocated. There is no custom over plough cultivation among the Mizos, Semas, Konyaks and so on, and yet women do not have access to land in these communities where tribal land under swidden agriculture is controlled and distributed by the chiefs. Not only that but a rudimentary form of social differentiation is generally associated with the state and private property formation. And yet such formation among the tribes, though at work well before the coming of the British, was confined to a few pockets or tribes. However, it is the incorporation of tribes into the larger social system under colonial rule and administration that accelerated as well as opened up new vistas of social differentiation among them. The nature of development pursued by the Indian state in the post-independence era has only accelerated and intensified the process at work during the colonial period. [. . .]

Conclusion: Emerging discourse

The People of India project launched on 2 October 1985 under the auspices of the Anthropological Survey of India enumerated 461 tribal communities of which 174 have been identified as sub-groups. Tribal communities in India are enormously diverse and heterogeneous. There are wide-ranging differences among them with regard to language, physical characteristics, demographic traits, modes of livelihood and cultural exposure, as also the treatment and position of women. Their roles, rights, privileges as well as constraints differ. Women continue to be governed by customary laws and norms. The data available on gender in tribal societies is sketchy, especially in the context of transformations that have been taking place. Given such heterogeneity, it is rather difficult to generalize on the position of women as a whole across tribal groups in India. What has been observed can at best be described as being illustrative and heuristic.

Despite such heterogeneity, they seem to share one point in common, that they are different from the dominant community of the region. Such persons have always been seen as alien and as outsiders and nowhere is this more pronounced than in situations of intense inter-community competition and conflict. In northeast India, such conflict not only resulted in the creation of tribal states but also an exodus of the non-tribal population from the sub-region. Yet such conflict still prevails, especially in states or regions where non-tribals continue to form a significant part of the population (Bhattacharjee 1982; Kumar 1995), as in the new state of Jharkhand. The outsiders here have invariably been described as exploiters and oppressors and are addressed by terms such as the *diku.* Even in Meghalaya, where the exploitation is less, a very strong term, *dakhar,* is used for the outsiders. There has been a steady erosion of the tribal life support system, of lands and the forest, leading to an increasing pauperization of the majority. There is also a loss of language, and a real danger of tribes becoming minorities in their own lands. Given all these factors, the construction of identity and community has taken on interesting dimensions. On the one hand there has been the movement against the influx of outsiders for fear of becoming a minority in their own state or region. On the other, there has been a demand for the establishment of an autonomous council in either the region or the state with a view to protect the social, cultural and economic interests of tribal people. Such articulations are more marked in the eastern and northeastern regions than the other regions of tribal India.

In all these arguments, traditions and customary law—and therefore even the gender issue—play a pivotal role. This has led to an interesting discussion on gender issues among the intelligentsia of many tribal groups. Questions raised have far-reaching consequences for the freedom of women on the one hand and the issue of equality on the other, particularly with regard to property rights in land. A lively discussion that has been going on in Jharkhand revolves around three points. One concerns tribal tradition or, to be more precise, customary tribal law. According to this law, land in many tribal communities is held by the lineage and not by individuals. Individual families have the right of use but cannot transfer it by sale or other means outside the lineage. This being the custom, the articulation of the demand for a share in ownership of land by women is considered misplaced and against the tribal ethos. The other two relate to transfer of tribal land from tribes to non-tribes and use of the provision of reservation by children born of inter-tribe marriages.

An important feature of change is a largescale alienation of tribal land from tribes to non-tribes. Several studies point to the massive land dispossession that began with British rule. This process has become accentuated in post-independence India despite enactment of the Land Transfer Regulation in states with a large tribal population. As of January 1999, the area alienated stood at over 900,000 acres. The states where this was most widespread were Andhra Pradesh, undivided Madhya Pradesh, Bihar (especially Jharkhand), Gujarat and Orissa. The methods by which tribal land has passed from tribes to non-tribes, are mainly fraud, force, enticement, encroachment and indebtedness (Government of India 2001, 119).

One of the ways by which non-tribals are acquiring tribal land is by marrying tribal women. In view of the fact that there is a restriction on the alienation of land from tribes to non-tribes, such methods have become fairly pronounced in areas like Jharkhand. In fact, K.S Singh refers to the large incidence of alienation of tribal land through marriage with tribal women who marry outside the community, and who are not only seen as aligning with the dikus but also as conduits of land transfer from tribes to non-tribes. Often, after such transactions, non-tribal men have deserted tribal women. This in itself is an emotive issue among tribes in view of the long struggle that they have waged against the alienation of tribal land. Coupled with this is the wider issue of tribal demography. Tribes in their own territory/locality are increasingly losing ground numerically with far-reaching economic and political implications. In the process, their survival as a group/community seems to be at stake. Hence anything that tends to jeopardize their land and population is viewed with a great deal of indignation, a case in point being reactions to women marrying outsiders, especially dikus. At such times there is conflict and tension between tribes and non-tribes, as the former mobilize against such marriage alliances. At times even coercion and intimidation have been used against young women who are being courted by men of non-tribal origin. Somewhat related is the issue of reservation. There has been a general tendency among families of mixed (inter-tribe) marriages to take advantage of reservation extended to the tribes. This raises the issue of whether children born of a tribal or non-tribal father are to be considered tribal or non-tribal.

This issue has two dimensions, the legal and the sociocultural. According to tribal customary law, lineage is invariably derived from the father's side, which makes the children's tribal status problematic. Even if they take their mother's totemic title and seek advantage of the legal provisions for tribes, they are still contravening customary law. And yet one finds children born of such wedlock taking full advantage of the reservation facilities, thereby depriving genuine tribals. As this phenomenon is fairly widespread in Jharkhand, it explains part of the resentment against non-tribals marrying tribals.

An equally interesting discourse in tribal society is over the issue of women's property rights, particularly inheritance. One section is in favour of property rights in land for women, despite resistence to the same in the name of custom and tradition. In the case of Jharkhand, for example, it is argued that, as per tribal tradition, there is no individual ownership of land. Rather, the tradition there is that of the *khuntkatti* system, where land is invariably held by the entire lineage. Hence the question of extending ownership rights in land to women does not arise. However, it may be of interest to note K.S Singh's observation on the matter. A higher sex ratio among the Ho tribe accounts for a large number of single women, many of whom claimed their customary right to maintenance. This was often questioned by their male agnates. Singh, as the commissioner of Chota Nagpur, disposed of a large number of cases regarding Ho women's right to maintenance according to custom (ibid., 3). Among the matrilineal Khasis, the ethnic identity issue is raised along with articulation of changes in the system of kinship, namely kinship roles and rules of inheritance (Nongbri 1998, 2000). Resistance to women's property rights is also related to the economics of land size. It is argued that women's entitlement will lead to further subdivision and fragmentation of already subdivided and fragmented land. In Jharkhand that will adversely affect farm efficiency and viability.

Issues such as these pose the problem of a woman as an individual and citizen on the one hand and as a member of a community on the other. As an individual and as a citizen, a woman is entitled to human rights provisions as well as of citizenship, that guarantee individual right to freedom. Yet there are provisions in the Indian Constitution that aim to protect and safeguard the interests of the tribes as a community. Taking a position either way can only be done at the risk of being accused of ignoring or overlooking the gender dimension of these issues. This is sure to be more problematic for non-tribal scholars or activists than for the tribals and the solution has to be provided by the community itself.

References

Bhattacharjee, J.B. ed. 1982. *Social tension in North-East India.* Shillong: North East Council for Social Science Research.

Government of India. 2001. *Report of the steering committee on empowering the scheduled tribes.* New Delhi: Planning Commission.

Kishwar, Madhu.1987. Toiling without rights. *Economic and Political Weekly* 22 (3): 95–101; 22 (4): 149–55; 22 (5): 194–99.

Kumar, B.B 1995. *Tension and conflict in North-East India.* New Delhi: Cosmo Publications.

Nathan, Dev. 1997. Gender transformations in tribes. In, *From tribe to caste*, ed. Dev Nathan. Shimla: IIAS, 247–86.

Nongbri, T. 1998. Gender issues and tribal development. RGICS Paper No. 47: Problems in Tribal Society–Some Aspects.

Nongbri, T. 2000. Khasi women and matriliny: Transformations in gender relations. *Gender, Technology and Development,* 4 (3): 359–95.

Sen, S. 1985. *Social and state formation in Khasi Jaintia Hills.* New Delhi: B.R Publishing Corporation.

Singh, K.S. 1988. Tribal women: An anthropological perspective. In *Tribal women*, ed. J.P Singh et.al. 3–10.

Unnithan-Kumar, Maya. 1997. *Identity, gender and poverty: New perspectives on caste and tribe in Rajasthan.* Oxford: Bergbahn Books.

∾

ETHNICITY AND GENDER:
IDENTITY POLITICS AMONG THE KHASI
Tiplut Nongbri

[. . .] This paper examines the effect of ethnicity on tribal women. Focused on the Khasi, a matrilineal tribe of northeast India, it seeks to establish how rising ethnic politics has had adverse effect on women. Since women's gender identity is generally treated as synonymous with ethnic identity, ethnic politics has the effect of reinforcing women's subordination. To counter the steamrolling effect of modernization and change and the threat these processes engender to their identity, men are increasingly using the state machinery to come up with measures that are not only detrimental to the interest of women, but also steeped in fundamentalist and patriarchal ideology. Women's traditional exclusion from politics effectively aided men in this regard. The paper observes that with the tribe's accession to the Indian Union and the political modernization of the northeastern region, the link between ethnicity, patriarchy and the state, which was lying dormant in the traditional political set up, has come to the fore. The unequal pattern of development, which exposed tribes to exploitation in the hands of outsiders, provided the immediate imperative for this tripartite partnership.

To contextualize my argument I will focus my attention on the Khasi Custom of Lineage Bill, 1997, a proposed legislation ostensibly to preserve the Khasi matrilineal system, but which in reality turns out to be an instrument to reconstruct and redefine their ethnic identity. [. . .]

Content and analysis of the Bill

The Khasi Hills Autonomous District (Khasi Custom of Lineage) Bill, 1997, (hereafter called the Bill) as passed by the Khasi Hills District Council on 13 March 1997, is yet to receive the governor's assent before it becomes law. Twice before (1980 and 1992) similar attempts were made but failed to materialize on account of the governor withholding assent to the Bill on each occasion. According to the Statement of Objects and Reasons, this exercise has been necessitated 'owing to the fact that a large number of people have been misusing the Khasi social custom of lineage for their personal advantage and self-interest thus jeopardizing and seriously disturbing the social and cultural life of the Khasi people. As such, it is felt expedient to provide a law for strictly following the prevailing Khasi social custom of lineage in order to keep and preserve the traditional matrilineal system of society of the Khasi and for the protection of their interest and at the same time to prevent claims of Khasi status by unscrupulous persons purely for the benefits, concessions and privileges conferred on the Khasi as members of the Scheduled Tribe under the Constitution of India'.

Due to these apprehensions and perceived threat to the stability of the traditional matrilineal system, the Khasi Hills Autonomous District Council, a representative body of the Khasi established under the Sixth Schedule of the Constitution and empowered to make laws, among others, on marriage, divorce and social customs, invokes state intervention by proposing a new legal regime in the form of a codified law supposedly to strengthen the existing customary arrangements of traditional Khasi society. As is inevitable in any process of codification, the traditional norms and practices get subjected to interpretations in the light of new and emerging sensibilities, experiences and needs of a given society and thus may involve substantial adjustments and accommodations. A perusal of the Bill under consideration would reveal that the new legal regime proposed is a restatement of what the traditional normative structure governing the Khasi social custom of lineage *ought to be* in order to contend with the changing realities of contemporary Khasi society.

The Bill at the very outset furnishes a legal definition of the term Khasi. According to section 2(h), a Khasi would mean 'a person belonging to Khasi tribe who may be a Khasi, Jaintia, Pnar, Synteng, War, Bhoi or Lyngngam, or who is recognized or deemed as such under the prevailing Khasi custom or this Act'. It would be pertinent to note that the proposed legal definition of the term Khasi goes beyond the traditional categories mentioned therein including those who are recognized or deemed as such under the prevailing Khasi custom, and seeks to introduce additional criterion provided by the Act itself. This becomes clearer as one moves on to section 3 of the Bill dealing with Khasi social custom of lineage, one of the hotly contested provisions, seeking to reconstruct the Khasi custom of lineage. According to this provision, a Khasi would belong to the *kur, jait* or clan of the mother if he/ she is born of a legal marriage and his/her

a) parents are or were both Khasi,

b) mother is or was a Khasi and the father a non-Khasi and if and only if the person and his/her Khasi mother fulfil the following requirements, namely:

   i)   they can speak Khasi, unless prevented from knowing the language by circumstances beyond their control;

   ii) they observed and are governed by Khasi matrilineal system of lineage, the Khasi law of inheritance and succession and the Khasi laws of consanguinity and kinship;

   iii) had not, at any time, in writing or otherwise voluntarily renounced the Khasi status;

   iv) had not adopted the personal law of the non-Khasi father or husband, as the case may be, or a personal law of a society incompatible with Khasi personal laws and customs; and

   v)   had not lost or been deprived of Khasi status by judgement or order of any competent court or by the operation of any such judgement or order, or under the provisions of this Act; or

c) whose father is or was a Khasi and the mother a non-Khasi and the Khasi father and every such person fulfil the requirements specified in five clauses above of clause (b) of sub clause (1) of this section shall be a Khasi belonging to such Khasi *kur, jait* or clan in accordance with the prevailing Khasi customs applicable to such Khasi father or belonging in such new *Kur, Jait* or clan as may be adopted under any prevailing Khasi custom applicable to the Khasi father or by '*Tang Jait*'.

What is significant about this construction of the Khasi custom of lineage as set out in sub clause (1) of section 3 above is that while it reiterates the traditional custom of lineage as firmly grounded in the principles of matriliny, according to which a child would always belong to his/her mother's *kur, jait* or clan, yet, if a Khasi woman or a man has a non-Khasi spouse, the offspring of such unions along with their Khasi parent, henceforth will be required to prove their bonafides in accordance with the prescribed standards in order to acquire/retain their identity as members of the Khasi matrilineal system. Although, the provision is couched in gender neutral terms, indeed at first glance the Bill appears to be favourable to women, given the cultural ideology of descent and the fact that it is women who bear children.

In order to fully understand the implications of the legal definition of the term 'Khasi', and the legal construction of the Khasi social custom of lineage, it would be useful to look at some of the other provisions of the Bill having a direct bearing on the issue of identity. One of the important provisions in this regard relates to divesting a person of his/her Khasi status. While section 3(4)(b) clearly envisages such a situation, section 10 specifically provides for the grounds on which a person may be deprived of his/her Khasi status. According to this provision, notwithstanding anything contained in any law in force, a Khasi person shall cease or deemed to have ceased to be a Khasi or shall lose or deemed to have lost or been deprived of Khasi status, on and from such date as may be specified in the order made by the registering authority, who voluntarily renounces his/her Khasi status or, fails to comply with any requirements or provisions of the Act or the rules or orders made thereunder, or fails to observe the Khasi matrilineal system of lineage or Khasi laws of inheritance, succession, consanguinity and kinship, or has adopted personal law of a society not compatible with Khasi personal laws and customs, or has lost or been deprived of Khasi status by the judgement or order of a competent court. The broad sweep of the already stringent requirements laid down in this provision gets further compounded by sub clause 5 which shifts the onus of proof that the person has not ceased to be a Khasi on the person who asserts it. Interestingly, as if to remove any ambiguity on this account and as a matter of abundant caution, the same principle has been reiterated in section 15 once again that the burden of proof, notwithstanding anything contained in any other law, shall be with the person who asserts that he/she is a Khasi. As such, a person may be divested of his/her Khasi status if he/she fails to satisfy the registration authority of their Khasi credentials strictly in conformance with the stipulated conditions. The complainant has no obligation under the Bill to prove that the person complained against is not a Khasi or that he/she has in fact lost his/her Khasi status/identity. An order depriving a person of his/her Khasi status can be made by the registration authority simply on a complaint, report or information by any person, authority, chief, headman, association, body or even on its own motion. The order of the registration authority will be final subject only to an appeal to the executive committee. Section 19 of the Bill clearly debars the civil courts from entertaining or dealing in any manner what so ever with any matter which is required to be settled, decided, dealt with or to be determined by the Registration Authority or the Executive Committee.

The Bill, however, is completely silent about the nature, character or composition of both these bodies who have been invested with extremely wide powers under its provisions and whose decisions can have far-reaching consequences with no judicial safeguards available to a person who may have to suffer loss of or is deprived of his/her Khasi status. The consequences entailed by a loss or deprivation of Khasi status thus would automatically divest a person of his/her right to inheritance or succession to any property, moveable or immoveable, and such a person will no longer be entitled to any privilege or concession for which a Khasi person would otherwise be eligible as a member of the Scheduled Tribe. Furthermore, such a person stands totally debarred from identifying himself/herself as a Khasi or as belonging to any Khasi *kur, jait* or clan or using any Khasi *kur, jait* or clan as a title or surname after his/her name for any purpose whatsoever. To add insult to injury, the Bill goes on to make it an offence punishable with imprisonment and/or fine for anyone who uses or continues to use Khasi *kur, jait* or clan as a title or surname or in anyway identifies himself/herself as Khasi after the loss or deprivation of Khasi status by virtue of an order passed by the registration authority or in appeal by the executive committee as the case may be. [. . .]

Emerging debate and the assertion of control over the woman's body

If the Khasi Custom of Lineage Bill contains a number of provisions which go against the spirit of liberal democracy the problem has further been compounded by the storm of controversies it has generated. Although some like the Seng Khasi expressed their agreement with the spirit of the Bill but refrained from supporting it 'in the present form and content', others are more categorical in coming up with reasons for their rejection of the proposed legislation. A perusal of the various memoranda of protests submitted to the chief executive member, Khasi Hills Autonomous District Council, and at the debates carried out in private discussions and the media show that the root of the controversy lies in the provision enshrined in Section 3.1 (b) which specifies that the offspring born of a Khasi mother and a non-Khasi father is a Khasi.

There is, however, nothing untoward about this provision as in accordance with the matrilineal principle, a child belongs to the mother's descent group and not that of the father's, making the above provision actually technically sound. This principle has been a longstanding one in Khasi society irrespective of the father's identity or status. As demonstrated in the earlier part of the discussion, this however is no indication of the paucity of a conception of paternity or of marriage regulations among the Khasi. Rather, as has been noted by Nakane, 'The Khasi have numerous prohibitions of marriage between near kin on both paternal as well as maternal sides. The first and second parallel cousins are avoided. Those related to father within three generations are avoided' (1967, 118). Neither is the father a peripheral figure within the Khasi family. Although religion defines the ritual unity of the sibling group, the household is primarily conjugal based. Nevertheless, for the purpose of group placement and kinship identity the role of the mother remains pivotal.

By assigning descent rights to the mother the Khasi gives cultural recognition to the woman's biological and reproductive role and highlights the crucial significance given to the nurturing role of the woman. Moreover, the fact that the woman not only carries the child/foetus in her womb for ten lunar cycles, but also nourishes it with her blood till it attains fetal maturity is deeply inscribed within the Khasi kinship ideology. The mother's nurturing role continues long after the child is born as she feeds it with her milk until it is old enough to subsist on a normal diet, thus the Khasi metaphor for common descent—'born of the same womb' and/or 'sharing the same blood.'

It is clear that the Khasi descent ideology fully supports the Bill's recognition that any child whose mother is Khasi is a Khasi even though she/ he may be fathered by a non-Khasi. So where does the problem lie?

At the root of the problem lies men's fear that recognizing children born of a non-Khasi father as Khasi would not only encourage the proliferation of inter-ethnic marriages, thus posing grave demographic and economic risks to the society, but would also endanger their ethnic identity. Viewing matriliny as detrimental to the interest of the community the Khasi Students Union (KSU) and the Syngkhong Rympei Thymmai (SRT), the two most radical organizations, called for the abolition of matriliny and replacing it with patriliny. Although not so categorical, this concern was also powerfully voiced by a number of participants at a workshop organized by the Hynniewtrep Endeavour Society (HES Report) in December 1997.

Although numerically small, the group powerfully argued that to recognize such women (and their children) as Khasi would not only expose the population to economic risks but would also tarnish their ethnic identity. Underlying the argument is the view that children born of mixed unions are of impure blood or 'half breeds', who undeservedly take up the benefits meant for the ethnic Khasi. Hence such children need to be de-recognized as Khasi in order to protect the interests of the genetically pure Khasi. In support of their argument, some of the participants conjured up scientific explanations. Indeed, one participant categorically stated, 'scientifically blood comes from the father and it was due to their ignorance that the Khasi attributed it to the mother' (HES Report, Panel 2, 4).

A close reading of the debate points to the emergence of a new cultural code which informs and redefines the Khasi matrilineal system and the position of women. The demand to forfeit women married to outsiders and their children of Khasi identity not only departs from the conventionally prescribed mode of reckoning descent but also reflects a militant strand of androcentric and racial bias. This fact is borne out by the manner in which some critics selectively target women while leaving out the men who are married to non-Khasi women. The KSU and the CRYF in particular, asserted that children born of a Khasi father and a non-Khasi mother are Khasi, therefore they need not go through the formality of *Tang Jait* to be recognized as Khasi (see Section 3, Clause 1 (c) illustrated above), whereas women who marry a non-Khasi should be disqualified from any claim to Khasi identity, thereby automatically rendering their children outsiders. By privileging the children of a Khasi father and non-Khasi mother, the KSU and the CRYF not only show their strong patriarchal orientations but also their prioritization of androcentric over ethnic interests.

What seems to have escaped the attention of many is that, in the name of protecting the ethnic purity of the Khasi and the interests of the 'pure blood' (Khasi *paka*) they overlook the interests of the castigated women and vulnerable family members who are reduced to the status of outsiders. Except for a note of caution from the Meghalaya Women's Alliance, which posed the question, 'whether we are ready to reject our own kith and kin and deprive them of their rights if they commit this breach of conduct', the discussion is dominated by those who view a woman's marriage to a non-Khasi as a slur to the image of the community. An unchallenged assumption that runs through the debate is that women married to outsiders are unpatriotic characters, devoid of any sentiment or attachment to their culture and tradition. Pointing to the 'evils' that marriage between a Khasi woman and a non-Khasi man purportedly brings into the society, the Central Riwar Youth Federation (CRYF) pointedly asked, 'Do they really love the Khasi community after marrying a non-tribal?'.

Implicit in the above question is the message that endogamous marriage, that is marriage between members belonging to the same community, is not only superior to an inter-ethnic marriage but is also expressive of ethnic loyalty. By linking endogamy with loyalty to the ethnic group this line of thinking not only seeks to secure a firm ideological base for their androcentric policy, it also undermines the legitimacy of the affected to mobilize and fight for their rights. This explains why many women who privately condemned the call to deny children of inter-ethnic marriages of their traditional social rights refrained from airing their dissent in public for fear of being accused of harbouring unpatriotic sentiments and values. Thus caught between the masculinist demand to establish their patriotic credentials and the humane call to protect the interests of their errant sisters and vulnerable family members they stayed out of the controversy by maintaining a stoic silence on the matter.

The keynote to the debate has been struck by Mr. Gilbert Shullai, eminent writer and statesman, who, in a private conversation, observed that the demand to forfeit women married to outsiders of their ethnic and social rights should be weighted against the importance of the clan in the Khasi society. As noted earlier, the clan is not only the basis of social and political organization, it is also the source of one's identity. For a family to escape from falling into social and physical oblivion, it must be able to perpetuate the existence of the clan, which means that its female members must marry, produce children and recruit them into the matri-clan. Failure to produce an heiress by the women of the family leads not only to the extinction of the family (*ing*) but also of the clan (*kur/jait*) which it represents. The cultural importance attached to the clan and the practical exigency that dictates the continuance of the family exerts heavy pressure on women to marry and bear children. So much so, that when a woman fails to get a suitor at the appropriate age, family and friends would urge upon her not to be too choosy, or else she would end up as an old maid and risk the possibility of terminating her family line. Numerous cases show that when the availability of potential mates within the group became restricted the Khasi were not averse to encouraging their daughters and sisters to accept a non-tribal as a spouse, provided he fulfills the social and moral requirements desirable in a life partner.

Another insight into the problem came from a casual conversation I had with a young female medical specialist working in Delhi who, in reply to my question about her marriage plans threw valuable light on the Khasi marriage system and its implications on the present generation. For her marriage is a distant possibility. As she had been away from home in pursuance of her education, she has had no opportunity of finding a suitor belonging to the community. Since there is no practice of arranged marriage in which the family finds a mate for their children she believes she would most probably end up remaining single. She disclosed that many of her batch mates who left home (i.e. Khasi and Jaintia Hills) for higher studies ended up marrying non-tribal boys, fellow classmates or colleagues whom they met in the course of their sojourn abroad, not a few of whom had to face the ire of their family and community members. Significantly she observed, 'Folks back home fail to realize that many educated girls end up marrying outside because of their inability to find a suitable match within the community, *as local boys usually prefer younger and less qualified girls and the absence of arranged marriage makes it difficult for them or their family to approach those of comparable age and educational background.*' [. . .]

Although inter-ethnic marriage occurs in many societies, in the present context it cannot also not be disassociated from the process of development carried out by the state. State-sponsored development, with its emphasis on building up the infrastructure, not only brought along with it a large contingent of labour and other personnel from outside, it also contributed to women's impoverishment by appropriating their land and forest resources, hence exposing them to economic and sexual exploitation by the outsiders.

Not so long ago, Roy-Burman noting the active movement of the migrant population in the northeastern states remarked:

> The presence of a large number of sojourners in its turn, coupled with growing imbalances in sex ratio, has serious implication for the quality of life. It means that there are a good number of male population from outside, without strong social moorings in the region. Social workers will have to address themselves to the consequential problem. (1990, 70)

What Roy-Burman obliquely notes as a consequential problem that requires the attention of social workers, apparently refers to the growing number of unwed mothers in the region, who were objects of exploitation in the hands of the non-tribal men. In their struggle for livelihood and security for their family many tribal women fell victim to non-tribal men, who under the pretext of marriage used them for their own benefit and then dumped them to their fate. However, instead of booking the culprit and tackling the problem at the socioeconomic and developmental level through raising of consciousness and eradication of female illiteracy, poverty and unemployment which are at the root of the matter, the state has done little in this regard other than impose strictures on the victims.

Also extremely significant by its silence is the state's attitude to persons who indulge in benami transactions, in which non-tribal businessmen used tribal men and women as fronts to secure licences, permits and other benefits to further their economic interests. It is a well-known fact that a large number of persons, many of whom hold important positions in the government, engage in illegal transactions with outsiders, allowing them to escape the arm of the law by lending their names to the latter's business. Though there is a law in the state which prohibits such transactions, no prosecutions have ever been launched thus far. It would not be far wrong to say that had the state been sincere in its intention to restrict misuse of benefits by the non-tribals it could have used the anti-benami law to root out this practice. This would have saved the state from coming up with a controversial bill like the Lineage Bill and also put a check on prospective exploiters of tribal women. Apparently, the fact that it is primarily men who engage in this kind of illegal practice may have been responsible for the state's inaction.

This power enjoyed by the decision-makers, to confine public policies and discourse to issues that are integral to their interests, not only projects a distorted picture of women but also enables the state to divert attention from its negative practices and push through its own ideological and political agenda. It would not be far wrong to say that the Khasi Custom of Lineage Bill and the debate that followed reflect a clear attempt by men to use both the state machinery and civil society to perpetuate their control over women. While women married to outsiders are the primary site of contestation, the implicit message is that women as a category are the property of the community, hence their sexuality, their children and their over all deportment and conduct are the concern of men who are its unchallenged protectors and custodians. Women themselves have little say in the matter, but are reduced to objects on which the laws and regulations are to be applied and enforced. Women's subordination is implied not only by their very absence from the official centres of decision making but also by their inability to resist even at the level of civil society. Interestingly, by projecting the Lineage Bill as a 'nationalist' agenda, directed at saving the Khasi culture and tradition from the threat of extinction under the influence of the cultural 'other', the state is able to stifle potential dissenting voices, who for fear of being branded as anti-national and/or unpatriotic have no option but to resign themselves to the regime of patriarchal control. [. . .]

References

Hynniewtrep Endeavour Society. *Ka Jingia phylliew Jingmut.* Shillong: HES, 1997/98.

Nakane, C. *Garo and Khasi: A comparative study of matrilineal systems.* Paris: Mouton, 1967.

Roy-Burman, B.K. Tribal population and development. In *Tribal demography and development in North-East India,* ed. A. Bose, T. Nongbri and N. Kumar. New Delhi: B.R. Publishing Corporation, 1990.

11

~

COMMUNALISM AND RELIGION

When the women's movement and women's studies emerged during the 1970s and early 1980s by making an impact in public life and higher education, questions of religious identity and a prior history of communal conflict were not on the horizon. One might recall Vina Mazumdar's comment when reviewing the frames of reference of the *Towards Equality* report twenty years after its production in 1994, that the authors of the report paid no attention to the politics of religious diversity. Perhaps the first major disturbance in taken for granted notions of secularism among many feminists was created by the Punjab crisis and the aftermath of the anti-Sikh riots in Delhi in 1984, when thousands of Sikh men were singled out by organized mobs for public lynching in the space of just three days. From the perspective of the history of the women's movement and for women's studies, however, the turning point came with the Shah Bano case of 1986. This event set the tone for the post-independence gendering of communalism, a process that has taken on many more dimensions in subsequent years, and shows few signs of abating.

It is therefore fitting that we begin this section with a discussion of the Shah Bano case itself, taken from Radha Kumar's book-length study of the women's movement. Two earlier essays—on the uniform civil code (in the section on Household and Family) and on Muslim women's education, have already introduced us to some of the issues involved. Radha Kumar outlines the rather unusual setting in which the question of personal laws and the UCC first re-emerged, namely the judgement passed in 1985 concerning Shah Bano, an old divorced woman, who filed for maintenance against her husband under the Criminal Procedure Code 125 (a law outside the purview of personal laws, intended to prevent destitution and vagrancy). The extraordinary trajectory of the case described in the essay produced far-reaching and deeply disturbing demonstrations of conflict between 'Islam', the 'nation' and 'women's rights'. It served to deepen the communalization of society against the backdrop of the parallel rise of the Ramjanmabhoomi campaign, and forced feminists to recognize the embattled location of Muslim women in particular, and the political salience of religion more generally, in contemporary society.

The next essay by Flavia Agnes was written in the wake of the riots that shook Bombay in the months following the demolition of the Babri Masjid at Ayodhya in December 1992 by the forces of the Hindu Right. It begins by looking back at the beginnings of the women's movement in the 1970s and early 80s, and the 'secularism' of those years. The substance of her critique, doubtless the product of hindsight, focuses on how the lines between the women's movement and communal groups could become somewhat 'smudged'. She goes on to document a number of legislations and other instances, where women's groups were not alert to their anti-minority implications. But it was after the riots that the deepest challenges to 'common platforms' across communities were encountered, and the question what women could be said to share beyond their respective communities came to be posed.

Flavia's provocative essay was thus a call to rethink the meaning of secularism in the movement. In an article written in the mid 1980s, a somewhat different voice has questioned the women's movement. According to Gabriele Dietrich, the women's movement has ignored the domain of religion (as distinct from questions of communalism), or as she would put it, has not been open to the significance of religious reform and the faith dimension of women within a secular movement. Efforts of genuine reform share little with communalism, and are necessary for building a more pluralistic secular culture, where rationalism and faith need not be mutually antagonistic. Much of Gabriele Dietrich's work has been concerned with developing this aspect of religious reform, drawing from feminist Christian theological scholarship as well as class- and caste-based critiques of women's lives.

Few domains have attracted such divergent approaches and differences among feminists. The next essay by Kumkum Sangari represents an intervention within the debate over personal laws. As the 1990s wore on, and the hold of the Hindu right deepened, women's organizations disagreed quite fundamentally over the very possibility of redeeming the idea of a common code for women. In her extensive essay, from which we have reproduced an excerpt, Kumkum Sangari sets out to question the elevation of religious definitions of community and cultural diversity, and the corresponding idea that gender justice should work within the sole legal framework of religious pluralism. Against those who argue that, in the current communal conjuncture, reform within different personal laws is the best strategy for feminists, Sangari claims that such an approach threatens to freeze identities within religious boundaries that have historically been in flux. Moreover, the special privileging of religious community cannot be sustained in the face of the multiple and cross-cutting categories of identity—based on class and caste, sect, language and region, among others—that characterize our diversity. Instead, she proposes that feminists train their attention on the multiple and overlapping patriarchies that structure women's lives.

If Sangari has critiqued the privileging of the category of religion as a unique marker of community identity, the final contribution to this theme on religion and communalism rethinks the relationship between the Hindu right and women. One of the developments to have deeply disoriented the women's movement during the 1990s was the emergence of militant, 'empowered' women leaders and members of explicitly Hindu rightwing organizations. In an early study in 1991, Tanika Sarkar offered a field-based account in the city of Delhi of the rise of the Rashtra Sevika Samiti in particular, the women's wing of the all-male RSS. Less than a decade later, Sarkar revisited members of this organization to discover that what had earlier been a vibrant, dynamic and public force, disturbing not only to women's organizations but also to the male parent cadre, had by 1999 declined and changed significantly. Sarkar believes that generalized fears of the rise of the Hindu right need to give way to more historically nuanced understandings of their fluctuating agendas and mass base.

These essays offer a sense of the different dimensions of the challenge represented by the rise of communalism and the meanings of religion. The political and social isolation and exclusion of minorities reached its height with the genocide in Gujarat in 2002, where Muslim women and children were specially and horrifically targeted. The heated debates over a uniform civil code have receded somewhat since the 1990s, and a series of focused legal campaigns have been the order of the day, such as to transform the Christian law on marriage and divorce, amend the Hindu Succession Act, and introduce a specific law on domestic violence. The difficult question of secularism, taken for granted in the early years, has since been subjected to enormous scrutiny and pressure. While it is clear that issues of religion or communalism cannot be privileged above other aspects of women's lives or the broader developments of the twenty-first century, these essays are also telling us that dismissing these spheres of meaning and control as only obscurantist or regressive cannot be the way forward either. Scholars in the field of women's studies today must, therefore, critique, explore and create new definitions of the secular in the battle of women's rights and gender justice.

∾

THE SHAH BANO CASE

Radha Kumar

[. . .] By the early 1980s, attempts to analyze the relationship of women to and within the family had led to examining the codification of women's rights in marriage, divorce, property, maintenance, etc. as in India most family law is differentiated on the basis of religion, as well as community. This entailed investigation into different 'personal' laws. (By a curious feat of meaning, the term 'personal' when conjoined with law means the different family laws of different religious communities).

The issue of personal law became especially controversial for feminists in 1985, with what is now referred to as 'The Shah Bano case'. On the 23rd of April, a five-member Constitution Bench of the Supreme Court led by Chief Justice Chandrachud, ruled that a 75-year old woman, Shah Bano, was entitled to maintenance by her husband under Section 125 of the Criminal Procedure Code. Shah Bano's husband, Mohammad Ahmed Khan, an advocate, had divorced her after roughly a half century of marriage. Ten years earlier, under pressure from her husband, Shah Bano and her children had moved out of the main house into a sort of annexe. For two years her husband gave her Rs 200 per month, and then abruptly stopped. In 1978 she filed an application in the Indore Magistrate's Court, under Section 125 of the Criminal Procedure Code (CrPC), asking that her husband be ordered to pay her maintenance. Intended to prevent vagrancy due to destitution, this section entitles destitute, deserted or divorced women to support from their husbands, provided they (the husbands) are not destitute themselves. Destitution thus defines the provisions in this section. The maximum amount allowed by it as 'maintenance' was Rs 500 a month, certainly not adequate for both shelter and subsistence. Shah Bano asked for the maximum, on the grounds that she was old and could not work to support herself. In other words, under Section 125 she had to show that she was destitute in order to claim support from her husband.

While Shah Bano's application was still pending, her husband decided to divorce her, using the triple *talaq*, which the Koran names the most lowly form of divorce. At the same time, he deposited Rs 3000 in court, claiming that he was returning the *mehr* agreed upon at the time of their marriage. According to Shah Bano, however, the *mehr*, a sum meant to be given to the bride as 'a mark of respect', was 3000 silver coins. Meanwhile, the magistrate ruled that Shah Bano *was* entitled to maintenance under Section 125, but fixed the amount at a ludicrous Rs 25 per month. She went on appeal to the Madhya Pradesh High Court, which raised the amount to Rs 179.20. Now Mohammad Ahmed Khan went on appeal to the Supreme Court arguing that the High Court judgement exceeded its jurisdiction and violated Muslim personal law as stated by the *Shariat*. In effect, several statements made up this contention: first, that as a Muslim he was bound primarily by Islamic law; second, that as maintenance from a husband related to the laws of marriage and divorce, which in his case fell under Muslim personal law, Shah Bano's application should be judged by this law and no other; and third, that if marriage, divorce and maintenance regulations fell under personal law, then criminal law should not enter the picture at all. In support of these arguments, he produced written statements acquired from the Muslim Personal Law Board, which said that under the *Shariat* the husband was not obliged to pay maintenance for more than three months after the divorce (the *iddat* period): with this, and with giving his ex-wife her *mehr*, his duties towards her ended. Moreover, said the board, the *Shariat* did not deal with the question of how the woman was to support herself after the *iddat*, and therefore the question was outside the purview of the court.

By the time the case was before the Supreme Court, therefore, the distinction between maintenance on destitution (section 125), and maintenance on divorce (which falls under personal law), was largely blurred. By virtue of this, the distinction between criminal and civil law was also blurred: at the same time, criminal law was banished from the territory of maintenance. Finally, the entire problem of female destitution was itself placed outside the purview of the court, on the grounds that the text of personal law did not deal with it.

Perhaps if the judgement of the Supreme Court on Mohammad Ahmed Khan's petition had ignored these points, it might not have been so controversial. It would, however, have been hard for them to do so, because these points *were* being argued before them, and countered by Shah Bano's counsel, who cited two verses from the Koran to show that the provision of maintenance was regarded as a duty for the 'righteous'. In any case, the five-member Constitution Bench, led by Justice Chandrachud, *did* go ahead and comment on abuses on women in the name of religion, and the advisability of a uniform civil code.

Basically, the judgement can be summarized as follows: firstly, it upheld Shah Bano's right to maintenance from her husband both under Section 125 and under Muslim personal law, quoting the two verses from the Koran which were cited by Shah Bano's counsel, Mr Daniel Latifi. Secondly, it asserted that Section 125 'cut across the barriers of religion', that is, it transcended the personal laws of the religious communities which any married pair might belong to. Thirdly, it was critical of the way women 'have been traditionally subjected to unjust treatment', citing statements by both Manu, the Hindu law maker, and the Prophet, as examples of traditional injustice. And finally, it urged the government to frame a common civil code, because the constitutional promise of a common or uniform civil code would only be realized at the initiative of the government.

Neither the upholding of Section 125 nor the criticisms of personal law as unjust to women were particularly new. Two earlier judgements upholding the rights of Muslim women to maintenance under Section 125 had been made, by the Supreme Court, in Bai Tahira *vs* Ali Hussain Fissali, 1979, and Fuzlumbi *vs* K. Khader Ali, 1980. Chief justice Krishna Iyer had delivered the judgements, and in both he had urged the need for judicial reform in Muslim personal law. Yet neither of the earlier two judgements used the 'in any case' arguments of the later judgement, which might have allowed misreading: for example, having decided that Section 125 was consistent with Muslim personal law, it was unnecessary to assert that, in any case, Section 125, being part of criminal law, cut across the 'barriers' of religion. Alternatively, having decided to uphold the jurisdiction of Section 125, as superceding personal law, it was unnecessary to interpret the *Shariat.*

Given that the judgement ruled that Section 125 CrPC and the *Shariat* were mutually consistent, it was certainly odd that a common civil code was urged on grounds which appeared to contradict the ruling:

> A belief seems to have gained ground that it is for the Muslim community to take a lead in the matter of reform of their personal law. *A Common Civil Code will help the cause of national integration by removing disparate loyalties to laws which have conflicting ideologies.* No community is likely to bell the cat by making *gratuitous* concessions on this issue . . . we understand the difficulties involved in bringing persons of different faiths and persuasions on a common platform. But a beginning has to be made if the Constitution has to have a meaning. (Emphasis added)

Put like this, it was clearly possible to infer that the judges were saying that Muslim personal law was bad, but 'the Muslim community' preferred unjust laws, so somebody (in this case the state) would have to impose justness on them. It was similarly easy to infer that imposition was to be made not for the sake of justice alone, but also for the cause of 'national integration'. And from this it was also easy to infer that national integration required Muslims to abandon 'loyalty' to Islam and Islamic personal law.

The judgement was widely criticized on a variety of grounds: overall, feminists, liberals and secularists were critical of it for having brought issues of religion and personal law into what was essentially a question of secular, criminal law. Further, said some feminists, instead of dealing with the general issue of personal laws and how they affected women's rights in any depth, the judgement focused on Muslim personal law alone. Commenting on this in an article, Madhu Kishwar concluded: 'By singling out Muslim men and Islam in this way, Justice Chandrachud converts what is essentially a women's rights issue into an occasion for a gratuitous attack upon the community.'

Muslim religious leaders concurred in the view that the judgement represented an attack on their community. The *ulema* (scholar priests) issued a *fatwa* (proclamation) that it was against the teachings of Islam. Wide publicity was given to the fatwa, and within a few months the whole issue took the form of a communal agitation, claiming that Islam was in danger. Muslim communalists demanded that the Supreme Court judgement be repealed and Muslim women be excluded from Section 125; jumping into the fray, Hindu communalists upheld the judgement, gleefully arguing that it supported their contention that Muslims were 'barbaric' and 'anti-national'.

In August 1985, a bill seeking to exclude Muslim women from the purview of Section 125 came up in Parliament. Sponsored by a Muslim League member of Parliament, G.M. Banatwala, the bill was clearly in response to the Shah Bano petition and the feminist espousal of her cause, for it was introduced while her case was being decided upon by the Supreme Court, just about a month before the judgement. The government decided to oppose the bill and briefed a Muslim Minister, Arif Mohammad Khan, to argue against it in Parliament, on the grounds that Section 125 was intended to prevent vagrancy and, as such, was not interfering with the personal laws of any community. Arif Mohammad, however, diverged from his brief, delivering an impassioned plea for a humane reading of the *Shariat.*

Muslim liberals, feminists and social reformers began campaigns all over India, but especially in Maharashtra, to publicize the upholding of Section 125 and to demand improvements in the legal rights of Muslim women against polygamy, and to maintenarce. At the same time outraged *ulemas* denounced Muhammad Arif Khan saying that as a layman he had no right to interpret the *Shariat,* and joined in a massively orchestrated campaign to repeal the judgement and support Banatwala's bill. Over one lakh people demonstrated in Bombay and at least as many in Bhopal, and there were a spate of smaller demonstrations all over the county; in Hyderabad there was a bandh; in Lucknow, the Muslim Personal Law Board announced that true Muslims should no longer go to the courts for redress, but should come to the *Shariat* courts which they were opening. As against this, only a few hundred demonstrated in favour of the judgement. Muslims who did so were often assaulted: the Talaq Mukti Morcha, which was launched in November in Kolhapur (Maharashtra), and which decided to march through the districts of Maharashtra publicizing the judgement with a poster exhibition, was forced to call off its march because the marchers had been assaulted in so many places. They were greeted by black flags in Miraj, threatened by a mob of four hundred in Parbhani, stoned at Nanded and Jalgaon, and in Ahmednagar they were surrounded by a mob of ten thousand, brandishing black flags, who stoned them, forcing them to call off the rest of the march.

To understand why the issue became so very heated, one has to look at the context in which it arose. The 1980s witnessed a steep rise in communal violence all over India, both Hindu–Muslim and Hindu–Sikh. The November 1984 riots were particularly alarming: not only was Mrs Gandhi's assassination treated as a communal issue by the Congress (I), but no attempt at all was made either to punish the guilty, or even to investigate the charges of political and police involvement in the riots. The sense that Hindu communalism was acquiring increasing legitimacy in the eyes of the state was further strengthened by the Ram Janmabhoomi agitation which was launched in Uttar Pradesh.

In October 1984, the Vishwa Hindu Parishad (VHP), a relatively new Hindu communalist organization, launched a full-fledged agitation demanding that a shrine in the precincts of the Babri Masjid in Ayodhya be declared the birthplace of Ram, and a temple built on the spot. The question of worship at the shrine-cum-masjid had been a source of conflict since the late nineteenth century and, pending a court decision on the issue, the whole place was locked up. The court case was revived by a 'Hindu' advocate, and in the meantime, the VHP led a 200,000 strong march to Ayodhya in 1984, to 'liberate' the shrine, and performed hundreds of fire rituals all over the Hindi-speaking belt in 1985, to mobilize around their demand for a Ram Janmabhoomi temple to be built within the precincts of the mosque. Alarmed by the growing strength of the VHP-led agitation and the threat it posed, several Muslim religious leaders and politicians formed a Babri Masjid Action Committee, to defend the status quo.

The Babri Masjid issue and the Shah Bano case began to be linked as representing a Hindu communal onslaught on Indian Muslims. Syed Shahabuddin, one of the leaders of the Babri Masjid Action Committee and a member of the Janata Party, shot to prominence as a leader of the agitation against the judgement, organizing a petition against it, which was signed by over 300,000 Muslims. In state elections in December 1985, Shahabuddin trounced his Congress (I) opponent from the Kishenganj constituency, despite an all-out Congress (I) effort to win Muslim votes by putting up the secretary of the Jamat-ul-ulema-e-Hind, and bringing two hundred *ulemas* to canvass for their candidate.

On February 1, 1986, the district magistrate, before whom the Babri Masjid–Ram Janmabhoomi case was pending, decreed that the shrine be opened to Hindus for worship. The VHP celebrated this with 'victory processions'. Muslims took out 'mourning processions' in retaliation, and soon clashes between the two groups began which escalated into riots in Delhi, Srinagar and various parts of Madhya Pradesh. Riots spilled over also to Pakistan. Alarmed by their loss in Kishenganj and seeing a further loss of credibility in Muslim eyes, the Congress (I) began to backtrack on their assurance of Muslim women's rights under Section 125, announcing that they were considering a review of the judgement and would introduce a bill on the lines of Banatwala's bill. To many, this announcement appeared as an utterly cynical willingness to sacrifice the rights of Muslim women on the anvil of political expediency. Immediately, Muslim reform groups and women's organizations began to lobby the government against this announcement but were unsuccessful. On the 25th of February, the Muslim Women (Protection of Rights on Divorce) Bill was introduced which excluded divorced Muslim women from the purview of Section 125, stating that the obligation of their husbands to maintain them ended with a three months *iddat* period, after which their families would have to support them or, failing this, their local waqf board.

The introduction of the bill caused a considerable furore. [. . .] Interestingly, the Muslim Women's Bill of 1986, which took away the Mulsim women's right to maintenance from their husbands (to the limited extent provided for by Section 125), also conferred a new right upon them which non-Muslim women do not have any equivalent of: the right to maintenance from the waqf board, that is, the body which administers communally held lands (granted for charitable purposes, or the benefit of the community). One of the not-so-odd fallouts of the agitation against the judgement has been that after the bill was enacted there have been a spate of lower and higher court judgements granting divorced Muslim women much higher sums of maintenance, payable by the waqf board, than have been granted before.

Not that this is in any way a justification of the bill-turned-act. By removing even the minor obligation which Section 125 imposed on husbands who had abandoned or divorced their wives, the act made it legtimate for Muslim husbands to simply leave their wives stranded. The curtailment of the jurisdiction of Section 125, moreover, not only set a precedent for doing away with any checks on mistreatment of women under personal law, it also laid the foundation for excluding specific groups or communities from culpability for acts which abet crimes relating to women. It is especially significant that it was in the course of this agitation that the demand for legalizing sati was first made.

Despite strong opposition to the bill, it was forced through Parliament on the 6th of May 1986, after an all night debate. The Congress (I) had issued a party whip instructing all its MPs to vote for the bill, no matter what their opinions on the matter were. This must have been the first time that a whip had been issued on a matter concerning women.

For feminists, the agitation around Muslim women's rights to maintenance consisted of a series of bitter lessons. Discovering the ease with which a 'community in danger' resorts to fundamentalist assertions of self, among which, invariably, control over women is one of the first such assertions to be made, feminists were confronted with the associated discovery of the ease with which the Indian state chose to accommodate communalism (by taking no action against the Ram Janmabhoomi agitation), and balance this by a concession to fundamentalism (allowing personal law to cut into the application of uniform laws such as Section 125.) [. . .]

∾

WOMEN'S MOVEMENT IN A
SECULAR FRAMEWORK: REDEFINING THE AGENDAS

Flavia Agnes

[. . .] Around the late 1970s and early 1980s the autonomous women's movement began to take shape mainly around the issue of rape and bride burning. The groups which mushroomed in various cities consisted of women from left and liberal backgrounds many of whom were professionals from the middle and upper strata of society.

Although the groups remained small in number, the movement was highly visible as it received wide media publicity. This acted as a pressure tactic and the state was forced to respond. Women's issues were placed on the agenda of state-sponsored developmental schemes, social work programmes and sociological research. The government set up anti-dowry police cells to help victims of domestic violence. There were also several cosmetic efforts at legislative reforms although the inadequately formulated laws did not have the desired effect.

The autonomous women's movement focused on issues which challenged the patriarchal power structures within a broad liberal framework. There were several instances where the movement addressed issues concerning dalits, tribals and landless labourers. The movement was also active in providing relief during communal riots and worked in broad secular forums. During community conflicts resulting in police excesses or during human tragedies it was able to place gender concerns on the agenda of human rights and civil liberties groups. But overall, it worked from a presumption that gender lines can be drawn up clearly and sharply in a patriarchal society and within these parameters sexual assault and domestic violence affect women equally across class, cultural and religious barriers.

Secular culture as an agenda

The leaders of this autonomous movement remained predominantly urban and upper class Hindu. Their work centered mainly in areas away and outside their own immediate neighbourhood and community context. In order to reach out to women from a different class, caste and culture and to propagate the new ideology of the strong and assertive woman, the movement adopted a populist approach and relied upon mythical symbols of 'Shakti' and 'Kali' to convey the newly constructed feminist ideology. The movement relied more upon myths and fictions rather than on the history of a pluralistic society, encompassing within its framework cultural idioms of minority communities. The intention of using symbols from the dominant culture was not to propagate Hindu ideology. But since the movement did not have 'secularism' as one of its prime objectives, no conscious efforts were made to evolve alternate symbols. Hence the cultural expressions familiar to the women who were in the forefront had surreptitiously crept into the women's movement.

The feminist movement also had to constantly counter the allegation that it was 'western'. So in order to establish the 'Indianness' of the movement it relied on Hindu iconography and Sanskrit idioms denoting woman power, thus inadvertently strengthening the communal ideology that Indian, Hindu and Sanskrit are synonymous. Within this social milieu of a high caste Hindu culture, the handful of minority women who were vocal and articulate had also internalized the dominant culture and hence did not protest against this trend. In order to prove their secular credentials they willingly divorced themselves from their own traditions and cultural symbols of women's strength and power and accepted not just cultural symbols but even food habits and dress codes of the dominant section.

With women's concerns gaining prominence in both governmental and non-governmental organizations during the 1980s, women's issues became an important agenda for all political parties. In Bombay, during the mid-1980s, the communal party Shiv Sena, which was gaining popularity among the lower middle class, was able to mobilize a large number of women around support activities like income generation, creches, mid-day meals for children, civic amenities, ambulance services and so on. The movement also appropriated cultural forums and public celebrations of Hindu festivals like Ganesh utsav and Satyanarayan pooja which had been popularized by Tilak during the nationalist struggle in the pre-independence era. In addition to the 'son of the soil' theory propagated by the Shiv Sena, it had also managed to attract women. As mothers of these sons of the soil, women were bestowed a special role and responsibility.

Through a systematic hate campaign, the Shiv Sena was able to whip up communal tensions among its women cadre. The image of the modern Hindu woman which was constructed while advocating a communal Hindu ideology was not the traditional subservient and docile domestic being, but a new modern Durga, the destroyer of evil, an angry and rebellious woman. This construction of the modern Hindu woman resembled very closely the Indian construction of the new 'feminist' woman. This new woman could come out on the street with men from the community to avenge wrongs. And in this action she had the blessings of the political party and the community leaders. Hence, women found this role not only exciting but also more comfortable in comparison to the protests against a violent husband or a rapist from within the community, because then they would not have the protective mantle of the party nor the blessings of community elders.

The smudging of lines between communal forces and women's organizations also found an expression through some of the more concrete demands raised by the movement. Obscenity is one such issue. Women's groups had taken up a campaign against obscenity in the media. The aim was to protest against using women's bodies as sex objects or in derogatory subservient roles. The campaign received the support of people from varied backgrounds, from Victorian moralists to Hindu revivalists. [. . .]

The second such issue is the demand for a uniform civil code. The women's movement has had a sustained campaign for reforms within the segregated and religion-based marriage laws and pressurized the state to evolve a non-sexist secular code. This demand found an echo in a similar demand by the communal forces. The family laws in India are termed as 'personal laws' and are divided along religious affiliations rather than territorial jurisdiction. Even after independence no effort had been made to evolve a uniform civil code, in spite of a constitutional mandate to do so. The ruling party, in order to lure the minority vote, continued to sacrifice the rights of minority women. Examples of this tendency can be found in laws governing Christian and Muslim minorities. The only exception is the recent reform in laws governing Parsis.

The archaic and anti-women Indian Divorce Act was enacted by the British in 1869 to facilitate the smooth functioning of the colonial regime. But today it is applicable to Indian Christians (who are referred to as 'native Christians' in the act). Under Section 10 of the act, while a man can get divorce only on the ground of adultery, the woman has to prove an additional ground such as cruelty or desertion. Repeated pleas to change this oppressive provision by Christian women's organizations as well as recommendations by the Law Commission have fallen on deaf ears.

In a similar vein, the Dissolution of Muslim Marriages Act of 1939 governing the divorce of Muslim women which has no provision for custody of children or for maintenance has remained unchanged. Further, the customary privilege of the Muslim male to a unilateral 'talaq' is held valid in spite of protests from Muslim organizations. But the most stark example of this tendency was the passing of the Muslim Women (Protection of Divorce) Act 1986. A judgement in 1985 popularly known as the Shah Bano judgement which reaffirmed the divorced Muslim woman's right to maintenance aroused the wrath of the leaders of the Muslim community because of certain adverse comments made by the judiciary against Islam. The adverse campaign led to the passing of laws which deprived divorced Muslim women of their hard won right to maintenance under a secular code.

It was not surprising that the demand for a uniform civil code raised by the women's movement aroused contradictory responses from fundamentalists depending upon whether they hail from the majority or the minority communities. It was opposed strongly by Muslim and Christian religious leaders who perceived it as a threat to their cultural identity and a violation of the fundamental rights guaranteed by the Constitution. But it became an important plank upon which hate for Muslims could be ignited. Through it, Hindu communal organizations were not only able to gain popularity among Hindu males who envied their Muslim counterparts the freedom to practise polygamy; they could also pose as the champions of the cause of women.

There was a very clear difference between the demands made by the women's movement which were based on a pro-woman, secular and non-sexist ideology, and the anti-Muslim demand of the communal forces. But this did not clearly manifest itself through well-publicized campaigns. Although most of the initiators of the movement were culturally Hindu, they perceived themselves as secular beings. Hence they did not focus sharply and minutely on the Hindu code and the sexist biases within it. At the same time, the movement could rally around important cases initiated by a few minority women challenging the biases within their personal laws. This resulted in the women's movement focusing primarily on lacunae within laws governing minority communities.

Perhaps a few examples of the extent of the sexist biases within laws governing Hindus are necessary to clarify the issue. The first and concrete example is the Hinduization of the Special Marriages Act. While the Muslim Women's Bill which deprived Muslim women of their right to maintenance under a secular code was strongly criticized, the amendment of 1976 to the Special Marriages Act of 1954 went unnoticed. This was the forerunner to the Muslim Women's Act and the first instance after independence when the trend towards a uniform secular code was reversed. A religious group was taken out of the purview of the secular code and placed within the purview of a code based on religion. By this amendment, if two Hindus married under the Special Marriages Act then the secular code which granted equal rights to men and women—the Indian Succession Act of 1925—would not apply to them and parties continued to be governed by the Hindu Succession Act which ensured male coparcenary rights, i.e. exclusion of daughters' from their father's ancestral property.

The amendment was both anti-women and anti-minority. It sought to protect the property interests of a Hindu male who married any woman within the broad Hindu fold by not depriving him of his coparcenary rights. Since the concept of coparcenary (through which a male member by birth becomes a partner in the ancestral property and a woman can never be a coparcener) per se is anti-women, this amendment was de facto against women's rights. At the other level it served as a deterrent to a Hindu male wishing to marry a women from a minority religious community because then he could be penalized by forfeiting rights to his ancestral property. This amendment aroused no public furore from progressive organizations. Perhaps it is apt to point out that this amendment was passed at a point in history when the legislature enacted major changes in laws governing women's rights, as a response to the Status of Women Committee report of 1974 *Towards Equality* and the International Women's Year, 1975.

Several other lacunae within the Hindu Code also went unnoticed. For instance, the procedure of solemnizing the Hindu marriage at one level remained brahminical but at the other level the code validated customary rituals and ceremonies. To this confusion the Hindi films have contributed their bit by creating a fiction that exchanging garlands or applying 'sindoor' to the forehead of the girl constitutes valid marriage. This confusion, coupled with non-registration of marriages, has enabled the Hindu male to contract a second marriage with impunity. [. . .] In divorce proceedings, a Hindu male can, at his whim and fancy, admit either his first or his second sexual relationship as a valid marriage. This makes the woman in a polygamous relationship extremely vulnerable, while it permits the man to enjoy the fruits of the relationship without any financial responsibility.

Only the Hindu Marriage Act permits the scope for ambiguity regarding the solemnization of marriage. Under other laws the officiating priest has to provide the necessary document by way of a 'nikha nama' or he is required to register the marriage with the Registrar of Births, Deaths and Marriages.

But unfortunately none of these and many other anomalies and anti-women biases within the Hindu Code have received wide media publicity. They remained hidden in statute books and legal manuals. The women's movement did not rally around litigations challenging these anti-women biases in its campaign for a uniform secular code. Hence the demand by the women's movement could not clearly position itself away from the sexist Hindu Code. [. . .]

With women's concerns gaining prominence, women's organizations will be forced to choose their political allies within the existing political set up. For instance, the recently constituted women's commissions both at the central and state level will be broad forums which include representations from women's organizations along with other political parties. While these will provide the opportunity to influence policy decisions, the representatives will have an option either to be co-opted by the ruling party or to form broad alliances with the opposition, including the communal organizations. The question which needs to be addressed is whether, in order to strengthen women's interests, it would be strategic to join hands with communal forces in broader forums, but which might amount to a tacit endorsement of their anti-Muslim propaganda. Or should commitment to secularism and minority rights be a pre-condition to forming coalitions for women's rights?

New challenges

While these issues have not been adequately addressed, the complexities of the post-riot situation (after the Bombay riots following the Babri Masjid demolition on December 6 1992), have brought minority concerns to centre stage. Some groups feel that women's issues can no longer be addressed merely within a patriarchal framework along gender lines but would have to be re-examined within the newer challenges to democracy, secularism and minority rights. The questioning is not limited to controversial issues like personal laws but has extended even to seemingly non-controversial issues like domestic violence.

Here is one example of the choices which were thrust upon women's groups in the context of the riots. Around October 1992, the Joint commissioner of police, R.D. Tyagi, issued directions to the subordinate police stations that cases of domestic violence should not be registered against women who do not bear visible marks of physical injury on their person. This direction was a set-back. It was through a sustained campaign that a social provision was incorporated within the Indian Penal Code which recognized both physical and mental violence against women within their matrimonial home. Although the officer later retracted his statement, to counter his allegation that women misuse the provision, a seminar was planned with police and legal authorities and was scheduled for January 1993. But the riots in December 1992 changed drastically the original context of the seminar. In the wake of the large-scale police brutality, where groups of young boys picketing the roads were shot down by police, the faith of the minority community in the law enforcing machinery had totally broken down. Large numbers of Muslim youth with bullet injuries were hiding in their homes haunted by the fear that they would be locked up were they to come near the vicinity of a police station.

In such a situation, where one whole community was being held at ransom, the issue of domestic violence had lost its earlier context. By organizing a seminar on domestic violence, we would be helping the police to defuse the more pressing issue of police excesses during the riots. Interaction with the law enforcing machinery in a forum on women's issues would amount to condoning their brutality towards Muslims.

Ironically, the social space which is denied to women in peace times was now being offered to them on a platter in the face of grave adversity. Women from both communities were being used or became willing martyrs in aid of the community, defying traditional norms and roles. In predominantly Muslim localities women became the buffer between police and community youth and hence suffered casualties. [. . .]

On the other side, the Shiv Sena was able to mobilize a large section of women to hold traffic blocks and demonstrations outside police stations to protest against the detention of community youth, even at midnight. Women slept on the roads to prevent army trucks from entering the area to rescue Muslim hostages or put out the blazing fires. Slogans which the left groups had used to strengthen collective actions were now used to whip up communal frenzy among violent mobs. For instance, the slogan—'Jo hum se takarayega, Mitti me mil jayega' (Those who confront us will turn to dust) rent the air. But sanction to oppose traditional norms did not imply that they would not be victims of sexual jealousy and domestic violence within their homes. So the women who threw stones at Muslim men who had been set on fire in the middle of the road would yet have to approach a women's organization for help in a personal problem.

With the Muslim community the equation was in reverse. The community leaders, who were fighting for legitimacy and the right to a dignified existence in a riot-torn situation, became our allies in anti-communal forums. But at that moment we could not dare to ask them their views on Muslim personal law. And even while we were being welcomed with open arms during peace rallies, we are apprehensive that riot time allies might become peace time adversaries. The same men may deny us access to women once normalcy returned, should we work on the issue of, say, maintenance to the divorced Muslim woman.

The riots dealt a severe blow to the premise that women have a separate existence apart from their communal identity, where problems of rape, divorce and maintenance could be discussed on a common platform. Clearly, the same issues affect different women in different ways at different times. We also realized that our allies and adversaries would change depending upon external realities. If social action means reacting to social reality, then, as this external reality changes, internal positions have to be redefined. Otherwise the movement itself would become redundant in the wake of the newer challenges.

In conclusion, it is necessary to emphasize that this critique of the women's movement has been made from within, as someone who has participated in all the different stages of its development. The contradictions and confusions are as much a part of it as are its gains, and are signs of a movement which is alive and growing, while reformulating its positions in response to external shifts in the configuration of power.

Analyzing such developments, one trade unionist felt that the Shiv Sena had been able to provide the space for the cultural assertion of the workers, however narrow and excluding in nature it might be. On the other hand, left organizations had rallied mainly around economic and political issues, which might have been limiting in its scope. Dalit and other caste-based movements also had to confront similar issues. The Mandal issue, which had divided the Hindu community along caste lines, appeared united as a cohesive Hindu force against the Muslims. Progressive organizations which had supported the Mandal campaign found that this alliance could not withstand the stress of communal pulls. Within the government bureaucracy, those who occupied reserved seats expressed deep-rooted communal biases, even while implementing government relief programmes. In Dharavi and other slums, corporators belonging to the Republic Party, a political forum of the dalits, led the riots against the Muslims. Shanta Dharia, a Republican Party woman corporator, was shot down by the police while leading a rioting mob.

A similar scrutiny of the earlier presumptions and premises of other social movements might help in building up a consolidated secular force which can stand the onslaught of rising communalism and counter its challenges effectively.

~

WOMEN'S MOVEMENT AND RELIGION
Gabriele Dietrich

Introduction

During the international women's decade, the question of women and religion did not come much to the forefront. The main emphasis was on women's deteriorating economic situation, declining work opportunities, victimization due to technological modernization, self-help through self-employment schemes and on sexual and other violence against women, like rape, wife beating, dowry deaths and so on. Attention was also paid to women's health situation, family planning schemes, the effects of certain contraceptives like IUDs, Depo-provera and NET-EN etc.

This does not come as a surprise since, in the feminist debate, patriarchy has been understood as exploitation of a woman's labour, sexuality and fertility. It is, therefore, only logical that primary attention should go to the economic aspects and to the actual physical subjugation of women. The only aspect where religion has come into the picture is the demand for a secular family code which has been raised on and off and, short of this, battles are today fought for Muslim women's rights to maintenance, for the right of Christian women to get a divorce, against extremes of discrimination in inheritance rights, for example, as in the Travancore Christian Succession Act. [...]

It is therefore, important to raise the question: What is the relationship of the women's movement to genuine religious reform? I do believe that this is a crucial question which has been ignored for far too long. I would like to define genuine religious reform as such a reform which enables individuals and groups to participate in secular political processes which are struggling for equality of all citizens and against economic, political and cultural exploitation, without being forced to abandon the faith dimension of their religious identity. Besides, genuine religious reform crystallizes the humanist content in a religion in such a way that non-believers or people of other faiths can relate to this humanist content in their own right. This latter dimension is an indispensable part of creating a rich secular culture.

This is a question which has not been raised in depth by the women's movement, probably for three reasons: First, the question of genuine religious reform is normally left out of the general debate on secularism. Religion is normally simply declared to be an obscurantist hangover which needs to be discarded. This year's (1986) independence day issue of the government-sponsored journal *Yojana,* under the title 'Why live with Nonsense?', is a striking example of this tendency.

Secondly, women, as primary victims of orthodox religion, have good reasons to be resentful of religion in general. It is, therefore, not surprising that, in the wake of the Delhi riots, the Saheli newsletter presented a very simplified reductionist view on religion and women which ends with the appeal: 'It is we who have to stop believing in gods and start believing in ourselves, our inalienable rights to a decent life on this earth. Our rituals have to be taken over by actions which lead to this. Our God has to be replaced by our love for humanity and our hatred for injustices.' A demonstration in Delhi on March 8 (International Working Women's Day), sponsored by different women's organizations, expressed their views on religion in a similar vein and was only questioned by a thoughtful article by Ruth Vanita in *Manushi.*

Thirdly, women, due to their position in society, have rarely been in the forefront of ideological production and especially of religions ideological production; women have rarely been theologians. A few have been famous mystics or poetesses. It is, therefore, not surprising if the domain of religious reform has normally remained controlled by enlightened male intellectuals who, at times, could have been creative enough to rethink women's position in their respective religions. The question is to what extent women actively need to intervene in religious ideological production. [. . .]

Rethinking women's position in religions: A methodological reflection

While the mainstream of the women's movement avoids entering into the subject beyond a general critique of religion as an oppressive force, there is also a fringe of the movement which uses religious symbols, for example, the women's publishing house 'Kali for Women'. While I have not heard of similar efforts among Muslim women, I have met individual Muslim women in the women's movement who wish to remain believers and who try to reconcile their faith with their religious commitment. Among Christians, attempts to develop a feminist theology are on the way.

The problem which arises is two-fold. On the one hand, one has to grapple with the problem of the use and reinterpretation of religious symbols in general. On the other hand, one has to deal with the problem of the use of scriptural sources in a way which takes socioeconomic historical conditions into account. Since the use of scriptures is the most obvious and widespread method, I would like to deal with it first.

This question of the use of scriptures naturally arises more in the explicitly scriptural religions like Judaism, Christianity and Islam, which have been called 'religions of the book'. In Hinduism, the vast heritage of *Sruti* makes religious traditions much more complicated. Yet, certain scriptural sources like the Vedas, Upanishads, the Bhagavadgita or Manu-Smrti are frequently referred to, and also the great epics like Mahabharata and Ramayana are often looked upon as being rather authoritative.

There is a certain tendency of religious apologetics which tries to maintain that 'originally' all religious were rather favourable to women and only 'implementation' was lagging behind. We are reassured by quotations for Manu: 'Where women are honoured, the gods rejoice,' or from the prophet Mohammed: 'Paradise is at the feet of mothers.' In such quotations, the praise of women remains entirely abstract, and the patriarchal family relations which form the prison of the home in which the woman is made the queen remain entirely unanalyzed and untouched. [. . .]

1. It is necessary to analyze religious sources as far as possible with methods of materialist history writing, i.e. connecting any statement on women with their actual position within the mode of production of the time in which the statement is made. It has also to be taken into account that most religious sources, and most history books, have been written by men and that this has ideological implications of its own.

2. Research on the position of women in religions cannot focus primarily on religious laws and ethical norms which ascribe to women a certain fixed position. Religious laws and ethical statements of this kind focus on marriage and family, and the whole aspect of women's education, public life, contribution to economic and cultural production and of women as self-reliant human beings tends to be narrowed down to her contribution as wife and mother. On the other hand, most religious sources also know of women who have lived lives in their own right, be they unmarried, married or widowed, and our attention has to focus on such women's roles which allows us to develop a wider perspective. Often, it is also necessary to draw on broader anthropological statements which are of general humanitarian value and to weigh them against oppressive role ascriptions. For example, the biblical statement that *all* human beings, women and men, are created in the image of God overrides other statements of subordination.

3. It is also important to understand the distortions and blatant contradictions in most conservative writings. On the one hand, a golden age of freedom and equality is projected while, on the other hand, women are pinned down to a subordinated life as housewives and mothers. For putting up with the contradiction, women are put on a pedestal. This kind of distortion comes indeed out of a material

contradiction which manifests itself differently in different modes of production. The need for production of life (i.e. child-bearing and child-rearing and maintenance work) which is seen as women's task in the family is in tension with the need to use woman's labour for the production of use and exchange value which requires women's work outside the house. The underlying problem here is one of the sexual division of labour, on the one hand, and maintenance of patriarchy (control of a woman's labour, sexuality and fertility), on the other. Religion has been one of the strongest forces to uphold the institution of the patriarchal family. Religious family laws mainly serve this supreme purpose. Likewise, the patriarchal family has strengthened institutionalized religion. To break through this alliance is a major task which the women's movement has not even tried to tackle.

These three guidelines which I have tried to evolve here, are, up to a point, also applicable to the use of religious symbols. It may not always be possible to fully trace the historic origins of a religious symbol but certainly it can be analyzed how it is appropriated by different classes. For instance, Sita, who was the symbol of the self-sacrificing wife in the eyes of orthodoxy, acquired the qualities of a self-willed courageous woman in the Gandhian interpretation and may be used as an outright symbol of protest if seen through feminist eyes. Bina Agarwal, in a recent Sunday edition of Indian Express, wrote a very moving poem under the title "Sita Speaks", in which Sita is encouraged to tell *her* side of the story.

As it is important to go into religious texts about women which go beyond the sanctified institution of marriage and family life, it is also important to go into the mythological heritage of religions in order to trace certain cultural assumptions about women which may be quite widespread in the public mind. There is, for example, a widespread assumption in Tamil culture that women are, in fact, bearers of supreme power and that this power needs to be controlled because it will turn destructive unless controlled. Thus, the power of women is supposed to be vested in their *karpu* (chastity) in order to ensure male control over women. If one takes the trouble to go through the temple myths of Tamil Nadu, one discovers an ancient layer of goddess religion in which the goddess is a virgin or a powerful independent entity in her own right. The *stala puranas* contain many versions which record the process of subjugation of the goddess, which usually ends up in sacred marriage. This process happens not only to the goddess but also to semi-historical figures like the Amazon queen Alli. Research into such historical backgrounds can unearth a protest potential as yet untapped.

Invariably, freeing women from the shackles of subordination involves making choices. In the same way as we constantly have to make choices between different roles offered in the family and in society at large, we also have to make choices between traditions and symbols offered: To *combine* an ideal of freedom and equality with women's exclusive destiny to be ideal wives and mothers is possible only in a hypocritical mind which tries to bamboozle us by means of cultural chauvinism. Real life and liveable values involve a more painful process of acceptance and rejection of contents which have to be tested in their potential to free or to oppress women. [. . .]

It is important to acknowledge that in communalism, in religious reform and in the women's movement a common question is raised but provided with different answers: the question of cultural identity. Communalism tackles the question by creating a false consciousness with the suggestion that people of the same religion automatically have the same socioeconomic interest, irrespective of class or patriarchy, and that the way to implement this interest is to politically organize on the ground of religion. Defence of a religious personal law is crucial to this approach.

The women's movement tends to build on the assumption that there is a certain community of interest between all women, and that the barriers of class, caste and community have to be overcome. While overcoming class barriers entails clear political choices in favour of poor and exploited women, overcoming of caste and communal barriers is often attempted in a somewhat voluntaristic way by simply declaring that they are artificial and, thus, somehow unreal.

Genuine religious reform deals with the matter in a more dialectical way by acknowledging the social reality of caste and communal cleavages, and identifying and contesting their religious sanctions. An active effort is made to overcome the meaning systems which give legitimacy to such cleavages. A leader like Dr M.M. Thomas declares wherever he goes that Christians cannot be communalists because they have to stand up for the new humanity in Christ and are, thus, responsible for safeguarding the humanness of every human being. He enables Christians to participate in secular political processes without abandoning their faith dimension, and he also makes the humanist essence of his faith accessible to non-believers. His other contention is that rationalism and religious faith in certain ways need each other in order to correct their mutual self-righteousness.

Since M.M. Thomas makes radical statements in religious language, he often suffers the fate of not being heeded by religious congregations (because of his political convictions) and by the secular political movement (because of his faith dimension). However, one does need to ponder the point that rationalism cannot always take its own rationality for granted (for example, the statement that religion is the greatest divider of mankind is not a rational statement), while a humanist faith can be quite rational within the parameters of the aim to build a human society.

An approach similar to that of M.M. Thomas is followed by Swami Agnivesh who was on the road in saffron robes instantly in protest against the anti-Sikh riots. He, like M.M. Thomas, openly theologizes on his option for the poor and on his political choices. At the same time, he makes it clear that political processes have to be free from the control of religious institutions. His saffron attire and religious language may alienate some people who are strict rationalists or those who feel that Vedanta can only be seen as reactionary. On the other hand, he reaches people with an emotional attachment to this particular religious tradition, and offers them identification with the poor, with human rights issues and anti-communalist religious tolerance which would otherwise remain beyond their horizon.

Among Muslims Asghar Ali Engineer has been untiringly recapturing the humanist traditions within Islam. He has paid a heavy price for his efforts even physically, being exposed to the violence of the reactionary forces in a very direct way. His reinterpretation of *jihad* for liberation, as opposed to *jihad* for aggression, opens up a social justice dimension suppressed by the conservatives. Faith to him means upholding the perspective of hope. God's sovereignty is not seen in competition to human initiative but, on the contrary, as a source of setting it free. While this kind of religious humanism is rare and comes under pressure from institutionalized religion, it is nevertheless an important ferment of cultural transformation. Since such enlightened individuals are open to the women's question, they may occasionally incorporate it. M.M. Thomas, in fact, has developed a growing awareness of it over the years. However, a feminist dimension of liberation theology has not yet evolved to any substantial extent.

There is an additional reason why the women's movement needs to go into the cultural question more deeply: The effort to give women a new sense of identity beyond family, caste and religion needs to grapple with the problem of cultural identity and continuity. It is comparatively easy to point out what has been oppressive and destructive of women in our cultural heritage. But, the question, what are the protest values and the humanist values of our cultural traditions also needs to be answered if shallowness is to be avoided. To work out the materialist and rationalist heritage is only one approach to this question, which leaves the reservoir of humanism within religion entirely untouched. The need to draw upon this reservoir also arises while facing the task of bringing up children in a meaningful way. Most activists confront the problem of having to relate to much more conservative and even very religious families in a constructive way. Their children have to bridge the gap between a non-descript culture in their own home and something very different in the homes of their friends and relatives. What does one finally believe in?

Alliance of anti-communist forces

Since secularism is not a sectoral demand, the women's movement cannot fight this struggle alone. It has to ally itself with other forces which are fighting for the same objective. However, the forces trying to build secularism in the present situation are by no means homogenous.

In Kerala, the CPI (M) has been able to champion the cause of a secular civil code to a certain extent. The fact that the party has a broad base in this state and that people's science movement has worked to build a scientific consciousness accounts for a more favourable situation here as compared to many other states. However, often enough, electoral considerations do weaken the left parties in taking a clear anti-communalist stand, as was obvious during the national election campaign of 1984.

Enlightened intellectuals in different religious communities also play an important role in creating an anti-communalist climate. It is important that the rationalist forces and the forces of religious reform which try to creatively work out a progressive faith dimension, do not become mutually antagonistic.

Dalit and tribal movements, which drastically attack caste and contest the domination of mainstream Hindu culture, have an important contribution to make towards a pluralistic secular culture. At the same, they may not always find it easy to come to terms with existing forces of religious reform of mainstream Hinduism. Take, for example, the reinterpretation of the terms *arya* and *dasyu* which Swami Agnivesh has to offer. This may not be acceptable to a Dalit perspective, while his involvement with bonded labourers or his participation in *ekta morchas* after the anti-Sikh riots are very important contributions towards the building of a secular humanist culture.

The women's movement may face its own difficulties in relating to all these forces because it may disagree with the party analysis of class and patriarchy, it may find the enlightened intellectuals to be paternalistic in dealing with women, it may find the champions of tribal and dalit culture to be romantics about women in Paleolithic times but not always helpful in a day-to-day interaction. Finally, as women in the women's movement, we may realize that we find it difficult to agree on issues of culture and religion. There are no easy answers but indications are that the perspectives on secularism, religious reform and a pluralistic humanist culture are deepening within the women's movement. If the challenge is taken up, women will be able to make the most crucial contribution towards building a truly humanist secular state.

As far as legislation is concerned, the women's movement needs to explore the possibility of contributing proposals for a secular family law, taking the existing personal laws into account. Such a law could offer an option for all progressive citizens to subscribe to and build their family life on a secular base. It is women who stand to gain the most from such an option.

∾

POLITICS OF DIVERSITY: RELIGIOUS COMMUNITIES AND MULTIPLE PATRIARCHIES

Kumkum Sangari

Should religion-based personal laws be maintained or should a uniform civil code be instituted? Among the numerous positions on this issue, those that are explicitly or implicitly based on some degree of genuine concern for gender justice and secularism range from briefs for legal uniformity to versions of legal pluralism. [. . .] The question of personal law hinges crucially and connectedly on notions of community, religion, state and cultural diversity, and the compatibility of each of these with gender justice. In the first part of the paper I will take up these in the form of a critique of the extant ideologies of religious community, of personal laws and their reform by either the community or the state. In the second part of the paper, I will discuss the ideology of cultural diversity and sketch an alternative notion of cultural diversity through a discussion of religious pluralism and legal pluralism, and then present a preliminary analysis of multiple and overlapping patriarchies in the last section. Religious and legal pluralism alongside multiple and overlapping patriarchies are in my view crucial coordinates in rethinking the question of gender justice outside the constrictive opposition between personal laws and a uniform civil code; a fresh understanding of these can help to formulate a material basis for new laws.

A substantial part of my essay discusses the concept of religious community for a number of reasons. Firstly, in various ways this concept underpins the defence of personal laws and plays into some liberal and majoritarian projects for a uniform civil code; in turn, the academic and the political discourses which privilege the idea of community are moulding and even setting the parameters for the present debate on laws. Secondly, community claims are not confined to minorities but are a central feature of pan-Indian Hindu majoritarianism. Thirdly, the prevailing definition of community is so reductive, static and essentialist that a defence of community in the name of social pluralism defeats its own declared objective of maintaining cultural diversity. [. . .]

I believe that a feminism which is based on a critique of biologism and of the sexual division of labour rests, definitionally, on the right to chosen political affiliation, and privileges social identities (as the terrain of contest, affirmation or remaking) above birth-bound ones; it cannot flirt uncritically with primordialism. Primordial claims cannot be a feminist principle because they are a principle of irrevocable division and will divide women by region, caste, religion and race. We can only take principled positions on the basis of non-primordial collectivities.

Thus, if it is true that religious community is at present to some extent a political identity (though an exclusionary one), it is equally true that there are political collectivities that do not insist on or trade in either the primacy or the exclusivity of primordial identities. In fact, most political parties appeal even now to identities other than the religious; so do numerous organizations and movements involving women, peasants and workers. Women's struggles within left-democratic frameworks rest on a view of women as bearers of a distinct political identity and a community of interests neither primordial nor biologistic, nor exclusive of class or cultural claims.

[. . .] It may be more productive, though less popular, to speak of communities not as 'given' on religious lines but to speak of the political, economic and electoral processes that are producing and privileging this particular sort of 'community' and facilitating specific types of ideological investment in it. It would then follow that secular feminist interventions could be directed at these processes, and not confined to finding just means of arbitration between 'given', pre-formed religious communities (a nagging reminder of colonial policies, even if partly justified by the present situation).

Religious and non-religious community claims

The question of religious community cannot of course exhaust the issue of primordial community. Primordial community claims coexist or intersect with claims to non-primordial collectivities—class, work and occupational identities, forms of contiguity in neighbourhoods and villages—which along with gender, have been the basis for non-community specific mobilization. Many contemporary 'community' claims are not for 'cultural autonomy' alone but are simultaneously a contest over the distribution and appropriation of resources and a feature of political organization. If the issues of material resources and political power were to be equitably resolved then the substantive content of 'cultural autonomy' would be different. The democratic assertions in some claims based on community, as in the case of dalits, in fact, intersect with and even rely on other forms of collectivity. Their invocation of 'material interests' is often a strong notation for, or empathetically indicates, identities premised on class-based, non-primordial aspects of social identity and the exploitation of labour.

Other forms of collective identity exist alongside, in tension or even in a struggle with primordial community claims precisely because the social, economic and political forces of capitalism in India pull in both directions. Should we strengthen those existing or possible political arenas where social inequities can be challenged without invoking or consolidating primordial religious identity and where primordial affiliations can be downplayed; or should we, as present community identity and communal politics would prefer, force them to remould or discard their agendas in favour of religious communities?

The question is further complicated by the fact that despite increasing communalization, even now religion is neither the only basis of primordial community claims nor the only practical and symbolic coordinate of political mobilization on primordial grounds. In fact religion does not have the foundational status ascribed to it by intellectuals and claimed for it by 'community spokesmen'. Politically volatile or active 'community' claims (that subsume myriad and diminutive primordial communities) on the basis of geographical territory or region, caste, tribal identity, broad linguistic distinctions (such as Hindi or Urdu), as well as narrower linguistic distinctions (such as local dialects), are being made alongside those based on religion whether configured as broad pan-Indian denominations such as Hinduism, Sikhism or Islam, or as smaller particularized sects.

Now if we were to imagine forms of 'decentralized' legal pluralism based on these primordial community claims, several problems would arise. Would a *single* basis for definition such as language or territory or caste or religion, be compatible with justice? And if so, what would be the rationale for suppressing all other conflicting claims? Why, for instance, should a caste-based community claim be less valid than a claim based on a major religious denomination? On what basis, if any, will any one of them be prioritized, and how many will such a prioritization satisfy? Even in the abstract, religion would not qualify as a contender for differential rights on the ground of unilateral past victimage and historical wrong. At present, the most dubious but vociferous claim of victimage and assertion of a violent 'righting' of historical 'wrong' is coming from Hindu majoritarianism, though by far the greatest historical wrongs have been to low castes and tribals.

Settling for legal pluralism based on any one primordial basis brings up the irresolvable paradox of differential rights; the notion of 'right' if it is to be legitimate must be potentially universalizable, for example, right to education, to work, to vote. So differential rights based on a primordial claim would keep creating new grounds for inequality and dissent even as they set out to resolve some existing areas of conflict. And in such a situation there would be, logically, no recourse to a language of common, potentially universalizable rights whether as basis for possible equality or as the *basis* for conflict resolution and arbitration or as basis for instituting the need for calling the state to account.

It is important to argue this because it would be literally *impossible* to institute a 'decentralized' legal particularism on the basis of *all* primordial community claims—religious, sectarian, linguistic territorial, caste or life-context. This would be a self-cancelling procedure, since the sheer multiplicity, even of politically articulated claims, would throw one back, ironically, on notions of individual rights.

Each and every basis or definitional category for primordial 'community' claims is fissiparous and open to further subdivision, either on the same lines, that is more particularized units of any one category, or through being undercut/crosscut by others categories. Thus a linguistic or religious community can fracture within the country on lines of dialects, sects, castes, region of origin or residence, class, language, and so on; while the diasporic location of Indians can further fracture primordial groups and set up new logics of differentiation on grounds of nationality and assimilation of local culture.

Again, few of these 'communities' will now or in future exist on co-residential, contiguous or interpersonal bases; not only are languages, castes, religions, etc, widely distributed over India and even internationally, but spatial distribution relocates them in different economies and in locally varied hierarchies. Not only does spatial distribution deterritorialize communities and communities' claims and in the simpler senses of dislocation or migration, but new forms of contiguity change the identities of persons thereby altering the meaning of a community's claims in its local register and substantive contents.

Such heterogeneity is not merely a jural or jurisdictional issue which can be solved on a passport model of portable identities that can be carried around. It challenges the very definition of community. This kind of heterogeneity within each nomenclature can be assimilated into a legally defined 'community' only through an artificial or pre-performed entity, and through *closure*—by making it impervious to change and indeed to the very liability of the continuous processes of identity formation.

Two major conclusions are inescapable. First, any single basis of 'community' will not only be ephemeral or provisional, liable to fragmentation by other cross-cutting affiliations, but it cannot represent the full spectrum of social divisions and locations, cultural diversities and aspiration. Second, if all except geographical territory is movable or mobile, if even claims to territory can be made at a long distance, if belonging does not involve presence, then 'community' claims are disguising a very real heterogeneity— they are in fact at this level hardly, or not at all, claims for recognition of existing cultural plurality. They are seeking homogeneity but are not *a priori* based on it. This is true as much of pan-Hinduism as of pan-Islamism.

Community, religion, women

The broad ideological conception of religious communities has uncomfortable implications since religious 'communities' are not only inegalitarian or class differentiated but are also specifically undemocratic regarding women. Community identities can be as much punitive as protective on patriarchal and proprietorial assumptions. If, as the more extreme arguments for reform of personal laws from 'within' seem to desire, communities were to legally govern, reform and adjudicate themselves, taking full responsibility for being either agents of change or protectors of the status quo, what will prevent them from trying to be self-legislating patriarchies; from strengthening local, interpersonal patriarchal control; and from continuing to hand power over to mullahs, priests, pundits or other chosen interpreters? There is little evidence to show that communities are committed to internal democratization of gender differences. And if such democratization will remain as pressing an issue (if not more pressing), even after communities have retained or achieved some measures of legal autonomy, then why not simply struggle for a thorough-going democratization on wider non-denominational principles of collectivity in the first place?

Women's own religious beliefs, consent to a religious identity and community as well as their agency in maintaining these, are often presented as the rationale for maintaining personal laws and reforming them only from within. This is a complex issue, partly because it can be argued for women from beleaguered minorities as well as from the chauvinistic majority.

In certain kinds of contemporary analysis overly anxious to establish that religion is not false consciousness, religion is simply turned into a matter of faith or belief alone, thus eliding the issue that religion prevails as an *institution* more than consciousness, true or false. This formulation not only serves as catchall for the complexity of the relations between gender and religion; it is then followed by the proposition that religious belief is giving agency to women. More often than not, the implication is that the presence of such an agency for women makes secular feminism questionable or even redundant. Thus a pernicious continuum is made between primordial denomination, women's belief and women's agency.

As a result, some serious questions are never asked. What is the nature of women's consent? When they consent to the punitive aspects of religious identity or community are they in fact consenting to the patriarchies with which these are meshed, or vice versa or both? Or, is their consent effectively consent to the host of other social factors in which both religions and patriarchies are enmeshed? Thus women's consent to religious definition may go beyond questions of individual faith and reflect the ways in which religions and patriarchies are articulating with other social structures. Should we confuse women's consent to patriarchal assertions of community, their inability or fear to step out of these in this particular political conjuncture, with the sum of their needs and aspirations? For instance, women's consent to Muslim community and to Hindutva enacts very different and antagonist relations of power; while women's active investment in Hindutva (a complex historical, political, economic, class/caste differentiated and conjunctural phenomenon), may have little to do with religious belief *per se*. Instead of conflating such consent with 'feminist agency' (a current preoccupation with some anti-communal feminists), a different type of consent to patriarchy has in the past and still does empower them for *selected* forms of social agency; further, this consent works through appreciating available hegemonic and/or legitimating languages into new ideological locales and pushes their previous proponents into more stringent political self-definition or at worst, into apology and retraction. Or to give another instance, many Muslim women are caught in a double emphasis: first, because a uniform civil code is seen to endanger the identity of physically endangered Muslims, the very claim to gender equality now implies disloyalty or antagonism towards the community; second, belief in Islam now appears to entail being prepared to accept patriarchal personal laws.

It is argued, in discussions and in writing, that opposing minority personal laws denigrates the laudable efforts as well as subsumes the initiatives of women involved in reforming personal laws from within. Undoubtedly, some Muslim and Christian women have religious yet reformist standpoints, oppose a uniform civil code, remove some gender inequities or 'corruptions' from their personal laws. I believe that the issues need to be posed differently— they should be disentangled from belief and concentrate instead on the nature and pitfalls of reform from within. Second, we have to determine if the strategies of religious reformism from within also have space for those other women who may or may not be believers, but find consent punitive, or who do not consent, or more to the point, who *need alternatives* in order to dissent in an effective way. This is important for two reasons. A feminist politics must account for women's consent to patriarchies, but it can scarcely afford to give political or theoretical primacy to women's will to consent to forms of social oppression *over and above* their will to contest these, since such a primacy is already on offer by a standard form of male conservatism. Nor can feminist politics take on board a divisive (or for that matter a unifying) politics based on essentialist identities, whether primordial or biologistic.

The question of representing 'other' women

In this context, confining women to the community identity and personal becomes a way of dismantling and preempting cross-denominational or extra-religious feminist collectivities. Against the potential dangers of representing 'other' women, that is women of other dominations, we must place the danger of refusing to represent each other. Refusal of a common ground of struggle is also a form of othering. Particularism can be segregationist in its logic. Unless universality is granted in principle (though not necessarily as a strategic mode of organization) as the possibility of mutual representation, feminist groups run the danger of replicating the structure of communalism.

The right to scrutinize and interrogate our entire social milieu is a democratic right for all and one that is particularly critical for feminists, and this cannot be confined to or reserved for one's own primordial denomination. If it is suspended in the name of religious community, then it will prevent women from critiquing a significant determinant of patriarchal operation in India, namely religion. Indeed it may altogether silence women—some in the name of belonging and loyalty to their religious group, and others because they have not the 'right' to speak of any religion but their 'own'. It is ironic too that inhabitants of a subcontinent, rich in irreverence, in both *comparison* and *critique* of religious philosophies, hierarchies, institutions and practices that were not limited by personal belonging, as well as rife with oppressions in the name of religions, should now be asked to piously desist from criticism of any but their own religion, within the rubric of a postmodernist politics of (self)-representation. Not only does this version of postmodernism, when transposed to the question of Indian personal laws, become unfaithful to its basic tenets of deconstructing the demarcation between within and without, but it ignores the material evidence of the fluidity of religions that I have discussed earlier. More significantly for feminists, this proposition of self-representation rests on a proprietorial view of religions (and as a corollary, even separate 'life-worlds'), as the exclusive property of particular groups, and as I will discuss later, one in which assumptions about owning religions 'naturally' extend to ownership of women.

The women who are (or are sought to be) united on the basis of systemic, overlapping patriarchies are nevertheless simultaneously divided along other lines. Three such divisions are pertinent to my argument: first, by class, overdetermined by caste, and the accompanying power to oppress other women and men; second, by consent to patriarchies and their compensatory structures and an accompanying delegated power to oppress other women; third, by the choice of rightwing politics that gives them a political armoury for 'othering' men and women from other religions. And here, the way in which feminists take up particular issues determines whether they are not classist, casteist, undemocratic or compromising with patriarchal arrangements. If they are, then and only then, do these turn effectively into divisions among women, instead of being, as they should be, divisions that must be *challenged* by feminism.

I do not think, however, that differences in religious faith can by themselves produce equally significant divisions between women. The particular reasons of belief need not by itself either constitute divisions along lines of power or alter the distribution of social power. To the extent that all religions are implicated in and enter into the broad process of social legitimation of patriarchies, challenges to patriarchies constitute a threat to specific forms of religious legitimation. In this regard religious affiliation makes a difference *to* women but need not produce a conflict between them; especially women who are willing to question the casteist or communal discriminations that inhere in some religious practices and are ready to consider that aspects of religions may be working to reconcile them to patriarchal oppression.

It is only when religious affiliation is translated into a politics and is aligned with institutions that it has the capacity to divide women. Thus, the institutionalization and communalization of religions have acted as a powerful force aggravated by the involvement of some women in entwining religion with the politics of the Hindu right. The rightwing appropriation of feminists' agendas or the language of citizenship and democracy is not unique to India and its function here as elsewhere is to divide and derail left, democratic, feminist agendas.

If this is an acceptable line of reasoning then the question arises as to why we should recede from a secular democratic agenda and from a commitment to common struggles. The divisions among women along lines of class, consent and political choices have to be fought through persuasion and/or political confrontation, not through a capitulative politics of difference, exclusivism or hyper-particularism.

One issue posed by feminists in the light of the recent riot-torn communal situation is whether gender unity can withstand communal hostility. Feminist groups, Flavia Agnes argues, are already over-inflected with 'Hindu' assumptions—an evidence of this over inflection is their past failure to mount a thoroughgoing critique of Hindu personal law—and cannot be isolated from the wider political contradictions; moreover she argues that in the aftermath of the riots, women do not have a separate existence away from their communal identity where legal issues can be discussed on a common platform. (See her essay in this cluster.) Her argument may fit well with another argument claiming that at present religious identities have acquired a preeminence and the only way to break out is by working within them or by 'negotiating' them. In practice this could mean that the patriarchal system operating in the country may henceforth have to be separately opposed by women from within different denominational groupings, while the range of these groupings could now extend beyond designated minorities and stretch to women opposing patriarchal practices from within the fold of Hindu communal organizations. If so, we will be unable to address the fact that the political play of denominational 'communities' with its logic of aggression and defence impedes women's individuation, and now being added on to inequalities in waged and unwaged work as well as in inheritance, is driving women further back.

I think the question of why women consent to religious definition and answers to this question, as well as the path to a common politics, hinge on our understanding of patriarchies: on the way patriarchies are embedded in or articulate with class structures, caste–class inequalities, religious practices, wider dialectics of social legitimation and other political formations. It is only if we see patriarchies as self-sufficient, unrelated to each other, isolated from wider social processes and determined by religion alone that we can support singular, separate struggles against them along denominational lines. If we see them as part and parcel of the wider social formation then we have to devise modes of organization and struggle that can encompass all the social inequities that patriarchies are related to, embedded in and structured or enabled by. Attacking patriarchal oppression is not a sectoral issue confined to women but central to any agenda for social change. Can we afford yet again to separate the 'women's question' from a wider struggle, and this time as victims of the divisions enforced by communalization? If feminism is to be an egalitarian, democratic and secular force allied with other such forces, then this, along with the very nature of patriarchies requires a common politics. [. . .]

∾

PRAGMATICS OF THE HINDU RIGHT: POLITICS OF WOMEN'S ORGANIZATIONS
Tanika Sarkar

The Rashtraswayam Sevak Samiti (RSS), founded in 1925, has steadfastly remained an all-male organization down to this day. Its founder Hedgewar had initially refused to consider the opening of a women's wing. However, in 1936, eleven years after its beginning, the RSS responded to the pleas of Lakshmibai Kelkar, mother of an important Sangh member. The Rashtrasevika Samiti was founded in 1936 with daily shakhas that provided physical martial arts as well as ideological or 'boudhik' training. It remained, however, a small and low-keyed affair. [. . .]

Around 1989–90, in a sudden and dramatic spurt of activities, the Sangh parivar threw up a large number of women's organizations and women leaders into dazzling prominence—the Bharatiya Janata Party's Mahila Morcha, the Vishwa Hindu Parishad's Maitri Mandal and Durga Vahini with their different regional versions. [. . .] I did some field work among Delhi-based women of the Hindu right between 1990 and 1993, at a time when the Sangh parivar was simultaneously engaged in a mass movement of violence against Muslims and in an electoral bid to capture state power at the centre. This was also the time when the Sangh began to flaunt its women for the first time in its history, in public places and roles. It was a special moment of spectacular growth and spread, a phase of mass mobilization and movement— all of which were new and heady departures for the Sangh and its women. At the Samiti office, office-bearers told me of an internal struggle that had preceded the Samiti's decision to allow and train women as karsevikas. They said that it had been the young members who forced the hands of the Samiti.

The Samiti was in an excited and hopeful mood, claiming credit for the growth of women's wings and activism. It was launched onto a course of developing a strong, wide-ranging and dynamic female cadre base for the

Sangh that would enjoy a powerful public identity and political function, and that would also claim equality in political work, without overtly claiming social equality. The enterprise was fraught with some tension since political equality already showed a few tentative signs of overspill into the social and the domestic. [. . .]

The tension, however, was structured by and contained within a generally conservative domesticity—a modernized and somewhat loose and flexible version of brahmanical patriarchy that allowed and encouraged education, employment and a more informed and activist politicization only on the basis of communal violence and commitment to an extremely inegalitarian social perspective. Male discrimination was questioned—if at all—in public spaces and in the workplace, rather than at home.

I found the field work a profoundly disturbing and disconcerting experience. As feminists, we had always celebrated the release of women from pure domesticity, their politicization had always been assumed to be an emancipatory possibility and the relationship between communal violence and women had been seen as one of male-inflicted violence and female victimhood. Recent experience confounded fond certainties and forced trajectories.

The last year of the century finds the Sangh parivar in significantly changed circumstances. The 'mass phase' of this fascistic formation—extremely limited and gestural as it was—is closing down, movements are being replaced with rhetoric and even their few feeble populist gestures are dying out fast. [. . .]

Going back to the women of the Samiti in April 1999, opened up new sources of disturbance for me. It, however, also brought a few crumbs of comfort. If we feminists had found the communalized public identity of Sangh women disturbing, the Sangh men seemed to have found it even more so, for different reasons. I went back at a moment of deliberate withdrawal of women's activism and a folding back of the public potential. [. . .]

I had hesitated to use the word 'fundamentalism' in the early 1990s, either about the Sangh's gender ideology, or about its women's organizations. I am convinced that the fundamentalist turn is now accomplished. I feel, moreover, that it was not my misrecognition that had earlier missed the point. It was something that has unfolded later, partly because of the dissonances and paradoxes that I could observe at that time. But above all, it happened because of a changed historical situation and its new logic.

Let me, first of all, establish my point about the retreat. The BJP has been in power in Delhi, till fairly recently, for five continuous years. It had ruled for more than a year at the centre. Yet, the Delhi Samiti membership seems to have been halved. It had stood at 2000 in 1991, according to Samiti reckoning. Now the same office-bearers put it at 1000, or a little more than that. The shakhas have gone down from sixty in the past year to a maximum of fifty-two at present. [. . .]

Socially and geographically, there has been stagnation and even decline in Delhi. On an all-India scale, the total membership has remained constant at two lakhs over the past decade, even though the Sangh parivar has seen a rapid growth in its power. The BJP Mahila Morcha has a membership of around thirteen lakhs, but it is to mobilize the women supporters of the BJP for electoral activities. It does not function as a women's organization. [. . .]

Secular feminists—haunted by the rapid growth of the right and a sense of guilt arising from failing to stem its growth—sometimes go on to an extreme to declare that the right has seized the initiative even in the women's movement from the hands of secular forces. This is paranoia, based on total ignorance of facts and figures. In fact, women's movements and organizations are one area where left and radical forces enjoy an overwhelming edge over the right—a fact that left parties probably will not like to advertise. The All-India Democratic Women's Association alone has a membership between 50–60 lakhs and it has grown rapidly in the last decade. The bulk of the force is recruited from rural women. Dalit women of AIDWA have been very active in the movement and the AIDWA too is active among the dalits. Recently, Brinda Karat led an anti-untouchability campaign in Tamil Nadu. The Samiti, on the other hand, admits that they still have to open an account in villages, and that they so far cover cities and district towns. They had said the same thing ten years back. Obviously, rural, poor or low caste women are not targeted as part of the potential female cadre base of the parivar to whom the Samiti brings the full benefits of Sangh education and training. Add to the AIDWA a very large number of autonomous women's organizations across the country that are engaged in radical movements and programmes, and we get numbers that are impressive by any count, certainly breathtaking by Sangh–Samiti standards. We need to remember that the growth in leftist women's organizations occurred in the teeth of adverse circumstances. While the last decade has been a fortunate one for the Sangh, left forces have not done well except in this sector. In contrast, even in Delhi, which has for very long been a Sangh stronghold, the membership stands static at about a thousand. The left, always very insignificant in the city, numbers about 47,000 in the CPM-affiliated Janwadi Mahila Samiti, more than doubling itself in the last decade, without the benefit of a corresponding growth in the strength of the parent organization. [. . .]

In the early 1990s, the Samiti was engaged in a variety of programmes. It ran a fairly substantial monthly magazine *Jagriti*, it provided orientation courses for wives of RSS men who had come from non-RSS families, it provided correspondence courses for newly married Samiti members who had joined non-RSS families and who found it difficult to attend shakhas, they were also meant for young girls who lived in areas which did not have shakhas. All these programmes have been discontinued. The only new addition has been to open discussion groups for old women. [. . .] Now the

Jagriti has been discontinued, replaced with an annual news-sheet, *Sevika*. The difference in nomenclature is interesting, for *Jagriti* (Awakening) had a dynamic, forceful ring to it that tried to merge into mainstream women's movement and its language. [. . .] The new news-sheet firmly puts the Samiti woman in her appointed place—that of service. It is concerned about distinguishing itself from the aspirations of the women's movement, not about appropriating and subverting some of them. The Samiti calendar for 1999 lists a ritual event for each day of the year, and most days, there are many more than one event. Many of them require a visit to the local temple, a pilgrimage and /or the intercession of a priest. There is no political event that is recognized on the calendar, not even December 6, though their women remain very proud of it. The point is that the women of the Samiti are now given a purely ritual identity, not really an overt, active, political one. [. . .]

The transiting to ritual/domestic from a public activist role does not bespeak a return to the so-called peaceful, maternal bosom of faith from the turbulence of modern politics. The urge for violence, destruction, revenge, for trampling over Muslims and Christians, is, if anything, even more strident today, but the Samiti transmits it in a different way.

[. . .] The heady hopes of going into war under the banner of the Samiti icon of Ashtabhuja Durga are no longer articulated. Samiti is content, as we shall see later, to remain a transmission belt for the RSS, conveying stories about Muslim and Christian 'atrocities' against Hindus. There is a retreat to older female functions and roles where women gossip about things that they have not seen themselves but have heard from their men.

Retreat from active violence or public politics does not mean an emphasis on women-centred work. Samiti office-bearers often refer to the 'social work' that their women do so well from their homes, but when they are pressed to specify, they fall back upon 'writing letters to newspapers about oppression of Hindus and about sex and violence in western movies and TV shows'. The Samiti celebrated its sixtieth year in 1996 with a national seminar on this theme. They also conduct workshops on the Vande Mataram hymn of Bankimchandra which the RSS considers to be the authentic national anthem for the Hindu nation. These workshops were held in public schools and in colleges like Shivaji College, Janaki Devi College and S.P. Mukherjee College in Delhi. The seminars and the letters to the editors seem to be the only other things that they do, apart from running shakhas. Despite five years in Delhi government and access to its funds, they have not set up shelters and counselling or legal help centres for battered women or significant schemes for employment generation or slum welfare. Elsewhere, too, a picture of minor, sporadic activity emerges. They run a girls' hostel at Nagpur, a new one has been opened at Jullunder in Punjab. [. . .]

Social questions are abhorred as divisive of national unity and they are avoided in the boudhik or ideological sessions of shakhas. Shakhas remain central to their enterprise. They see them as mobilizing points for entire localities, since through intimate relations with the women they gain entry into their homes. Since each shakha trains 20–25 women at the most, relations are warm and close, spiced with 'enjoyable' activities like storytelling and games. Parents who do not subscribe to Sangh ideology would still like to send their daughters to shakhas since they teach deference and obedience, they inculcate conservative values like arranged matches, good home keeping, modesty in dress and behaviour, and diligent service to men and elders. Girls themselves like to go because of the physical training programmes which are invaluable ways of gaining a control over their own bodies when they have control over so little. The sense of physical well-being, strength and empowerment remain valued resources, even when no other kinds of empowerment are offered. Also, the ideological instructions about services to a militaristic, aggressive Hindu nation, of vengeance against its enemies, about heroic qualities of legendary men and women who resisted 'enemies' of the nation, fulfil aspirations for a life above pure self-interest, release frustrations built up through being girls in orthodox families. Moreover they are not told anything that offends mainstream patriarchal, Hindu nationalistic values and myths. Although they do admit that young girls are not the most enthusiastic members, they do not prohibit all the new pleasures in the name of fighting western culture. Girls are encouraged to look good the modern way. They can visit beauty parlours and spend money on buying beauty products—provided most of them are home manufactured. Though mini-skirts and shorts are out since they expose the body, jeans are all right if they have the right figure, then they must cultivate one. These are important concessions. The new consumerist self-absorptions of the middle class woman, fanned by the ad-culture and the flood of beauty-aids, cosmetics and household gadgets, are encouraged, since they provide the economic survival of much of the country's manufacturing trading classes. And this class is also the major basis for the political support of the Sangh parivar.

What cannot be tolerated, however, and what is powerfully and continuously denounced as the fruit of the western poison tree, is the notion of equal gender rights. [. . .]

The old *Jagriti* was equally silent about problems within the family. But it had a lot to say about discrimination in public spaces, in state agencies, in the workplace. The sevikas now refuse to discuss even that. When I ask 'pracharika' Poonam Gupta what she would consider to be the biggest problem for Indian women, she could not think of a single issue to say but for the well-worn theme of alleged Muslim lust for the pure Hindu woman. (A pracharika is a woman pledged to strict celibacy, who is a full-time activist and who supervises the functioning of the shakhas.) Similarly, when I asked Asha Sharma, (the 'karyavayika' or organizing secretary, Delhi for the last ten years), the same question, she mentioned the British education policy which closed women's eyes to questions of 'nationality, patriotism, culture and motherhood' by teaching them about 'struggles, law, fighting men'. She shrugged off my queries about dowry and domestic violence impatiently as things that do not merit a discussion. At length, she said that rape was a problem of great proportions.

Of course, the new phase of the left-secular feminist women's movement consolidated itself around rape as a symbol of the most violent expression of patriarchal values, of the complicity between the state and the violent man. The founder of the Samiti, Lakshmibai Kelkar, had also urged for shakhas for women when she saw a wife being assaulted in the presence of her husband and concluded that since Hindu men cannot defend their wives, the wives must learn to protect themselves. The present reasoning of the Samiti is different from both understandings. Rapes occur, they say, since women have forfeited their older modes of honour and motherhood status by being addicted to struggles and enmity with men. Moreover, the western films and cable TV programmes have created a vulgar preoccupation with sex and desire that was unknown to Hindu society of past. The resolution, unlike that of their founder, is not physical empowerment of threatened women. It is the retrieval of past honour by the recuperation of the motherhood ideal and by the banning of the media products. [. . .]

Sevikas are home and neighbourhood based, insulated from contamination from lesser social circles. There is only one major exception to this. Some of them—mostly the unmarried pracharikas—work with the Sangh's slum rehabilitation programmes under the Seva Bharati scheme. Some others train the teachers who work in the RSS schools under Vidya Bharati. Both are huge growth areas of the Sangh—the Vidya Bharati competing with the government chain of model schools, and Seva Bharati running 1,700 centres in Delhi alone. Most teachers in the Vidya Bharati scheme are women, and Seva Bharati work of rehabilitation would seem to require 'womanly' nurturing services. Yet, Samiti participation even here is highly restricted. The Samiti at best is an auxiliary to certain fronts under the Sangh.

The Sangh parivar appears to have launched on a curious course of action. It proudly forefronts elected women members in the higher legislative and executive bodies. In this respect, its record is far better than that of the Left. On the other hand, women who are thus exalted do not come from women's organizations, nor do they have prominent bases among the women of their own political clusters. They are quite indifferent to women's issues, problems, demands. What is the implication of this split between the women's organizations and women in electoral politics? Incidentally, the same pattern is repeated among the women of the Shiv Sena in Mumbai. [. . .]

The need to field women candidates is obvious given a steadily growing women's constituency, reinforced by extremely vocal and active women's movements. Also, reservation of seats for women in local and state-level elected bodies makes it indispensable. The interesting thing is the careful insulation of such candidates from women's issues and organizations even within the Sangh parivar.

I would argue that the need to push women into electoral politics is counter pointed deliberately by efforts to ensure that this does not add an edge to gender concerns or to empowerment of women within the Sangh parivar. Women enter electoral politics and earn the party some kudos for progressive attitudes, without a concomitant compulsion for the Sangh parivar as a whole to sensitize itself to women's needs. Moreover, women MPs or MLAs of the BJP cannot enter the sanctum sanctorum of decision-making—the Sangh itself, which remains exclusively male. Nor are women members of the central organizing committee of the Shiv Sena. The implications of their prominence in public politics are thus clipped at both ends. Women's organizations, on the other hand, cannot borrow the lustre of their elected sisters who, on the other hand, are individuals unconnected with organized women as a front within the parivar. I found it interesting that Samiti office-bearers and pracharikas were quite contemptuous about the issue of women's reservation in Parliament, arguing that it denoted a tragic dilution of the principle of merit. One can perhaps make the same point about the left parties which have a remarkable absence of women in their central decision-making bodies. At the same time, their women's organizations are vibrant, dynamic, burgeoning, innovative and creative fronts, in sharp contrast to the rather moth-eaten Samiti of the Sangh parivar and the Mahila Aghadi of the Shiv Sena.

If the Samiti is now a small, bounded, non-expansive affair, like the good, modest, non-competitive Hindu women, then what is the significance of the new accents and stresses within them? I believe that the pattern has a great relevance. These women are the custodians of essential Sangh values, of its authentic ideology, that the other fronts have somewhat diluted and imperilled in the current war games over electoral power. Since electoral preoccupations will continue to grow, the conservation of older values becomes all the more crucial. Hence the Samiti is important as both a guarantee as well as a mirror.

Secondly, if the battle over electoral power is ever decisively won, then the Samiti will be the nucleus of the new Hindu domesticity. Its women will be the exemplars, living models for the pattern to be realized in the Hindu rashtra of the future. Therefore, precisely at a moment of expected triumph did it need to contract its activity and affirm its purity, domesticity and conservatism at the cost of its public activism.

We will be quite misled to believe that it is an entirely imposed change enforced by the male Sangh. Women have genuinely invested in this commitment. They see a bright future for themselves as the soul of the Hindu rashtra, as the defender of tradition against the west, as partners in an internal colonization over the Muslim and the Christian.

Finally, the convictions that the Samiti expressed go beyond gender—or rather, gender is the pattern, the inspiration for relations between castes and classes. Since it can mystify its operations of power with intimacy, it is the most effective argument for all hierarchies. The battle against equality and rights that the Samiti had undertaken in the name of Hindu traditions is also a larger, unnamed struggle that the Sangh is engaged in to re-orient the discursive order of power relations in the Hindu rashtra of its dreams.

12

~

SEXUALITIES

If there is one subject that has burst forth as a fresh site of engagement over the last decade or so, it is that of sexuality. Even though the national conference of women's movements did address sexuality in its Patna conference in 1988, it was only in the subsequent national conference held in Tirupati in 1993 that issues of sexuality, including lesbian sexuality, found its way into the sessions and final resolutions. For its part, the Indian Association of Women's Studies had a sub-theme on sexualities as late as 2005. However, it would simply be a distortion to therefore claim that issues relating to sexuality have hitherto been suppressed by the women's movement and women's studies.

How, then, should we look at this thematic? To start off with, we might miss the fact that questions of sexuality have structured the very conceptualization of the rights and wrongs of women in our context, from the first public debates on widowhood, marriage and education, all of which shook up the nineteenth century. Questions of sexual purity could be decisive for the re-marriageability of the widow; the debate surrounding raising the age of consent for a girl in marriage hinged on her age of puberty and readiness for sexual intercourse, and even opposition to women's education was often couched in terms that hinted at the sexual impropriety that would attach to women capable of reading and writing. Though so much has been said about the social shaping of women's issues during the colonial period, we are still at the early stages of unpacking the new sexual norms and senses of selfhood that were effectively produced and contested, which formed a kind of undertow to the official naming of women's issues during this time.

The first two contributions to this section are examples of how feminists have interrogated the legacies of history. Indeed, it is worth noting that the first major interventions within the field of sexuality by scholars were historical rather than contemporary. In the opening excerpt from her longer essay, Kumkum Roy examines the *Kamasutra*, India's classic treatise on matters pertaining to sexual desire and pleasure, from a feminist perspective. She tracks the history of this text from the Sanskrit version through a succession of modern translations, to show how far it is from being an unrestrained exposition on sexual permissiveness and freedom, an index of our erotic 'golden age'. The next essay by Janaki Nair is a contribution to a larger body of scholarship on the devadasi system which flourished in parts of south India till its decline in the early decades of the twentieth century. Literally meaning god's servant, the devadasi became a subject of reform largely due to new perceptions about the problematic sexual nature of her work as a dancer and singer attached to the temple complex. Janaki Nair discusses the special case of the princely state of Mysore, which, unlike the neighbouring Madras Presidency, did not come under direct British Rule. As she points out, it was the modernizing bureaucracy—rather than social reformers or feminists—who were at the forefront of ensuring that the devadasi would have no future state patronage of her art.

All the remaining essays in this section have a contemporary focus. There are other pieces in this reader that deal with sexuality—in the next section on literature and the media, for instance, we have the example of feminist writers in Telugu, who were attacked in the early 1990s for writing ostensibly 'pornographic' poetry. Again, in the earlier thematic section on the law, Ratna Kapur had queried proposals to implement sexual harassment for their potential to curtail freedom of sexual expression. Thus, there clearly have been sites such as the law or women's writing where women's sexuality has been critical. However, what is different now is that much of the new energy and controversy in the last decade can be pinned to the public emergence of non-normative sexual subjects, whose very presence and voice at the margins of the women's movement have given sex and sexuality meanings they did not have before.

The next piece introduces one such voice, in the form of the 'Sex Workers Manifesto'. On the one hand, it could be argued that sex work is hardly new—indeed, the debate around the devadasi tradition became inextricably tied up with questions of prostitution, and the acute victimization suffered by the devadasi-turned-prostitute. On the other hand, not unlike contemporary international controversies, newly formed sex workers' organizations in India have raised a set of demands that have upset 'mainstream'—including most feminist—views of the nature and problems of prostitution. The Sex Workers Manifesto formed the theme paper of the First National Conference of Sex Workers, organized by the Durbar Mahila

Samanwaya Committee in 1997 in Calcutta. It addresses the stigmatization and oppression suffered by sex workers, but from a perspective that believes that sex work must be recognized as a legitimate occupation, and indeed, that commercial sex can be a source of pleasure for women, at least under the right conditions. While there has been some debate on the legal history of regulating prostitution, such as the Immoral Traffic (Prevention) Act of 1986, and ongoing concern over the spread of HIV/AIDS through sex work in the field of health, only a small beginning can be said to have been made among women's groups and in women's studies. In spite of the presence of sex workers' organizations at recent conferences of the women's movement and women's studies, serious engagement between feminists and sex workers is still in its infancy.

A different set of voices constitutes the excerpted pieces from 'Lesbian Emergence', taken from a special dossier prepared by the Campaign of Lesbian Rights or Caleri in 1999. This campaign was made possible by the publicity and controversy that surrounded the commercial screening of the film *Fire*, the subsequent attacks on the film by Hindu rightwing organizations in Mumbai and Delhi, and the counter-protests that followed. At the heart of the controversy was the lesbian relationship between the two female protagonists of the film. Diverse positions on and readings of the film filled newspapers and journals (one of which has been included in the dossier here). Questions of lesbianism took on a public life in the wake of this controversy, marking a new phase in the history of gay, lesbian and alternate sexualities in our context. The number of groups committed to upholding the rights of lesbian women multiplied in cities and towns across the country, sometimes with close links to prior feminist organizations. A subsequent campaign, also included in the dossier, has been the demand for the repeal of Section 377 of the IPC, which prohibits sexual acts 'against the order of nature' and has been used to harass and target gays and lesbians. This demand to repeal Section 377 has, so far, been rejected by the courts. The politics of sexual orientation—which was certainly part of the women's movement from the 1980s, but in a less public form—has acquired greater visibility in some women's groups and among women's studies scholars, especially given the violence experienced by lesbians at the hands of their families and society. We have yet, however, to gain a perspective on the deeper structures of heterosexual normativity and its forms of exclusion, beyond the everyday experiences of homophobia.

Our next essay is a contribution to a very mainstream subject—that of the media. Media images of women were questioned by the very first women's groups in the 1970s and 80s, who felt the powerful impact of such images in sustaining women's subordinate status as objects of male sexual gratification. The strategy of banning or censoring problematic images—on hoardings and advertisements, and especially in popular films—has therefore been at issue for quite some time. In this excerpt from her longer essay, Shohini Ghosh, in turn, questions most feminist engagements with such censorship by seeing how it differs from mainstream and rightwing anxieties about obscenity. She argues that feminists have often conflated sexism with sexual explicitness, and have selectively criticized the use of women in advertising. Feminist attacks on obscene representations run the risk of suppressing or curbing freedom of expression and women's agency on sexual issues, so 'missing the wood for the trees' according to Ghosh. From the debates and campaigns of the 1990s over events like the Miss World beauty contests and in popular media images, the question of censorship continues to divide women's organizations. The most recent issue focused on the closing down of dance bars in Mumbai city in early 2006, where protests against women's degradation as bar dancers clashed with the right to work. Here, too, we are discovering how issues of sexuality throw up unanticipated tensions around new subjects.

Our final contribution in this theme is an indication of how existing critiques of institutions such as the family are being taken onto new terrain by emergent queer positions. On a platform organized on the occasion of a gay and lesbian film festival in 2004, Marxist, feminist, dalit and queer critiques of marriage and family revealed the profound roles these institutions have played in ensuring class, caste and gender subordination. Rinchin's contribution to this discussion, included here, argues that an institution like the family is not just a contradictory space of both care and violence (as feminists have long recognized), but deeply exclusionary in its effects. Alternate ways of cohabiting, and many significant relationships—whether sexual or not—that make up one's life, are relegated to the margins by the dominant place occupied by the marriage relationship in contemporary culture. Gays, lesbians and bisexuals, in particular, are under constant pressure to change themselves in order to enter into the more familiar relationships of marriage and family, and even then, can be subjected to further violence.

Questions of censorship and sexual agency, sex work and non-normative sexualities are thus posing new questions to women's studies and all those committed to gender justice. If the scholarship that inevitably accompanies the emergence of new subjects and campaigns is still in formation, we can expect the years to come to see much more thought and action at the intersections of feminist and sexual politics.

≈

UNRAVELLING THE *KAMASUTRA*

Kumkum Roy

The blurb of one of the most recent English translations of the *Kamasutra,* that by Danielou, describes the text as 'the world's oldest and most widely read guide to the pleasures and techniques of sex'. Further:

> Realistic and pragmatic in its approach, the *Kamastura* deals without ambiguity or hypocrisy with all aspects of sexual life—including marriage, adultery, prostitution, group sex, sadomasochism, male and female homosexuality and transvestism. The text paints a fascinating portrait of an India whose openness to sexuality gave rise to a highly developed expression of the erotic. (1994)

In a sense, this eulogy summarizes some of the most widely accepted readings of the text, many of which have crystallized over the past century or so.

The *Kamasutra* was highly visible some years ago in an advertising campaign for a condom. The images which accompanied the text almost invariably depicted a jean-clad man (whose face was barely visible) embracing a young woman, whose eyes were more often than not closed (presumably in ecstasy) and who was more obviously exposed to the gaze of the (male?) observer. While the imagery deliberately and somewhat obviously modernized the text, it also captured one of its dominant strands, namely, its definition of gendered sexuality.

More recently, the *Kamasutra* provided the title (and, it would seem, little else) to Mira Nair's controversial film, which was not released in India at the time of writing. Going by available information, it was initially titled *Tara and Maya* after the two main women protagonists. Supposedly set in the sixteenth century, at least a thousand years after the *Kamasutra* was compiled, Nair's film 'is about female friendship and female rivalry, but is ultimately about female solidarity'(cited in the *Telegraph*, 1 December 1996). These are themes that can be read into the Sanskrit text with great difficulty, if at all. That the film was so renamed and then censored is in a sense suggestive of the meanings attributed to the text, which is both perceived and portrayed as being synonymous with notions of sexuality, at once unrestrained and sophisticated.

Undeniably then, the *Kamasutra,* a text which was probably compiled at least one thousand five hundred years ago, is still with us. The text can be located within the tradition of *sutras* or *sastras* of early erotic literature, and within the contemporary context, where the proliferation of translations of the text has, in a sense, transformed it. [. . .]

Questions of context and form

The *Kamasutra* was probably composed or compiled between the second and fourth centuries AD in north India. While it is traditionally ascribed to Vatsyayana, it is in all likelihood a composite work, a feature fairly typical of Sanskrit texts. It was probably composed after, and in connection with, two other major works, the *Dharmasastra* ascribed to Manu (also known as the *Manusmrti)* and the *Arthasastra* assigned to Kautilya. Stylistically, the *Kamasutra* is particularly close to the latter text.

[. . .] The programme of the author(s) of the *Kamasutra* seems to have been at least two-fold. On the one hand, kama or desire was to be accorded legitimacy by being made the subject of a sastra. This is evident in the very first, introductory statement: 'Salutations to dharma, artha, and kama,' (*Kamasutra* I.1.1.) a statement in consonance with the customary invocation of the gods which marks the beginning of most Sanskrit works. Thus, at one stroke, kama is located in conjunction with dharma and artha and elevated through an implicit equation of all three with the gods. More explicitly, Vatsyayana states that some sages felt that whereas dharma and artha, given their complexity, were legitimate subjects for discussion, kama was natural and universal and hence did not require codification.

Repudiating this, Vatsyayana argues that women, unlike females of other species, do not have a specific mating season. Consequently, unions between the sexes are governed by other considerations (*upaya),* which need to be regulated. In Vatsyayana's understanding then, human sexuality is socially constructed rather than rooted in the natural order. At the same time, desire is understood to be basic to human existence, comparable to food.

On another level, and more obviously, the text focuses on the legitimation of a (or some) particular form(s) of desire, that is to say, it delimits the contents of kama, in effect recognizing and centralizing the heterosexual desires of upper class men vis-à-vis all women (directly) and lower class men (indirectly). Desires, thus constructed, are no longer amorphous or inchoate— in fact, we are faced with 'Desire', which acquires definitional status and in terms of which other manifestations are classified as subordinate, irrelevant, or even disruptive. Clearly then, the definition of desire codified in the *Kamasutra* was integrated, ideally, into relations of power, so that it could be viewed as an expression of power.

As an extension of this, positions within the realm of desire are carefully located—one is either capable of experiencing desire or being an object of desire, a man or a woman, powerful or powerless. The specific desire which is privileged is embedded asymmetrically—that is to say, women are differentiated almost ad infinitum, from men and from each other, whereas powerful men are consolidated into an almost homogeneous category.

Yet this neat hierarchizing tendency had its problems as well. An attempt seems to have been made to make the text comprehensive and universal. As a result, a wide range of sexual practices attributed to different regions are listed. While the normative thrust of the text ensures that such practices are ordered hierarchically, the very process of listing would have accorded recognition to diverse practices, which need not necessarily have been in harmony with one another.

Moreover, to acquire validity, any code had to be implemented. This in turn rested on its ability to persuade and/or coerce women and men who were denied access to the process of codification to believe that its end product, normative sexual behaviour, was indeed applicable and valid for all. In other words, the contents of each code had to be communicated and enforced.

The text as available at present is divided into seven sections. The first deals with general practices and precepts (*sadharana*), the second with heterosexual intercourse (*samprayogika*), the third with obtaining a bride (*kanyasamprayuktaka*), the fourth with the duties of the wife (*bharyadhikarika*), the fifth with relations with wives of other men (*paradarika*), the sixth with courtesans (*vaisika*) and the last with secret formulae (*aupanisadika*) designed to ensure success in sexual activities. Not surprisingly, the second section, with its vivid if somewhat monotonous details on physical positions, has attracted the most attention in recent years, in spite of the fact that this comprises approximately only a quarter of the text. An analysis of the text suggests that the second, sixth and seventh sections were probably independent of each other and of the remaining sections. These were collated in order to arrive at a comprehensive definition of sexual relations.

While the text is both composite and complex, there is a central concern with defining desire in order to develop a specific understanding of gender relations. This in itself was by no means easy, and its transmission, in particular, may have been fairly complicated.

The first section of the *Kamasutra* lays down, amongst other things, channels for the proper communication of its contents. Access was granted to both men and women. This is somewhat surprising in view of the general tendency to exclude women from sastric knowledge. What is interesting is the argument advanced for opening up the text to women: they ought to acquire knowledge of the sastra as they were involved in its practice. However, women's access to the text was simultaneously circumscribed. A married woman could acquire knowledge with the permission of her husband, whereas others had to learn it from trustworthy people, specifically married women, kinswomen, or servant women.

Clearly, women could not be taught by men versed in the Sanskrit sutra version of the text, as the very proximity of women and men outside certain regulated contexts would have opened up the possibility for alternative expressions of desire. If women were to be taught by other women, who were by definition excluded from direct access to the sastras and Sanskrit learning, the complexities of the text in terms of both style and content would have had to be simplified. In other words, the text would have to be converted into oral formulae or dicta, suitable for transmission to a non-scholastic audience. However, once this was undertaken, the introduction of non-sastric elements was possible within the framework of the text. In fact, the text may have been modified in the process of communication, by less 'scholarly' men as well as women. Thus circumscription was possible only up to a point, beyond which both access to and the construction of the text could become relatively open-ended activities. [. . .]

Locating socio-sexual relations

The *Kamasutra* is primarily directed towards the *nagaraka* (citizen), who is often equated with the *nayaka* or actor. While the *nayaka* is by definition male, he is also expected to be prosperous and 'cultured'. Besides this, his caste affiliations are considered to be relatively unimportant; any man, if sufficiently wealthy, could aspire to proficiency in the precepts and practices advocated in the text.

The structure of the text can, in fact, be envisaged in terms of concentric circles, centering on the *nagaraka* and moving outwards through wider social relations. The work begins by constructing the ideal life style of the male protagonist, and follows this up by defining the norms of heterosexual intercourse. This is then located within the context of marriage, defined in terms of stratified relations between men and women. Control over women within the patriarchal household is extended to control over women in other households. Finally, the prostitute is accommodated, although, as we shall see, this is somewhat tangential to the perspective of the text.

The construction of the *nagaraka* as a man who is the focus of socio-sexual relations and in control of them required as its corollary that women, as the object of such relations, be classified and objectified. This resulted in defining ideal women in terms of physical and mental attributes, and classifying them according to region. There is a striking dichotomy between the construct of the *nagaraka* or *nayaka*, where the ideal seems to be a single, uniform, universal man, and the sheer plurality and diversity of types of women enumerated. Not surprisingly, there is no feminine equivalent for the *nagaraka*.

Besides, while we do have references to *nayikas* (the female counterpart of the nayaka), the attributes and roles of the two categories are not envisaged as identical. The former were classified according to their relationship with men—they could, for instance, be virgins, remarried women, or prostitutes. What differentiates women from one another, and from men, is whether they are accessible to a single man, to two men, or to all men. Thus, the basic definition of women as accessible to men is elaborated. Further, the construction of the *nayakas* as the embodiment of masculinity was reinforced by the classification of eunuchs, defined as the *trtiya prakrti,* literally the 'third nature', the first two types being men and women. Eunuchs could be feminine or masculine in attire and manner, but were defined as feminine vis-à-vis the *nayakas.*

Distinct constructions of masculinity and femininity are also evident in the description and classifications of forms of physical intercourse. The naming of kinds of genital contact seems to be almost exclusively in terms of the position or role ascribed to the female partner. Some of the names suggest a passive construction of female sexuality; for instance, the *irmbhitaka* or the yawning position was so named as it involved holding up the legs of the woman. Other names, such as the *vadavaka* or mare-like position, in which the woman was expected to hold the penis firmly, suggest an understanding of more active female participation. However, such activity was implicitly viewed as exceptional; the woman astride the man was classified as *purusayita,* literally the woman who assumes the position of the man. On a more basic level, the male partner was defined as the doer (*karta*), with the female counterpart as the *adhara* or base. We are assured that both experience pleasure through their complementary roles.

As important as the kinds of genital contact which are named are those which are either not named or viewed with a certain amount of ambiguity. These include same sex genital or anal intercourse. References to lesbian relations, for instance, occur not in the context of kinds of sexual unions but in the section dealing with the means of winning over the wives of others. Further, lesbian sex is defined in terms of categories of heterosexual intercourse, with one of the women involved being classified as *purusavat,* literally, man-like. Thus, at one level, such relations were either obliterated or marginalized from the discussion. While at another level, recognition was accorded by assimilating them to heterosexual roles which were legitimized within the dominant tradition. [. . .]

On yet another level, violence within sexual relations was both recognized and structured. This is evident in the terms used to classify sexual contact. A particular type of kiss, for instance, required the forcible pulling of the virgin (*kanya*) towards the man. The woman is described as forcibly engaged (*balatkarena niyukta*). Besides, the beating of a woman by a man was recognized as a legitimate part of sexual intercourse. This was justified on the understanding of sex as *kalaharupam* or combat. While men were permitted to indulge in four or possibly eight types of beating, women were expected to respond with various kinds of shrieks and other sounds. Thus, the outcome of the combat was ideally regulated. More insidious was the understanding that if a woman protested against being beaten, this was simply what was expected of her in the game. Thus, her cries could be viewed not as expressions of pain but as indications of conforming to the code. At the same time, the *Kamasutra* warns against the 'excessive' use of violence which could and evidently did occasionally result in the death of the woman.

While violence was recognized as intrinsic to masculine sexuality, women's anger was permissible only within limits. This is evident from the range of actions permitted to the *nayika* who lost her temper; she could shout, scream, even kick the *nayaka*, but was then expected to go to the door and cry and permit the *nayaka* to conciliate her. [. . .]

If the construction of wifehood rested implicitly on an acceptance of violence as a possibility within sexual relations, the wife's subordination was envisaged in less dramatic ways as well. She was expected to treat her husband as a god, look after the household, maintain a garden, serve her husband by dressing for him, cooking according to his tastes, sleeping only after he had slept, waking before him, performing rituals for his welfare, seeking his permission before going out, avoiding the company of 'disrespectable' (and possibly threatening) women, including mendicants, renouncers of the world, witches, fortune-tellers and unchaste women. The dependence of the wife was foregrounded particularly in the context of polygyny. The *Kamasutra* urges women not only to accept, but to actively forge, relations which would underscore their subordination. For instance, a childless woman was expected to encourage her husband to remarry, while the junior bride was advised to defer to her senior.

The preoccupation with desire was not explicitly connected with concerns of procreation. This may seem somewhat surprising, given the sastric status accorded to the text. However, it is perhaps explicable within the overall framework of sexual relations envisaged within the text. The potential or actual availability of women to the male protagonist would have ensured procreation. Besides, given that even in texts such as the *Manusmrti* there is no notion of absolute illegitimacy, but of more or less legitimate offspring, any progeny produced through the satiation of kama could have been accommodated.

[. . .] While women were defined as accessible, access to women was construed as an index of male status. Thus, the village chief was supposed to have access to village women, and could have intercourse with them while they were engaged in forced labour, when they entered the granary, when they were transporting, buying or selling things, when they were working in the fields or cleaning the house. In other words, such women could be subjected to sexual advances during virtually all their routine activities. The officer in charge of cattle was permitted similar access to wives of shepherds and so on.

Not surprisingly, such access was envisaged as most complete in the case of the king. If he desired a woman, a slave woman and/or his wife were expected to assist him in his pursuit. However, the king was warned of the dangers of attempting to enter another man's house and of other men gaining access to his own harem. The latter situation was one where the neat ordering of hierarchies evidently collapsed. Were high status women defying their covertly powerful husbands in inviting low status men? If so, this constituted an explicit challenge to gender stratification. On the other hand, if the problem was posed in terms of low status men gaining access to high status women, a gender-based hierarchy would remain inviolable. However, the king's power over his male subjects would be called into question. Neither possibility was perceived as desirable. The solution offered was pragmatic, and consisted in guarding women.

The sixth section of the text was supposed to have been compiled at the request of the courtesans of Pataliputra (modern Patna). This section is somewhat intriguing, in that the protagonist is no longer the *nayaka* but the prostitute, and the issue at stake is not the fulfillment of kama but the question of profits. The prostitute was advised to observe a semblance of wifehood. This included pretending to learn the sixty-four erotic arts from the man, as well as adopting his likes and dislikes. These were recognized as strategies for extracting wealth from her sexual partner. As such, the prostitute merely appeared wife-like. [. . .]

Translation and modernity

Texts related to or explicitly derived from the *Kamasutra* continued to be composed till the seventeenth century. However, many of the later versions omitted the section on prostitution and genital-oral contact elaborating instead on the second section:

> Thus we come across as many as 50 varieties of union in the supine posture, 12 in the sidal, 13 in the sitting, 17 in the standing, 21 in the bent and 12 in the opposite. (Bhattacharya 1975, 102)

Burton's translation of the *Kamasutra* launched the text into an entirely new level of popularization. Born in 1821, Richard Burton traveled widely through France, Italy, Arabia and India. He evidently combined a 'love for the Orient' with an aversion for 'the rigid hypocrisy of Victorian sexuality' possibly stemming from his own interest in homosexuality. Besides the *Kamasutra,* he translated the *Arabian Nights,* and an Algerian text, *The Perfumed Garden.* The diverse reactions which Burton's work aroused point to the complexities which surrounded (and continue to surround) discussions on sexuality. On the one hand he was knighted in 1886; on the other hand, his wife burnt the manuscript of his translation of the section on homosexuality in *The Perfumed Garden* after his death.

Burton was probably the first to define the *Kamasutra* as a 'work on love'. He may also have begun the process of representing the subject of the text as 'natural'. This in turn provided the basis for universalizing its message. We are told that 'the human nature of today is much the same as the human nature of long ago'. Moreover, the text was recommended a 'work that should be studied by all, both old and young'. The actual dissemination of the contents of the text on an unprecedented scale was made possible through the medium of print. The process of printing also ensured that the text was standardized in a way which was not possible with a handwritten and/or orally transmitted work. [. . .]

Some of the strategies which underlay Burton's endeavour continue to be resorted to by Indian translators of the *Kamasutra*. Once again, they raise questions of sexuality, but locate this within a variety of other concerns such as those of science, modernity, or even salvation. Virtually every translation contains an introduction which encloses the text and attempts to circumscribe the meanings we are expected to read into it. For instance, Upadhyaya's translation, which is explicitly meant for 'members of the medical and legal professions, scholars, and research students of Indology, Psychology, and Social Sciences' is accompanied by an introduction designed to collapse the distinctions between a specific definition of desire and a more universalistic notion of love. This is achieved by juxtaposing a number of statements on the *Kamasutra* by Indologists and sexologists, and on love by Mahatma Gandhi and Rabindranath Tagore. A cheap version of the text (priced at Rs 12.50) and explicitly meant 'for youth on the threshold of married life' includes in its introduction comments by highly placed government officials and academicians evidently intended to serve a similar purpose. [. . .]

Given the preoccupation with projecting the *Kamasutra* as scientific, it is alarming to note that some present-day commentators tend to justify sexual violence as natural. We are informed that 'males now definitely know that the manifestation of tears and cries in a female are quite normal . . . and inwardly she desires the opposite of what she expresses by tears and cries and her withholding of favours from the male'(Upadhyaya 1961, 22) . Simultaneously, female sexuality is understood in almost mechanistic terms. Thus, clitoral stimulation is discussed in terms of the 'adequate amount of pressure on that electric button which normally sets the whole mechanism in operation'(Ibid., 19). [. . .]

There have also been some ingenious attempts to link kama with *moksa* or salvation, the privileged goal attributed to and claimed for diverse early and (by extension) contemporary Indian traditions. According to Mulk Raj Anand, for instance, knowledge of the *Kamasutra* was expected to 'lead not only to healthy enjoyment of the variegated pleasures of the body but also clarify the mind of all filth attached to the secret act. Also no hidden longings should remain in the mind of the seeker after *moksa*' (1958, 26).

Most printed versions of the *Kamasutra* tend to be illustrated. This is especially true of the more expensive, glossy, coffee-table editions. What is interesting is that even the professedly scholarly or academic translation produced by Upadhyaya contains as many as fifty plates, apart from other illustrations. There are two striking features about these illustrations. First, they are assembled from diverse traditions of sculpture and painting. We have, for instance, depictions from the sculpture of the 3rd century Nagarjunakonda as well as Pahari paintings of the eighteenth and nineteenth centuries. We have representations from Khajuraho and the Deccan as well as from Konarak and Bikaner.

This focus on and reworking of the text through illustrations blurs the distinction between the erotic and the pornographic, and is obviously useful as a sales strategy. Then again, the illustrations have the effect of valorizing, and to an extent isolating, the heterosexual dyad from the web of social relations within which they are embedded. As such, the translation implicitly appeals to the individual/heterosexual pair, and legitimates a certain 'modern' individualism by creating an illusion of social sexual relations.

With the growing accessibility of translations, the fate of the Sanskrit version has been one of steady marginalization. [. . .] Not surprisingly, the study of the *Kamasutra* in Sanskrit is not open to students in most modern departments which teach the language. The reason, ostensibly, is the nature of the text. Thus, access to and understanding of the text are structured. In effect, the Sanskrit text has become increasingly inaccessible, especially for women.

For all practical purposes, we are now left with translated versions of the text which project it as both ancient and modern, peculiarly Indian as well as universal, scientific as well as aesthetic. The weight the text has acquired means that if we feel uncomfortable with what it says we run the risk of being labelled as antiquated or too modern, unscientific, petty, un-Indian, crude, unsophisticated, irrational. Thus, at long last, the text becomes truly prescriptive. [. . .]

To an extent, the fate of the *Kamasutra* is symptomatic of that of questions of sexuality in general. Having attained a certain visibility, sexuality is often viewed as symbolic of liberal attitudes, yet in the process of acquiring this visibility, its social context has often deliberately been obscured. It may not be possible to retrieve the potential for critique and contestation inherent in oral transmission, but we need to create its equivalent so as to ground our discussions on contemporary sexualities within a complex reality.

References

Bhattacharya, N.N. *History of Indian erotic literature.* New Delhi: Munshiram Manoharlal, 1975.

Burton, Richard. *The Kamasutra and the Perfumed Garden.* England: Omega Books, 1987.

Danielou, Alain. *The complete Kamasutra*. Rochester: Park Street Press, 1994.

Kamasutra. Edited by Madhavcharya. Bombay: Laxmi Venkateshwara Steam Press, 1934.

Khanna, G. *Kamasutra: Its relevance today*, Bombay: Jaico Books, 1985.

Upadhyaya S.C. tr. *Kamasutra of Vatsyayana*. Bombay: Taraporevala, 1961.

≈

THE DEVADASI, DHARMA AND THE STATE
Janaki Nair

In 1929, Muthulakshmi Reddy, the first Indian woman legislator and an indefatigable campaigner against the devadasi system, moved a bill to end the dedication of women to temples in the presidency of Madras. In her statement of objects and reasons for the bill, Reddy complained of the inadequacy of Sections 372 and 373 of the Indian Penal Code in preventing such dedication, and insisted that 'a legislative enactment is therefore necessary in dealing with the practice of dedication *per se* . . .' (*Stri Dharma* 1930) Deploring the fact that the agitation of 'high minded Hindus' for devadasi abolition since 1869 had not yielded legislation, she praised the princely state of Mysore for setting a good example by passing a government order for complete abolition as early as 1909. Since Mysore was also a Hindu state, this was a clear indication, she said that 'Hindu religion does not sanction immorality in either man or woman'.

The abolition of a practice which 'in the name of service to God has condemned a certain class of women to a life of either a concubine or prostitute' only became law in 1947 in Madras. Yet what took years of active campaigning and effort by feminists such as Reddy was achieved by mere administrative fiat in Mysore state. The Mysore government did not labour under the same constraints as the alien colonial authority in rewriting Indian tradition; their policies neither provoked alarms of religion in danger nor accusations of ignorance of the sastras.

In fact, the Mysore government's order of 1909 only represented the final stage in a process of producing a new moral order that had begun in the early 1890s. This was when the first steps were taken to align notions of dharma—morality or law with persuasive power, a moral order which the maharaja protected—with an emerging colonial judicature by a bureaucracy pledged to developing and expanding forms of justice that were no longer embedded in, or derived from, cultural forms characteristic of the pre-colonial order.

[. . .] Persistent demands in the Mysore Representative Assembly after 1883 for reforms in temple management led the Mysore government to appoint a special officer as muzrai superintendent or Secretary. (The word 'muzrai', which was derived from the Persian word Mujra, meaning deductions or allowances, referred to allowances granted for religious and charitable purposes.) The new officer, A. Srinivasacharlu, briskly went about the business of introducing new budgets and sanctions, appointing *dharmadarsis* (temple managers equivalent to the dharmakarthas of Madras), revising and regulating tasdik pattis, all of which aimed at restoring the original grants made to temples, 'to impart to the worship and rituals therein more impressiveness and solemnity by a stricter conformity with the spirit of the Hindu religion as expounded by accepted authorities'. An opportunity to effect a serious and irrevocable change in the political economy of the temple presented itself soon after he assumed charge. The muzrai secretary was presented with a bill of 12 rupees 5 annas and 4 paise as payment to a woman called Ramamani who had performed *tafe* (dancing) services at the car festival of Bhoganandeswara Temple at Nandidurg, Chikkaballapur. He only reluctantly agreed to pay, saying that such *tafe* services were an unnecessary waste of money that could be better spent on 'improving sanitation'. Promising to issue a circular outlining the legitimate services of devadasis in temples, Srinivasacharlu categorically asserted that it did not include *tafe* or dancing.

We do not know the basis on which the muzrai secretary made his categorical decision, that is, knowledge of the scriptures or familiarity with temple custom, but it may have been prompted in part by the growing clamour in the neighbouring Madras Presidency of the anti-nautch (literally anti-dance) campaign conducted largely by educated upper caste Hindus. For the most part, Mysore appears to have escaped any such vociferous campaign. In 1891, however, the *Vrittanta Chintamani*, echoing the fears that were voiced in the Madras press, conceded that the concern for the abolition of the devadasi system was rooted in fears of female empowerment within the new colonial dispensation. Thus, it noted that some dancing girls of Madras were very rich, lived in large houses, kept carriages and paid large amounts of municipal taxes; this entitled them to vote in municipal committees. The paper suggested that these rights be withdrawn to reduce the embarrassment faced by respectable gentlemen who had to beg these 'low women' for their vote. To some extent, such upper caste discomfort with these cultural traditions was an indication of the success of missionary critiques of 'bad' Hindu practices.

The Mysore muzrai secretary did not issue the promised circular in 1892, but waited until 1898 to implement his decision during the revision of the tasdik pattis of the Nanjangud and Melkote temples (which were among the largest of the temple institutions in Mysore). On that occasion, he directed that *tafe* women should not be admitted to any kind of duty in the two temples, and although they could continue to be paid while they were alive, their posts should not be filled up after their deaths. Even in 1898, there appears to have been no sustained discussion of what constituted the 'legitimate services' of devadasis: the muzrai secretary was obviously secure in his belief that the 'immorality' of devadasis was too self-evident to warrant discussion. [. . .]

The muzrai secretary was quite determined to put an end to the practice of dancing in temples and temple processions. In this, he was amply aided by public opinion opposed to the continued indulgence of the maharaja in practices that were an embarrassment to the moralities of the middle class. The muzrai secretary therefore issued strict orders disallowing the 'detestable creatures' from accompanying the maharaja's procession on his tour of Sivaganga and Melkote temples in 1900. A more lasting solution to the embarrassment of seeing devadasis continue their role in temple rituals than mere official disapproval was to cut at the source of their livelihood, i.e. suspend payments and resources that sustained the devadasi and her arts. The muzrai secretary recognized this when he ordered that positions that fell vacant in muzrai temples after the death of a devadasi should not be filled. Not only did this represent a far greater incursion into the traditional duties and rights of devadasis, it ensured that the change was irreversible.

The first spirited challenge to the new situation came from the twelve devadasis who worked for the Srikanteswara temple at Nanjangud, a prominent temple complex that had long enjoyed princely patronage. In two emotional petitions which cited the authority of the sastra and customary practice, the women reminded the sovereign of his duty towards protecting hereditary occupations such as theirs.[. . .] In a recognition of the shifting relations of power, the devadasis' next petition was addressed to the muzrai commissioner as well, requesting reinstatement as per family traditions, but now expressing a willingness to adapt to the changed circumstances. Their overriding anxiety was to preserve not just their livelihoods but their skills in music and dancing which, they said, should not be allowed to languish and die for want of state patronage; the devadasis therefore offered to perform at state gatherings if necessary.

The Mysore officials who could no longer rely on government fiat to initiate social change on this scale, sought a reference to the sastras as the indisputable word on the duties of devadasis. [. . .] The agamiks entrusted with the task masterfully demonstrated that devadasis did indeed have specific services to render in the temple. From the moment they woke up, bathed and put on fresh clothes and adorned themselves with flowers, they spent the day participating in temple rituals. They concluded their comment with the sly suggestion that although this was what the sastras said, the government should do whatever was appropriate. Attention was now trained on the 'personal purity and rectitude of conduct and celibacy which were considered essential in case of female servants of god'. The sastric authorities were once again summoned to adjudicate on the question of whether strict *brahmacharya* was expected of devadasis.

The agamiks in their second memo of 16 August 1907 complied with the expectations of the authorities by reiterating the need for strict *brahmacharya* among devadasis 'even though they have tied the *thali* (necklace that is the sign of marriage)', that is, even though they were married to the deity. They raised the spectre of a world turned upside down, which it was the duty of the government authorities to set right. The Mysore administration was now confident that the decision to discontinue with the services of devadasis could even be turned to their advantage. If the devadasis could be shown as having violated sacred traditions, this would cast the Mysore administration in a new light, not merely as protectors of true Dharma, but restorers of a previous standard of purity:

> Whatever may have been the original object of the institution of the Devadasis, the state of immorality in which these people are now found appears to justify the action taken by the government in removing them from the sacred institutions like temples.

Devadasis who held land directly, and possessed deeds to prove that, were confirmed as the owners of that property in perpetuity on the payment of quit rent. Even in those cases where lands were not directly held by the women but by the temples, the government could not resume land; lands donated to temples could only be resumed if services for which they were endowed were not performed. Devadasis could hardly be dispossessed for non-performance of their duties when such non-performance was no fault of theirs. By making celibacy, and not just the performance of dance rituals, a condition of their continued enjoyment of temple grants, the state adroitly contained the crisis produced by its own illegality in ending local law-ways. The irony is inescapable, since in most cases, as we have seen, the women had received land grants from male patrons for services which combined artistic and sexual skills. [. . .]

The second councillor, K.P. Puttanna Chetty, commended the 'high moral courage' of the government in excluding devadasis from their temple services. Yet it was not just women who had been found lacking in the morality appropriate to temple offices; the venality of male *archakas*, 'men of little learning and not of high moral character', was legendary. However, there is no further reference to this lapsed tradition in the final government order of 1909 which abolished the employment of devadasis in muzrai institutions. [. . .]

Through the suppression of the polyvalent roles of the devadasi, the Mysore authorities had begun drawing the lines between respectable and disrespectable female sexuality, a distinction that was consonant to a large extent with dominant nationalist discourse, especially in the period of Gandhian nationalism. Perhaps the most striking instance of the distantiation of the nationalist elite from disreputable women was Gandhi's refusal to allow nearly two hundred prostitutes of Barisal from participating in the non-cooperation movement until they publicly renounced their profession (Kishwar 1985). The new morality which was concretized by Gandhian nationalism signified a shift from the nationalist response of the last decades of the nineteenth century. The cumulative effects of the implementation, and then repeal, of the Contagious Diseases Acts in British cantonments in India, the intermittent use of lock hospitals to regulate urban prostitution throughout the nineteenth century, and the gradual growth of leagues of social purity and temperance committees consisting of missionaries as well as Indian anti-nautch campaigners, had produced something of a backlash. Indigenous male elites increasingly felt themselves reduced to the level of clients when they had once been patrons, and portrayed the surveillance measures of the British authorities, who were unable to distinguish family women from others, as a violation of community honour. Once more, the resistance to colonial intrusion into the private domain was articulated as resistance to colonialism itself: the 1888 Congress annual meeting therefore passed a resolution seeking to abolish British laws regulating prostitution on the grounds that the honour of respectable Indian women was at stake.

In the period of Gandhian nationalism, however, chastity in 'thought, word and deed' were seen as critical for the development of the moral force of a satyagrahi. Thus, undergirding Muthulakshmi Reddy's campaign to enfranchise devadasi inams and delink it from service to the temple was a certain puritanism which was at odds with her anxiety to develop women's independence. She therefore resolved the troubling question of devadasi sexuality within the parameters set by male nationalists by encouraging them to marry and domesticate themselves. For the most part, references to female sexuality in journals like *Saraswathi,* edited by R. Kalyanamma, remained muted. On one occasion when it was discussed, as in the profile of Yamini Poorna Tilakamma, reference was to the reformed sexuality of a fallen woman who responded to the call of Gandhi. Tilakamma, whose 'moral weakness' in her early childhood in Guntur led her to the life of veshya/devadasi, continued as a prostitute for 18 years until in 1923, in the 'sacred age of Gandhi', she set up an institution, Yuvathi Sharanalaya, devoted to the eradication of prostitution, and an end to the devadasi system. Credit is given not only to Tilakamma but to 'the Andhra leaders who made her take up this work' (*Saraswathi* 1923).

A sign of the shift from a defence of certain forms of sexuality in the name of 'tradition' to a more active distantiation from such traditions was the fate of the reprint of *Radhika Santwanam* (Tharu and Lalita 1991). *Radhika*

Santwanam was a book written by an eighteenth century courtesan of the Thanjavur court, Muddupalani. It was a subversion of traditional erotic genres in that it centred on women's sexual pleasures. In 1910, Bangalore Nagaratnamma, herself a learned woman, renowned musician and courtesan and a gayaka (a member of one of the endogamous groups from which devadasis were drawn), was entranced by the sophistication and literary merit of Muddupalani's work, as well as its attempt at subversion, and published a fresh edition of the book. Responding to the outrage of some reformers who declared the poem obscene and vulgar, the colonial authorities seized all copies of the book in 1911 under Section 392 of the Indian Penal Code. It was clear that, on the critical question of subordination of female sexuality, the interests of empire and nation were not necessarily in opposition.

The gradual erosion of the material support for the artistic abilities of the devadasi resulted in her decline as a professional dancer, producing in its place a proletarianized sex worker, with nothing to trade but her sexual services, which were now a threat, rather than an adjunct, to the patriarchal household. In many ways the devadasi became indistinguishable from her urban counterparts, and from the basavis in the rural areas. Beginning in the 1930s, the expanding markets for prostitutes in cities such as Bombay found ready recruits among the devadasis and basavis of Mysore.

Bangalore Nagaratnamma's own survival as a skilled musician and the patronage she continued to receive were exceptional rather than the rule. Not only had the Mysore government invented a split between respectable and disrespectable sexuality, it had realigned access to property along such axes as well. Once the critical relation between new patriarchal definitions of female sexuality and women's rights to property was redefined, it became possible, especially in the 1930s, to legislate against immorality on the one hand (evidenced by the passage of the Suppression of Immoral Traffic in Women and Girls Act of 1937) and for the rights of women to property on the other. As the devadasis were symbolically and materially deprived of their resources, and consequently unable to practise their artistic skills, they were reduced to the status of proletarianized sex workers. When the extension of Hindu women's rights to property did take place, with the relatively uncontested passage of the act amending women's rights under Hindu Law in 1933, it was middle class, upper caste women, whose sexuality was reined in to the domain of domestic monogamous life, who stood to gain. Having declared women's rights to property under Hindu Law an anomaly when it was linked to non-patriarchal forms of marriage and family, the state could now bestow rights on women within the framework of the patriarchal household.

What new codes of morality did new nationalist patriarchy propose for men themselves? Here the Gandhian ideal of celibacy was far less pervasive, and not surprisingly, one of the persistent demands of first wave feminism was an end to the moral double standard. Even the ideal of companionate marriage pursued with such vigour in colonial India was not one that necessarily entailed strict monogamy of men. While there was certainly a contraction of legitimate spheres of male sexual fulfillment, the growth of prostitution in an illicit subterranean sphere, suppressed from public view, ensured the 'natural' promiscuity of men a continued mode of expression. Writing in 1930, Ananthakrishna Iyer speculates on the origins of the devadasi system thus: 'the founders of this institution made this an outlet for safeguarding family women for the good of the country'. This understanding resonated in the arguments made by opponents of proposed strictures on the practice of prostitution during debates on SITA in the 1930s.

If strains of democracy within the emerging conception of modernity may be traced at all, it is the yearnings of male nationalists for a companionate marriage in which wives consented to the 'natural' promiscuity of men, provided it did not occur at the expense of domestic arrangements. In his brief sketch of Bangalore Nagaratnamma included in a collection of writings on the luminaries of Mysore, D.V. Gundappa (DVG) speaks at length of the virtues of one of her patrons, a Mysore high court judge, Narahari Rao (Gundappa 1987). Narahari Rao attended her performances daily, and resolved to become her patron. DVG reconstructs a dialogue between Narahari Rao and his wife that bears detailed quotation:

> When Narahari Rao desired to become a patron of Nagaratnamma, he first sought the permission of his lawful wife (Dharmapatni). He called his wife and said:
>
> Narahari Rao: Listen, I want to ask you something. I need your permission.
>
> Wife [who remains unnamed]: Will anyone believe that you need my permission [for anything]? Tell me what you want me to do.
>
> N: It's not that way. This is a special situation. I have become enamoured of Nagaratnamma's music for several days now. She sings very well. I wish to be able to listen to her music now and then. If you have any objections, tell me now and I shall let go of this interest.
>
> W: It is my desire that your desires be fulfilled.
>
> N: I will ensure that you are not inconvenienced by this.
>
> W: How can it be an inconvenience to me? You have done your duty by the family. Our children have grown and are standing on their own feet. Our daughters are married. Our sons are educated. Now it is our duty to keep you happy.
>
> Thus this noble woman (Mahathayi) gave her permission. Only then did Narahari Rao go ahead with his plans.

We do not know whether such a conversation did take place, but it is interesting that DVG reports this exchange just before he speaks of the embarrassment caused by Narahari Rao's patronage of Nagaratnamma to the government of Mysore, whose employee he was. When the dewan learned of the daily visits of Narahari Rao to Nagaratnamma's quarters in the official government carriage, replete with the regalia of the princely state, he decided to intervene. He requested Narahari Rao not to sully the image of the government by visiting Nagaratnamma in the official vehicle. Narahari Rao was suitably chastened, and readily complied by ending his use of the government vehicle, though he continued his patronage of Nagaratnamma.

It is striking that the moral objection to Narahari Rao's actions came from the government rather than the wife. It is also interesting that a split was achieved between the spheres of the public and the private. The granting of patronage to a devadasi was a public expression of power by zamindars, notables, chieftains in pre-colonial India, in return for religious honour and sexual services, which were inseparable. In modernizing Mysore, however, such patronage had to be privatized, marked off from the public world where the façade of a new morality was maintained. Only as long as their patronage of public women such as Nagaratnamma remained a private matter could public men, judges such as Narahari Rao, uphold and dispense a new order of justice delinked from princely forms of power and authority. Meanwhile, the modernity of the middle class woman was expressed in the form of her consent to a form of patronage that recalled an older extended sexual order. Her 'modernity' consisted in permitting the continuation of a reformed patriarchy; promiscuity was a privilege of the modern male as long as he remained attentive to his duties as a father.

The ease with which the Mysore bureaucracy displaced monarchic institutions is an indication of the material ineffectuality of monarchical rule under paramount colonial power. Colonial rule had however enabled the Mysore bureaucracy to extricate recognizably patriarchal elements from a pre-colonial order that legally extended female and male sexuality beyond the domain of the conjugal family. What was put in its place, both in the nationalist imagination and in bureaucratic practice, in the name of a new, abstract legality, was a more thoroughly patriarchal family order which maintained the illusion of mutual respect and companionship.

References

Stri Dharma 13, March 1930.

Kishwar, Madhu. October 1985. Gandhi on women. *Economic and Political Weekly* 20–40 and 41.

Saraswathi 6, no. 3. 1923.

Iyer, Ananthakrishna. 1930. *Mysore tribes and castes* 4. N.p.

Gundappa, D.V. 1987. *Kelavu mahaniyaru.* Bangalore: Gokhale Institute of Public Affairs.

Tharu, Susie and K. Lalita. 1991. *Women writing in India.* Vol. 1. *Sixth century B.C. to the present.* New Delhi: Oxford University Press.

≈

SEX WORKERS' MANIFESTO

Durbar Mahila Samanwaya Committee

A new spectre seems to be haunting society. Or maybe those phantom creatures who have been kept in the shades for ages are taking on human form—and that is why there is so much fear. For the last few years, the sex workers movement has made us confront many fundamental questions about social structures and relations, interlinkages between class, gender and sexuality, about politico-moral ethics. We think an intrinsic component of our movement is to go on searching for the answers to these questions and raise newer ones.

What is the sex workers' movement all about?

We came together as a collective community through our active involvement as health workers, the Peer Educators, in a STD/HIV Intervention Programme which has been running in Sonagachhi, one of the oldest and largest red light areas of Calcutta since 1992. The programme provided the initial space for building mutual support facilitating reflection and initiating collective action among us, sex workers. Very early in the life of the Sonagachhi Project, we, with the empathetic support of those who had started the project, clearly recognized that even to realize the very basic project objectives of controlling transmission of HIV and STD among sex workers and our partners, it was crucial to view us in our totality—as complete persons with a range of emotional and material needs, living within a concrete and specific social, political and ideological context which determines the quality of our lives and our health—and not see us merely in terms of our sexual behaviour.

To give an example, while promoting the use of condoms, we soon realized that in order to change the sexual behaviour of sex workers it was not enough to enlighten us about the risks of unprotected sex or to improve our communication and negotiation skills. How will a sex worker who does not value herself at all think of taking steps to protect her health and her life? Even when fully aware of the necessity of using condoms to prevent disease transmission, may not an individual sex worker feel compelled to jeopardize her health in fear of losing her clients to other sex workers in the area unless it was ensured that all sex workers were able to persuade their clients to use condoms for every sexual act? Some sex workers may not even be in a position to try and negotiate safer sex with a client as they may be too closely controlled by exploitative madams or pimps. If a sex worker is starving either because she does not have enough customers or because most of her income goes towards maintaining a room or meeting the demands of pimps, madams, local power-brokers or the police, can she be really in a position to refuse a client who cannot be persuaded to use condoms?

And what about the client? Is a man likely to be amenable to learn anything from a woman, particularly an uneducated, 'fallen', often poor woman like a typical prostitute? For him, does not coming to a prostitute necessarily involve an inherent element of taking risk and behaving irresponsibly? In which case are not notions of responsibility and safety completely antithetic to his perceptions about his relationship with a prostitute? Does not a condom represent an unnecessary impediment in his way to 'total' pleasure? Moreover, in most cases this male himself may be a poor displaced man. Is he in a position to value his own life or has he enough motivation to take steps to protect his own health?

Then again why does a sex worker who is ready to use condoms with her clients seldom agree to have protected sex with her lover or husband? What fine balance between commercial transaction and love, caution and trust, safety and intimacy engenders such behaviour? How do ideologies of love, family, coupledom and motherhood influence our every sexual gesture?

Thus, thinking about such an apparently uncomplicated question of whether a sex worker can insist on having safe sex, made us realize that the issue is not at all simple. Sexuality and the lives of sex workers are intrinsically enmeshed in the complex social structure we live within and the powerful dominant ideologies which shape our moral ethical values. In 1995 we came to form the Durbar Mahila Samanwaya Committee, a forum exclusively of sex workers and their children to share experiences and plan strategies for struggling against our conditions of material deprivation and social stigmatization. This was the first time that a group of sex workers rallied together and explicitly spoke of the rights and wrongs of our profession at a public forum and attempted to inscribe our self-defined and self-conscious identity as sex workers in the public sphere.

We believe that like any other occupation sex work too is an occupation, not a moral condition. If it is one of the 'oldest' professions in the world that is because it must have continued to meet an important and consistent social demand. But the 'prostitute' is rarely used to refer to an occupational group of women who earn their livelihood through providing sexual services, rather it is deployed as a descriptive term denoting a homogenized category, usually of women, which poses threats to public health, sexual morality, social stability and civic order. Within this discursive boundary, we systematically find ourselves to be targets of moralizing impulses of dominant social groups through missions of cleansing and sanitizing both materially and symbolically. If and when we figure in political or developmental agendas we are enmeshed in discursive practices and practical projects which aim to rescue, rehabilitate, improve, discipline, control or police us. Charity organizations are prone to rescue us and put us in 'safe' homes; developmental organizations are likely to 'rehabilitate' us through meagre income generation activities which in any case never help to erase out the stigma as 'former' prostitutes and the police are bent upon regularly raiding our quarters in the name of controlling immoral trafficking.

Even when we are inscribed less negatively or even sympathetically within dominant discourses we are not exempt from stigmatization or social exclusion. As powerless abused victims with no resources, we are seen as objects of pity. Otherwise we appear as a self-sacrificing and nurturing supporting cast of characters in popular literature and cinema, ceaselessly ready to give up our hard earned income to our clients, our 'sinful' ways and finally our lives to ensure the well-being of the hero or the society he represents. In either case we are refused enfranchisement as legitimate citizens or workers and are banished to the margins of society and history.

The kind of oppression that can be meted out to a sex worker can never be perpetrated against any other regular worker. The justification given is that sex work is not real work, it is morally sinful. As the whole structure and mechanisms of the sex industry are kept hidden behind the façade of sexual morality and social order, unlike other professions, there is no transparency, legitimacy or scope for any discussion about the demands and needs of the workers of the sex industry.

People who are interested in our welfare, and we acknowledge many are genuinely concerned, often cannot think beyond rehabilitating us or abolishing prostitution altogether. However, we know that in reality it is perhaps impossible to rehabilitate a sex worker because society never allows to erase our identity as prostitutes, as morally violated and threatening. Then, is rehabilitation a feasible or even desirable option for us? In a country where unemployment is of such gigantic proportions, where does the compulsion of displacing millions of women and men who are already engaged in an income earning occupation which supports themselves and their extended families come from? If other workers in similarly exploitative occupations can work within the structures of their profession to improve their working conditions why cannot we, sex workers, remain in the sex industry and demand a better deal in our work and life? [. . .]

Do men and women have equal claims to sexuality?

Societal norms about sex and sexuality do not apply similarly to men and women. If at all there is any acknowledgement of sexual needs beyond procreation, it is only for men. Even if there are minor variations from community to community and if, in the name of modernity, certain sexual mores have changed in some places, it is still largely men who have enjoyed the right to be polygamous or seek multiple sexual partners. Women have always been expected to be faithful to a single man. Beyond scriptural prohibitions too, social practices severely restrict the expression of female sexuality. As soon as a girl reaches her puberty, her behaviour is strictly controlled and monitored so as not to provoke male lust. In the name of 'decency' and 'tradition' a woman teacher is prohibited from wearing the clothes of her choice to the university. While selecting a bride for the son, the men of the family scrutinize the physical attributes of a potential bride unabashedly. Pornographic representations of women satisfy the voyeuristic pleasures of millions of men. From shaving creams to bathroom fittings, products are sold through attracting men by advertisements depicting women as sex objects.

In this political economy of sexuality there is no space for the expression of women's own autonomous sexuality and desires. Women have to cover up their bodies to protect themselves from the male gaze and at the same time bare themselves for male gratification. Even when women are granted some amount of subjecthood by being represented as consumers in the commercial media, that role is defined by their ability to buy and is normed by capitalist and patriarchal strictures.

Is our movement anti-men?

Our movement is definitely against patriarchy, and men as a collective group who derive their social power over women from patriarchal institutions, but not against all individual men. As it so happens, apart form the madams and landladies, almost all people who profit from the sex trade are men. But what is more important is that their attitudes towards women and prostitution are biased with strong patriarchal values. They generally think of women as weak, dependent, immoral or irrational—who need to be directed and disciplined. Conditioned by patriarchal gender ideologies both men and women in general approve of the control of the sex trade and the oppression of sex workers as necessary for maintaining the social order. The power of this moral discourse is so strong that we prostitutes too tend to think of ourselves as morally corrupt and deprived. The men who come to us as clients are victims of the same ideology too. Sometimes the sense of sin adds to their thrill, sometimes it leads to perversion and almost always it creates a feeling of self-loathing and guilt among them. Never does it allow for confident, honest, sexual interchange between consenting adults.

It is important to remember that there is no uniform category of men. Men, like women, are differentiated by their class, caste, race and other social relations. For many men, adherence to the dominant sexual norm is not only impracticable but also unreal. The young men who look for sexual initiation, the married men who seek the company of 'other' women, the migrant labourers separated form their wives who try to find warmth and companionship in the red light areas cannot all be dismissed as evil and immoral. To do that will amount to dismissing a whole history of human search for desire, intimacy and mutual pleasure. Such dismissal creates an unfulfilled demand for sexual pleasure, the burden of which, though shared by men and women alike, ultimately weighs more heavily on women. Sexuality—which can be a basis of an equal healthy relationship between men and women, between people—becomes the source of further inequality and stringent control. This is what we oppose.

Next to any factory, truckers' check points or markets there have always been red light areas. The same system of productive relations and logic of profit maximization which drives men from their homes in villages to towns and cities makes women into sex workers for these men.

What is deplorable is that this patriarchal ideology is so deeply entrenched and the interest of men as a group is so solidly vested in it, that the women's question hardly ever finds a place in mainstream political or social movements. The male workers who organize themselves against exploitation never address the issues of gender oppression, let alone the oppression of sex workers. Against the interests of women these radical men too defend the ideology of the family and patriarchy.

Are we against the institution of the family?

In the perception of society we sex workers and, in fact, all women outside the relation of conjugality, are seen as threats to the institution of the family. It is said that, enticed by us, men stray from the straight and narrow, destroy the family. All institutions from religion to formal education reiterate and perpetuate this fear about us. Women and men too are the victims of this all-pervasive misogyny.

We would like to stress strongly that the sex workers' movement is not against the institution of the family. What we challenge is the inequity and oppression within the dominant notions of an ideal family which support and justify the unequal distribution of power and resources within the structures of the family. What our movement aims at is working towards a really humanitarian, just and equitable structure of the family which is perhaps yet to exist.

Like other social institutions, the family too is situated within the material and ideological structures of the state and society. The basis of a normative ideal family is inheritance through legitimate heirs and therefore sexual fidelity. Historically the structures of families in reality have gone through many changes. In our country, by and large, joint families are being replaced by nuclear ones as a norm. In fact, in all societies people actually live their lives in many different ways, through various social and cultural relations—which deviate from this norm, but are still not recognized as the ideal by the dominant discourses.

If two persons love each other, want to be together, want to raise children together, relate to the social world, it can be a happy, egalitarian, democratic arrangement. But does is really happen like this within families that we see, between couples we know? Do we not know of many, many families where there is no love, but relations are based on inequality and oppression? Do not many legal wives virtually live the life of sex slaves in exchange for food and shelter? In most cases women do not have the power or the resources to opt out of such marriages and families. Sometimes men and women both remain trapped in empty relations by social pressure. Is this situation desirable? Is it healthy?

The whore and the Madonna—divide and rule

Within the oppressive family ideology, it is women's sexuality that is identified as the main threat to the conjugal relationship of a couple. Women are pitted against each other as wife against the prostitute, against the chaste and the immoral—both represented as fighting over the attention and lust of men. A chaste wife is granted no sexuality, only a de-sexed motherhood and domesticity. At the other end of the spectrum is the 'fallen' woman—a sex machine, unfettered by any domestic inclination or 'feminine' emotion. A woman's goodness is judged on the basis of her desire and ability to control and disguise her sexuality. The neighbourhood girl who dresses up cannot be good, models and actresses are morally corrupt. In all cases female sexuality is controlled and shaped by patriarchy to reproduce the existing political economy of sexuality and safeguard the interest of men. A man has access to his docile home-maker wife, the mother of his children, and the prostitute who sustains his wildest sexual fantasies. Women's sexual needs are not only considered to be not important enough, in most cases its autonomy is denied or even its existence is erased.

Probably no one other than a prostitute really realizes the extent of loneliness, alienation, desire and yearning for intimacy that brings men to us. The sexual needs we meet for these men is not just about a mechanical sexual act, not a momentary gratification of 'base' instincts. Beyond the sex act, we provide a much wider range of sexual pleasure which is with intimacy, touch and compatibility—a service which we render without any recognition of its significance. At least men can come to us for their sexual needs—however prurient or shameful the system of prostitution may be seen as. Women hardly have such recourse. The autonomy of women's sexuality is completely denied. The only option they have is to be prostitutes in the sex industry.

Why do women come to prostitution?

Women take up prostitution for the same reason as they may take up any other livelihood option available to them. Our stories are not fundamentally different from the labourer from Bihar who pulls a rickshaw in Calcutta, or the worker from Calcutta who works part time in a factory in Bombay. Some of us get sold into the industry. After being bonded to the madam who has bought us for some years we gain a degree of independence within the sex industry. A lot of us end up in the sex trade after going through many experiences in life—often unwillingly, without understanding all the implications of being a prostitute fully.

Why do we end up staying in prostitution? It is after all a very tough occupation. The physical labour involved in providing sexual services to multiple clients in a working day is no less intense or rigorous than ploughing or working in a factory. It is definitely not fun and frolic. Then there are occupational hazards like unwanted pregnancy, painful abortions, risk of sexually transmitted diseases. In almost all red light areas housing and sanitation facilities are abysmal, the localities are crowded, most sex workers are quite poor and on top of it there is police harassment and violence from local thugs. Moreover to add to the material condition of deprivation and distress, we have to take on stigmatization and marginalization, the social indignity of being 'sinful', being mothers of illegitimate children, being the target of those children's frustrations and anger.

Do we advocate 'free sex'?

What we advocate and desire is independent, democratic, non-coercive, mutually pleasurable and safe sex. Somehow sex seems to imply irresponsibility and lack of concern for other's well-being, which is not what we are working towards. Freedom of speech, expression of politics all come with obligations and the need to acknowledge and accommodate other's freedom too. Freedom of sexuality should also come with responsibility and respect for other's needs and desires. We do want the freedom to explore and shape a healthy and mature attitude and practice about sex and sexuality, free from obscenity and vulgarity.

We do not yet know what this autonomous sexuality will be like in practice; we do not have the complete picture as yet. We are working people, not soothsayers or prophets. When, for the first time in history, workers agitated for class equity and freedom from capitalist exploitation, when the blacks protested against white hegemony, when the feminists rejected the subordination of women, they too did not know fully what the new system they were striving for would exactly be like. There is no exact picture of the 'ideal' future—it can only emerge and be shaped through the process of the movement.

All we can say is that, in our imagination of autonomous sexuality, men and women will have equal access, will participate equally, will have the right to say yes or no and there will be no space for guilt or oppression.

We do not live in an ideal social world today. We do not know when and if ever an ideal social order will come into place. In our less than ideal world if we can accept the immorality of commercial transaction over food or health, why is sex for many so unethical and unacceptable? May be in an ideal world there will be no need for any such transactions—where material, emotional, intellectual and sexual needs of all will be met equitably and with pleasure and happiness. We do not know. All we can do now is to explore the current inequalities and injustices, question their basis and confront, challenge and change them.

Which way is our movement going?

The process of struggle that we, the members of Durbar Mahila Samanwaya Committee, are currently engaged in has only just begun. We think our movement has two principal aspects. The first one is to debate, define and re-define the whole host of issues about gender, poverty, sexuality that are being thrown up within the process of the struggle itself. Our experience of Mahila Samanwaya Committee shows that for a marginalized group to achieve the smallest of gains, it becomes imperative to challenge an all-encompassing material and symbolic order that not only shapes the dominant discourses outside but, perhaps more importantly, historically conditions the way we negotiate our own locations as workers within the sex industry. This long term and complex process will have to continue.

Secondly, the daily oppression that is practised on us with the support of the dominant ideologies has to be urgently and consistently confronted and resisted. We have to struggle to improve the conditions of our work and the material quality of our lives, and that can happen through our efforts towards us—sex workers—gaining control over the sex industry itself. We have started the process—today, in many red light areas in cities, towns and villages, we sex workers have come to organize our own forums to create solidarity and collective strength among a larger community of prostitutes, forge a positive identity for ourselves as prostitutes and mark out a space for acting on our own behalf.

Male prostitutes are with us too

The Durbar Mahila Samanwaya Committee was originally formed by women sex workers of Sonagachhi and neighbouring red light areas, and initially for women prostitutes. However, within two years of our coming into existence, male sex workers have come and joined us on their own initiative. These male sex workers provide sexual services to homosexual men primarily. As our society is strongly homophobic, and in fact penetrative sexual act between consenting adult men is still legally punishable, the material and ideological status of male sex workers is even more precarious. We therefore had welcomed them in our midst as comrades in arms and strongly believe that their participation will make the sex workers' movement truly representative and robust.

The sex workers' movement is going on—it has to go on. We believe the questions about sexuality that we are raising are relevant not only to us sex workers but to every men and women who questions subordination of all kinds—within the society at large and also within themselves. This movement is for everyone who strives for an equal, just, equitable, oppression-free and above all a happy social world. Sexuality, like class and gender, after all makes us what we are. To deny its importance is to accept an incomplete existence as human beings. Sexual inequality and control of sexuality engender and perpetuate many other inequalities and exploitations too. We are faced with situation to shake the roots of all such injustice through our movement. We have to win this battle and the war too—for a gender just, socially equitable, emotionally fulfilling, intellectually stimulating and exhilarating future for men, women and children.

∾

LESBIAN EMERGENCE
Campaign for Lesbian Rights

Introduction

The Campaign for Lesbian Rights (Caleri) coalesced in the days following broadbased protests against the Shiv Sena's attacks on the film *Fire* in December 1998. The individuals and groups who met after the protests decided to develop a year-long activist effort aimed at pushing forward the issue of lesbian rights at the level of the people, through a public campaign. The focus on lesbian rights was for a reason—to articulate and nurture the troubled connections of lesbians in/with the women's movement, to talk about the social suppression of women's sexuality in general, and to address the aspects of lesbian lives that make our struggles distinct from the gay men's movements.

When we discussed the idea of bringing out a publication to document the first half of our campaign, several of our constituent groups expressed some scepticism. 'Isn't it premature?' some wondered. 'Who would it be for?' As the discussion progressed, we agreed that unless we documented our processes now, it would never be done. And we believed that these processes would be valuable for other activist efforts devoted to the rights of lesbian and bisexual women in India, and could contribute to sustaining and inspiring actions elsewhere. Furthermore, we also needed to put together resource material for the groups of lawyers, journalists, college students and others who had got in touch with us after reading the leaflets we distributed around Delhi, asking us to conduct public meetings to talk about the issue in greater depth, and this seemed like a good way to combine both objectives, and bring out a publication that was both report and manual. We hope not only that it will be useful for other groups working on their own, but that it will encourage them to contact us for collaborative actions. We hope also that it will advance our own efforts towards greater transparency and accountability.

This report consists of pieces written by the Working Group of the Campaign (anonymous, in the spirit of collectivity, but marked with the initials of the individual author in the interests of accountability) as well as pieces by constituent organizations, supporters, and a few excerpts from published texts. The pieces offer many different perspectives on lesbian rights, some divergent or even in conflict with each other, but the purpose of this report, like the purpose of the Campaign, is to try to create a space for open debate, where we can all talk about advancing the cause in our own ways. [. . .]

A lesbian critique of *Fire* by V.S.

Today it has become impossible to separate the politics of protest, sexual rights and artistic expression from the actual images of the controversial film *Fire* which supposedly is and is not about lesbianism, depending upon who is attacking or defending it. The Canada-based director herself has skillfully adopted the politics of convenience, selling her product through gay and lesbian channels in the West, where the film has received awards and accolades for its supposedly progressive depiction of women rebelling against hetero-patriarchal oppression. However, here 'at home' in India, the director explicitly denied that the film had a lesbian theme, quickly clarified to the press that she was heterosexual, and reportedly said that she would be devastated if her daughter turned out to be lesbian.

The director's hypocrisy, defensiveness and retreat into the safe shelter of her heterosexuality have not deceived Indian lesbians and gays for even a moment. We are well aware that we have been rigorously exploited and commodified as subject matter. The fallout of the demonstration outside New Delhi's Regal Cinema on December 7, 1998, and the fractures and dissension within the solidarity of those who participated, has been discussed elsewhere in this report. I will restrict myself to a brief comment on my experience of viewing the film itself, which in many ways is as problematic as the Shiv Sena's homophobic assaults on its screenings. As frame followed frame, I began to experience a sense of growing alienation from the narrative being played out on the screen. This may have been because it swiftly became obvious that the director was alienated from the central dilemma of the 'non-lesbian' sisters-in-law around whom the plot is centred. There was absolutely no exploration of the immense frustration and tension that comes from the overwhelming strain of trying to nurture an intimate sexual bond in a crowded household without privacy, autonomy or mobility, as is the case in so many families where doors cannot be locked or separate beds claimed. Most gays and lesbians in the Indian social context will testify to the psychological repercussions of being denied a reasonable space in which to spend sexual time with a lover.

Nor does *Fire* attempt to probe the profound guilt, shock, fear, anger, shame, crippling ambivalences and equivocations and other anarchic and threatening emotions that accompany sexual practices generally considered perverted, criminal and taboo. The critical question of what constitutes the lesbian/gay/transgender/transsexual 'self' (if there is such a thing), and how we work these selves into our daily existence as social and political creatures, a question we queers grapple with all our lives, simply glides past the consciousness of our screen 'non-lesbian' 'lesbian' lovers shackled in their respective sexless and loveless marriages. The sisters-in-law are too busy looking beautiful as they spread saris to dry on their terrace while the exoticized tapestry of congested, ritual-ornamented middle-class life somehow stitches itself into being within the household and in the lanes below. The director carefully keeps our heroines at a lyric distance from the anguish and the euphoria of lesbian social realities, as well as from each other (the brief sex scene was as appealing as watered milk), from their uncaring husbands, and most of all from the excruciating but essential project of claiming some kind of stable selfhood once the layers of illusion, and the illusory protections these offer, are peeled away, violently, unpredictably, and often invisibly.

The director's commitment to inauthenticity becomes even more transparent through her rampant use of 'othering' devices. The film opens and closes with the image of Muslim monuments in imperial marble and common stone—the Taj Mahal, a legendary celebration of heterosexual love, and the Sufi dargah of Nizamuddin Auliya, refuge of the destitute and the despairing, as well as of poets and agonized emperors. The director inserts parodic representations of scenes from the Ramayana in various fragmented forms as a comment on the 'realistic' narrative, throughout the film. The characters are further 'othered' by being depicted as victims—through class (the blackmailing, masturbating servant who exposes the lesbian love affair to the household), through infirmity (the mute, paralyzed, old mother-in-law, privileged witness of the servant's ejaculations), or through the addiction to modes of excess (the brutal younger brother rents out pornographic videos while his 'oriental' mistress dreams about emigrating to the Far East), the tormented elder brother fixates on a guru and arbitrarily imposes Gandhian experiments in celibacy upon his wife). The sisters-in-law are excessive, of course, because they are 'non-lesbian' 'lesbians'.

Where are the fully fleshed, psychologically convincing individuals in this tableau of two-dimensional pathologies? Where is the reliable index of 'normalcy', empathetic and balanced articulation, nuanced logic, sensitive descriptions of queer realities? Perhaps as a disempowered minority we simply do not matter to the director except as compelling and profitable subject matter.

As a lesbian spectator I found the film so plastic, the aestheticism so deliberate, the satire so laboured, that to argue whether *Fire* is lesbian themed or not is as circuitous and futile as insisting that a doughnut is defined by its fat ring of fried pastry, not its hole. [. . .]

Lesbians and the Law: Section 377 of the Indian Penal Code

Memorandum submitted on 26 February, 1999 to the Committee on the Empowerment of Women: Appraisal of Laws relating to Women (Criminal Laws)
Subject: Repeal of Section 377 of the Indian Penal Code

The Campaign for Lesbian Rights submits the following memorandum:

1. The Campaign for Lesbian Rights is a group of individuals and organizations who feel strongly that discrimination on the basis of sexual orientation/identity is a violation of basic human rights.
2. We submit that Section 377 of the Indian Penal Code is now obsolete and must be struck down by this Committee as being unconstitutional and violative of the fundamental rights guaranteed to every citizen of India for the following amongst other reasons:

    (a) The expression 'carnal intercourse' used in Section 377 is extremely vague and ambiguous, lending itself to diverse and unfortunate interpretations—for example, it has been used to justify discrimination against women engaging in consensual lesbian relationships. Women have been harassed, attacked, blackmailed, coerced into marriages and sexual relationships; have lost their jobs, housing rights, family property, etc. and have been prevented from protesting by being threatened by police and their immediate social milieu with the use of Section 377. It is pertinent to mention here that this particular section was introduced in a rushed manner by the Law Commission in 1937, with practically no debate on the issue. Many criminologists and law enforcement experts have expressed the view that sexual activities between consenting adults in private should not be subject to criminal law.

(b) A plain reading of Section 377 makes it abundantly clear that homosexual identity per se is not an offence, while an act of sodomy (whether heterosexual or homosexual) can however be classified as a crime under Section 377 of the Indian Penal Code. However, this section is used to harass and threaten gay men, and also heterosexual couples who might wish to engage in anal intercourse. Through misinterpretation, it has also been used to target and discriminate against lesbian and bisexual women, through assertions that by analogy, all same-sex contact is 'unnatural' and an offence. We wish to make it clear that while we are against all forms of forced sexual activity, whether homosexual or heterosexual, and strongly condemn them, consensual adult homosexual acts cannot be clubbed together with forced sodomy.

(c) In Kharak Singh's case the Supreme Court of India held that the right to privacy is part and parcel of the fundamental right to life and liberty guaranteed by Article 21 of the Constitution. Article 21 has also been given a very wide interpretation in the case of Francis Coralie vs Union of India (AIR 1981 SC 746) wherein the Court observed through Justice Bhagwati (page 753) that 'we think that the right to life includes the right to live with human dignity and all that goes along with it. Every act which offends against or impairs human dignity would constitute deprivation pro tanto of this right to live.'

(d) The right to privacy has also been recognized by the International Convention on Human Rights 1948. Article 12 of the Universal Declaration of Human Rights made by that Convention, ratified in 1978 states: 'No one shall be subjected to arbitrary interference with his [sic] honour and reputation.'

(e) Drafted in 1833, the Indian Penal Code is in many respects archaic and absurd. In 1957, the British Committee on homosexual offences and prostitution under the chairmanship of Sir John Wolfenden recommended that adult consensual homosexual acts be decriminalized. Such a change had been recommended more than 50 years earlier by Havelock Ellis, eminent British sexologist and author of the path-breaking study, 'The Psychology of Sex'. In 1958 the Homosexual Law Reforms Society of Great Britain began campaigning for such a step. National debate in the UK centred around the question of whether the state should regulate morality. This long campaign resulted in the descriminalization of private adult homosexual consensual acts in England and Wales through the Sexual Offences Act 1967.

(f) The British had passed sodomy laws in all their colonies. India is now one of the few former colonies that continues to keep such an anachronistic law in its books. For example, in July 1990, Hong Kong decriminalized adult consensual homosexual acts. In fact, India, Pakistan, Malaysia and Singapore are the only Asian former colonies that still have sodomy laws.

(g) After years of lobbying and negotiations by European gay rights organizations, respected international organizations like Amnesty International have in recent years taken a stand on violations of the human rights of lesbian women and gay men.

(h) Section 377 is violative of Article 14 of the Constitution since it encourages discrimination against persons purely on the basis of their sexual behaviour. The idea that sexual relations must take place only within a prescribed sexual format shows bias, ignorance and lack of tolerance.

(i) According to established medical opinion such as that of the American Psychiatric Association and the World Health Organization, female and male homosexuality and homosexual acts are perfectly normal, reflecting a different sexual orientation and pattern of loving and cannot be considered abnormal anymore.

(j) According to the Kinsey Report on Human Sexuality, published in 1948 and 1953, 2% of women and 4% of men have been exclusively homosexual for a substantial part of their lives, and a much larger percentage (13% of women and 37% of men) have had consensual homosexual experiences. While the percentages may appear to be small, in practice this means that millions of people all over the globe and even in India possess a different sexual orientation and have different patterns of loving.

(k) It is totally erroneous to propose that homosexuality is essentially a western phenomenon which was 'exported' to India. In fact, ancient Indian art and sculpture in India testifies to the prevalence of homosexuality in this country to a greater or lesser extent. It is in fact the criminalization of homosexuality which is a western import.

(l) Even in the Kamasutra, an authoritative text on sexuality by the sage Vatsyayana, an entire chapter has been devoted to the subject of homosexual relations.

(m) According to Article 25(1), all persons have been guaranteed freedom of conscience, which must be understood to mean the right to have a certain sexual orientation.

In the context of the above, the Campaign for Lesbian Rights makes the following demands:

i. Repeal of Section 377 of the Indian Penal Code as it is ultravires of the Constitution, in order to protect the fundamental and legal rights of sexual minorities in general, and to ensure that women who have a different sexual orientation are not discriminated against.

ii. Redefine the offence of rape and sexual violence in the Indian Penal Code to include all coercive sexual acts, so that after Section 377 is repealed, all non-consensual sexual acts (e.g. child abuse) continue to be an offence under the law. Rape law should be made applicable to both men and women, irrespective of whether the acts are homosexual or heterosexual. [. . .]

~

THE TROUBLED EXISTENCE OF SEX AND SEXUALITY: FEMINISTS ENGAGE WITH CENSORSHIP

Shohini Ghosh

Cultural transition and urban anxieties

India has a rapidly changing media situation today. Satellite broadcasting and an increasing number of television channels disseminate an unprecedented amount of programming. The state-controlled TV's exclusive monopoly over viewers has firmly been displaced. The 'liberalization' of the skies has provided viewers with access to a large amount of both Indian and international programming. Concurrent with larger socio-political and economic shifts, the new developments in the media scenario have also created newer anxieties. [. . .]

Double trouble: Sex and television

In 1993, the Bharatiya Janata Party (BJP) and Shiv Sena launched an assault on Bombay cinema by disrupting films in mid-screenings, banning stars of Pakistani origin and boycotting 'anti-national' stars like Dilip Kumar and Shabana Azmi for attending Pakistan Day celebrations. The resultant 'treaty' between the BJP and the Film Makers Combine (FMC) recommended steps to curb the 'deterioration of cinema culture' by prohibiting 'insult to the Hindu faith', promotion of 'anti-national elements' or 'body exposure'. The Hindu right was perhaps quicker to sense the subversive potential of popular cinema.

The first major controversy around 'obscenity' was articulated through major representational shifts concerning women: the blurring of distinction between the 'bad' vamp (westernized, sexy and promiscuous) and that of the 'good' heroine (chaste and virtuous). Like most non-conventional 'disruptions', it appeared first in the song and dance sequences and was celebrated unabashedly in *'Choli ke peechey kya hai?'* (What's behind the blouse?) from the film *Khalnayak* (The Villain, 1993).

The *'choli'* controversy debated whether or not the song was vulgar and obscene. The Hindu right attack against the song was led by the Shiv Sena in Bombay and the student wing of the BJP, Akhil Bhartiya Vidyarthi Parishad (ABVP) in Delhi. A petition was filed in the Delhi High Court asking for the deletion of the song from the film and a ban on audio cassettes sales. The petition alleged that the song was 'vulgar, against public morality and decency'. After dismissal of the case by the trial court, the petitioners went to the High Court with the appeal that, left unchallenged, the court's decision would be an incentive to depicting increasing vulgarity on screen, which in turn, would lead to increasing sexual harassment. The High Court dismissed the petition in a 14-page order on grounds that (a) film viewing was a matter of choice with no coercion involved; (b) that it was 'sheer imagination' that the song would lead to eve-teasing; and (c) the alleged vulgarity was acceptable to society in keeping with 'latest developments' in the film world.

Khalnayak features two versions of the *'choli'* song. The allegedly 'indecent' version is sung by two women (Ila Arun and Alka Yagnik) and performed by two women (Madhuri Dixit and Neena Gupta) who pretend to be prostitutes. The second version, with identical lyrics and music, is sung and performed by men. This version culminates in the heroine being intimidated and physically assaulted by the male protagonist. Ironically, both the petition and the protestors chose to ignore this version. The anxiety regarding 'increasing sexual harassment' not withstanding, the protesters demanded censorship not of the version that actually depicted violence against women but one that represents sexual agency on their part.

The ritual of outrage and anxiety around the *'choli'* song was re-enacted around subsequent songs like *'Sexy, sexy , sexy, mujhe log bole'* (.People say I am sexy, sexy, sexy) from *Khuddar* (Self-respecting Person, 1993), *'Mera pant bhi sexy'* (My pant is sexy . . .) from *Dulaara* (The Loved One, 1993); *'Sarkayleo khatiya jara lage'* (Bring your cot closer, I am feeling cold) from *Raja Babu* (His Lordship, 1993) and similar songs with double entendres. The word 'sexy' placed both the songs from *Khuddar* and *Dulaara* in trouble. The Central Board of Film Certificate (CBFC) asked the director of *Dulaara* to replace the word 'sexy' with 'fancy'. Despite All India Radio's ban the song topped all popularity charts. *'Sexy, sexy, sexy, mujhe log bole'* ended up being re-recorded as *'Baby, baby, baby . . .'* even though all private television channels continued to broadcast the 'sexy' version.

Organizations that protested against 'obscenity and vulgarity' in film songs included the National Human Rights Commission (NHRC), the Centre for Media Studies, the National Commission for Women (NCW), the Parliamentary Standing Committee and the CBFC . Anurag Chaturvedi of the Marathi paper *Mahanagar* and member of the examining committee constituted to look into these songs told the press that 'unless this trend is checked more songs will be written in the language of the *Kamasutra*. Eve-teasers will be singing them on the streets and there will be no one to stop them.' Justice Ranganath Mishra, chief commissioner of the NHRC, called film songs 'the worst violators of human rights'.

This outrage and panic around 'obscenity' received an impetus with the release of the Media Advocacy Group (MAG) report titled *People's Perceptions: Obscenity and Violence on the Small Screen* (1994). Targeting film songs as the 'worst offenders', the report claimed that parents 'angry and disgusted' at the rising levels of obscenity in the media are unable to control the viewing habits of their children. It identifies the 'low-income group male' as the most vulnerable to 'negative effects' and assumes that media 'impacts' directly. Assuming the classic 'culinary fallacy'—that people consume wholly and uncritically whatsoever appears on TV—the report constructs the viewer as a vulnerable and passive non-agent.

The reportage of this report in newspapers generated more anxiety by carrying the 'image blaming' process a step further by concluding that 'obscene and vulgar' film songs 'increased eve-teasing and harassment' (Rai 1994; Ninan 1994; Kazmi 1994), that 'there seemed to be a greater fear that young women might start imitating the clothes and morals depicted on the screen'.

Pressured by these groups and following a furore in Parliament, the Information and Broadcasting (I&B) Ministry recommended revision of the CBFC Guidelines in order to curb 'obscenity and vulgarity'. The consequent 'revision' added to the already existing list of 'objectionable visuals' under categories titled Violence and Vulgarity that merits being quoted in its entirety.

1. Selectively exposing women's anatomy (e.g. breasts, cleavage, thighs, navel) in song and dance numbers, through suggestive and flimsy dresses, movements, zooming particularly in close-shots [sic].
2. Double meaning dialogues referring to women's anatomy (e.g. breasts or apples or some other fruits).
3. Stimulation [sic] of sexual movements (e.g. swinging of car, cot).
4. Man and woman in close proximity to each other or one over the other and in close proximity and making below-the-waist jerks suggesting copulation.
5. Pelvic jerks, breast swinging, hip jerks, man and woman mounting on each other, rolling together, rubbing women's body from breasts to thighs, hitting/rubbing man with breasts, sitting on each other's

thighs and waist with entwined legs, lifting and peeping inside a woman's skirt [sic], squeezing woman's navel and waist.

6. Vulgar kissing on breasts, navel, buttocks upper part of thighs.
7. Coins, etc. being put inside blouse and other types of eve-teasing as there is invasion of privacy of women's body.
8. Disrobing women.

Sexual reorientation and women's bodies

In all the controversies around the representation of women's bodies, the most frequently used terms by women activists and feminists have been 'objectification', 'commodification' and 'degradation'. The feminist opposition to obscenity questions 'the use of women as sex objects, as commodities meant to be consumed. In the language of pornography, women are not in control of their sexuality, but objects of male desire. Moreover, the use of the female body to sell consumer goods reinforces the notion that the woman is an object' (Menon 1995). Here, 'object' and 'commodity' are used interchangeably. It is important, however, that the two be separate.

If 'commodification' means to sell 'consumer goods', then we must ask *why* certain images of the body that transgress the more traditional representations of women (like the *choli* song, Anjali Kapur's *Fantasy* cover, the Tuff shoes ad, Hussain's Saraswati, rape and love-making sequences in the *Bandit Queen*, and finally the Miss World contest) are considered more 'problematic' than, say, the more pervasive representations of the sari-clad housewife selling detergents, washing machines, bathing soap, moisturizing lotion, microwaves, refrigerators, music systems, computers, clothes or even sanitary napkins? To my mind, the sexism of ads showing women selling domestic appliances is far more problematic because they permanently place women in the kitchen. This usually never causes outrage because it reinforces women's role in the family. If the objective of selling all consumer products is profit, can we say that selling certain 'consumer goods' like cosmetics, constitutes more 'degradation' than others? Does it follow that the more successful the company, the greater the profit, the more the commodification and thereby the worse the degradation? Moreover, the women who choose this profession use their bodies not just for somebody else's profit but also their own. They are successful professionals themselves for whom 'beauty' is business.

Feminists need to ask why only women's bodies are criticized for 'commodification'. In a rapidly commodifying world, what makes the commodification of women's bodies worse than commodification of anything or anybody else? Why, for instance, are sports professionals not indicted for commodifying their bodies to sell credit cards, music systems, shampoos, beers, cigarettes and also cosmetics? Why are certain musicians not condemned for commodifying their music in order to sell consumer products? Why are heart surgeons not indicted for commodifying life-saving skills?

It is equally true that commodification is rarely decried when profits accrue from works of art. India's top painters sell their paintings for enormous sums of money. However, this is rarely called commodification. The charge of commodification is inevitably made with reference to images with a popular appeal or what is patronizingly considered to be for mass consumption. Therefore, the popular image of Madhuri Dixit singing *'Choli ke peechey'* is more likely to be condemned than Hussain's paintings of her, even though the contents of the latter may be more sexist than the former.

Similarly, it is assumed that objectification leads to degradation even though neither term has been adequately explained. There are two critical contentions here: *when* is a woman objectified and 'degraded' and *who decides* when she is degraded and objectified? Feminists have observed that image-blamers often contend that sexual imagery may not cause harm but is harm itself because it objectifies and degrades women. How is this 'radical critique' by feminists different from the 'traditional values' argument of the religious right?

The difference is hard to determine as both groups (though motivated by different impulses) seem to rely on conservative notions of female purity and a good girl/bad girl sexual double standard. Therefore, a woman who 'degrades' herself by posing as a sex object is 'cheap' and 'vulgar'. It would hardly matter whether she was the object of sexism, misogyny and/or violence, or whether she was the object of desire. The conflation of discrimination and desire, coercion and consent have resulted in all representations that denote and connote sex to be labelled 'bad', and consequently damned. The immediate loss here is the crucial difference between sexual explicitness and sexism.

Much of the anxiety of the moral panic lies along blurring the lines between the good and bad girl. *'Choli ke peechey'* is sung by a good girl (the heroine) who occupies, momentarily, the space of the bad girl (the vamp). Similarly, the outrage against Anjali Kapur began with the photographic juxtaposing of two occupations: one decent (as lawyer) and the other indecent (as model). Working with this logic, the Shiv Sena criticized Milind Soman for posing in the nude, and 'degrading' someone who was to become his wife (model Madhu Sapre).

Undergirding this unease of blurring dichotomies is a strong women-blaming impulse. Good girls deserve respect while bad girls do not—because they are 'asking for it'. As one secular critic wrote:

> Personally, I find the artistic depiction of Saraswati distasteful and the arguments of its defenders greatly flawed . . . If Hussain faces himself—which he has probably forgotten to do—he will realize that his paintings caused serious hurt. He will realize that while he can afford to play around

with Madhuri, he should leave Saraswati alone. (*The Times of India*, 13 October 1996)

Feminists have observed that the 'objectification' argument is not too different from the 'tight sweater' excuse that rapists have resorted to. Under image-blaming the woman is still to blame. If not the women in the sweater, then the woman in the magazine.

Given the lack of consensus on understanding terms like obscenity, vulgarity, pornography, objectification, commodification and degradation, who has the right to decide how women are to be represented? Advocates of state intervention must know that ultimately it is the state that will have the power to decide what falls into the category of suppressible materials. It is the state that will decide how women are to be represented. In a situation where the BJP is in power, it is the Hindu right that will try to determine how women are to be represented.

Representations that have historically been censored under obscenity laws have included famous paintings and sculptures by classic masters; photographs by renowned photographers; works by women and feminist artists; family photographs; erotica produced by women for women; non-sexual cartoons with satirical political comments; news coverage of female victims of sexual violence; materials containing information on health, reproduction, contraception and disease control; and critiques of women's subordination and marginalization (Strossen 1995).

Suppression of sexually explicit material has frequently resulted in censoring sex-related information about critical feminist issues like clitoridectomy, HIV/AIDS, child sexual abuse, marital rape, contraception, reproduction, safe sex and women's health. Under the same law, material relating to sexual minorities has been censored. Seen in many parts of the world, anti-pornography laws are used most often to suppress material relating to sexual minority groups. The Hindu right has consistently opposed sex education in schools on grounds of obscenity.

Throughout the history of the women's movement, freedom of speech and expression has been the foremost weapon in fighting sexism, discrimination and violence. It is ironical that today the same right is being curtailed in the name of women's rights.

All the controversies discussed above seem to arrive at one conclusion: that all speech and representation that implicate sex and sexuality is bad because sex itself is bad. The feminist argument here does not seem very different from that of the right wing, especially as sexism ends up being equated with sexual explicitness. This collapse of sexuality and sexism only invites dangerous appropriations of the feminist critique by those who are inimical to feminist interests. Feminists against censorship feel that there is a need to insist that sexism is not exclusively located within sexually explicit representations. The problem with pornography is not that it is sexually arousing because 'stimulating desire is as worthy as an artistic goal as stimulating social anger or aesthetic admiration', but because it is sexist (Stam 1989). It cannot be assumed that this varied and diverse genre is uniformly sexist.

Feminists have argued that any representation that naturalizes the strategic claim that women are inherently inferior to men is a sexist one. This could be found in a 'religious text, a literary classic, a silence in a corporate boardroom, a popular television show, a rock opera or rap lyric, an insult traded between two gay men, or a government bill' (Smith 1995). Sexism may exist in myriad discriminatory images across myriad cultural forms. A sexually explicit sexist representation simply takes this basic theme and recodes it around sexual imagery: it disempowers women by legitimating the notion that women are by nature not equal to men within sexual relationships. All the more reason why feminists must insist, against the religious right, that the problem with sexist pornography is not that is it 'explicit, kinky, anti-family . . . or pro-queer' but that, like sexist representation in other cultural forms and practices, it erases alternative representations. In fact, there is little difference between sexist pornography and religious fundamentalism as both discourses naturalize women's subordination. Moreover, both disempower women by reinforcing socioeconomic inequality and compulsory heterosexuality. Mahesh Bhatt comes uncomfortably close to the mark when he says that the anti-pornography scare is led by 'self-appointed moral guardians' who are 'repressive, anti-sex, anti-play and anti-pleasure'. By throwing the 'baby of consensual erotica out with the bathwater of machismo' feminists may end up throwing out the 'baby of pleasure with the bathwater of ideology' (Stam 1989). This refusal of pleasure and female desires may run counter to the interests of the very women feminism purports to serve.

Censoring representations of sex and sexuality in the Indian cinema context has its own unique problems. While CBFC guidelines do not explicitly prohibit kissing, screen kisses have been judiciously disallowed except in rare circumstances. Consensual erotica has rarely been represented with sexual explicitness. The resultant use of suggestive imagery has prompted writer Shobha De to remark that 'a sex scene in [Indian cinema] is two birds kissing, two flowers meeting in midstream, a bush violently shaking'. This paradoxical relationship of erasing consensual sex in favour of violent sexual assault is a point that feminists need to ponder. The oft quoted feminist lament that Indian cinema is replete with sex and violence needs to be rethought as far as the bit about 'sex' is concerned. In this context, feminists need to introspect about whether implicit in their protest is an assumption that 'sex' equates 'rape'.

It would seem to make more sense for feminists to demand space for greater sexual expression on the part of women. There has to be a conscious attempt to struggle to create space for consensual erotica in which women are willing and active agents. Targeting sex in place of sexism is simply missing the wood for the trees. The emergent narrative shifts and disruptions are neither wholly progressive nor uniformly retrograde. But they have served to prise open new spaces, often fleeting and transitory, that help articulate women's pleasure, desire and fantasies. Our feminist endeavour then is to both critique and celebrate while encouraging a 'pleasurable danceable, political, artistic praxis'.

References

Rai, Usha. 1994. Raunchy songs take eve-teasing to new heights. *The Indian Express,* 11 May.

Ninan, Sevanti. 1995. DD's porno show. *The Hindu,* 8 May.

Kazmi, Nikhat. 1994. Six bad apples spoil the whole bunch. *The Times of India.*

Menon, Nivedita. 1995. Feminism and the pin-up syndrome. *The Times of India,* 23 February.

Strossen, Nadine. 1995. *Defending pornography.* New York: Scribner.

Stam, Robert. 1989. *Subversive pleasures: Bakhtin, cultural criticism and film.* London, Baltimore: The Johns Hopkins University Press.

Smith, Anna Marie. 1995. By women, for women and about women. In *A queer romance: Lesbians, gay men and popular culture,* ed. Paul Buston and Colin Richardson. London, New York: Routledge.

~

QUERYING MARRIAGE AND FAMILY
Rinchin

Recently, two young girls living in a slum in Bhopal were in the news—with headlines like 'Girl-friends shun family for each other', 'They want to stay together like husband and wife' (*Hindustan Times,* August 2004). The newspapers talked about one girl's (forced) marriage to a man, about how her 'girlfriend' ('who acts like a boy') disrupted the marriage and brought her back, so that the two could be together. They also reported that the girl's parents filed a police complaint against them, and that the police and counsellors spent hours counselling the girls to return to their 'families' and to have 'normal families' of their own.

While the papers went to town talking about one girl's digression from gender norms and the couple's strange affinity to each other, many questions were raised, but many others ignored. The reports implied that by doing what they wanted to, that is, not being in a heterosexual marriage and rejecting the demands of their families (use of words like 'shun'), the girls had not been loyal to their families, caused them pain (constant projection of helpless and pained parents) and brought shame upon them and the community because of their choices (invocation of guilt—they did not even think about their old parents). The family's act of forcibly marrying the girl against her wishes to a man and the validity of that marriage were never brought into question. The act was seen more as a desperate and legitimate attempt to plant the girl within a 'normal' family.

Speculations about the nature of the girls' relationship were of course the most highlighted aspects of the story, and gossip spread fast. There were many assumptions being made. That they wanted to live together was clear, that they did not want the option of the families presented to them, was also evident. Clear, too, was the fact that the police could not and had no legal right to separate them (both were adults) or to make them return to their families.

But what was also assumed was that they wanted to live as husband and wife, and that their relationship was the same as a married or to be married couple, except that both were women. It was also assumed that the girls placed their sexual relationship above all their other relationships; their queerness was only in relationship to each other, and the choice of how they wanted to lead their lives was not a matter of self-expression but a result of sexual and gender confusion. This would lead us to believe that if they could marry, they would. We really do not know—they might want to, but they might not either.

But, then, what are the options—even in our own lives when it comes to marriage and family? What vocabulary do we have to speak about alternatives and what gives us even a sliver of a concept to build another reality on?

While presenting this critique on marriage and families, this paper attempts to see how families are also a context of violence, oppression and restriction; how the overemphasis of family and marriage does not allow for the true exploration of any other relationship; how the institution of family and marriage restricts and denies all forms of existence; how other relationships are actively suppressed; and what other forms of relationships and families might be, as well as the lack of security and legitimacy they face.

Family is seen as a space to imbibe and learn, as also a place for disciplining, coercion and restriction. Members of the family are burdened with the duty of replicating the structure, and if that does not happen, there is guilt for defiance or failure. The family is also often considered a space for caring, nurturing and sharing, and most importantly, the sharing of property. As seen now, the family is bound by invocation of loyalty, blood and inheritance and forcibly obliges members to place it above everything else. All other relationships are seen as feeding into the family, but lesser somehow. Families are also not open for any and everyone, as the gates for entry are birth and marriage. The use of force and violence for submission and compliance is not unknown. There is documented evidence of forced marriages, unlawful confinement, excommunication, desperate suicides and killings of many who have gone against the prevalent norms of caste, class and sexuality, including lesbian suicides (Fernandez 1999; Gopal 2002).

One of the major points of debate and concern in recent times has been the mainstream cultural or community space that queer, marginalized sexualities have occupied. The perception has been that these groups have their own different and alien culture and that they have to move out of the 'cultural space of the family' to another cultural space. But to move out of a structure is not to move out of a cultural space. A cultural space can move beyond the formally recognized structures; unfortunately, just now, the monolith of marriage and a typical family set-up that is born out of it dominate the cultural space. If this is not the only space, then why is it the most broadcasted and rigidly policed? Because it is a familiar cultural space, one which has sanctity and acceptance, and seems like a natural place to be, a 'comfort zone'. Is this why we are unable to seek and find other moulds, even words to describe ourselves, and the others whose lives interweave into our own? Who are the husband, wife, mother and father in the relationship is the common question. These definitions restrict our lives, term as frivolous all other choices, make multiple partners promiscuous and lifestyles so precarious that violence within and outside leads to the questioning of their very validity and existence. Within the family, violence is seen as a serious concern, but never as a threat to the validity, relevance and existence of the institution itself. So while we mistrust what we do not understand (different lifestyles and choices), there is little interrogation of that which we trust because of its familiarity and apparent inevitability. Therefore, rape and issues of family violence, especially dowry, became major issues of campaigns and concern and led to changes in legislation, but the validity and existence of the structures within which they happen did not come into question. There have been changes, however, that saw the broadening of these concerns: the issue of single mothers and legitimizing of children outside of marriage have been some of the positive legal changes in the past decade, in terms of providing security to those who live outside the boundaries.

Is marriage changing, or are other relationships becoming more acceptable and secure? Will heterosexual or gay marriages change the structure of the heterosexual marriage itself? The outcry against gay marriage (one of the issues on which George Bush supposedly won the elections) and the fear that it will sully and destroy the sanctity of the institution suggests that it will, in a way, subvert marriage from within. The other question that arises is why, when there is a strong queer feminist critique of marriage as a problematic institution, are we supporting gay marriages? In the given context, where the only legally and socially sanctioned institution for cohabiting is marriage, and family through that marriage, it is what people will choose to be able to live legal and secure lives, at least in terms of the law. As for whether these moves will strengthen or subvert marriage, we can only wait and watch.

But then are gay marriages enough? Does the queer and feminist critique of marriage end just at the fact that marriage, as an institution, is exclusive? I believe not. If married gays become the norm, and if the validity and purity of relationships are measured by the normative standards of monogamy, marriage and 'stability', it becomes problematic. Because our queer experience does not only place us in a marginalized position, but also allows us to recognize the process of marginalization, it becomes important for us to examine whether trying to fit into already existing structures leaves others out. Even the critique and interrogation of these institutionalized systems and structures will help us to see other existing or emerging structures.

Psychiatrists still tell 'confused bisexuals' that to turn heterosexual or marry a person of the opposite sex (because they can! They are not totally gay, are they!) is their chance to have a normal family. There are sociological and psychological studies that talk of 'promiscuity' and 'unstable relationships', of 'not of being able to have fulfilling and meaningful relationships', of 'infidelity', as some of the ill effects of sexual abuse, violence and other trauma. These words in themselves are subjective. A clear understanding and questioning of these terms, and their connection with the prevalent perception of the stable and monogamous marriage (or similar relationships) as the final actualization of love and care, will help us to grasp better other lifestyles that bewilder us, and also force us to look for other parameters to define what is 'fulfilling' and 'healthy'. This will also help us to understand the difference between what we may actually want and desire, and what we have been taught to want.

Demarcated roles

There is also a binary in relationships with clearly demarcated roles of the sexual and non-sexual. These sexual liaisons are valued over others and the one sexual relationship, in which sex becomes secondary after a while and 'love and care' take over, is the culmination of our quest—marriage. Non-sexual relationships are looked at as pure, but not potent or fruitful, rather as infertile, as seedless or barren fruit—the last resort for those who have failed to have sexually based relationships. Therefore, friends, siblings or others sharing home and life together will always be seen as living in limbo, waiting for the real important relationship to happen. The importance of these people and the role they play in each other's possessions are never recognized. Even the census does not give such units recognition as households or families. Their place in each other's biological families is always that of an outsider; 'just a friend', 'like family' are words that to my ears sound insulting to these relationships, marking them as lesser. On the other hand, relationships based on sex outside of marriage are seen as highly sexualized, passionate and consuming, without care and responsibility and, above all, indulgent. Therefore, they become the target of revulsion and disgust. The violation of rights of people in such relationships is unquestioned and violence is seen as the natural outcome of such a lifestyle. The recent murder of Alexander Pushkin and the media outcry and public horror against the 'dark underbelly of Delhi's gay culture', 'cruising', 'pickups' and 'casual sex' was a case in point. Terms like 'loose', 'promiscuous' and 'dangerous' lifestyles have been used to justify the violation of the rights and dignity of people, be it extortion, rape, expulsion from work, discrediting their voices or even murder. Even now we all like to push at long-term relationships, marriage-like unions and fairy tale romances of same-sex love. In this way, all other and different forms of living and relationships are denied.

Creating new families

Rebelling against the family and putting other people above blood relatives has always been guilt ridden. Not being close to the family of birth is seen as loss and emptiness and even adoption is seen in the same way, the second best to having your own biological child. There is a difference in the way we see the relationships we cherish and having to measure them or fit them into the form of structured relationships or bonds of monogamy and marriage. Many structures that do not fall into any of the familial safety nets like communities of sex workers, hijra people, street children, multiple partner relationships and many others that we may not know of are seen as either based on money/material needs or the lack of choice. This is even as the most substantial lack of choice and question of property (money) remain within marriage and the family, and stand unquestioned.

While we struggle to find peace with the families we are born in, we are also creating new families that may not be similar. The objective is to have acceptance of our gender, sexualities and lives in the former; it is also to create, not acceptance or tolerance, but a rightful space for the latter, as units or non-units that may be beyond clearly defined structures. I am looking for a space to explore different relationships and would like to see that they get importance and social significance. I do not want all my relationships to be confined to blood /sex binaries or units. It makes me wonder whether if I adopted a child (only married people can adopt as a couple, others would have to adopt as single women, so no one else could legally be the child's parent or guardian), in what way would I allow my lovers, friends and persons who closely support me to have a role in her life? What would be their legal and social standing in relationship to my biological family, and who would be her next of kin? The description of parents as being in a set of two (and for an unmarried person that is not an option, even if she wanted it to be) itself can be stifling and thwarting. How would I create an atmosphere that will allow them space to explore and grow bonds? It is clear that relationships have their own paths, but the social context and prevalent norms determine even what relationships get a chance to develop. Sentiments such as loyalty, guilt, legalities of inheritance, insurance, pension, property, even social gifts (how much we spend on whom?) are all connected to the way we perceive family. So while I try to create an emotional space for such bonds to grow, there is another set of matters that one confronts: how do I become the nominee on my friend's bank account; how does one add someone who is not the biological next of kin into a credit card: how does a 'non-blood' or non-marital relative become the beneficiary of my life insurance policy; will my 'significant others' get a share of my family property if I die?

The gay movement in the past two decades has focused on these issues, of getting legitimacy for the partner in gay relationships, with major victories on issues like health benefits, etc. in countries like Canada and the US. Countries like Sweden already recognize gay unions but these have still not been able to deal completely with the larger issues of non-monogamy and the unstructured family (Thompson 2004). And now, and in the future, these are the questions that we will have to deal with. In India, we are confronted with a situation where Section 377 still exists and only relationships of blood and marriage are given legal recognition for social and other purposes.

In literature and in many other hidden or invisibilized forms, we have seen different kinds of relationships that have either been kept hidden because of fear, or ignored and suppressed within the larger canopy of the traditional family. Bhupen Kakkar's short story of a 'typical family' within which multiple lovers exist, but from the outside, is one example (Vanita and Kidwai 2001). The many descriptions of Mir Taqi Mir and his unique relationship with his father and his father's disciple (Ibid., 184) , the films *Tehri Lakir* and *A Womb of One's Own* (screened at the Larzish film festival in 2004) and many more such examples bring out plural and unique ways of living.

The practical difficulties of trying to live out such relationships come at every level: from nominees on bank accounts, to life insurance policies, to who is next of kin and takes charge of your life and death by default. Even commercial transactions, medical decisions, etc. go to the next of kin who are defined only as relatives by blood or marriage. One would look for spaces, for the recognition and importance of all relationships, outside and within these confines. This can happen only with the broadening of the whole concept of family, rather than going back into it, by interrogating and dismantling marriage, or by relegating it to one way of living rather than the only one. The more family ties are loosened, the more air there will be for other bonds to blossom.

It is also important to see how these ideas and lifestyles are being perceived. Alternative sexualities and families cannot simply be defined in relation to the 'other' or the mainstream, but must be seen as ways to seek or negotiate relationships based on particular perspectives. They could be seen as interrogating and moving beyond the present structure rather than simply resisting the normative models of relationships. When we talk of resistence, we place one model over the other, but what is needed is probably an appreciation of the difficulties involved in exploring and negotiating such relationships. For some, such choices may not be a form of resistance but the expression of a desired way of life; they become acts of defiance simply because they go against the norm. The need may be to understand them, to recognize, nurture and make them secure rather than to valorize them. I would like to try not to fall into seeing everything as 'gay resistance' and deny subjectivity and agency to individual choice.

Love and relationships are not political acts, but for people to live beyond the boundaries, and for others to be able to critique the system and see other options through that living, is a difficult path with little social and legal security. The people who do this unwittingly or wittingly have the difficult task of making the unfamiliar familiar. The personal is personal, lived experiences are what start the politics of thought and resistance. Then it becomes the job of politics to protect all kinds of personal plurality, to ensure its survival and to nurture it with rightful security and dignity.

References

Fernandez, Bina. 1999. Protection from violence, joint suicides too many. In *Humjinsi: A resource book on lesbian, gay and bisexual rights in India.* Mumbai: India Centre for Human Rights and Law.

Gopal, Meena. 2002. The time is now: Need for liberating perspectives on the critique of the family. Paper presented at 10th national conference, Indian Association for Women's Studies, Bhubaneshwar.

Thompson, Susan. 2004. The queer argument against marriage: The end of gay liberation? www. Rabble News.org.

Vanita, Ruth and Saleem Kidwai, ed. 2001. *Same sex love in India: Readings from literature and history.* New Delhi: Macmillan.

13

~

LITERATURE AND MEDIA

The fields of literature and the media have already made their presence felt in the preceding sections of this volume. Whether it be a discussion of Indian nationalism, the education of women, marriage relations, the politics of caste, or issues relating to sexuality, we have seen how canonical writings, women's magazines, dalit fiction and mainstream cinema have become critical objects of attention for activism and scholarship. Already in the 1970s, when the first stirrings of a fresh phase of the women's movement became visible, the Progressive Organisation of Women based in Hyderabad, for instance, took up campaigns against the depiction of women in film hoardings along with anti-dowry and sexual harassment issues. In 1981, the feminist faculty of the department of English literature at Indraprastha College for Women in Delhi organized a seminar on women and culture, some of whose path-breaking presentations found their way into the volume *Recasting Women: Essays on Women in Colonial India*. The women's journal *Manushi* (recall the article from its inaugural issue on campaigns against dowry deaths in the first sub-theme of this volume) has been carrying film reviews as a regular feature.

Methodologies and subjects associated with literature and the media are thus considered essential for understanding and combating women's oppression. Interestingly, feminists in the field of English literature soon used their insights to develop fundamental critiques of the very discipline in which they were housed—the first such disciplinary intervention of its kind. The 'crisis of literature' evident in the 1990s brought with it both a restructuring of literature itself—Indian texts, women's writings, popular media alongside or even in place of the English canon—and new objects of analysis altogether.

New fields of inquiry, embodied in existing disciplines like history and sociology, but also in newer fields like comparative literature, media and film studies, cultural studies and women's studies itself, have therefore become enmeshed with the study of literature in innovative ways.

The selection of pieces in this section provides a glimpse of the range of interventions by scholars and activists drawing on texts and media representations. The opening essay is itself indicative of changing concepts of the text itself. Nabaneeta Dev Sen discusses her research into alternative Ramayanas, composed by women in different languages, often in oral form, and with extraordinary variations in style and content from the 'original'. Beginning with Chandrabati's *Ramayana* from the sixteenth century, to a range of contemporary women's songs and narratives found in Bengali, Marathi and Telugu, Dev Sen focusses on their evocations of Sita and the ways in which they reflect the concerns of rural women's lives: These include themes such as the 'orphaned' status of the girl child, child marriage, pregnancy and child-bearing, abandonment and survival. Our next piece is a book review by Susie Tharu of two autobiographical texts by Binodini Dasi, as rendered into English and contextualized by Rimli Bhattacharya. A century ago, Binodini Dasi was both the most popular actress on the stage of Calcutta, and a critical figure in the making of the modern Bengali theatre. Tharu's essay opens up the contradictions between Binodini's successes as an actress—drawing large crowds by her talent in bringing a range of lofty characters to life—in sharp contrast to her own destiny. Not only were her 'lowly' origins never forgotten and repeatedly remarked upon, but Binodini herself experienced the worst of betrayals precisely because she dared to expect otherwise. The autobiographical texts themselves are therefore as much a searing critique of Bengali society as an account of one woman's personal life.

The next two contributions bring us to contemporary southern India. The first of these has been taken from a longer essay by Rajeswari Sunder Rajan "Life after Rape", which is a comparative analysis of a Tamil short story by the popular writer Anuradha Ramanan. In the essay from which this has been taken, Sunder Rajan juxtaposes this story with certain 'master-texts' of 'first world' literature, namely *Clarissa* (1748) amd *A Passage to India* (1924) to bring out the resources of a comparative method. The story in question— "Prison"—tells of a brahmin woman who is raped by a profligate (lower caste Christian) landlord. Abandoned by her husband, the protagonist then takes up a separate residence in the rapist's household, gradually chastising him, to become increasingly powerful in her own right. Sunder Rajan brings into relief the unavailability of a simple feminist narrative of victimization and empowerment—rather, it is her brahmin status and maintenance of ritual and sexual purity that function as central levers in the protagonist's life after rape. The next contribution by Vasanth Kannabiran and Volga takes us into a significant moment in the political history of the women's movement in the state of Andhra Pradesh. In the early 1990s, a number of literary critics, including some from the left, attacked the work of Telugu feminist writers, notably their poetry, for being pornographic. The article begins with a sample of the new poetry that brought fresh issues about women's lives into the public sphere, disrupting not just mainstream conventions, but those of the revolutionary left as well. Tracing the reactions and responses as they unfolded, Kannabiran and Volga also show how feminists were able to turn the tables in a way by then bringing out a special volume of their writing under the title 'Blue Skies'.

The last three pieces collected here deal with different forms of popular media—cinema, advertising and the newspaper, and from different vantage points. Tejaswini Niranjana's essay examines the distinctiveness animating the major film hit *Roja*, originally produced in Tamil by Mani Ratnam, which won a National Integration Award and came to be billed as a 'patriotic love story'. Set in Kashmir riven by militancy and the counter-insurgency of the nation state, what sets the film apart is also the strong audience identification with (rather than mere admiration for) the hero and heroine. Niranjana's analysis reveals the deep relationships between *Roja*'s narrative and filmic structure and the rise of a newly self-confident middle class bolstered at once by a liberalizing economy and the rise of Hindutva. Less obvious but nonetheless significant is the problematic trajectory of the heroine, as her agency and actions shift in the course of the film. The short piece by Kalpana Sharma (originally a newspaper article from *The Hindu*) echoes some of the concerns discussed by Shohini Ghosh in her essay on censorship in the previous section. The early 1990s (also the years of hit films like *Roja*) constituted a watershed for the advertising industry as it responded with alacrity to the new opportunities of liberalization and the growth of the market. Kalpana Sharma is at pains to show just how misplaced the call by the Maharastrian government was to ban a particular advertisement for jogging shoes in which a male and female model pose together in the nude. Rather she asks her readers to recognize the force of advertising in its promise of glamour through transformed social relations. Activists themselves may fall short of realizing the stakes involved when asking for bans against 'bad' sexist ads, since the industry itself is only too ready to use intelligent, funny, and even feminist ideas of equality and empowerment to promote their products. How, then, does one approach the advertising industry?

Our final contribution is an excerpt from a larger study on the representation of women's issues and women politicians in the news, here that of the press. Sonia Bathla looks in particular at the coverage of two major politicians (Sushma Swaraj and J. Jayalalitha) in three select newspapers (the *Hindustan Times, Hindu* and *Pioneer*) during the twelfth Lok Sabha elections in 1998. Once again, it is the power of the media in shaping reality—here, the world of electoral politics—that is foregrounded. More specifically, Bathla does a close content analysis of the representation of these politicians to show

how they received 'positive' and 'negative' coverage in terms of the construction of feminine virtues. The overall marginalization of women and agendas linked to them (such as the ongoing impasse besetting the campaign on reservations for women in Parliament) in the medium of the press requires a deeper analysis of the construction of politics itself.

Here, then, are seven essays that show us just how pervasively mediated our world has become. Questions of representation—whether by women themselves textually or orally, and especially the arenas of entertainment, advertising and news coverage—are raising fresh challenges for women's studies. It is amply clear that we must go beyond an older approach of good and bad representations of women. The work of critique and of creative thought and action may wish to learn from women's retellings of a patriarchal narrative like the Ramayana and from several critics' warning that feminist visions of empowerment have been coopted by many. More than anything else, however, these essays demonstrate that women's studies is not staying still but is itself in a process of reinvention, prepared to ask hard questions when answers are not yet forthcoming.

~

ALTERNATIVE INTERPRETATIONS OF THE RAMAYANA: VIEWS FROM BELOW
Nabaneeta Dev Sen

Just as the Rama myth has been exploited by the patriarchal system to construct an ideal Hindu male, Sita too has been built up as an ideal Hindu female to help serve the system. Sita remains the ideal woman through whom patriarchal values may be spread far and wide, through whom women may be taught to bear all injustice silently.

But there are always alternative ways of using a myth. If patriarchy has used the Sita myth to silence women, village women have picked up the Sita myth to give themselves a voice. They have found a suitable mask in the myth of Sita, a persona, under which they can express their tensions, and critique patriarchy in their own fashion, among themselves.

Ten years ago I gave my first lecture on this topic in this very room, all excited about my first encounter with an alternative text, a woman's Ramayana, not recognized as such, and rejected by scholars till then. That was by Chandrabati, a sixteenth-century Bengali woman. Chandrabati's is clearly a woman's text; she begins with Sita's birth instead of Rama's, ends with her death, and in the middle, repeatedly steps in to make uncomplimentary comments about Rama's flaws, criticizing the hero. Her Rama is a far cry from the *sthitadhi* image that Molla, her Telugu contemporary, presents, following the dominant male tradition. Chandra is constantly questioning Rama's wisdom, his integrity, both as a husband and as a ruler. Both Molla and Chandra subvert the epic in their own ways, with different intentions. Chandra uses the Rama myth to speak up for the collective tragedy of the unrewarded 'virtue' of Indian women, while Molla has a different agenda. Rebelling against her prescribed space outside the mainstream—doubly damned for being a woman and low caste—she uses the Ramayana to gain recognition as a court poet. Hence, Molla identifies with the male brahminical tradition, while Chandrabati chooses the women's oral tradition, rejecting the canon.

In women's oral tradition in India, never mind where you are, you are all sisters in sorrow. Though the singers may wear different clothes, cook very different food, speak different languages, when they sing the story of Rama, they echo one another. Translated into English, the songs sound startlingly similar. I have used women's work songs and ritual songs from Marathi, Telugu, Maithili and Bengali in this lecture.

While weeding, sowing, husking or grinding, or preparing for a wedding, women all across the subcontinent sing these songs. These are connected with different moments of a woman's life, and here Sita is the name of the one who grows up in neglect, attains puberty, gets married, gets pregnant, is abandoned and gives birth. They call it the Ramayana but it is of Sita that they sing.

In women's retellings, the Rama myth is blasted automatically though probably unwittingly. Here, Rama comes through as a harsh, uncaring and weak-willed husband, a far cry from the *maryada purushottama,* but Sita is no rebel; she is still the yielding suffering wife, though she speaks to her friends of her sufferings, of injustice, of loneliness and sorrow. Even Chandrabati, who chastises Rama under her own name lets Sita remain the timid Hindu heroine.

The topics that interest men do not interest women. They leave out the details of war, Rama's glory, the details of brahminical rituals, etc. and sing of abandonment and injustice, and of weddings, pregnancy and childbirth. Naturally, the songs centre around Sita, rather than Rama. The Ramayana sung by the mainstream bards has little in common with the women's songs. Women sing privately for themselves, male bards sing for the public. Their approaches to the epic and to the act of singing are totally different. The professional bard sings of Rama. The village woman sings of Sita. We shall touch upon a few selected themes derived from these songs which are highly relevant to women's lives in India today, especially rural women.

  i. Sita, the foundling. The girl child as the essential orphan.
 ii. Child marriage and its concerns, the giving-away songs.
iii. The in-laws and the bride, the nature of domestic abuse.
 iv. Pregnancy—the cravings, the desire to be spoilt a bit.

v. Childbirth under dire conditions.

vi. Abandonment and survival.

Incidentally, there are several other themes, which we will leave for another occasion.

The foundling: The girl child as the essential orphan

We begin with the theme of Sita as the foundling. Here is a Marathi song— Sita, in forest exile, talking to the birds and trees, she has no one else to talk to: 'Sitabai says, "What kind of a woman am I? I was given away to Rama when I was five years old. What sort of mother's love have I got? . . . Dear plum tree, dear babul tree, Sita is telling you the story of her life. Please listen . . . "' Here is the girl child as the essential orphan, one can feel the eagerness of an isolated woman to communicate. This feeling of being utterly alone and unloved is echoed in other languages. I quote Sita from Bengali:

> *I have no father, no mother*
> *I was found at the tip of a plough*
> *I don't know who my parents are*
> *Or who my brother is*
> *Like moss in a stream*
> *I float from shore to shore . . .*

I am tempted to compare a Munda tribal song here, Sita's sighing again: 'On the grassy uplands, the ploughmen found me/They took me to the King's palace/ . . . I grew up like an edible fruit/Though Janaka gave me in marriage to Rama/I didn't forget my sufferings . . . /Never have I known happiness . . .'

Why is it that all these women choose to sing of Sita as an orphan rather than a princess? The commonest epithet for Sita in Bengali (also found in Maithili) is 'Janam-dukhini' (born to suffer). There is a fundamental insecurity underlining their lives; all of these songs see the universal woman essentially as an orphan, as a being without an identity, an ever-alienated self in exile.

Child bride

Coming to the theme of the child bride, in songs where the women are getting Sita ready for her in-laws, we can hear the heart beat of rural Indian women. They lament for a very young girl, not yet ready to start an adult life, being sent away in marriage, into alien surroundings. Take this Telugu song: 'The tiny girl is only as tall as seven jasmine flowers/She can stand neither the heat nor the rain/ . . . Such a lovely child is being given away in marriage, to Rama, today.'

Then this song from Bangladesh: 'Little by little pour the water, let us dry her hair with a towel, or Sita might catch a cold.' Sita's aunts are bathing her—the basic paradox of child marriage is exposed in this song. A mere child who is not yet even physically capable of taking care of herself, is being forced to take up the social responsibility of wifehood.

Giving away

From the child bride, we move to the theme of giving away the bride. The tension and the anxiety of the parents come out sharply in these songs. In one Telugu song, King Janaka takes Dasaratha, Rama's father, to the wedding hall and shows a small child, Sita, sleeping in a huge wedding bed. 'Look, how helpless she looks in that flower-bed! She is still an innocent child.' Here is a clear hint of the possibility of marital rape; the bride's father is gently trying to make the groom's father aware of the cruelty involved.

In another Telugu song, Sita's mother Bhudevi has a woman-to-woman talk with Rama's mother: 'From today Sitamma is truly your daughter/She knows nothing/ . . . teach her to boil milk/to make ghee from butter/ . . . She has not been taught the household chores as yet.' And here is the advice she gives Sita when she leaves her mother's place:

> *Never leave your hair open in the street*
> *Don't laugh showing all your teeth*
> *Don't look around when you are in a crowd*
> *Keep your eyes lowered in public'*

And the most important advice of all, 'Never offer flowers to any man other than your husband.' The song still has its place in Andhra weddings even among urban women, since the mother's advice is the same.

Sasurbas (marital home)

In spite of all the lessons taught, the child bride has a tough time at her in-laws. In Marathi, the *sasurbas* songs of Sita give a clear picture of the torture of the bride by her mother-in-law. It is the story of a girl born with a crooked fate line. I quote: 'Brahma was in a hurry/Drawing the line of fate/On Sita's forehead/The line became crooked.'

Here is a taste of Sita's sasurbas:

> *Ram gave Sita his love*
> *On a tiny tamarind leaf*
> *Kaikeyi poured poison in Rama's ears*
> *Like a scorpion.*

The description gets pretty graphic from time to time:
> *Sita was tortured by one and all*
> *They fed her only bitter neem leaves for 12 years*

They didn't let her wear kumkum for 12 years
Her hair is all tangled up
For 12 years they didn't let her wash it.

A clear picture of domestic abuse, both physical and mental. She is not allowed to eat, nor to groom herself, she is not allowed sexual pleasure either.

Sita has been in exile
Right inside her bedroom
Rama didn't share her bed
For 12 years
Rama is absorbed in his own business
Poor Sita's youth is wasted away.

The story is not unfamiliar to Indian homes.

Pregnancy cravings

To come to a lighter note, women singers pay a great deal of attention to Sita's desires during her pregnancy. They ask a question that neither Sita's husband Rama nor the epic poet Valmiki ever concern themselves with: What does Sita, the individual, desire for herself? In this Telugu song, Sita is three months pregnant. 'What does Sitamma's heart desire?' Well, she wants nothing less than paneer made from tiger's milk! So, Lakshmana, her devoted brother-in-law, gets it for her from the forest. 'But, brother Lakshmana I have one more desire in my heart.' 'What is it now?' 'In the middle of the blue ocean lies a distant sandbank/In the middle of the sandbank stands a single teakwood tree. From that teakwood tree hangs a special honeycomb/ With that honey I wish to eat sada dosas.' Thus the women laugh at themselves, asking for the unattainable and settling for the ordinary. On hearing this wish, mother-in-law Kaushalaya comments, 'I too had my babies, but did I ask for such ridiculous stuff? All I wanted was tamarind and coconut! '

Sita's exile

Moving to unpleasant areas again, let us talk about Sita's exile now. In this Marathi song, Rama is lamenting for Sita after he has exiled her. But what is his lamentation? Rama wipes the corners of his eyes with the end of her shawl and wails:

Where can I find a queen like Sita now?
Who can sprinkle the floor with water as well as she can?
Who will give me my dhotis?
And who can serve me good meals as Sita can?
Sita is in exile, who will make a fine royal bed for me now?

And make the sandal paste?
Brother Lakshmana, let us shut down the pleasure palace.

And he stands his cot up on its side with his foot while tears gush down his cheek like water from rainwater pipes. Now that Sita has been driven out, Rama has lost a maid, a cook, a bed-maker, a housekeeper and a pleasure-giver. A terrible loss, no doubt.

In a wish-fulfilling Bangladeshi song Rama's lament reaches the point when he repents having sent Sita into exile and begs Lakshmana to bring her back as she is the breath of his life.

Let us see now how Sita prepares for exile. Here is a Marathi song:

Sita is going to the forest
She is pouring out her heart
Only to you and me (saying)
'Rama has no compassion
I am five months pregnant.'
Sita is leaving home
She is sharing her sorrow with you and me (saying)
'No one felt any pity for me here
I am carrying a little baby in my belly.'

We can hear the voice of disenchantment and criticism, which only women can share among themselves.

In Bangladesh, too, the exile songs are heartrending, but not necessarily softly worded. For example: 'Five months pregnant, Sita was in the royal palace, a heartless Rama sent her off to the forest!' In another song, Sita takes a few steps and looks back a few times: 'But oh! The palace of that sinner Rama still rises high. To call someone who is known as *karunasindhu* ruthless (*pashanda*) takes a great deal of accumulated anger. But to brand the *pattiapaban*, as a sinner (*papishthi*) himself, goes that unbelievable step further.' And Chandra had written, unabashedly, '*Ram go tomar buddhi hoilo nash!*'

Childbirth in exile

Exile is mentioned as a part of the birthing songs. Take this one from Maithili:

Sita walks to her forest exile
Girls, exile is written for Sita
Sita goes one mile, she goes two miles, girls
In the third mile the pain arises
Now life wishes to be born, girls,
Call the midwife, quick!
The tree came out of the forest

So, you are my friend, my well-wisher?
You take my golden bangle then
And cut the cord of the baby . . .

This Maithili song brings out the terrible loneliness of a pregnant woman, who has no one to help her in the moment of distress, thrown out of her secure home. And the next one is a Marathi song, giving us the postpartum story:

Sitabai has given birth
Where will Sita find nourishment?
There is no one to cook her a meal
Sita is in exile
There is no cradle for her babies.

Sitabai has given birth
The hills and the forest are rejoicing
She has no one else to call her own.

This is how the women of our subcontinent sing themselves into their Ramayana:

Sita's exile
How many times will it happen?
Sita's exile
Is happening every moment, everywhere
When leaving for the forest
Sita distributed it amongst us all
Bit by bit.

It is a lone struggle for Sita, expressed so well in this Marathi song:

How did they do it?
It melts our blood into tears . . .
Who is fighting so bravely in the forest?
Who is all alone?

Rama is reading about Sita's exile
In a book . . .

The alienation of Rama's reality from Sita's hits us directly. When women sing the Ramayana, Rama is not part of the book, but outside it.

Tribal Ramayanas

To see how far our Ramayana tradition can move away from Valmiki, let us take a quick look at the tribal Ramayanas. Although the very idea of singing the Rama legend is itself a form of sanskritization of the tribal culture, the tribals identify with the disempowered, some even claiming their origins from Ravana, the vanquished hero and some from Hanuman. Kumbhakarna is their great sage. Usually they have fragmented songs, very few claim to have a complete Ramayana. When they do, like the Karbis of the northeast region, they quite unabashedly call it *Sabin Alum* or *Sita Kengri Alum,* that is 'Song of Sita'. Like women of the mainstream culture, the tribals all over India share their sympathies with Sita.

They look upon Sita as the essential orphan and see Rama as the oppressor. Whether he is a king or a god, Rama remains distant, inaccessible and unaccountable for his acts. Rama is the representative of the brahminical-feudal system, whereas Sita is a child of nature, just like the tribals themselves. In the Munda tales, Ravana is described as a noble hero belonging to one of their clans, the Timling. Rama's treatment of Sita draws adverse comments and she remains the symbol of suffering in Munda poetry. In the Munda song quoted earlier, Sita is an abandoned tribal girl, found in a tribal village in a year of drought. And Janaka is a peasant. Sita is abducted by Ravana when she is grazing goats. Mundas claim Rishyashringa was a tribal priest who actually fathered Rama and his brothers, and the three queens return to him at the end of the epic. Just as the brahminical tradition has Hinduized them with myths, they too have tribalized the Ramayana in their own fashion.

The Mundas are not alone in claiming Ravana as their clansman; a group of Gonds call themselves Ravanavamsi. The Korkus consider Ravana and Meghnada as sacred deities who guard them against all diseases and disasters. The Kuskos and the Bhuiyans consider Kumbhakarna as a great sage practising deep penance. And in the Bhilodi Ramakatha, the Adikavi Valmiki himself is appropriated, he appears in the beginning of the tale as Valio, a Bhil.

But there are other, livelier versions of the Rama tale among the tribes. For example, the Pardhans have songs describing a physical intimacy between Lakshmana and Sita. This is not so shocking, as among many of the tribes of central India (like the Gonds, Murias, Parajas, Bhataras and Paharias) an intimate relationship between the younger brother and the elder brother's wife is permitted. Here is another tale where the Baigas (a sub-tribe of the Gonds who originally came from Dravidian culture) make poor Lakshmana go through the fire ordeals, not once but twice, to prove his chastity when Rama wrongly suspects he had an illicit relationship with Sita. After passing the two fire tests a desperate Lakshmana prays to mother earth for shelter, and she does receive him into her heart. In this most unconventional tribal story, the roles of Sita and Lakshmana are reversed.

It is interesting to note how the concept of power changes in the tribal versions. In Mizoram, where Lakshmana and Hanuman play more important roles than Rama, the epic heroes threaten each other with guns. Bows and arrows are obsolete. But in the Dubla tales another, even more modern, source of power can be seen. When he marries Sita, Rama is nine years old, going to school with a slate and an inkpot. Education, of course, is the ultimate source of power. Therefore, Rama, the tribal boy, is sent to school. The Dublas, incidentally, are a nomadic tribe and do not normally send their children to school.

The Karbi Ramayana, which is called the 'Song of Sita', is regarded as the very first song of the Karbis (the adikavya as it were). It has several versions in different parts of the northeast. In one intriguing version, Rama has to perform a certain puja, during the epic battle for which there were only two capable priests on earth, Bali and Ravana. Bali had already been killed, Ravana was the only priest left. So Rama requests him with all due honour to do the puja and Ravana accepts. Rama prostrates himself before Ravana when he comes to perform the puja and Lakshmana is extremely annoyed at the gesture. But Rama explains that it was not to his enemy but to his priest that Rama was paying respect. Ravana, the priest, blesses Rama saying that victory will be his. Here is another instance of using the brahminical value system itself to subvert the classical relationship between Rama and Ravana in order to make Rama bow down to the generosity of Ravana. This is a rather sophisticated story where the concepts of enemy, priest and individual person are all separated. It is a most intriguing way of using brahminical tradition to subvert the classical text.

In yet another Karbi version, after marrying Sita, Rama happily stays on in King Janaka's palace, because in the matrilocal social system of the Karbis, this is expected. But Dasaratha pleads with Janaka that Rama must return after one year, because he is the heir to his throne. So, prince Rama stays on for one year as a *gharjamai* to assist Janaka in *jhum* cultivation, a typical Karbi agricultural practice, and keeps Lakshmana to help him.

There is a beautiful conclusion to the 'Song of Sita'. After Sita's descent into the earth, Rama dreams of Sita. He wakes up in the morning and walks down to the sea and asks it to give way, so that he can unite with Sita. The sea obliges, and the loyal Lakshmana keeps him company, the two enter the netherworld to meet Sita. So ultimately it is Sita's song.

I will wind up this section with a Mech Ramakatha which was collected in 1958 in the northeast region. In this rather unusual Ramakatha, the tribal people have ultimately traced the communal conflict between the Hindus and the Muslims back to the Ramayana. In their version, Lakshmana had eaten beef, which made him a Muslim. As a Muslim, Lakshman had two sons, Hassan and Hussein, whom Rama's two brave sons Lava and Kusha fought and killed. This is the Mech Ramayana.

Now, there we have a Ramayana from below indeed! Fratricide was not the theme of this epic, but thanks to the view from below, it is. We wanted to see how far our Ramayana tradition can move away from Valmiki, and we have seen it. [. . .]

~

BINODINI DASI: AN ACTRESS IN THE DRAMA OF PUBLIC MODERNITY IN INDIA

Susie Tharu

It is hard to accept (though, I suppose, not surprising) that the non-Bengali reader has actually had to wait for close to a century for a full translation of these two quite stunning autobiographical texts by one of the first professional actresses in modern Indian theatre. Histories of literature and indeed of the arts more generally, are focused on the work of upper caste male (and occasionally female) artists; canonical criticism has engaged primarily with the world as it took shape around them and their kind; scholarly and critical mindsets have been tuned to recognize and value the drama of those subjects. Little surprise, therefore, that a text by a non-brahmin working woman from the 'prostitute quarters' of late ninetteenth-century Calcutta should lie forgotten, or that when it surfaces, it does so in hazardous waters.

Translations like these are among the many everyday reminders of the impoverishment of our elitist scholarship. Binodini herself is aware of the problem when she writes in 1912: 'Let them not read it who will despise or ridicule this insignificant piece of writing. Let them refrain from sprinkling salt to further irritate the deepest wound in a woman's life' (04). And later: 'Because I have no relations, I am despised. I am a prostitute, a social outcast. There is no one to listen or to read what I feel within. That is why I have let you know my story in pen and paper' (107). This is a text aware that it must await a reader who will recognize its value and bring it to life.

No small part of the achievement of Rimli Bhattacharya's thoughtful and erudite translation and editorial framing (the introduction, notes, history of the public theatre, photographs, appendices) is the alertness to the challenge posed by this extraordinary text. In a serious sense therefore, there are three books under review here: two by the nineteenth-century writer and one by a contemporary of ours. All three, I suggest, are of critical importance to a renewal of our understanding of Indian modernity.

Binodini Dasi was eleven when she began work in the public theatre in Calcutta in 1873 and 'retired' when she was only in her mid twenties. Yet, during those few years, she played over eighty major roles, worked in close association with the leading playwrights and directors of the time, and was instrumental in the setting up of the legendary Star Theatre. Indeed, by the 1880s, she had already become something of a celebrity. People thronged to see her on stage. Theatre directors spoke of her work as a rare and happy combination of talent, intelligence and diligent professionalism, often adding that her talent quite belied her humble origins. Men offered fabulous sums to have her move into their 'protection'. Ramakrishna Paramahamsa, the late nineteenth-century spiritual figure, not only visited the theatre to see Binodini at work, but also blessed her after the performance. (It was a blessing-cum-promise-of-purification that would haunt her for the rest of her life.) *My Story* was written in 1912–13 at the request of Girishchandra Ghosh, Binodini's mentor, 'father of the modern Bengali theatre', and a leading intellectual of the time. He hoped that the process would help bring under control her unruly heart and contain her pain. The text she produced did not live up to his expectations. *My Life as an Actress* (1925) would perhaps have better fitted them.

Binodini Dasi died in 1941 at the age of seventy-nine. Much of the significance of Binodini's life, and indeed that of her career as an actress, arises from the fact that it coincides with the consolidation of the public theatre in Bengal. The term 'public' here combines the sense of a theatre that was open to the public at large (as against private performances that took place in temples or zamindari households) as well as that of the theatre—and indeed literature and the arts generally—as a key institution in the shaping of a new civil-societal public sphere in Bengal. Its charge was the envisioning, and indeed the making, of this sphere and a cognate public. It was a theatre, therefore, that was concerned as much with the pleasure that would draw and persuade its audience, as with the intellectual, moral and aesthetic improvement of national character. The best known figures of the time were involved in the process, and clearly regarded themselves as part of a cultural vanguard. For example, Girishchandra Ghosh not only wrote plays and adapted the novels of contemporaries such as Bankimchandra Chatterjee for the stage, but also wrote on women's education, *bhakti*, the relationship between religion and physics, and so on. Ishwarchandra Vidyasagar, who had been on the committee of the Bengal Theatre, had resigned in protest in 1873 when it was decided to get women from the prostitute quarters to act female roles, but continued to be closely associated with it through his friend Michael Madhusudhan Dutt. Binodini reports that Vivekananda himself frequently graced her performances.

Binodini's role in this larger project was critical. 'I must acknowledge quite openly,' Girishchandra Ghosh wrote, 'that *I am totally indebted to* her multi-faceted talents: plays such as my *Chaitanya Lila, Buddhadeb, Bilawamangal* and *Nala-Damyanti* earned the respect of the audience partly because Srimati Binodidi has played the main role in each of these plays and has achieved the *supreme conceptualisation* possible for each of these characters . . . [the performance was] illuminated with such purity that it did not seem as if she were acting; her performance appeared to be *a real event*' (208; emphases added) . 'Her Chaitanya,' the critic Shambhunath Mukhopadyay observed, 'showed a wonderful mastery of the forces dominating one of the greatest of religious characters who was taken to be the Lord himself and is to this day worshipped as such by millions.' As for her depiction of Bilasini Karforma, 'the woman graduate', it 'exhibited so as to say an iron grip on the

queer phenomenon, the Girl of the period as she appears in Bengali society'
(100). Binodini is repeatedly described as bringing these characters 'to life'.
It is as if her acting was the alchemy whereby the disparate dimensions of the
new ideological configuration were transformed into an image of such sterling
quality that it not only carried conviction, but also compelled belief. As an
aesthetic achievement, this is similar in scope, it seems to me, to the
Renaissance invention of the vanishing point in perspectival art, the invisible
yet controlling narrative of the nineteenth-century realist fiction, the modern
subject-agent or indeed the rational, consenting, citizen of the liberal polity.

The tributes cited, however, open out onto two further issues. First, the
persistent sense of amazement that despite her lowly origins, despite her lack
of breeding as it were, Binodini is able to enter these 'lofty' roles and recreate
them in a manner that is not simply realistic, but uplifting. Shambhunath
Mukhopadyay calls it a miracle; Girishchandra Ghosh attributes it to her
completely forgetting herself. The more interesting issue, however, is that of
Binodini's inspired feel for the pulse of the audience. She is praised, we
should note, not simply for acting well in some abstract way, but for *bringing
alive* a Chaitanya that the people 'adored', the queer figure of the woman
graduate 'as she appears in Bengali society', and so on. Both these astute
critics draw our attention to what is in fact happening: the *event*, the *miracle*,
is the fine-tuned, indeed sublime (in the full Kantian sense of the term)
recreation of figure and world for a historical audience. *My Story* is in part
an elaboration of what went into this feat. We find there a textured sense of
the dedication, the untiring industry, the erasure of her unworthy self, the
rigorous disciplines of body and intellect that were necessary to 'bring alive',
to give bodily form as it were, to the dramatic conflicts, the personae, the
sentiment, the devotional fervour, that would be the very soul of the new
public sphere. As Walter Benjamin points out in his famous essay on
translation, and as Binodini demonstrates, the creation of life is not a
question of biology but of history. To create life (or to translate/modulate
modernity in such a manner as to compel belief from an Indian audience?)
is also to be finely attuned to the visible and invisible specificities of the
historical moment of the Bengal Renaissance.

However, there is another side to Binodini's autobiography. If the
theatre was able to conjure a 'life' for an Indian people, it was also an
institution that consistently, and in many different modes, debarred the
outcast(e) 'prostitute' Binodini from that very 'life'. A multitude of questions
arise. Let us ask but one: What are the implications of a life story written by
one who is debarred from life? Well, for one thing it creates dissonances that
put into jeopardy the very genre of autobiography. We might sense this in
Girishchandra Ghosh's unease with *My Story*. It was, he felt, too personal, too
bitter a social critique, not concerned enough with acting as profession/skill/
technique. Binodini's text—as indeed her person—is at once excessive and

inadequate; the authority of the norm against which it is measured beyond question. This unease may also be found in the continued critical observation that the narrative does not flow well, that it is a patchwork, that her angst is altogether too ontological, and so on. Ghosh, we remember, attributes the problem to Binodini's 'unruly heart'. Indeed, Binodini herself is sometimes haunted by the fear that something may be wrong with *her* (though what is remarkable is her confidence in her position and the repeated protest against being pathologized). Indeed, if, as Gramsci suggested, the task of the cultural historian is to make an 'inventory of the self', then the genius of the autobiographical mode—which in some sense it shares with history—is that it makes this inventory, yet presents it not as list but as event. As something that *happens* (to me). And it is in the recounting of exactly what happened, that we have access to hope, expectation and disappointment—in other words, to the dimensions of meaning and significance that constitute the historical subject.

The irony is that while the 'event' in Binodini's famous performances is something that *happened* (and this would hold true also in the dutiful accounting of canonical autobiographies and elite histories), the event in *My Story* is the opposite: a *not-happening*. What she hoped for, the expected, did not happen. It is, in other words, an event in which several strands in the history of modern India—genealogies of sexuality, the aesthetic, the public sphere, as also of class, caste and gender —are condensed into an autobiographical moment that stages them as deception, and further, as betrayal. 'The talented, the wise and the learned write in order to educate people, to do good to others. I have written for my own consolation, perhaps for some unfortunate woman who taken in by deception has stumbled on to the path to hell' (107). Such an event, far from being a testimony to the contract of modernity, is that very contract staged as breach of promise. The betrayal is at once personal: 'I wondered afterwards, was all their love and affection only a show of words in order to get some work out of me?' (89–90); it is social: 'utterly despicable and degraded in our status in society' (104); it is ontological: 'My restless heart asks time and again, "what is my work in this world? . . . in which part of the Lord's scheme have I ever been of any use?" (56). Her scepticism grows out of reflection on her experience and involves a loss of faith in both man and god: 'You say that if you heard the entire story of my life you would be able to explain to me how I have been created for the Lord's work. I too will unfold these incidents to you from beginning to end. If you listen you would understand how unbelief has only deepened and how impossible it would be to uproot it' (60). Her worn-out body now lies abandoned 'in some corner of the world in a state of torpor' (59).

There is much to say for Rimli Bhattacharya's admirable translation—it really warrants a separate review. Of course, not knowing Bangla, I am in no position to conduct the acid tests of how close it is to the original, where Rimli has made a mistake, where I could have done better and so on. But frankly, I am of the school that feels that the test of a translation is not merely the pleasure of one who can read the original in any case. I am enthusiastic about this translation because of the intellectual seriousness with which it addresses the task of making this historical text available to a contemporary reader. I have enjoyed the care that has been lavished on detail: the obvious attention to tropes, to diction, to the logic of sentences, to the mechanics of editing and, beyond that, to all the subtleties that combine to make the agile and historically grounded English into which she has translated this text. As for the outwork: though there is much in Rimli's editorial presentation (the obscuring of the caste issue, the constraining of these autobiographies into the frame of theatre history, the recounting of theatre history as the activities of the *bhadralok)* that I would take issue with, I also hope that she has set the standard now for serious translation. I hope that we will see more texts presented with the documentary and critical framing that enables an informed reading of a text from another language.

References

Bhattacharya, Rimli, ed. & trans. 1998. *Binodini Dasi:* My story *and* My life as an actress. New Delhi: Kali for Women.

∼

LIFE AFTER RAPE: NARRATIVE, RAPE AND FEMINISM

Rajeswari Sunder Rajan

[. . .] Anuradha Ramanan is a prolific writer of fiction, both short stories and novels, for popular mass-circulation Tamil magazines (published mainly in the state of Tamil Nadu, in south India). "Prison" first appeared in one of these magazines, *Ananda Vikatan*, in 1984, as the prize-winning entry in a short-story competition; it was subsequently filmed, and then included in an anthology of Ramanan's short stories.

"Prison" is a post-rape narrative concerned to show how the female protagonist, Bhagirathi, survives the fear and humiliation of her rape by a stranger and her subsequent abandonment by her husband. Bhagirathi comes to a small village in Tamil Nadu as the 18-year-old bride of the temple priest Raghupathi. She catches the eye of Anthony, the rich and rakish village landlord, who immediately plots to catch her alone. The story begins with his easy, insolent rape of Bhagirathi, in broad daylight, at a time when the priest is offering prayers at the temple.

Bhagirathi, shocked and frightened, seeks her husband's protection. He spurns her in anger, and walks out of the house, never to return. Bhagirathi wanders the streets, becomes a byword as a fallen woman.

She then comes to a decision. She goes to Anthony's house, announces that she is going to live there, and forbids him to touch her again even though he has already raped her once. Anthony is stunned and remorseful. At her insistence, he arranges for her to have her own living quarters and her own cooking utensils. After some years he remonstrates with her at her confined existence, and offers to find her husband for her. She mocks his naivety, and insists that he too must share her punishment—her continued presence in his house will be his bane.

They spend thirty years in this fashion, living in the same house, hardly talking to each other. She proudly goes every day to the river to fetch her own water, braving the villagers' taunts. Anthony leaves more and more of the management of his lands to her, and she is meticulous in her dealings. He is a Christian, and she a brahmin. But she places flowers every day at his shrine of the Virgin Mary. Her presence in his house inhibits his drinking and womanizing.

Finally, Anthony lies ill. When he goes into a fit of coughing and gropes for a basin to spit into—there is no attendant—Bhagirathi hears him and offer him the basin, speaking her first direct words to him in all their years together. He is moved at her offer of service but considers himself unworthy of her attentions.

Anthony dies shortly thereafter. He has left her his house and enough money to live on comfortably. The rest of his wealth goes to orphanages. At his death, Bhagirathi realizes that he has cared more for her than the husband who made his marriage vows to her. She takes off her *thali* (the symbol of marriage worn round the neck), and places it on the butt of Anthony's gun. Better to live as the widow of Anthony than the wife of Raghupathi, she decides. She lies down weeping, to mourn him.

The question that irresistibly offers itself is: What impels Bhagirathi's social and sexual rebellion? If I chose to read "Prison" as a feminist text, it is in spite of a complete absence in the story of any feminist 'solution' to the issue of rape. Among the possibilities that the story ranges over on behalf of Bhagirathi—her vagrancy, her suicide, her return to her rapist, or her reclamation by her husband—there is, on the contrary, not even a suggestion of recourse to women's groups and their strategies of resistance. Ramanan does not consider that an activist women's group might have provided Bhagirathi with legal aid so that she might prosecute her rapist or seek out her husband to claim maintenance from him. Nevertheless, a certain feminism (here, western liberalism and a 'liberated' sexual code) is implied in any attack on religious orthodoxy in the Indian social context. In this situation, Ramanan gives the initiative and resources for coping entirely to Bhagirathi though she is a product of a culture that largely negates any meritocratic individualism and envisages an entirely subordinate role for women. Needless to add, Bhagirathi's rebellious celibacy has little to do with modern sexual liberation. But destitute and socially outcast though she is, Bhagirathi still retains her identity as a superior caste subject, and deploys it to intimidate her rapist, first into accepting her in his house, and then into leading a life of chastity with her.

There are two ironies here. The first is that a brahmin is male by definition; a brahmin woman is neither formally initiated into the rites of castehood, nor does she follow any separate practices of brahminhood except as they relate to her connection with the male brahmin. A brahmin is born into his caste, a brahmin woman is born his daughter. 'Brahmin woman' is a derived identity.

The second irony is that in today's Tamil Nadu, brahminism has been stripped of virtually all its traditional material and political claims to power— the religious supremacy of the priesthood, and its monopoly over learning— in large part due to a vigorous Dravidian (non-Aryan) political and cultural movement in this century.

Yet it is through laying claim to one of the standard practices of brahminism—ritual purity—that Bhagirathi secures her safety. On the grounds that she would be contaminated otherwise, she commands her own living quarters and her own cooking utensils, and fetches her own water. She cows Anthony, more powerful than her in every other way, by asserting her superior caste status. The semiotics of purity bear further scrutiny. We notice how within this situation Bhagirathi invokes one standard of purity (caste) to modify or displace another (female sexuality), by claiming for the former higher validity and broader social import. Taking into account the complexity of the social procedures by which both caste and female chastity are invested with power, Bhagirathi plays off one against the other.

Why and how does her strategy work? The most important of the reasons is the supremacy that 'brahminism' as a cultural and ideological value still retains in contemporary Tamil Nadu. In spite of successfully curbing institutional brahmin influence in the region, the Dravidian political parties have not successfully forged a counter-culture. Their early ideological struggles for atheistic rationalism and a reformist language policy aimed at de-Sanskritizing the Tamil language, have in recent years largely lost their force. The upward class and caste mobility of non-brahmin groups has instead been directed towards, precisely, Sanskritization.

But where is the locus of these superior values? Not in the brahmin male, marginalized in the economic and political spheres: it is precisely his emasculation that the rape of his wife emphasizes. Instead the Brahmin woman now assumes and deploys 'brahmin' values in the context of an identity crisis. The separation, in "Prison", of ideological value from political/

economic power, and its correspondence to the separation of the brahmin woman from the brahmin male, dramatizes a crucial historical warp. A realignment of gender positions is inscribed via the crisis in caste identity.

I wish to emphasize that only the configuration of brahminism and femininity at this specific historical juncture allows Ramanan to grant Bhagirathi access to the power of asserting caste status. Nothing in the traditional content of brahminism—or Hinduism, broadly—would encourage Bhagirathi's negotiation with her sexual violation in this way. She ironically recalls the legendary figures of Ahalya and Sita from Hindu mythology, women raped or abducted, who are forced to establish their chastity through miraculous tests or prolonged ordeals. As traditional narrative models, these legends propose purification for the violated woman through symbolic death (transformation into a stone, passage through fire) to resolve the crisis of rape or attempted rape. The social imposition of tests/ordeals through which women must pass in order to qualify for their re-entry into 'society' gives Bhagirathi no reason to suppose that she can defy sexual mores with impunity.

Nevertheless, the 'rewards' of these processes of sexual violation—test/ordeal—survival are great for the women who undergo them. Ahalya and Sita become triumphant and enduring cultural symbols of *pativrata*, or husband worship; their legendary and heroic chastity has retained a powerful ideological hold on the Hindu imagination. Thus, in a narrative that is structured as a series of escalating shocks aimed at the Hindu bourgeoisie—first the woman's return to her rapist, then the brahmin woman's cohabitation with a lower caste Christian—the greatest blow lies in the story's ending, when Bhagirathi blasphemes *pativrata* by casting off her *thali* (her symbol of marriage) and drapes it over the butt of Anthony's gun (an equally transparent symbol of physical and sexual power). Confounding marriage and rape, she sees marriage as a prolonged sexual domination by the male, and rape as a momentary violent aberration, but both as compensated by, and entailing, the man's responsibility for the woman. The familiar and somewhat clichéd polemic against sexual double standards also involves her in a more complex judgment of the two men: 'The man who lived with me for six months cast me off in an instant. And here is this man who committed a moment's folly, and has cherished me ever since without any expectation of return . . .!' As long as the identity of 'wife' allows her to maintain also the identity of 'brahmin woman' and thus create a zone of safety, she holds on to it. But with Anthony's death she can repudiate this identity and become 'Anthony's widow', a woman without a man. Wife/widow, brahmin/not-brahmin, protection/autonomy are alternating and opposed states and identities that Bhagirathi adopts as circumstances warrant them, with the goal, at one level, of mere survival, but at another that of social interrogation and critique as well.

Bhagirathi's foregrounding and deployment of her caste and marital identities are not, however, built upon a transcendence or obliteration of Anthony's sexual violation of her. Instead Bhagirathi presents herself to Anthony *as* the woman he has raped:

> The woman who stood before him gazing so fiercely . . . was that a woman's gaze . . . how was it that he hadn't fallen before it earlier? . . . No woman he had raped had ever come to stand at his door like this before, with a gaze that pierced like a spear.

Within Ramanan's frame, the female victim of rape narrative becomes the subject of a second narrative, scripted by her, that escapes past models offered by male narratives ('no woman . . . had ever . . .'). Bhagirathi never allows Anthony to forget that the defining act of their relationship is his rape. Her insistent thrusting of her fallen status upon Anthony results in that foregrounding of the 'sexual differential' that Gayatri Spivak has emphasized in her discussion of the raped woman, the eponymous protagonist of the story "Draupadi": an act that turns her enemy into a 'powerful 'subject'', 'a terrifying superobject'(1982: 387).

The identity of a 'raped woman' that Bhagirathi embraces is not based, it must be emphasized, upon a conventional acceptance of the *loss* of chastity, and thereby the diminution of 'full' womanhood. Ramanan allows Bhagirathi to make an appropriative, revisionary reading of the religious texts of Hinduism to apply to her situation. When Raghupathy, the priest, returns home from the temple, he is murmuring the opening invocation from the Upanishads:

> *Purnam adah, Purnam idam, purnat purnam udacyate*
> *Purnasya purnam adaya purnam evavasisyate*

> (That is full and this is full.
> Out of that eternal whole
> Springs forth this eternal whole
> And when the whole is taken from the whole,
> There still remains the complete whole.)

This description of godhead as a metaphysical plenitude is taken by Ramanan as a description of human including female, selfhood; and she finds sanction in it to repudiate the metonymic social definition of chastity as a woman's precarious 'possession' that can be lost, or as a 'component' of sexual integrity.

Though the identity that Bhagirathi retains/adopts after her rape—as superior caste subject, as another man's wife, as raped woman—is achieved within the subject-constitutive boundaries of her religion and culture, there is room for her to grow, improvise and assert herself within the 'prison'. One instance of this is her daily act of placing flowers at the feet of Anthony's statue of the Virgin Mary—and whether this is construed as an act of worship, a gesture of female solidarity, or a dignified concession to and recognition of Anthony's god, it is a deliberate and freely performed action. Another space of development is her growth into the role of manager of his property. Though not by her own calculation—it is Anthony who delegates power to her—she comes to handle all the produce and sale of his land; and when he dies she inherits part of his wealth. This inheritance is ultimately what prevents Anthony's death from becoming a second abandonment. She is compensated for her loss of social and caste status by acquiring economic power—as, precisely, 'Anthony's widow'.

Anthony's role in the 'charade' is not played only in response to the rules set by her; his is an active reformation whose model comes from his own religion. A strong if sentimental sense of sin leads him to piety, penance and charity. His celibacy is dictated by his characteristic conversion of the woman he has raped into the sexless maternal figure, the type of the Virgin Mary. Bhagirathi's relationship to the Virgin is not, of course, one of identity. The Hindu models of female chastity available to her are, as pointed out earlier, not sexless figures but heroic and 'innocent' married women. The dialectic between two sets of religious values, Hindu and Christian, as mediated by their norms of female purity, is a complex one here. Anthony's Christianity, we must note, is also encoded by Ramanan in social, as opposed to merely religious, terms. Indian Christians, especially in rural south India, are for the most part converts form lower caste Hindu groups. Ramanan tacitly reinforces the stereotype of the rapacity of their 'original' caste identity (as non-brahmin men), even while she grants them the 'redeeming' values of their new religious identity (as Christian men).

It is clear that the ideological structures that the story both operates within and strains against, in its construction of the raped woman as subject, are shaped by the realities of its social, religious and cultural limits: but included in these realities is a certain liberalizing, modernizing discourse of 'feminism'.

There is a danger, in both story and criticism, of idealizing Bhagirathi's feminist individualism. Her choices cannot be *themselves* valorized as feminist: as a destitute woman, she seeks not independence but male protection; when she repudiates her identity as Raghupathy's wife, it is only to take on the designation of 'Anthony's widow'; she enforces Anthony's chaste behaviour towards her only at the cost of laying waste her own sexual life; above all, she succeeds in securing her safety and purity only by entering a 'prison', as Anthony ruefully points out.

Ramanan explores the concept of the 'prison' creatively. Sociologists have observed that Indian women experience social space in such binary oppositions as private/public, danger/safety, pure/polluted. Ramanan deconstructs these oppositions by blurring spatial designations. Bhagirathi is raped in a 'safe' place, her home—paradoxically no place is considered more safe than a house whose doors stay open—which Anthony enters 'as if he owned it'. Bhagirathi herself is caught napping, 'her head pillowed on the threshold', and it is at the threshold that Anthony 'looms'. The threshold is, of course, the open space that confounds the inside of the house with the outside. After her rape, Bhagirathi is, literally, errant, a homeless woman forced to spend the nights in the porch of her husband's locked house, or the temple courtyard—spaces which are both within and without enclosures, marking her own indeterminate subject status. The people of the village pronounce her a vagrant, a woman 'of the streets', that terrifying ejected, antisocial female element, a bogey for 'good' girls.

The discourse of crime and punishment invariably foregrounds the concept of the 'prison' as the incarceration of the individual wrongdoer in the interests of the larger social good. But Bhagirathi's entry into purdah does not fit into this moral scheme—her re-entry into the domestic sphere is performed as an act of violent intrusion, not one of discreet disappearance. Her occupation of the woman's space that is designated purdah, or the inner rooms, is a form of territorial conquest. Purdah, in certain western feminist analysis, has been equated with 'rape, forced prostitution, polygamy, genital mutilation, pornography, the beating of girls and women', as instances of 'violations of basic human rights' (Hosken 1981: 15)). But in such analyses, as Chandra Mohanty has argued, 'the institution of purdah is . . . denied any cultural and historical specificity, and contradictions and potentially subversive aspects of the institution are totally ruled out'(1984, 347) . In "Prison" the experience of purdah is precisely rewritten in terms of its 'contradictions and . . . subversive aspects'. Segregation works both ways: Bhagirathi's occupation of the inner rooms confines Anthony to the hall—for her only a passage of transit (just as her expulsion from her husband's house has meant also his disappearance into a perpetual diaspora). Bhagirathi's entry into Anthony's house is a parody of his entry into hers.

Further, Bhagirathi refuses literal imprisonment, risking public exposure every day by going to the river to fetch water. Here Ramanan plays the private/public opposition into narrative and subject-constitutive areas as well. Bhagirathi becomes a public figure in the small village community, is ironically referred to as Anthony's 'woman', and is made the subject of ribald speculation and rumour. What remains a private matter is the truth, the chaste relationship of the man and woman. In the modern female *bildungsroman,* the development of an individualistic female selfhood—as the example of Hawthorne's Hester Prynne so dramatically represents—builds upon such a polarity of private integrity and public opprobrium. When a woman's consciousness of individualistic identity is forced into existence through social isolation brought on by the stigma of sexual impropriety—as a Bhagirathi's or a Hester Prynne's is—it stands in contrast to the politics of feminism. Terry Eagleton has confidently asserted, for instance, that 'a modern Clarissa would not need to die' (1982: 94) because of the access she would (presumably) have to the help that women's groups would extend to her. Victimhood, in such an argument, also provides the female subject with access to a sense of collective gendered identity based upon a shared oppression. In the absence of such organized resistance—and I have pointed out how Ramanan rules out such a solution within the terms of the narrative's discourse (its setting in a small rural community, in an unspecified past time, makes this entirely 'natural')—a tenuous individualism shapes the female subject's resistance. Ideally, this selfhood constitutes for the female subject existential freedom, space for growth and change, a full 'inner life', and some access to power, even if it ends as a costly or self-defeating venture. Clearly, the exercise of choice cannot be a sufficient condition of a woman's freedom when her choices are both limited and severely determined.

I have therefore tried to show how the female protagonist of this Tamil short story must both deploy her 'superior' identity as brahmin woman and foreground her abject destiny as raped woman; how she is complicitous in a politics of caste as well as isolated by the brute reality of rape; how she *chooses* her prison as well as chooses a *prison*. The claims of a certain 'realism' do not permit more than this even-handed distribution of gains and losses for the oppressed female subject within the short story's narrative mode. Nevertheless, the politics of the story—its irony towards and polemic against sexual morality, its overt purpose to *epater le bourgeoisie*—results, inevitably, in a valorization of Bhagirathi's individualistic, even antisocial, will to survive. A feminist critical enterprise is therefore obliged, even while it is constantly aware of the story's balance of forces, to strategically privilege its incipient utopian gesture towards the reclamation of the raped female subject.

References

Eagleton, Terry 1982. *The Rape of Clarissa: Writing, Sexuality and class struggle in Samuel Richardson*, Oxford: Blackwell.

Hosken, Fran. 1981 "Female Genital mutilation and human rights" *Feminist Issues* 1, 1981.

Mohanty, Chandra Talpade. 1984. "Under Western eyes: Feminist scholarship and colonial discourse' *Boundary* vol.2 no.3, pp.333-58.

Spivak, Gayatri 1982. "Draupadi" in Elizabeth Abel ed., *Writing and Sexual difference*, Sussex, Harvester Press.

TELUGU FEMINIST POETRY

Vasanth Kannabiran and Volga

Advaita

I cannot write of joy
I can only speak
of the joy I feel
my body
brightening to a moonbeam
softening to a dab of butter
rising into a fragrance of flowers
arching into a rainbow
flying light and free
carving out impressions
in a continuous flow of movement
springs within and without
bursting all dams
dancing in frenzied joy
there is no world outside my body.
My body swells and is the world
wondrous feeling as if I were
falling in love again
and again a first birthing

—Volga

Labour Room

See! It strikes you like a 3D film
The violence of reality
the reality of violence.
Step into the labour room
Framed in seductive white of
sensuous silk-scented jasmine
sweetened milk.
You see alienation
bondage
exile
each table turbulent with suffering
The walls wet weary
tremulous with tears

sobs screams save me O god
splitting at the seams
living actions like
walking, talking, laughing
assume a different meaning here.
Does the body scream or moan
legs splayed apart
vulgar vulnerable waiting
for the gathering pain to break
like a copper coin poised on the rails
like sawdust spiralling around the saw
grating midway through the log
How now!
release comes with greater and greater pain
Does a fish turning on a spit
singed by the hot flash of red hot coals
feel like this.
Do cows muzzled for slaughter
feel trapped like this.
Patience
the clock has to strike twice more
There is yesterday's case, her pulse failing
This one has a foetus lying crosswise
her BP steadily rising
No space to think.
Not a razor's edge between life and death
Sounds of taxis searching
rickshaws jingling
footsteps thundering
Look
a woman hugely pregnant
a saline bottle slung upside down
mocking her
is oozing out her life
drop by drop
MOVE OVER.

—*Kondepudi Nirmala*

Suicide is My Protest

Unable to bear
the gentleness of my husband
who softly spreads firewood

and stones
my petal soft heart
I set myself ablaze
that then is my protest.

To escape the
wolves that would
roast and eat me
I lay my head on the lap
of the husband
who cooks and consumes me
and burn myself
that then is my protest.

Like a globule of spit
collected and spat
in the face of this justice
that chokes my very breath
I tighten the noose
around my neck
That is the only protest I know.
These tears and anger
smash against
this world that will not let me grow
and this time that will not let me live
is my fearful protest.
This my death
a resounding slap
in the face of your values
and this my dying declaration
did it reach you?

—Ravulapalli Sunitha

Mother

Huge black eyes sear the dark
as your bronze bell metal voice soars
forth on those rare summer nights
sending old uncles and aunts
nodding in the courtyard
remembering forgotten passions
murmuring child child
sing another one
and you burst forth effortlessly

into yet another song
Bewildered I watched
those intense coal black eyes
that voice searing the darkness
stoking buried embers
on that summer night
puzzled
having only seen you
scrub your pots
slice vegetables
season curry
little understanding at seven
the passion your throat would pour forth
never once dreaming
that passion could actually
be your own.

Your bosom was to cushion
my rage and desire
never did I glimpse
the furnace roaring
beneath those liquid eyes
and cool calm palms.
Your arms would lock
and cushion
my children in love
releasing me
in search of myself.

Hating you loving you fighting you
hacking at the chord
that binds me to you
I realise in sudden shock
that soon I will lose you
and a blackness shrouds and chokes me
as a single thought
hammers unrelenting at my heart
if only I could go back
and glimpse those
buried griefs and desires
that inarticulate longing
that long betrayal
of marriage and motherhood
through which I

your daughter
devoured you
as much
as everything else.

—Vasanth Kannabiran

Untitled

My daughters shall not
Grow up beautiful
But they will inherit
The wealth of my story
Neither will they be happy
For the hour of their days
Shall be counted
By ten times the troubles I now bear
But they will not weep
Nay, theirs shall be a countenance
Of firm defiance.

—Ratnamala

There is an old Indian fable of a wolf that threatened to devour a lamb for drinking water in a stream and polluting the water, making it unclean for the wolf. The lamb then pointed out that it was drinking downstream and the polluted water could not flow upwards to the point where the wolf was drinking. The wolf then charged, 'Well, one of your fore fathers must have drunk upstream and polluted the water and you must pay the price.' The bitter and venomous criticism of women's poetry brings to mind this fable. There is no rationale, no material basis, no logic underlying the attack. As if it is not enough that women exist, they actually presume to write. However carefully you search you can only find hate and fear.

Modern Telugu literature has been dominated for the last two decades by a strong and energetic school of revolutionary poetry. Turning towards Naxalbari and the Armed Struggle as providing a hope for the future, this school of poetry set out to further the revolution and cast a shadow over other Telugu writing by its sheer volume and strength. However, in the 1990s this school was getting repetitive and had lost its initial vitality—perhaps also because of the changed political social reality it was rooted in.

The last decade, however, has seen feminist politics raise for discussion issues of patriarchy, gender oppression and the politics of housework. Feminist politics has problematized gender relations and laid bare its critical role in our society. Largely as a result of the women's movement and the issues it raised, women began to write poetry that flowed from their lived reality. The freshness and power of this poetry coupled with its startlingly unconventional subject matter loosened a wave of shock and horror in mainstream Telugu literature.

When we consider why women write poetry we find that writing poetry is often less demanding in terms of time and privacy than writing fiction. Publishing a poem in any one of the literary pages of most dailies is also comparatively simpler. It was when the number of occasional poems grew that one literary critic Tripuraneni Srinivas brought a collection of women's poems together in a small anthology *Guri Chusi Pade Pata* (Songs Striking a Target), thus creating a genre. The women poets in this volume—such as Kondepudi Nirmala, Volga, Ghantasala Nirmala, Jayaprabha—about fifteen in number, were writing about their lived experience with a vivid directness hitherto unheard of in Telugu poetry. This resulted in two visible reactions, one sometimes masking the other. It was evident that a hitherto untapped source of poetry was now on the literary scene. Its creative power and energy made a lot of contemporary poetry seem lifeless and second rate. This outpour had to be stopped. At the same time, the fact that women were articulating their fears, hopes, desires and disappointments in love, marriage, motherhood and the family shocked the patriarchs of Telugu poetry to the core. It was alright to raze a society to the ground, or a government, but to question the sanctity of the family, or motherhood? Daring to discuss menstruation or abortion as experience was unbearable, anarchic and individualistic. It was a convenient weapon to destroy the newly emerging trend and see that the claim to excellence remained a patriarchal prerogative.

Questions of social purpose, of what the suitable subject matter for poetry might be, and what language is fit for poetic use were raised, followed by a concerted attack on feminist writing, dubbing it trashy, obscene, pornographic, vulgar, 'blue'. 'A trend that is devoid of social responsibility,' one critic thundered. 'These women are without virtue,' another proclaimed and the self-righteous anger poured out, an anger exalted by its self-righteousness and in turn justified by it. The assumptions underlying most of this criticism were based on the 'natural' role of women, their social responsibility for motherhood and the impropriety of women speaking about the body, sex and sexual relations. The concrete result of this persistent and virulent attack was that women writing poetry began to feel threatened and isolated. Began to wonder whether they should write or stop.

Asmita, a women's resource centre, then organized a two-day workshop (in 1994) to discuss why women write and why men feel so threatened when women write. What emerged from the discussion at the workshop was that there was no philosophical or theoretical basis to the criticism. For instance, the objection to the use of words or phrases like, a shower of semen, vagina, nocturnal emissions, menstrual blood are all phrases that have been used by ancient writers and by progressive and revolutionary poets. And yet the thought of women daring to use words like these brings forth an outpouring of rage. The anger and abuse that was used to silence women who are speaking out is evidently an attempt to censor women into propriety, ensure that sexuality and reproduction are discussed only within certain parameters and to preserve the gendering of literary discourse. This workshop then brought out an anthology of women's poetry entitled *Neeli Meghalu* (Blue Skies).

The title mocked at the term 'blue' (signifying the pornographic) that was used by the critics and enlarged it. The volume has been dedicated to Audre Lorde and quotes her lines saying poetry is no luxury and pastime for women, it is our very existence. The volume also includes excerpts from the criticism so that it 'is not lost in the dustbin of history'.

The volume *Neeli Meghalu* has received great praise and has been rated as one of the two most significant literary volumes of the century in Telugu. Ironically, this public acclaim has reversed the trend of criticism so drastically that now there is a rush to translate, republish and research these poems. Careers and academic ratings are being earned on the very writing that was reviled and marginalized before the volume appeared. It is as if quantity had suddenly become quality and a concerted defiance has suddenly brought the poems respectability.

If we look closely at some of the comments that have been published in literary pages the underlying fears can be seen only too clearly:

> They project revolting bodily functions and natural discomfort as issues of identity.
>
> Natural cycles of life, menstruation, and physical filth have become literary symbols and entered the marketplace. Instead of portraying the miracle of birth as rebirth and the sacred struggle to give life, "Labour Room" dares to depict this as the inconvenience of being women.
>
> Symbols of the body, bodily functions, the process of reproduction, are creating 'blue' poetry.
>
> It is distorting and demeaning to reject social responsibility from the standpoint of physical existence.
>
> It is true that in modern Telugu poetry the Digambara school of poetry used vulgar language without inhibitions. But their purpose was social. The 'bleeding' poetesses of today have a purely personal purpose.
>
> This so-called feminist poetry does not represent the whole race of women. It represents only the desires of overfed, self-indulgent, urban upper class women.

The positions vary as one can see. Some are of moral outrage, some are 'Marxist' criticism, some literary aesthetic, some anti-feminist. But whatever the stance, one can sense the insecurity that lies beneath it.

It is paradoxical but true that while the material conditions of women's lives have changed, and everyone, including these critics, accept such change, they find it difficult, if not impossible, to accept or allow any change in the ideology that circumscribes women's lives. So while women are in fact often deciding not to bear children or not to dress in clothes that veil the body, a poem that looks at the myths of birthing or at the modesty of the sari, which says

> *this sari*
> *reminds me of chastity . . .*
> *its borders clutch*
> *my heart heavily*
> *bowing me down . . .*

is attacked severely.

Women, however, have begun to write in a political context. And they are speaking to each other, forging a language to speak their angers and passions. The language of women's poetry is defined within and against their reality. As they speak, they refuse to be defined and eroticized, for brains and ideas crippled and bound as women's feet were in the past. And that change is significant. And the critics are justified in fearing the collapse of a patriarchal order if women speak at all.

Now that women have expressed their resistance through poetry and tasted triumph, feminist concerns have begun to appear in several other forms. Other arts like painting and sketches by women are also emerging. An interesting fact, however, is that all this creative outpouring is met with critical silence. There is no criticism, no praise, no response—just a censoring silence.

∼

INTEGRATING WHOSE NATION?
TOURISTS AND TERRORISTS IN 'ROJA'

Tejaswini Niranjana

January 1993. A cinema hall in Hyderabad. The Telugu version of Maniratnam's film *Roja* is being shown. Every show displays the 'house full' board, and every seat in the theatre is occupied. From the opening minutes of the film, the morning show audience (mostly male, middle and lower middle class, possibly college-going) indulges in loud cheering and shouting, their slogans calculated to strike a special chord after the destruction of the Babri Masjid just a few weeks previously: Jai Sri Ram, Pakistan Murdabad, Bharat Mata Ki Jai.

November 1993. Another cinema hall in Hyderabad. *Roja*, which has won the National Integration Award, is showing in its dubbed Hindi version.

The house full board has been put up. The dress circle audience is more restrained now, although there is seemingly spontaneous and sustained clapping on several occasions throughout the film, which is now billed as 'a patriotic love story'. Perhaps it is entirely a coincidence that the Hindi version has been released just after the Hazratbal siege, during the parliamentary elections in the northern states, and just before the first anniversary of the Babri Masjid's demolition.

This is surely a phenomenon—a box-office hit (in urban markets, at least) film that evokes from its audience not whistles and comments on the heroine but displays of 'nationalistic' fervour. The response is enabled in part by identifying the nation with the heroine, who is then alternately motherland and lover/devoted wife. It is also enabled by the imaging of the really modern (read secular) as the truly Indian, an imaging which presents the middle class Indian male not as someone we want to emulate but someone who *is* us. The sighs of admiration invoked by some of the hero's actions (as in the scenes with the militants), which are 'realistic' rather than superhumanly heroic, seem actually to be satisfactory sighs of self-recognition. Not so much 'We won't be able to do what he did.' but a righteous 'We would do exactly the same thing those circumstances.'

In quite a few of his films (*Geetanjali, Anjali, Mouna Raagam*), Maniratnam has cultivated an audience primarily composed of the newly articulate, assertive and self-confident middle class that is also claiming for itself the spaces of nation and secularism premised on Hindutva. What are the complicities of the mode of cinematic realism adopted by Maniratnam with the aspirations of this newly visible class? It is a realism that has for its immediate ancestors, the middle-brow Hindi films of the 1970s. But whereas the 70s film (*Rajnigandha, Guddi,* etc.) presented wistful and affectionate pictures of middle class relationships (no grand passions, no melodrama), *Roja* deploys the mode very differently. The 'ordinary' middle class person is suddenly inserted into a national conflict, and what helps him/her is just being who they are: simple, decent, patriotic people who successfully appeal to the 'human' in both militants and army officers. Maniratnam's films are also different from another kind of middle-brow film, an example of which would be Saeed Mirza's *Albert Pinto ko Gussa Kyoon Aata hai,* where the (lower) middle class protagonists are often portrayed as initiating or participating in some kind of social critique of existing inequalities. Maniratnam's middle class characters are unapologetic in every way, and the films celebrate rather than criticize their lifestyles and aspirations.

Hindu as secular

The celebration of the 'new' middle class (and here our texts could range from commercial cinema to the pronouncements of the proponents of liberalization) has as a focal point the question of national integration. As the

Hindutva forces reoccupy the discourses of liberal humanism in India, an anti-colonial bourgeois nationalist project is refigured and the secular subject is reconstituted. The project is now one that bestows citizenship on the Hindu *as Hindu,* the supposed 'tolerance of Hindusim' allowing it to function as 'truly secular'; in the demarcation of this new space of the secular, the 'communal Muslim' is defined through a process of exclusion. What everyone is now being urged to integrate into is the hegemonic Hindu nation, and all the groups which are out of the 'mainstream' are said to engage in violent activity intended to destroy the nation—the common project, as the media would have it, of the Kashmiri militants, Khalistanis, ULFA, PWG, LTTE and others, a project in which it is claimed that these groups actually work together. The hegemonic definition of the nation today may not overtly manifest itself as Hindu; I would like to contend, however, that the claiming of the nation by the new middle class and the series of exclusions (of dalits, of Muslims) it produces as *natural* feeds into the agenda of the forces of Hindutva, and that the portrayal of 'mainstream' and non-exceptional characters in commercial cinema provides one point of access to this complex configuration.

Appropriately for what it sets out to do, *Roja* has two beginnings. One shows the Kashmiri militant Wasim Khan being captured by Indian army soldiers after a fierce gun battle and a chase; in the haunting soundtrack another theme is picked up: beauty of nature, as in birdsong, fading into gunshots, and followed by a generic middle eastern—read Islamic—keening. The other opening sequence depicts, with an eye straight out of *National Geographic,* the waterfalls and coves and shining green fields of the village of Sunder Bhanpur (somewhere in India), with the heroine Roja singing and romping through the landscape. In this rapidly presented sequence—its slickness that of a TV commercial—we see Roja sometimes with her youngest sister, driving a tractor (for fun, since they do not 'work'), playing pranks on the older villagers, dressing up in men's clothes, wearing a graduate's convocation robes, and dancing through a field where women are transplanting seedlings (as in other Maniratnam films, actual labour serves as a backdrop that enhances the lightheartedness of the heroine). Then we see her and the other girl driving a flock of goats down a hill (not work, but play again) and across the road to block the vehicle of the hero and his mother so that he can be scrutinized before he enters the village. As I had argued in an earlier article on Maniratnam's *Geetanjali,* his heroines appear to be uninhibited, high-spirited, self-assertive, never at a loss for words. These are women whom in a certain sense feminism has made articulate, but they are recuperated into the very spectacularization that feminism would like to challenge. Interestingly also, Roja's high spirits, like Geetanjali's, seem to be made possible by the exemption of the heroines from 'real work'.

Rishi Kumar, the urbane hero, has come to 'see' Roja's sister, since he wants to marry 'a girl from a village'. Not only that, he would like his bride to be from the beautiful village with which he has fallen in love ('I love the very soil of this place,' as he says later). But clearly he will not marry just anyone—when the match with Roja's sister falls through because she wants to marry someone else, he turns immediately to Roja, whom he has glimpsed twice up to then. Roja addresses her father as daddy, has a television set at home, is accustomed to talking on the telephone; except that she does not know English, she is quite at ease in urban surroundings, adapting without difficulty to Rishi's upper middle class home and milieu. Roja is not therefore in the genre of the 'village belle' of Hindi and other regional cinema. Her old world and her new one are in an almost seamless continuum rather than opposed to each other. Given the rapid urbanization of the rural upper class/ castes, English is no longer a sufficient marker of cultural difference or even a marker of non-Indianness. Instead, 'English' can be acquired through the training in consumerism; what is more curious, English is closely associated not with the non-Indian but that which is not only assertively Indian but clearly nationalist: as indicated by the words which signify Rishi's profession and his daily activity, a point to which I will return.

Neo-traditionalism

What the village stands for in Rishi's eyes is clearly a newly formulated traditionalism: the 'ethnic' wedding (so much unlike the hotel or function hall reception now seen as so tasteless by the upper middle class), the colourful clothes of the old women who dance for the couple, or the sexual frankness of the 'rustic' wedding song (which is sung in playback partly by the rap musician Baba Sehgal). All this ethnicity is not at variance with Rishi's cosmopolitan modernness; on the contrary it helps strengthen its self-confidence. Except for the dhoti-kurta of his wedding day, Rishi usually appears only in jeans and shirt or sweater. On the other hand, the Kashmiri militants always appear in clothes marked as ethnically Muslim; their ethnicity reveals them as anti-modern (therefore anti-national or anti-Indian), intolerant and fundamentalist, while Hindu ethnicity as displayed by the chief protagonists is merely part of the complexity of being Indian. The Hindu wedding rites are normalized so that we do not even notice them or mark them as 'religious', just as we do not really see Roja's frequent attempts to pray to her idols as significant to the story. The militants, especially Rishi's main captor Liaqat, however, are always shown praying—an action shored up by inter-cutting and by the soundtrack in such a way as to make it seem not only an assertion of religious difference but a menacing or sinister portent. Whereas their religiosity is always portrayed as grim and humourless, Roja's prayers are funny and endearing, inviting the audience to identify with her hopes and anxieties.

Rishi's occupation is 'cryptologist', a word uttered in English and left unexplained, until he tells Roja in passing that she should get 'security clearance' since he deals with 'confidential matters' involving 'coding and decoding' (all these phrases uttered in English). Rishi is shown a few times in front of a computer monitor and keyboard, ostensibly working on decoding a message. His work, directly related to the security interests of the country, is presented to us as truly nationalist and, interestingly, his nationalism is not anti-western but (although never stated) is anti-Muslim. When Rishi's boss, who is supposed to go to Kashmir to help the army, falls seriously ill, he asks Rishi to take his place. His 'You don't mind going, do you?' is answered by Rishi's 'Of course, not. I'll go anywhere in India. Isn't Kashmir in India'? (Loud audience applause.) Roja insists on accompanying her new husband, although she has initially rejected all his advances due to a misunderstanding. So like many earlier Hindi film honeymooners, they arrive in 'Kashmir'. But to an official welcome, to be put up in a five-star hotel where there are obviously no other guests. As they are driven through deserted streets, Roja asks why the town looks so empty and Rishi merely answers 'curfew'. When asked why there should be curfew, he uses a favourite word: 'security'. No other explanation is necessary or even expected, either by the plot, the heroine, or the audience. Hardly any ordinary Kashmiris are shown in the film, except for a newspaper boy and some people selling souvenirs. In two fantasy/song sequences, we do see Kashmiris—either women or children dressed in elaborate costumes. All the other Kashmiris (with one exception) are militants, and male.

The romantic song sequence—snow-capped mountains, placid lake, green fields—functions as a double allusion: an allusion to loss, evoking previous Hindi films set in Kashmir (the industry now being deprived of a locale that could be used in any film to create instant magic); and indicating to the middle class tourists from other parts of India that they can no longer visit Kashmir, a place of ravishing natural beauty—as the camera insistently points out—that should be rightfully 'ours' but has now been made inaccessible by the activity of anti-nationals. A person like Roja who is visiting Rishi cannot freely look around like the tourists could. As the palmist-guide Chachchu Maharaj says: '*Tum tourist ho ya terrorist ho?*' adding himself that only terrorists come here now. When Roja breaks open a coconut as offering to the temple idol, the sharp sound brings security guards running. Roja's comment is telling: 'Can't even break a coconut in Kashmir'.

Coming in search of Roja, the hero is kidnapped by the militants who have been following him, and who demand in exchange for his release their captured leader Wasim Khan. Roja has already gone to the police along with Chachchu the palmist, to report that *raakshas jaise aadmi* took away her husband, who is a *deshpremi*. The aid of the state is invoked for the 'good citizen' against the militant 'demons'. Roja, although all she demands is her husband's return ('I don't care about the country'), is patriotic by implication, through her representation of both Rishi and the militants. As she screams at the army officer who is in charge of the case when she hears that Wasim Khan is not to be released, 'Would you say the same thing if a *"mantri ki beti"* had been taken hostage? Is a *mantri ki beti* more important than my husband?' The audience is appreciative of the allusion to recent history, for was not the minister concerned both Kashmiri as well as Muslim whereas the 'Indian' Roja and Rishi are neither?

Rejection of the state

Rishi's patriotism is driven home through two dramatic acts performed by him in captivity. First, when his captors want him to speak into a tape recorder and ask for the release of Wasim Khan, all he says into the machine is a firm 'Jai Hind'. Even after repeated blows which leave his face bleeding, he continues to say the phrase over and over again, making the audience cheer aloud. When the news arrives that the government has refused to release their leader, one of the militants picks up an Indian flag and rushes outside holding a flaming torch, with which he sets fire to the flag. Rishi leaps through a window, shattering a glass pane, knocks over the militant, and throws his body onto the burning flag, driving the audience delirious. Having put out the fire, Rishi rises to his feet, partially aflame. In his jeans and sweater, with the flames licking his clothes, he looks uncannily like the full-colour pictures with which the media glorified the upper caste/class anti-Mandal agitators in 1990, agitators who claimed that they were truly secular because they did not believe in caste but only in merit. Whereas in the anti-Mandal agitation, caste difference was coded as lack of merit, in *Roja* religious or ethnic difference (specifically Islamic) is portrayed not only as anti-national but as lack of humanity. It is the burden of the film to create the convergences between the *human,* the *secular* and the *nationalist.* As Rishi 'burns', the soundtrack rises to a crescendo, the words (from a poem by the nationalist writer Subrahmanya Bharati) blending into a triumphant chant. Throughout this sequence inter-cut shots show the militant leader Liaqat deep in prayer inside the building, unconcerned about the struggle over the burning flag outside.

Another mark of Rishi's patriotism is his effort to convince the militants that their activities are misguided. In a series of conversations with Liaqat, he elicits the true cause of the militants: *'Yeh jihaad hai, Kashmir ki azaadi ke liey,'* he is told. Much later, Liaqat again declares to him: *'Jihaad—holy war hai—Hindustan ke saath.'* Not only do 'they' not use the secular name 'India', they also constantly invoke the name of god and religion in support of their actions. 'If you try to escape', says Liaqat, 'I'll kill you, *khuda ki kasam.'*

At the end, however, Rishi does escape, with the help of Liaqat's sister (mute throughout the film, but always depicted as shocked/weeping/distressed at the militant's rough treatment of their captive, and at the death of her youngest brother). In spite of Roja's determined appeals to the army and to the minister who arranges to have Wasim Khan released, the exchange of prisoners does not take place, and Rishi, although he is an employee of the state, does not depend on the state for regaining his liberty. Roja pleads with the minister who is inspecting the army in Kashmir: 'My husband is not a big man, but *'Bharat ki praja to hai'*, and we need security.' The middle class, in claiming its complete identification with the nation, has to demonstrate that demands made on the state are not met. The new class has to show its self-reliance instead, for the state apparatus is out worn, out of date, however large and impressive it may seem. This middle class imperative to detach itself from the state to mark its coming to maturity can also be seen as a rejection of the Nehruvian state which had been compelled to write into its policies a vision of democracy and egalitarian socialism. Among the consequences of these failed policies, the middle class would argue, is the situation in Kashmir, which can no longer be dealt with by the state but only by individuals like Rishi who has shaken Liaqat enough to let him go even when the militant has a rifle trained on him. Liaqat is shown to have been made *human*, through suffering and through Rishi's goodness (i.e. patriotism). 'Go,' he says, *'Ugravaadi aansu ponchega.'* Rishi's patriotism, I would contend, is not state centred; in fact, the state in this film is one that has failed in all respects—it cannot defeat the militants, cannot rescue its employee, a failure that can be made to justify a middle class rejection of it in favour of liberalization and free enterprise.

And what of Roja? In spite of the film bearing her name, the central character is clearly the cryptologist Rishi Kumar. But Roja is integral to Rishi's vision of love for the nation. In the song *'Roja jaaneman'*, for instance, in Rishi's reverie the rose (red/green) he sees outside his cell merges into the figure of his bride (who is especially towards the end of the film dressed in green sari/red or saffron blouse or red sari/green blouse). In turn the beauty of the Kashmiri landscape blends into the physical beauty of the heroine, who appears in this particular song-sequence dressed in Kashmiri clothes and jewellery, followed by little children also wearing Kashmiri dress. The early autonomy and assertiveness shown by Roja before marriage all but disappears in the sober woman who attempts to win back her husband's life, and whose agency actually comes to naught. Rishi appears to have chosen well: his bride has enough English to understand his 'I love you' and enough domestic skills to make *malai ke laadu* for his boss. 'Modernity' and 'tradition' come together unproblematically in/for the authentically secular new middle class (Hindu) subject who—marked as 'Indian'—has transcended communal difference just as she transcended caste; reserving the isolated second term 'tradition' for those who can then only be fundamentalist, communalist or casteist.

~

THE MEDIUM IS THE MESSAGE
Kalpana Sharma

With Enron out and Swadeshi in, the Maharashtra government is clearly striving to lead the way in promoting 'true' Indian culture and values, whatever they might be. Unfortunately, the road to this goal is paved with many unexpected potholes, in the form of the state's own offspring laughing in the face of such values.

Thus, when two middle class Maharashtrians, Madhu Sapre and Milind Soman, who have made it big in the world of modelling thanks to their beautiful bodies, posed in the nude together, for an advertisement for jogging shoes, all hell broke lose. Reprints of the ad were burned, there were demands for its ban, the editor of the magazine which published it was made to apologize and eventually even Madhu Sapre said she was sorry. Milind Soman, however, remained unrepentant.

But this deluge of apologies appeared to have settled the issue. The deviants were repentant, they would not do this again and thus all was well. Public opinion had won, immorality had been vanquished, even if temporarily. More important, Indian womanhood had been saved from being demeaned. But is that really what happened? Maharashtra's minister for transport and culture, Mr Pramod Navalkar, was quoted stating in an interview, 'I was particularly upset about the Madhu–Milind ad because they are going to get married. How can we allow anyone to pose in the nude with his wife?' The key words in this reaction are 'how can we allow'. Who are 'we'? The government? Mr Navalkar and his party? Or men? And what does he mean by 'allow'? That men can pose in the nude with other women but not with their wives? Or perhaps one should not expect logic when people's sensibilities are apparently outraged. Of course, the fact that Madhu Sapre is a well-known model in her own right, is financially independent and just happens to have decided to marry an equally successful male model appears to have escaped the attention of Mr Navalkar. That apart, regardless of whether one finds the controversial ad tasteless or aesthetic, the fact that the man and woman come across as equals is inescapable. The posture clearly does not seek to demean either sex. The advertiser has been clever because the product being sold is unisex, something people of both sexes can use. And the message is that if you use this particular product, you will be more desirable. John Berger in his book *Ways of Seeing* has some interesting things to say on this subject. Those working up a head of steam over the Tuffs shoes ad would do well to read this perceptive book. Berger writes, 'Publicity increasingly uses sexuality to sell any product or service. But this sexuality is never free in itself; it is a symbol for something presumed to be larger than it: the good life in which you can buy whatever you want. To be able to buy is the same thing as being sexually desirable.'

He points out: 'It is important here not to confuse publicity with the pleasure or benefits to be enjoyed from the things it advertises . . . publicity can never afford to be about the product or opportunity it is proposing to the buyer who is not yet enjoying it. Publicity is never a celebration of a pleasure-in-itself. Publicity is always about the future buyer. It offers him an image of himself made glamorous by the product or opportunity it is trying to sell. The image then makes him envious of himself as he might be . . . publicity is about social relations, not objects. Its promise is not of pleasure, but of happiness: happiness as judged from the outside by others. The happiness of being envied is glamour.' This is the pivot on which all advertising turns. Therefore, it is important not just to view the image but to read the message. And, in fact, the message is often far more offensive than the image. Today, in India, advertising stares us in the face from almost every surface. The all-pervasive nature of this medium, combined with the magic mantra of liberalization, makes for a pretty heady mix. Advertisers are having fun. They were always important, now they are more important. There is a greater range of products to sell, the competition is a little more fierce and technology has given them the tools to manipulate and change images at will. At the top end of the spectrum, Indian advertising has demonstrated its ability to produce aesthetic and tasteful advertisements, both in print and on film. Humour is another attribute that has been used effectively in some of these ad films.

But, unfortunately, for every one such 'good' ad, there are dozens of 'bad' ads. These are either imitative of western ads, or use cheap tricks to attract attention, or are obviously in bad taste. How should one react to the latter? In the early 1980s, some women's groups had taken to tarring hoardings that depicted women as sex objects. In discussions with leading figures in advertising on this issue, one was constantly reminded that such advertisements were merely 'bad' advertising and not sexist; that using a woman's body to sell an unrelated product was a tactic of the past which had long been discarded by the 'good' professional advertising agencies. There is no doubt that public reaction to such poor advertising did put some pressure on advertising agencies to pull up their socks and create better campaigns. But the very nature of advertising, its fundamental motivation—which is to entice the consumer to buy on the promise that mere possession of a product will somehow transpose them to a higher plane—guarantees that there will always be plenty of irrelevant and even objectionable advertising around.

Thus, whether it is nudity or depicting the strong, independent, Indian woman, advertising will use any tactic to lure the consumer. Having endorsed the right of producers to sell their products, it is difficult to draw a line on this issue.

Ultimately, the only check on racist, sexist or communal advertising can be public opinion. For every one person who objects, there will be at least another with the opposite point of view. The real reason why the objectors succeed, however illogical or reasonable the nature of their objections, is not because the advertisers accept their point of view but because they cannot afford to be seen in a negative light. In most cases they think it prudent to withdraw an ad and try again, rather than ignore public opinion.

This is an advantage that can be selectively used. But the line between imposing one particular set of 'values' on a multicultural society and checking the power of the advertiser is a very fine one.

$\sim$

GENDER CONSTRUCTION IN THE NEWS MEDIA
Sonia Bathla

Media, in a democratic society in particular, assumes a significant role during election time. Needless to say, for most of us, the election process may have little reality beyond its media version. We rely on the media for most of our information—who are the contestants? What are the issues on their agenda or manifesto? What kinds of policies are they proposing for the various problems facing the people and the country? Which constituencies are they trying to reach? Further, is the media playing the role of a facilitator or mediator between the public and policy makers? Are they carrying citizens' concerns or those of various constituencies to the policy makers? Such efforts on the part of the media, gain much more importance in a pluralistic society, where different groups with different interests contest political definitions and decisions.

In the process, some issues, groups, parties, newsmakers and themes dominate coverage, while others get ignored or marginalized. In that sense, what we see is not 'the reality', but its media version. Election news depend upon various factors or decisions made by news organizations about what to observe, what to report and what emphasis to place on various parts of the coverage. It is certainly a difficult task to figure out such factors due to the non-transparent relationship between the news organization and its sources, the complexity of the relationships between politics and the mass media, the internal working within a media organization and the perception of media persons towards various issues, and so on.

This study is concerned with the extent to which women's political participation figured as an issue for the media. More specifically, I am interested in news media representations of women politicians during the 12th Lok Sabha elections held in early 1998, when the then United Front government lost the support of Congress (I). [. . .]

To understand the approach of the press towards women politicians, I selected news items in the print media focusing on two key figures, J. Jayalalitha and Sushma Swaraj. While Jayalalitha headed the All India Dravida Munnetra Kazhagam (AIADMK), a regional party in Tamil Nadu (TN), Sushma Swaraj was the spokesperson of a national party, that is, the Bharatiya Janata Party (BJP), which has by and large been labelled as a communal party or a Hindu party within the Indian political system. In terms of personal background, both leaders are poles apart. Jayalalitha, the daughter of a film actress, started her career in Tamil films at a very young age. During her career, she was known as the 'mistress' of the famous film star M.G. Ramachandran. MGR, as he was popularly known, founded his own party and became the chief minister of Tamil Nadu. After his demise, Jayalalitha managed to become his heir despite strong opposition from his party members and his wife. Within Tamil Nadu, Jayalalitha 'has established herself as the reigning queen of the AIADMK' (Kishwar, 1999). She is an extremely powerful female political leader, and in fact she *is* the AIADMK. This is in spite of her alleged involvement in various corruption cases.

On the other hand, Sushma Swaraj, a lawyer by profession, enjoys a 'clean' image and, in fact, is a strong pillar of the BJP. She has been actively involved in politics for over twenty years. She fought her first Lok Sabha election in 1996 from the south Delhi constituency and emerged as a winner. Sushma Swaraj's father-in-law was a politician in Haryana and her husband is a senior bureaucrat at the centre. By all accounts, Sushma Swaraj has a non-controversial married life.

The objective of analyzing the media coverage of Jayalalitha and Sushma Swaraj was to find out how they were they perceived and presented by the media. What issues were they associated with? And what can be concluded from that coverage? I must mention that I did not compare their coverage against any male politician, as such an exercise would have been too elaborate. It was also difficult to find appropriate equivalents for these female politicians. [. . .]

Media coverage of Sushma Swaraj and Jayalalitha: A qualitative analysis

A considerable amount of research has gone into understanding the problems that women face in politics, the factors that obstruct their participation in political life, and so on. Some general conclusions that can be drawn from the western secondary literature are that women receive less representation in the media; the coverage associates them with domestic/private concerns (i.e. family and children) even when they are active in the public sphere, thereby indicating what their primary concerns should be; women get to be identified with social, welfare and women's issues—an extension of their domestic roles; and the media are more concerned with women's personal characteristics, traits and feminine aspects, with gendered frames commonly employed for defining and describing women politicians.

Results and analysis

The Indian press made no attempts to corner women leaders within the private sphere. Both Jayalalitha and Sushma were completely engaged in the political arena, with no apparent obligations to domestic/private concerns. This appears to be particularly the case for Sushma Swaraj, who has combined both her family and career. Furthermore, the leaders were not found to be associated with social, welfare or development issues. However, a great deal of coverage focused on their personal characteristics, traits, mannerisms, attire, looks and feminine aspects. Further, the effect of gender was produced through the positive coverage given to Sushma Swaraj and the negative coverage given to Jayalalitha. This drastic difference in the treatment meted out to the two women may be attributed to our cultural and gendered contexts.

I shall elaborate upon the findings as follows. As stated above, the media did not associate selected women leaders with private/domestic issues (in terms of family or children). This is particularly relevant for Sushma Swaraj, since she is married and has still been active in the political arena. While the probability of the media being inquisitive about how women combine their 'homely roles' (as wife and mother) with their professional career or demands of an election campaign may be greater in the case of newcomers, a mention of that at any stage of a woman's political career cannot be ruled out. In that sense, the stereotypical association of women with the private did not emerge in the coverage, indicating that women leaders are welcomed or acceptable within the public sphere. It may be an exaggeration to corroborate this conclusion on the basis of the study of just one leader. However, one can say with a certain surety that the Indian English press normally does not focus on leaders' private sphere(s).

Yet, the effect of gender surfaced in a clear and significant way through the particular coverage of the two leaders, suggesting biases in favour of feminine virtues. A major observation that came through was that Jayalalitha received an extremely negative coverage while Sushma was projected in a fairly favourable light by the media. Both the leaders were projected at extreme ends. The three newspapers examined (the *Hindu, Hindustan Times* and *Pioneer*) had very little to say about the positive aspects of Jayalalitha and the negative aspects of Sushma Swaraj. Regarding Jayalalitha, one could gather from her coverage that she was a popular leader who could attract large crowds, was emboldened, determined and had improved her support base. Otherwise, she generally came across as opportunistic, extremely corrupt, strategic, calculated, pragmatic, clever, harsh, arrogant, high-handed, a sinner, and much more. She was a woman who was obsessed with adornments like jewellery, gems, watches, pearls, etc. a special mention may be made of a statement passed by a respondent and carried in the *Hindu*. It said: 'I thought being a woman, she will rule well. But after her lavish wedding expenditure, I have voted for the DMK this time.' Further, Karunanidhi posed, in a story in *The Pioneer*: 'Ask her if there is another woman in history who has indulged in so much plunder and loot . . . Beware of this lady; she is out to invoke sympathies through plain hoodwinking.' She got equated with cholera and virus and her rule was described as a dark period in the history of Tamil Nadu. She was also projected as a sobbing and grieving woman suffering at the hands of Karunanidhi. In some situations, she could fret, fume, get angry, shout, sulk, and even be venomous and develop personal animosity. All in all, Jayalalitha was projected as an oddity, an anomaly, a deviant or an uncontrollable and unnatural phenomenon, particularly if one judges her coverage against that of Sushma's. She was portrayed as a gang member who knows how to play her game well. Her ways of speaking and campaigning were also ridiculed, even though she is a good orator and a successful and powerful politician.

On the other hand, Sushma appeared to be very agreeable, that in itself setting the definition for an 'ideal woman'. In short, she was presented as being smiling, pleasant, beaming, suave, charismatic, an iron lady with a high profile, diligent, an able administrator and a star campaigner. She held a responsible and respectable status, and closely identified herself with women and their issues. She was projected as a champion of women's rights, although she positioned herself within the liberal framework, with a number of leaders vouching for her. She had a number of pictures portraying her favourably, like performing some *hawan* ceremony, hugging a burqa-clad woman, being felicitated in her constituency, and so on. She received tumultuous welcomes at crowded public meetings. An item in the *Hindustan Times* mentioned her birthday and on this occasion a 'large number of women and young girls flocked to garland her in different colonies, while others rushed to the jeep with sweets'. She was a 'behanji' next door, winning people, and particularly women and young girls, with her charm. The *Pioneer* wrote: 'Jat women with their *pallus* covering their face jostled to garland and embrace Ms Swaraj.' Positive references were also made to her way of dressing. The *Hindustan Times* commented at one time: 'decked up in a saffron silk sari and gold jewellery, a smiling Mrs Swaraj signed the papers'. In short, the media provided complete legitimacy to her ideas, her words and her images, and there was a clear bias in her favour. While it is true that not all the opinions printed in a paper are held by journalists, or statements carried are passed by reporters, every news item goes through 'gatekeepers' before it is published in a paper. In that sense, it is endorsed by the paper and acquires legitimacy. The reporters writing on Jayalalitha may not have personal grudges against her but as a matter of fact she got projected in a negative light. Similarly, though reporters may not be personally fond of Sushma Swaraj she, nonetheless, received a positive portrayal.

Why did Jayalalitha and Sushma receive such divergent coverage? Did Jayalalitha's negative coverage have to do just with her being corrupt? Similarly, is her clean record responsible for Sushma's positive image? If negative coverage has to do simply with being corrupt, then there is an urgent need to examine the coverage of male politicians who have been equally corrupt and unprincipled in order to determine the treatment they receive from the media. However, I would rather suggest that there could be a close linkage between the perceptions of the media and the personal backgrounds of the two women leaders. In other words, there seems to be a greater probability that both leaders' coverage has to do with their personal life/background rather than just their political or professional life. Corruption or bad administration is not exceptional to Jayalalitha. What is exceptional is her non-conformity to the social (patriarchal) order— the fact that Jayalalitha started her career as an actress, became the 'mistress' of MGR, and did not live the conventional life of a woman. On the other hand, Sushma is an ideal Hindu woman who visibly conforms to the social system in terms of her commitment to her married family, her ways of dressing, her identification with other women, her commitment and loyalty towards her party, which is for women's 'empowerment' and not for women's 'liberation'. Otherwise, Sushma's positive coverage may surprise one against the backdrop of her belonging to a party which was by and large labelled as 'communal' by the media, the intelligentsia and most other political parties. Keeping that in view, one may contextualize Jayalalitha's negative coverage in terms of a backlash against a woman who has not lived up to social norms.

However, it is important to ask from where the media's perceptions originate. What are those cultural contexts within which gender is produced and its frameworks deployed? It is not within the scope of this study to go into the details of specific cultural contexts, as I am dealing mainly with 'how' the media has responded to women politicians, and not 'why'. Still, one does need to go beyond the visible to the framing of the 'ideal/good woman' and the 'bad woman' from within the discourses of India's colonial and nationalist history. The nationalist project did not bar women from entering the public domain and yet, it perceived them as representatives of the private sphere and expected them not to lose their spiritual essence and feminine virtues (Chatterjee 1989). This framework could provide a starting point for understanding the differences in the media's perception of two leaders. The results also suggest that conceptions of the private and public realms work differently in the western and Indian contexts, all of which call for further investigation.

References to feminine virtues and personal appearance also indicate that the biology of a female or the fact of her being a 'woman' politician, rather than just a politician who happens to be a woman, remained at the centre of media coverage. Sushma's hyper-womanly identity and Jayalalitha's anti-womanly identity presented them as 'the other' or 'the unusual' within the male dominated political system. Sushma was 'presented' as a 'woman politician' who identified herself, however loosely, with women and vice versa, whom women loved, who had all the feminine qualities, who knew how to dress up properly, who was pleasant, always smiling, who seemed committed to every aspect of feminine identity etc. She was an icon of Indian womanhood. She was neither viewed as a policy expert nor as an authority on important national issues.

Similarly, Jayalalitha was a corrupt 'woman politician', who could indulge in plunder and loot, who could sulk when people preferred to listen to other leaders' speeches, who was obsessed with jewellery, saris, gems, soaps, watches, etc. and who could wail, sob and grieve for the wrongs done to her because she was a woman first and a politician later. In this sense, both the leaders were presented to the reader as 'the other', the 'unusual' within the political system. Evidently, the media was carried away by Sushma's hyper-womanly identity and Jayalalitha's harshness and aggressiveness, which indicates how the media functioned within existing norms. It is paradoxical that while on the one hand, Jayalalitha was a tough and aggressive politician, on the other, she appeared as a fragile person, indicating how even a successful and clever woman politician is first of all a 'woman' with 'natural' weaknesses, rather than a politician. She was attacked simultaneously for being too aggressive and too emotional and impulsive.

A microanalysis of the stories with regard to the issues revealed that, by and large, no linkages were suggested between Jayalalitha and women's issues or even broader issues of development and social welfare. In the *Hindu*, she was generally projected as being caught up in the petty politics of making alliances with other parties, her differences with the BJP, seat-sharing arrangements, and conflicts with the DMK and the Tamil Maanila Congress (TMC). The stories focusing on her were engaged in making calculations, predictions about alliances, number games, analyzing internal politics of parties, etc. The *Hindustan Times'* stories focused on Jayalalitha's rally, her alliance with the BJP, her manifesto, her way of campaigning, her sobbing and wailing, the conflict between her and Karunanidhi, her party's stand on Ayodhya, Mathura and Kashi, the election scene in Tamil Nadu and prospects of various parties in the elections, her mannerisms at public gatherings, the conflicts between Jayalalitha and P. Chidambaram, alliances between Subramanya Swamy and Jayalalitha, unprincipled alliances and dying ideology. Brief items focused on seat sharing, conflicts between local parties, alliances, criticism by leaders of each other, personal attacks, etc. Similarly, the *Pioneer* focused on personal attacks between leaders, seat distribution, alliances and predictions about who would win and lose. Issues like the eradication of poverty, problems of the minorities and women, and the Jain Commission Report did not get a mention in even one sentence.

Even Sushma Swaraj was not associated with the broader issues of development and social welfare. She generally appeared as a spokesperson of her party and hence raised only those issues that existed on its agenda. In the *Hindu*, the issues associated with Sushma include the revival of the economy, full statehood for Delhi, and crime and law and order in Delhi. In the *Hindustan Times*, the issues noted were the failing external value of the rupee, the centre's wasting financial resources, full statehood for Delhi, rising crimes in Delhi, land management and housing, the development of mass rapid transit system and so on. However, all these issues were touched upon briefly in terms of space. The *Pioneer* focused on conflicts, winning/losing, criticism, campaign activity, filing papers, how politicians should dress up, how it had become so important for politicians to attend weddings during elections, etc. Sushma was found criticizing Sonia for the Blue Star Operation and the 1984 massacres. However, all the papers certainly perceived her as a champion of women's rights and concerns and she was projected as a women's leader.

It may be observed from the above discourse that both leaders were generally not associated with so-called social and welfare issues or projected as agents of change, as has been the case in the west. In fact, an analysis of the stories revealed that the media hardly touched upon larger issues, whether hard or soft, in the selected stories. This observation needs to be contextualized within a broader context of the general political culture of the country, indicating how gender holds an insignificant status in certain situations and that the media function within their own agendas.

Over the last few years, the Indian political system has gone through various changes. One of the drastic changes which occurred was the breakdown in the monopoly of dynastic rule of the Congress (I), followed by the development of a multi-party system, coalition governments and so on. Further, marginalized groups also staked their claim within the political system, the result of which is that the struggle for power has increased. Since coalitions are also formed on the basis of narrow interests and gains, it became difficult for them to survive the normal tenure of five years. One person or party within a coalition holds the power to disrupt the government, and the moment one government collapses, other parties immediately indulge in negotiations and bargains to find coalition partners to form a new government at the centre. As a result, India has seen a number of elections in the last few years. The situation still remains unstable and fragile. Concerns over the broader issues of governance and development find little place.

Looking at the coverage of the two key politicians in the preceding sections, it is easy to observe that the media seems to be operating within the framework of a 'horse race'. They were least bothered about the bigger issues facing the country and the agenda of the leaders. The focus of the stories, by and large, remained on individuals and party politics, alliances, seat distribution, backbiting and personal criticisms by politicians of each other. This was particularly observed in the coverage of Jayalalitha. Within the news stories, larger issues were touched upon only in passing and did not analyze the leaders' position on them. Even the articles focusing on, for example, unprincipled alliances, legacies and ideologies were mainly concerned with party politics and predictions about winners and losers.

Finally, it must be said that the coverage of Jayalalitha and Sushma Swaraj revealed that both the leaders were under-represented, in terms of both space and place in the media. The number of stories recorded was not significantly high either. The highest number recorded was about Jayalalitha, who was covered in thirty-four items in the *Hindu*, and yet it did not give her an average of even one item a day. The analysis of their coverage in terms of variables like their status as primary actors, as speaking subjects, as interviewees and their appearances on important pages also indicated that they did not receive considerable attention from the media.

References

Chatterjee, Partha. 1989. The nationalist resolution of the women's question. In *Recasting women: Essays in colonial history*, ed. Kumkum Sangari and Sudesh Vaid. New Delhi: Kali for Women.

Kishwar, Madhu. 1999. Indian politics encourages Durgas, snubs women. *Manushi*, March–April, 111.

NOTES ON CONTRIBUTORS

Bina Agarwal is Professor of Economics at the Institute of Economic Growth, New Delhi. She has written widely in the fields of feminist economics, agriculture and environmentalism, including *A Field of One's Own: Gender and Land Rights in South Asia* (1994); and more recently *Psychology, Rationality and Economic Behaviour: Challenging Standard Assumptions* (co-edited, 2007); and *Capabilities, Freedom and Equality: Amartya Sen's Work from a Gender Perspective* (co-edited, 2005).

Flavia Agnes is a women's rights advocate, activist and researcher, and a co-founder of MAJLIS, a legal and cultural resource centre, in Mumbai. Among her many writings on feminism, law, secularism and identity politics are an autobiographical book *My Story Our Story . . . Of Rebuilding Broken Lives*, and *Law & Gender Inequality: The Politics of Personal Laws in India*.

Indu Agnihotri is currently Senior Fellow, Centre for Women's Development Studies, New Delhi. Before this she was Reader, Department of History, Vivekanand College, University of Delhi. She has been actively involved with the women's movement in India.

Jasodhara Bagchi was the founder Director of the School of Women's Studies and Professor of English at Jadavpur University. She is currently Chairperson of the West Bengal Commission for Women. Recent publications include the co-edited volumes *A Space of Her Own: Personal Narratives of Twelve Indian Women* (2005); *The Changing Status of Women in West Bengal, 1970–2000: The Challenge Ahead* (2005); and *The Trauma and the Triumph: Gender and Partition in India* (2003).

Vineeta Bal is a member of Saheli Women's Resource Centre in New Delhi and works as a scientist at the National Institute of Immunology. She is closely associated with issues concerning women's health and the status of women practitioners of science.

Narayan K. Banerjee is an anthropologist and was Director of the Centre for Women's Development Studies. He worked with the Indian Census for some years before joining Centre for Women's Development Studies. His interest areas are organizations of rural women, women's rights to natural resources and gender-balanced development. He has been working with women's organizations in the CWDS Bankura Project for the last two decades.

Nirmala Banerjee was Professor of Economics at the Centre for Studies in Social Sciences, Kolkata. Previously she worked as an urban planner, and retains an interest in urban economy and industrialization, apart from her research on women's issues, particularly women's work experiences. She is deeply involved in the women's movement in India, and is a founder member for SACHETANA, a Kolkata-based voluntary women's organization. She has authored many books on socially relevant issues.

Sonia Bathla worked as a Junior Fellow at Centre for Women's Development Studies from 1997 to 2004, in the fields of gender and the print media. Her study *Women, Democracy, and Media: Cultural and Political Representations in the Indian Press* was published in 1998. A poet at heart, her book *Pehchan* was published shortly before her untimely demise.

Upendra Baxi is Professor of Law, University of Warwick; he was Vice Chancellor, University of Delhi and University of South Gujarat. His most recent publications are *The Future of Human Rights* (3rd edn, 2008*)*; and *Human Rights in a Posthuman World: Critical Essays (*2007).

Kamla Bhasin is a social scientist by training, and has been involved with issues related to development, education, gender and the media since 1972. She has worked with the Food and Agriculture Organization's (FAO) Freedom from Hunger Campaign/Action for Development, and is presently the Advisor to the South Asian Network of Gender Activists and Trainers (SANGAT). She is a well-known gender trainer and has written extensively on participatory training, women, feminism and sustainable development. She has also written many songs on all these issues.

Dipta Bhog is at present Co-director of Nirantar, A Centre for Gender and Education, based in New Delhi. She has worked intensively with rural women and girls on issues of development. She has specialized in issues of literacy and adult education, curriculum development, and the critique and production of school textbooks. She was also a member of a committee set up by National Council of Educational Research and Training to write the focus paper on Gender in Education for the New Curriculum Framework 2005.

Urvashi Butalia is a publisher, writer and activist. She was the co-founder of Kali for Women Press, and later founded Zubaan Press, an imprint of Kali for Women. She has written widely on many issues relating to women and gender, communalism, conflict and peace, and history. Her publications include *The Other Side of Silence: Voices from the Partition of India* (1998); *Speaking Peace: Women's Voices from Kashmir* (ed. 2002); *Poster Women: A Visual History of the Women's Movement in India* (ed. 2006); and *A Sense of the Past: Women's Writings on Partition* (ed. 2008).

Campaign for Lesbian Rights (Caleri) is a New Delhi-based non-funded autonomous coalition of individuals and organizations and is not affiliated to any political party.

The Campaign for Lesbian Rights coalesced in the days following broadbased protests against the Shiv Sena's attacks on the film *Fire* in December 1998.

Uma Chakravarti is a feminist historian who taught history at Miranda House, University of Delhi, for over four decades. She has been associated with the movement for women's rights and democratic rights since the 1970s. She lives and works from New Delhi. Her most recent publication is *Everyday Lives, Everyday Histories: Beyond the Kings and Brahmans of 'Ancient' India*, 2007.

Karuna Chanana was Professor at the Zakir Husain Centre for Educational Studies, Jawaharlal Nehru University, New Delhi. Her specializations are sociology of education and sociology of gender. Among her writings are *Interrogating Women's Education: Bounded Visions, Expanding Horizons*, most recently *Inclusion and Exclusion: A Study of Women and Men in Delhi Police*, 2005 (co-authored).

Partha Chatterjee is Professor of Political Science, Centre for Studies in Social Sciences, Kolkata, and Professor of Anthropology, Columbia University. His more recent publications include *A Princely Impostor? The Kumar of Bhawal and the Secret History of Indian Nationalism* (2002); and *The Politics of the Governed* (2004).

Maitrayee Chaudhuri teaches sociology at the Centre for the Study of Social Systems, Jawaharlal Nehru University, New Delhi. She is currently Director, Women Studies Programme at JNU. She has written widely in the areas of gender, culture, globalization and media; and the changing practices of sociology. Her books include *Feminism in India*, (2004); *The Women's Movement in India: Reform and Revival* (1993); and *The Practice of Sociology* (2003).

Prem Chowdhry taught history at Miranda House, New Delhi and was a Fellow of the Nehru Memorial Museum and Library, New Delhi. She has published widely and her most recent publication is *Contentious Marriages, Eloping Couples: Gender, Caste and Patriarchy in Northern India* (2007). She is also an avid painter.

Durbar Mahila Samanwaya Committee is a group of 60,000 sex workers first established in Kolkata in 1995. The Committee has been active in demanding the decriminalization of prostitution and in promoting the rights of sex workers and their children.

Bhargavi V. Davar is a social science researcher in mental health. Her publications include *Psychoanalysis as a Human Science: Beyond Foundationalism*; *Mental Health of Indian Women*; and *Gender and Mental Health*. She is presently researching and writing on indigenous healing and mental health.

Vasudha Dhagamwar was Professor of Law, University of Delhi, worked as Director, MARG and is currently Chairperson, PRAKRITI. She has been actively involved with women's issues and the law, and recently authored the book *Role and Image of Law in Rural India* (2005).

Neera Desai, the founder Director of the Research Centre for Women's Studies, was formerly Professor of Sociology at the SNDT Women's University, Mumbai. She is one of the founder members of the Indian Association for Women's Studies. Her publications include *Women and Society in India* (co-authored); *Indian Women, Change and Challenge in the International Decade: 1975–1985* (co-authored); *A Critical Review of Women's Studies Research in India 1975–1988*; and *Feminism as Experience: Thought and Narratives* (2006).

J. Devika teaches and researches at the Centre for Development Studies, Thiruvananthapuram. Her publications include *Her-Self: Early Writings on Gender by Malayalee Women* (2005); *En-Gendering Individuals: The Language of Re-form in Early Modern Keralam* (2007) and *Individuals, Householders, Citizens: Malayalees and Family Planning 1930–1970* (2008).

Gabriele Dietrich is Professor at the Centre for Social Analysis, Madurai, and has worked with women's movements and people's movements for many years. She has published widely on development issues, women's movements, Dalit issues, religion and cultural perspectives.

Leela Dube is a social anthropologist, and has written in the areas of gender, kinship, caste and culture. She was Senior Fellow of the Nehru Memorial Museum and Library, and Chairperson, Commission on Women, the International Union of Anthropological and Ethnological Sciences. Her publications include *Matriliny and Islam; Women and Kinship: Comparative Perspectives on Gender in South and South-East Asia*; and *Anthropological Explorations in Gender*.

Nandita Gandhi is an activist of the contemporary women's movement and founder member and Director of Akshara, a women's resource centre working for gender equality. She has written *The Anti Price Rise Movement in Mumbai, Maharashtra* and co-authored with Nandita Shah *Issues at Stake: Theory and Practice in the Contemporary Women's Movement in India* and *Contingent Workers: Women in Two Industries in Mumbai*.

V. Geetha is an independent scholar who writes in both Tamil and in English. Among her books are *Gender; Patriarchy*; and with S.V. Rajadurai, *Towards a Non-Brahmin Millennium: From Iyothee Thass to Periyar* (1998). She is Editorial Director, Tara Publishing, Chennai.

Anita Ghai is a Reader in the Department of Psychology, Jesus and Mary College, New Delhi. Disability issues are central to her life both professionally and personally. Her recent publications include *(Dis) Embodied Form: Issues of Disabled Women* (reprint 2006); and *The Mentally Handicapped: Prediction of Work Performance* (co-authored). She acts as an Overseas Editor for the journal *Disability and Society*.

Shohini Ghosh teaches and researches at the Mass Communication Research Centre, Jamia Millia Islamia, New Delhi. She is a member of the feminist film collective Media Storm, and has been a co-director of the Centre for Feminist Legal Research. She has written widely on issues related to cinema, media and representation, gender and sexuality.

Nandita Haksar is a human rights lawyer and women's activist. Her publications include *Demystification of Law for Women* (translated into major regional languages);

Framing Geelani, Hanging Afzal: Patriotism in a Time of Terror. She has evolved and taught courses on human rights in various universities.

Zoya Hasan is Professor of Political Science at the Jawaharlal Nehru University and is currently a member of the National Commission for Minorities. Her recent books include *Unequal Citizens: A Study of Muslim Women in India* (co-authored); *In a Minority: Essays on Muslim Women in India* (co-edited); *Transforming India: Social Dynamics of Democracy* (co-edited); and *Democracy in the Muslim World: The Asian Experience* (edited).

Devaki Jain founded the Institute of Social Studies Trust, and is a founder member of the Indian Association for Women Studies, and Development Alternatives for a New Era, DAWN. Her latest publications are *Are We Knowledge Proof? Development as Waste* (2003); *A View from the South: A Story of Intersections* (2004); *Women, Development and the UN: A Sixty-years Quest for Equality and Justice* (2005); and *Women, Public Policy and the New World Order.*

Mary E. John is currently Senior Fellow and Director at the Centre for Women's Development Studies, New Delhi, and was Associate Professor at the Women's Studies Programme, Jawaharlal Nehru University. She has written widely on feminism and women's studies. Her publications include *Discrepant Dislocations: Feminism, Theory and Postcolonial Histories* (1996) and more recently *French Feminism: An Indian Anthology* (co-edited, 2002) and *Contested Transformations: Changing Economies and Identities in Contemporary India* (co-edited, 2006).

Sharmila Joshi is an independent journalist based in Mumbai, who writes extensively on gender issues. Her academic background is in historical sociology, and she is currently working on a PhD in the field of gender and development.

Kalpana Kannabiran is a founder member of Asmita Resource Centre for Women, Hyderabad, and Professor of Sociology at NALSAR University of Law, Hyderabad. She is co-author of *De-Eroticising Assault: Essays on Modesty, Honour and Power* (2002); co-editor of *The Situated Politics of Belonging* (2006); and editor of *The Violence of Normal Times: Essays on Women's Lived Realities* (2005).

Vasanth Kannabiran specializes in gender and development issues and is a founder member of Asmita Resource Centre for Women, Hyderabad. She has co-authored *De-Eroticising Assault: Essays on Modesty, Honour and Power;* co-edited *Web of Deceit* (2003), and *Mahilavarnam/Womanscape: Women in Andhra Pradesh,* 2001.

Ratna Kapur is the Director of the Centre for Feminist Legal Research, New Delhi, and currently the Senior Gender Advisor for the United Nations Mission in Nepal. She has written and published extensively on feminist legal theory, postcolonial feminism, international law and human rights. Her latest book is *Erotic Subjects: Law and the New Politics of Postcolonialism* (2005), and her forthcoming book is *Gender, Migration and Law* (2007).

Brinda Karat belongs to the All India Democratic Women's Association (AIDWA), and has been its General Secretary from 1993 to 2004. She is a Central Committee Member of the Communist Party of India (Marxist), and a Member of Parliament

(Rajya Sabha, 2005–2011). She is the author of *Survival and Emancipation: Notes from Indian Women's Struggles.*

Malavika Karlekar has been a university teacher and is now a researcher, author, editor and curator of archival photographs. At present she is based at Centre for Women's Development Studies and is the editor, *Indian Journal of Gender Studies* and Curator, Re-presenting Indian Women 1875–1947: A Visual Documentary.

Saleem Kidwai is an independent researcher, living in Lucknow. He taught history at University of Delhi for twenty years. He co-edited *Same-Sex Love in India: Readings from Literature and History* (2001) with Ruth Vanita.

Madhu Kishwar is a Senior Fellow at Centre for the Study of Developing Societies and Founder of Manushi Sangathan. She is also the founder Editor of *Manushi: A Journal about Women and Society* founded in 1978. She has written widely on women's issues. Her forthcoming books are *Zealous Reformers, Deadly Laws: Critical Review of Laws to Strengthen Women's Rights* (2008); *The Quintessential Oneness of* Amar, Akbar, Anthony: *Bollywood's Portrayal of Minority–Majority Relations in India.*

Maithreyi Krishnaraj was Professor and Director of Women's Studies at SNDT Women's University. She has been a guest editor for the Review of Women's Studies in the *Economic and Political Weekly* since 1986. Her recent publications include *Between State and Market: Human development in India* (2007); *Gender, Food Security and Rural Livelihood* (2007); and *Women Farmers of India* (2007). Forthcoming work includes *Motherhood, Mothers and Mothering;* and *Food Security, Agrarian Crisis and Rural livelihoods: Gender Implications.*

Radha Kumar is Director of the Mandela Centre for Peace and Conflict Resolution at Jamia Millia Islamia University, and trustee of the Delhi Policy Group. Her books include *Making Peace with Partition* (2005); *Divide and Fall? Bosnia in the Annals of Partition* (1997); and *A History of Doing: Movements for Women's Rights and Feminism in India, 1900–1990* (1993). She has edited or authored many reports, of which the most recent are among the Delhi Policy Group publications.

K. Lalita is co-author of *We were Making History: Life Stories of Women in the Telangana People's Struggle* (1989); co-editor of the two volumes of *Women Writing in India: From 600 BC to the 20th Century* (1991, 1993); and co-author in Telugu of *Savalaksha Sandehalu.* She was founder President of the Progressive Organisation of Women, and founder coordinator and current Vice-President of Anveshi Research Centre for Women's Studies. She is also Director of ThinkSoft Consultants and Yugantar.

Manimala is an independent journalist known for her reports on human rights. She heads the publishing organization, Books for Change, which publishes books on many issues of contemporary social concern. She has an MSc (Zoology), MEd, LLB and a PhD in mass communication.

Ruth Manorama is President of the National Alliance of Women's Organisations. She is also an activist and writer on many issues. She founded the organization

Women's Voice in Bangalore which took up slum dwellers' and domestic workers' rights. She has been active in the women's movement and in mobilizing on Dalit rights, and became a founder member of the National Federation of Dalit Women in 1994. Ruth Manorama received the Right Livelihood Award in 2006.

Vina Mazumdar was founder Director of the Centre for Women's Development Studies, New Delhi, and a co-founder of the Indian Association for Women's Studies. She has written widely in the field of women's studies. Currently she is National Research Professor in Social Sciences, Government of India, and is also Coordinator and General Editor of a series of volumes on *Women, Equality and Governance: Landmarks in the Indian Story,* a documentation/archival project from the pre-Independence period till the end of the twentieth century.

Nivedita Menon teaches Political Science at University of Delhi. She works on contemporary politics with a feminist lens. She is the author of *Recovering Subversion: Feminist Politics beyond the Law* (2004). Her recent books are an edited volume, *Sexualities* (2007), and a book co-authored with Aditya Nigam, *Power and Contestation: India after 1989* (2007).

Ritu Menon is a publisher and writer, co-founder of Kali for Women Press and later, founder of Women Unlimited. Her recent publications include *Unequal Citizens: A Study of Muslim Women in India* (2004); *Educating Muslim Girls: A Comparison of Five Indian Cities* (2005); and *From Mathura to Manorama: Resisting Violence against Women in India* (2007). She has also edited *No Woman's Land: Women from Pakistan, India and Bangladesh Write on the Partition of India* (2004), and several anthologies of stories by Indian women.

Asok Mitra, formerly of the Indian Civil Service, was Professor of Population Studies, Jawaharlal Nehru University, New Delhi. He was Registrar General and Census Commissioner of India between 1958 and 1968. His book *India's Population: Quality and Control* was published in 1978.

Manoranjan Mohanty was Director of Developing Countries Research Centre, and is Professor of Political Science, University of Delhi. He edited *Class, Caste, Power* (2004); and his forthcoming books are *Right to Participate: Local Governance and Grassroots Democracy in India and China*; and *Rural Reforms in Wuxi.*

Janaki Nair is Professor at the History Unit of the Centre for Studies in Social Sciences, Kolkata. Her most recent publication is *The Promise of the Metropolis: Bangalore's Twentieth Century* (2005). Her research interests include feminism, urban studies, visual cultures and modern Indian history.

Annie Namala completed her masters in Social Work from the Madras School of Social Work, and has been working with Dalit organizations and collectives for over two decades in Andhra Pradesh. Over the past three years, she has shifted to New Delhi, and does research and policy advocacy on the exclusion and discrimination of Dalit children. She is currently with the Indian Institute of Dalit Studies.

Tejaswini Niranjana is Senior Fellow at the Centre for the Study of Culture and Society, Bangalore. Her most recent book is *Mobilizing India: Women, Music and*

Migration between India and Trinidad (2006). She has lectured and published widely on feminist theory, cultural studies and women's issues more generally.

Tiplut Nongbri is Professor of Sociology at the Centre for the Study of Social Systems, Jawaharlal Nehru University, New Delhi. Her publications include *Development, Ethnicity and Gender: Select Essays on Tribes in India* (2003); *Gender, Matriliny and Entrepreneurship: The Khasis of North-East India* (2008).

Gail Omvedt, born in Minneapolis, United States of America, has been living in India since 1978, settled in the village of Kasegaon in southern Maharashtra. She is Research Director of the Krantivir Trust and Visiting Professor and Coordinator, School of Social Justice, University of Pune. Among her numerous books are *Seeking Begumpura: The Social Vision of Anti-caste Intellectuals* (2008); *Ambedkar: Towards an Enlightened India* (2005); *Buddhism in India: Challenging Brahmanism and Caste* (2003).

Rajni Palriwala is Professor at the Department of Sociology, University of Delhi. Her research and writings have been within the broad areas of gender relations, work, kinship, women's movements and feminist politics, fieldwork methodology, and more recently care, citizenship, and the state. Her recent books and edited collections include *Care, Culture and Citizenship: Revisiting the Politics of Welfare in the Netherlands* (co-authored, 2005); *Changing Kinship, Family, and Gender Relations in South Asia: Processes, Trends and Issues* (1994); and *Marriage, Migration and Gender* (co-edited, 2008).

Kumud Pawde is Professor of Sanskrit and has published widely on issues relating to the Vedic *Smritis* and classical literature. She writes on the women's movement and Dalit movements in Maharashtra. She is the President of the All India Progressive Women's Organisation which was established in Nagpur in 1974. She brought out a second edition of her highly acclaimed autobiography *Antasphot* in 1995.

Imrana Qadeer was Professor at the Centre of Social Medicine and Community Health, Jawaharlal Nehru University, New Delhi. She has been active in health and women's movements. Some recent publications are *Socioeconomic and Political Determinants of Health*; and *Status of Health Services in India: An Overview*.

Rajeswari Sunder Rajan is Global Distinguished Professor in the English Department at New York University. She is the author of *The Scandal of the State: Women, Law and Citizenship in Postcolonial India* (2003); *Real and Imagined Women: Gender, Culture and Postcolonialism* (1993); and has edited several collections of essays, most recently, with Anuradha Needham, *The Crisis of Secularism in India* (2006).

Mohan Rao is Professor at the Centre of Social Medicine and Community Health, Jawaharlal Nehru University, New Delhi. A medical doctor specialized in public health, he has written extensively on health and population policy and on the history and politics of health and family planning. He is the author of *From Population Control to Reproductive Health: Malthusian Arithmetic* (2004); and has edited *Disinvesting in Health: The World Bank's Health Prescriptions* (1999) and *The Unheard Scream: Reproductive Health and Women's Lives in India* (2004). He is currently a member of the National Population Commission.

Sharmila Rege teaches at the University of Pune and writes in English and Marathi on feminist sociology, dalit feminisms and popular culture in Maharashtra. Her current research interests focus on the booklet and music cultures of Ambedkarite counterpublics. Her most recent publication is *Writing Caste/Writing Gender: Narrating Dalit Women's Testimonies* (2006).

Rinchin presently lives and works in Bhopal. She is associated with peoples groups and organizations, and writes on related issues.

Kumkum Roy teaches ancient Indian history at the Centre for Historical Studies, Jawaharlal Nehru University, New Delhi. Her publications include *The Emergence of Monarchy in North India, as Reflected in the Brahmanical Tradition* (1994). She has also edited an anthology titled *Women in Early Indian Societies* (1999).

Saheli is an autonomous non-funded women's group since 1981. Activities include campaigns and struggles against violence against women, discrimination in law, coercive population policy, hazardous contraceptives, sex determination, communalism, militarization and war. Saheli works in solidarity with democratic rights groups, lesbian, gay and dalit movements. Saheli publishes occasional monographs and reports, and a newsletter in Hindi and English thrice a year.

Kumkum Sangari taught English at Indraprastha College for Women, University of Delhi and was a Professorial Fellow at the Centre for Contemporary Studies, Nehru Memorial Museum and Library, New Delhi. She is at present William F. Vilas Research Professor of English at the University of Wisconsin at Milwaukee. Amongst her many writings, she has authored *Politics of the Possible: Essays on Gender, History, Narratives, Colonial English* (2001); and *The Names of Violence*, 2008.

Stree Shakti Sanghatana was an activist women's organization based in Hyderabad, engaged in research as well as campaigning, legal aid and counselling, mainly among urban women. The group brought out in Telugu *Manaku Teliyani Mana Charitra* (1987); and in English *We were Making History: Life Stories of Women in the Telangana People's Struggle* (1989).

K. Saradamoni, a social scientist who worked for many years with the Indian Statistical Institute, Delhi Centre, is currenly living in Thiruvananthapuram. Concerned about women and society for nearly six decades, she has written numerous books and articles. She writes in Malayalam and English. Her main research interests have been land and labour, inequality and social transformation. She is currently President of the National Federation of Indian Women.

Lotika Sarkar was Professor of Law at the University of Delhi, and a founder member of the Centre for Women's Development Studies. She has written extensively on law and gender issues. Her recent publications include *Women and Law: Contemporary Problems* (co-edited, 1994); and *Between Tradition, Counter Tradition and Heresy: Contributions in Honour of Vina Mazumdar* (2002).

Tanika Sarkar is Professor of History at the Centre for Historical Studies, Jawaharlal Nehru University, New Delhi. She has authored several books and monographs. Her recent publications include *Hindu Wife, Hindu Nation: Religion, Community Culture* *and Nationalism* (2001); and the two volumes of *Women and Social Reforms* (2008) co-edited with Sumit Sarkar.

Nabaneeta Dev Sen was Professor of Comparative Literature at Jadavpur University, Kolkata. She is the founder President of the West Bengal Women Writers' Association. Her first collection of poems, *Pratham Pratyay*, was published in 1959. She has published numerous books in Bengali—poetry, novels, short stories, plays, literary criticism, personal essays, travelogues, humour writing, translations and children's literature.

Nandita Shah has been active in the women's rights movement for the last twenty years, as activist, teacher, gender trainer and writer. Currently she is Co-director of Akshara, a women's rights organization based in Mumbai, and is active in the international team organizing the World Social Forum. She has co-authored *Issues at Stake: Theory and Practice in the Contemporary Women's Movement in India* (1992); and *Shadow Workers: Women in Home-based Production*.

Kalpana Sharma is currently an independent journalist and columnist based in Mumbai. In over three decades in journalism she has held senior editorial positions in *The Hindu, Times of India* and *Indian Express*. She is author of *Rediscovering Dharavi: Stories from Asia's Largest Slum* (2000); and has co-edited *Whose News? The Media and Women's Issues* (1994/2006); and *Terror, Counter-Terror: Women Speak Out* (2003).

Kumud Sharma was former Director and is currently Vice-Chairperson at the Centre for Women's Development Studies. Her publications include *Women in Focus; National Specialised Agencies and Women's Equality: A Case Study of Central Social Welfare Board.* She has worked on the sociology of development, women's studies, women in the political process, and so on. She is currently working on issues related to gender and poverty, gender and environment and women in local self-government.

Veena Shatrugna trained as a biochemist and is a Senior Researcher and Deputy Director at National Institute of Nutrition, Hyderabad. She is a founder member of Anveshi Research Centre for Women's Studies, Hyderabad. She has researched and published widely in the fields of women's health and nutrition.

Vandana Shiva is a physicist, philosopher and ecofeminist, and is the director of the Research Foundation for Science, Technology and Ecology (RFSTE). She has established Navdanya, a movement for biodiversity conservation and farmers' rights. Her most recent books are *Biopiracy: The Plunder of Nature and Knowledge;* and *Stolen Harvest: The Hijacking of the Global Food Supply.*

Shodhini was born as a collective effort to create an alternative for women's health. It sought to empower women by validating their traditional knowledge and enhancing its status to increase women's control over their own bodies and their own health by training local women in gynaecology, technology and resources by growing medicinal plants.

Jaya Srivastava, former Director of Ankur, Society for Alternatives in Education, has been working with women, young people and children in the slums of New Delhi, for over two decades. She has been active in the women's movement and in numerous campaigns. She provides training inputs to various organizations, and has presented papers at national and international conferences, and contributed to various magazines and volumes on relevant issues.

Susie Tharu was Professor in the School of Critical Humanities at the Central Institute of English and Foreign Languages, Hyderabad, is a founder member of Anveshi Research Centre for Women's Studies, Hyderabad. Her publications include the two volumes of *Women Writing in India* (co-edited, 1991, 1993); and *Subject to Change: English Studies in the Nineties* (ed. 1997). Currently she is at work, in collaboration with K. Satyanarayana, on a collection of documents from the Dalit upsurge of the 1990s in south India.

Patricia Uberoi was Professor at the Institute of Economic Growth, New Delhi, and is currently Director of the Institute of Chinese Studies located at the Centre for the Study of Developing Societies, New Delhi. She has researched extensively on family, kinship, marriage and gender, and on aspects of popular culture and social policy with reference to both India and China. Her most recent books include *Freedom and Destiny: Gender, Family and Popular Culture in India* (2006); *Anthropology in the East: Founders of Indian Sociology and Anthropology* (co-edited, 2007); and *Marriage, Migration and Gender* (co-edited, 2008).

Sudesh Vaid was one of the founding members of the People's Union of Democratic Rights (PUDR), an organization that has worked vigorously for the preservation of the democratic rights of Indian peoples for over two decades. She taught for over twenty-five years at Indraprastha College for Women, University of Delhi, and was responsible for setting up the first IP College Women's Cell. Her publications include *The Divided Mind: Studies in Select Novels of Defoe and Richardson* (1979); and *Recasting Women: Essays in Colonial History* (co-edited, 1989).

Ruth Vanita was formerly Reader, University of Delhi, and is now Professor at the University of Montana. From 1978 to 1990 she was founding Co-editor of *Manushi: A Journal about Women and Society*. She is the author of *Sappho and the Virgin Mary: Same-Sex Love and the English Literary Imagination* (1996), and co-editor (with Saleem Kidwai) of *Same-Sex Love in India: Readings from Literature and History* (2001); *Love's Rite: Same-Sex Marriage in India and the West*; and *Gandhi's Tiger and Sita's Smile: Essays on Gender, Culture and Sexuality*.

Virginius Xaxa teaches Sociology at Delhi School of Economics, University of Delhi. He is the author of *Economic Dualism and Structures of Class in Plantation and Peasant Settings in North Bengal* (1997); and co-author of *Plantation Labour in India* (1996).

INDEX